# Napoleon

# GEORGES LEFEBVRE

# *Napoleon*

BOOK ONE

From 18 Brumaire to Tilsit

1799–1807

*Translated by Henry F. Stockhold*

BOOK TWO

From Tilsit to Waterloo

1807–1815

*Translated by J. E. Anderson*

*Introduction and Further Reading*
*by Andrew Roberts*

LONDON

The Folio Society

2009

*Napoleon* by Georges Lefebvre was first published as *Napoléon*, volume XIV of the series 'Peuples et Civilisations', by Presses Universitaires de France, the first three parts in 1935 and the second three parts in 1936. The first translated edition, based on the fifth (1965) edition, was published in two volumes by Routledge & Kegan Paul Ltd in 1969, as *Napoleon: From 18 Brumaire to Tilsit, 1799–1807*, translated by Henry F. Stockhold, and *Napoleon: From Tilsit to Waterloo, 1807–1815*, translated by J. E. Anderson. The text of this combined, single volume follows that of the first translated editions, with minor emendations.

This edition published by The Folio Society Ltd
44 Eagle Sreet, London WC1R 4FS
www.foliosociety.com

This edition is published by arrangement with Routledge
and Columbia University Press.

© 1936 Presses Universitaires de France
Translation © 1969 Columbia University Press

Introduction and Further Reading © 2009 Andrew Roberts

*Frontispiece*: David's idealisation of Napoleon Bonaparte crossing
the Alps by the Great St Bernard Pass in May 1800

Second printing 2010

Typeset in Ehrhardt with Bulmer display at The Folio Society.
Printed on Abbey Wove paper at Memminger MedienCentrum AG,
Memmingen, Germany. Bound by Lachenmaier, Reutlingen,
Germany, in cloth blocked with a design by Neil Gower

# CONTENTS

# BOOK TWO
# FROM TILSIT TO WATERLOO, 1807–1815

# ILLUSTRATIONS

*The First Kiss this Ten Years!* Hand-coloured etching by James Gillray,
1803. LC-USZC4-8778.
(*Library of Congress, Prints and Photographs Division*)

Meeting of the deputies of the Cisalpine Republic. Oil painting by
Nicolas-André Monsiau, 1808.
(© *Châteaux de Versailles et de Trianon/Daniel Arnaudet/RMN*)

Attempt to assassinate Napoleon. Coloured engraving by a French artist,
1800–1. (*Bibliothèque nationale de France, Paris/Lauros/Giraudon/The
Bridgeman Art Library*)

Cadoudal's conspirators. Watercolour by Armand de Polignac, *c.*1804.
(*Musée de la Ville de Paris, Musée Carnavalet, Paris/Archives Charmet/The
Bridgeman Art Library*)

Execution of Georges Cadoudal. Watercolour by Armand de Polignac,
*c.*1804. (*Musée de la Ville de Paris, Musée Carnavalet, Paris/Archives
Charmet/The Bridgeman Art Library*)

Emperor Napoleon in his study at the Tuileries. Oil painting by Jacques-
Louis David, 1812. 1961.9.15. (*Image courtesy of the Board of Trustees,
National Gallery of Art, Washington*)

Empress Josephine. Oil painting by Pierre-Paul Prud'hon, 1805.
(© *Gérard Blot/RMN*)

*Allegory of the Concordat of 1801.* Oil painting by Pierre Joseph Célestin
François, 1802.
(© *Châteaux de Malmaison et Bois-Préau/Droits réservés/RMN*)

Napoleon visiting the Sevene brothers' silk factory in Rouen. Coloured
lithograph by Jean-Baptiste Isabey, 1804.
(*Châteaux de Versailles et de Trianon/The Bridgeman Art Library*)

Napoleon at the Battle of Jena. Oil painting by Horace Vernet, 1836.
(© *Châteaux de Versailles et de Trianon/Droits réservés/RMN*)

*A Rosey Picture of the Times.* Coloured etching by William Emes, 1812.
(© *Hulton-Deutsch Collection/Corbis*)

Napoleon visiting the battlefield of Eylau. Oil painting by Antoine-Jean Gros, 1808. (© *Musée du Louvre, Paris/Daniel Arnaudet/RMN*)

Meeting between Napoleon and Tsar Alexander I of Russia on the Niemen River. Oil painting by Adolphe Roehn, 1807.
(© *Châteaux de Versailles et de Trianon/Gérard Blot/Jean Schormans/RMN*)

The three monarchs: Emperor Francis II of Austria, Tsar Alexander I and King Frederick William III of Prussia. Watercolour by J. G. Mansfeld and Johann Adam Klein, 1816. (*Albertina, Vienna*)

### BETWEEN PAGES 370 AND 371

Manuel de Godoy, duke of Alcudia. Oil painting by Francisco de Goya y Lucientes, 1801. (*Museo de la Real Academia de San Fernando, Madrid/The Bridgeman Art Library*)

Joseph Bonaparte, king of Spain. Oil painting by François Pascal Simon Gérard, *c.*1810. (© *Mairie, Ajaccio/Gérard Blot/RMN*)

Surrender of Baylen. Oil painting by José Casado del Alisal, 1838.
(*Prado, Madrid/The Bridgeman Art Library*)

Interview at Erfurt. Oil painting by Nicolas Gosse, 1838.
(© *Châteaux de Versailles et de Trianon/Gérard Blot/RMN*)

Assault of the monastery of San Engracio, Saragossa. Oil painting by Louis François Lejeune, 1827. (© *Châteaux de Versailles et de Trianon/Daniel Arnaudet/Jean Schormans/RMN*)

Marshal Lannes mortally wounded at the Battle of Essling. Oil painting by Albert-Paul Bourgeois, 1810.
(© *Châteaux de Versailles et de Trianon / Gérard Blot / RMN*)

Marshal Soult at the Battle of Oporto. Oil painting by Joseph Beaume, 1839. (© *Châteaux de Versailles et de Trianon / Daniel Arnaudet / Gérard Blot / RMN*)

*John Lagobe, English Manufacturer: Goddamit, No One Bought My Bales.* Coloured engraving by an unknown English artist, *c.*1808.
(*Graphic Arts Division. Department of Rare Books and Special Collections. Princeton University Library*)

*The Happy Effects of That Grand System of Shutting Ports Against the English.* Hand-coloured etching by George Cruikshank, 1808. LC-USZC4-6235. (*Library of Congress, Prints and Photographs Division*)

*Divorce of the Empress Josephine.* Oil painting by Henri-Frédéric Schopin, 1846. (*By kind permission of the Trustees of The Wallace Collection, London*)

Marriage procession of Napoleon and Marie-Louise in the Tuileries gardens. Oil painting by Etienne-Barthélémy Garnier, 1810. (© *Châteaux de Versailles et de Trianon / Daniel Arnaudet / Hervé Lewandowski / RMN*)

Napoleon presenting the king of Rome to dignitaries of the Empire. Oil painting by Georges Rouget, 1812.
(© *Châteaux de Versailles et de Trianon / Droits reservés / RMN*)

Napoleon hunting in the forest of Compiègne. Oil painting by Carle Vernet, 1811. (*Photograph © The State Hermitage Museum / The State Hermitage Museum, St Petersburg*)

Napoleon with his nephews and nieces at Saint-Cloud. Oil painting by Louis Ducis, 1810.
(© *Châteaux de Versailles et de Trianon / Gérard Blot / RMN*)

Battle of Leipzig. Oil painting by Alexander Ivanovich Sauerweid, *c*.1813. (*State Central Artillery Museum, St Petersburg/ The Bridgeman Art Library*)

Napoleon bidding farewell to the Imperial Guard. Oil painting by Antoine Alphonse Montfort, 1825. (*Châteaux de Versailles et de Trianon, Paris/ Lauros/ Giraudon/ The Bridgeman Art Library*)

*Battle of Waterloo: the Charge of the Second Brigade of Cavalry*. Oil painting by Denis Dighton, *c*.1815.
(*The Royal Collection © 2009, Her Majesty Queen Elizabeth II*)

Return of Louis XVIII to Paris. Watercolour by an unknown French artist, 1815. (*Musée de la Ville de Paris, Musée Carnavalet, Pars/ Lauros/ Giraudon/ The Bridgeman Art Library*)

Congress of Vienna. Sepia wash on paper by Jean Baptiste Isabey, 1815. (*© Musée du Louvre, Paris, D.A.G./ Christian Jean/ RMN*)

*War. The Exile and the Rock Limpet*. Oil painting by Joseph Mallord William Turner, 1842. (*© Tate London, 2009*)

# INTRODUCTION

There is a paradox that lies at the heart of Georges Lefebvre's magisterial biography of Napoleon Bonaparte, published in this fine edition by Folio for the first time as a single volume in English. The author, who held the Chair of the History of the French Revolution at the Sorbonne from 1937 until 1945, was one of the great Marxist intellectuals of the second quarter of the twentieth century; indeed it was he who invented the soubriquet 'History from below'. Yet his two-volume *Napoléon*, first published in 1935–36 and translated into English in 1969, is emphatically of the 'Great Man' school of history so despised by Marxists. It is pure history from above, and accepts that the actions and will of a single extraordinary man could counteract those of the proletarian masses that Lefebvre himself idolised. So how could this be?

Born to relatively poor parents in Lille in August 1874, Georges Lefebvre attended the local *lycée* and only matriculated into the University of Lille by means of a series of scholarships that were early testaments to his burgeoning intellect. He became a teacher after graduating in 1898 and began writing in 1904, but it was not until 1925, when he was over fifty, that he published his doctoral thesis, *Les Paysans du Nord pendant la Révolution Française*. This posited the thesis that it had been the peasantry that ignited, supported and sustained the French Revolution, which he depicted as developing through four distinct phases between the Fall of the Bastille in 1789 and Napoleon's Brumaire *coup* ten years later.

In 1935 – the year of the publication of this life of Napoleon – Lefebvre was honoured by becoming the president of the Société des Études Robespierristes (he admired the 'Sea-Green Incorruptible' for his frugality, integrity and application) and also the director of the *Annales Historiques de la Révolution Française*, home of the *Annales* school that was to dominate French historiography. Two years later he was raised to his professorship at the Sorbonne, which he held until his retirement from active teaching in 1945.

The Marxist interpretation which Lefebvre applied to the French Revolution was fully developed in his book *Quatre-vingt-neuf*, which was published in English as *The Coming of the French Revolution* in time for its 150th anniversary in 1939, but the Second World War intervened before it could become well known in France. Although Lefebvre survived the German Occupation, *Quatre-vingt-neuf* was banned by the Vichy regime, and its initial print run of eight thousand copies was burned. After the war, the two volumes of his history of the Revolution before and after 1793, with their concentration on dialectical materialism as the central explanation for its causes and course, were published in 1951 and 1957. These books, utterly dominant in their day, sought to impose a classical Marxist dialectic on the French Revolution, whereby the monarchy and nobility were initially overthrown by the bourgeoisie and clergy, who were themselves toppled by the workers and peasants, a conceptual framework that has since been comprehensively deposed by successive waves of revisionists. Lefebvre died in Boulogne-Billancourt on the outskirts of Paris on 28 August 1959.

In Pieter Geyl's historiographical masterpiece *Napoleon: For and Against*, published in 1949, the final chapter was devoted to Lefebvre's life of the emperor, which was lauded as 'free from *parti pris*. He has an eye for the positive achievements and above all he can appreciate the greatness of the figure … He writes vividly and to the point and shows himself a man of imagination … The portrait as a whole shows a remarkable tact and a fine balance.' This encomium still stands. Geyl was impressed by the way that although Lefebvre pointed out that Napoleon was indeed bent on world domination,

> The beauty of Lefebvre's book consists in the fact that he is able to present, and continually to recall, this general vision upon Napoleon and his regime, without neglecting the endless multiplicity of facts which determine and modify each particular instance. English imperialism, Austrian reaction, the personal policy of [Tsar] Alexander, none of these is blurred in order to make Napoleon stand out with more sharpness.[*]

Lefebvre criticised Napoleon's hatred of free speech and his willingness to close down newspapers that indulged in it too freely, but this may well have reflected the author's contemporaneous view of Adolf Hitler, who had been Chancellor of Germany for two years by the time of the

[*] Geyl, *Napoleon: For and Against* (London, 1949), pp. 421–2.

publication of *Napoléon*, and who had already closed down newspapers, imprisoned political opponents, withdrawn from the League of Nations and set Europe on the path to war.

Described by Robespierre's biographer Colin Haydon as an 'austere republican',[*] Lefebvre also took Napoleon to task for his lack of trust in the French people, pointing out the paradox in the emperor's attitude towards the general will, and likening it to that of Frederick the Great. 'The fewer obstacles he met, the more jealous and irritable he became,' wrote Lefebvre. 'Like Frederick II, he continually emphasised the personal character of his government. Judging by the constitutions he gave to the realms of Naples and Westphalia, his intention was to eliminate finally the elective principle. However, neither the electorate nor the assembly did anything to hinder him.'

Lefebvre highlighted the Treaty of Lunéville of February 1801 as the moment when the true interests of France began to diverge from those of her First Consul, a date far earlier than most of Napoleon's other biographers. 'Bonaparte had slashed the Gordian knot with a single blow,' he states when summing up the treaty. 'The victory over Austria had done far more than confirm and consolidate the conquest of the natural frontiers ... he clearly indicated that he intended to keep Austria out of Italy altogether ... The pacification of Europe, pursued along these lines, could only result in a temporary truce.' In such strictures against Napoleon's hectoring and bellicose foreign policy it is again hard not to discern contemporaneous criticism of Adolf Hitler.

Yet even that needs to be seen in the context of Lefebvre's equivocating conclusions about Napoleon back in 1935, because when considering whether 'Napoleon's work was doomed to fail', the author wrote: 'It would perhaps be salutary for all would-be Caesars and for the good of the human race if this judgement could be held beyond a doubt. But this cannot for one moment be admitted.' For, Lefebvre argues, Tsar Alexander I's 'will-power might well have failed at Moscow, and the allied army might have been destroyed at [the Battle of] Lützen. The only solid certainty is that the risks were tremendous, and that France, hazarding her all, lost all that the Revolution had conquered in her name.'

Lefebvre sees Napoleon's second tragedy as stemming from the breakdown of the Anglo-French Peace of Amiens in May 1803, and it is hard to disagree with him. Fierce historiographical battles have been fought

[*] Colin Haydon and William Doyle (eds), *Robespierre* (Cambridge, 2006), p. 6.

ever since, not least by Napoleon himself in his memoirs dictated on St Helena, over whether Britain or France was primarily responsible for the second outbreak of war since 1793. Some British historians such as J. Holland Rose believe they could prove without doubt that Napoleon's lust for conquest doomed the Treaty of Amiens, while others – often French – have blamed a bellicose English government with equal vigour and certitude, often using the same archives and documents to support their case.

Lefebvre is probably not far off the truth when he concludes that during the fourteen-months of peace:

> If Bonaparte's provocations are undeniable, nonetheless it is a fact that England broke the treaty and took the initiative to wage preventive war from the moment that she could hope for Russia's collaboration. Britains justification was the preservation of the European balance of power, but this grave concern did not extend to the sea, since in her eyes God had created the oceans for the English. The conflict between Bonaparte and England was in reality a clash between two imperialisms.

British foreign policy had indeed long been one of opposition to any single power dominating the European Continent – and thus the Channel 'invasion' ports – as Philip II of Spain and Louis XIV of France had previously seen, and Kaiser Wilhelm II and Adolf Hitler were to find subsequently. It was a policy of self-preservation as much as imperial expansion, but Lefebvre was right to assume that the two imperialisms could not mutually thrive.

Because Napoleon is extremely hard to pin down in class and nationalist terms, Lefebvre considers him 'something of the uprooted person' who had only become French relatively late, without having identified himself with the traditions and interests of France during his youth. Lefebvre also describes him as 'something of the *déclassé* ... He was neither entirely a gentleman nor entirely common. He served both the king and the Revolution without attaching himself to either.' As well as of course making him all the more interesting a political phenomenon as a result, Lefebvre spotted how this helped Napoleon in placing him above the political parties of his day, so that 'neither in the *ancien régime* nor in the new order did he find principles which might have served as a norm or a limit.' With this extraordinary hybrid human, Lefebvre seems to be arguing, anything was possible, which makes for a biography that is almost as much a personal adventure story as an intellectual treatise.

Where Lefebvre, at least to English eyes, does seem to have had a blind spot is in his overall negative depiction of Napoleon's nemesis, the duke of Wellington, whom he sees merely as a cold martinet without a scintilla of Napoleon's genius. His description of the Iron Duke as coming from 'the aristocratic morgue' is perhaps the dominant one amongst French historians, who on the whole do not ascribe martial glory to the man who nonetheless soundly defeated Napoleon on the only field of battle where the two men met. Lefebvre was perfectly capable of accepting that Wellington 'had a clear and precise mind of a positive cast, with good organising ability', and 'was a man of cool and tenacious will-power, though this did not exclude an ability to take bold and calculated risks', but these qualities were not enough for Lefebvre to consider Wellington a great man, and it is hard not to conclude that this was primarily for class reasons, since Wellington was the son of an Anglo-Irish earl.

'His expression was marked by an aristocratic pride', writes Lefebvre of Wellington,

> hardened still further by his long years among the Indians. He treated his officers with a haughty disdain, and had an unlimited contempt for the common people, and for his own soldiers … At any rate his pride of country bound him closely to his own social caste and to the land in which they were, in his view, the lawful owners, and his only thought was to serve them. With a hard and dry character in which imagination and affection were equally wanting, he was at any rate preserved from the romantic individualism that was the ruin of Napoleon, but his talent lacked the unending fascination exercised by the genius of the emperor.

So much as a glance at Elizabeth Longford's two-volume life of Wellington – still the best biography of him after four decades – shows us that in fact the duke was indeed proud, but also romantic and affectionate, and served far wider interests than merely the narrow ones of the Anglo-Irish Protestant Ascendancy from which he sprang.

Lefebvre's Marxism enters his life of Napoleon, but it never infects it to the detriment of the narrative. Like all enlightened despots,' he wrote,

Napoleon always devoted great attention to economic progress; not, indeed, because it improved the lot of mankind and permitted the common people to share in the fruits of civilisation, but simply for political reasons. He was interested in sound finance, in the growth of population and the consequent fresh supply of recruits to the army, and in 'order', that is, a minimum of idleness and an abundance of commodities.

This is classic Marxist analysis, but coincidentally also the correct one. Although many of the *Annales* school of French historians sought to represent Napoleon as 'a prisoner of the demographic and social structures he encountered', Lefebvre was far less ideologically strait-jacketed, merely stressing, in the words of a recent study, 'Bonaparte's dependence on his inheritance from the bourgeois revolution'.[*] This, too, makes sense. Jules Michelet, whose history of the Revolution was published in 1847, stated that '*l'acteur principal est le peuple*'. He was, along with Jules Guesde and Jean Jaurès, a powerful intellectual influence on Lefebvre, but in *Napoléon* the principal actor was always the emperor. In that sense this is emphatically not a Marxist work.

The love-hate relationship that Lefebvre had with his subject stemmed from the emperor's many fascinating contradictions, summed up in the following lines, which should serve to whet the appetite of any reader for the pages that follow:

A successful soldier, a pupil of the *philosophes*, [Napoleon] detested feudalism, civil inequality and religious intolerance. Seeing in enlightened despotism a reconciliation of authority with political and social reform, he became its last and most illustrious representative. In this sense he was the man of the Revolution. His headstrong individuality never accepted democracy, however, and he rejected the great hope of the eighteenth century which inspired revolutionary idealism – the hope that some day men would be civilised enough to rule themselves.

That Napoleon did not believe in this millennial concept is clear from

[*] Malcolm Crook, 'Time for a Hero?': Reappraising Napoleon on the Bicentenary of his Rise to Power', *History*, vol. 87, no. 288 (2002), p. 544.

Lefebvre's work, but the extent to which that is because Napoleon genuinely thought democracy impossible, or merely recognised that it would hamstring his personal ambitions, is not so clear. Lefebvre presents us with the facts and, like all good historians, stands back to allow us to use them to make up our own minds.

Napoleon himself defined history as 'a myth that men agree to believe', but Lefebvre enjoyed digging below the surface of Napoleonic myth-making, and stayed remarkably free of making value judgements, even in the conclusion of his work. 'The moralist must praise heroism and condemn cruelty,' Lefebvre is quoted as having said, 'but the moralist does not explain events.' That is done by the historian. I believe that Lefebvre refused to inflict his Marxist views on this biography because he was simply too good and too honest a historian. He was also a Frenchman, who could write of how Napoleon's 'springs of action, his unconquerable energy of temperament, arose from the depths of his imagination'.

Lefebvre eschewed imposing a determinist rationale on the life and achievements of Napoleon partly because he saw the absurdity that resulted when Leo Tolstoy had tried to do the same thing in his notorious passage in *War and Peace*, but also because, as he himself admitted, 'Marx clarified the dominant influence of the mode of production, but it was never his intention to exclude other factors, especially Man ... It is Man who makes history.' Of no-one could that be truer than of Napoleon Bonaparte, as this well-written, scholarly and – thanks to the Folio Society – highly attractive volume so conclusively demonstrates.

ANDREW ROBERTS

*May 2009*

# TRANSLATOR'S NOTE[*]

This book is a translation of the first three parts of Georges Lefebvre's history of the Napoleonic era. The original work was published in 1935, and this translation is based on the fifth (1965) edition.

Throughout, my primary object was to fashion a clear and readable English translation. This was not always an easy task. By confining himself to a one-volume history, Lefebvre was forced to compress an enormous quantity of factual material into relatively little space. He was impatient in his attention to narrative detail, often reducing the findings of his massive research efforts to a succession of clipped, laconic statements. This sometimes made it difficult for me to convey a sense of continuity because parts of the historical narrative were insufficiently developed. However, it is only fair to point out that it was not the author's purpose to describe at length that which could readily be found in many another period history. Lefebvre was a historian's historian, and he simply assumed that his readers would possess an easy familiarity with his subject. His demands upon his readers were as severe as his sweeping synthesis and vision of the whole through its variegated parts were magnificent.

In endeavouring to strike a just balance between readability and strict adherence to the original, I felt compelled to take certain minor liberties with the text. Interminably long paragraphs were broken up, and in a few instances the order of sentences was rearranged for the sake of greater clarity. Occasionally a connective was added, when dictated by reasons of sense and style. Christian names of less well known personages were frequently supplied, and obvious errors involving names, dates and quotations were silently corrected. Attempts, although not always successful, were made to reproduce quotations in their original wording whenever they emanated from an English source. Certain foreign terms and expressions were thought better left in the original, whether by virtue of their acceptance into contemporary English usage or because they defied translation into precise English equivalents: *Sturm und Drang, corvée, octrois, receveurs généraux, rescriptions, biens nationaux, amalgame*. In such

[*] To Book One.

cases, explanatory footnotes were provided wherever deemed necessary.

I wish to express my profound gratitude for the invaluable assistance I received from my dear friend Wilson Robert Augustine of York University. For his painstaking scrutiny of the entire manuscript, for the countless hours which he devoted to it and for his many penetrating criticisms and expert suggestions I am indeed deeply indebted. I am also indebted to Professor Leon Smolinski of Boston College for his generous help on passages dealing with fiscal and monetary policy, and to Dr James Friguglietti of Harvard University for his thoughtful letters in which he called my attention to numerous textual errors in the French printings of this work. Finally, I owe a great debt of gratitude to my mother, Rose Ruth Stockhold, without whose constant encouragement and support this translation might never have been completed.

HENRY FREDERIC STOCKHOLD

*New York*
*January 1968*

# FOREWORD

At the time when Napoleon Bonaparte assumed control of France, Europe and the French Revolution had been at war for over seven years, and except for a brief interruption, this conflict was to last until 1815. The 18 Brumaire did not in itself mark the end of an epoch. It might be more logical to say that the period of peace which followed the Treaty of Amiens was the dividing point between two eras. True, when considering the internal history of France, one sees that the *coup d'état* of Brumaire opened the way for the restoration of personal power. In this respect, the contrast between the Napoleonic and revolutionary periods is well defined, but their essential unity cannot be ignored. It was to the Revolution that Bonaparte owed his marvellous destiny. He was able to force himself upon republican France precisely because an internal necessity fated that country to dictatorship as long as the partisans of the *ancien régime* strove to re-establish the monarchy with the help of foreign powers.

In his methods of government, Bonaparte had more in common with the Committee of Public Safety than writers are generally willing to admit. It was because he respected the social legislation of the Constituent Assembly that he was able to remain the leader of France. His military victories assured that the work of the Constituent Assembly would endure and become permanently rooted in French society. More than that, his victories enabled French ideas to sweep over the Continent with a rapidity and an efficacy which neither propaganda nor spontaneous diffusion could have equalled. Had he not implanted the fundamental principles of the modern state and society in all the countries which he dominated, no trace would have ever been left of his lightning campaigns. In vain did he attempt to create a new legitimacy and a new aristocracy. His contemporaries always saw him as the soldier of the Revolution, and it was as such that he made his mark upon European civilisation.

All this notwithstanding, from the moment that Bonaparte became master of France, he was elevated to a place in the very centre of universal history. And so, despite the fundamental unities linking his reign with the tragedy that was the Revolution, the traditional dividing point – his accession – has much to be said for it, and is the one used in this work.

It is hardly necessary to point out that this book is not a biography of Napoleon. An attempt has been made to cast light not only on the essential features of the collective life of the French people and those who were subjugated by the emperor, but also on the operation of forces independent of his will and on the distinguishing characteristics of nations which escaped his domination. England and the United States maintained their liberal tradition; capitalism continued its progress; and the bourgeoisie, growing in strength, was well on its way to assuming complete political power. Religious life followed its course, and Napoleon was unable to modify it. Nations reacted against the universal empire whose foundations he was laying. Above all in Germany, Romanticism fostered new ways of feeling, thinking and acting; and Latin America threw off the Spanish yoke. Even the Far East, in a negative way, experienced repercussions of the great conflict, for it would have been subjected to European assaults much earlier had not the Napoleonic Wars monopolised the energies of Europe. The nineteenth century, so shifting and varied in its character, was visible beneath the apparent uniformity which Napoleon's genius tried to impose. But during the course of this period, otherwise so brief, everything seemed to yield before him. It was he who dominated history. What then could be more natural than that this volume should bear his name?

*Napoleon*

# BOOK ONE

From 18 Brumaire

to Tilsit

1799–1807

# I

# The Legacy
# of the Revolution

# CHAPTER ONE

# The Conflict between the *Ancien Régime*
## and the Revolution

THE PASSAGE OF TEN YEARS, and, above all, war, had profoundly modified the course of the French Revolution. The map of Europe had already undergone a marked change, and the expansion of French territory to the 'natural frontiers' had clearly upset the European equilibrium. Such was the inheritance of Bonaparte, and it weighed heavily on his policies. It will be advisable therefore to describe some of the features of that heritage, even if we disagree with Albert Sorel's contention that Bonaparte was more the creature of his destiny than its maker.

Of these features, the most deep-seated was the conflict which had been going on since 1789 between the Revolution and Europe. Above all, a social conflict existed between the privileged classes and the bourgeoisie, who were supported by the rest of the Third Estate. A political conflict existed also because royal despotism, like privilege, had been condemned, and kings, having taken the aristocracy under their protection, ventured the risk of perishing with it. Finally, there was a religious conflict arising from the common understanding of the Revolution as the offspring of Cartesian rationalism, whose merciless critique had destroyed the mysteries and traditions which were regarded as comprising the foundation of the *ancien régime*. The rivalry of nations, each aspiring to hegemony, blurred these conflicts but did not obliterate them from the consciousness of contemporaries. Unyielding, they dominated the history of the Napoleonic era.

## THE SOCIAL AND POLITICAL CONFLICT

The ebbing of the Revolution had been evident since 9 Thermidor. The Constitution of Year III (1795) had brought to power a bourgeoisie genuinely attached to the new order, yet hostile to democracy, which it did not distinguish from Jacobinism. Along with Madame de Staël and the *Idéologues*, it favoured an oligarchy more modern than that of England but essentially analogous to it – an oligarchy which would strike a balance between the interests of the rich and men of talent. Meanwhile, the bourgeoisie gradually set about destroying the work of the Mountain [extreme revolutionaries], and did not even spare that of the Constituent Assembly. They abolished family courts and courts of arbitration, and reinstated imprisonment for debt and notary fees. The retroactive features of the inheritance laws of Year II disappeared, and the rights granted to bastards were fiercely attacked. The sale of the *biens nationaux** no longer benefited anyone but the rich, and in Year VII those who held mortgaged *biens nationaux* were gratuitously given an unencumbered title. The division of communal lands was suspended, and attempts were once again made to drive the peasants from the forests, which they had used freely since 1789.

But what basic significance did all this have for the European nobility? Strive as the Revolution might for bourgeois ideals, it nevertheless remained a revolution for civil equality. Wherever its armies had penetrated – Belgium, the Rhineland, Holland, Switzerland – the Revolution had undertaken the destruction of the *ancien régime*. The pope was a prisoner; the prince of Orange, the Rhenish electors and the Swiss patricians were in flight. Suvorov's victories alone had reconquered Italy and had restored its legitimate princes. The states neighbouring France were being secretly permeated with subversive propaganda and the news of the liberation of French peasants and the victories of the Sansculottes was spoken of everywhere. Less effective were the efforts of writers and journalists, most of whom had been either disillusioned by the excesses of the Terror or else forced to be silent. One could point to men everywhere who wished to make a compact with the French, as, for example, in South Germany. Even in Prussia the refusal to perform *corvée* and to pay feudal dues became more frequent. It was rumoured that the king would abolish these exactions, and Frederick William III was besieged with petitions on his accession. Across the sea, Antonio Nariño had translated the Declaration of the Rights of Man, and in the United States, Washington's party suspected Jefferson and the Republicans of having been contaminated by the egalitarian mania.

* Literally, national property. The property confiscated by the state from the clergy, nobility and others during the Revolution. TRANSLATOR.

Everywhere, even among the great Whig families, the aristocracy was frightened and rallied around the throne; everywhere, governments tightened their controls. Except for Russia, stooped under the atrocious despotism of Paul I, the prize went to Austria, where henceforth Colloredo became the living spirit of an obscurantist police state for which Metternich later claimed credit. In Prussia, Wöllner, who up until the death of Frederick William II had attempted to install the same system, had only recently been dismissed. At Jena, Fichte, accused of atheism and abandoned by the duke of Weimar, had been forced to surrender his chair in 1799. In England, habeas corpus had been suspended since 1794, and 'seditious' associations and publications had been prohibited. In 1799 Pitt made printers profess their allegiance, and he had members of illegal societies sent to penal colonies for seven years. In America, the Federalists, profiting by their rupture with the Directory, voted an Alien Bill aimed at French democrats, and a Sedition Act to deal with associations and newspapers. In Latin America, the cause of liberty already had its martyrs. While not entirely groundless, the fears inspired by 'Jacobins' were exaggerated. The rare admirers of France, like Kant, Fichte and the youthful Hegel, who set out to criticise the Bernese patriciate and the oligarchy of Württemberg, took great care to stipulate that they placed their faith solely in legal and peaceful progress. No nation imitated France spontaneously; rather, it was her armies that spread the principles of the Revolution.

Lively though the reaction was, it could not be said to have condemned all reform. Enlightened despotism had shown that some reforms were reconcilable with absolute monarchy and an aristocratic society. Recognising that not all of the work of the Constituent Assembly was contemptible, governments of the *ancien régime* envied France for its administrative unity and for its suppression of fiscal privilege. The example of England further demonstrated to the agricultural countries of the Continent the advantages of enclosure and the drawbacks of serfdom. Nevertheless, it was only in Germany, notably in Bavaria and Prussia, that reforms were undertaken which would permit Western influences to combine with national traditions.

The *Aufklärung* [German Enlightenment], while it had lost its prestige among the *literati*, had nonetheless schooled the bourgeoisie and officialdom. Count Montgelas, who had recently come to power in Bavaria, was one of its disciples. In Berlin, the Austrian ambassador bitterly remarked that the Prussian bureaucracy criticised the enemies of France for wanting to 'banish from the earth the rule of reason', to which Prussia owed her greatness. The Prussian higher civil service, which was organised into colleges and recruited by co-optation, maintained a strong *esprit de corps*. It had watched with displeasure the ceaseless royal extension of cabinet power, whereby everything was decided by the king and his *camarilla*; such personal administration of Silesia and the Polish provinces by crown and non-ministerial advisers ('cabinet') had incurred disastrous results in the reign of Frederick William II. These lofty civil servants would have willingly subjected their king to the rule of law, and Wilhelm Carmer, who finished drafting Frederick's law code in 1794, included provisions for personal liberty, permanence of tenure for judges and religious toleration. They also realised that the Frederician state, with its peasant serfdom, its provinces jealous of their particular institutions and divided from each other by customs barriers, each considering itself autonomous, did not form a single nation. Finally, like all coastal Baltic states, Prussia had been for a quarter-century a major exporter of grains and textiles, and enlightened individuals took notice of the introduction into Denmark of English agricultural methods by Albert Thaer, the Saxon agronomist. The Prussian civil servants were equally interested in the economic liberalism of Adam Smith, which was taught in Hamburg by Johann Büsch, in Vienna by Watteroth, and notably in Königsberg by Christian Kraus, who exerted a great influence on two eminent administrators of the monarchy, Schön and Schrötter. The people most inclined to accept new ideas, however, were officials whom Prussia had drawn from Western Germany or abroad: the Franconian Karl Altenstein; the Hanoverian Karl von Hardenberg, who governed Ansbach and Bayreuth; Johann Struensee, who came from Denmark; and most important of all, Heinrich Baron von und zum Stein, a scion of the Rhenish *Ritterschaft* [Imperial Knights], who before taking office in 1804 had administered the provinces of Cleves and Mark where the 'Prussian system' had never been introduced.

Nor was this all. Contrary to certain historical accounts, Stein and other statesmen examined the French experience closely and concluded from it that the government could increase its power and prestige by giving the nation some voice in questions of law, taxation and administration. Nevertheless, since they defined the 'nation' as the nobility and rich bourgeoisie, it was on England that they concentrated their attention.

Under Pitt's guidance that nation appeared to have reconciled royal prerogative with constitutional law, party rivalry with the maintenance of order and stability, aristocratic supremacy with bourgeois ambition, and the interests of the nobility with those of the whole commonwealth. Pitt humoured the lords, whose 'pocket' and 'rotten' boroughs assured him a parliamentary majority, but he did not share their prejudices. Among the ninety-five peers he appointed were a number of 'new men', captains of banking and commerce who rejuvenated the aristocracy and helped it to remain rich and able. Thanks to Burke, this miracle of balance and wisdom had won the adherence of numerous enemies of the Revolution, particularly those of middle-class and Protestant origin, like Mallet du Pan and François d'Ivernois. There were admirers of England even among the French émigrés. German anglophilia naturally abounded in the Hanseatic towns, and in Hanover it flourished at the University of Göttingen. August Rehberg and Heinrich Brandes acquainted Stein with English ideas, and he used them in his own political thought. One can find evidence of them in the individualistic teachings of Wilhelm von Humboldt, who would have left the state with only police and military power, abandoning the other spheres of government, as in England, to the spontaneous organisation of society. This, he believed, would have served to subject the social order to the patronage of the aristocracy.

The great majority of the privileged classes abhorred these bureaucratic reformers as much as they did the 'Jacobins'. In the face of their protests, sovereigns faltered or fell back. Pitt himself was an example. Without repudiating his early projects, he deferred them until a later time. In Austria, the agrarian reforms of Joseph II had been suspended by Leopold II, and in 1798 his successor Francis II ended by retaining the feudal dues and the corvées. In his Livonian provinces, Paul I contented himself with wresting certain mitigations of serfdom from the Diet, and his commissioner in the Danubian principalities, Paul Kiselev, went no further. In Prussia, the Junkers had already imposed a revision of Frederick's code upon Frederick William II, and Frederick William III soon renounced his plan to suppress fiscal privileges, a reform which he had contemplated in 1798. True, he resolutely continued to liberate peasants and reform the agrarian economy in his vast personal domains, but he did not dare extend these enterprises to the seigneurial *Gut*. The Prussian nobility retained its monopoly of high positions and ranks. In 1800 there were only 695 commoners out of six or seven thousand officers. Stein himself was unable to effect more than technical reforms in finance, and he failed to abolish the internal customs barriers.

Thus the reformers outside France were almost as ineffectual as the Jacobins. It was the ruling hand of Napoleon, or the rude impact of his armies, that would rejuvenate the Old World. And France had never ceased to be the *bête noire* of European monarchies and aristocracies. 'I am not, nor can I ever be, sympathetic to the French,' wrote Maria Carolina of Naples; 'I shall always regard them as the assassins of my sister and of the royal family, and as the oppressors of every monarchy.' Stolberg called them the 'Western Huns', and Nelson, although he was not born noble, contemptuously referred to them as the 'French villains'. The conservatism of the Consulate and Empire never succeeded in appeasing them except superficially.

The anti-French Coalitions have been traditionally explained in terms of national interests, and the entire drama has been reduced to the question of the balance of power, or, as Pitt said, of security. This conclusion is not unreasonable since ill will towards the French never once prevented sovereigns from dealing with France when they found it expedient; but for all that, they did not cast off their inflexible enmity, and their entourages persisted in proclaiming their hatred of France. This is an incalculable factor which cannot be disregarded. Only in order to conciliate the Whigs did the Tories publicly deny the intention of imposing on France a government of their own choice. Lord Grenville was revealing his real feelings when on 22 December 1795 he included amnesty for émigrés and the restitution of their estates among the numerous conditions of the peace. In January 1800 he added the restoration of the monarchy. This noble lord was revolted by the necessity of negotiating with republicans, whom he could not even regard as gentlemen. Nor would Pitt rejoice at having to stomach the man of whom he would speak on 3 February 1800 as 'this last adventurer in the lottery of revolutions'.

## THE CONFLICT OF IDEAS

Political and social reaction naturally found their reflection in the world of thought. Authority and tradition once again came into fashion, and an increasing number of writers and publicists passionately applauded its return. Some were motivated by conviction, others by self-interest – for governments recognised the value of propaganda and appropriated money for that purpose. Important among the voices of reaction were French and Genevan émigrés like Rivarol and Abbé Barruel, François d'Ivernois and Mallet du Pan. In England, Canning joined the list with the publication of his periodical *The Anti-Jacobin*. Usually, events in France were exploited in order to terrify the population. Abbé Barruel resumed Hoffmann's charges against the *Illuminati* and Freemasons with never-failing success. But certain writers made it a point of honour to raise the level of the debate by offering a new defence of traditional thought in opposition to the rationalist critique.

There was nothing original in this, for during the course of the eighteenth century, English empiricism, having become conservative with Hume and even more so with Bentham, had aspired to restore authority and moral conventions. It was argued that just as reason was able to govern the physical world by searching for natural law and conforming to it, so reason could observe social life and discover that traditional institutions, by virtue of their prolonged existence, were in harmony with the 'nature of things'. In Burke, this pragmatism had been complicated by the addition of a social vitalism borrowed from medical science, such as had been taught in eighteenth-century France at the school of Montpellier and by Marie-François Bichat during the period of the Directory. Man was thought to be the fruit of a spontaneous and progressive germination caused by an irrational force called life. Similarly, Burke spoke of society as a plant or animal, the individual being only one of its organs, so that social authority was imposed on him as a condition of his existence which he could no more repudiate than his physical needs. This experimental rationalism, mingled with a mysticism which gave it some affinity to Romanticism, passed from England to Germany, where it made a strong impression on Rehberg and Brandes. It has been said that Friedrich von Gentz, who translated Burke's *Reflections* as early as 1793, and even Metternich derived their political philosophy from this school of thought.

Very close to these ideas were two French political philosophers, Louis de Bonald and Joseph de Maistre. In 1796 there appeared the simultaneous publication of the former's *Théorie du pouvoir politique et religieux* and the latter's *Considérations sur la France*. They too subordinated the individual to society, and Bonald frequently referred to the nature of things, but they substituted the working of Providence in place of the vital life source. According to the autocratic and authoritarian

Bonald, who cherished the royalist tradition as much as he did Catholicism, the structure that God had set for society remained immutable. For Joseph de Maistre, who had a sense of history and who, as a good Ultramontanist, was somewhat indifferent to forms of temporal government, the Creator limited himself to preserving society by infinitely wise and flexible means. Thus man had to bow before the facts.

On occasion, even political economy was not above attacking lofty reason. Observing the England of his time, Malthus in 1798 maintained that the notion of unlimited human progress was but a chimera, because in spite of technological efforts, population tended to increase much faster than the means of subsistence. Thus every social improvement which helped to increase the species merely resulted in aggravating the evil; it was disease, 'vice', famine and war which redressed the balance. Yet Malthus, who was fundamentally liberal, found an escape by advising that the poor resign themselves to chastity. The traditionalist thinkers, however, were unanimously convinced that he had struck a fatal blow at the hopes of Condorcet and Godwin.

Having identified the Revolution with rationalism, the traditionalists did not delay in turning against it the most dreaded enemy that rationalism had ever encountered, namely the movement inimical to the primacy of reason. This movement, which had inspired Rousseau and the *Sturm und Drang*, was in the process of flowering, towards the closing years of the century, into what is usually called the first German Romanticism. Cartesian rationalism had promised that intellect would be able to solve the riddle of the universe, and it commanded that reason defend its freedom against instinct and feeling, which were under the sway of matter operating atomically and mechanically. It was a philosophy of endeavour in which science and happiness were the rewards. But there are always mystics waiting to experience the mystery of an inspiration which is pure grace; there are always unruly spirits hoping that chance may bring them happiness, or taking pleasure in risk itself; and there are always artists with an inclination for imagination and fantasy. The wheel of time now brought forward a new generation in quest of something original in order to win its place in the sun. So it rehabilitated the emotions and outlined a metaphysics that endowed emotion with the ability to attain the absolute through intuition while denying reason such access. There were philosophers who were entirely of the same opinion. Kant, in particular, destroyed the Cartesian metaphysic, after which he constructed another by predicating the existence of an ethical sense, which was divine intuition in essence.

Mysticism, which had never been stifled by rationalism, enjoyed an extraordinary vogue at the end of the century. It achieved popularity through the occultism of Swedenborg, de Pasqualis and Saint-Martin, and began to seep into Freemasonry and Illuminism, since it claimed to rest on scientific theories and discoveries. From medicine it, too, borrowed vitalism, and from physics it borrowed magnetism, which was also considered to be an irrational force. Mesmer's tub, like somnambulism, brought the mind to a state of entranced unconsciousness, at which point it made contact with the supernatural world. Even Catholicism was unable to protect so loyal a son as Joseph de Maistre from its seductive lure.

Nevertheless, the depth of any such movement is not readily evident if its ideology alone is considered and if no allowance is made for the temperament and social condition of its adherents. For the most part, these mystics were either unable to adapt themselves to the social milieu or had not yet succeeded in doing so. They included the sick, or unstable, whose helplessness doomed them to melancholy and even to suicide; the young, thirsting for independence and pleasure and incensed by social restrictions; and yet others who were trying to make their way in the world and who collided with the privileges of rank, fortune or established reputations. It is not surprising that these people tended to idealise the Robin Hood figure, the righter-of-wrongs, nor that with age or success many of them became wiser. There have always been 'romantics', but the eighteenth century witnessed their proliferation because the rise of the bourgeoisie dislocated social groupings and a growing number of talented but poor young men became irritated and desperate.

Literature and art more or less capitulated to the anti-rationalist reaction. In the name of reason, the French imposed tyrannical aesthetic rules which greatly restricted opportunities for originality. French works became models everywhere, and critics, especially in Germany, had every opportunity to denounce this 'classic' art as a foreign importation. In this domain, the successes of undisciplined individualism far outweighed risks, while actually promising renown. Originality was sought everywhere – in nature, in little-known islands, in the Orient, China, America and in the works of the forgotten past. The English and Scots ecstatically welcomed the spurious poems of Ossian, and the French invented the troubadour style. Shakespeare was used to justify all the attacks on the three unities of time, place and action in French classic drama, as well as the attacks on the distinction of literary genres. Even Hellenism, which was just being discovered, was invoked in order to repudiate seventeenth-century tastes.

The plastic arts, less flexible, did not enjoy the same degree of emancipation. The end of the century again witnessed the triumph of the classic spirit, which sought its sources in antiquity and in the Italian Renaissance. It was owing to the genius of David and Canova that this triumph was possible. On the other hand, the new spirit was given a powerful stimulus by the development of instrumental music, a modern art form which created its own rules, and which was pre-eminently Romantic in that it suggested rather than described, and was essentially sensual and emotional in its appeal.

In many ways it seemed that the revolutionary upheaval ought to favour this new spirit. The Revolution had emancipated the individual, declared war on all traditions, proclaimed freedom of the press and theatre, and suppressed the privileged groups whose task it had been to assure the maintenance of classical disciplines. It had inflamed human passions, and its numerous and terrible vicissitudes affected a good many people who were to develop a morbid taste for the unstable and the horrible – as the success of Ann Radcliffe's novels aptly demonstrated. Finally, it revived a sense of tragedy arising from the spectacle of so many misfortunes and of man's struggle against the implacable forces of nature and fate. Nevertheless, the effects of the movement were not everywhere the same.

For the time being, southern Europe was scarcely affected; even in France and England Romanticism had not made much headway. Despite William Cowper and the Lake Poets, it was the classicism of William Hayley which set the fashion in England around 1800, while George Crabbe remained faithful to a discreet and restrained realism. In France, the revolutionary fever had inspired the writing of speeches and hymns, but it had revitalised neither the theatre, poetry nor the novel. The most likely explanation is a political and social one. In both countries young men found spheres of action other than the realm of thought and the arts. In England, they were attracted to business and politics, and the struggle against France gradually reinforced the trend towards conformity. Wordsworth, Coleridge and Southey finally gave in under the pressure of the social ostracism inflicted on them. In France, youth either entered the service of the Revolution or emigrated. Until 1815 war captivated their imagination and their craving for fame and fortune. Napoleon himself was a Romantic poet who became a man of action, and it was not for lack of trying that Chateaubriand did not undergo the same metamorphosis.

Things were different in Germany, still imprisoned within its medieval casing. The enthusiastic and impulsive Friedrich Schlegel was a kind of Vergniaud who would have nothing to do with revolution, and even the war did not attract him. German patriotism, which was not yet political, was the affair of princes and nobles. Germany's two outstanding poets, Goethe and Schiller, settled down after a hectic youth: the former became minister to Charles Augustus of Weimar, and the latter, professor at Jena. They claimed by studying Greek antiquity to have discovered how man's divergent inclinations could be brought to harmony in the realm of art – the *élan vital* and passion reconciled with reason. Their new humanism summoned the individual to isolate himself in order to develop his own 'totality'. It approached a pantheistic position in philosophy and exercised a keen attraction for a while. Works like *Wilhelm Meister* (1794–6), the *Wallenstein* trilogy (1798–9) and 'The Song of the Bell' (1799) enchanted the reading public. Wilhelm von Humboldt joined the classical movement, and Friedrich Hölderlin was no stranger to it.

Nevertheless, the attraction was short-lived, and quite naturally so, for in no other country was mysticism so powerful. It stood at the very core of Lutheranism, and through Pietism and the Moravian Brotherhood one could trace the connection between Jacob Böhme, the shoemaker and theosophist of the seventeenth century, and the Romantics. Böhme had been read by scholars like Abraham Werner, Karl Ritter and Franz Baader, who in turn imparted the most unexpected symbolic interpretations to their own positive understanding of his works. After Kant, intuitionism had continued to occupy an ever-increasing place in German philosophy, and had finally brought that philosophy to a position of transcendental idealism. In his *Theory of Science* (*Grundlage der Gesammten Wissenschaftslehre*) which appeared in 1794, Fichte had, in a spiritual insight, seized upon *ego* as the unique reality, which manifests itself in pure activity. He then erected *non-ego* in order to provide *ego* with a motive for seeking to absorb *non-ego*. Later, Schelling endowed *non-ego* with an independent, albeit purely idealistic, existence. He believed that nature and *ego* were but two aspects of the absolute, whose unconscious unity was disassociated by reflection, but which artistic genius could grasp through intuition, and to which it could give expression in its works. Finally, music flourished in Germany as never before. The art of Haydn, who was then producing his greatest works, *The Seasons* and *The Creation*, still breathed the radiant and confident optimism of the eighteenth century. On the other hand, the tragic spirit of Beethoven was already stirring in some of his first sonatas.

The century had not yet come to a close when a group of men, separating themselves from Goethe, and still more from Schiller, took as their banner the words *Romantic* and *Romanticism*, and thereby derived their success. In 1798 Friedrich Schlegel, together with his brother August, launched a review in Berlin called *The Athenaeum*. It lasted three years. In Dresden in 1798, then in Jena (where August taught) in 1799, they met with Novalis (whose real name was Baron von Hardenberg), Schelling and Tieck. Tieck had just published *The Outpourings of a Lay Brother Friend of the Arts (Herzensergiessungen eines Kunstliebenden Klosterbruders)*, which had been left to him by his friend Wilhelm Wackenroder, who had died while still young. Together they outlined a philosophy which Friedrich Schlegel incorporated into his literature course in 1804, but which never took a systematic and coherent form. Inasmuch as they were disciples of the classics, they at first conceived of the world as an inexhaustible flux, continually changing the creations of the life force. Under the influence of Schelling and other savants, they introduced into their philosophy the concept of a 'universal sympathy', which manifested itself, for example, in chemical affinities, magnetism and human love. Having been moved by the religious effusions of Schleiermacher, they later borrowed from Böhme the idea of a *Centrum*, which was the soul of the world and the divine principle. In any event, it was only the artist of genius who had access to the true reality, through his powers of intuition or even by means of dreams and magic. In him, this mysterious experience transmuted itself into a work of art. This was a philosophy of miracles in which the poet was high priest. Unfortunately, it cannot be said that the miracle was ever really accomplished, since these Romanticists left no great works, the best being those of Novalis, chiefly his *Hymns to the Night* (1798–9).

They did, however, sow some fertile ideas. A major role was played by August Schlegel's lectures, given in Berlin between 1801 and 1804, in which he defined Romanticism and proclaimed art the highest form of expression in the life of a nation – the very symbol of its spirit. Schlegel taught history a valuable lesson: that beauty knows no universal, and that art must be studied and appreciated primarily in relation to the circumstances under which it is created. Nations, for their part, deduced the corollary that nothing is more valuable to the process of attaining complete national self-consciousness than the study of the monuments of their past. It was through the Romantic movement that Germany, already on the threshold of a political and social revival, became, in addition, one of the centres of European thought. Its effects on France came at a later time, but its influence in England was immediate. Coleridge, who had already discovered the virtues of intuition, came into contact with the philosophy of Romanticism while travelling in Germany and embraced it wholeheartedly.

Romanticism in itself was not a political doctrine, but since it relied on sentiment in politics as in every other area, its adherents were left without clear principles to follow. With reaction triumphing, and the careers of the Romanticists still ahead of them, they were not long in becoming ardent counter-revolutionaries. Moreover, looking into the past, they discovered the Holy Roman Empire and the papacy, as well as the moving quality of Catholic liturgy and music. As early as 1799 Novalis extolled Christian unity, which had done so much credit to the Middle Ages, and composed a hymn to the Virgin. He himself remained Protestant, but since Austria had many posts to fill, and offered a sterner resistance to Napoleon, many of Novalis's friends entered Austrian service and were converted to Catholicism.

However interesting these ideas may be, their influence on public opinion must not be exaggerated. The majority of those who abhorred the Revolution were not inspired by philosophical motives, and if they felt any such need, they looked for it in religion. The closing years of the eighteenth century witnessed a religious renaissance which conservative pragmatism and sentimental intuitionism favoured, but which had its own origins. Aristocracy, just as it had rallied to the side of monarchy, increased its solidarity with state churches and concurred in the opinion that the first of the Jacobins had been none other than the Devil himself. Besides, great catastrophes and protracted wars have always brought the restless and frightened masses back to the altar.

The revival of religion filled a pressing need of Catholicism, which had been the principal victim of disaffection. Both France and the countries she occupied were no more than 'mission lands'. In Germany a new disaster was imminent: the treaties of Basle and Campoformio presaged a general policy of secularisation, and Protestants, even counter-revolutionaries, enthusiastically envisaged 'driving the black army from the Rhine'. In addition, enlightened despotism maintained its tutelage. In Germany and Austria, it was the state which trained the clergy in its universities and regarded the *curé* as an instructor rather than a priest. In Spain, Godoy's successors, Francisco de Saavedra and Mariano Luis de Urquijo, had been posing as *philosophes* ever since 1798; in 1799 appeals to the papal court in Rome were forbidden, and there was some thought of seizing ecclesiastical properties in order to procure money. Pius VI had just died a prisoner of the Directory, and Austria scarcely concealed her eagerness to divide the temporal domain of the Holy See with the kingdom of Naples. Yet contrary to the expectations of her enemies, the misfortunes of the Church turned to her advantage, for they brought her sympathy. England welcomed with open arms the deported French priests, who were to sow the first seeds of an English Catholic renaissance. Then, too, in order to conciliate the Irish, Burke had never stopped urging that they be granted religious liberty. In Münster, a small zealous group gathered around Franz Fürstenberg and Bernhard Overberg. It was called the 'Holy Family', and in it, such personalities as Princess Galitsin and the marquise de Montagu (sister of Madame de Lafayette) occupied a shining place. For them, Stolberg's conversion in 1800 portended much. Emperor Paul I of Russia also inspired great hopes. He had been persuaded by Joseph de Maistre and Father Gruber to insist on the re-establishment of the Jesuits, and he had taken under his protection the Order of Malta, to which he was elected grand master.

Protestantism, which until then scarcely had been touched by the Revolution, derived nothing but benefit from the religious renaissance. In Germany, Schleiermacher revitalised its mystical fervour in his *Reden über die Religion*, which appeared in 1799, while Wilhelm Wackenroder and the Romanticists were finding their way back to religion by way of aesthetic intuition. At Emkendorf in Holstein, Fritz von Reventlow was the guiding spirit of a circle of piety which was the counterpart to Münster's 'Holy Family'. Stolberg stayed there before his conversion, and even Portalis, a Catholic and future minister of cults after the Concordat, was associated with the group. In England, Wesley, who died in 1791, had brought Methodism closer to the Church of England by creating, alongside the lay preachers, a hierarchy which co-opted its members. In 1797

this resulted in the first schism within Methodism, but the sect nevertheless continued to grow by encouraging mysticism among the masses.
Methodism exercised a profound influence over the Dissenters. The Baptists advanced by copying Methodist ways, while the Socinian and rationalist Presbyterianism of Priestley and Price were rapidly disappearing.
Even in the Anglican Church there formed a small core of evangelicals
who tried, although unsuccessfully, to revitalise the Church, the most
notable of them being Wilberforce. The Dissenters now abandoned their
sympathies for the Revolution, and even if their conservative influence
over the masses has been exaggerated, it still appears to be indisputable.

France seemed to remain the bastion of rationalism in the world, at least
in the critical sense, hostile to tradition and Christianity as in the eighteenth century. Its spokesmen – Destutt de Tracy, Cabanis, Daunou, Volney – were entrenched in the Institut and in the great establishments of
higher learning, which had been founded by the Convention. They controlled the *Décade Philosophique* through Ginguené, and their disciples
taught in the *écoles centrales*, which had been organised in almost all of the
départements. Rationalism, however, was undergoing changes. Most of the
few remaining materialists among the *Idéologues* were no longer concerned
with metaphysics. Influenced by the sciences, they limited themselves to
the study of phenomena, and leaned towards experimental positivism.

The sciences were flourishing in France because the Revolution had
given them a prominent place in public education. Destutt de Tracy and
Cabanis intended to formulate a science of the mind, a psychology
detached from metaphysics but linked to physiology. Political economy,
under Germain Garnier and J.-B. Say, laid a less well-founded claim to
the dignity of an experimental science. It was a movement fertile in ideas,
but did not make great strides until much later. Moreover, this positivism, reflecting as it did the spirit of the Encyclopaedists, differed
greatly from English empiricism. It appears again in Laplace's *Système du
Monde*, in Lamarck's attack on vitalism and in Charles Dupuis's *Origine
de tous les cultes*. Although the government and the republican bourgeoisie tried to become socially conservative, they in no way lessened
their hostility to Christianity. Among the masses, religious habits were
certainly very much weakened, for Ercole Consalvi would write at the
time of the Concordat that 'the majority of the people are indifferent'.

It should not be forgotten, however, that the philosophy of rationalism
in the eighteenth century, far from being embraced by all Frenchmen,

had been attacked by numerous writers generally lacking in talent but not in readers. Instead of abandoning their convictions in the revolutionary turmoil, the champions of tradition had become firmer in their beliefs. Their ranks were swelled by a part of the old bourgeoisie, which had been ruined by the inflation and so had developed an aversion for new ideas.

Nor was France spared from mystical and sentimental doctrines of intuition. Occultism had collected its faithful there, and began to flourish around 1800, notably in Lyon with Jean Willermoz and in Alsace where Jean Frédéric Oberlin combined it with German influences. It was in France, in fact, that Romanticism found its most illustrious and by far most influential protagonist, for Rousseau's spell had never lost its force. On the contrary, those who repudiated his political theories were precisely the ones most eager to grant sentiment a leading place in literature and religion, Chateaubriand being a celebrated example. Finally, like everywhere else, some Frenchmen returned to Catholicism, whether from feeling, like Joseph Joubert; from conservative convictions, like Louis de Fontanes; or simply to find comfort, like Bancal des Issarts, the friend of Madame Roland. When at a later time Bonaparte did an about-face, these men would provide him with support for concluding the Concordat, in spite of the opposition of those who had brought him to power, and against the will of his own army.

If rationalism had thus reached its limits, the cause is not to be found in counter-revolutionary pragmatism, since the works of Bonald and de Maistre, appearing abroad, had not made any inroads in France. The same was true of German thought. Romanticism in France had no philosophy; it had not even supplanted classicism in art. Literature of the North was read only to discover themes to exploit, or for its picturesque elements, or for its emotional content. The current fashion was Ossian, who had been translated into French by Marie-Joseph Chénier, and from whom Antoine Arnault had drawn his *Oscar* and *Chants galliques*. Bonaparte, too, became infatuated with Ossian. But in 1800 Madame de Staël for the first time contrasted the literature of the North with that of the South, and advised French classicists to borrow from the former its mood of melancholy and sadness. The better part of the French public continued to be indifferent to the conflict between philosophical rationalism and tradition, and surely nothing can better account for Bonaparte's success. The new bourgeoisie of *nouveaux riches*, who had risen to wealth through the sale of the *biens nationaux*, speculation and government contracts, and who were totally ignorant, cared but little for what Beugnot called 'the sickness of principles'. In this respect, former nobles in the government, like Barras and Talleyrand, who were avowed embezzlers and experts in the art of treachery, displayed a cynical disdain. The high society that haunted the fashionable salons – those of Mesdames Tallien, Hamelin or Récamier – thought only of pleasure. More serious still was the fact that the younger generation, which had grown up in the midst of turmoil, was poorly informed and did not trouble itself about it. The members of this generation were realists, and dreamed only of making their careers. The military provided the path to success, and courage was a sufficient qualification. But even if these realists gave Bonaparte a free hand, as long as he was victorious, they by no means wished for a return to the *ancien régime*. Indifferent to ideas, they accepted the achievements of the Revolution as a *fait accompli*, at least to the extent that they profited from it. Thus the majority of the nation remained loyal to the work of the Revolution, and the gulf between France and Europe continued to exist.

## THE AWAKENING OF NATIONALITIES

There was a universal quality in the conflict between the Revolution and the *ancien régime*. It was a war of class against class, and at first national sentiments did not appear to have been brought into play. Such feelings, moreover, were not considered important in the eighteenth century. Monarchs and the diverse elements of the aristocracy formed a cosmopolitan society of rulers who parcelled out peoples among themselves like flocks, without regard for their national origins. There existed states, but no nations. Although the enlightened bourgeoisie was well aware that the human race admitted of variety, fundamentally they envisaged it as one, capable of attaining a common civilisation; and although rationalism had secularised the concept of Christendom, it had also perpetuated it. The Revolution once begun, Louis XVI made an appeal to the solidarity of all monarchs, and the émigrés made an appeal to all aristocracies. This call was not made in vain. Ever since 1790 Burke had advocated a crusade, and so did François d'Ivernois around 1800. By the same token, all men were brothers to the revolutionaries, and all tyrants were their enemies. Until 1815 the struggle retained something of this quality. France maintained friends abroad up to the very end, while at home, irreconcilable enemies remained.

Having called upon men to govern themselves, the Revolution, according to the same canon, summoned nations into being. Partisans of the Revolution proudly styled themselves 'patriots', and to them France was 'the nation'. At first, however, they believed that all would welcome France's gospel, and that in this way civilisation would preserve its universal character. Steeped as they were in the belief that tyrants alone made wars and that democracy would bring peace and brotherhood to all people, it never occurred to them that nations might become enemies. Conversely, monarchs and aristocracies were hostile to the national idea, because it seemed to be tied to principles of popular sovereignty and civil equality – *Nation, das klingt jacobinisch* ('Nation, that sounds Jacobin'). In the Low Countries, the nobility and the clergy preferred to fall back under the yoke of Austria rather than lose their privileges. Similar fears weakened the national cause in Poland. In Hungary, the magnates remained faithful to the Habsburgs, even allowing themselves to be partly Germanised once they were allowed a free hand over the peasantry. As for monarchs, they continued to pursue their own anti-national interests. They succeeded in partitioning Poland. The Hungarian Diet in vain asked for concessions from Vienna: Magyar as the official language, customs advantages and access to the sea through the annexation of Dalmatia or Fiume [Rijeka]. But despite the recommendations of the regent, Archduke Joseph, Emperor Francis II turned a deaf ear to these demands. In Ireland, the insurrection of 1798 persuaded Pitt to end what remained of her independence, and the government and parliament in Dublin were suppressed. One hundred Irish members and thirty-two Irish Lords were henceforth to sit in Westminster. The island kept its debt and its domestic taxes, but was to contribute two-seventeenths of the imperial expenditures. It was given reason to hope for the opening of the English market. Above all, Pitt, with the support of the lord-lieutenant, Cornwallis, and the first secretary, Robert Stewart, Viscount Castlereagh, disclosed his intention of repealing the Test Act, which prohibited Catholics from sitting in Parliament. He even hinted at the possibility of 'establishing' the Catholic Church in Ireland, provided the government had the right to supervise the choice of bishops – to which ten bishops concurred. This alone sufficed to turn a number of Irish Protestants against the union, men who had at first rallied to the project out of fear. Pitt was forced to resort to bribery by distributing peerages and large sums of money which were, moreover, charged to the Irish debt. Union was finally voted in Dublin on 5 February 1800, and ratified in London in May.

It was the war which gradually brought about a change from cosmopolitanism to nationalism. Attacked on all sides, the French were the first to develop a sense of their own uniqueness. They scorned those who would remain enslaved, and prided themselves on being *La Grande Nation*. The Republic, when it turned to conquest, exploited these feelings by appealing to pride and self-interest. But thus severed from their revolutionary idealism, such sentiments lost some of their purity. From the very beginning, Bonaparte favoured this development, which so greatly contributed to his ascendancy.

England, too, finally caught the national fever from warring with France. At first, the remnants of the Whig Party under the leadership of Fox had ranged themselves on the side of popular sentiment, and had regarded the war as the affair of Pitt and the Tories. But when France made preparations for a descent on Ireland, and when she conquered Egypt, feelings began to change. The invasion of Switzerland converted Coleridge who, in 'France: An Ode', condemned the impious and perfidious enemy, the fickle and cruel race. From then on, Pitt was able to ask of the nation an effort which was greater than prudence would have allowed prior to the change in public feeling.

Meanwhile, France was establishing the principle of territorial and national unity by uprooting the remnants of the *ancien régime* in Holland, the Cisalpine and Switzerland. This did much to promote the awakening and growth of local national sentiments. The French intervention benefited Italy in particular, where the nationalists, more numerous than is often believed, suddenly became aware of themselves. But pressed by the necessity of war, France treated these countries like military marches. Charged with the burden of supporting the French army, they soon came to realise the price of independence. Thus, by a fatal reversal that Robespierre had once predicted, France brought about their hostility. When the Russians and Austrians invaded Italy in 1799, they were hailed as liberators.

The danger was still not great, because Germany had not yet been affected. Although the magnificent flowering of arts and letters, and the return to the past which Romanticism had aroused, had succeeded in exalting a feeling of national consciousness in the literate public, it had not yet assumed political form. In contrast to politically organised peoples and their barbaric struggles, Germany, the *Kulturnation*, was by her very weakness considered superior and endowed with a divine mission. This proud attitude did not survive the invasion.

In France, the nation rested to all intents and purposes on a contract. With due allowance for the natural and historic conditions which influence individual preferences, the nation had established its federation on the basis of free choice. In contrast to this revolutionary concept of the nation, a different view evolved in Germany. Herder, and after him the Romantic movement, regarded the German nation as a living being, born like all others out of the unconscious operation of a life spirit – the *Volksgeist*. Customs, traditions, language, folk songs and art were but manifestations of this force. Once again we find Germany the centre of future European development. She would become the rallying point against revolutionary France, not only through her emergence as a nation, but also by preaching a different concept of nation – a collective being in which the individual loses all claim to autonomy, and in which freedom, as with the mystics, lies in the cheerful acceptance of submission, and which, repudiating a rationalist and a universal civilisation, places a supreme value upon its own needs and passions.

A similar development was taking place in Japan at about the same time. There, Chinese mandarins had previously imparted a critical and rationalistic strain to their teachings. They contested the solar ancestry of the Mikado, and they declared that the gods did not recognise differences among men. But ever since the middle of the eighteenth century, under the leadership of Kamo Mabuchi and his disciple Motoori Norinaga (who died in 1801), there had developed a mystical and Romantic revival which had a high regard for Buddhism and its moral precepts and which restored Shintoism and the prestige which the nation had enjoyed in the past. The political consequences of this movement were most significant. According to these innovators, the emperor once again became the son of the gods, the shogun a usurper, and the Japanese a chosen race destined to dominate over a world empire. After the authoritarian and reforming regency of Sadanobu Matsudaira, which ended in 1793, the shogun Ieharu achieved a reconciliation with the court in Kyoto. Nevertheless, the seeds of an imperial revolution had been sown. It is not surprising to find once again the alternation of two eternal courses in the history of human thought. Since, however, there existed as yet no intellectual relations between Europe and the Far East, this similarity between the two ends of the world is well worthy of notice.

# CHAPTER TWO

## The Consequences of the War
## and the Terms of the Peace

QUITE APART FROM the issue of national enmities, there were traditional aspirations of states which, from the beginning, complicated the conflict between France and the rest of Europe. In going to war, the Coalition was not aiming merely to crush the Revolution. The continental powers planned to dismember France, while England hoped to seize her colonies and destroy her commerce and navy. This would advantageously terminate the Anglo-French duel begun in the time of Louis XIV and restore British hegemony upon the seas – a superiority that had been recently compromised by the American Revolution. But not all of the problems which had brought the powers into conflict during the eighteenth century were resolved as yet: the Prussian–Austrian alliance would eventually founder over the Polish question; Russian designs in the East and in the Mediterranean worried Pitt; and Spain continued to be apprehensive about England. The allies never succeeded in co-ordinating their efforts, and the disparity of their separate gains only served to accentuate their division. The continental powers were beaten, and France was able to negotiate with Prussia, win Spain over to an alliance, and attain and surpass her 'natural boundaries'. The Second Coalition had recaptured Italy and a part of Switzerland in 1799, but, like the First Coalition, it was already disintegrating. And while England might triumph on the sea, lacking an army she could not by herself subdue France. Nor was her economic position without its weaknesses. The question was whether France, profiting from these European divisions, could achieve victory and secure a lasting peace that would preserve her 'natural boundaries'. All historians of Napoleon regard this as the fateful issue controlling his destiny.

## THE CONTINENTAL POWERS

The European monarchs were a singularly mediocre lot. In Austria, Francis II was a solemn nonentity who kept his brother Charles in the background and insisted on conducting all affairs with his devoted but not very intelligent chief *Kabinettsminister*, Count Colloredo. In Prussia, Frederick William III was honest, well-meaning and not too bright; and although indecisive, he was very jealous of his authority. In Russia, there was Paul I, half-mad, inconstant and cruel. Even the war had not taught these monarchs anything. Austria, for example, still recruited soldiers by impressment, or by drawing lots among the peasants, and they were still enlisted for life. The officers, almost all of them nobles, continued to purchase their posts. In 1798 Archduke Charles had planned to regroup his regiments into divisions, but the war had forced him to give up the project. Neither tactics, nor strategy, nor logistics had undergone any changes.

The continental powers were not lacking in men. It has been estimated that between 1792 and 1799 their losses numbered 140,000 killed, 200,000 wounded and 150,000 prisoners – a large figure no doubt, but their manpower remained far from being exhausted. What was mainly lacking was money. In Austria, despite an increase in taxes, the annual deficit soared from twenty million guldens (or florins)* at the end of Joseph II's reign, to ninety million in 1796. The government had to resort to forced loans, and the debt rose from 390 million in 1793 to 572 million in 1798. England granted subsidies to Austria, and, in addition, guaranteed or authorised private loans in London. Nevertheless, financial solvency could be maintained only by issuing paper money, the *Banko-zettel*, the value of which had to be pegged by decree in order to finance the campaign of 1800. The amount of paper money in circulation rose from twenty-seven million in 1793 to two hundred million in 1801. From then on, the Austrian florin began to depreciate. In 1801 it had lost sixteen per cent of its par value on the Augsburg exchange. Weaker still was the Russian rouble, which was being exchanged at sixty per cent of its par value in Leipzig. The Russian debt, which had been contracted primarily in Holland, rose from forty-three to 132 million florins under Paul I, and the government issued fourteen million new paper roubles every year. Sweden also resorted to printing paper money, which lost over twenty-

* This monetary unit was worth about fifty French *sols*.

five per cent of its value in 1798. It would have indeed been difficult for the Coalition to keep the war going without English subsidies. But did a coalition still exist?

Paul I made a great show of his hatred for the French Revolution: he sheltered Louis XVIII at Mittau, and supported Condé's army. But it had taken the Egyptian campaign to convince him to enter the war. This was because the Eastern question was coming to assume an ever greater importance for Russian foreign policy. Catherine II, not content with dismembering the states of the sultan, had won a privileged position in them – certain rights over the fate of the sultan's Christian subjects, and free passage for her merchant ships through the Dardanelles. This privilege was accorded to England only in 1799, and to France in 1802. The disintegration of the Turkish Empire promised fresh gains. Since 1793 Selim III had striven to organise a modern army, but in many provinces he exercised only nominal authority. Ali Pasha (Tepelini) was carving himself a fief in Albania and Epirus; Pasvan Oglu had seized Vidin, named himself pasha and was marching on Adrianople; Djezzar controlled Syria; and Abdul Aziz, leader of the Wahabis, had conquered the entire Nejd and now threatened the holy cities and the pasha of Baghdad. The Greeks, and particularly the Serbs, were also causing concern. The former, taking advantage of the war, were spreading throughout the Mediterranean, thanks to Turkish neutrality. They penetrated the Black Sea in Russian ships and began forming colonies in every large port. They had heard about the French Revolution through the writings of Adamantios Koraés and Rhigas Pheraios, and they had seen the tricolour streaming over the Ionian Islands. The call of Hellenism had indeed been aroused. The Serbs, exasperated by the depredations of the Janissaries, had given their assistance to Austria in the last Turkish War. Their leaders, Karageorge and Nenadovich, were only waiting for an opportunity to resume hostilities on the side of Russia.

Russia gained access to the Mediterranean Sea as a result of Bonaparte's Egyptian expedition. Paul I became an ally of the sultan, and had the Straits opened to his warships. Together with the Turks and the pasha of Janina, he occupied the Ionian Islands, making them a republic under his protection. Elected grand master of the Order of Malta, Paul planned to rule over the island, and on 3 November 1799 Grenville had to promise him that should England seize Malta from France, she would not remain there. Paul also coveted Corsica, landed his troops in the kingdom of Naples, and promised to restore the king of Sardinia. Thus by reversing traditional Russian policy towards Turkey, he was able to acquire a degree of influence in the Mediterranean never again equalled by his successors. England, intent on recapturing Egypt, was willing to ignore the spread of Russian influence. But Francis II had no intention of letting the Russians have their way in Italy, and Paul, ascribing Suvorov's defeat at Zurich to Austria's treachery, recalled his army. This put an end to Russian participation, since Rostopchin, hostile to the idea of a Coalition, had triumphed over Panin and had been named head of the department of foreign affairs. Paul's defection resulted in isolating Austria, but, more than that, the way was now open to a conflict with England, should she in the future consider herself free to retain Malta. Had not Catherine II once before mobilised the neutrals against England's naval hegemony and prevented her access to the Baltic, which was of paramount importance to British commerce?

Meanwhile, Austria had to bear the brunt of the war alone. Officially, the Reichstag supported the war, but ever since the Peace of Basle, the Holy Roman Empire seemed no more than a shadow. Prussia guaranteed the neutrality of Northern Germany and Hanover. To the north of the line of demarcation – the 'enchanted circle' as it was called by the Austrian Hudelist – the German states enjoyed the advantages of peace and large commercial profits. Prussia's prestige was much enhanced, and Frederick William was rapidly becoming a 'lodestar', an 'anti-emperor'. It was quite unnecessary for Gentz, in 1799, to advise Frederick William that he persist in this policy of neutrality, for he was already well set on the idea. Indeed, he counted on becoming the leader of a North German confederation, and he dreamed of territorial expansion. He waited impatiently for secularisations, coveted Hanover and manoeuvred to annex Nuremberg. Austria then, driven from the north, felt discredited in the south by the loss of the left bank of the Rhine; and she also felt betrayed in her designs on Bavaria, although Maximilian Joseph, who succeeded Charles Theodore in 1799, momentarily feared for his succession. As for the duke of Württemberg, Frederick II, he was embroiled in a chronic conflict with the provincial estates who, on their own account, had already despatched emissaries to Paris. In these circumstances, the South German princes followed Austria out of fear alone, and they were only waiting for an opportunity to accommodate themselves with France. A union of the German states against France thus became impossible, and the very disappearance of the Holy Roman Empire seemed so likely that Görres had already ironically drawn up its death certificate. Chancellor Thugut of Austria was not worried about it, and he regretted the loss of the Low Countries even less. He did not neglect to seek indemnification in Poland, but like his eighteenth-century predecessors, his interests were cast primarily in the direction of Italy. After absorbing the Venetian states, he hoped to supplant the French in the peninsula from which they had just been driven. In that case, he calculated, not without reason, that Austria would have little cause for complaint in the end.

Would the French win over the Russians and neutralise Austria by abandoning Italy to her? If so, the least that could happen to England was that she would be left without allies.

## THE ENGLISH WAR EFFORT

Britain's administration had undergone no changes. It remained antiquated, complex, encumbered by sinecures and inclined to corruption. Nevertheless, parliamentary government attested to a stability and continuity of purpose that continental despots might well have envied. England's ruling oligarchy did not abound in talent, but it regarded the nation as its patrimony and defended it with tenacity and discipline. Their leader, William Pitt, had been unlucky in his undertakings, but they admired his perseverance and cautious empiricism, which had spared England constraints and sacrifices. Recognising the danger at last, they began to cry out for a reversal of policy. England began to impress sailors and recruit soldiers for the war effort, both drawn from the poorer classes of society. These men were then led by volunteers from the aristocracy, who purchased their commissions. Bodies of fencibles were formed for home service, and the militia was gradually raised to one hundred thousand men. In principle, they were to be chosen by lot, but in practice, those chosen were allowed to purchase substitutes, and parishes generally bought their contingents for a price. So common had this practice become that the recruitment of regulars eventually dried up. Between 1794 and 1799 the latter were used in the colonies, and the allies, encouraged by English subsidies, were left with the burden of creating a continental diversion which would further England's interests. Grenville frankly admitted that he much preferred to pay the continental powers than to send them reinforcements, which would have deprived industry of its manpower. Besides, the money was not lost since it was spent on the British market for supplies which the armies needed.

This was a costly policy. Expenditure rose from £26* million in 1792 to £91 million in 1801. Pitt effected a slight increase in indirect taxes, which in 1797 provided seventy-five per cent of the revenue, but this was insufficient. Revenues covered sixty-eight per cent of expenditures in 1792, and less than twenty-nine per cent in 1797. The Bank of England discounted exchequer bills only cautiously: £8.5 million in 1792, £17 million in 1797. With the suspension of gold payments, the Bank became more obliging, so that this floating debt surpassed £24 million in 1801. But the most important resource was the consolidated bonds, whose principal rose from £9 million in 1792 to £36 million in 1801. Pitt's ability to maintain the rate of exchange while amortising the debt shows to what degree the English aristocracy had confidence in its own future, and it also proves that England was already drawing vast sums from her trade and her colonies. Nevertheless, England's staying power depended on credit. Since the activity of her capitalists also depended on it, it is understandable that this hitherto unknown system appeared artificial and rickety to the French. It was on the basis of that judgement that France waged its economic war during the entire period.

When, after 1794, war on the Continent took a turn for the worse, the British government made every effort to urge the nation on to new sacrifices. The decisive change did not come, however, until after the Treaty of Campoformio, when England found herself isolated, attacked in Ireland and threatened in Egypt. With the suspension of gold payments in 1797, Pitt insisted on financial reforms to limit inflation. This time the landed gentry and the middle classes were not completely spared: the land tax was increased and an income tax was introduced. Direct taxes brought in £10.5 million in 1801, compared to £3 million in 1792. But their importance must not be exaggerated, for in 1801 indirect taxes still represented sixty-five per cent of receipts, and loans over sixty-five per cent of expenditures. It became evident at this time that a renewed effort would be required to continue the war.

Recruitment proved far more difficult to improve. In 1794 it was easy to find home volunteers by the tens of thousands, for until an actual inva-

* In 1791 £1 sterling equalled twenty francs (one *louis d'or*), thirteen marks, eleven Dutch florins, eight roubles and 4½ American dollars. The 1791 £1 would be the equivalent of about £5 5s today.

sion they remained in their homes and were excused from service in the militia. They were organised by private initiative, and they agreed to fight within a certain radius fixed by themselves. It was expected that they would wage war as in the Vendée, but, in fact, the only thing they had in common with the volunteers of the French Revolution was their name. Luckily for England, they were never put to the test. Meanwhile, the situation in the regular army became so critical that in 1796 country parishes were required under penalty of fine to provide fifteen thousand regulars drawn by lot. The attempt failed completely, because they preferred to pay the fine. Finally, in 1798 it was proposed that militiamen enlist in the regular army in consideration of a bounty. But the idea encountered strong opposition from the lord-lieutenants of the shires, who named the officers of the militia and maintained it on the revenues of the land tax, and thus considered the militia their preserve. Nevertheless, this system was finally adopted on 12 July 1799, and it lasted until 1815. The militiamen answered the call and took part in the expedition to Holland, and later in Egypt. Pitt went no further, not daring to institute compulsory military service.

Nor did he put an end to the confusion in the military administration, which was divided between Dundas, Windham, the duke of York and the Home Office. In reality, operations were directed by Pitt, Grenville and the king. But some progress was made in military technology: mounted batteries were created in 1797, and the artillery was made an independent corps in 1799. Apart from garrisons, the English expeditionary force numbered only about ten thousand men, and, not counting the expedition to Holland, which failed pitifully, the army fought only in the colonies between 1794 and 1805. First the French islands, then the Dutch, then Trinidad; and in 1801 the Swedish and Danish Antilles fell. But 7,500 men perished in San Domingo, which had to be evacuated in 1798, when Toussaint L'Ouverture allied with Sonthonax to drive the English from the island. These successes were naturally due to the action of the fleet, which constituted England's main contribution to the Coalition.

The fleet had grown much larger, although not without difficulties, since the merchant marine was expanding at an even swifter rate. As early as 1793 it became necessary to permit seventy-five per cent of the crews of English vessels to consist of foreigners. Sailors of all nations, prisoners of war, convicts, strikers and political suspects were all impressed indiscriminately. Since shipboard life remained unbearable, mutinies were frequent. In 1797 they degenerated into a widespread revolt, which was put down by setting a few examples, but chiefly by increasing pay and prize money. Naval technology scarcely changed. The standard ship of the line remained two hundred by fifty feet at midship beam, equipped with seventy-four guns, two fighting decks and a six-hundred-man crew; still, the number of towering three-deckers gradually increased. Lord Spencer, First Lord of the Admiralty until 1801, encountered no major obstacles in construction. The English oak and the fir or Norway pine of Scotland were still accessible. Timber from the Baltic region, which the French could no longer buy, as well as American white pine, were also used.

Until 1796 the naval war was pursued ineffectively. Howe and Bridport kept their ships in port during the winter months, thus suspending the blockade. Then the rupture with Spain led to the abandonment of Corsica and the Mediterranean. A resurgence began in 1798 when Admiral Jervis, earl of St Vincent, organised permanent cruises at a short distance from the coasts, coupled with a supply service and staggered reliefs. The cruising fleet was ordered to rally at the entrance to the Channel if the French attempted to run the blockade. In the same year, Pitt decided to force his way into the Mediterranean to save Naples. He failed, but managed to seize Sicily and Minorca. Meanwhile, the British fleet was joined by the Neapolitan and Portuguese navies. The Dutch fleet was captured in 1799, and Nelson had already destroyed Brueys's squadron at Abukir. The Army of Egypt was bottled up, and Malta was besieged. It looked as if, barring intervention by Paul I, the Mediterranean would fall to England. But the French had not yet been eliminated: in April 1799 Admiral Bruix was able to leave Brest, reach Toulon and return to his home port. At least the British admirals were able to safeguard their lines of communication, put a check on the activities of the corsairs and destroy the enemy's merchant marine. Thanks to the use of convoy escorts, shipowners lost only five hundred ships in an average year. This constituted three per cent of the total British complement, hardly more than the usual hazards at sea. Marine insurance rates, which had climbed to fifty per cent during the American War of Independence, did not now exceed twenty-five per cent, and after the peace in 1802 dropped to twelve per cent. England captured 743 privateers and, as early as 1798, held twenty-two thousand sailors as prisoners. The French were left with two hundred merchant vessels of more than two hundred tons, only one-tenth of their effective strength in 1789.

Of all the Coalition powers, England alone had achieved her ends. Her allies realised this and criticised her for not having sent them troops; this did not strengthen the Coalition. But England had yet to learn that her navy alone could not force France to capitulate, and that ultimately victory would have to be won on the Continent.

## FRANCE AND HER ALLIES

With the Coalition powers disunited, France certainly occupied a very strong position on the European Continent. In addition to Avignon, Montbéliard and Mulhouse, she had annexed Belgium, Maastricht and Dutch Flanders, the left bank of the Rhine (at least up to a line which, leaving the Rhine below Coblenz, reached and followed the course of the Roer), the ancient bishopric of Basle (which comprised Porrentruy, the valleys of Saint-Imier and Moutier, and Bienne), Geneva, Savoy and Nice. France was still the most populous country in Europe. The war had cost her around six hundred thousand casualties, dead and missing. These losses, however, which were considered unparalleled, had not compromised her strength, which, used sparingly, could undoubtedly repulse any assault. Moreover, France was no longer isolated as in 1793.

Compulsory military service, which had been adopted as a temporary expedient under the name of *levée en masse*, was now established as a permanent principle of recruitment by the Jourdan Law of 19 Fructidor, Year VI (5 September 1798). Except in the case of invasion, this law limited its demands to a fixed body of men, chosen either by lot or by conscription. But in Year VII young men who were about to be drafted were given the opportunity to evade the law by jointly recruiting volunteers to make up the contingent of their communes. Bonaparte would add only the privilege of individual replacement, a measure which had been granted and later suppressed by his predecessors. The Directory had, in addition, perfected the *amalgame*,* appreciably improved the cavalry and reorganised the officer corps: the election of officers by soldiers was greatly reduced by the Law of 14 Germinal, Year III (3 April 1795).

* A process whereby raw recruits were immediately mingled with seasoned veterans and were expected to learn the essentials of war while marching on their way to the front. Thus, by dispensing with formal military training, the French armies were able to obtain the men needed to fill the ranks in the shortest possible amount of time. This principle, first tried in 1793, was used with increasing frequency by the later republican governments and during the time of the Consulate and Empire. TRANSLATOR.

The spirit of the army had undergone a change. As in civilian life, love of glory and even of money had gradually replaced revolutionary ardour. Yet, despite mutinies instigated by royalist propaganda, the army continued to be the shield of the Revolution. As an instrument of war, it was incomparable. Rapid promotion for bravery remained the popular symbol of equality, and attracted the ambitious and fighting young men. The importance given to individual worth, which the Revolution made the essential principle of the modern world, showed its value; this superior social principle gave the French army a decided edge on those of the *ancien régime*.

For France, no less than for her enemies, the weak point lay in the increasing difficulty of financing the war. Bankruptcy had forced the Directory to liquidate paper money and revert to specie. Reduced to tax receipts alone, the Directory was also ever-increasingly exposed to the usual embarrassments of deflation: changing prices, economic paralysis and a decline in revenues. This financial situation, for which it was not responsible, prevailed throughout its history, and accounted for its unfortunate reputation. The Directory actually made great efforts to improve the financial situation. It ameliorated the direct tax base and even created a new one; it urged, with some degree of success, the drawing up of tax rolls; and it tried to expedite methods of collection, without, however, going so far as to deprive the elective municipal and provincial bodies of those functions. It also increased indirect taxes, and placed them in Year VII under the permanent regulation of the registration, stamp and mortgage departments. Finally, it established a tax on the use of public conveyances, instituted highway tolls on wagons and beasts of burden, and provided assistance to the towns by authorising them to institute *octrois*.* The Directory fully realised that important consumer goods (salt, for example) would have to be taxed in order to secure abundant and regular revenues, but these were measures which it did not consider itself strong enough to risk. Consequently, it was left with no alternative but to cut expenditures, which in turn forced it to repudiate two-thirds of the public debt and to neglect public services.

Had the Directory succeeded in balancing the regular budget, it would still have been obliged to finance the war, and this could have been done only on credit. For political reasons, however, forced loans were the

* Taxes on commodities which were brought into towns. Hence, municipal tolls. TRANS-
LATOR.

only means of borrowing. There were no bankers willing to advance the government the money necessary to keep the treasury going. Since the tax collectors kept their funds as long as possible in order to turn them to profit, there was talk of re-establishing *rescriptions*, that is to say, promissory notes made by the tax farmers of the *ancien régime* against future tax receipts. But who would discount them? The bankers did indeed propose the creation of a state bank, but one which would discount their own paper. In short, the Directory was compelled to pay the *rente*,* pensions and salaries in bearer bonds, which made it thoroughly detested, and it was forced to hand over the provisioning of the military to private companies who fleeced the government, and who were reimbursed in shares of *biens nationaux*, timber, future taxes or in drafts that no bank could cash.

These expedients, which constituted disguised inflation, provoked a wave of frenzied speculation. They also demoralised many government officials and politicians to whom contractors offered bribes in the hope of getting paid. The army suffered terribly, and was enraged at these 'intercessors'. Since the police lacked the means to combat thievery, law and order became increasingly compromised as the economic crisis steadily worsened. The life and morals of the nation were not the only things affected: the penurious Directory exploited Holland and expanded into Italy and Switzerland in order to support its armies. Purveyors, generals and war commissioners zealously pursued their own selfish interests. The army, and even the state, lived on war; this was the origin of a war party whose incarnation was Bonaparte.

The restoration of public order and finances required time, as the Consulate would demonstrate, but most important of all, a strong hand was needed. The Directory organised its work well (its 'secretariat of state' was later taken over by Bonaparte, as was its Ministry of Police, which Fouché had joined in Year VII), but it failed to consolidate its power. In the first place, the Constitution of Year III had re-established decentralisation on a wide scale, and had created a separation of powers in Paris which deprived the national executive of the initiative that war demanded. The executive did not have control of the treasury, and was impeded in its work by insoluble conflicts with the legislative chambers, or between the chambers themselves. In the second place, as long as the

* Various kinds of government obligations, such as bonds, annuities and other securities (and the interest paid on them) – all of which constituted the public debt. TRANSLATOR.

former privileged classes resisted the new order, there survived in France
a stubborn core of seditious opposition, civil war and treason, which
weakened the government or drove it to violence. In Year VII the west of
France had again taken up arms, the south-west was in rebellion and an
uprising in Provence and Franche-Comté was being prepared for the
spring, with foreign connivance and English money.

The counter-revolution could not be expected to subside as long as it
retained the support of part of the Catholic clergy. On 18 September
1794 the Civil Constitution of the clergy had disappeared along with the
religious budget. Priests were required only to swear loyalty to the
Republic, but many of them refused. These were hunted down and
interned on the prison ships at Rochefort or Île de Ré, and then deported
to Guiana. They were to some degree in contact with Rome and with the
former refractory bishops, most of whom lived in England and were subsidised by Pitt. Whether they so desired it or not, their faithful followers
were likely recruits for the insurrection.

The priests who had submitted to the laws, and the former constitutional clergy who had reorganised their churches after the Reign of Terror, were unfavourably disposed to the Directory, for, like the bourgeois
republicans and the *Idéologues*, the Directory had lost no opportunity in
showing its hostility towards Catholicism. It had sold many churches,
imposed the observation of the *décadi* (Tenth Day), forbidden by law all
public religious observances and introduced into the churches themselves Tenth Day worship and theophilanthropy in rivalry to Catholicism. After 18 Fructidor the Directory began to attack the 'free schools',
which were chiefly Catholic. They were to be closed down unless instruction in civic virtue was assured, and public officials were forbidden to
send their children to these schools. Had the Republic abandoned this
hostile attitude and practised a sincerely neutral policy towards religion,
it would undoubtedly have won over the constitutional and the juring
clergy and weakened the prestige of the refractory priests. This, however,
would have required a far-sighted policy. It would have been necessary to
come to terms with the pope to obtain immediate results, but having
already imprisoned and deported him, the Directory would have had too
much ground to regain. In any event, its supporters would never have
permitted it. The state might have found a bulwark in the attainment of
national unity, real or apparent, but such an ambition presupposed a state
already strong.

Among France's allies, Spain, who alone truly deserved the name, did what she could; one of her squadrons was even anchored at Brest. But the war was proving disastrous for her. Her fleet, defeated at Cape St Vincent, had been unable to prevent the loss of Minorca and Trinidad, and the silver of the Indies arrived only with difficulty. There were fears for the Americas, and the fate of the pope and the Bourbons of Parma and Naples saddened Charles IV. Meanwhile, the Directory increased its demands. It had nothing but contempt for the home of the Inquisition and for a king cuckolded by his foreign minister, Godoy. It coveted Louisiana, and it protested against the consideration shown to Portugal – without even noticing that Talleyrand, having been bribed by the Portuguese, was a responsible party. Exasperated, Spain ended by listening to English proposals. All was not yet lost, but it would have been necessary to conciliate this *ancien régime* monarchy, whose means were limited, and which was capable of acting only very slowly. Her finances were also in a pitiful state: in 1799 a fixed rate of exchange was given to the *vales reales*,* which were being quoted at fifty per cent of par. With the help of François de Cabarrus, founder of the Banco de San Carlos in Madrid, the French financier Ouvrard had already contracted to provision the Spanish fleet, and he dreamed of grandiose speculative schemes in that country, which the French regarded as an Eldorado.

In addition to the Spanish ally, there were the vassal republics. The Italian ones were lost, and at the Battle of Zurich, Masséna was able to save only half of the Helvetic Republic. The Batavian Republic had almost been lost, and the English had seized its ships. Both of these satellites provided supplies for the French troops and offered important strategic positions. To provide more than this would have required the existence of stable governments, something the Directory failed to establish.

There was also a social problem. The privileged classes either emigrated or kept aloof because the French had proclaimed the end of the *ancien régime*. The bourgeoisie was more disposed to participate in the government on condition that it be granted political power, which was also claimed by the only true francophiles, the Jacobins. Both these parties intrigued with the representatives of the French Republic to bring about *coups d'état*. Schimmelpenninck, the leader of the moderate Dutch

* Interest-bearing royal bonds circulated as legal tender and issued by the Spanish government to meet its current obligations. TRANSLATOR.

bourgeoisie, wished to create a government which would be agreeable to France, until the time when peace would bring independence. It was only in July 1798 that he was able to organise a definitively constituted Batavian Directory, and it was still not stable. In Switzerland, La Harpe had been able to impose his dictatorship, thanks to the war, but the moderates were planning his overthrow.

Burdened by the military occupation, the masses were hostile in Holland and hesitant in Switzerland. To win them over, it would have been necessary to favour the peasantry, as in France. In Holland, nothing was done. In Switzerland, the personal feudal rights of the gentry and the lesser tithes were abolished without indemnity in 1798, but feudal dues and the great tithes were made redeemable. Although the state undertook to pay a share of the indemnity, it planned to do so in *biens nationaux*, which could therefore hardly pass into the hands of the peasantry. In addition, a land tax was introduced before the old feudal dues were abolished. Finally, French rule annoyed everyone. In these countries, too, government reform was deemed desirable. This was what the Directory thought, and it even proceeded to make certain attempts in this direction that it would never have dared try at home. But it did not have the authority to carry them through. What France lacked most of all in its struggle with Europe, was a government with the energy of the Committee of Public Safety.

### THE BLOCKADE AND THE NEUTRALS

The war on the Continent ended French hopes of successfully contesting England's hegemony of the seas. Consequently, France gave the economic struggle a new direction: she tried to turn against the English the very methods that they had previously perfected. During the eighteenth century, while a blockade might prove bothersome to an enemy, it could hardly paralyse him. In accordance with the principles of mercantilism, the maritime powers saw the blockade primarily as a means of suppressing the enemy's exports in order to seize his markets and corner the supply of specie. Even so, there were still advantages to be had in buying certain raw materials or, given the opportunity, foodstuffs from the other side. Nor, according to mercantile theory, were there any reasons for refusing to sell goods to the enemy, apart from the contraband of war. Thus England applied the blockade with a judicious empiricism, granting licences when convenient even for ports actually closed by her squad-rons. Since the number of these ports could never be great, the neutrals had every opportunity to get around the blockade. England had also worked out a maritime law in her own inimitable fashion: enemy goods were declared fair prize even when carried in neutral bottoms, and all or any part of the enemy coast was considered to be under a 'paper blockade' – so that any vessel coming from or sailing towards it was regarded as a blockade runner. Finally, the system was enforced by boarding all mer-chantmen on the high seas. Thus, the ocean was turned into an English imperium.

The neutrals particularly resented the regulations aimed at the colonies. Colonial traffic had always been foremost in international com-merce, and in time of peace every mother country claimed a monopoly of trade with her colonies. But France, and later Spain, being at war with England, renounced these exclusive rights and opened their colonies to neutral shipping. After 1793, as in 1756, England forbade neutrals to reap the benefits of this windfall, intending to bring her own ships to the enemy colonies. Nevertheless, in order to pacify the Americans, who considered themselves the most injured party, England permitted neu-trals who were destined for neutral, non-European ports, to load in the West Indies and later re-export the cargo once it had become their own property. This was known as the 'circuit'. Soon thereafter, the British Navigation Act was suspended, owing to a shortage of ships and a desire to use neutrals to export goods to France. In 1798 neutral vessels were granted permission to carry on trade in the West Indies for England or for their own countries. Thus, while retaining a virtual monopoly over colonial products, England turned the neutrals into auxiliaries.

England also granted licences to neutrals in keeping with her needs. In this way her commerce assumed, to a certain extent, the aspects of a con-trolled economy. Despite their grievances, the neutrals – Scandinavians, Prussians, Hanseatics and Americans – made huge profits. Hamburg took the place of occupied Holland as the intermediary between England and Germany, and became the largest banking centre on the Continent. It was through the House of Parish that subsidies reached the Coalition. Ameri-can sales, of which half were in colonial products, rose from $20 million in 1790 to $94 million in 1801. They supplied the Antilles and Spanish America, carried wood and grain to England and won an important place in the French market and in Hamburg. Americans were perfecting the science of naval construction, and the Baltimore clipper came to be regarded as a model. Finally, because the neutral nations prospered, their businessmen and financiers became resolute anglophiles.

It was now up to France whether she should preserve a large part of her maritime commerce, even with England; all the more so, since the neutrals did their best to evade the British regulations. During the American Revolution, France had accepted the formula which stated that except for contraband, a neutral ship had the right to protect merchandise (*le pavillon neutre couvre la marchandise*). This had allowed her to continue trading, and had won her the Dutch alliance at a time when the League of Armed Neutrality was being formed against England. The Convention had later reversed this policy, the underlying reason being the treaty of 1786, which had subjected French industry to English competition. The war had provided an excellent opportunity for a countermove. The cotton manufacturers clamoured louder than anyone for a return to protection, and Fontenay, the great merchant from Rouen, became their spokesman. They guided the Convention just as they would later guide Napoleon. Furthermore, the belief persisted that England's economy, and consequently her credit, depended on exports, and that the hardest blow one could strike would be to deprive her of France, her best customer. Such was the reasoning of Brissot and Kersaint in January 1793, and such would be the reasoning of the emperor at a later time. On 9 May a decree declared enemy property in neutral holds to be lawful prize, and on 9 October a prohibition was placed on English goods.

As long as neutrals were allowed to trade with France, these measures were illusory, since England permitted the neutrals to do so precisely in order to dispose of British goods. Besides, the people regarded the neutrals with disfavour since their purchases forced prices to go up. An embargo was declared in August, and France thereby gave the blockade an airtight character which the English themselves did not.

Shortages of colonial products and raw materials, beginning with cotton, were not slow in making themselves felt. This was not what the businessmen had intended. The blockade was supposed to be flexible like that of the enemy, for the convenience of the mercantile interests. Anxious about provisioning the army, the Committee of Public Safety reopened the ports to neutrals, and the Thermidorians restored their treaty privileges. English goods immediately reappeared. But after the Treaty of Campoformio, when England remained the only enemy and when overland trade was resumed, the protectionists returned to the offensive. The Directory once again forbade British products, and on 29 Nivôse, Year VI (18 January 1798), adopted an unprecedented measure against the neutrals: their vessels were to be considered lawful prize if they were found carrying any items whatsoever of British origin or if they had merely called at an English port. Neutral vessels no longer appeared, but the United States broke off diplomatic relations with France.

Smuggling, however, continued actively, and France's allies also engaged in it. It was partly in order to check the flow of contraband that Geneva and Mulhouse were annexed in 1798. France and Holland, which together absorbed eighteen per cent of British exports in 1792, still accounted for twelve per cent in 1800. The Directory was fully aware that for such an economic policy to be both effective and bearable, France would need a vast continental market. Conquest became in part a necessity of the economic struggle. The occupied countries and Spain were closed to the English, and it was pointed out that the occupation of the Hanseatic towns would ensure control over the German market. The continental blockade was beginning to take shape, and the world was already being divided into two very unequal parts: France and her allies on the one hand, England and all other countries on the other. The two principal belligerents were now forced to consolidate their respective positions in order to survive.

France had suffered serious losses. The most terrible blow had been the loss of her colonial trade, which had accounted for a third of her imports and a fifth of her exports in 1789. A part of the Continent remained closed to her, and she had not been able to recover her former position elsewhere. Despite the fact that she had increased in size, her sales fell from 441 million *livres* in 1789 to 272 million in 1800. The revolutionary crisis had affected every industry, and some had recovered only with difficulty. More than half the looms were idle in Lyon, and cloth manufacture had been reduced by more than two-thirds since 1789. After having succumbed to a runaway inflation, France now found herself a prey to the ills of deflation, which added to the general feeling of insecurity. Metallic currency continued to be scarce, and credit was non-existent. Interest rates varied from three to seven per cent per month. The decline in prices paralysed industry. A succession of good harvests, which in itself should have had a calming effect, provoked a further decline in prices, and reduced the buying power of the peasantry. The

Directory could do nothing except redouble its encouragements. But this was only a passing crisis. Given a government with renewed strength, and given the re-establishment of peace on the Continent, metallic currency would gradually reappear, new avenues of trade would emerge and production would recover.

The French Revolution had created conditions favourable to economic progress: freedom, thanks to the abolition of guilds, and unity of the national market, through the suppression of internal customs duties, the reduction of tolls and the adoption of the decimal system. It had also opened new vistas in the annexed lands, where French metallurgy, for example, could avail itself of the resources of Belgium and the Saar. There was still an abundance of labour in the countryside. The blockade, if it had been applied for expediency rather than for purely warlike ends, would have had only salutary results, by providing the protection necessary for nascent capitalism. It did in fact exercise a favourable influence on the metallurgical, chemical and especially the cotton industries. Cotton continued to be the most innovating industry, and the most alluring for capitalists. The manufacture of spinning jennies increased greatly, and Christoff-Philipp Oberkampf had already begun operating the first calico printing machine in 1797. Several captains of industry made their appearance and founded factories: Boyer-Fonfrède in Toulouse, Richard and Lenoir in Charonne, and Bauwens in Passy and Ghent. Machinery was only in its infancy, and was still unknown in the manufacture of cloth; William Cockerill, an English industrialist who had crossed over to the Continent, had only just been called to Verviers. Silk was still being spun by Vaucanson's method, and Jacquard had not yet perfected his weaving loom. Metallurgy registered no progress. Except in the Anzin mines, no use was made of steam power until Bauwens adopted it in Ghent in 1799. But since France was sheltered from English competition, she could afford to mechanise at leisure.

In any event, the French Republic – where the great majority of the population were peasants who practised mainly a form of natural economy – could have lived, if necessary, from her own resources. Agriculture, which had also been released from its fetters, improved, but slowly. The rural community retained its practices of compulsory crop rotation, common pasturage and other time-worn rights. In fact so strong was this attachment that no one in the revolutionary assemblies ever dared to suggest that a redistribution of land be imposed to uproot these customs. Nor had much of the common land been divided. While artificial pasturage, tobacco, chicory and potatoes made small gains, land reclamation, irrigation and planting declined; roads continued to be in bad repair, and a rural police simply did not exist. Yet the social structure of the countryside had improved, and thus increased the country's powers of resistance. The number of small landowners had grown considerably, at least in certain regions: by thirteen thousand in the Moselle, by twenty per cent in the Côte-d'Or and by ten thousand in the Nord. At the same time, large-scale farming generally declined in favour of more moderate holdings. Naturally there remained many landless day labourers, more or less condemned to begging, and the stability of the rural population depended on the harvest as always. But ever since the disappearance of the tithe and feudal dues, the government had no more to fear than passing disturbances.

England could no more defeat France with the blockade than with the guns of her fleet. Moreover, should the Republic succeed in restoring peace on the Continent, her economic position could once again become satisfactory. The question of knowing whether England was, in this respect, exposed to collapse is far more complex.

## THE STRENGTH AND DANGERS OF BRITISH CAPITALISM. EUROPEAN EXPANSION IN THE WORLD

England profited from an enormous advance in capitalistic production. Its growth continued to be favoured by the rise in prices, which had begun around the middle of the eighteenth century and which persisted throughout the revolutionary and Napoleonic periods until the second decade of the nineteenth century. The basic cause for this rise is to be found in the great increase in currency, due first to the increased production of the American mines, but also to the appearance of fiduciary money in a number of countries such as Denmark, Sweden, Russia, Austria, France, Spain and the United States. The issue of paper money was generally accelerated by the war.

By driving out fortunes, the revolutionary crisis caused the metallic supply of foreign nations to increase. Much French specie found its way to England, Holland, Prussia and Hamburg. An international syndicate (with which Napoleon would later have to cope) involving Baring of London, Hope and Labouchère of Amsterdam, Parish of Hamburg (not to speak of Boyd, established in both England and France), and foreign bankers in Paris, notably Perregaux, were making enormous profits by speculating on the *assignat*, usually selling it short. Little is known about the consequences of the inflation on the European Continent. The prices of colonial products increased greatly in Hamburg from 1793 to 1799, but it appears that the abundance of money operated to increase speculation rather than production. In any case, it was England which most profited from the inflation.

The Bank of England was the only bank issuing notes that inspired confidence, and after the occupation of Holland, England became the surest refuge for capital. In 1794 the Bank purchased £3.75 million worth of precious metals, instead of the average £650,000. Its banknotes in circulation rose from £11 million in 1790 to £15 million in 1800. Until 1795 it discounted commercial paper at less than three per cent. The rate increased only after the suspension of the gold standard in 1797: in 1800 it rose above six per cent. Moreover, England was the only country where banking developed in the provinces. In 1792 there were 350 banks issuing notes without any sort of control. They financed local businesses, so that the monetary inflation was accompanied by an inflation of credit. Momentarily compromised during the panic of 1793, these banks prospered afterwards more than ever. In 1804 they numbered nearly five hundred. Prices rose almost continuously. Taking as an index 100 for the year 1790, they reached 156 in 1799. Wheat, priced on the average at forty-five shillings a quarter between 1780 and 1789, leaped to fifty-five shillings in the following decade. Wages rose proportionally far less, so the margin of profits increased. Since the inflation made money cheap, everything stimulated the spirit of business enterprise.

The rise in prices might have resulted in hindering exports, but for the suspension of the gold standard. The abundance of money had made it possible for Pitt to obtain loans, and he had thus been able to deal with the Bank. But he was still forced to make the Bank discount an increasing quantity of exchequer bills. In 1795 the Bank held exchequer bills totalling nearly £13 million at a time when its cash reserves were less than £5.5 million. Then, too, since Pitt was forced to pay in cash for the expense of the expeditionary forces, for the grain purchases of 1796 and for the foreign subsidies (a total of more than £28 million from 1793 to 1799), he compelled the Bank, despite the law, to advance him a part of its cash reserves which, early in 1797, did not exceed much more than

£1 million. Its banknotes were then declared inconvertible, and remained so until 1821. Since the Bank of England was the keystone of the entire credit structure that sustained the economy, the consequences of this action could have been disastrous. But there was no panic. The people, unacquainted with the methods of John Law or the *assignats*, never realised that the pound was in danger. Pitt also reassured the capitalists, persuading them by means of an energetic fiscal reform that he had no intention whatsoever of resorting to paper money. With peace restored on the Continent, he spent only £2 million in 1797 and 1798 for the support of the armed forces in Europe, and for foreign subsidies. The pound sterling was at a premium, and the Bank's cash reserves were brought to £7 million in 1799. In fact, the Bank henceforth accepted a far larger quantity of exchequer bills, and there was some governmental inflation, but it was moderate enough not to ruin the currency as in France, and it spared England the deflation which had overwhelmed the Directory. But this was only a lull in the storm. In 1799 the war was resumed on the Continent, and scarcity compelled the government to make new grain purchases which cost nearly £3.5 million. The Bank's reserves fell off, and this time the rate of exchange dropped. The pound lost eight per cent of its face value in Hamburg and five per cent in Cadiz in 1799. Although it was not long before this crisis impaired the nation's morale, the decline of the pound, in itself, benefited the capitalists: they were paid in cash for exports, while they themselves paid wages in depreciated paper currency. England's monetary and financial policy, by its empirical methods, attested to a degree of expertness of which no other country was then capable.

The industrial revolution owed its progress to this policy, but it advanced more slowly than has sometimes been believed. In the cotton industry, which was the most advanced, weaving was still done by hand. Edmund Cartwright's power loom was first adopted only in 1801 in Glasgow, and its use spread only after William Radcliffe's invention of the dressing machine around 1804. The woollen industry was still in its trial stage; it made little use of the spinning jenny, and Cartwright's machine for spinning wool combings was not perfected until 1803. Coal mining remained backward despite the growing expansion of rails and the use of steam engines. With the exception of a few cotton mills, the steam engine was not yet used in industry. Most cotton mills were still content with the water-frame. In communications, interest was still centred on canal construction, and there were few good roads. The slowness of transportation and the constant decline in wages enabled traditional manufactures to hold out energetically, and capital continued to be concentrated in commerce rather than in the creation of factories. Some contemporary captains of industry like David Dale, who was the father-in-law of Robert Owen, and Radcliffe of Stockport began with the putting-out system. But Crompton's spinning mule, although not in use everywhere, gave to cotton spinning an irresistible force. Knitted goods and loom-made lace prospered. Metallurgy was extensively modernised, and engineers, the most famous of whom was Bramah, inventor of the hydraulic press, were rapidly increasing the number of machine tools. In all branches of production where it became established, the machine guaranteed England world supremacy.

According to official valuations of the customs house, based on a scale of prices which had prevailed at the end of the seventeenth century, Britain's balance of trade should have been constantly favourable. In 1799, for example, the balance of payments surplus came to £5 million. Industrial progress has always been cited as the cause. In reality, reference to the real value of imports and exports suggests the contrary conclusion, that except for a very few years – only one, 1802, between 1798 and 1815 – Great Britain's balance of trade showed a deficit: £10.5 million in 1799, and almost £20 million in 1801. If industrial exports increased in quantity, their prices also declined, a factor, moreover, which allowed England to retain and win new markets in spite of the difficulties presented by the war. England became nonetheless wealthier. The balance of accounts was redressed by freight charges, insurance, commissions and above all by the exploitation of overseas territories – the Negro slave trade, the funds invested in plantations, the salaries and pensions of officials of the East India Company, the colonial speculations of private traders, the riches which the 'nabobs' brought back from the colonies and the return on capital invested there.

The rise in prices also benefited agriculture. England at this time no longer produced enough grain for its home consumption, and the war made purchases so expensive that the Corn Laws lost their effectiveness, as long as wheat prices remained so high. The result was that more wheat was planted, since it became more profitable than stock farming. Enclosures were also extended on a larger scale than ever before, making this a golden age for landlords as well as for farmers. Improvements in agricultural methods continued, and in 1793 Sir John Sinclair and Arthur Young were placed at the head of a Board of Agriculture. The agrarian revolution had also affected Scotland. There the clan chiefs, who were landlords and who wished to devote their estates to stock raising, evicted the Highland tenant farmers, who were left with no choice but to emigrate. In regard to her food supply, this agricultural prosperity strengthened England and made her less vulnerable. It also enabled small landowners to hold out and even increase in numbers in certain counties. Actually there were not many left, but at least they were content with their lot, and along with the farmers they constituted an element of stability.

English capitalism, despite its progress, did not yet entertain the idea of free trade. Far from renouncing the Corn Laws, both landowners and farmers demanded that they be strengthened. Manufacturers remained faithful to mercantilism to the point of prohibiting the exportation of machinery. But at home they increasingly evaded the regulations limiting the number of apprentices and authorising the establishment of a minimum wage. Workers, on the other hand, continued to invoke the statutes of labourers and backed up their demands with blacklists and strikes, which were forbidden in principle, but which the justices of the peace were reluctant to condemn – inasmuch as the employers themselves set the example in breaking the law. Also worthy of note was the Combination Act of 12 July 1799. Enacted at a time when the authorities allowed the laws favourable to workers to fall into abeyance, the act punished every kind of strike, as well as workingmen's associations and collections of funds intended to support strikes. The employment of foundlings, women and uprooted peasants, plus the advances made by mechanisation depressed wages, which trailed far behind rising commodity prices. In addition, the truck system and the imposition of arbitrary fines helped to reduce wages even more. Beginning in 1795, however, wages were supplemented out of the receipts of the poor tax, such assistance being calculated in relation to the price of bread. This accounts for the relative resignation of the working classes.

Aside from France, English industry was almost unrivalled. Except for a few mining works and the great Silesian metallurgical industry – a monopoly of a few magnates, or of the state – capitalism on the Continent ignored the steam engine and remained commercial. The cotton industry prospered in Saxony, Switzerland and Swabia, but it was not until 1786 that the spinning jenny was introduced in Chemnitz, and the knitting machine appeared only in 1797. Besides, the war affected traditional industries, such as Silesian linen, which was completely ruined.

In agriculture, the Baltic states, which produced for export, began to imitate England. Above all this meant dissolving the village community and reconstituting the divided land strips into unified plots capable of escaping the system of obligatory crop rotation and common pasturage – in short, working towards enclosures. The states also sought to abolish serfdom and to arrange the redemption of the tithe, feudal dues and corvées so as to transform the peasant into a landowner or a wage-earning day labourer. This reform had been operating in Denmark ever since 1781, and it was extended in principle to Schleswig-Holstein in 1800. In Prussia the king applied it to his own domains.

As an importer of grains, England could not help but profit from these reforms. She likewise regarded favourably the advances made in the United States, still purely agricultural, and was particularly pleased by the progress of sea-island cotton, which had been brought over from the Bahamas in 1786. It had been introduced in Glasgow for the first time in 1792, and had been immediately acclaimed by cotton spinners. No sooner had the problem of ginning been solved by Whitney's invention in 1793 than exports reached eight million pounds in weight, and by 1798 this figure had already doubled. It was a development of far-reaching significance to the United States, for slavery thenceforth became a fundamental institution in the South, and planters began to covet Florida and Louisiana. For the time being, however, the North saw in it only an opportunity to put its capital and ships to work. The introduction of English technology was still in its very beginnings, and the great fortunes of the Astors and the Girards were being built by trade, shipping and speculation in land.

Deprived of the markets controlled by France, yet relieved of French competition, England compensated at the expense of her allies and the neutrals. It was through the Hanseatic ports that she entered upon the economic conquest of Germany. Her exports to Bremen and Hamburg increased sixfold between 1789 and 1800. At the Frankfurt and Leipzig fairs she came into contact with Swiss, Austrians, Poles and Russians. Her cotton goods and her yarn in particular drove out Swiss and Saxon products. The world of finance looked to London. The elector of Hesse invested his capital there, and it was by helping him to do it that Meyer

Amschel Rothschild of Frankfurt extended his business; in 1798 his son, Nathan, established himself in England, and became wealthy soon after. The Baltic region also became an English preserve of great importance for supplies of naval stores, grains and textiles. At the beginning of the nineteenth century, seventy-two per cent of British imports came from Prussia and Russia, seventy-five per cent of her grain from the port of Danzig alone. French resistance fared better in the Mediterranean. She embarrassed England by conquering Italy, but she failed to eliminate her. After 1798, however, France was driven from the Levant.

The naval struggle increased the importance of the continental routes between the Mediterranean and the northern seas. The closing of the Rhine had seriously imperilled communications across France, Italy, Switzerland and Holland, which, until then, had been more or less secure. Ever since 1790 France had interrupted traffic along the left bank by bringing her customs posts to the river, and the occupation of the Rhineland and Holland was a new blow to this trade route. With the mouth of the Rhine closed, Cologne's trade was reduced to less than a third of its previous volume by 1800; only a portion trickled through Emden to Frankfurt. To the south, Switzerland was cut off from Genoa. As in the time of Louis XIV, the transcontinental route receded towards the east. Henceforth it would pass through Hamburg and Leipzig in order to reach Venice, or preferably Trieste.

We possess only problematic estimates based on customs house valuations (official values) to indicate the fluctuations of British commerce up to 1798, but the trend is clear. Exports would have risen from £20 million in 1790 to £35 million in 1801, and taken together with imports, the volume would have increased from £39 million to £67 million. In terms of real values, exports rose from £42.6 million in 1798 to £52.3 million in 1800, and taken together with imports, the volume increased from £99.1 million to £118.8 million. The tonnage of departing ships increased by a third, reaching almost two million tons. It was during the war that the London docks were constructed and equipped with bonded warehouses. The cotton industry, more than any other, profited from this rise. Its exports soared from £1.5 million to £6 million in 1800; and imports of raw cotton rose from £734,000 in 1797 to £1,663,000 in 1800. That same year (1800) two million tons of coal and 1½ million tons of wrought and cast iron were exported.

England also doubled her shipments to the United States. Like the latter, her eyes remained fixed on Spanish America, where her occupation of Trinidad served primarily for smuggling. The unrest there promised great prospects. United States independence, the suspension of the *exclusif** and the abolition of slavery in the French Antilles had shaken the whole colonial system. Above all, the Creoles wanted freedom of trade, as did Belgrano in Buenos Aires, and Spain had been forced to admit neutrals into her colonial ports. Some of the colonies were also beginning to aspire to political independence. In Mexico and in Venezuela, conspiracies resulted in bloody repressions. After first having made his appeal to France, General Francisco Miranda turned to England when Spain changed sides in the war. In London he met Nariño and O'Higgins, and was to have founded a 'Lautaro Lodge' to prepare a general insurrection. In any case, in 1798 he solicited the aid of Pitt in the name of a committee formed in Spain at his instigation, but Pitt referred him to the United States, which had for the moment broken with France.

England, mistress of the seas, was now in other parts of the world the only nation capable of imposing the authority of the white man. It was a task to which she was not much disposed. Although the mercantile view had not adopted Bentham's hostility towards colonies, the example of American independence did not encourage further colonisations. Rather, England's imperialism was commercial. Still, the British Empire continued to grow. The French Antilles were there for the taking. Enormous amounts of capital were invested in Dutch Guiana, resulting in a tenfold increase in production. The navy needed anchorages like the Cape of Good Hope. Colonial administrators, who descended from the nobility, satisfied their yearning for action by spontaneously pushing for further conquests. In Africa, the colony of Sierra Leone was founded in 1792, Mungo Park explored the Niger as far as Timbuktu, and the Cape was taken from the Dutch. In Australia, Captain Arthur Phillip had landed the first gang of convicts at Sydney in 1788.

But it was in India above all that the English expanded, after the arrival of Richard Wellesley, earl of Mornington, afterwards Marquess Wellesley. He annexed part of Mysore following the death of Tippoo Sahib in 1799, and in 1800 established his protectorate over the Nizam,

---

* A term denoting a system of exclusive colonial trading rights, whereby a mother country prohibited its colonies to raise or manufacture anything that might compete with its own goods, to trade with other countries or to use any ships other than its own in foreign trade. TRANSLATOR.

sovereign of Hyderabad, who had obtained the rest of Mysore. Then he attacked the Marathas. He kept a close watch over the Punjab, where Ranjit Singh had forced the Afghans to cede Lahore in 1794. Finally he attended both to Persia, where Sir John Malcolm secured a treaty in 1801 that opened the Gulf coast to the English, and to the Red Sea, where Perim was occupied in 1798 and where Sir Home Popham was later despatched to obtain the Arabian coffee monopoly and to prepare an expedition of sepoys against Egypt.

Had it not been for the war in Europe, the Far East would very probably also have fallen prey to European encroachments. In Indochina, Bishop Pigneau de Béhaine helped Nguyen Anh recapture Cochin China from the rebellious Tayson mountaineers, and he remained Nguyen's counsellor until he died. Nguyen then gradually reconquered Annam and Tonking, where the Le-Loi dynasty had been dethroned, and he assumed the crown in 1803 taking the name of Gia Long. Nevertheless, French influence had fallen to nothing. In China, the Manchu dynasty reached its peak under Ch'ien Lung, who died in 1799 after having conquered the frontier provinces. Not content with colonising these provinces, the Chinese were already spreading in numbers into Cochin China and the Philippines. They reached as far as Siam and Bengal, and were the only foreigners admitted into Japan. At home they traded with Europeans only at the Portuguese trading post of Macao, which was frequented by hardly any but the English and Americans after the dissolution of the Dutch East India Company. Sent to Peking in 1793, the Irishman George Macartney was unable to obtain any concessions. But after the death of Ch'ien Lung, his cruel and dissolute son Chia Ch'ing (1796–1820), who was threatened by revolts fomented by secret societies, was no longer in a position to resist anyone attacking in force. The English, however, were busy elsewhere. Japan was even more tightly closed. Unable to feed her population, which was continually being decimated by famine, Japan nevertheless prohibited the importation of grain and forbade emigration. Each year she admitted only a few Chinese junks and one Dutch vessel to which she sold some copper at Nagasaki. Quite weak militarily, Japan witnessed with misgiving the arrival of English and especially Russian ships in Sakhalin, the Kuriles and even Ezo in 1792.

Missionaries have often paved the way for merchants and soldiers, but at this time they were primarily concerned with America. In China, Ch'ien Lung persecuted the Lazarists, who were successors to the

Jesuits, and their mission, whose recruitment had been interrupted by the Revolution, disappeared in 1800. A new development was the entry into the lists by the Protestants, who had hitherto been represented by only a few Moravian Brothers. It was, in fact, England which changed the situation. The first incursions were made by the Baptists in 1795; and in 1799 Joshua Marshman landed in Bengal, where he was given a very bad reception by the East India Company.

Emigration among the whites came almost to a standstill. It was rather through an excess of births that the settlers of North America multiplied and advanced towards the West, pushing back the forest. In the United States, Kentucky and Tennessee were admitted as states in 1791 and 1796, Ohio in 1803. But in 1800 the West still numbered only 370,000 inhabitants out of more than five million. Vancouver explored the Pacific coast from 1790 to 1795, and the Russians had begun to appear there, but between the Atlantic and Pacific there existed no connection other than the trading posts of the Hudson's Bay Company, which had reached as far as the Columbia River. In 1793 Alexander Mackenzie still preferred to venture into the solitude of the Arctic regions.

With Latin America no more than a hope, Europe and the United States constituted the markets on which the existence of England depended. That these markets might sooner or later be threatened was considered not entirely impossible. On the Continent, industry could not help but feel the effect of British competition. To save their spinning industry, Switzerland and particularly Saxony were forced to modernise their equipment – the first water-frame machine appeared at Chemnitz in 1798. Thus an embargo on British goods would have been as useful to them as it was to France. Then, too, the British blockade continually gave rise to diplomatic difficulties. In 1794 Denmark and Sweden had drawn up a new league of neutrals. Alone they were powerless, but if Russia joined, Prussia and North Germany would follow suit, and the Baltic would be closed. The United States presented an even more obvious danger to British commerce. To the question of the blockade had been added that of the American sailors whom England purposely confused with the nationals she sought out and impressed from aboard neutral vessels. Washington and the Federalists confined themselves to protests, but in 1801 Jefferson became president, and it was likely that he would prove less accommodating.

Nor must it be forgotten that, because of the war, the conditions of world trade were not entirely sound. In London, Amsterdam and Hamburg, speculation on colonial commodities took the form of reciprocal credit arrangements, and capital was immobilised in stock accumulation. As the Elbe froze over and shipments stopped late in the winter of 1799, prices rose to dizzy heights in Hamburg. When the thaw set in before the spring fairs, ships began to pour in and a drop in prices followed, reaching as much as seventy-two per cent in sugar. At the same time the war resumed, and in August, on the eve of the invasion, Amsterdam bankers cut off credit. In Hamburg, 136 firms failed, and the House of Parish lost over a million marks. The crisis had its repercussions throughout Europe, and especially in London, where at least twenty merchants went bankrupt. The cotton industry was considerably shaken, and factories either shut down or cut wages. It was in order to curb the labour unrest that the Combination Act was then passed. As it happened, the financial and monetary situation was growing worse, and finally the harvests of 1799 and 1800 proved exceptionally bad. The quarter of wheat rose from forty-nine shillings at the beginning of 1799 to 101 shillings in February 1800.

France failed to attain her goal by shutting out the English, for British commerce found new markets and prospered more than ever. In believing England's economic structure to be weak and artificial, the French were mistaken because they overlooked the wonders of the credit system. Yet it is true that England's economic structure was a delicate mechanism, automatically subject to intermittent checks, and capable of breaking down through a combination of external circumstances such as the policies of other states and bad harvests. Precisely such a threat was looming in England, and it was quite possible that a time would come when, disheartened, she would consent to make peace.

## THE TERMS OF THE PEACE

To profit from such an occasion, the Republic had to restore peace on the Continent. She would have to fight and conquer once again, and then, when the treaty was signed, re-establish internal order and disarm the counter-revolutionary forces. Otherwise, their persistent appeals abroad would bring about a renewal of hostilities at the first crisis. Success also depended, however, upon just which of its conquests France intended to keep.

After 9 Thermidor French policy had gradually turned to the acquisition of natural frontiers. In the Constitution of Year III, the Thermidorians had forbidden the surrender of any territory whatsoever. At that time (August 1795), French territory had included, by reason of conquest, only Savoy and Nice. But on 9 Vendémiaire, Year IV (30 September 1795), the Convention annexed Belgium, and this acquisition was held to be sanctioned by the constitutional plebiscite. Henceforth, the plebiscites of 1793 were also invoked to justify France's claim to the left bank of the Rhine, contrary claims to which were abandoned by Prussia at Basle, by Austria at Campoformio and by the Holy Roman Empire at Rastatt. Carnot, a member of the Directory until 18 Fructidor, did not approve such aggrandisement, and the *Idéologues*, who propelled Bonaparte to power, were of virtually the same opinion. On 1 November 1799 one of them, probably Daunou, declared in the *Décade Philosophique* that the Constitution of Year III, by fixing the territorial limits of the Republic, had decreed 'eternal warfare and the total annihilation of the French people'. This did not mean that the republicans would have to negotiate on the basis of the 'old limits', as the royalists were made to promise by France's enemies. France could still expand into Walloon Belgium and into the Saar.

The majority of the nation would surely have approved this moderation. What it wanted above all else was peace, as the article in the *Décade*, which was destined to prepare the *coup d'état*, indeed proves. Nevertheless, the difficulties of such an attitude must not be disregarded. In its struggle against royalism, the Directory had never ceased to appeal to national feeling, so that the republicans developed the habit of identifying the Revolution with the conquest of the natural frontiers. Consequently, they prided themselves on having completed the work of the monarchy. The army would not have looked favourably upon the loss of its conquests. If the army secured peace by means of fresh victories, how could the government be less demanding than its predecessors?

The Directory had let Bonaparte set a dangerous precedent by his formation of the Cisalpine Republic beyond the natural frontiers. It was an act which he subsequently repeated in Rome and Naples. He established himself in Piedmont, made the canton of Valais a republic in order to control the Alpine passes, and behaved like an overlord in Holland and Switzerland. Still, it could be argued that the war justified such a policy. With the peace signed, France would assuredly not lose interest in what took place along her natural frontiers, but it did not follow that she would have to maintain her armies in these adjacent lands. She might well content herself with guaranteeing their independence in conjunction with the other powers. There is no doubt that public opinion would have supported the government in this respect. After so many disappointing experiences, the Girondins' enthusiasm for revolutionary propaganda had faded, and no one would blame Bonaparte for not having re-established the Roman or Parthenopean Republics.

A lasting peace was impossible as long as France went beyond her natural frontiers, but assuming she went no further than that, would the continental powers have granted her even that much? It has been denied, but without convincing reason. For Prussia, only the promise of indemnities in Germany mattered, and Russia had not gone to war for the sake of the left bank of the Rhine. Austria would be the most recalcitrant, but would have been pacified by territorial compensations, especially by a renunciation of French claims in Italy.

There remained England. Pitt had stated at various times his refusal to negotiate without a full guarantee of England's security, and that this could not be obtained as long as France occupied the Low Countries. He further stated that France would have to be deprived of at least the major part of the left bank of the Rhine which, added Grenville in 1795, would then be reunited with a Belgium in Austrian hands. While it was not true that England's security was their only concern – they also wished to deprive France of Savoy – nevertheless it cannot be denied that one of the cardinal points of England's foreign policy had always been to preserve the Low Countries from French domination. Only now the Low Countries would have to be recaptured, and this was an undertaking in which England could not succeed without the help of her continental allies. If France came to terms on the Continent, it would then be a matter of a war of attrition. Economic circumstances might then induce England to resign herself to the situation, especially if the seas and the colonies were left to her uncontested. The crisis of 1797 had forced Pitt to suggest such an accommodation, and in 1799 all signs were pointing in the same direction. The danger, however, was that France might attribute England's difficulties to nothing other than the blockade she had imposed to counter that of her rival. In such a case the temptation might arise to contest England's rule of the seas as well, by increasing the pressure through an extension of the blockade to all of Europe. Then the war on the Continent would have begun anew and would have truly become a *guerre éternelle*, not because France would have reached her natural frontiers, but because she would have overstepped them.

If wisdom had prevailed in France, it would have meant that Europe, so intensely hostile to the regicidal Republic, would have for ever renounced the idea of recovering all or part of France's prodigious conquests. But this is not the way to look at the question. In 1799, as always, the problem for a statesman was not how to arrest the course of history. Rather, it was a matter of knowing whether France had a chance to secure peace for a decade or two, while retaining her so-called natural frontiers, and to regain her strength in order to prepare to defend them with still more energy than before. That the answer was 'yes' cannot be doubted; but would the republican members of the Directory have been capable of it? This is by no means certain, but at the end of 1799 the decision was no longer theirs. They had placed it by their own choice in the hands of a single man.

# CHAPTER THREE

# The Coming of Napoleon Bonaparte

T HAT THE FRENCH REVOLUTION turned to dictatorship was no
accident; it was driven there by inner necessity, and not for the first
time either. Nor was it an accident that the Revolution led to the
dictatorship of a general. But it so happened that this general was Napoleon Bonaparte, a man whose temperament, even more than his genius,
was unable to adapt to peace and moderation. Thus it was an unforeseeable contingency which tilted the scale in favour of *la guerre éternelle*.

## THE DICTATORSHIP IN FRANCE

For a long time the republicans had wanted to strengthen the central
authority. One need only look at the constitutions they gave to the vassal
states: in Holland, the members of the Directory controlled the treasury;
in Switzerland, they appointed government officials; in Rome, they
appointed judges as well. In the Helvetic and Roman Republics every
department already possessed a 'prefect'. All this is not to mention the
Cisalpine Republic, which was Bonaparte's personal fief. Unfortunately,
in France the amending procedure prescribed by the Constitution of Year
III required a delay of at least seven years. The *coup d'état* of 18 Fructidor
had provided the occasion sought by Sieyès, Talleyrand and Bonaparte,
but they let the opportunity slip. In Year VII, however, they hoped to
bring about a new one. Without realising it, the republicans were giving
way to a tendency which, ever since the start of the civil and foreign wars,
was pushing the Revolution in the direction of a permanent and all-
powerful executive, that is to say towards dictatorship. It was this social
revolution that drove the dispossessed nobility far beyond insurrection.
Subsidised by enemy gold, it exploited the wartime hardships – that
inexhaustible source of discontent – and particularly the monetary and
economic crisis, thereby intending to turn the people against the government. The French did not want a return to the *ancien régime*, but they

suffered and they held their leaders responsible for it. At every election the counter-revolution hoped to regain power. It was awareness of this danger that led the Mountain in 1793 to declare the Convention in permanent session until the peace. The Thermidorians had intended to restore elective government, but they immediately returned to Jacobin expediency by passing the Decree of the Two-Thirds. Next, the Directory, overwhelmed by the elections of 1797, re-established the dictatorship on 18 Fructidor. Yet as long as the Constitution of Year III continued to exist, this dictatorship, put to the test each year, required a host of violent measures and could never be brought into working order. So it was still necessary to revive the principle of 1793 and invest it with permanence until such time as peace, settled once and for all, would persuade the counter-revolution to accept the new order. It was in this respect that Napoleon's dictatorship became so much a part of the history of the French Revolution. No matter what he may have said or done, neither he nor his enemies were ever able to break this bond, and this was a fact which the European aristocracy understood perfectly well.

In 1799, as in 1793, the Jacobins wished to establish a democratic dictatorship by relying on the Sansculottes to push it through the councils. Taking advantage of the crisis preceding the victory at Zurich, they succeeded in forcing the passage of several revolutionary measures: a compulsory loan, the abolition of exemptions from military service, the law of hostages, a repeal of assignments on public revenues which had been granted to bankers and government contractors, withholdings on the *rente* and on salaries, and, finally, requisitions. These measures constituted a direct attack on bourgeois interests and brought that class to action. Thus it was symbolic that assignments on public revenues were restored the very night of 19 Brumaire. The *Idéologues* who gathered around Madame de Condorcet at Auteuil or in the salon of Madame de Staël wanted neither a democratic dictatorship nor even a democracy. Writing in 1799 on the means to 'end the Revolution' and on 'the principles fundamental to the Republic' (*Des circonstances actuelles qui peuvent terminer la révolution et des principes qui doivent fonder la république en France*), Madame de Staël expressed their desire: to devise a representative system of government which would assure power to the moneyed and talented 'notables'. Sieyès, who had become a director, took his inspiration from the Decree of the Two-Thirds. Together with his friends he wanted to select the membership of the newly constituted bodies which would then expand themselves by co-optation, leaving to the nation only the role of electing candidates. Furthermore, those already in office saw in this plan the chance to keep themselves in power.

The people having been eliminated as an obstacle to the dictatorship of the bourgeoisie, only the army remained. The Directory had already sought its help on 18 Fructidor, Year V, and had managed to keep the upper hand, despite serious inroads. Now, however, the situation was very different in that steadfast republicans, not royalists, were to be driven out. Only a popular general could have carried it through, and Bonaparte's sudden return destined that it should be he. The will of the nation which was invoked to justify 18 Brumaire played no part in the event. The nation rejoiced at the news that Bonaparte was in France because it recognised an able general; but the Republic had conquered without him, and Masséna's victory had bolstered the reputation of the Directory. Consequently, the responsibility for 18 Brumaire lies on that segment of the republican bourgeoisie called the Brumairians, whose leading light was Sieyès. They had no intention of giving in to Bonaparte, and they chose him only as an instrument of their policy. That they propelled him to power without imposing any conditions, without even first delimiting the fundamental character of the new regime, betrays their incredible mediocrity. Bonaparte did not repudiate the notables, for he too was not a democrat, and their collaboration alone enabled him to rule. But on the evening of 19 Brumaire, after they had hurriedly slapped together the structure of the Provisional Consulate, they should not have harboured any more illusions. The army had followed Bonaparte, and him alone. He was complete master. Regardless of what he and his apologists may have said, his rule was from its origins an absolute military dictatorship. It was Bonaparte alone who would decide the questions on which the fate of France and Europe hinged.

## NAPOLEON BONAPARTE

What sort of a man was he? His personality evolved in so singular a manner that it defies portrayal. He appeared first as a studious officer full of dreams, garrisoned at Valence and Auxonne. As a youthful general, on the eve of the Battle of Castiglione, he could still hold a council of war. But in the final years as emperor, he was stupefied with his own omnipotence and was infatuated with his own omniscience. And yet distinctive traits appear throughout his entire career: power could do no more than accentuate some and attenuate others.

Short-legged and small in stature, muscular, ruddy, and still gaunt at the age of thirty, he was physically hardy and fit. His sensitivity and steadiness were admirable, his reflexes quick as lightning and his capacity for work unlimited. He could fall asleep at will. But we also find the reverse: cold humid weather brought on oppression, coughing spells, dysuria; when crossed he unleashed frightful outbursts of temper; over-exertion, despite prolonged hot baths, despite extreme sobriety, despite the moderate yet constant use of coffee and tobacco, occasionally pro-duced brief collapses, even tears. His mind was one of the most perfect that has ever been: his unflagging attention tirelessly swept in facts and ideas which his memory registered and classified; his imagination played with them freely, and being in a permanent state of concealed tension, it never wearied of inventing political and strategic motifs which mani-fested themselves in unexpected flashes of intuition like those experienced by poets and mathematicians. This would happen especially at night during a sudden awakening, and he himself referred to it as 'the moral spark' and 'the after-midnight presence of the spirit'. This spirit-ual fervour shone through his glittering eyes and illuminated the face, still 'sulphuric' at his rise, of the 'sleek-haired Corsican'. This is what made him unsociable, and not, as Hippolyte Taine would have us think, some kind of brutality, the consequence of a slightly tarnished *condottiere* being let loose upon the world in all his savagery. He rendered a fair account of himself when he said, 'I consider myself a good man at heart,' and indeed he showed generosity, and even kindness to those who were close to him. But between ordinary mortals, who hurried through their tasks in order to abandon themselves to leisure or diversion, and Na-poleon Bonaparte, who was the soul of effort and concentration, there could exist no common ground nor true community. Ambition – that irresistible impulse to act and to dominate – sprang from his physical and mental state of being. He knew himself well: 'It is said that I am an ambi-tious man but that is not so; or at least my ambition is so closely bound to my being that they are both one and the same.' How very true! Napoleon was more than anything else a temperament.

Ever since his military schooldays at Brienne, when he was still a poor and taunted foreigner, timid yet bursting with passion, Napoleon drew strength from pride in himself and contempt for others. Destined to become an officer, his instinct to command without having to discuss could not have been better served. Although he might on occasion have sought information or opinion, he alone was master and judge. Bonaparte's natural propensity for dictatorship suited the normal practice of his profession. In Italy and in Egypt he introduced dictatorship into the government. In France he wanted to put himself forward as a civilian, but the military stamp was indelibly there. He consulted often, but he could never tolerate free opposition. More precisely, when faced with a group of men accustomed to discussion, he would lose his composure. This explains his intense hatred of the *Idéologues*. The confused and undisciplined, yet formidable masses inspired in him as much fear as contempt. Regardless of costumes and titles, Bonaparte took power as a general, and as such he exercised it.

Beneath the soldier's uniform, however, there dwelled in him several personalities, and it is this diversity, as much as the variety and brilliance of his gifts, which makes him so fascinating. Wandering about penniless in the midst of the Thermidorian festival, brushing past rich men and beautiful women, the Bonaparte of 1795 burned with the same desires as others. Something of that time never did leave him: a certain pleasure in stepping on those who had once snubbed him; a taste for ostentatious splendour; an over-tender care for his family – the 'clan' – which had suffered much the same miseries as himself; and a few memorable remarks of the citizen-turned-gentleman, as on the day of his coronation when he exclaimed, 'Joseph, if only father could see us!' But even much earlier there lived in him a nobler trait, a passionate desire to know and understand everything. It served him, no doubt, yet it was a need which he fulfilled for its own sake, without any ulterior motive.

As a young officer he was a tireless reader and compiler. He also wrote, and it is obvious that had he not entered the royal military academy at Brienne, he could have become a man of letters. Having entered into a life of action, he still remained a thinker. This warrior was never happier than in the silence of his own study, surrounded by papers and documents. In time he became more practical, and he would boast that he had repudiated 'ideology'. Nevertheless, he was still a typical man of the eighteenth century, a rationalist, a *philosophe*. Far from relying on intuition, he placed his trust in reason, in knowledge and in methodical effort. 'I generally look ahead three or four months in advance to what I must do, and then I count on the worst'; 'all work must be done systematically because left to chance, nothing can succeed.' He believed that his insights were the natural fruit of his patience. His conception of a unitary state, made of one piece according to a simple and symmetrical plan, was entirely classical. At rare moments his intellectualism revealed itself by his most striking characteristic: the ability to stand off from himself and take a detached look at his own life, and to reflect wistfully on his fate. From Cairo he wrote to Joseph after having learned of Josephine's infidelity, 'I need solitude and isolation. I find grandeur tiring, my feelings drained and glory dull. At twenty-nine I am completely played out.' Walking with Girardin at Ermenonville, he would exclaim shortly thereafter, 'The future will tell if it would not have been better for the sake of world peace had Rousseau and I never been born.' When the state councillor Roederer remarked, while visiting the abandoned Tuileries Palace with Napoleon, 'General, this is all so sad,' Bonaparte, already First Consul for two months, replied, 'Yes, and so is grandeur.' Thus by a striking turnabout, this firm and severe intellect would give way to the romantic melancholia characteristic of Chateaubriand and de Vigny. But these were never more than flashes, and he would pull himself together at once.

He seemed to be dedicated to a policy of realism in every way, and he was, in fact, a realist in execution down to the slightest detail. During the course of his rise, he made the rounds of human emotions, and well did he learn to play upon them. He knew how to exploit self-interest, vanity, jealousy, even dishonesty. He knew what could be obtained from men by arousing their sense of honour and by inflaming their imagination; nor did he for a moment forget that they could be subdued by terror. He discerned ever so clearly what in the work of the Revolution had captured the heart of the nation and what fitted in with his despotism. To win the French people, he declared himself both a man of peace and a god of war. That is why he must be ranked among the great realists in history.

And yet he was a realist in execution only. There lived in him an *alter ego* which contained certain features of the hero. It seems to have been born during his days at the military academy out of a need to dominate a world in which he felt himself despised. Above all he longed to equal the semi-legendary heroes of Plutarch and Corneille. His greatest ambition was glory. 'I live only for posterity,' he exclaimed; 'death is nothing, but to live defeated and without glory is to die every day.' His eyes were fixed on the world's great leaders: Alexander, who conquered the East

and dreamed of conquering the world; Caesar, Augustus, Charlemagne –
the creators and the restorer of the Roman Empire whose very names
were synonymous with the idea of a universal civilisation. From these he
did not deduce a precise formulation to be used as a rule, a measure or a
condition of political conduct. They were for him examples, which stimulated his imagination and lent an unutterable charm to action. He was
stirred less by the accomplishments of his heroes than by the consuming
spiritual zeal which had engendered their work. He was an artist, a poet
of action, for whom France and mankind were but instruments. How well
he expressed his sense of grandeur when, in St Helena, he evoked memories of the victory at Lodi and the awakening in his consciousness of the
will to power! 'I saw the world flee beneath me, as if I were transported in
the air.'

That is why it is idle to seek for limits to Napoleon's policy, or for a
final goal at which he would have stopped: there simply was none. As for
his followers who worried about it, he once remarked, 'I always told them
that I just didn't know,' or again, more significantly, despite the triteness
of his expression, 'To be in God's place? Ah! I would not want it; that
would be a cul-de-sac!' Here, then, we see that dynamic temperament
which struck us at first glance in its psychological manifestation. It is the
romantic Napoleon, a force seeking to expand and for which the world
was no more than an occasion for acting dangerously. But knowing the
disposition of one's means alone is not the mark of a realist. On the contrary, the realist also fixes his goal in terms of the possible, and although
his imagination and his flair for grandeur push him on, still he knows
where to stop.

That a mind so capable of grasping reality in certain respects should
miss it in others, as Louis Molé* so accurately observed, can only be due
to Napoleon's origins as much as to his nature. When he first came to
France, he considered himself a foreigner. Until the time when he was
expelled from Corsica by his compatriots in 1791, his attitude had been
one of hostility to the French people. Assuredly he became sufficiently
imbued with their culture and spirit to adopt their nationality; otherwise
he could never have become their leader. But he lacked the time to iden-
tify himself with the French nation and to adopt its national tradition to

* Comte Louis Mathieu Molé was prime minister of France from 1836 to 1839. Under
Napoleon I he held various important prefectural and ministerial posts, and he was an
*auditeur* in Napoleon's Conseil d'État. TRANSLATOR.

the point where he would consider its interests as a limitation upon his own actions. Something of the uprooted person remained in him; something of the *déclassé* as well. He was neither entirely a gentleman nor entirely common. He served both the king and the Revolution without attaching himself to either. This was one of the reasons for his success, since he could so easily place himself above parties and announce himself as the restorer of national unity. Yet neither in the *ancien régime* nor in the new order did he find principles which might have served as a norm or a limit. Unlike Richelieu, he was not restrained by dynastic loyalty, which would have subordinated his will to the interest of his master. Nor was he motivated by civic virtue, which could have made him a servant of the nation.

A successful soldier, a pupil of the *philosophes*, he detested feudalism, civil inequality and religious intolerance. Seeing in enlightened despotism a reconciliation of authority with political and social reform, he became its last and most illustrious representative. In this sense he was the man of the Revolution. His headstrong individuality never accepted democracy, however, and he rejected the great hope of the eighteenth century which inspired revolutionary idealism – the hope that some day men would be civilised enough to rule themselves. He did not become cautious through a concern for his personal safety, as were other men, because he was indifferent to it. He dreamed only of greatness through heroism and danger.

What about moral limits? In spiritual life he had nothing in common with other men. Even though he knew their passions well and deftly turned them to his own ends, he cared only for those that would reduce men to dependence. He belittled every feeling that elevated men to acts of sacrifice – religious faith, patriotism, love of freedom – because he saw in them obstacles to his own schemes. Not that he was impervious to these sentiments, at least not in his youth, for they readily led to heroic deeds; but fate led him in a different direction and walled him up within himself. In the splendid and terrible isolation of the will to power, measure carries no meaning.

Unaware of Bonaparte's romantic impulse, the *Idéologues* believed him to be one of their own. Perhaps they could have succeeded in restraining this elemental urge by keeping him in a subordinate position under a strong government. But by pushing him to supreme power, the Brumairians precisely renounced any such precaution.

# I I

# The Pacification of
# France and Europe
# (1799–1802)

# CHAPTER FOUR

# The Organisation of the
# Dictatorship in France

HAVING SEIZED POWER, Napoleon immediately set about organising his dictatorship. A part of his work was destined to endure, and still forms the administrative backbone of France today. The fruits of this long and exacting labour which continually preoccupied him until his downfall, could only appear gradually. Meanwhile, preparation for the campaign of 1800 brooked no delay. Napoleon was therefore forced to improvise at whatever risk. These two features would continue up to the very end. He never stopped building for the future, but bent as he was upon doing the impossible, he was forever condemned to improvising every one of his enterprises.

## THE PROVISIONAL CONSULATE AND THE
## CONSTITUTION OF YEAR VIII

On the evening of 19 Brumaire, Year VIII (10 November 1799), several deputies hastily sanctioned the establishment of a provisional government, which was charged with the task of drafting a new constitution. Both executive and legislative power was placed in the hands of three consuls: Bonaparte, Sieyès and Roger Ducos. On the twentieth they agreed to take turns presiding, but actually Bonaparte took complete control from the very beginning. Two commissions of twenty-five members, each divided into three sections, were substituted for the Council of Ancients and the Council of Five Hundred and were to assist only in the preparation of the new constitution.

This development did not give rise to any serious opposition, since neither the Revolution nor the Republic seemed to be called into question. It was just another *coup d'état*. A barely enthusiastic France watched Bonaparte at work – who even knew whether he would last? Still, a leftist and a rightist minority began to take shape immediately. The Consulate was anti-Jacobin in its origin, since the motive for the Brumaire *coup* had been, after all, an alleged 'anarchist' plot. It was the left which had opposed the meeting of the Councils at Saint-Cloud and offered resistance in certain sections of the country. Sixty-one deputies had been excluded from that sitting, fifty-six of them Jacobins, of whom twenty were later exiled to Guiana and the Île de Ré, and many others had been arrested. The terroristic measures of 1799 – the compulsory loan, the law of hostages and the requisitions – were rescinded; it was a victory for the merchants and the bankers. Now that 'respectable citizens' professed their satisfaction, so too did the royalists in their publications and in the theatre. In Bonaparte they hoped to find a second Monk, a restorer of the monarchy, and a strong clerical upsurge was evidenced everywhere as the refractory clergy no longer remained in hiding. But Bonaparte lost no time in repudiating the counter-revolution, and he was able to repress it without much trouble since the departmental administrations of the Directory were retained and placed under the control of delegates appointed by the consuls. Fouché, the minister of police, from the first took the side of the left; he rescinded the proscription of the Jacobins. True to the spirit of Brumaire, Bonaparte ruled along with the notables, who were either allied or committed to the work of the Revolution.

Meanwhile, the drafting of the constitution continued under the care of the two sections of the legislative commissions who were specifically assigned to this task. They consulted Sieyès, but the Oracle, as he was called, declared that he had not yet prepared anything. He voiced his views, however, the essence of which has been preserved by Boulay de La Meurthe, Daunou and Roederer. Even though their reports differ to some extent as to what was actually said, two points are worth noting. First, the Brumairians were to be installed in the constituted bodies, which would then proceed to recruit additional members by co-opting from among the notables. Public officials would likewise no longer be elected, since authority, said Sieyès, would have to come from above. He added, however, that since confidence must come from below, the people – who were to be made sovereign by virtue of universal suffrage – would be allowed to choose candidates from among the notables to make up the electoral lists. This would not in any way have impeded the realisation of the idea which had given birth to 18 Brumaire – a dictatorship of the notables. Power, on the other hand, was to be thoroughly divided. The legislature was to consist of three assemblies; and executive power was to be divided between a grand elector appointed for life, but subject to 'absorption' by the Senate, and two consuls appointed by him – one for domestic affairs, the other for foreign affairs. Within their respective spheres of authority, both consuls and their separate ministers and the state council were to enjoy complete independence. Here then were Sieyès's real intentions. By designing these complex provisions he sought to protect freedom of individual action from state despotism. But in so doing, he underrated the need to strengthen the authority of the government, which had been the second motive for the *coup d'état*, and he also underestimated the extent of Bonaparte's ambitions.

Bonaparte naturally offered no objection to the disappearance of elective government or to the creation of numerous assemblies, but he categorically demanded executive power for himself alone. A meeting of Bonaparte and Sieyès, arranged by Talleyrand, only served to embitter the conflict between the two consuls. The members of the two sections dealing with the constitution put an end to the dispute by pronouncing themselves against Sieyès. They declared themselves in favour of a First Consul who, although assisted by two lesser consuls, would be invested with pre-eminent authority and the power to appoint all officials. They did not even spare the rest of Sieyès's plan, and they decided to re-establish both a limited suffrage based on property qualifications and the elective principle, probably realising that the assemblies would otherwise be left powerless before Bonaparte.

As soon as the draft had been written down by Daunou, Bonaparte assembled the members of the two commissions in his apartments. New deliberations ensued, during which Sieyès managed to restore into the constitution the principle of co-optation, the Lists of Notability, and universal suffrage, apparently without any trouble since Bonaparte could not but approve them. Bonaparte in turn considerably increased his own powers. His two colleagues found themselves reduced to a consultative voice, and he alone acquired the power to promulgate laws. The Tribunate was deprived of any legislative initiative. The final product thus appeared to be a compromise, but, in fact, what Sieyès had obtained could only have benefited Bonaparte, once the latter had concentrated complete executive power in himself. Doubtless some of the Brumairians went along with him in order to tie themselves to his rising star; others, however, supported him out of principle, sincerely believing that the well-being of the Revolution necessitated a strong leader.

Because of the informal nature of these proceedings, legal debate should now have been left to the Council of Five Hundred and the matter then referred to the Council of Ancients. But the general feeling was to terminate these deliberations, and when, on the night of 22 Frimaire (13 December), Bonaparte requested the deputies to indicate their assent by signing the articles, and proceeded then and there to insert the names of the three consuls (Bonaparte, Cambacérès and Lebrun), no one protested against this new *coup d'état*. The constitution offered to the French people for approval was carried in a national plebiscite by a vote of 3,011,107 against 1,562. Having already undergone irregularities in its preparation, the constitution was subjected to yet another illegality by being put into effect on 4 Nivôse (25 December) before being ratified.

This Constitution of Year VIII, comprising ninety-five articles hastily tossed together, made no mention of the rights of the citizen other than a guarantee against nocturnal house searches, and it was very incomplete in its organisation of public powers. In its brevity and obscurity, the constitution conformed to Bonaparte's desire to preserve a free hand for himself. Above all, it established the omnipotence of the First Consul, and except for the right to make peace or war, which was of little consequence at this time, Napoleon held complete executive power. He appointed the ministers and the other high government officials; only the justices of the peace were to be elected. His ministers, being responsible, were subject to prosecution by the Corps Législatif, but this only increased his control over them. The First Consul and his hand-picked functionaries, except for the ministers, were responsible to no one, and could only be prosecuted by the Conseil d'État, whose members Bonaparte himself appointed. He alone possessed the right to initiate legislation. The legislative power was reduced to a mere deliberative process and to a 'yes' or 'no' vote on bills introduced by Bonaparte after listening to the opinions of the Conseil d'État. Even so, discussion and voting were kept separate: the hundred-member Tribunate discussed, while the Corps Législatif – the three hundred 'mutes' – voted. Finally Bonaparte exercised without a check decree powers which revolutionary assemblies had accorded in the past to the executive for applying the law, the details of which were left for him to fill in and to interpret. Another body, the Sénat Conservateur, could annul laws deemed unconstitutional, but in reality the office of senator was a sinecure since its functions were mainly electoral.

It has rightly been said that the constitution reflected the work of Bonaparte, but there is another factor of major importance which serves to explain the complete ineffectiveness of the assemblies – namely, the abolition of the elective principle. Henceforth, members of the assemblies were chosen without popular participation. The two departing provisional consuls and the new second and third consuls appointed the first thirty-one senators who, in turn, chose the other twenty-nine senators; in the future, the Senate would continue to recruit its full complement of members by co-optation. The Senate was to name the tribunes and legislators as well as the consuls at the expiration of their ten-year terms. Subsequently, however, all of these nominations were supposed to be made from among the notables who were to be elected in a number of stages by universal suffrage. In each 'communal district' (*arrondissement communal*) the electors chose a tenth of their number, and these candidates on the 'communal list' of notables then selected a tenth of their number to form the departmental list. The same procedure was again applied by the notables on the departmental list to form a national list of candidates eligible for public office. Just what the 'communal district' was intended to be no one now knows. In any event, the system turned out to be inapplicable, and the lists finally prepared in Year IX were, for all they were worth, hardly used at all.

The nation was sovereign, of course, but it was no longer consulted. The Brumairians were satisfied – they now sat as the government. Yet they represented no one but themselves, and Bonaparte wasted little time in telling them, 'I alone represent the people.' Although they formed so-called representative bodies, they remained a group of notables which was summoned by the executive to collaborate in government only to the extent to which it might suit him. The king, under the Restoration, admitted as much. At first the Brumairians thought differently. Since they fully mastered the Senate, which Sieyès had filled with hand-picked candidates, they also controlled the Tribunate and the Corps Législatif, and so believed themselves in a position to force their collaboration upon Bonaparte. And in fact, the assemblies did manifest a tendency to resist, but since the constitution offered no means of resolving these conflicts, they evolved by way of successive *coups d'état*, which only Bonaparte had the means to carry through. The history of the Consulate and even of the Empire is in part the steadily increasing subjection of the legislative power. From the very first, Bonaparte encroached upon its rights. On 5

Nivôse, Year VIII (26 December 1799), he empowered the Conseil d'État with the function of interpreting laws by issuing 'opinions'. Nor did he hesitate at times to modify or circumvent the laws according to his need by means of executive decree. The Constitution of Year X permitted him to deprive the Tribunate and Corps Législatif of all authority by investing the Senate with *consultum* powers. Thus, by abusively enlarging the scope of his regulatory power (*pouvoir réglementaire*), Bonaparte eventually began to legislate directly by decree.

The contention has been advanced that Bonaparte and Sieyès filled the assemblies with Jacobins – the so-called 'safe Jacobins'. Not so at all. Rather, they favoured the moderates far more. Second only to the Institute, the Senate became the bastion of the *Idéologues*. The Tribunate was filled with writers and orators such as Daunou, Chénier, Ginguené, Say, and above all Benjamin Constant. Those less known were diverted to the Corps Législatif. A total of 330 members had previously occupied seats in the councils of the Directory, fifty-seven in the first three revolutionary assemblies. The Jacobins and the loyal nobility numbered but a small minority. Under these circumstances – this being the personnel upon which Bonaparte himself depended – it would have been impossible for him to impart a significantly different colour to the Conseil d'État and ministries. It explains the fact that even the Conseil d'État tended towards a certain degree of independence. In his choice of the two junior consuls, however, Bonaparte revealed his true inclination. Cambacérès had been a member of the Plain in the Convention. Stately and ceremonious, he was loyal and he did his best to exercise a moderating influence on Bonaparte. Lebrun, a former secretary under Chancellor Maupeou, had kept himself aloof during the Revolution, and Bonaparte knew him to be a royalist. In finance, he called upon the services of Gaudin and Mollien, both of whom had been employed in the office of the Contrôle Général. The result was a symbolic fusion of the revolutionary bourgeoisie and the men of the *ancien régime* who were now reconciled to the new order. Then, by gradually increasing the proportion of ex-royalists in the government, Bonaparte aligned his personnel in harmony with the evolution towards monarchy.

## THE ORGANISATION AND EXTENSION
## OF BONAPARTE'S POWERS

Bonaparte moved into the Tuileries Palace on 30 Pluviôse, Year VIII (19 February 1800), and immediately retired to his private study so as to work undisturbed. The only people permitted access to his presence were his secretaries for dictation, Bourrienne at first, then Méneval or Fain. Whenever he wished to confer with his collaborators, he would move to an adjoining room. The very thought of the *ancien régime* monarchy, however, filled him with a mistrust for ministers and their encroaching ways. He accustomed them to communicate with him in writing. It was not long before he had in his hands reports periodically submitted to him in the form of ministerial 'portfolios', information on the state of affairs in the Ministry of War, and at a later time, the accounts of the *domaine extraordinaire* (the extraordinary internal and external receipts). He retained the office of the Secretariat of State, which had been created by the Directory, and changed it into a ministry, placing it under Hughes-Bernard Maret. It acted as a central bureau for collecting the dossiers of the various governmental departments and offices, and it communicated to them Bonaparte's orders, which Maret received day and night. Thus the ministers were transformed into mere clerks.

Bonaparte also increased their number: to the existing Ministry of Finance he added a separate Ministry of the Public Treasury in 1801; while alongside the Ministry of War, he created a separate Ministry of Military Affairs in 1802. Moreover, he established within certain ministries themselves independent bodies* entrusted to councillors of state who acted as his direct agents and were to deal with public worship, public education, national property, forests, and bridges and highways. This was the origin of our present-day department heads (*directeurs*). The ministers took offence, but these rivalries delighted Napoleon, as they had Louis XIV before him. Only Talleyrand, the minister for foreign affairs, enjoyed the privilege of working together with the master. On his part he affected an air of downright adoration of Bonaparte. Although Napoleon scorned him, he was also reluctantly deferential to Talleyrand – the deference of a parvenu to the blue-blooded aristocrat steeped in the

---

* The author is referring to the General Boards (*Directions Générales*), which were established partly to minimise the importance of the ministers and partly to facilitate the business of administration. TRANSLATOR.

kind of etiquette which inspires respect by its very loftiness and makes one feel the presence of a great personage. Since the ministers were shorn of the authority to make decisions, and since they did not in themselves constitute an organised body, Bonaparte alone, as Beugnot remarked, 'kept everything together'. Like Frederick II, he ruled from the depths of his study.

Having never been schooled for this kind of work, Bonaparte lacked much of the requisite technical know-how for it. Tales of his instant, all-pervading comprehension are pure legend. He managed to teach himself a great deal, but his real talent lay in the ability to recognise the value of the men who had ruled during the Revolution, to consult them frequently, and to use them for his own purposes. From the inception of his term as consul, these were the kind of men he chose to make up the majority of the twenty-nine-member Conseil d'État. Except for Brune and Réal, the backgrounds of these men marked them as moderates. Their ranks numbered but three ex-members of the Convention, of whom only one, Berlier, had been a regicide, and even he had favoured a postponement of execution. Alongside these were men like Champagny, Fleurieu and Moreau de Saint-Méry, who left no doubts about their royalist sympathies and who had regarded the passing of the *ancien régime* with considerable regret. These two groups grew unevenly during the years to follow: to the former were added Thibaudeau and Treilhard; to the latter, Barbé-Marbois, Portalis, Dumas, Bigot de Préameneu and Muraire. They did not all enjoy their master's trust. When Bonaparte returned from Marengo on 7 Fructidor, Year VIII (25 August 1800), he effected a change which enabled him to dismiss without public scandal any councillor who might have incurred his displeasure, for he considered it politically unwise to attract too much attention to such situations. Henceforward, Bonaparte prepared two lists every three months, one containing the names of councillors engaged in ordinary service, the other, the names of councillors extraordinary, that is to say charged with specific missions and thus kept out of the meetings of the Conseil d'État, although retaining both title and honours. Their mission accomplished, nothing dictated that they should be reinstated, and so it sufficed to transfer a councillor from one list to the other to conceal a disgrace.

The Conseil d'État was divided into five sections which functioned separately but which periodically assembled at general meetings, usually under the presidency of Bonaparte. It also had a General Secretariat which was placed under the direction of Locré. Appointed as they were by the First Consul and subject to dismissal, the councillors lacked the kind of independence which in the royal Conseil d'État had resulted in venality, fixity of tenure and an *esprit de corps* engendered by social and professional ties. Since the council lacked decision-making authority, it merely expressed opinions which were in no way binding on Bonaparte.

The role of the Conseil d'État was nonetheless considerable, especially during the first years. It boasted many famous administrators, such as Roederer, Chaptal, Crétet, Fourcroy, Portalis, Berlier and Thibaudeau, and it was in the council that the great organic laws and codes were drawn up. As a court of supreme administrative jurisdiction, the council, sitting in disputation, was in a position to regulate little by little the operation of the entire administrative machine. Bonaparte took great pleasure in this work. He allowed the councillors to express themselves freely and, feeling very much at home, would himself expatiate with inexhaustible verve. He excluded from these discussions only political questions, notably the Concordat and the Law of 18 Germinal, Year X, which he knew would encounter strong resistance.

Bonaparte never granted the council a monopoly on advice, however. He also provided a stimulus to other advisory groups whose gatherings were improvised at first but later became more regular. To these so-called 'administrative councils' he would summon the interested ministers and their department heads, several state councillors and even certain officials, specially invited, from the provinces. Although not as well known as the Conseil d'État, these last-mentioned groups played a role almost equal in importance.

The new government, like the Directory, was from the very first day haunted by the deplorable condition of the treasury, which it had found almost empty. Consequently, the government was forced to make almost daily appeals to bankers for loans by mixing threats with soft words. Then, too, administrative reforms were first introduced in the realm of finances, and it was in this area that centralisation scored its first success. Early in Frimaire before the completion of the constitution, Gaudin, the new minister of finance, undertook certain decisive measures to raise revenues and to replenish the treasury. His first act, initiated on 3 Frimaire (24 November 1799), was to deprive local officials of the power to assess and in part collect direct taxes, reserving this responsibility for agents of the central government. At the head of the new central organisation stood a general director for direct taxation and deputy directors for each département. Below them were auditors (*contrôleurs*) and inspectors (*inspecteurs*) in charge of apportioning taxes among the taxpayers in each commune. Although these deputy directors appointed local tax assessors (*répartiteurs*) to aid them, they alone were responsible for drawing up the tax rolls. But no one gave much thought to the new assessments for the time being, and the auditors set about preparing the tax lists in arrears and those of Year VIII (the current year) by copying the previous ones. Other government appointees included a treasurer and a paymaster in each département, revenue agents called *receveurs généraux* and *receveurs particuliers*,* as well as tax collectors (*percepteurs*) in towns where the tax rolls exceeded fifteen thousand francs. Elsewhere, municipalities retained the right to collect taxes and generally awarded the office to the lowest bidder. Finally, on 6 Frimaire, the annual rescriptions of the *receveurs généraux* were re-established.† They were to be issued in twelve monthly instalments, but were actually made payable over a period of twenty months. The chief bureaux in the Ministry of Finance – those dealing with property, customs and the debt – rapidly acquired directors, the treasury department being the first to do so; on 1 Pluviôse (21 January 1800), it was placed under the direction of Dufresne, who had been a treasury employee before 1789 and at the time of the Constituent Assembly. A separate Ministry of the Public Treasury was created in Year X and was placed under Barbé-Marbois.

The great problem was to market the promissory note issued by the *receveurs généraux*. In order to back them up, Gaudin established a Security Bank (Caisse de Garantie), which he funded by returning to the practice of bonding officials of the fisc and by putting the bank in charge of warehouses and consignments. Placed under Mollien's direction, this bank was also to maintain the price of government bonds by carrying out open-market purchases in order to reduce the rate of interest and place the treasury on a better footing. Thus it soon came to be known as the

---

* The *receveurs généraux des finances* were a traditional agency surviving from the *ancien régime*. They comprised important government officials who acted as representatives and banking agents of the treasury. The *receveurs particuliers des finances* were created on 18 March 1800. They too acted as treasury agents and were in charge of collecting direct taxes, fines, etc. TRANSLATOR.

† These rescriptions were advances based on anticipated revenues, and issued by the *receveurs généraux* to the treasury in the form of notes promising payment at a future date. The notes were then discounted for the treasury by bankers. TRANSLATOR.

Sinking Fund. The discounting of promissory notes, nevertheless, still depended on the bankers' good will. The Revolution had made it possible for them, in agreement with leading manufacturers, to organise several issuing institutions for their personal needs. Chief among these were the Bank of Current Accounts (Caisse des Comptes Courants) established in Year IV and run by Perregaux, Récamier and Desprez, and the Commercial Discount Bank (Caisse d'Escompte du Commerce) founded in Year VI. The former possessed the funds to come to the aid of the treasury, although a state bank would have been preferable. This was precisely what the directors of the Bank of Current Accounts wanted – a state charter which would enable them to expand their business. It was in this manner that their final agreement with the regime was sealed. On 24 Pluviôse (13 February 1800), their bank was transformed into the Bank of France with a capital of thirty million francs in one-thousand-franc shares. The two hundred leading stockholders elected fifteen governors (*régents*) and three directors (*censeurs*); the governors then appointed three out of their number to be in charge of granting commercial loans and establishing the discount rate. The Bank of France contracted to include in its portfolio rescriptions amounting to three million francs. In return, half of the Sinking Fund's security bonds were placed into Bank of France stock, and the other half was made available to the Bank outright. Finally, the Bank was to manage government annuities and pensions. Nevertheless, the Bank was not granted a monopoly of issuing notes in the belief that it might then choose to discount notes only for its own shareholders, thus forcing businessmen everywhere to come to its counters. That, in fact, was one of the tacit assumptions upon which the agreement was based.

Much as Gaudin's work deserves to be admired, to forget that for months it constituted but a mere façade would be to misconstrue the history of the Consulate. The tax rolls were not prepared until the end of Year VIII, and only a small part of the rescriptions was in fact ever discounted by the Bank. Had the Bank accepted all of the rescriptions that were issued, the proceeds would still not have been sufficient to cover the state's expenditures. Like the Directory, Bonaparte remained for a long time at the mercy of the bankers and purveyors.

The reform of the provincial administration, which was an indispensable adjunct to that of the central government, produced results more quickly. It was initiated by Bonaparte in January and culminated in the

Law of 28 Pluviôse (17 February 1800), prepared under the chairmanship of Chaptal. The départements, cantons and communes were retained – these last regaining their divisional autonomy owing to the abolition of the cantonal municipalities which had been created in Year III. Between the communes on the one hand and the départements on the other, the new intermediary administrative unit became the *arrondissement*, a revived district, but of larger area. Every administrative division was placed under the direct responsibility of a single magistrate. A prefect assisted by a general secretary replaced the older 'central administration' in every département; a subprefect was despatched to every *arrondissement*; and a mayor together with one or more deputies was sent to every commune. As with the central government, the main point of the reform was to abolish popular election. Henceforth all officials were appointed by the government. The authority to choose mayors and deputies in communes with less than five thousand inhabitants was delegated to the prefects. Although local councils were retained on the departmental, district and communal levels, their members were also chosen by the central government or by a prefect. Furthermore, their sessions and functions were vastly reduced: local councils listened to financial reports, and on the departmental and district levels they assessed direct taxes, voted additional sums of moneys (centimes) to meet local needs, and were permitted to formulate resolutions; on the municipal level, they regulated the use of communal lands and provided for the upkeep of municipally owned buildings. As for questions relating to the centime and to loans, the Municipal Council was to register only an opinion. Thus the communes were reduced to a state of tutelage. The administrative divisions which had been created for the large municipalities in Year III were abolished. Lyon, Marseille and Bordeaux were to be administered by a single council, but until Year XIII they remained with several mayors. In Paris, the twelve districts and their municipalities were retained, almost all of the administrative powers were transferred to the Prefecture of the Seine, and a General Council took the place of the Municipal Council.

Bonaparte did not know enough about the political personnel to draw up the list of prefects himself. That task was left mainly to his brother Lucien, the minister of the interior, or, more accurately, to Lucien's secretary, Beugnot, a former member of the Legislative Assembly. But Cambacérès, Lebrun, Talleyrand and Clarke also put forward proposals, as did certain members of the assemblies, like Chauvelin and Crétet for the

Côte-d'Or. As a rule, Bonaparte followed Lucien's choice of candidates. Most of the prefects were appointed on 11 Ventôse (2 March). Once again, the choice fell principally on the moderates, of whom about half had served in former revolutionary assemblies. Letourneur had even been a director of the Committee of Public Safety, and Jeanbon Saint-André – whose Jacobin views offered a marked contrast to the general tenor of choices and who was assigned the annexed département of Mont-Tonnerre – had been an active member of that committee. To the prefectures were added generals and diplomats. All of the prefects were men of wide experience, and most were very capable. The prefectoral corps, which did so much to enhance Bonaparte's reputation, was one of the legacies of the French Revolution. As in the case of the central bureaucracy, it was destined to take on characteristics of the *ancien régime*.

In no instance were these prefects recruited locally – unlike the minor officials and members of local councils who were actually appointed by prefects and local politicians. Generally, the prefects too observed a preference for moderate notables who had sat in the local assemblies or headed technical bureaux during the Revolution. In the département of Seine Inférieure, half of the members who had participated in the general council of 1790 were restored in 1800. It was the villages that presented the greatest problem. The Revolution had unearthed but few villagers well enough educated and cultured to possess a sense of integrity and of public interest. The fact that the prefects encountered the same difficulty was frequently used as an argument for handing over the communal administration to the nobility.

Although the principle of centralisation of power constituted the single most important feature of Bonaparte's reform, it was also a step towards the division of bureaucratic functions among officials who were independent of each other and were directly responsible to the central authority. Their technical proficiency was bound to increase at the expense of a further weakening of local autonomy. The Revolution had given administrative bodies control over matters in litigation, direct taxation and the police. The Law of 28 Pluviôse now conferred the first upon the council of prefecture, over which the prefect in effect presided. Gaudin took away the administrative bodies' power to tax; and the municipality soon lost the power to judge over infractions of the law.

The logic of the system was such that Bonaparte also separated the police from the administration in order to transform the police into a centralised institution. Towards this end he retained the Ministry of General Police, which was reorganised by Fouché with the help of Desmaret, a former revolutionary priest and functionary during the Directory, who as head of the secret section of the Ministry of General Police became Fouché's indispensable assistant. In Paris, the restoration of the former Lieutenancy of Police under the name of Prefecture of Police on 17 Ventôse (8 March 1800), provided Fouché with a coadjutor. The prefect of police was charged with maintaining order in the capital, and was later subordinated to the Municipal Guard, created on 4 October 1802. Dubois, a former attorney in the *parlement* and a tool of Fouché, became the first prefect of police for Paris. In the provinces, the Ministry of General Police did not have permanent representatives. The creation of general commissioners of police in the large towns and on the frontier, which replaced the local authorities, did not begin until 5 Brumaire, Year IX (27 October 1800). Several special commissioners were also appointed, as in Boulogne. Other than that, in most of the départements the only permanent agents of the ministry were the prefects, who possessed the authority to issue search and arrest warrants as had the *intendants* in times past. They were not, however, responsible to the minister of police alone. Furthermore, since prefects lacked trained subordinates, they often received their directions from the minister himself, or from agents whom he despatched to the provinces. The *gendarmerie*, which was carefully reorganised under the command of General Moncey, functioned separately alongside the police.

These sundry institutions wielded excessive powers from the start. Fouché scattered a blanket of police spies and informers everywhere, who were recruited from within even the highest classes of society. The *cabinet noir*, headed by Lavalette, kept a close surveillance over correspondence. Arbitrary arrests became widespread, and the prefects themselves issued *lettres de cachet* not only against political suspects, but also against persons charged with having violated the law who were either guiltless or had already been acquitted, and also in the interests of certain influential families. That the police system lacked the degree of unity and centralisation which characterised the rest of the government was undoubtedly due to Bonaparte's mistrust of Fouché, who was the most invaluable, feared and independent of ministers. Asking little in the way of a budget, he had his own sources of revenue which he derived from the closing down of gambling houses, the rights to issue passports and firearm permits, confiscations of conspiratorial funds, and many kinds of arbitrary contributions exacted from brothels. Thus, in order to keep him in check, Bonaparte favoured the existence, side by side, of several police organisations. He had his own private police, not to mention a host of informers like Fiévée, Madame de Genlis and Montlosier; and he also allowed Dubois to dabble in politics and set himself up as a rival to Fouché. As a result, these competing police bodies strove to outdo each other at the expense of a citizenry deprived of all redress.

The reorganisation of the administrative system had hardly been set into motion when that of the judiciary system was also effected by the Law of 27 Ventôse, Year VIII (18 March 1800). On the civil side, the commune retained its local magistrate (*juge de paix*), and every *arrondissement* received a court of the first instance – as had formerly been the case with the district. A novelty was the establishment of twenty-nine courts of appeal, which brought back memories of the *parlements*. As to the criminal courts, the instrument of justice became the police court, while the court of the first instance and the court of appeal were given the authority to pronounce sentence. The criminal court of the département was to be retained, but henceforth staffed with its own judges. The law also provided for the retention of grand and petty juries, commercial, military and maritime courts, as well as the court of cassation. The manner in which legal officials were to be chosen was subsequently worked out. Bonaparte continued to appoint the notaries (*notaires*); and he reserved to himself the choice of bailiffs (*huissiers*), except those of the justices of the peace, and the choice of *procureurs* to whom he restored the title *avoués*, without, however, making their employ compulsory. The profession of *avocat* alone remained open.

Changes in the judiciary hierarchy did not constitute the most important feature of the Ventôse Law, however. In the first place, except justices of the peace and those of the commercial courts, judges were no longer elected. Aside from the Court of Cassation magistrates, who were appointed by the Senate, the First Consul named all other judges. True, they were irremovable, but they depended nevertheless upon the state for their salaries and promotion. It must have pleased Lebrun to have seen the realisation of Maupeou's reform, and it is likely that he had a hand in it. In the second place, the office of the public prosecutor (*ministère public*) was entirely reconstituted. Here lay the real basis of public order which had brought about the reform. The question was not merely one of purging the judicial personnel and of assuring its loyalty, but was also one of intensifying the use of repressive measures in a troubled land. The functions of the prosecuting magistrate (*accusateur public*) were merged with those of government commissioners who had always been representatives of the central power; that is, the prosecutor was to manage the judicial police officials. The justice of the peace and the officer of the *gendarmerie* retained their authority to issue warrants and to initiate pre-trial hearings. Then, as in the past, these preliminary judicial enquiries were taken up by the president of the court of the first instance who was head of the grand jury but nonetheless appointed by the state. The process of consolidation was still incomplete, but it did not remain so for long.

The choice of magistrates entailed greater difficulty than that of the prefects because they were considerably more numerous and had to be recruited locally. Therefore Bonaparte was obliged to rely on the advice of others. Circulars requesting nominations were sent to the regional assemblies, and many very different persons of distinction were solicited for information. Abrial, minister of justice, prepared the lists of candidates according to districts; Cambacérès then examined them with the assistance of regional politicians. But despite these precautions, the formation of the courts was attended by a certain degree of confusion and resulted in certain choices which were to be regretted. Here, too, men of the Revolution were favoured and made irremovable, thanks to which the judicial personnel evolved less rapidly than others in the direction of the *ancien régime*.

The administrative and judicial reforms of Year VIII occupy a position in the history of France second in importance only to the work of the Constituent Assembly of 1789, to which it was greatly indebted, however. The Constituent Assembly had abolished privileges and intermediary bodies, and it had achieved national unity. Bonaparte had but to affix his stamp, and that is why he was able to succeed so rapidly. After all, he did no more than resume the precedent set in Year II. The Committee of Public Safety had not had the time to carry out the policy of centralisation as thoroughly, but its intention had been the same. Saint-Just had envisaged a single magistrate in every département or district, acting as agent of the central authority, and Chaptal spoke as Robespierre might well have done when he said, 'The strength of an administrative system lies completely in the certainty that the laws and acts of the government will be executed without reservation . . . The chain of execution extends downward without interruption from minister to those who are to be administered and transmits the laws and orders of the government to the very last branch of the social order with the speed of electricity.' This was the comparison which the Sansculottes were so fond of making.

The laws of Year VIII have often been ascribed to a design on the part of Napoleon to increase his own authority, and not without reason. No mention had ever been made in the constitution of the abolition of popular elections for local assemblies, and Bonaparte's contemporaries were fully aware that his dictatorship had made a giant step forward. And yet behind these laws there lay deeper causes which discouraged resistance to them. The policies of decentralisation carried out by the Constituent Assembly had imperilled France during the war, and had created a state of affairs which continued as long as the war lasted. It was in response to this situation that the Committee of Public Safety had seized the reins of government – reins that had slackened under the Thermidorians until finally Bonaparte seized them once again. He turned a temporary expedient into an ideal of government. That he should have thus satisfied his personal instinct for domination was made possible only because the ideal fully tallied at that time – and the Brumairians were as one in this opinion – with the interests of revolutionary France.

While occupied with the task of reshaping the nation, Bonaparte nevertheless felt compelled to defend himself against criticism. The notables had been delivered from the 'democratic' danger and were in possession of all the important positions. But since they no longer decided anything, they nurtured a discontent which Madame de Staël, who had hoped to govern France through the intermediacy of Bonaparte or at least Benjamin Constant, did not bother to hide. It was in the Tribunate, which certainly offered the means for it, that opposition broke out. The Tribunate sat permanently, elected its executive officers (*bureaux*), and chose Daunou as its president. It could make resolutions, discuss petitions, lay charges against ministers and denounce government measures which it deemed unconstitutional to the Senate. Above all, the Tribunate was a place for making speeches, and Benjamin Constant took full advantage of this opportunity, starting on 5 January 1800, when the very first bill was presented to the Tribunate for discussion. Upon hearing of this, Bonaparte became enraged and everyone took cover. Sieyès departed for his country house, accepting an endowment, much to his discredit. To tame the moderates, Bonaparte had only to ask, 'Do you want me to abandon you to the Jacobins?' The Jacobins naturally felt even more disaffection. Throughout the countryside and especially in the west of France they were kept in check by the menaces of the 'Whites'. The installation of prefects took away support for the Jacobins in former administrative bodies. They frequently rioted, as in Dijon and Toulouse, and were not really put down until the summer. As for the royalists, they changed their tune because Bonaparte, during an interview with their representatives Hyde de Neuville and d'Andigné, refused to accede to any of their demands. Controlling as they did most of the newspapers, they made a great outcry against the new assemblies, demanding an immediate purge. But on 17 January 1800 Bonaparte took advantage of this disturbance to shut down in one blow sixty out of the seventy-three existing newspapers. Others stopped publication later, and by the end of 1800 there were only nine. The *Moniteur* had become the official government organ after 27 December 1799, and was under the direction of Maret. Censorship, although not officially re-established, was in fact carried out by Fouché, and on 5 April 1800 Lucien Bonaparte instituted it in the theatres. Of course the leftist press was also swept away by the purge.

With legal opposition impossible, extremists began to think in terms of violence. During the month of Germinal, there was again talk of a Jacobin plot. But the only serious danger could have arisen from the army, where there were still many republicans and even more malcontents, for there was no general who did not feel himself cut out to be First Consul. Bonaparte used circumspection. He appointed Carnot minister of war, and he greatly increased the number of concessions to Moreau, who commanded the Army of the Rhine. His most fearful enemies remained the royalists, at least those who were resolved to turn down all concessions. Yet they could agree neither on principles, since some advocated constitutional monarchy, nor on a method of action. Living in Mittau with d'Avaray and Saint-Priest, Louis XVIII combined negotiation with conspiracy. A royal agency in Paris, in which Royer-Collard figured, was instructed to sound out Bonaparte, and handed him two letters from the pretender which were left unanswered. In Swabia, a bureau directed by Précy and Dandré and subsidised by Wickham was preparing an invasion of Provence by émigrés. Moreover, this bureau corresponded with royalists in Lyon, Toulouse and particularly Bordeaux where the Institut Philanthropique of Year V had struck deep roots. The comte d'Artois, who resided in England, maintained agencies both in Jersey and in Paris where the plots of Hyde de Neuville were uncovered in May. The royalists' main strongholds were in the west, however. There the *Chouannerie* had resumed in Year VII, but soon degenerated into a form of brigandage which, with the arrival of government troops in October – Hédouville north of the Loire and Travot in the Vendée – was promptly reduced. Hédouville entered into negotiations with the *Chouan* chieftains, and they agreed to an armistice on 4 January 1800. Bonaparte, who wished to turn all of his forces against Austria, was very anxious to pacify the west. Unlike the Thermidorians, however, he had no intention of dealing with the rebels as equals, and he was determined to disarm the peasants. Consequently, he offered amnesty to those who would lay down their arms. But receiving no answer, he despatched Generals Brune and Lefebvre to the west, suspended the constitution in those départements, and ordered anyone apprehended with arms or preaching rebellion to be shot. Actually there was little fighting. The nobles d'Autichamp and Bourmont surrendered in January. The popular leaders held out somewhat longer in Brittany, Cadoudal being the last to submit on 14 February. In Normandy, Frotté, who had come to Alençon to negotiate under promise of safe conduct, was arrested during the night of 15–16 February. At Verneuil on 18 February, the detail which was taking him to Paris encountered a courier with orders to set up a court martial, and Frotté was executed that same day along with six of his companions. In his struggle against partisanship, Bonaparte continued to act in the tradition of Year II: he was a terrorist pure and simple. 'Not since the time of Robespierre have laws been so severe,' noted an annalist from Chinon.

Bonaparte took good care not to make a habit of these methods, however. He was more skilful than the Jacobins in these matters, and he did not go beyond making examples; at the same time he welcomed all offers of surrender. Not waiting for the peace to disarm the counter-revolution, he undertook measures to hasten his summoning of the nation. Thus he was sure to please a great many people, for an end to disorders would bring a return to prosperity and would calm those who had profited from the Revolution. True, it was to be feared that the rallying together of the diverse elements of French society was not all that genuine, and Bonaparte never harboured any illusions on that score. But what did it matter so long as he continued to be victorious?

The great difficulty was to make the republican bourgeoisie and particularly the army accept measures which were favourable to the refractory clergy and émigrés. Until Marengo, however, Bonaparte kept to moderate enough enactments. On 28 December 1799 he confirmed to Catholics the full use of non-alienated churches. He also granted them freedom to worship every day, even Sundays, except on the *décadi* – a reservation which turned out to be of little importance since he abandoned in effect the religion of patriotism and almost all the revolutionary festivals. He merely demanded from the priests a promise of loyalty to the Constitution of Year VIII. It seems that for a time he believed they would seize this opportunity to submit. Nothing came of it, however. The majority of those who had refused the earlier oaths continued to do so now, despite the advice of Abbé Émery. Religious worship in secret continued and the ringing of church bells and religious processions remained the subject of numerous conflicts. Bonaparte quickly realised that in order to break the resistance of the clergy, he would have to come to terms with the pope. Moreover, the Conseil d'État declared that the constitution implicitly abrogated the exclusion of ex-nobles and parents of émigrés from public office. However, it also decided to retain the laws proscribing the émigrés themselves. But on 3 March 1800 it was decided that only those who had fled before 25 December 1799 were to be included on the émigré list, and a commission set up with the object of reviewing émigré applications for re-entry into France accepted a great many such requests. The ex-terrorists Barère and Vadier, those who had been proscribed in Fructidor and members of the old 'patriotic' party of the Constituent Assembly, such as Lafayette, were all recalled without argument. The émigrés on the list numbered 145,000, however, and the work of the commission proceeded slowly. Fouché himself advised the recall of émigrés en bloc, aside from a few exceptions. But the time was not yet. To undertake such a risk, as in arranging a concordat, Bonaparte would first have to enhance his prestige by achieving both victory and peace.

## THE IMPROVISATION OF THE CAMPAIGN OF 1800

Bonaparte prepared energetically for the campaign on which the retention and extension of his power depended. Manpower was not a problem, for on 8 March the entire yearly contingent of recruits was placed at his disposition. But he opposed the methods used by the Jacobins and the Directory. This was decidedly not the time to imitate the great military conscription of Year VII; besides, money was lacking. Moreover, Bonaparte realised, if we are to believe a historian who was very partial to him, that a 'nation's enthusiasm for war grows inversely to the number of soldiers called upon to go to war', and so he contented himself with thirty thousand men. The well-to-do were easily managed, since they were given the right by law to find substitutes. The Army of the Rhine having been made ready, it remained to put together a fresh Army of Reserve. This entailed making use of all available means, emptying military depots, recalling the veterans of the Army of the West, creating an Italian Legion, and marching conscripts who had not yet learned to load their rifles. Bonaparte employed little in the way of cavalry, and even less artillery. Given these conditions, it required an incredible amount of audacity and self-confidence for Bonaparte to plunge into the conquest of Italy.

The main problem was to finance the campaign. About sixty-five million francs were needed. The irregular war subsidy, which had taken the place of the compulsory loan, and the measures used to expedite the collection of revenues did not meet the immediate needs; all the more so since obligations could be discharged in notes and drafts which had been issued by the Directory and were now valueless. In addition, private contractors who were again entrusted with the commissariat insured their deliveries with chattel mortgages. Gaudin wished to resort to indirect taxation, but Bonaparte, still somewhat unsure of his strength, limited himself to standardising municipal tolls (*octrois*), which were to be earmarked for poorhouses and the municipalities themselves. Expenses were cut to the limit, but the Consulate was obliged in the end to resort to the same expedients as the Directory. The government discontinued the contracting system and re-established requisitions. But the certificates of receipt could not be used to discharge tax obligations. The government then decided on a partial deferment of payments: every ten days the little that was left over in the treasury was distributed to the various ministries. Other than that, the government issued drafts which were irredeemable. In the end it resorted to bankers and contractors who agreed to discount the notes at five per cent per month. The government also turned to financiers abroad, such as in Geneva and Hamburg, who, under pressure and compulsion, advanced 6½ million francs.

The only novel feature instituted by this authoritarian government in its financial dealings was its high-handedness. The private contractors, who were not being paid, were nevertheless alerted to hand over fifty-two million francs if they wanted to be reimbursed in new debt certificates (*assignations*), which immediately lost fifty per cent of their face value. Gabriel Ouvrard, the famous financier who had been thrown in prison, was forced to give the government fourteen million francs. Consequently, survival became a daily problem. Although the government's efforts were indeed prodigious, it would be a mistake to delude oneself about the results. The Army of the Rhine, which received preferential treatment for political reasons, was granted altogether 6,200,000 francs, and in Pluviôse was owed fifteen million francs' back pay. The Army of Reserve ambled on without pay or provisions other than those got along the way from the peasants. As in the Revolution, the enormous gaps in the preparation of the campaign were made up at the expense of the troops. In finance, as in politics, everything hung on victory. The war effort could not be kept up for long without demanding from the nation the kind of sacrifices which had made the Convention and the Directory so unpopular.

This, at least, was how people reasoned, and everyone prepared himself accordingly. When Bonaparte left Paris on 6 May, the Brumairians began contemplating the range of possible solutions in the event that he should fail to return. Sieyès reappeared in Paris, and there was talk of a directory, of a new First Consul – Carnot, Lafayette, Moreau. Mention was also made of the duc d'Orléans. Bonaparte's brothers, Joseph and Lucien, were burning with desire to be of service. Given the situation, some speculation was to be expected; but it is difficult to believe that there were not many prominent persons who looked forward to defeat with complacency. The liberals and certain Jacobins were left with no other hope. 'I wished for Bonaparte's defeat because it was the only means left to stop the advance of his tyranny,' wrote Madame de Staël some time later. The royalists, for their part, did their best as usual to help the enemy: Cadoudal returned from England on 3 June to revive the *Chouannerie*. The defeat of Bonaparte would have surely meant the fall of the nation and of the Revolution. France could no longer hesitate to choose between Napoleon and his rivals.

# CHAPTER FIVE

# The Pacification of Europe

MUCH AS IT WAS in Bonaparte's interest to wage battle and dictate peace, it was just as important for him to convince the French people that he was not responsible for the war. He would willingly have concluded an armistice in order to complete his preparations, and above all to rescue the army in Egypt, whose loss would constitute an irreparable setback for France in the Mediterranean and in the East. But to make peace on the basis of the natural frontiers was for him unthinkable. He later remarked that to abandon Italy 'would have dampened imaginations', that is to say, undermined his prestige. Nor would he listen to the proposals of the king of Prussia who told Beurnonville that the conditions of a genuine desire for peace would be the evacuation of Holland, Switzerland and Piedmont. Perhaps *The State of France in Year VIII*, which was shortly to be published by d'Hauterive, Talleyrand's right-hand man, best reflected the political ideas of Bonaparte. It proposed that Europe substitute for the traditional policy of balance of power a kind of league of continental states under the hegemony of France.

The enemy, however, did Bonaparte the service of rejecting his peace offers. Actually, Thugut, the Austrian chancellor, was diplomat enough to enquire into the conditions for peace, but when Talleyrand mentioned the territorial limits established at Campoformio, Thugut objected vehemently; and when the present limits were suggested as a basis of understanding, he dodged the entire question. For as long as he remained in power, Thugut longed to reconquer Nice and Savoy in order to force the king of Sardinia to cede in return part of Piedmont to Austria; the Austrian archduke Charles, who counselled treating with France, lost the command of the Army of Germany. To the English Thugut suggested that they might make conquests in France to finance the restoration of the monarchy. At least he had the intelligence not to say anything publicly. Pitt and Grenville, however, committed the blunder of openly disclosing the secret aspirations of the aristocratic Coalition. They declared before the House of Commons that a treaty with Bonaparte would not guarantee the future, and they pronounced, with impertinence to the French Republic, that the best assurance would be 'the restoration of that line of princes which for so many centuries maintained the French nation in prosperity at home, and in consideration and respect abroad'. The Prussian publicist Friedrich von Gentz, who was in their pay, suddenly became possessed with an intense zeal for a counter-revolutionary crusade. Consequently, there was nothing left for France but to fight.

## THE CAMPAIGNS OF 1800
## AND THE TREATY OF LUNÉVILLE

Russia had withdrawn from the struggle, and Frederick William III could not have wished for better than to reconcile her with France, thereby securing himself from all risk. But it could not have suited Bonaparte to have chosen him as a mediator. Resuming the policies of Dumouriez and Danton, themselves heirs to the anti-Austrian tradition in French diplomacy, Napoleon offered Frederick instead an alliance which would have turned Prussia into an auxiliary. The king refused, and so the war became a duel between France and Austria.

Thugut, whose mind was fixed on Italy, kept General Kray in his defensive position behind the Rhine. To General Melas in Italy, whose forces were reinforced with great difficulty to something over one hundred thousand men, he issued orders to attack the French, who had withdrawn behind the Apennines in the vicinity of Genoa since November, and to march into Provence where Willot and the marquis de Puyvert were to provoke an insurrection. The Austrians counted on the help of the English in Minorca, but, as usual, Dundas was unable to gather a sufficient force. Sir John Stuart, having been given only five thousand men, tendered his resignation, and his successor, Sir Ralph Abercromby, did not arrive until after the Battle of Marengo. Melas now scattered half of his forces across the plain and below the Alpine passes. Seizing the offensive with the other half, he split the French forces in two on 6 April, laying siege to Masséna in Genoa and driving Suchet back to the banks of the Var. The result of Thugut's military strategy, based as it was on purely political considerations, was that the Austrian army drove the French towards the south-west, and obtained nothing decisive. The French, on the other hand, remained in control of Switzerland and were consequently in a position to take the two Austrian armies from the rear.

At first Bonaparte deployed the various parts of his Army of Reserve between Chalon and Lyon. In March he attempted to persuade Moreau to cross the Rhine near Schaffhausen with his entire force in order to cut Kray's communications and so beat him in detail.* According to this plan, the Army of Reserve would then have entered Switzerland and, reinforced by a part of the victorious Army of the Rhine, would have carried out the same operation against Melas, crossing the Alps as far east as possible, no nearer than by the St Gotthard Pass. But Moreau completely failed to grasp the value of this thunderbolt strategy, and in the meantime, Melas began his attack. Leaving Moreau to his own devices, Bonaparte concentrated his Army of Reserve in the lower Valais region towards the end of April. On the twenty-seventh of that month, on the basis of information gathered by his engineers, he decided to lead the army to the Great St Bernard Pass which, having been crossed in 1798 and 1799, was a passage familiar to French armies. On 5 May he ordered Moreau to send him General Moncey with twenty-five thousand men by way of the St Gotthard. Moreau, however, was unwilling to send more than fifteen thousand men. This did not weaken him any the less during his offensive which had just begun, and the decisive blow was reserved for Bonaparte. It was the starting point of their falling out.

The crossing of the Great St Bernard, begun on the night of 14–15 May, was completed on 23 May. Since the troops were forced to defile laboriously past the great guns of the fortress of Bard, only ten cannons were able to get through, and until the army reached Milan this made up the entire artillery. Lannes, who was in the vanguard, captured the fort and town of Ivrea located at the head of the plain of the Po. From there, Bonaparte could have rallied Turreau's forces which were descending the Mont Cenis and Mont Genèvre passes and marched on Genoa. But then Melas would have been free to concentrate his men and to fall back on Lombardy if he were beaten.

The alternative course was to march on Milan and so cut his line of retreat. A victorious encounter would then be decisive and would deliver Italy to the French. Yet the risk was great. As long as the army in Milan had not secured a line of operations – an assured retreat across the St Gotthard – Melas would be in a position to cut its communications by

---

* Divide the enemy into separate, isolated pockets, and then defeat each one successively. TRANSLATOR.

undertaking an offensive north of the Po. Bonaparte needed a victory, an immediate victory. He therefore chose the latter course, perilous, but bound to produce a stupendous effect if successful. The main army, covered by Lannes, turned eastward and reached Milan on 2 June, where it was joined by General Moncey and his reinforcements. The Austrian general Vukasovich had fallen back behind the Oglio River and the Austrian forces found themselves separated into two very unequal masses. The French divisions then headed south, crossed the Po, converged towards the west, seized the defiles of the Stradella Pass where Lannes took Montebello on 9 June, and then debouched on to the plain of Marengo. On 13 June the advance guard, led by Victor, reached the banks of the Bormida within view of Alessandria. Bonaparte had combined the advance of his divisions with a sureness that was truly amazing. He arranged their grouping into autonomous corps, keeping them as concentrated as possible. Meanwhile, Masséna had been obliged to evacuate Genoa on 4 June, and had rejoined Suchet, who was driving back Elsnitz and inflicting great losses on the Austrians. Bonaparte thought that they would be able to take Melas from the rear. Although they failed to do so, they were nevertheless able to draw off a sizeable part of the enemy's cavalry.

Out of the seventy thousand men still left to him, Melas concentrated only thirty thousand at Alessandria. He had taken a great gamble by leaving himself without cavalry, but he still had almost two hundred cannons. Bonaparte was ignorant of his precise whereabouts, but he realised that the Austrian force might try to cross the Po or slip away along the Apennines. Consequently, on 13 June he despatched one division north of the river and two more under Desaix's command towards the south, keeping only twenty-two thousand men and twenty-two or twenty-four cannons. Moreover, he committed a cardinal mistake by failing to cut the bridges of the Bormida. On 14 June, at 9 a.m., his advance guard was attacked by twenty thousand Austrians. Two divisions hurried to the rescue, but were outflanked by the enemy's left, and the French fell back in disorder, leaving their artillery behind. Fortunately for them, the Austrian divisions on the left and on the right were advancing separately in marching column, concerned only with what lay before them and not seeking to envelop the French forces. Bonaparte hastened to recall the divisions which he had sent out to bar Melas's escape, but only Boudet's force (five thousand men and five cannons) was brought back by Desaix in time. Having rallied together the remnants of the French army, Desaix attacked the front of the advancing Austrian column. The battle was still undecided when Kellermann with four hundred cavalry charged the Austrian flank. The enemy panicked and broke into a rout, but the Austrian left and right kept order and covered the retreat. Desaix had been killed in the midst of the fighting, unnoticed.

This, then, was the victory which Bonaparte had wanted. It was indeed the crowning point to an admirable campaign, but considering the manner in which the battle began, he should have lost; he later took pains to spread a falsified account of the battle which misled historians for a long time. Had he lost, the army could have extricated itself because it had maintained a line of retreat, but Bonaparte's career would undoubtedly have been finished. Never in war as in the life of man (genius or not) has the unforeseeable been more clearly manifest. The defeat did not bring the Austrian army to the point of despair, because the French forces were exhausted and short of munitions, but Melas became totally demoralised. 'His appearance was as doddering as his physique,' said Count Neipperg, a man who was destined to gain some renown as one of the Austrian officers sent to negotiate with the 'rabble'. Under the terms of the armistice, which was signed on 15 June at Alessandria, the Austrians withdrew to the line of the Mincio River, keeping Tuscany and the Papal Legations.

Moreau, meanwhile, was slowly advancing in Germany. After his left wing made a diversionary feint on Kehl, the main army crossed the Rhine at various points from Breisach to Schaffhausen on 28 April–1 May. He then proceeded to march across the Black Forest in the direction of General Lecourbe, who commanded the French right wing. This entailed a considerable loss of time, and the separate forces failed to concentrate for combat. Only Moreau, with the centre, managed to support Lecourbe. Kray had been surprised, however, and was unable to collect his army to take advantage of the disarray. At Engen and at Stockach on 3 May, and at Messkirch on 5 May, Moreau kept the upper hand, thanks to the steadfastness of his soldiers. He continued his advance towards the Iller River and the Vorarlberg, driving a wedge between Kray and his left which occupied the Tyrol. Kray then fell back on Ulm. Moreau, who was weakened by the loss of fifteen thousand men whom he had sent to Italy, had only ninety thousand soldiers against the Austrian's 140,000, and so began to manoeuvre his forces, not daring to attack. Finally, on 19 June

Moreau forced a crossing of the Danube at Hochstädt, compelling the Austrians to abandon Ulm from the north. The enemy made their way back across the Danube, trying to establish a line of defence on the Isar, but the French dislodged them by occupying Munich, throwing them back on the Inn. On 15 July an armistice was signed at Parsdorf.

On 16 June Bonaparte had again written to Francis II inviting him to negotiate a peace. But the proposal came at a bad time. On 20 June Thugut concluded a treaty with Lord Minto in which England granted Austria a subsidy provided she did not sign a separate peace. In order to gain time, the Austrian court nevertheless despatched Count Saint-Julien on an unofficial mission to Paris, the purpose of which was to make enquiries into the proposed conditions for peace. Outwitted by Talleyrand and threatened by Bonaparte, Saint-Julien allowed himself to be induced into signing a preliminary draft of a treaty ceding the entire left bank of the Rhine in return for certain unspecified compensations in Italy. Upon his return to Vienna, he was discredited and thrown into prison. Meanwhile, in order to play along with Austria's game, England declared herself ready to participate in a conference, at which point Thugut agreed to negotiate officially. Since the armistice conventions were nearing their term, Bonaparte took advantage of this offer to demand a general suspension of hostilities and the right to reprovision Malta and reinforce his position in Egypt. This Grenville refused; besides, Malta capitulated on 5 September. The price of this stalemate was paid for by Austria, since Bonaparte had only agreed to prolong the armistices on condition that she surrender Philippsburg, Ulm and Ingolstadt. Meanwhile in Vienna, there raged a fierce struggle between the advocates of war and those for peace, viz., between Thugut, who was supported by Maria Carolina of Naples and the empress on the one hand, and Archduke Charles on the other. Thugut refused to ratify the agreement signed by Saint-Julien and he resigned as chancellor. He was succeeded by Louis de Cobenzl, who had negotiated the two last partitions of Poland in St Petersburg. Thugut nevertheless maintained his influence through the instrumentality of Colloredo, since Cobenzl personally departed for Lunéville to negotiate the treaty. Having first been summoned to Paris by Napoleon, Cobenzl was unable to begin his talks with Joseph Bonaparte, France's representative at Lunéville, until 5 November 1800. Anyway, these conferences in Lunéville came to naught because the First Consul remained vague on the subject of French concessions in Italy. All the while, Napoleon proceeded to establish himself in the Cisalpine Republic, Genoa and Piedmont. It was there that Murat led the Third Army of Reserve. In addition, General Dupont occupied Tuscany under the pretext that the English were in Leghorn [Livorno]. With this act, which was in direct violation of the armistice, the winter campaign began.

The French forces in Italy now numbered one hundred thousand, of whom only fifty-seven thousand were under General Brune, the new commander-in-chief of the army in Italy. Brune held the line of the Mincio opposite the Austrian general Bellegarde, who commanded eighty thousand men deployed between the Vorarlberg and the Po. Macdonald, who with the eighteen thousand soldiers of the Second Army of Reserve occupied the Grisons, had received orders to cross the Splügen Pass, thereby extending Brune's left in an attack through the Tyrol. In Bavaria, Moreau led an army of ninety-five thousand men, which the Austrians opposed with one hundred thousand, who were nominally under the command of the young archduke John, but in reality were led by General Lauer. On the Main stood Augereau with sixteen thousand French and Dutch troops. It would have been only natural to have combined the forces of Augereau, Macdonald and even Murat with those of Moreau for a drive on Vienna, but Bonaparte counted on dealing the mortal blow himself in Italy.

The campaign was decided in much less time than Bonaparte had thought possible. Preparing to cross the Inn with sixty thousand men, Moreau had deployed his divisions along the river when suddenly Lauer, with sixty-five thousand men, took the offensive, manoeuvred to the right, and skilfully began threatening the French left at Ampfing. As the two armies turned to face each other, Moreau rushed to gather together all the available forces along the edge of the forest of Hohenlinden. There the battle took place on 3 December. The Austrians, advancing through the woods in separate, unconnected columns, found themselves unable to debouch from the defiles of the forest into the clearing. Meanwhile Decaen and Richepanse flanked and turned the Austrian left. Then Richepanse went on to take the Austrian centre from the rear, causing them to break into a rout. The Austrians lost twelve to fifteen thousand men and one hundred guns. This time Moreau hurried to the pursuit, chasing after the dislocated enemy and capturing twenty-five thousand prisoners. In order to avoid losing Vienna, Austria signed an armistice at Steyer on 25 December, and agreed to conclude a separate peace. While this was taking place, Macdonald had reached the upper Adige after a remarkable campaign across the mountains, and Brune was finally able to begin his attack. Brune, however, handled the crossing of the Mincio very badly, and at Pozzolo on 25 December General Dupont escaped disaster only because the enemy forces were equally poorly commanded. With the Adige and Brenta having been crossed, the armistice signed at Treviso on 15 January 1801 pushed the Austrians back behind the Tagliamento River. Thus it was Moreau who had put an end to the war, and for this Bonaparte never forgave him. As for Murat, he invaded Tuscany and at Lucca drove out the Austrians, and compelled the Neapolitans to sign a convention at Foligno.

In Lunéville, Cobenzl did his best to resist Bonaparte's demands, giving in step by step as the news grew steadily worse. Having agreed to negotiate in the name of the Holy Roman Empire and having abandoned Mantua, he attempted to salvage Tuscany. But England was powerless to help in this matter, and Paul I had definitely broken with England and begun his rapprochement with France. The peace was finally signed on 9 February 1801, exactly as dictated by the First Consul. The Holy Roman Empire consented to cede, pure and simple, the entire left bank of the Rhine, subject to certain indemnities which were to be distributed among the dispossessed princes at the expense of lands belonging to the Catholic Church. The duke of Modena was awarded the Breisgau, and the duke of Tuscany was also compensated in Germany. France seized control of northern and central Italy: the boundary of the Cisalpine Republic was extended to the Adige thereby including the territories of Verona and Polesina; the territory of Novara, taken from Piedmont, had already become part of the Cisalpine Republic so as to open the route of the Simplon Pass; finally, the Papal Legations were also incorporated into the republic. The treaty made no mention of the kings of Sardinia and Naples, nor of the pope. Hence their respective fates were left to Bonaparte's discretion. True, the treaty did guarantee the independence of the Cisalpine and Ligurian Republics, Holland and Switzerland. But then, what was this promise worth?

Precisely what was going to be in store for Italy soon became apparent. Even then the Cisalpine Republic was reorganised by Bonaparte, who gave it first a *consulta* or legislative assembly and then a triumvirate of his own making. In Genoa, he established a governing commission. The refusal of Charles Emmanuel IV, king of Sardinia, to return to Turin led to Bonaparte's establishment of a provisional government in Piedmont. The Russian negotiations with the French ambassador Saint-Marsan over the future of Piedmont – negotiations which had been pursued out of deference for the tsar – were broken off immediately after the death of Paul I. Piedmont was transformed into a French military province, divided into départements, and subjected to the same administrative and financial rule as France. King Ferdinand IV of Naples signed the Treaty of Florence on 28 March, according to which he evacuated Rome, ceded the island of Elba and the principality of Piombino, agreed to close his harbours to English vessels and authorised the occupation of Otranto and Brindisi for one year by French garrisons who could use them as ports of embarkation for Egypt. Lucca became a republic. Tuscany was to be Bonaparte's trump card in his Spanish and colonial politics. On 21 March 1801 the Treaty of Aranjuez awarded the grand duchy of Tuscany (which had been converted into the kingdom of Etruria at Lunéville) to the duke of Parma's son, who was the nephew of the Spanish queen and husband of a Spanish infanta. This gift to Spain was considered payment for her cession of Louisiana to France, made on 1 October 1800. In addition, France was to obtain Parma from Spain, but the ageing duke of Parma turned a deaf ear on the bargain and Bonaparte did not press matters until his death. Bonaparte's representatives carried great authority everywhere: Brune in Milan, Jourdan in Turin, Dejean in Genoa, Saliceti in Lucca, Clarke in Florence, Moreau de Saint-Méry in Parma, Alquier in Naples and Murat in Rome where Pope Pius VII, elected in February 1800 by the Venetian conclave, had established himself the summer before. Like the other princes of the peninsula, the pope lay at Napoleon's mercy, and Marengo, like Marignano 285 years before, would open the way to the negotiation of a concordat under advantageous circumstances.

Bonaparte had slashed the Gordian knot with a single blow. The victory over Austria had done far more than confirm and consolidate the conquest of the natural frontiers. As the creator of the Cisalpine Republic, it would have been personally difficult for Bonaparte not to have recaptured it. But far from stopping there he clearly indicated that he intended to keep Austria out of Italy altogether. Finally, the Treaty of Lunéville provided the means for contesting the Austrian claims in Germany. The pacification of Europe, pursued along these lines, could only result in a temporary truce.

## THE LEAGUE OF ARMED NEUTRALITY
## AND THE ENGLISH CRISIS

While Bonaparte was depriving England of her allies, he also strove to threaten her directly, and with the help of Paul I he began making plans for an anti-British federation of continental states – preliminary shades of the system later adopted at Tilsit.

During the course of the year 1800, Bonaparte began reorganising the naval administration and developing the armament, especially at Brest. After Lunéville he formed a camp at Boulogne with the intention of invading England. In England, public opinion, if not the government, immediately reacted with alarm. In August 1801 Nelson attacked the French flotilla commanded by Admiral Latouche-Tréville on two separate occasions, but he was repulsed with heavy losses. With Holland unable to do any more on the sea, Bonaparte redoubled his demands on Spain. It was partly in order better to control that country that he extended himself in Italy, for Bonaparte himself later declared that whoever held Italy also held Spain. It was all very reminiscent of eighteenth-century politics and of the Family Compact of 1761, but it was not Bonaparte's fault that the Bourbons of Naples were not committed to the revival of this policy. However, in 1802 the occurrence of a double marriage between the son of Ferdinand IV and a Spanish infanta on the one hand, and the prince of Asturias and Marie-Antoinette of Naples on the other, offered some hopes in this respect.

Bonaparte unfortunately had no other ideas on Spain than had the Directory before him. He too despised that country of the Inquisition, along with its king and queen and their favourite, Manuel de Godoy – Godoy had just recovered his control over the affairs of state by having his cousin Don Pedro de Ceballos installed as first secretary of state after Urquijo's disgrace on 13 December 1800. Bonaparte therefore treated them with contempt. Believing the kingdom enormously rich, his demands on it were great, and he attributed its traditional dilatoriness to bad will. Meanwhile, his entourage looked on Spain as an object of prey. Talleyrand extorted immense bribes which he divided with Berthier, never missing an opportunity to manifest his hatred of Charles IV, who had not been able to conceal his contempt for him. Ouvrard was also looking out for fortunes to be made in Spain and maintained close contact with Hervas, a Spanish banker residing in Paris whose daughter married

Michel Duroc, the future duke of Friuli. The Spanish fleet by itself would have been ineffective against England, and its principal squadron, commanded by Admiral Gravina, continued to remain at Brest. Beyond Spain, however, Portugal, a British 'fief', was vulnerable, and Lucien Bonaparte was sent to Madrid to persuade the Spaniards to undertake a joint expedition. The affair turned out to be sheer comedy. Godoy, who harboured his own suspicions, did not bother to wait for the French army. He captured the fortress of Olivenza on 16 May 1801, laid siege to Elvas on 18 May and having thus brought to an end the 'war of the oranges', he immediately proceeded to sign a peace, the conditions of which were the cession of the province of Olivenza by Portugal and the promise to pay Spain an indemnity of fifteen million francs. As an accessory to this scheme, Lucien returned to Paris with immense plunder. Talleyrand was also involved, being in the pay of Portugal and as a former lover of Madame de Flahaut, whose second husband was the Portuguese ambassador. Even England was prepared to profit from the situation, if necessary, by seizing Brazil. She had refused to grant military assistance to Prince John, who was regent of Portugal in the name of his insane mother, and to his minister, Coutinho, counselling them to sue for peace in order to avoid occupation. Duped on all sides, Bonaparte raged, but to no avail as he was unable to do more than raise the amount of the indemnity to twenty million francs.

Assistance came principally from Paul I, whose hostility towards England was steadily mounting, and also from the neutrals who followed in Russia's wake. Towards them, Bonaparte exhibited a degree of moderation which contrasted with the policies of the Directory and which in no way portended the continental blockade. From the month of December on he abolished the radical measures of his predecessors, returning to the attitude adopted by France during the American War of Independence. He also made certain changes in the area of laws governing prizes at sea. The emissaries from the United States, whom President Adams had agreed to send in his anxiety to avoid war, soon arrived in France. Since France recognised the principle of freedom of enemy goods in neutral ships, except contraband (*le pavillon neutre couvre la marchandise*), an agreement was easily reached and concluded at Mortefontaine on 30 September 1800. The Americans were especially desirous that Bonaparte no longer insist on the alliance of 1778, so that they might be free to pursue the policy of no entanglements which Washington had always advocated.

Bonaparte's attitude made that of England appear much more irritating
to the Scandinavians, the Prussians and the Russians. Besides, Paul I was
growing increasingly worried about the fate of Malta. On 29 August he
declared an embargo on all English vessels in Russian ports, and did so
again upon learning that Malta had capitulated; in addition, Grenville, on
17 October, decided in favour of keeping Malta. Finally, on 16 December
1800 Sweden and Denmark, following Russia's lead, formed, together
with her, the Second League of Armed Neutrality, Prussia joining on 18
December. England was now shut off from the Baltic Sea; the Danes
entered Hamburg, and Prussian troops occupied Hanover, on the pretext
of preventing a French occupation. British shipping was thus effectively
barred from the German rivers and the Hanseatic towns. England was
now deprived of its two essential markets, Germany and the Baltic states.

It was Bonaparte's treasured hope that Paul would consider these
steps as only preliminary to a more far-reaching alliance between France
and Russia which would officially unify the Continent against England.
Ever since July 1800 he had offered to restore to the tsar, without ransom,
the Russian prisoners who had been detained in France, and not on a
basis of exchange, since the Russians held no French prisoners. Towards
this end General Sprengporten was despatched to France. In December
a simultaneous exchange of friendly letters passed between Paul and
Bonaparte: the latter ordered the suspension of hostile acts against Russian vessels; the former expelled Louis XVIII from Mittau. Then, in
March 1801 Kolychev was sent to Paris to sign the peace and to discuss
terms for an alliance. Paul, very much at odds with England, decided to
embark on the conquest of India, and marched off an advance guard of
cossacks towards the steppes of Central Asia. But for all that he had no
intention of renouncing the gains which he had already won or even those
which he contemplated, such as Rostopchin's proffered European project
entailing the partition of the Turkish Empire between Russia and Austria
and the creation of an immense Greek state under Russia's protection.
Paul still coveted Malta; he expected that the kingdom of Naples would
be evacuated and the king of Sardinia restored; and he also maintained his
protection over Germany. But Bonaparte, who had refused to surrender
Italy to Austria (it would have assured the peace), was not about to hand
that country over to Russia. Nor was he about to deliver her the Grand
Turk. How then was Bonaparte to win Russia over to his side without in
effect granting her anything? The problem was all the more difficult since

Kolychev, like Markov who succeeded him in July, was the inflexible representative not only of Paul I but of a Russian aristocracy still very hostile towards France, and he had made it a point of honour to defend the interests of the Italian princes. A choice had to be made. But as far as England was concerned, the prospects were not becoming any the less perilous.

England was experiencing severe difficulties. Her industry had suffered from the crisis of 1799, and famine had been rampant ever since the harvest of that same year. Between 1800 and 1802 England imported nearly 3½ million quarters of wheat. Neither of these blows, however, was as harsh as the one dealt her by the League of Armed Neutrality. The stoppage of shipments from the Baltic caused a panic on the corn exchange, and the quarter rose to 151 shillings on 25 April 1801. A pound of bread sold for up to more than five pence, or the equivalent of seven French *sous*. Even though Parliament decreed the usual measures for such eventualities, disturbances erupted here and there which were blamed on speculation, and the farmers did in fact unite to keep prices high. Threatening placards, which were ascribed to Jacobinism and to French propaganda, such as those calling for 'bread or blood', inflamed public opinion. At the same time the financial situation appeared disquieting: gold was at a nine per cent premium in 1801, and silver at seventeen per cent; the cash reserves of the Bank of England fell once again to £4½ million; subsidies amounting to £5,600,000 together with the cost of maintaining garrisons (£2,800,000) and grain purchases accounted for £23 million which flowed out to the Continent in 1800 and 1801. The rate of exchange on the pound lost nearly sixteen per cent in Spain in 1801, and thirteen per cent in Hamburg. And yet neither the aristocracy nor the merchants countenanced the idea of raising the income tax. Given these conditions, peace, as in 1797, soon became the cry of the day, and Fox took advantage of it. On 9 October 1800 William Grenville's brother, Thomas, wrote: 'The scarcity of bread and the consequent distress of the poor, if it continues, will, I believe, force you whether you will or no to make your peace with France.' And the *Monthly Magazine* (October 1800) pointed out that 'As the humane and laudable policy therefore of starving the French nation cannot be realised, perhaps it would be sound policy to try to prevent our own people from starving by making peace.'

It would have been difficult for Pitt and Grenville to accept this fact had not an incident in domestic politics spared them that humiliation.

The Union with Ireland having been accomplished, it still remained to honour the promise tacitly given to the Catholics to abolish the Test Act. On 30 September, however, the lord chancellor, Loughborough, had declared himself opposed to its abolition. His sentiments were promptly echoed by the entire Protestant coterie, and the king pronounced himself publicly as being of the same opinion. The cabinet became divided over the issue, and Pitt tendered in his resignation on 5 February 1801. The king then called on Addington, a man of mediocre talents, to form a government, thereby assuring himself more influence in the conduct of affairs. As a result of these troubles, George III succumbed to another fit of insanity, but he quickly recovered and blamed Pitt for his illness. Eager to resume his office, Pitt unabashedly promised never again to raise the Catholic question during the king's lifetime. Grenville, however, refused to have any part in this recantation, and since Addington was not willing to step down, Pitt was forced to resign on 14 March. Political circumstances being what they were, it may be assumed that Pitt's disappointment was to some extent mitigated. Lord Hawkesbury, the new foreign secretary, had approached France with offers to open peace negotiations as early as 21 February. And although Addington's administration, which in fact depended for its continued existence on Pitt's tolerance, received Pitt's approval on its policies as far as the signing of the Peace of Amiens, it is quite possible that Pitt, seeing that a peace was inevitable, was only too happy to have escaped the responsibility for its making.

The negotiations between Hawkesbury and Talleyrand immediately ran afoul over the question of Egypt. Hawkesbury was not opposed to letting the French stay there; he even sent a countermand to the expeditionary force already on its way to Egypt, which arrived too late, however. But as compensation he wanted to retain most of the British conquests, whereas Talleyrand calmly contented himself with offering India! Actually, England's willingness to treat only reinforced the hopes of Bonaparte, who counted on crushing her with the help of Russia. Addington, on the other hand, although resolved to negotiate, hoped for a somewhat better settlement should the ventures then in progress turn out favourably. As it happened, the respite benefited Great Britain.

## THE PEACE OF AMIENS (25 MARCH 1802)

Two events occurring almost simultaneously shattered the dream of a continental coalition. During the night of 23 March 1801, Paul I was assassinated. That should not have come as a surprise. The Russian nobility, already exasperated by his sanguinary fickleness which threatened all of the officials, had been driven to it because the break with England would have deprived them of a market for their grains and timber. The plot was engineered by Count Nikita Panin and Count Peter Pahlen in collusion with Alexander. It appears that the grand duke had stipulated that no bodily harm should befall his father, and he was later overcome by grief, but his illusions, if that were the case, were naïve to say the least. One of the first things Alexander did was to seek an accommodation with England.

The other event occurred on 28 March when a squadron under Sir Hyde Parker, with Nelson second in command, forced the passage of the Sound. Copenhagen was shelled, and the Danish fleet severely damaged. Denmark concluded an armistice, and upon hearing of the tsar's death, signed a peace on 28 May; Sweden had already done as much on 18 May, and Alexander followed suit on 17 June. The Second Armed Neutrality was no more. Formed during the course of the winter, it had not inflicted great material losses on England, but it did leave an impression not soon forgotten. There was nothing left for Bonaparte to do but come to terms with Russia. On 8 October Alexander agreed to re-establish the peace officially. He secured recognition of the situation which his father had acquired, both in the Mediterranean where he retained a protectorate over the seven Ionian Islands and a garrison at Corfu, and in Turkey where Bonaparte accepted him as the sultan's mediator. France also consented to evacuate Naples after a settlement of the Egyptian question and to treat the king of Sardinia with the consideration called for by the situation. Finally, the affairs of Germany were to be arranged by common agreement. In short, Bonaparte conceded to Alexander very nearly all that he had wrangled out of Paul, and that without obtaining in exchange anything more than a peace treaty. For Napoleon it was a resounding failure.

The Egyptian venture turned out to be another setback. On departing from Egypt, Bonaparte had appointed General Kléber to succeed him. The latter was determined to follow Bonaparte back to France as soon as possible by signing a convention of evacuation. Kléber, the grand vizier Yussef, who commanded the Turkish army advancing through Syria, and Sir Sydney Smith, an English commodore, met on 24 January 1800 at El-Arish, where they negotiated an agreement; but Admiral Keith, the commander of the English fleet, refused to ratify it. The grand vizier resumed his advance on Cairo, but Kléber completely routed the Turkish army at Heliopolis on 20 March. Unfortunately, Kléber was assassinated on 14 June. His successor, General Jacques-Abdallah Menou, lacked Kléber's authority, and his conversion to Islam had not increased his prestige. He continually quarrelled with his subordinates, and used his soldiers as judges. In an effort to save the Army of the Orient, Bonaparte sent a squadron under Admiral Ganteaume to reinforce Menou. It sailed from Brest on 23 January 1801, and would have encountered little in the way of enemy opposition, but Ganteaume timorously put in to port at Toulon. When he resumed the attempt towards the end of March, the British expeditionary force had already set sail for Egypt, and Ganteaume once again begged off. In a final attempt he put out to sea at the end of April and tried to land his reinforcements in Tripoli, whose pasha had consented to a treaty, but confronted there by Arab hostility Ganteaume abandoned the whole project. At that moment the fate of Egypt was already decided. Shortly after the capture of Malta, Henry Dundas, the secretary of state for war, had ordered preparations for the sending of an expeditionary army to Egypt under the command of Sir Ralph Abercromby. It landed on 6 March and repulsed Menou's attack on 21 March at Canopus. With Popham's fleet now in control of the Red Sea, six thousand sepoys sent from India by Marquess Wellesley landed at Kosseir; meanwhile, twenty-five thousand Turks emerged by way of the Isthmus. Cairo fell on 28 June, and Alexandria on 30 August.

Late in July, after the break-up of the Second Armed Neutrality and the failure of his attempt on Portugal, Bonaparte held out new peace proposals according to which the belligerents were to restore to each other their respective conquests. The only exception was that Holland would lose Ceylon and would open the Cape to international traffic. In short, France was to relinquish Egypt – a condition about which Bonaparte affected calm acceptance, but which made its loss nonetheless certain. On the other hand, France would retain all her continental conquests. England was to abandon Malta, Minorca, Elba, Trinidad, the French Antilles and, in effect, Egypt, keeping only Ceylon. Although her position had already become favourable enough to make this glaring inequality appear offensive, England was content to demand only the retention of Trinidad in addition to Ceylon. Concerned over her relations with Alexander, England raised no objection to the restitution of Malta, although she could have pleased him by demanding guarantees for Naples and Sardinia. No efforts were made towards that end, however. Only in regard to Holland did Lord Hawkesbury try to obtain assurances, and he also demanded that Malta be given a garrison furnished by a great power, which would thus become the guarantor of its neutrality. This provided France with an excellent opportunity to advance the candidacy of Russia and so revive her rivalry with England. But Bonaparte spurned the chance, and when he threatened to break off negotiations if these preliminaries of peace were not signed, Hawkesbury gave in on 1 October 1801, without so much as demanding an indemnity for the prince of Orange or a commercial treaty.

It has been argued that this capitulation was caused by Addington's incompetence as prime minister, but that reason is simply not adequate. After all, the British government continued to labour under the pressure of the crisis which had characterised the early months of the year and whose effects were still being felt throughout the country. More than anything, the government wanted to economise, and it believed that peace would provide a return to prosperity. The intense rejoicing with which the public reacted to the news of peace attests to the fact that such was the dominant opinion. Nevertheless, there were protests and reservations made both in Parliament and in the press. William Windham cried out against the 'fatal treaty' which he regarded as 'the nation's death warrant' and which, he claimed, would allow Bonaparte to undertake fresh conquests. Addington retorted that since a new coalition was for the moment impossible, it would be better to try a policy of peace which a contented France might after all take to heart. Should the case prove different, England would always find allies again. Castlereagh, in a letter, expressed the same opinion. Pitt, who had approved the government's policy, defended it on 3 November on the surprising ground that Trinidad constituted a more valuable gain than Malta, the retention of which would have made peace impossible anyway, and that Ceylon seemed preferable to the Cape. He placed great value on Trinidad for the sugar it produced and as an important base for the contraband trade with Spanish America. Here one can distinguish an expression of the mercantilistic attitudes on the objectives of war which had always dominated the policies of Britain's ruling oligarchy. In England the peace was regarded not only as a truce but also as a businessmen's experiment.

It was not long before perspicacious individuals realised that the chances for a lasting peace were indeed quite poor. Bonaparte was already engaged in sending an army to San Domingo (December 1801), and in January he became president of the Cisalpine Republic whose name was changed to Italian Republic. In discussing the final settlement of the treaty, Bonaparte refused to consider a commercial agreement, and he laid claim to certain colonial concessions, the opening of India to free trade, and a station in the Falkland Islands. These demands were rejected, but created quite a sensation. Nevertheless, Addington persisted in his course. It is quite certain that in the negotiations which followed at Amiens, British interests suffered once again from the incompetence of the government and its representative, Cornwallis – an honest man, a good soldier but a pitiful diplomat. France's allies, who bore the cost of the peace, and particularly Schimmelpenninck, would have gladly lent Cornwallis their support; but it was not until they had agreed to the preliminaries that Bonaparte admitted them to the conferences.

The discussions centred principally on the French conquests and Malta. Bonaparte wanted England to recognise the new republics, a gesture to which she was not altogether opposed provided that some concessions were granted to the king of Sardinia. Obtaining nothing on that score, England refused. Bonaparte then declared that she should have no grounds for complaint if 'in consequence her commerce suffered' and if one of these states should choose to incorporate itself 'with a major continental power'. It was a bad omen! As for Malta, England accepted Talleyrand's proposal for a collective guarantee of the great powers, but refused to agree to a general dismantling of its fortifications, insisting that the island receive a Neapolitan garrison until such time as the reconstituted Order of St John could itself procure adequate forces to maintain its independence. Having torn Malta away from England, Bonaparte saw his success confirmed. Still, Malta's surrender was made dependent on so many conditions that England too should have been reasonably satisfied and could await developments. Cornwallis had been instructed to hold fast on two other points: the cession of Tobago in exchange for the cost of maintaining French prisoners, and an indemnity for the prince of Orange. However, Bonaparte was adamant in his refusal to surrender any French territory, and as for the 'Orange-Nassaus', he observed that negotiations regarding an indemnification were going on in Berlin. The heir to that house, a great admirer of the First Consul, displayed his willingness to deal directly with Bonaparte and left England. Cornwallis then signed the peace on 25 March 1802.

Public opinion in England, although somewhat cooler than before, remained satisfied, and a great many islanders flocked to France out of curiosity for a country transformed by such momentous developments and ruled by such an astonishing figure. Although critics in political circles were rapidly becoming more numerous, Parliament still accorded the government its confidence.

As chief of state, Bonaparte had attained the crowning achievement of his destiny by signing the Peace of Amiens. Europe had agreed to lay down its arms without contesting his claim to the natural frontiers. But his indomitable will to power, which he was unable to bridle with each succeeding opportunity, prevented him from ever being satisfied in a way that France might have been, had she but been her own mistress guided by national tradition and interest alone. Still, all would not have been lost had Bonaparte stopped harassing England on the seas and in her colonies, agreed to reopen the French market to English trade, and consented to exercise in neighbouring countries that legitimate amount of influence which his power allowed and which the security of France's frontiers required. Even before the Peace of Amiens had been concluded, however, Napoleon had given proof that this was not the way he understood matters to be.

## THE REORGANISATION OF THE VASSAL STATES

Actually, France could not abandon her neighbouring states and those she occupied to their own devices without first making sure that they were in a position to defend and govern themselves. Now, after the political and social changes to which she had subjected them, they would have been hard put to organise themselves on their own. In many of the vassal republics, the unionist advocates of strong central government were unable to agree with the federalists on the very principles of government. Such was the case in Holland, in the Cisalpine – where the inhabitants of the département of Olona, that is to say, the Milanese, who followed Count Melzi, quarrelled with the Oltrepadani (the inhabitants of the states south of the Po), also known as Emilians, led by Albini – and above all in Switzerland, where the cantons passionately regretted the loss of their autonomy.

More serious still was the social conflict. Jacobin democrats were becoming very active, agitating in their clubs and jeering at nobles and priests at every opportunity. Being but a minority, they were on the best of terms with the French, to whom they had appealed for help, and were quite willing to do their bidding. Representatives of the bourgeoisie, like Schimmelpenninck in Holland, Usteri and Rengger in Switzerland, Corvetto in Genoa, and those of the nobility who were reconciled to republican government, like Count Melzi d'Eril in the Cisalpine, approved with more or less vigour the unity and the new social order; but they were hostile to democracy and hoped that, as in Consulate France, the notables would be assured a position of pre-eminence. Nevertheless, they were not always at one – in Switzerland especially – on accepting the Constitution of Year VIII in so far as it suppressed the normal functioning of elective government. If they felt the need to depend on France, they were also less obedient. In Holland and in Switzerland they appealed to France to preserve the integrity of their country; everywhere, they wished for the evacuation of French troops and for independence. As for the aristocracy, they hoped for the downfall of France so that they might restore the *ancien régime*. To achieve this they would have delivered their country without scruple to other foreigners, but since the French were there, they played the role of patriot. They were willing to keep quiet for the time being as long as Bonaparte left them alone.

In addition to this kind of party strife, normal government was also made impossible by budgetary difficulties. The cost of the war and the occupation had from the very start ruined finances and crippled economies. The Cisalpine, with its four million inhabitants, paid thirty-three million francs to the French army, and it furnished French troops with requisitions in kind whose total amount was estimated at 160 million francs. Then, too, the military arrogated to itself additional levies at will, and generals, notably Murat, subjected the authorities to high-handed treatment. The same can be said of civilian officials, like the marquis de Sémonville in Holland. Both the military and civilian officials intervened in local politics and supported this or that candidate according to their preferences. Consequently, petitioners came to Bonaparte from every direction requesting that he reorganise the state as he saw fit or that he lighten their burden and bring his own subordinates to justice. Bonaparte was as free to act among these factions as he was in France. He hated the democrats, distrusted the moderates whom he considered too independent in regard to France, and he did not want to re-establish the aristocracy. As long as the Concordat remained to be concluded with the pope who, for his part, still hoped to recover the Papal Legations, and as long as the war with England continued, Bonaparte acted with circumspection, and this he did to advantage. For as the situation worsened, so did his task become easier, and as long as the occupation lasted, his troops cost him nothing. It was only after the preliminaries of the maritime peace were signed that the changes began.

In Holland, where there appeared some signs of disobedience, Sémonville, the French representative, prepared a constitution with the approval of the Dutch Directory. It was designed to place power in the hands of trustworthy men. He submitted it, on his own prerogative, for popular ratification, but the legislative chambers refused to sanction it on the ground that the procedure had been illegal. General Augereau then dissolved the two chambers, and the constitution was placed before a national plebiscite. A majority vote was obtained by declaring that the abstentions had been taken as a sign of approval, and the constitution was promulgated on 6 October 1801. It created a *Staatsbewind* or reigning council invested with legislative initiative and executive power, including the nomination of officials, and a legislative body to be renewed one-third at a time by means of elections in two stages. In fact, the Directory itself named seven of the twelve regents, the remainder being co-opted; it also chose the members of the legislative chamber. The new government, just as Bonaparte had hoped, worked to unify factions, but it did so by getting rid of the democrats and by giving all of the official posts to the notables.

In Italy, which Bonaparte himself intended governing, the work of reorganisation took a little more time. During the month of July 1801 a deputation from the Cisalpine Republic arrived in Paris to complain about the intolerable situation at home. In October it was arranged that a 'commission' gather in Lyon in order to establish a new government. The commission was made up of lawyers, representatives of the army and of the national guard chosen by the government, and of elected members of the courts, chambers of commerce, universities, and departmental and municipal administrative bodies. In addition, these choices were made under the watchful eye of Murat. On 29 December 1801, 442 deputies met in Lyon. Talleyrand, who arrived on the eve of the meeting, divided them into regional sections for the purpose of studying the constitutional project and drawing up lists of trusted candidates from which the new personnel would be chosen. In so doing, he fanned the flames of particularism so that Bonaparte might step in and arbitrate over a divided assembly. The latter made his appearance on 11 January 1802. He proceeded as usual to make his personal enquiries, and settled everything himself. He considered Joseph for the presidency of the Cisalpine, but that important personage refused because he was not being offered Piedmont as well. On 21 January the committee in charge of selecting chief magistrates chose Count Melzi and Count Albini. They both refused. On 24 January Bonaparte was offered the presidency and he accepted, taking Melzi as vice-president. Two days later, he substituted the name 'Italian Republic' for that of 'Cisalpine', thus giving rise to great hopes. The date set for the official installation of the new government was 9 February 1802. The executive authority was accorded the same prerogatives as in Paris; it included a secretary of state and various ministers. In addition, the executive chose the members of the legislative council from among the candidates nominated by the three electoral colleges. On this occasion, however, Bonaparte himself elected the members of the legislative council and the colleges. Finally, the Italian Republic was given an original institution called the State Council: it was irremovable and was to deal with foreign affairs and matters of state security. In Genoa, a constitution drawn up by Saliceti in October 1801 was promulgated in June 1802. There, Bonaparte named the members of the Senate and a doge who formed the executive authority. A *consulta*, which should have been chosen by three electoral colleges, was never formed. Lucca submitted to a similar reorganisation on 28 December.

The history of the Helvetic Republic was considerably more turbulent. The *coup d'état* proposed by Frédéric-César de La Harpe to his colleagues in the Directory in November 1799 did not receive their approval. The legislative councils, having been warned, countered by voting the dissolution of the Directory on 7 January 1800, entrusting power to an executive committee in which Dolder exerted the leading influence. The executive committee soon also fell to quarrelling with the councils and appealed to Bonaparte. On 7 August 1800 the councils, surrounded by French troops, capitulated and formed a provisional government from among their own ranks, charged with the task of preparing a new constitution. The *coup* was the work of moderate unionists, that is to say, that party which favoured strong central government and a unitary state. Above all, they were advocates of government by notables. As enemies of the Jacobins, they sought the support of the aristocracy and reintroduced tithes, ground rents and feudal dues which had previously been abolished. True, these were made redeemable, but at the expense of the peasantry. In January 1801 these moderates submitted to Bonaparte a constitutional project markedly unionist in character, according to which the members of the constituted bodies were to be co-opted. Seeing that the unionists were intent upon laying claim to the Valais and to the bishopric of Basle (the Bernese Jura), the federalist-minded representative of the French government in Switzerland, Reinhard, suggested fomenting a new revolution with the support of the aristocracy. This, however, Bonaparte would not permit. He simply rejected the constitutional proposal, and on 29 April 1801 substituted for it a counter-project called the 'Constitution of Malmaison', which foreshadowed the later Act of Mediation. Bonaparte felt that federalist sentiment was too deeply rooted not to grant a large degree of sovereignty to the cantons. It is also likely that since he intended to evacuate Switzerland in order to benefit from its neutrality, he was not favourably disposed to the creation of a centralised Switzerland which would have made that country too powerful. By the Constitution of Malmaison, the seventeen cantons were given considerable autonomy, and were authorised to frame their own constitutions with a proviso that suffrage be limited to property holders. The federal Diet elected a Senate consisting of twenty-five members who in turn chose two leading magistrates from among themselves bearing the title of *Landammann*: one presided over the Senate; the other formed, along with four other senators, a small council which was to exercise the executive authority. The central federal authority now possessed extensive powers, particularly in its appointment of the cantonal prefects (*Statthalters*).

This solution pleased no one. The unionists assured themselves a majority in the Diet, and excluded from the Senate the federalists who seceded. The unionists then refused to apply the Constitution of Malmaison, voted for a new one, and, to crown it all, openly defied Bonaparte by accepting into their ranks the deputies from the Valais. On 28 October 1801 the French agent, Verninac, and General Choin de Montchoisy declared the Diet dissolved and set up a provisional government under the rule of Aloys Reding, the ablest of the aristocrats. Reding purged the administration, suppressed freedom of the press, amnestied the émigrés, abolished the land tax and reopened the monasteries. Bonaparte refused to recognise him, demanding that he make a place for the moderates. This naturally created discord within the council. Reding journeyed to Paris, but received nothing for his trouble; he returned to Switzerland, and proceeded on his own authority to promulgate a new constitution on 26 February 1802. During the Easter recess, however, Verninac took advantage of Reding's absence from Berne to have it annulled by his enemies. An assembly of notables was summoned, and it finally approved the Constitution of Malmaison on 29 May 1802 and appointed Dolder *Landammann*. The Valais was constituted as an independent republic, and the valley of Dappes was ceded to France.

There exists an obvious connection between these changes and those which took place in France. Everywhere, the Constitution of Year VIII had encouraged notables to lay claim to authority by much the same processes. Everywhere, the executive power had undergone strengthening, thus holding out the promise of order and stability. And everywhere, Bonaparte demanded that democrats be brushed aside and that efforts be made to win over moderates and well-intentioned aristocrats. But it was in Italy, where he regarded himself as master rather than arbiter, that Bonaparte revealed his real predilections, which he never dared to make the rule in France, still less in Holland or Switzerland, where he was to maintain genuine elections in the future. In the Italian constitutions, the electoral colleges were not in any way founded on suffrage, even of a kind limited to property holders. They were simply professional groupings: the first consisted of a certain number of landed proprietors (*possidenti*), the second of merchants and manufacturers (*commercianti*) and the third of members of the professional classes (*dotti*). The first two of these colleges co-opted their members; the third, being naturally suspect of harbouring 'ideology', i.e., subversive ideas, was limited to offering the government a list of candidates. To perfect the scheme, only one step remained to be made: simply to confer upon the chief of state the power to appoint the members of the colleges.

In itself, the reorganisation of the states that bordered France did not offer Europe any cause for concern. Quite the contrary: it was to be hoped that France, having made it possible for these states to govern themselves, would recall her troops and give them the independence which she had promised them – barring the details – in the Treaty of Lunéville. Bonaparte did in fact give the order to evacuate Switzerland in July 1802; and he also consented to reduce the number of soldiers stationed in Holland – the prince of Orange having renounced his claims to the stadholdership on 24 May, in exchange for the cession of Fulda and Corvey to his son. At any rate, it was good enough to pass as a promise of future evacuation. Melzi, in the Italian Republic, hoped to obtain a similar advantage sooner or later: Bonaparte's presidency could only be temporary. How very illusory these hopes appear to us today! But without these illusions, the road upon which Addington and Pitt decided to venture would have lacked all *raison d'être*.

## CHAPTER SIX

# Bonaparte Consul for Life

VICTORY AND PEACE made Bonaparte a hero of the nation, and he used the occasion to increase his personal power and to further his personal ambitions. The country, satisfied with his accomplishments, was willing to follow him; but there were feelings of regret and anxiety when he heightened his dictatorship at the very moment when peace promised a return to liberty. In any event, opposition increased, and it was only by fresh applications of force that Bonaparte was able to subdue the resistance.

### THE CRISIS OF YEAR IX

After Bonaparte's departure for Italy, France experienced a period of anguish. His defeat would probably have resulted in an invasion by foreign troops, and most certainly in new uprisings inasmuch as bread prices had risen ever since the harvest of Year VII; during the course of a riot in Toulouse, the mob forced merchants to lower the price of grain. On the Paris exchange, prices were falling. Then suddenly, as if by magic, the news of the military victory at Marengo restored public confidence and magnified Bonaparte's popularity a hundredfold. Appreciating the power of the press and possessing an instinct for public relations, Bonaparte had assumed that such indeed would be the effect. In his mind, pride and ambition spontaneously transformed truth into legend. He published a *Bulletin of the Army of Reserve* which, along with the *Moniteur* and other more or less official newspapers, glorified his entire campaign. Moreau's victory at Hohenlinden came too late to attenuate his prestige, and besides, he took good care to stifle its repercussions. Ironically, had the truth about Marengo been known, Bonaparte's halo would surely have been even brighter, for men are seduced still more by the workings of chance than by sheer genius (and it inspires in them a certain superstitious awe). The throw of the dice at Marengo could hardly have detracted from a man who, on two occasions, had miraculously escaped the English cruisers.

In the meantime, Bonaparte, having heard what was being said and plotted during his absence, hastened to return to Paris, and he entered the city on 2 July 1800. He returned an embittered man, full of rancour against his entourage, with a hostile distrust for the generals who had been waiting for the chance to succeed him. And he was seized with a feeling of melancholy now that the effort was spent and the danger past – and now that the tragic side of the adventure dawned on him with the full realisation of how close he had come to disaster.

The royalists collapsed at once. Only a few bands of brigands remained from their preparations for an insurrection. Wickham returned to England, and the agency in Augsburg dispersed; some of its members tried to regroup in Bayreuth, but Fouché had them thrown into prison by the Prussian police. England stopped subsidising Condé's corps of émigrés, which had entered into its pay, and disbanded it. On 7 September 1800 Bonaparte at last made his reply to Louis XVIII saying, 'Your return to France is not a thing to be wished for; it could only be accomplished over the bodies of one hundred thousand men.' Expelled from Mittau, the king took refuge in Warsaw, then later went to England. Their rupture was complete.

The republicans, too, were well aware that Bonaparte's victory would rivet their chains. There were many in his entourage who had secretly contemplated his death or downfall. Now they became all the more anxious to convince him of the necessity to stabilise his authority by restoring the hereditary monarchy to his own advantage. Most illustrious among them were Roederer and the Feuillants. They had rallied to the Republic, but remained monarchists at heart. Talleyrand naturally supported them. Lucien Bonaparte, always turbulent, fearlessly said what no one else dared to say when he launched a pamphlet entitled *A Comparison between Caesar, Cromwell, Monk and Bonaparte*, which was probably written by Fontanes. The path of fortune had been marked for Fontanes ever since the First Consul had returned to France and designated him to deliver a eulogy on the occasion of Washington's death, not to mention the fact that he was already Elisa Bonaparte's lover.

Nevertheless, all these manoeuvres encountered resistance. Fouché remained hostile to all monarchical projects until 1804. For Fouché, although widely connected and valued even in the Faubourg Saint-Germain for personal services rendered *sub rosa*, was still regarded as the leader of the left. And not without good reason. True, he was a sceptic who bore no illusions about men, an egotist whose passions were money and power. But his attachment to his revolutionary past was greater than one might suppose. Witness his domestic life, simple and familial, his cool vigour and determination, and his preference for terroristic methods, which, although wisely tempered, quite naturally suited his functions as chief of police. Then there was his sincere desire to save what he could of the work of the Revolution and to prevent the aristocracy from regaining control of the state. Finally, and above all, there was his hot temper, concealed under a phlegmatic exterior, resulting in his habitual irreverence, his caustic tongue and his nostalgic regret for the time when, as representative on mission of the Convention, he too had spoken with absolute authority in the name of the sovereign people. Bonaparte valued his talents and feared him, feeling that Fouché might assert his independence at any time.

Fouché found support in Bonaparte's immediate circle. Josephine, having failed to produce an heir, feared that the establishment of a hereditary line of succession would lead to a divorce. Bonaparte could hardly have been pleased by the insatiableness of his family clan; he fully expected a raging tempest if circumstances forced him to choose between his brothers. But he did not intend to have his hand forced, and he considered any talk of monarchy premature at this time: the peace had not been concluded, the reorganisation of the country had to be completed, and the parliamentary bodies still had to be cowed. And so Lucien was dismissed; he ceded his post as minister of the interior to Chaptal, and became an ambassador.

Bonaparte was waiting, nonetheless, for the chance to increase his own power. The uncovering of several conspiracies furnished him with just such an opportunity. These plots were still another consequence of the victory at Marengo: after that battle, the Jacobins and royalists lost all hope, and some became desperate enough to try their hand at assassination. In the closing days of Year VIII and shortly thereafter, three Jacobin plots were uncovered: on 14 September three persons were arrested; this was followed by the arrest of Aréna, Topino-Lebrun and two others on 10 October; and finally, Chevalier and an alleged accomplice on 8 November. Whether or not these conspiracies were genuine has never been settled. The second seems to have been uncovered behind Fouché's back, and Fouché, feeling his position endangered, made a great fuss about the third so-called conspiracy. Just as the government was working on a project to proscribe the Jacobins, the royalists came on the scene and greatly facilitated this task. In June Cadoudal had sent several *Chouans* from Brittany to organise a plot in Paris. The police, who kept track of their movements, were only able to apprehend a certain chevalier de Margadel, whom they shot. Three of the conspirators – Saint-Réjant, Limoélan and Jean Carbon – managed to construct an infernal machine which they exploded in the rue Saint-Nicaise the evening of 24 December on Bonaparte's route from the Tuileries to the Opéra. Twenty-two people were killed and fifty-six were wounded, but Bonaparte escaped unharmed. The consensus was that this had been the work of Jacobins. Bonaparte, who was already near enough to the throne to loathe regicides above all else, also appears to have believed it. On 25 December, while the parliamentary bodies were congratulating him on his fortunate escape, he thundered furious imprecations on 'those who have dishonoured the Republic and sullied the cause of liberty by all kinds of excesses, and especially by the part they played in the September days and the like'. 'Blood must run,' he declared in the Conseil d'État on 26 December. And indeed, the previously accused Jacobins were either shot or guillotined on 13, 20 and 31 January 1801.

The upshot of the affair was the wholesale arrest of Jacobins which now followed, and their subsequent deportation without trial. Fouché had laid the blame on 'English gold' ever since the night of the attempt – indeed, he knew who the true culprits were. Limoélan was kept in hiding by the Jesuit Clorivière and by the sister of Champion de Cicé until he finally managed to escape to America where he became a model priest; Carbon was arrested on 8 January, and Saint-Réjant on 28 January. But it was too late to save the victimised Jacobins, and besides, Bonaparte could not have been swayed from his goal. The Conseil d'État refused to pronounce on the proscription, declaring that it was not a legislative matter. Then on 5 January the Senate was called upon to ratify the act as a 'measure tending to preserve the Constitution'. Among the 130 deportees were Choudieu and two former deputies, Talot and Destrem, whose vehement opposition on 19 Brumaire Bonaparte had never forgiven. There were also some well-known revolutionaries: Fournier l'Américain, Rossignol and Lepeletier. Fouché managed to save about a third of them by playing for time. Twenty-six were not sent to Guiana until 1804, and sixty-eight were shipped out to the Seychelles after 1801. More than half died in exile. In addition, many more republicans were placed under surveillance. Fouché also arrested about a hundred royalists, whom he condemned to prison or interned without trial. Carbon and Saint-Réjant were tried at last, and succumbed to the guillotine on 21 April.

The Bonapartist terror had once again struck the left and the right. 'It was the only kind of impartial justice from which he never wavered,' wrote Madame de Staël; 'thus he made friends out of those to whose hatreds he ministered.' The blow had been directed primarily against the left, and one might even say that it had been completely crushed. But the Jacobins were not the only ones affected. The assemblies had not been summoned to vote on the law of proscription, because it was not absolutely sure that they would accept it. Bonaparte's pronouncement on 26 December, that 'the metaphysicians are the cause for all our troubles', very clearly constituted a threat to the assemblies. After that, he turned to the Senate which, as 'guardian of the constitution', invested itself tacitly with the power to modify or violate that constitution. Consequently, the decree of 13 Nivôse, Year IX (5 January 1801), stands as the first in a series of *senatus consulta* which were to make it possible for Bonaparte to legislate personally without the legal assistance of the assemblies, and so to revise to his own advantage the Constitution of Year VIII, which had not provided for any such procedure.

During and after the month of November 1800, while the proscription of the Jacobins was going on, Bonaparte contemplated certain repressive measures which, although less spectacular, would exercise a still much greater influence on the general condition of the country. The problem, as he saw it, was to put an end to the *Chouan* uprisings and to brigandage with one blow. Cadoudal, having revived the *Chouannerie*, was scouring the countryside in Brittany. He was continually being hunted down and was forever eluding capture. Using the good offices of the royalist Bourmont, Fouché finally succeeded in bribing certain persons involved in the *Chouannerie* to kill or deliver Cadoudal to the police. But the Breton royalists had an extremely active counter-espionage network which extended into the government ministries. Thus, when the two renegade *Chouans*, Becdelièvre and Duchatellier, were sent to murder their former leader, Cadoudal, informed of the situation, had them killed. The prefect of Ille-et-Vilaine, Borie, may himself have betrayed Duchatellier.

The exploits of the *Chouans* exasperated Bonaparte. On 23 September 1800 Clément de Ris, former administrator of Indre-et-Loire, senator and important purchaser of the *biens nationaux*, was kidnapped from his château at Azay-sur-Cher, while on 19 November Audrein, bishop of Finistère, was assassinated. Convoys carrying treasury funds were continually being raided and pillaged by various bands of insurgents. As in Year VIII, Bonaparte had recourse to extreme measures. On 18 Floréal, Year IX (8 May 1801), three columns accompanied by military tribunals were despatched under the command of General Bernadotte. The mopping-up operations proceeded rapidly. By the end of the year, Cadoudal returned to England. Even so, there still remained some isolated bands of *Chouans*. Aside from a few sincere individuals, the majority were irregulars who looked upon rebellion as a way of life.

Whether or not the brigands invoked the name of religion or the king, they existed to some extent everywhere. Certainly they were not restricted to mountainous regions, such as the Alps and Apennines where the *Barbets* carried on a smuggling trade; they were also to be found in wealthy places such as Nord and Beauce. People called them *chauffeurs* (furnace men) because they tortured their victims by fire to extract their money. This was nothing new; the rural population abounded in day labourers, who were unemployed part of the year, and peasants who were unable to live on the meagre harvest from their lands, especially during the bad years. The countryside was always swarming with beggars and vagabonds, and it was inevitable that some of them became outlaws. The evil had been seriously aggravated by internal troubles as well as the war, which upset the economy and disorganised the rural police. The peasant has always valued his security even more than the urban dweller, because he has always been more exposed. And since security is the basic condition of sustained and productive labour, nothing could have been of greater service to the nation than its re-establishment. Consequently, nothing could have heightened Bonaparte's reputation more, as was indeed the case with Henri IV and Louis XIV.

The problem was not just one of apprehending the brigands – that could have been done by letting the army reinforce the *gendarmerie* – but of obtaining their conviction. Both witnesses and juries knew that they were open to reprisals, and so the one kept quiet and the other acquitted the culprits. Numerous cases of misdemeanours had already been brought before the courts in Year VIII, and prefects had been given the right to supervise the choosing of juries by the justices of the peace. The results remained poor. Moreover, the slowness with which the repression

was carried out deprived it, in part at least, of its efficacy. Under analogous circumstances, the monarchy had had recourse to the provostal
court, a special legal instrument which summarily condemned and executed: 'caught and hung'. As an exceptional measure, Bonaparte resorted
to military tribunals in the west, in Provence and in the Rhineland. He
had not the slightest intention of renouncing them, but he also wished to
revive the expeditious methods of the *ancien régime* on a permanent and
regular basis.

Such, then, was the object of the law of 18 Pluviôse, Year IX (7 February 1801). It authorised the government to establish, in each département
where Bonaparte thought it advisable (he decided on thirty-two), a
special criminal court composed of a president, two judges from the
regular criminal court and five other persons (three from the military,
two civilians) all appointed by the First Consul. They were to pronounce
final judgement, without appeal, on vagrants and habitual criminals,
*ratione personae*, and on a great number of crimes pertaining to brigandage: burglary, highway robbery, murder, arson, counterfeiting, seditious assembly and illegal possession of weapons. The following year, on
23 Floréal, Year X (13 May 1802), another special court was established
in every department dealing with crimes of forgery, but which, in the
absence of a special criminal court, could also take cognisance of many
crimes of brigandage.

On 26 Vendémiaire, Year XI (18 October 1802), the jury system was
suspended in a large number of départements by a *senatus consultum*;
henceforth, criminal court judges were set up into a kind of special court
without any intervention on the part of the military, however. In short,
Bonaparte did away with the jury system in a great many parts of France,
and these newly created judicial bodies continued to function until his
downfall. The same law did away with the grand jury, since the special
courts now delegated the preliminary judicial inquiry to one of their
members. Finally, the regular judicial process, wherever it continued to
exist, was given new strength by a change in the office of public prosecutor and by a reform in procedure. On 7 Pluviôse, Year IX (27 January
1801), a 'criminal magistrate' (*magistrat de sûreté*) took the place of the
government commissioner in the courts of the first instance, and he was
empowered to draw up the indictments; the judicial inquiry became in
part secret, witnesses being heard in the absence of the accused. Thus the
grand jury had to decide from indirect evidence, since the accuser and

witnesses were excused from appearing in court so that they might be kept out of reach of the felons' vengeance.

Despite all of these measures, one should not conclude that Bonaparte succeeded in immediately re-establishing perfect order in the country districts. Regardless of what he may have thought or done, the suppression of mendicity and vagabondage did not depend on him entirely. It was a long time before outright banditry was overcome. In the Rhineland, it was a difficult task to capture Schinderhannes, a veritable 'Cartouche'* whom people regarded with some complacency because he was particularly fond of attacking Jews. Nevertheless, by the early years of the Empire it was apparent that conditions had become incontestably better. Since the special courts were not used for political ends – they touched only the abject and delinquent members of society – they were not condemned by public opinion. As for political suspects, Bonaparte dealt with them through the military tribunals of which he made much use. Although the judicial reforms were severe with respect to professional criminals, they also served to check the poverty-stricken elements that despair might otherwise have driven to riot, as in 1789. 'Decent', law-abiding citizens drew no distinction between starving mobs and felons, nor did the law of Year IX. Such must have been Bonaparte's wish surely, for according to Chaptal, he feared nothing quite so much as a bread riot.

The establishment of the special courts, coming on the heels of the proscription of the Jacobins, caused a good deal of concern among the republicans in the assemblies. Debate in the Tribunate became very heated, and a vote in the Corps Législatif resulted in eighty-eight 'nays' as against 192 'ayes'. No longer bearing any illusions about Bonaparte, the republicans did not miss this opportunity to remonstrate. Nevertheless, one must do them justice: these notables had favoured strong government, but not an arbitrary one, and they were unable to regard these exceptional measures as being any more consonant with principles under the Consulate than at the time of the Convention under the Mountain. Bonaparte, however, would not be blocked by any law, not even a constitutional one. Speaking before the Conseil d'État in Year X, he came straight to the point: 'A constitution must not interfere with the process of government, nor be written in a way that would force the government to violate it . . . Every day brings the necessity to violate constitutional laws; it is the

* Cartouche was the leader of a notorious band of robbers in the early eighteenth century. TRANSLATOR.

only way, otherwise progress would be impossible.' 'Government does not have to be tyrannical . . . but it cannot avoid committing certain arbitrary acts.' Briefly then, the Constitution was a screen for enlightened despotism. Debates in the Tribunate also aroused Bonaparte's fury. 'In the Tribunate are a dozen or so metaphysicians only fit for the garbage heap. They are vermin on my clothes. I am a soldier, a son of the Revolution, and I will not tolerate being insulted like a king.' The crisis of Year IX thus rendered official the breach between Bonaparte and the republican bourgeoisie, which had carried him to power. But now he wanted them to ratify the Concordat, and of all his projects, it was precisely this one that they least approved.

This parliamentary opposition found no support in the rest of the country. The various interest groups were satisfied, and peace and public order favoured a resumption of business. A new bank of issue was created in Paris: a commercial bank known as the Caisse Jabach. Notes issued by the Bank of France and its rivals permitted speculators to dispose of currency in the provinces where it stimulated the economy. A series of bad harvests brought about an unprecedented increase in the price of agricultural products, and so strengthened the buying power of the landowning peasantry or farmers. After the deflation, which had made them so unhappy under the Directory, they were delighted with this windfall. They were grateful to the First Consul who exhibited, moreover, an avid interest in the national output, and so they spared him no encouragements. An amelioration in the condition of public finance was also becoming noticeable. The military conquests had helped to lighten the burden on the budget, since the French armies were now able to maintain themselves outside France. Taxes were being collected regularly, and in Year X the budget actually revealed a small surplus of receipts over expenditures. In large towns the tax on movable personal property was gradually being replaced by municipal tolls (*octrois*), to the satisfaction of the rich. As for taxes on landed property, a study was being conducted to determine ways of arriving at a more equitable distribution of the burden among the communes. Later, in Year XI, cadastral surveys of the extent of cultivations, land boundaries and valuations of soil productivity were undertaken in a number of communes in every département.

The state of the treasury continued to be a matter of concern. An attempt was made to eliminate some of the middlemen (*faiseurs de services*) in the ministry's operations by creating, on 18 August 1802 (30

Thermidor, Year X), an association or syndicate of *receveurs généraux*. The idea was to force them to discount their own obligations, but the attempt failed. The notes continued to be negotiated at a loss. For the public, however, the major event was the liquidation of the debt. As in the time of the Directory, it was achieved by means of bankruptcy. The highly depreciated 'two-thirds' bonds issued in 1797 were freely exchangeable at one-twentieth of their face value for consolidated government annuities bearing five per cent interest, unless the bearer chose to redeem them, as before, for payments in *biens nationaux*. Bonds issued in Year VI and paper obligations in arrears were consolidated into government bonds at three per cent and five per cent interest with extreme slowness. Still, creditors were happy that this enactment of 30 Ventôse, Year IX (21 March 1801), had at least brought them something; but the main impression resulted from the resumption, at the end of Year VIII, of the cash payments of government salaries and annuities. Purveyors to the state continued to be paid at Bonaparte's pleasure.

This is not to say that confidence in French finances was fully restored. In spite of manoeuvres on the part of the Sinking Fund, the value of government bonds on the Bourse remained weak. After the Peace of Amiens, the five per cent French consolidated government bonds were quoted at forty-eight to fifty-three francs, while the three per cent British Consols fluctuated between sixty-six and seventy-nine. Still, if the bourgeoisie felt itself at the mercy of any new crisis that might have arisen, it did not wish to precipitate one by creating difficulties for Bonaparte. The lower classes alone suffered. After the harvest of Year VIII, the price of a four-pound loaf of bread rose to thirteen *sous* (sixty-five *centimes*) in Paris, and by 1801 the rise in prices affected all commodities and so lessened the good feeling brought about by the Treaty of Lunéville. The harvest of Year XI was quite poor, even in areas of large-scale farming; during the course of that winter, bread rose to eighteen *sous* in Paris, and as high as seven *sous* per pound in small towns and the countryside – as much as in England. Brittany, no longer able to export, remained the only exception.

In order to meet the crisis, Bonaparte turned to methods which had been used by the *ancien régime*. The prefect of police reorganised the bakers along corporate lines, and compelled them to set up a reserve granary. This resulted in driving many small bakers out of business. On 17 November 1801 Chaptal was instructed to purchase grain abroad, but since the government was short of money, it again became necessary to approach the bankers: five were commissioned to procure fifty thousand quintals monthly. This turned out to be insufficient, and in Floréal, Year X, Bonaparte brought the financial wizard Ouvrard out of disgrace and obtained his promise to do what was necessary to relieve the situation. Success was such that Paris was kept supplied, and the price of bread was maintained at eighteen *sous*. A million quintals of grain and more were needed to do this, at a cost of over twenty-two million francs; the grain was then resold at a loss of 15½ million francs to the state. Outside the capital, the countryside was once again dotted with familiar scenes: bands of beggars, requisitions on farmers, incendiarism and raids on markets. That this agitation did not become so menacing as in 1789, when bread was almost as expensive, was due only to the absence of political and social troubles and to the efficient reorganisation of the repression that had just been introduced. Here, then, were the fruits of the law of 18 Pluviôse, Year IX. In any event, popular disturbances could only have brought about a still closer attachment of the propertied classes to Bonaparte. He became the bulwark of society. The crisis attained its height during the summer of Year X, at the very moment that Bonaparte was preparing to assume the Consulate for Life, and so served his purposes well.

## THE CONCORDAT

In order to re-establish order once and for all, it was still essential that the counter-revolution in France be disarmed, and Bonaparte had long considered that this could be done only through a reconciliation with the Roman Church. The refractory clergy continued to be intractable. 'Peace with the non-juring clergy is not to be expected,' wrote de Redon, one of the Consul's special commissioners.

One might well ask what the future of France would have been had Church and State remained separate? The Roman Catholics would not have recognised the secular character of the state or liberty of conscience; at best, they would have resigned themselves to tolerance at the price of a privileged position. Only on these terms would they have agreed to disarm, at least temporarily. And so Bonaparte decided to make the best of it. On 30 Thermidor, Year VIII (17 August 1800), in the presence of Roederer, he began reproving those who 'believe that the priests should be ignored as long as they keep still, and arrested whenever they step out of line. It is as if one were to say: You see these men with torches camped around your house? Leave them be. If they set fire to it, arrest them.' What was to be done? 'Win the leaders over by appealing to their interests,' but first and foremost, choose them well. 'Fifty émigré bishops subsidised by England', he would later say to Thibaudeau, 'are now running the French clergy. Their influence must be destroyed, and to accomplish this requires the pope's authority.' This, then, was the reasoning behind the Concordat.

To call upon the pope to dismiss the French bishops, as Louis XIV had once thought of doing, was tantamount to dealing a death blow to ecclesiastical Gallicanism, one of the oldest of French traditions. This tradition was totally foreign to Bonaparte, whose sole interest was monarchical, not clerical, Gallicanism. The only argument which might have moved him had been Thibaudeau's remark: 'You will never truly win them over to the Revolution.' Bonaparte overrode this judgement. Like all others who had invoked the assistance of the Roman Church, he believed himself strong enough to keep it under his control.

Disarming the royalists by denying them the support of the clergy was not the only advantage to be gained from the Concordat. Although there was no issue of counter-revolutionary affection for the Bourbon cause, in such newly acquired provinces as Belgium and the Rhineland, the support of the local clergy was still much to be desired. These people had no national political institutions, and their primary loyalties lay with their priesthood. Consequently, to win over the priests was to win over their flocks. Another point that did not escape Bonaparte's attention was that even among ardent supporters of the Revolution, there were many who retained their ties with traditional religion and who deeply regretted the schism. Would they not have covered with gratitude the man who would effect a reconciliation, even an apparent one, between the Church and the principles of 1789? And what possessor of Church lands would not have been overjoyed to hear that the clergy had for ever renounced its attempts to reclaim them?

Bonaparte also foresaw an advantage to be reaped in the future. Wishing to win the aristocracy and counter-revolutionary bourgeoisie to his side, he could hardly ignore the religious renaissance they were now experiencing. At the beginning of 1801 Father Delpuits-Bordier founded the Congrégation de la Vierge, which was to acquire much renown; it was not long in attracting such personages as Mathieu de Montmorency and his brother, as well as Laënnec. Charitable congregations also began to re-appear; they were readily patronised by Chaptal in Paris, and certain pre-fects such as J.-A. de Bry in Besançon. Religion was once again considered good form in society, and it was reflected in the literature of the day. Writers were delighted at the opportunity to renew religious themes and give direction to the intellectual fashion. Madame de Genlis, the self-styled 'mother of the Church', was prolifically turning out her novels of virtue; Chateaubriand, sensing the trend, was in the process of writing *Le Génie du Christianisme*, which would appear on the eve of the Easter Te Deum of 1802 celebrating the conclusion of the Concordat, and would prove the truth of Catholicism by its aesthetic merits. Writers like Fontanes, who were more political in their thinking, saw a good deal more deeply into the situation: restoration of the cult was socially significant in that it would support the new class division. And since it was precisely Bonaparte's intention to consolidate this class division, he fully agreed with them. As he told Roederer and would later repeat to Molé, 'There can be no society without material inequality, and there can be no material inequality with-out religion. A starving man watching another stuff himself cannot accede to their differences if there is no authority to tell him "God wills it so"; the world must consist of rich and poor alike; but there will come a day when for all eternity, man's lot shall be decided differently.' Fontanes, too, sharply observed that the government would also benefit from an agree-ment. 'No religion, no government,' he wrote to Lucien on 18 April 1801. 'Successful conquerors have never quarrelled with priests. They can be kept in check and made use of . . . One may laugh at the augurs but it would be impolitic not to join them in eating the sacrificial birds.'

Although winning over the pope did not seem to be the most difficult of tasks, it was really not an easy thing to do. While passing through Vercelli on 25 June 1800, Bonaparte had made overtures to Bishop Mar-tiniana, who in turn transmitted them to the pope in Rome. Pius VII was not the fighting pope that his predecessor had been; he was a gentle soul and somewhat weak-willed. Still, he baulked at making peace with the Revolution and especially at abandoning the old episcopate who pro-claimed that they had sacrificed themselves for the pontiff. Then, too, there was the risk of alienating Louis XVIII and the Catholic powers. In August 1800 the cardinals, who regarded the prospect of a concordat with little favour, declared the oath of fidelity to the constitution illicit. It was a decision that Pius VI had never dared to make, and which Pius VII wisely kept secret. On the other hand, it seemed impossible to reject an offer so advantageous to the Church and so profitable to the papacy. This last consideration was most assuredly a weighty factor in its favour. In the first place, the French army could still come to Rome, and Pius VII distrusted both the Neapolitans who occupied his capital and the Austrians who were still in possession of the Legations. Secondly, by deposing the Gallican bishops, the pope would gain an unprecedented victory over Gallicanism.

This point having already been granted by Bonaparte for his own reasons, Cardinal Spina left for Paris with instructions to demand, as a preliminary, the restoration of Catholicism as the 'dominant religion'. Arriving on 6 November, he immediately met with Abbé Bernier, Bonaparte's negotiator. The former spiritual leader of the Vendéans, Bernier had just crossed over to Bonaparte's camp in the firm hope of becoming archbishop of Paris and being elevated to the office of cardinal. Naturally the French proposals made no mention of a state religion, but at Spina's insistence, Bernier gave way and Bonaparte saw no harm in it. There was a misunderstanding, however, for Bonaparte had failed to realise the technical implications of such an avowal. By calling Catholicism the state or dominant religion, he only intended to confer on the Church an endowment and a privileged position over all other sects. Talleyrand and Hauterive quickly opened Bonaparte's eyes to the fact that this would do away with such basic revolutionary gains as the liberty of conscience and the secular character of the state. From then on Bonaparte recognised Catholicism only as the religion of the majority of Frenchmen, a position from which he refused to budge.

The other point of contention was that the non-juring French prelates were to be forced to resign their dioceses. The pope, despite his scruples, had too much at stake for Spina not to have finally ceded to Bonaparte's demands. If the negotiations dragged on, it was because the Curia was awaiting the outcome of the war; but the occupation by the French armies of the Legations and of Rome itself left no alternative but to yield. At the end of February 1801 the tempo of the negotiations increased, and Bonaparte sent Cacault to Rome to pursue the matter. Since the Curia procrastinated, Bonaparte directed Cacault on 19 May to demand an unreserved acceptance of the French terms and to break off negotiations in case of a refusal. The cardinals had already rejected the French proposals, however, and Pius VII had just sent the First Consul a letter suggesting certain modifications when Cacault, returning to Paris, took it upon himself to bring Cardinal Consalvi, the papal secretary of state, back with him. Arriving on 2 June, Consalvi proceeded to dispute the treaty article by article, but finally signed it on 16 July 1801 at two o'clock in the morning.

According to the terms of the Concordat, Catholicism was declared the religion of the majority of the French people as well as that of the consuls. It was further stipulated that should a non-Catholic accede to the head of the government, negotiations would have to be opened for a new concordat. The Church was to enjoy freedom of public worship, subject to certain police restrictions which the temporal authority might deem necessary in the interest of public safety. The state, for its part, agreed to pay salaries to bishops and to as many parish priests as there were justices of the peace (3,000–3,500 by the law of 8 Pluviôse, Year XI – 28 January 1801); it authorised the restoration of cathedral chapters and diocesan seminaries, without, however, being obliged to endow them; and it granted Catholics permission to make pious foundations. The pope undertook to exhort refractory bishops to renounce their sees, failing which he would dismiss them. Bonaparte was to make identical demands of the constitutional clergy, thus putting an end to the schisms. No mention was made of the monastic orders, which, therefore, remained completely under the direct authority of the pope. The power of the bishops was also considerably increased, in the spirit of the Edict of 1695: they were given the right to appoint parish and chapel priests – a privilege which they had not enjoyed under the *ancien régime*. In return, Bonaparte obtained a new episcopate of his own choosing, an oath of fidelity to be taken by the clergy, public prayers for the Republic to be recited at the end of divine services, the promise of the Church not to contest the sale of its confiscated lands, and to accept a redrawing of ecclesiastical boundaries. Bishops were to be nominated by the First Consul and canonically instituted by the pope. This was the essence of the matter for Bonaparte: he believed that by controlling the bishops he would be controlling their priests and, fearing the refractory element, he preferred placing the parish clergy under the thumb of the episcopate rather than watching over them himself. As for the monastics, he intended to tolerate their independence only to the extent that it would prove profitable for him to do so.

The pope ratified the Concordat and sent Cardinal Caprara to Paris as his legate to supervise the practical details of its application. Meanwhile, on 7 October, Bonaparte appointed to the post of minister of public worship his councillor of state, Portalis – a man whose fervent piety was combined with definite Gallican leanings, but who nevertheless lost no time making numerous further concessions. The constitutional bishops, who had held a council in 1801, submitted without resistance despite the severe criticism of the Concordat by their most illustrious representative, Abbé Grégoire. Such, however, was not the case with the non-juring bishops: thirty-six of the eighty-two refused to submit, as did one of the thirteen bishops from the newly annexed territories (*pays réunis*). These recalcitrants protested against the dispossession of their sees, and in this they were followed by a number of their faithful. The result was that in several dioceses there continued to exist, and does to our own day, a Church opposed to the Concordat – the so-called Petite Église – although its adherents were never numerous.

In spite of the opposition, a list of new bishops was immediately prepared. Since the provisions of the Concordat did not specify any specially reserved places for the constitutional bishops, Rome claimed the right to refuse their institution, and it took all of Bonaparte's firmness to carry through the appointment of twelve ex-constitutionals, among whom Grégoire was noticeably absent. Also appointed were sixteen of the former refractory bishops who had sent in their resignations, which included Champion de Cicé at Aix, Boisgelin at Tours and d'Aviau at Bordeaux. To these were added thirty-two new bishops drawn largely from among the priests who accepted the agreement. The entire settlement was imperilled at the last moment by Caprara's insistence that newly appointed ex-constitutional bishops retract their late errors and by the latter's staunch refusal to make amends. Bernier, who was negotiating for the French government, managed to save the situation by making use of an equivocation, as had been done in 1668 to reconcile the pope with the Jansenist prelates: he simply assured Caprara that the schismatics had made a satisfactory oral declaration of their errors. It should be added that this over-cunning individual only received the bishopric of Orléans for his services.

All that remained now was to have the treaty ratified by the assemblies. The Conseil d'État was frankly hostile to it, and its session on 12 October was very stormy. Bonaparte had just prohibited all gatherings of theophilanthropists, a move hardly calculated to assuage feelings. On 22 November the Corps Législatif elected as its president Dupuis, author of the anti-religious book *L'Origine de tous les cultes*; on 30 November the Senate chose the constitutional bishop Grégoire to fill a vacancy. In the Tribunate, opposition to the Concordat was fairly unanimous, and the *Idéologue* Volney was subjected to a celebrated dressing-down by Bonaparte. Opposition in the government found two opportunities to manifest its annoyance: in the peace treaty with Russia which the opposition criticised roundly because the text made mention of 'French subjects' rather than 'French citizens', and in the Civil Code, of which the first 'Titles' were voted down on 28 December, except for the one dealing with the public registry, because it explicitly excluded any state religion. There was not the least doubt as to the sentiments of the army, and on 20 July, the morrow of the signing of the Concordat, Fouché directed that recalcitrant priests were to be sought out and arrested; Bonaparte had to make him withdraw the order. It seemed as if the Concordat was headed for certain defeat.

Talleyrand advised making some concessions to the opposition, and he himself pointed the way, observing that the literal execution of the Concordat would necessitate certain supervisory regulations. Appearing as *Articles organiques du culte catholique*, these regulations were then added to the Concordat without the knowledge of the pope, who, upon hearing of their inclusion, did not dare protest. The articles made Gallicanism a general law of the state: seminarists were to be taught the four Gallican articles of 1682; and the publication of bulls, the holding of general councils, the ordination of priests, the creation of seminaries and the editing of catechisms were all made subject to the approval of the government. The temporal authority further arrogated to itself the right to regulate bell-ringing, processions and priestly dress. The articles also fixed the new ecclesiastical divisions and the salaries, from which pensions granted by revolutionary laws were to be deducted. Communes were permitted to grant lodgings or to pay chapel and parish priests if they so desired.

This was not all. In order to ensure that Catholicism would not again become the state religion, provisions for Protestants were drafted under the title of *Articles organiques des cultes protestants*. Reformed and Lutheran ministers were also to be salaried; Calvinists were to be administered by local consistories comprising the most heavily taxed members of the congregation and placed under the presidency of the oldest pastor; Lutheran Churches were to be provided with general consistories. This Protestant charter was joined to the Concordat, framed by the 'Organic

Articles', and so constituted a single and unique law. It was not certain that even so modified, the agreement with the papacy would have found favour in the assemblies. But Bonaparte had taken precautions, especially since he harboured other designs which were sure to encounter opposition. A new *coup d'état* sufficed to bring about the capitulation of the assemblies.

## THE TRIBUNATE PURGED AND THE
## LIFE CONSULATE ESTABLISHED

On 4 January 1802 Bonaparte withdrew all the bills that had been submitted to the assemblies, and put them, as Portalis had predicted, on a 'law-making starvation diet'. Three days later the Conseil d'État declared that the session of the assemblies should therefore be considered terminated, and that it would now be possible to proceed with the first renewal of a fifth of its representatives, which had been scheduled for Year X. Since the method of selecting the outgoing members had not been defined in the Constitution, the matter was referred to the Senate. Clearly, these members should have been chosen by lot, and one might well have thought that the Senate would have acted accordingly since it, no less than the other assemblies, entertained certain qualms. But the Senate was probably threatened with force, and it may have been promised new advantages as an inducement to submit. In any event, the Senate itself decided, by a vote of 46 to 13, to designate the members who were to be retired, and in so doing, it removed the most prominent *Idéologues* in the Tribunate, to wit: Benjamin Constant, Marie-Joseph Chénier, Daunou, Ginguené, Laromiguière and Jean-Baptiste Say. They were replaced by men of lesser consequence, officers and civil servants. Carnot alone remained. Lucien Bonaparte became a tribune, and so re-entered politics to play the same role as at Brumaire. He presented to the Tribunate a measure which was adopted on 11 Germinal, Year X (1 April 1802), dividing that body into three sections which were henceforth to deliberate *in camera* on laws and articles of the Civil Code. This was soon followed by a consular decree which ruled that the laws under preparation were to be examined first by competent section heads and state councillors in special councils presided over by the First Consul. Thus it was highly improbable that any disagreement would ever be aired at an open session. 'There must not be any opposition,' said Bonaparte. 'What is government? Nothing, if it does not have public opinion on its side. How can it hope to counterbalance the influence of a tribune if it is always open to attack?' The Conseil d'État, likewise suspect, was also affected by these changes since it no longer exercised control over the final drafting of laws; in short, it was in the specially created councils composed of his trusted appointees that Bonaparte now set about preparing his ambitious programme, the results of which were only submitted to the Conseil d'État as a mere formality.

The assemblies having been subdued, there remained only the danger of a military revolt. Advantage had been taken of the peace to scatter and purge the dangerous elements of the several armies; a corps destined for Portugal had been supplied by the Army of Italy; troops sent to San Domingo had been provided by the Army of the Rhine. Nevertheless, a good deal of discontent persisted, for the army's pay was not being met regularly, and soldiers, especially in these times of scarcity, longed for the profitable adventurous life which was so much a part of every campaign. Paris was literally swarming with idle generals who envied their chief. They were the men who least believed in his military genius and would only admit to the workings of chance. 'There is not one among them who does not fancy himself as deserving as I,' Bonaparte would say. They all put themselves forward as republicans, but their civism was open to great doubt. They spoke of dividing France into separate commands; had they succeeded, they would have soon fought among themselves and the country would have fallen into a state of anarchy. Given the fact of military dictatorship, a single dictator was the only logical possibility, and the French nation, on this score too, endorsed Bonaparte.

Foremost among the generals hostile to Bonaparte were Moreau and Bernadotte. Moreau was definitely on bad terms with his rival. His wife and mother-in-law even urged him to break off all social contact with Bonaparte; the *Moniteur*, for its part, insinuated that Moreau had been malfeasant in Germany. But he was even more indecisive in civilian matters than in military life. Bernadotte, on the other hand, was more energetic, and as commander of the western forces at Rennes, he would have been in a position to issue a manifesto. Actually, in spite of his blustering ways, he was much too concerned for his own interests not to have carefully weighed the risk involved in such an act. As minister of war, he had missed his chance to seize power in the summer of Year VII, and circumstances now were much less favourable. Before he would compromise himself, he insisted that the Senate take the first steps. In Paris, from March to June, numerous secret conspiratorial meetings were held, and certain civilians were sounded out, including Fouché. Meanwhile, three officers were arrested on 7 May, one of whom was General Donnadieu. On 20 May General Simon, Bernadotte's chief of staff, secretly despatched two inflammatory proclamations to the army, attacking Bonaparte. These fell into the hands of Dubois, the prefect of police in Paris, who rejoiced at having caught his minister napping. Fouché then arrested General Simon and his accomplices in the 'libel plot'. Bonaparte hushed the matter up for he did not want it said that the army was against him. The officers in question were kept in prison without trial; the Eighty-second Regiment of the line was shipped out to San Domingo and remained there permanently; and the generals Richepanse and Decaen were sent to the colonies – Lannes to Lisbon, and Brune to Constantinople. General Lahorie was retired and General Lecourbe was put on half-pay. Bernadotte continued to be spared out of consideration for his wife Désirée Clary, Bonaparte's former fiancée whom he had abandoned for Josephine, but he nevertheless lost his post. Nothing ever did more to heighten Bonaparte's so-called anti-militarism, which was only a distrust of his former comrades. This wariness dated from his famous declaration to the Conseil d'État on 4 May 1802, when he said, 'Pre-eminence lies incontestably with the civilian authority.' And on this occasion, he regarded himself as such. Politicians who found themselves compromised were advised by Fouché to take cover. Madame de Staël left Paris for her château at Coppet in Switzerland, and when, in 1803, she attempted to return, Bonaparte ordered her expulsion from France.

Bonaparte's misgivings could not have been too serious, for in no way did they slow down the course of events. The Peace of Amiens, signed on 25 March 1802, acted like a signal. In less than two months, from 8 April to 19 May, the regime underwent a complete change: the Republic was transformed into a monarchy, the counter-revolution was officially won over, and the power of the notables was increased. On 18 Germinal, Year X (8 April 1802), the law comprising the Concordat and the Organic Articles was passed by the Corps Législatif. Ten days later the performance of a Te Deum at Notre-Dame celebrated the reconciliation of the Revolution with the Roman Church. This was followed on 6 Floréal (26 April) by a *senatus consultum* (actually prepared two weeks earlier in a special council) granting amnesty to émigrés provided they returned to France before 1 Vendémiaire, Year XI (23 September 1802), and agreed to swear fidelity to the Constitution. Only the most compromised émigrés, a number not exceeding one thousand, were to be denied amnesty. On 11 Floréal (1 May) a law reorganising the system of public education authorised the establishment of *lycées*. It was hoped that a distribution of grants would promote the growth of a body of civil servants and of the professional classes in a direction favourable to the government. Then, on 29 Floréal (19 May), a law created the Legion of Honour. It was to consist of fifteen 'cohorts', each numbering 350 legionaries appointed by Bonaparte from among the notables, both civil and military. A grant of two hundred thousand francs to each 'cohort', defrayed out of the *biens nationaux*, held the promise of salaries, lodgings and convalescent homes for legionaries who in turn swore 'to dedicate themselves to the service of the Republic', 'to combat . . . all attempts at restoring the feudal order' and 'to unite . . . in the preservation of liberty and equality'. The Legion of Honour was indeed a host of meritorious citizens, and not a national decoration, as its members were not even given a distinctive medal at this time. Finally, between 8 and 14 May, the rule of Bonaparte was transformed into the Life Consulate.

Although the capitulation of the Senate and the purge of the Tribunate robbed the Brumairian bourgeoisie of all hope, a certain amount of resistance continued to make itself felt. The Legion of Honour was harshly criticised in the Conseil d'État, and the law by which it was created passed in the Corps Législatif by a vote of only 166 to 110. As for the Constitution, Bonaparte succeeded in overthrowing it, but only by means of successive violations of his own authority and with the collaboration of the monarchist-minded members of his entourage – Cambacérès, Roederer, Talleyrand and Lucien. On 6 May the Treaty of Amiens was sent to the Senate, and that body was asked to determine what token of the 'nation's gratitude' could most fittingly be bestowed upon the First Consul; but on 8 May, when a senator proposed consulship for life, the assembly contented itself by passing a resolution that 'Napoleon Bonaparte' be re-elected for an additional period of ten years. This, incidentally, marked the first appearance of Bonaparte's famous first name in official documents.

The attempt to circumvent the constitution having proved a failure, Bonaparte, acting upon the advice of Cambacérès, picked up the thread again by replying, on 9 May, that he would accept the Senate's generous offer 'if the will of the people' directed him to do so. A special council then drafted two questions which were to be submitted to the French people for a vote. Framed by Roederer, the resolution proposed, in addition to the Life Consulate, that Bonaparte be granted the right to designate his own successor. Although there was nothing to justify such a procedure legally, the Conseil d'État, to which the matter was referred, passed the resolution; Fouché did not attend the session, and five or six councillors absented themselves. Presented with the draft referendum, Bonaparte cautiously struck out Roederer's provision for the succession. The Tribunate and Corps Législatif, having no power to intervene in the revision of the constitution, approved the plebiscite on the Life Consulate. The Senate, thus pushed aside, ironically saw itself charged with the task of counting the popular vote which, as in Year VIII, was cast publicly. On 14 Thermidor (2 August) the Senate proclaimed Bonaparte Consul for Life.

Without wasting any time, Bonaparte dictated a new constitution which was approved by the Conseil d'État and the Senate, without discussion, on 4 August. One of its articles empowered the First Consul to present for the Senate's approval his choice of a candidate for the succession. This could be done by testament, or for that matter, at any time. In the event that the Senate did not agree, Bonaparte could name two other candidates, *seriatim*, of whom the third only could not be rejected. Bonaparte had thus arrogated to himself a right which he had declined to ask from the people. The difficulties initially inherent in choosing a likely successor have often been cited as an explanation for this tortuous course of events. As long as Bonaparte remained childless, Joseph and Lucien quarrelled over the succession as if, Lucien remarked, it had been 'their own late father's inheritance'. To have favoured a Brumairian would have incurred the bitter resentment of others. The problem might have found its solution in Charles, son of Louis Bonaparte and Hortense de Beauharnais. Napoleon had in fact contemplated the possibility of eventually adopting a nephew from that marriage; but Charles was not born until 10 October. It would therefore seem that, notwithstanding his subjection of the press and the assemblies, Bonaparte saw danger in submitting to a plebiscite a proposal altogether too monarchical. Consequently, he took by force what he had not dared solicit. It has also been argued that the men of the Revolution, who had linked its destiny to that of Bonaparte and who looked upon him as the only man capable of defending the natural frontiers, found themselves logically obliged to make him a monarch in order to obtain the stability to which they aspired. But, as

Thibaudeau foresaw only too well, the Life Consulate and the hereditary succession were no more than illusory guarantees. Bonaparte's rule – essentially a military dictatorship founded on victories – had no real need of these measures as long as he remained triumphant on the field of battle. As Bonaparte himself remarked, 'What meaning would these *senatus consulta* have if ever the Coalition powers entered Paris?' And once dead, who would care about his will? Had the testament of Louis XIV ever been respected? France, which revered him, and the Brumairians, who were his prisoners, yielded to his demands. Neither the glory that comes from being the nation incarnate and the foremost of its citizens would gratify Bonaparte, who alone conceived the desire to become king, without even deceiving himself about the ephemeral nature of his improvised greatness.

Still, it must be noted that the republican bourgeoisie, while a party to his demands, continued to remind him discreetly of the pact made in Brumaire. Roederer himself, among others, had spoken of important bodies representing the predominant social interests which would be linked to the government and given constitutional guarantees; no doubt this meant granting the assemblies, and especially the Senate, some real control. These republicans also pointed out that the executive power was now strong enough to restore to the citizenry a certain degree of liberty. Chabot de l'Allier made a timid allusion to this necessity when he presented Bonaparte with the law on the plebiscite (it was the same Chabot who had moved in the Tribunate to reward the First Consul on behalf of the nation): 'The greatness and munificence of Bonaparte's conceptions will not let him depart from the liberal principles which made the Revolution and established the Republic. His devotion is too great ever to permit him to blemish with abuses of power the immense glory which he has already acquired.' The *Idéologue* Camille Jordan expressed his thoughts more plainly in *The True Meaning of the Plebiscite for the Life Consulate*, a pamphlet which was promptly confiscated.

The master would not forgive. Fouché fell into disgrace on 26 Fructidor (13 September), and his ministry was reattached to the Department of Justice. Roederer was eventually deprived of both the presidency of his section in the Conseil d'État and of his direction over matters of public education. For the time being, Bonaparte emphasised the necessity for dictatorship: in England, the opposition had a place in the constitutional order; in France, it was to become the province of the counter-revolutionaries and the Jacobins. Now that he had restored to the former their civil rights, Bonaparte could fairly remind the republicans that a return to elections would not necessarily benefit them. 'Government must remain in the hands of the men of the Revolution; that is the only thing they have.' Bonaparte's collaborators did not contest this, but they pointed out that it had been their understanding that they would be sharing the business of government with him.

The *senatus consultum* of 16 Thermidor, also known as the Constitution of Year X, reduced the extent of their participation instead. The First Consul invested himself with the power to make treaties and grant pardons, with the exclusive right to designate candidates to the Senate, the Court of Cassation, the office of second and third consul, and to select justices of the peace from among candidates proposed by the electors. Above all, he reserved the right to define or interpret the constitution by organic *senatus consulta*. This would later permit the establishment of the Empire to proceed without any of the difficulties which had been incurred in the creation of the Life Consulate. He also assumed the right to suspend the constitution, dissolve the Tribunate and Corps Législatif, and annul decisions of the courts by regular *senatus consulta*. Drafted by a privy council which he created and whose members he appointed before each sitting, these *senatus consulta* provided him with the sole power to initiate legislation. The Senate, invested with this exorbitant authority, was appropriately reconstituted. Although its members continued to be co-opted, the First Consul was given the right to present candidates for seats created by the Constitution of Year VIII and the right to appoint forty additional senators directly. Presently, on 14 Nivôse, Year XI (4 January 1803), Bonaparte secured their appointment. At the same time, he created a *sénatorerie* in each of the administrative districts of France, which were themselves based on the territorial jurisdiction of a Court of Appeal. These *sénatoreries* were endowed with national lands and seigniorial residences which Bonaparte bestowed upon the more compliant senators as a bonus to their existing salaries. Finally, the new constitution authorised senators to hold, in addition to their seats, ministerial positions and various high government posts. The powers of the other assemblies, on the other hand, were reduced. The Corps Législatif lost the right to hold regular sessions and to elect its own president. The Tribunate was reduced to fifty members, and a provision that condemned it to silence was incorporated in the constitution. The Conseil d'État yielded its precedence to the

Senate, and saw itself rivalled by the Privy Council. Although Bonaparte did not cease to submit new laws in the Conseil d'État, he could now dispense with it and legislate by *senatus consulta*.

Another major change was the abolition of the *Listes de Notabilité*, which the Senate had only just published in March. Bonaparte's pretext was the difficulties which had been encountered in drawing them up, while in fact he felt that they allowed too great a latitude of choice to the assemblies. No doubt he also wished to please the notables by restoring to each département its own body of representatives. He therefore instituted a system of electoral colleges to take the place of the *Listes de Notabilité*. At its base, the cantonal assembly, composed of all citizens in the canton, presented candidates for the office of justice of the peace and for seats on the municipal councils. It also nominated the members of the district and departmental colleges from among the six hundred most highly taxed citizens, so that the tax rolls finally appeared. The district colleges nominated two candidates for each vacancy in the Tribunate and Corps Législatif; the colleges of the départements nominated two candidates for each vacancy in the Corps Législatif and Senate. The assemblies were thus made regionally representative. Since the colleges were obliged to choose at least one of the two candidates outside their own ranks, they were not completely oligarchical. The First Consul exercised a powerful influence on these colleges since he not only appointed their presidents but could add ten members to the district college, twenty to the departmental college, and he authorised public functionaries to take part in their proceedings.

Given the fact that the members of the assemblies were chosen for life terms, and that vacancies were not filled until an assembly fell below a third of its original number, elections were reduced to a minimum. Moreover, until Year XII, notables who had recently been chosen to the communal lists alone made up the cantonal assemblies, and the colleges which they in turn constituted continued to function without change until the end of the Empire. The monopoly of the notables was thus confirmed and even strengthened. Hearken to Lucien as he lectured to the college of the département of Seine on 24 March 1803: 'The principles of our new electoral law . . . are no longer founded on chimerical concepts but on the very basis of society, property, which arouses in us a desire to preserve public order. Today, the electoral privilege has by gradual and temperate means become the exclusive prerogative of the most enlightened and civic-minded class of our society.' But in reality, it was to Bonaparte that this class would henceforth owe its place.

## BONAPARTE'S SOCIAL POLICY

The major enactments of Year X were not just limited to the extension of Bonaparte's personal power; they also foreshadowed the social schemes which were taking shape in his mind. Speaking before the Conseil d'État, Bonaparte lashed out against the individualistic society which had been born out of the French Revolution. He characterised it as so many 'grains of sand', and he stressed the necessity 'to erect some pillars of granite upon the soil of France', so as to 'give the French people a sense of civic direction'. Plainly stated, Bonaparte wanted to create clusters of interests attached to the regime, who, in return for advantages and honours, were expected to secure the loyalty of the populace by virtue of their influence upon the wage-earning classes. This was tantamount to a revival of the kind of intermediate or corporate bodies that had been prevalent under the *ancien régime*, with the added safeguard that they should no longer be able to oppose the state or degenerate into oligarchies. Bonaparte cleverly pointed out that this would directly benefit the bourgeoisie. He argued that 'while we lack unity', the aristocracy was a block bonded by blood, class prejudice and ecclesiastical hierarchy, and that the Legion of Honour would serve 'to bring together the partisans of the Revolution'. The creation of these social bodies, however, would be left to him and to him alone; the penal code even went so far as to subject all organisations numbering more than twenty persons to his authority. So it was perfectly clear to everyone that his power would grow.

The assemblies constituted one such body, the Legion of Honour another, the electoral colleges yet another. Added to these was the newly swollen bureaucracy, graded according to a table of ranks. Drawing initially from the financial middle class, Bonaparte created, by a decree of 19 Germinal, Year XI (9 April 1803), a new set of officials: the *auditeurs*.*

---

\* These *auditeurs* were groomed for positions as future state councillors, judges and other high administrative officials. As such, they provided an administrative link between the ministers and the Conseil d'État on the one hand, and the assemblies on the other. They were charged with presenting reports to the meetings of the sections of the Conseil d'État. They were also allowed to attend sittings of the general assemblies, but were denied the right to speak other than in answer to points requiring explication. TRANSLATOR.

Sixteen were appointed at first, but this was only a beginning. They were attached to the ministries and to the Conseil d'État and were to form the nucleus of a high administration free from ties with the Revolution or the *ancien régime*. Judges occupied a place of honour in this scheme. Being poorly paid, they were drawn perforce exclusively from the well-to-do middle class. The Constitution of Year X gave them a hierarchy and a discipline that was professional. Officials of the legal establishment were also organised into corporations: chambers of solicitors (*avoués*) had existed since Year VIII; notaries (*notaires*) and public auctioneers (*commissaires-priseurs*) had been associated since Year IX. Nor were the businessmen forgotten: chambers of commerce and manufacture, brokerage houses and the reappearance of commercial agents were not only a response to technical needs but part of a definite social plan. Had it been left entirely to Bonaparte, one would surely have witnessed the rebirth of guilds.

As Bonaparte conceived it, then, the social hierarchy was to be founded on wealth. It could not have been otherwise, since he had seized power with the sanction of the bourgeoisie. True, by making free education available to all, the *Idéologues* had intended to introduce men of talent, as well as men of fortune, into leading government positions. But wealth once acquired tends naturally to reserve this privilege for itself. Moreover, Bonaparte shared the distrust of the rich for 'men of talent' as long as they were poor, regarding them as revolutionary tinder; and so it was generally agreed that they would only be employed in technical positions, as in the time of the former aristocracy and absolute monarchy. Whenever Bonaparte proclaimed himself the representative of the Revolution, he always reduced that movement to the abolition of privileges of which the rise of the propertied bourgeoisie was a direct consequence. One only has to remove his personal despotism to appreciate the fact that the social enactments of Year X laid the foundation for the July Monarchy.

The Civil Code became the bible of the new society. On 12 August 1800 a committee of four legal experts – Tronchet, Portalis, Bigot de Préameneu and Maleville – was appointed to prepare a draft of the *Code Civil*. The project was completed in January 1801, but Bonaparte's conflict with the assemblies led to the suspension of open debate on the laws until 1803. The various articles were finally promulgated as a single law on 21 March 1804, under the title of the Civil Code of the French People, and only later became known as the Code Napoléon. Bonaparte took personal part in the preparation of the Code, but only on those sections dealing with family law. He was intent on strengthening the authority of the father and the husband in the home, on depriving illegitimate children of their heritage unless they had been legally recognised (in which case their share was to be reduced anyway), and on retaining divorce, for his own reasons.

Like all of Bonaparte's achievements, the Code was dual in character. On the one hand, it confirmed the disappearance of the feudal aristocracy and adopted the social principles of 1789: liberty of the individual, equality before the law, secularisation of the state, freedom of conscience and freedom to choose one's profession. This is why it swept through Europe as the symbol of the Revolution, and heralded, wherever it was introduced, the fundamental laws of modern society. Tarnished though this quality may have become in our time, the failure to depict the Code in all of its original freshness would play false the history of the Napoleonic years, and it would prevent us from ever grasping the full significance of the French hegemony. But, on the other hand, the Code also confirmed the reaction against the democratic accomplishments of the Republic. Conceived in the interest of the bourgeoisie, it was concerned primarily with consecrating and sanctifying the rights of property which it regarded as a natural right, anterior to society, absolute and belonging to the individual, and it gave the possessor the title to ownership. Sections regulating contracts dealt almost exclusively with property, with services being relegated to two articles. To a large degree, the family itself was regarded in this light. Consequently, the scrupulously detailed regulations governing the marriage contract made of it a moneyed transaction, and behind the Code's extensive interest in filiation lay the question of inheritance.

The idea that the laws should promote the interest of the state, as understood by Bonaparte and his jurists, was the other guideline employed in the preparation of the Code. It was Bonaparte who, in a certain measure, limited the rights of landed proprietors in matters of subsoil use and eminent domain, and above all in their freedom of testamentary disposition. The family was of great value to the state, for it constituted one of those social entities which disciplined the behaviour of individuals. The *patria potestas*, which had been weakened by the Revolution, was thus restored once again: a father could imprison his children for six months on the strength of his word alone; he had complete control over their property; similarly, he could administer his wife's property and, joint ownership being part of the common law, he could dispose of it as often as not. But, as with all groups, there was always the possibility that the family might become too powerful as against the state, and especially so since its cohesiveness was by nature very strong, thus giving rise to the restoration of an independent aristocracy. For this reason, the state placed the family under its tutelage: the testamentary powers of the father were modified by re-establishing the principle of 'legitimacy', and the question of inheritance was declared to be a matter of public interest and was made subject to the regulation of law. Viewed in this light, the Code was bitterly criticised by the former nobility and by a part of the bourgeoisie, whose powers it limited in that it assured the division of patrimonies.

As regards those who possessed nothing, the Code kept silent except to protect their personal freedom by prohibiting the lease or hire of services in perpetuity. Proclaiming the freedom of labour and the equality of citizens before the law, it in fact abandoned the wage earner, as had been the wish of the Constituent Assembly, to all of the hazards of economic competition, and it treated labour as just another commodity. It repudiated the idea, conceived in 1793, of recognising the citizen's right to a livelihood. Since only the employer was taken at his word in matters of wage disputes, the Code even departed from the principle of juridical equality by discriminating against wage earners. Moreover, the state used its police powers to enforce labour discipline, because the Code could not offer sufficient protection to employers: since the poor possessed nothing, they would have been effectively immune to punitive law suits. The law of 22 Germinal, Year XI (12 April 1803), renewed the ban on workers' associations, and on the following 1 December a decree obliged workers to carry a workbook supplied by the local authorities, without which it was forbidden to employ them.

The Code, then, was the product of the evolution of French society in so far as it created the bourgeoisie and carried it to power. When one considers the Code in its detail, the imprint of history upon it becomes even more apparent. The Napoleonic jurists drew largely from the works of Domat and Pothier, both of whom had already embarked upon a rational codification, the latter devoting himself to the written Roman Law of the Midi, the former to customary law. By combining this legacy with the work of the Revolution and weeding out the contradictions, they succeeded in making the Code a compromise. Another manifestation of the

Code's historic character was its extensive preoccupation with landed property, which was still the principal form of wealth, whereas it neglected industrial wealth, business organisations and credit. In short, it cannot be said that the Code was a product of theoreticians who wished to impose arbitrarily on a society an abstract set of laws remote from living reality, and the criticisms levelled by Savigny and other German jurists were completely unfounded. These critics were inspired by aristocratic sentiments of which the Code was the very negation.

Bonaparte's idea of public education was that it should be in keeping with the established social order and the authoritarian nature of the regime: it must, he said, 'embrace the nation' and be the 'first concern of the government'. The decree of 11 Floréal, Year X (1 May 1802), drafted by Fourcroy, whose proposal was substituted for that of Chaptal (which was thought too ambitious), left the elementary schools (*écoles populaires*) to the care of the municipalities, just as under the *ancien régime*. Like Voltaire before him, Bonaparte and a large number of the middle class believed that to educate the poor was politically and socially inconvenient. Not so with regard to secondary institutions of learning which were to educate future leaders. These were patterned on the Prytanée, formerly known as the Collège Louis-le-Grand and the only such school preserved by the Revolution: under the Directory it had again become a school of resident students, unlike the *écoles centrales*, and it was remodelled in Year VIII (22 March 1800) by Lucien Bonaparte, then minister of the interior. Every appeal court district was to have a state-supported *lycée*. It was also intended that there would be secondary schools, privately administered but government-authorised and -controlled; in Year XII the state began appointing their teachers. Six thousand four hundred scholarships were created for the *lycées*, of which 2,400 were awarded to the sons of military officers and government officials, and the remaining four thousand were set aside for the best pupils in the secondary schools. To a degree, these grants met the wishes of the *Idéologues*; but being in fact beyond the reach of the poor, they constituted an endowment only in favour of civilian and military officials and were an inducement to bind the *petite bourgeoisie* to the notables and to seduce its most talented elements: as public servants or as leaders in the nation's economic life, they would no longer be a ferment of unrest. Institutions of education which were not administered by the state continued to exist in principle, although in Paris at least, Frochot, prefect of the Seine, claimed the right to authorise and supervise them. The Catholic clergy immediately benefited from this tolerance; the Frères des Écoles Chrétiennes became active once again and founded an institute at Lyon in Year XII. Bonaparte never created any obstacles for the clergy when it came to primary education, and because he attached no importance to the education of women, he permitted the restoration of several sisterly teaching orders. The *lycées* and the clerical secondary schools for boys soon came into conflict with each other, however, and in the end, Napoleon was driven towards the establishment of a government monopoly over all forms of public instruction.

Even as he sanctioned its social ascendancy, Bonaparte evidenced his distrust of the middle class. In the Conseil d'État he spoke harshly of wealth: 'Affluence carries no merit. The rich are often a pack of undeserving idlers, and a rich merchant usually gets his wealth either by selling dear or by outright thievery.' More critical still was his attitude towards men of finance. Clearly, his was not an attack upon all forms of wealth, but one directed against the masses of liquid capital which were precisely the origin of bourgeois fortunes. First, it was a wealth not readily seizable, be it to tax or to confiscate. Then, too, it produced at every turn individuals who, taking pride in not being indebted to anyone but themselves and being all the more determined to preserve their independence, tended to shatter the social structures which Bonaparte strove to establish. In his pursuit of the throne, Bonaparte evidently contemplated a monarchy based on the support of a landed aristocracy, in return for which the monarch would guarantee the servitude of the peasantry. This ideal was not to be realised, and Bonaparte did not even consider restoring a nobility at this time; but he found himself guided by preference even more than by the national interest in bringing about a reconciliation with the counter-revolution. In the months following the establishment of the Constitution of Year X, what struck contemporaries most was the very progress of this reconciliation.

The application of the Concordat followed its course. Caprara, the papal legate, was conciliatory, and Portalis endeavoured to please him without completely concealing his own attachments to Gallican traditions. By the nature of things, the refractory priests began to play an increasingly important role in the new clergy. The government recognised the inevitability of the situation and forced the constitutional bishops to accede to it, for even had circumstances been otherwise, they

would have been unable to find a sufficient number of priests who had
taken the oath. In the département of Bas-Rhin, for example, Bishop
Saurine was unable to appoint more than sixteen 'constitutionals' out of
351 priests to parishes and chapels, making less than five per cent; as for
the former refractory bishops, La Tour d'Auvergne in the Pas-de-Calais
and Caffarelli in the Côtes-du-Nord, they awarded the 'constitutionals'
seventy-eight positions out of 634, and forty-three out of 340 respectively, or about twelve per cent. Then again, a number of bishops
imposed an oath of submission, which amounted to a retraction, on the
juring clergy of 1791, and when the prefects objected, they succeeded at
best in making the wording of the formula somewhat less precise. The
constitutional bishops were exposed to the insolence of their subordinates, and the case was worse for ordinary priests.

Fouché insisted in his circulars on maintaining liberty of conscience,
and he presumed, not without impertinence, the right to treat bishops as
if they were government officials or police auxiliaries, a sort of spiritual
*gendarmerie*. He fell into disgrace, however, and Portalis, the director of
cults, almost always sided against the prefects. In order to pacify the
bishops, the prefects of the Pas-de-Calais and Bouches-du-Rhône were at
last removed. The Organic Articles, no sooner promulgated, encountered many a snag. Prelates were addressed as Monseigneur; ecclesiastical
garb reappeared; religious processions and bell-ringing were freely
restored; and bishops were allowed to add to their title, 'by divine mercy
and by grace of the Holy See'. Contrary to his personal feelings, Portalis
refused to make the observance of Sunday obligatory, believing that habit
would see to it soon enough. He did, however, permit the revival of marriage banns, and above all he supported bishops in their efforts to secure
the right to watch over government officials. 'You are in a better position
than anyone else', he wrote to Champion de Cicé, 'to inform the government on all that touches upon the public interest.' The subprefect of
Boulogne, Masclet, although distrustful of the clergy, nevertheless
instructed his mayors that no matter what their personal convictions,
they were still obliged by virtue of their office to conform to religion.

The lower (non-beneficed) clergy immediately complained of their
wretched condition. The peasants were not hostile to them, merely
indifferent, and no one wished to support them. Although the Organic
Articles made religious worship free of cost, charitable donations were to
be divided among parish priests (*curés*) and curates (*vicaires*), and this

practice was promptly revived. Bishops began to publish schedules of expected contributions, and they set about establishing church councils which were intended to assure the material well-being of the parishes. But the non-beneficed clergy still were accorded neither lodgings nor salaries by their congregations, and Bonaparte in Year XI began to press the administrative bodies to deliberate upon these matters; he also restored to parishes non-alienated Church lands. These measures were not truly effective but under the Empire the State became increasingly open-handed to the Church. And so the Concordat became a point of departure for a development which prepared the Catholic clergy for the later triumphs of the Restoration.

The return of the émigrés did not give rise to any debates such as those generated by the Concordat, but it made a deeper impression still, and it is worth mentioning that if Bonaparte did receive numerous compliments on the occasion of the Life Consulate, he did not receive a single one apropos the amnesty. The amnesty put the émigrés under the surveillance of the police for the next ten years, and they, like others, could be incarcerated by simple administrative action. Consequently, the émigrés exercised great caution as a rule, but this did not stop them from behaving like masters in the villages or from seeking to force upon the purchasers of their alienated properties a restitution or a settlement. The purchasers of national lands took alarm, especially since Bonaparte ordered an audit of the accounts on 23 July 1803, to determine the balance of their payments outstanding. This provoked all manner of chicanery and even some frantic speculation, the impression being that the sales themselves might be called into question. Had the choice been left to Bonaparte, the decree of 17 July 1793, which had abolished without indemnity the feudal seigneurial dues (*rentes foncières*), might have been revised so as to have provided a compensation to former landowners as well as revenue to the treasury – these landed rents being largely tied in with the national lands. However, Bonaparte did not venture to override the decision of the Conseil d'État which declared on 19 February 1803 that the law could in no way be revised. Already a number of émigrés had taken positions in the regime: Louis-Philippe Séguier had been appointed to the Conseil d'État; Séguier sat in the Court of Appeals of Paris, and the duc de Luynes sat in the Senate; and in 1804 Joseph-Marie Gérando became chief of a department in the Ministry of the Interior. Bonaparte also married several of his top-ranking officers — Junot,

Lannes, Augereau, Savary – to daughters of the nobility. Others, Duroc and Marmont for example, preferred money.

The reconciliation was most apparent at the court of the First Consul. The Tuileries Palace, more than Malmaison, rapidly took on the flavour of the old monarchy. Duroc was already governor of the palace. In November 1802 Josephine received an official rank and was henceforth surrounded by four ladies-in-waiting chosen from the old nobility. It was in this company that she travelled with Bonaparte to Belgium. There seemed to be no end to the minute refinements of etiquette. The populace was again dazzled by the spectacle of costumes, carriages, liveried attendants, festivities and fancy-dress balls at the Opéra. When General Leclerc, Pauline Bonaparte's husband, died in San Domingo in January 1803, ceremonial mourning was reintroduced at the court. A new saint's day, the festival of St Napoleon, was instituted on 15 August 1802, and the republican holidays of 14 July and 1 Vendémiaire were celebrated, until 1804, only for the sake of appearance. Finally, in 1803, coins were struck in Bonaparte's effigy.

The salons eagerly followed the tone set by the court. This newly emerging aristocracy kept the *nouveaux riches* and men of finance at a distance. Bonaparte prescribed for it a certain decorum which had not been characteristic of the pre-revolutionary aristocracy. He took Josephine away from her former friends, Madame Tallien and Madame Hamelin, and he recalled women to a sense of propriety. But this austerity of morals was never more than a façade, and Bonaparte was never one to deny himself the pleasures of indulgence. His sole concern was that outward appearances be maintained, and in this he himself set the prime example. The fact of the matter was that this society was still thoroughly middle-class, and it condemned the ease and abandon of the eighteenth-century nobility for its lack of 'considerateness'. Moreover, its transformation was far from complete, as the fate of the Legion of Honour clearly demonstrated: having violated his own law by appointing the members of the Legion's 'Grand Council' (they should have been elected), Bonaparte proceeded to postpone the nomination of the legionaries. Already this institution which he had designed seemed to him too closely tied to the Revolution.

By the end of 1802 many indications left no doubt as to Bonaparte's real intentions. Thus from the standpoint of national policy Bonaparte reached his pinnacle with the Treaty of Amiens. More than anything the French people wanted peace, and Bonaparte gave it to them; they were attached to the social accomplishments of the Revolution; and Bonaparte had preserved them. Satisfied and proud of their leader, they had not yet begun to realise that he was abusing his power and that he contemplated objects inimical to their own interests. But they did not want their leader to become king, and they wanted still less that he create a nobility, while Bonaparte in his heart had broken with the Republic and with the notion of *égalité*. Pleased with having secured the natural frontiers, they did not in the least desire to go beyond them, but their master had already done so, making war inevitable. The French people still saw him as a hero of the nation at the very moment that he had ceased to be one.

# I I I

## Imperial Conquest to
## the Treaty of Tilsit
## (1802–1807)

CONTEMPORARIES AND EARLY CHRONICLERS of Bonaparte attributed the imperial conquests and the Empire itself to what they called the 'ambition' of Napoleon. Not that ambition was the only factor. Opportunities did present themselves, but even then the national interest would have counselled a prudent refusal. For many historians of a later time, such an interpretation seemed too simple. Some wished to see him only as the defender of the 'natural frontiers': they argued that the republicans had made him a consul and then an emperor for this very purpose, but that this task, the baleful legacy of the Revolution, compelled him to conquer Europe and at last destroyed him. These historians were merely transposing, in an obvious way, the idolatrous myth of the Old Guard, to which Napoleon himself, while at St Helena, gave wide currency – a soldier of the Revolution, he had done no more than to defend himself against monarchy and Old Europe. Other historians, loath to diminish the role of the individual in history and refusing to regard Napoleon as simply an instrument of destiny, persisted in seeking in his character the wellspring of his policy, thinking it could be found in some grand unifying design. There were those for whom the thematic idea was the struggle with England over maritime supremacy; and for these, the period after the rupture of the Treaty of Amiens was the apotheosis of the struggle begun under Louis XIV and had its roots in the old history of France. There were others for whom it was the 'oriental' mirage that lured him towards the precipice. For still others, Bonaparte was more European than French, and endeavoured to re-create the Carolingian, and later the Roman, Empire – the well-ordered world of Western Christian civilisation.

In each of these interpretations there is a piece of the truth, but all are insufficient. It is true that Bonaparte's sponsors wished to hold on to the 'natural frontiers', and that to defend them one might have been tempted to venture beyond them; but this was neither the surest nor the only means of protecting them; nor is it clear that he had only the interests of the nation in mind in extending his conquests. It is true that England was his constant and tenacious enemy, and that in beating him, she triumphed over France once and for all; but if, in accordance with a maturely considered plan, he was aiming at England alone, his continental policy would have been greatly different – the blockade itself, of which so much has been made, was much more the offspring of the Grand Empire than its cause. Nothing would have pleased the new Alexander so much as a thrust towards Constantinople or India, but most of his enterprises were only ephemerally connected with this dream. It is a fact that he compared himself to Charlemagne and to Caesar, and that he aimed at a political federation of the Western world, but it was not an intellectual desire to restore the past which drove him to action. The legend of the hatred of the Coalition powers for the soldier of the Revolution contains a keen insight, and it is surprising that so many historians should have forgotten it. But there was more to Bonaparte's policy than justifiable self-defence.

The truth is, no unifying concept can be found that will rationally explain Napoleon's foreign policy; he simultaneously pursued ends that were contradictory. In the last analysis, we must return to his 'ambition'. Contemporaries were blinded by the crude and gaudy theatrical apparatus, the wanton adventures, the quarrels of a rapacious family and the malversations of officials. While appreciating Napoleon's genius, they depreciated his ambition to the common level of humanity. With time's perspective, the dimness of his image has been brought to focus and his mystery unveiled: the heroic urge to take risks, the magic lure of the dream, his irresistible force of character.

# CHAPTER SEVEN

# France and England: The Struggle Renewed (1802–1805)

A T NO TIME were the traits of Napoleon's personality better revealed than in the critical years between the Treaty of Amiens and the War of 1805. The treaty with England did not last much over a year. But so long as the struggle on the Continent was not renewed, the political arrangement which had been possible in 1799 – a victorious but peaceful France, facing England, mistress of the seas – had not been completely discarded. After the Peace of Pressburg, this solution was no longer possible.

## BONAPARTE'S ECONOMIC POLICY AND THE RUPTURE OF THE TREATY OF AMIENS

It would be difficult to disprove Prime Minister Addington's serious resolve to try the experiment of peace and his faith in its substantial duration. He repealed the income tax and cut naval expenditures by £2 million. St Vincent, First Lord of the Admiralty, suspended ship construction and dismissed the workers in the naval dockyards. The timber trust broke with him after he initiated an investigation of their peculations, and supplies to the dockyards dried up. Nevertheless, the government encountered opposition in its own party. Convinced that the peace would permit France to rearm for a new assault against the British Empire, the Tory dissidents preached war to the death, as had the Whigs a hundred years earlier. The Tories controlled part of the press, and the French émigré Peltier assisted them in vituperating the Revolution and the military dictatorship of Bonaparte.

The business community hesitated between these two policies. Peace endangered many interests: the war industries were grinding to a halt; English merchants were on the point of losing their monopoly of commerce in the Baltic and in Germany, not to mention the harm to the colonial trade; the restitution to France of her lost colonies was a material loss to England, the trade of Dutch Guiana alone being valued at £10 million. Finally, after the signature of the Treaty of Amiens, world prices fell to such a point that even the neutrals, and especially the United States, regarded the peace as a calamity. Nevertheless, it was generally thought that these evils were only temporary. The tocsin rung by the Tories left some impression, but on the sea and in the colonies, the peril did not seem imminent. As for the Continent, English opinion was not overconcerned. The relevant question was whether Bonaparte would open the vast market of France and her satellites to British commerce, for England would not tolerate the treaty for long if profitable business relations did not quickly ensue. In May 1802 the foreign minister Hawkesbury stated that it would be necessary to hasten the re-establishment of commercial relations in order to win over the greatest possible number of people to the peace. The key to the problem thus lay in the economic policy of the First Consul.

Like all enlightened despots, Napoleon always devoted great attention to economic progress; not, indeed, because it improved the lot of mankind and permitted the common people to share in the fruits of civilisation, but simply for political reasons. He was interested in sound finance, in the growth of population and the consequent fresh supply of recruits to the army, and in 'order', that is, a minimum of idleness and an abundance of commodities. Yet he was more receptive to some branches of production than to others. Military by nature, he distrusted business and finance, which were cosmopolitan and closely linked with England. He was interested in industry, especially to the extent that it consumed native raw materials. He was inclined to regard agriculture as the strength of a great military state, of a Sparta or a Rome. Thence came the soldiers, and thence the capacity, if necessary, to be economically self-sufficient. In this his ideas were physiocratic, and to the extent that he turned from the bourgeoisie and envisaged the re-creation of a landed aristocracy, he approached that school of thought from a second direction. But, as always happened when he ran into concrete difficulties, he did not trouble himself with pursuing a single theory. Although he favoured agriculture, he continually carped at the right to export grain, because the masses stirred with every increase in the price of bread as the experience of Year X had confirmed. For reasons of state, he shared the popular prejudice against speculators in the grain trade and cultivators who sought to reap undue profits. Industrial crises, when they threw workers out of jobs, caused similar problems; and so it was necessary for him to keep a close watch over the cotton industry, despite the fact that it utilised an imported raw material.

Of all the practical considerations which Bonaparte faced, it was the monetary problem which demanded his greatest attention. While England was giving way to a mild, controlled inflation, one which kept prices at a high level and stimulated production, France, apart from the limited issuances of banks, was saddled with a metallic currency that was persistently being hoarded, and she experienced a continued shortage of *louis d'or*. This inconvenienced her economy because capital continued to be scarce and expensive. Bonaparte never ceased reproving the Bank of France for its extreme caution in discounting commercial paper, and he would have wanted to see it branch out into the provinces making credit widely available. The scarcity of coin also affected public finances adversely by placing a great burden on the treasury. After the fiasco of the *assignats*, Bonaparte was loath to return to paper money; such an attempt would surely have incurred a loss of prestige. Like Colbert in analogous circumstances, he was converted to mercantilism and so to the belief that France had to protect her supply of specie by purchasing little from abroad and by creating metal inflows either through increased exports or simple conquest.

The Consulate also took pains to encourage manufactures, particularly of luxuries. A Bureau of Statistics, created in 1800, resumed the investigations begun by the Committee of Public Safety and François de Neufchâteau. Working through the prefects, it undertook an economic and demographic census of France, and in the course of the following years, a substantial part of its findings was published. An attempt was made to unify the French economy by adopting the decimal-metric system which, however, only gradually gained acceptance. On 17 Germinal, Year XI (7 April 1803), the ratio between silver and gold was set at 1 to 15.5, but owing to a lack of resources an insufficient number of coins were struck to replace the old currency. The new regime stood firmly behind its money; the franc was legally defined in terms of silver (4.5 grams of pure silver, or five grams of silver 9/10 pure). Since the *livre* had never been legally defined, money of account and metallic currency became identical in value for the first time.

The regulation of commerce was entrusted to a general council, and with the advent of the Empire it was brought under the jurisdiction of a section of the Conseil d'État. On 19 March 1801 the exchanges were reorganised; on 24 December 1802 Chambers of Commerce reappeared; on 28 April 1803 sixteen seaports were designated as ports of international trade and were accorded the right to establish bonded warehouses. At the close of 1801 a 'Society for the Encouragement of National Industry' was formed under the presidency of Chaptal; as minister of the interior, he revived the practice (begun at the time of the Directory) of holding industrial exhibitions. On 12 April 1803 Chambers of Manufacture appeared. The Paris Agricultural Society had already been reconstituted in 1798.

Like Colbert, Bonaparte was by nature inclined to regulate by means of corporations. Artisans would gladly have recovered their monopoly, and certain merchants would have welcomed regulations against cottage industry and hired labour. Using 'public order' as an excuse, the prefect of police managed to reorganise the bakers and the butchers along guild lines. The First Consul did not dare go further for the moment, however, because the bankers and leading industrialists, supported by the Conseil d'État, were strongly opposed to any restrictions on freedom to work. The Law of 22 Germinal, Year XI (12 April 1803), confined itself to the establishment of a system of copyright for trade marks and designs. Then, too, the state of the fisc did not permit public works to be undertaken as would have been desirable. Nor did it allow scope for the encouragement of private enterprises. Even later when funds were available, Napoleon refused to give direct assistance to industry; he only gave them contracts and, in times of crisis, loans, in order to avoid stoppages in the production of goods. All that remained to complete a Colbertian system was the addition of a protective tariff.

There were many powerful reasons recommending this last step. Laissez-faire economics, as preached by Jean-Baptiste Say, was far from being universally accepted. In a work published in 1805, *Du gouvernement considéré dans ses rapports avec le commerce*, Ferrier remained faithful to the mercantilism of Colbert. Even before the Peace of Amiens, English smuggling was constantly denounced, and more so when the war ended. The cotton manufacturers were vociferous in stating that a return to the treaty of 1786 would engender a repetition of the grave crisis which followed it. Weaving continued to prosper, and although spinning was making some progress (the annual importation of cotton bales rose from an average of five million kilos in the preceding decade to nearly eleven million kilos in Year XII), it fell short of expectations. For high-count thread especially, English manufacturers defied all competition. Bonaparte had not revoked the ban against English merchandise pronounced by the Directory; what is more, on 19 May 1802 he authorised a temporary raising of tariff rates, and taxed colonial articles of English origin at least fifty per cent higher than similar articles from the French colonies.

On the other hand, Bonaparte had not yet discarded the possibility of a commercial agreement with England. Coquebert de Montbret and a number of other commercial agents were sent to London and were offered a return to the Treaty of 1786 along with safeguards which would permit France to take temporary measures to protect its home industry. In the summer of 1802 the Council of Commerce came out firmly against the prohibition of English imports, and Chaptal advised the government to accept London's offers and to demand that the English market be opened to French silks as well as wines on the same basis as port and sherry. He also counselled against a high French tariff. 'I am waiting', he said, 'for our manufacturers to begin screaming.' This plan could have been withstood by dispensing appropriate favours. Coquebert, on the contrary, advised that British cargo be accepted only to the extent that French products of equal value were admitted to the British market. Chaptal replied that such a proposal would mean issuing licences and creating a monopoly of foreign trade for the benefit of a few private individuals. This system of licences, which Chaptal characterised as 'absurd', was in fact instituted in 1811. Between the extremes of free trade and embargo there was room, given English consent, for a policy of moderate protection as advocated by Chaptal, and of which French industry was so much in need. Between the demands of industrial entrepreneurs and the national interest (which called for peace), it remained for Bonaparte to decide. In the end, he chose to support the side of total protection.

Bonaparte was simply not interested in keeping the peace. 'A First Consul', he told Thibaudeau, 'cannot be likened to these kings-by-the-grace-of-God, who look upon their states as a heritage . . . His actions must be dramatic, and for this, war is indispensable.' He was careful not to speak these thoughts in public, for the nation would have disapproved. 'I have too much at stake to let foreigners take the initiative,' but, he added, 'they will be the first to take up arms.' With such an attitude it was natural that he should encourage them. In any event, by assuring an accumulation of coin, the embargo hastened the military build-up to the point where it became a weapon of war – as it had been during the Revolution.

It seemed more than ever before that the economy and financial structure of England, based on borrowing and inflation, were vulnerable. Such sentiments were repeated by Hauterive in Year VIII, the chevalier de Guer in 1801, Lassalle in 1803, and by the *Moniteur* itself. Although there existed no doubt of the perils menacing France, the mistake of believing that France, unassisted, could bring the English to economic ruin, was again committed. Bonaparte was over-ready to share this illusion, since he, a soldier and a dictator, held in contempt this oligarchy of merchants who were without an army and without a government. He would have played both Cato and Scipio to England's Carthage. No more was said of a commercial treaty: vessels were seized because they were found carrying articles of British origin. Meanwhile, France's foreign trade rose from 553 million francs in 1799 to 790 million in Year X. The English capitalists learned that the economic struggle would continue, and they became disgusted with a peace which profited them nothing.

Since colonial goods were essential to her foreign trade, it became incumbent upon France to salvage the Antilles which were still left to her. The Peace of Amiens had not yet been signed when Bonaparte despatched an expedition to San Domingo. Toussaint L'Ouverture was by now in control of the entire island, and had, on 9 May 1801, promulgated a constitution granting himself governing powers under the purely nominal authority of France. Although he surrendered in good faith to General Leclerc, who headed the French expedition, he was arrested on 7 June 1802 and deported to France, where he died in the fortress of Joux on 7 April 1803. At the same time, Richepanse reoccupied the smaller West Indian islands. If these Antillean conquests were not worth troubling about, the English were nevertheless truly concerned over Bonaparte's Louisiana project: an expedition was being prepared on the coast of the North Sea to send General Victor to the Mississippi. The flotilla was scheduled to depart in March 1803, but it was delayed. In the meantime, Spain closed the Mississippi to American traffic. Since France and Spain were allies, and Holland a French satellite, the Gulf of Mexico appeared to be at Bonaparte's disposal. And, consequently, so did the contraband of the Spanish Indies, where the French were now in a position to extract advantageous concessions. Nevertheless, these prospects vanished without England having to interfere. The United States, which had for some time coveted Spanish Florida, had no wish to see the French established in New Orleans. The newly elected president, Jefferson, with his secretaries Madison and Gallatin, tried to pursue a Republican programme of peace, disarmament and reduced expenditures. Even though Jefferson was well disposed towards France, and had been pleased with the signing of the Treaty of Mortefontaine, he could not hold back the tide of public opinion. And so he let it be known that if France remained in Louisiana, the United States would join England in the coming war. On 12 April 1803 Jefferson's ambassador, James Monroe, arrived in Paris with a proposal to which Bonaparte had already decided to agree: the purchase of the Louisiana Territory. The ensuing treaty, signed on 3 May, brought Bonaparte eighty million francs, of which only fifty-five million remained after deducting indemnities owed to the United States and the commissions paid to Hope and Baring, the bankers who handled the transfer.

Insurrection, resulting from the re-establishment of slavery, had already become widespread throughout San Domingo. In Bonaparte's immediate circle, where the advocates of the white planters were many (not to mention Josephine herself), the slave system was being upheld as the most expedient way to revive production quickly in the colonies. However, it was not imperative that there be slavery, since even in the colonies where the decree of 16 Pluviôse, Year II, had been applied, both the commissioners of the Directory and Toussaint L'Ouverture himself had already instituted forced labour. Bonaparte was at first inclined to keep this system, limiting himself to the retention of slavery in the islands where it already existed – the Mauritius island group where the Convention decree was considered a dead letter, and Martinique which, having been under English occupation, had never received the decree. Finally, Bonaparte gave in. Indeed, the law of 20 May 1802 explicitly stated that slavery would be 'maintained' in the colonies, from which one might have deduced that it was not to reappear in places where it had been abolished. But Bonaparte, deciding otherwise, commanded Richepanse to reintroduce slavery in Guadeloupe, thereby provoking a revolt. In San Domingo, Leclerc declared the measure premature. But the blacks could see what was in store for them, and in September Toussaint's lieutenants, Christophe and Dessalines, had no trouble raising the island in revolt. The French force, decimated by yellow fever, was rapidly exhausted.

Leclerc died. His successor, Rochambeau, a supporter of the planters, lost everything by attacking the mulattos, whom Bonaparte had already alienated by prohibiting them entry to France and marriage with whites. Port-au-Prince fell on 19 November 1803, and a few besieged garrisons managed to drag out a miserable existence until 1811.

If the English were displeased to see France re-establishing her colonial empire, they might nevertheless have delayed going to war to prevent her from doing so. But to threaten English possessions was altogether another matter, and this was precisely what Bonaparte did. A new grand concept prompted him in the direction of the Mediterranean, that is to say, Egypt. The Treaty of Amiens had at last convinced the Turks to make peace with the French (26 June 1802) and to open the Dardanelles to French trade. A French agent, Ruffin, immediately set about restoring the consulates in the Levant. Also, pacts had been concluded with the pasha of Tripoli in 1801 and with the bey of Tunis in 1802. In August 1802 a flotilla compelled the dey of Algiers to follow suit. Constantinople was already very concerned about French intrigues in the Peloponnese, in Janina and among the Serbs, and there were fears of a possible partition. At the end of August Colonel Sébastiani embarked on a mission of observation to Egypt, by way of Tripoli, and then went on to Syria, seeking everywhere to establish ties with the native chieftains. Cavaignac had been sent to Muscat, and Decaen sailed for India on 6 March 1803 with a sizeable staff capable of forming sepoy regiments. All this led England to conclude that Bonaparte was planning to launch a new attack against Egypt and India, and that prudence demanded that he be stopped from completing his preparations. Under the circumstances, a British surrender of Malta was unthinkable. But that decision was a clear violation of the Treaty of Amiens.

Bonaparte's continental policy gave the English the pretext they needed. Despite Schimmelpenninck's repeated demands, Bonaparte refused to evacuate Holland, alleging that the conditions of the treaty had not been fulfilled. Although he abandoned the Neapolitan ports and the Papal States, he annexed Elba in August 1802, Piedmont in September, and occupied Parma in October, following the death of its duke. In Switzerland, the last of the French troops had no sooner withdrawn when Alois Reding led a rising of the small mountain cantons on the night of 27 August 1802. A rebel Diet was gathered at Schwyz. Zurich, Berne and Fribourg fell under its sway. The legal government, seeking refuge in

Lausanne, desperately granted the rebel peasants of Vaud the abolition of feudal dues, and promised to compensate the proprietors out of public lands: but in vain. The government was thus forced to appeal to Bonaparte for help. The First Consul intervened as mediator on 30 September, and imposed a general disarmament. Ney marched into Switzerland, and the Diet, obtaining nothing more substantial than fine words from England and Austria, dispersed. Reding was arrested. A consultative assembly was summoned to Paris on 10 December, and a commission of ten of its delegates was appointed to discuss Bonaparte's project for a constitution with four French senators. Bonaparte ordered the commission to draft constitutions for the several cantons, and these were then embodied in the final product, the Act of Mediation of 19 February 1803. Each of the nineteen cantons received its own constitution providing for a limited, property-based suffrage in most cases, particularly in the old aristocratic cantons where it ensured that the rule of the pre-revolutionary urban patriciate would continue. The cantons recovered a large measure of autonomy, the freedom to dispose of public lands, and the right to regulate feudal dues and religious affairs. Reaction was thus enabled to triumph nearly everywhere, religious liberty being guaranteed only in the districts where it had previously existed. All that remained of unity was the equal rights of the cantons, which were forbidden to form alliances, the liberty of the Swiss to dwell and own property throughout the confederation, and the abolition of internal tariff barriers. The feeble central government was composed of a Diet, where each canton had one or two votes depending on its importance, and a chief magistracy, the office of *Landammann*, which revolved among the leaders of the six main or 'directorial' cantons, viz. Berne, Basle, Lucerne, Zurich, Fribourg and Solothurn. Bonaparte appointed the first *Landammann*, Louis d'Affry, a former officer of the French Swiss Guards, who represented Fribourg. On 27 September 1803 the Helvetic Confederation signed a defensive treaty of alliance with France for fifty years and renewed the stipulations for the recruitment of four regiments of four thousand men each. But the confederation was left without a standing army, and Bonaparte did not even permit the formation of a general staff.

Meanwhile, in Germany, French influence was making giant strides towards a settlement of the indemnities promised by the Treaty of Lunéville to the dispossessed princes of the left bank of the Rhine. The Reichstag had refused to let the question be settled by the Holy Roman

Emperor, and had empowered a committee to discuss the indemnity with France. In vain did the Austrian foreign minister, Cobenzl, attempt to influence France with an offer of an alliance. Bonaparte and Alexander of Russia had already agreed to regulate the affair together. Actually, all the German princes, headed by the king of Prussia, negotiated at Paris and bribed Talleyrand with a combined sum of ten to fifteen million francs in their separate efforts to obtain choice lands. George III himself accepted the bishopric of Osnabrück. Dalberg, elector of Mainz, eagerly took part in the sport. Saxony, having no rightful claim, alone hung back. On 3 June 1802 France and Russia invited the Imperial Diet to ratify the plan worked out at Paris. Austria expressed her disapproval and took hold of Passau, which had been destined by the settlement for Bavaria; but she had to pull out in the face of unanimous protests. It was Bonaparte who rescued Austrian prestige in the end by reserving a place for her in the concluding agreement on 26 December. On 25 February 1803 the Reichstag ratified the Imperial Recess.

The new imperial constitution abolished the ecclesiastical principalities and reduced the number of free cities from fifty-one to six, thus completing the process of secularisation which had taken place in 1555 and 1648. Prussia acquired the bishoprics of Paderborn, Hildesheim, Erfurt and a substantial part of Münster; Bavaria received the bishopric of Freising, and part of Passau; Baden obtained the towns of Mannheim and Heidelberg, and the right-bank territories of the bishoprics of Speyer, Strasbourg and Basle; other states participated in shares proportionate to their size. Austria, which was least favoured of all, ceded the Breisgau and Ortenau to the duke of Modena, but gained the bishoprics of Brixen and Trent and part of the bishopric of Passau; through Austria's influence, the grand duke of Tuscany received the archbishoprics of Salzburg and Eichstädt. Austria confiscated the lands and funds of princes dispossessed in her territories.

For the Catholic Church, the Recess was a catastrophe comparable to that of the sixteenth century: the Church lost nearly 2½ million subjects and twenty-one million florins in annual revenue; eighteen universities and all monasteries were secularised; and of the clerical electors, only Dalberg of Mainz survived the redistribution, his seat having been transferred to Ratisbon [Regensburg]. Austria, apart from her loss of prestige, was forced to contemplate the imminent doom of the Holy Roman Empire because the princes of Württemberg, Baden and Hesse-Cassel became electors, thus making the Protestant states the new majority in the electoral college as well as in the Diet. The *Ritterschaft* and the knightly orders were also destined shortly to disappear despite Austria's attempts to save them. France could only profit from this reshuffling of German territories, since all of the South German states had turned towards her to oppose the Habsburgs. Prussia gained much but failed to fulfil all of her aspirations, having to turn down Hanover and a proffered French alliance in order to avoid falling out with England. With the advent of peace, Prussia had lost her domination over Northern Germany. Frederick William III met the Russian tsar in Memel on 10 June 1802, this marking the beginning of Alexander's loving friendship with Queen Louise, which bound him ever after to the Hohenzollerns. But the Prussian king sensed that he was the protégé, rather than the ally, of Russia, and so felt slighted.

England was an impotent witness to these upheavals, which, while they did not violate the Treaty of Amiens, were in her eyes clearly contrary to its spirit. Since Russia and Austria were concerned with the fate of Switzerland, and since Austria was disconsolate over the loss of Germany and Italy, the English were comforted and irritated at the same time: as Addington had foreseen, England would find allies. Until October 1802 relations with France remained satisfactory. Addington, who had complaints of his own about the *Moniteur*, even took cognisance of Bonaparte's protests and began civil action against the émigré journalist Peltier. As late as 10 September instructions received by Whitworth, the English ambassador in Paris, were still wholly peaceful. But the annexation of Italian territory, and above all the intervention in Switzerland (which made quite as much of a stir as it had in 1798) caused an about-face. Hawkesbury expressed his 'profound regret'. 'Although we wish for peace ... we must depend on the co-operation of the French government.' 'England desires for the Continent the status quo as of the time of the Treaty of Amiens, and nothing but that.'* In his mind, the idea was being formed that every French gain would necessitate a *quid pro quo*.

The best interests of France were, at the very least, to play for time. She had only forty-three ships of the line, and while she planned to build twenty-three more, they would not be ready until 1804. Bonaparte anticipated

---

* The translator has failed, despite extensive efforts, to locate the source of these quotations, and so has been unable to render them in their original English wording. TRANSLATOR.

war in his instructions to Decaen, but not before the autumn of 1804. Nevertheless, he impolitically replied that England 'should have the Treaty of Amiens, and nothing but the Treaty of Amiens'. Talleyrand's threat that 'the first cannon shot could suddenly bring into being a Gallic Empire' and persuade Bonaparte to 're-establish the Empire of the West' only added fuel to the fire. Even so, Hawkesbury did not press matters and allowed the French and British ambassadors, Andréossy and Whitworth, to return to their posts. This apparent weakness only served to excite the First Consul more. On 30 January 1803, at the very moment that England was completing its evacuation of Egypt, he published in the *Moniteur* a report by General Sébastiani containing the notable remark that 'six thousand men would suffice to reconquer Egypt'. This kind of provocation is hard to explain. Although he would tell Lucien that he was thus counting on goading 'John Bull to fight', he was well aware that France was not ready. In October Talleyrand had also stated that if England was leading the world to believe that 'the First Consul had refrained from doing any particular thing because he had been prevented, he would do it forthwith'. Such statements were as subversive of the national interest as they were irrational.

Actually, Hawkesbury's peaceful posture was purely temporary. 'It would be impossible, under present circumstances, even supposing it were wise policy,' he wrote to Whitworth on 25 November 1802, 'to engage England in a war over one or another of France's recent aggressions. Our policy must seek to use these aggressions to build a defensive system of alliance for the future, together with Russia and Austria.'* As early as 27 October he had tendered Russia a definite proposal of alliance for the preservation of the status quo in Europe. Alexander was then preoccupied in arranging German affairs together with France, and so at first turned a deaf ear. But Bonaparte's Eastern policy at last moved him too: as with the earlier French expedition to Egypt in 1798, it brought Russia and England closer together. Alexander reasoned that if he could not have Malta, it would be better for the English to have it than the

* See the previous note. The diplomatic correspondence between Hawkesbury and Whitworth can be found in Oscar Browning, *England and Napoleon in 1803: Despatches of Lord Whitworth* (London, 1887). However, this collection neither contains any passages even remotely resembling the above quotation, nor is a despatch by Hawkesbury dated 25 November 1802 to be found anywhere in the book. Hawkesbury wrote to Whitworth on 14 November and on 14 January, but these despatches make no reference to a defensive system of alliance with Russia and Austria. TRANSLATOR.

French. On 8 February 1803 Hawkesbury therefore learned that the tsar wished the evacuation of Malta delayed. The news, coming as it did following the publication of Sébastiani's report in the *Moniteur*, could not have been better timed. On the ninth, Hawkesbury instructed Whitworth that before evacuating Malta England would demand 'a satisfactory explanation' of the conduct of the French government.

There ensued a series of stormy interviews between Bonaparte and the British ambassador, and on 20 February, in a message delivered to the Corps Législatif, Bonaparte denounced the schemes of the war party in London. On 8 March George III replied in a speech from the throne by drawing attention to French armaments; Parliament responded by calling up the militia. For the moment, England was committed to staying in Malta since the conditions stipulated in the Treaty of Amiens had not been fulfilled: Alexander was clouding his guarantee with reservations that presupposed a rewriting of the terms of the treaty, and Prussia followed suit. But Addington, having decided now to keep the island, took this opportunity to give events a sharp turn. On 15 March he demanded occupation of Malta for ten years, as compensation for French territorial gains. Talleyrand replied by offering to negotiate within the framework of the Treaty of Amiens. Meanwhile, Hawkesbury learned on 14 April that Russia, while declining a new alliance, had promised its support if Turkey were attacked, and that Alexander had repeated his advice over Malta. On the twenty-sixth Whitworth presented Bonaparte with an ultimatum.

This sudden resolve on the part of the English upset Bonaparte's entourage. Fouché was to tell him in the Senate, 'You, like us, are a product of the Revolution, and war places everything in doubt.' In March it was whispered in Whitworth's ear that in consideration for a bribe the First Consul's family could be persuaded to appease Bonaparte, and that Talleyrand would help provided he received his share. Bonaparte too was upset by Russia's fears: on 11 March he wrote to the tsar to reassure him and to entreat him to pacify England. He now requested Russian mediation, and proposed to leave Malta in the hands of Great Britain for a year or two, after which time it would be turned over to Russia. Addington replied that this was unacceptable, and Whitworth left Paris on 12 May. The British government reserved the option of treating the diplomatic break as a declaration of war, contrary to continental custom. British men-of-war began to capture French commercial vessels at sea without prior warning, an act which was regarded as one of unqualified piracy on the part of 'perfidious Albion'.

Alexander had in fact accepted the offer of mediation; aside from being flattered, he was well pleased with the prospect of occupying Malta, thus keeping both England and France out of the East. To Vorontsov, who demanded explanations, Addington answered that he had not had time to consult the king. This unyielding attitude, so contrary to previous policy, could only be explained by the intervention of the war party, and perhaps Pitt. It did not create a good impression at home, and the Whigs outdid themselves in denouncing it. It took some time for England to become equal to the occasion, but Bonaparte was so dangerous that national unity was welded much more quickly than it had been at the time of the Revolution.

The responsibility for the rupture has been a subject of much passionate argument. If Bonaparte's provocations are undeniable, it is nonetheless a fact that England broke the treaty and took the initiative to wage preventive war from the moment that she could hope for Russia's collaboration. Britain's justification was the preservation of the European balance of power, but this grave concern did not extend to the sea, since in her eyes God had created the oceans for the English. The conflict between Bonaparte and England was in reality a clash between two imperialisms.

## THE ESTABLISHMENT OF THE EMPIRE
### IN FRANCE (1804)

The war, while benefiting neutral shipping, impeded English trade and caused a decline in the value of the pound sterling. It affected French trade even more. Bonaparte retaliated against attacks on French merchant vessels by sequestering enemy goods and incarcerating British subjects. Although he regarded British seizures of French merchantmen as justification, such counter-measures were considered outrageous and offered no practical help to French businessmen. After the Treaty of Amiens, entrepreneurs had gone heavily into shipbuilding, and many lost their fortunes, including Barillon, a governor of the Bank of France. All of the banks were either directly or indirectly involved with maritime investments, and so were threatened with ruin. The stock exchange was also affected: five per cent bonds fell from sixty-five in March to forty-seven at the end of May. Bonaparte, aware of the danger ahead, had reorganised the Bank of France by the law of 24 Germinal, Year XI (14 April 1803). Mollien, director of the Caisse de Garantie, unceasingly clamoured against the shareholders of the Bank, who enjoyed the privilege of discounting their own notes, and who paid themselves fat dividends and then speculated on the rise of the Bank's shares. Dividends were limited to six per cent by the new legislation, and the discount operation was entrusted to a committee of merchants, but without any real improvement as events in 1805 were to show. For Bonaparte, it was essential that the position of the Bank be strengthened. Its capital stock was raised to forty-five million francs, and a reserve fund was created. It was granted the monopoly of issuing banknotes in Paris, and it absorbed the Caisse d'Escompte du Commerce (Commercial Discount Bank), a rival bank. In return, the Bank agreed to discount all the rescriptions of the *receveurs*, which were collectable after one or two months. Both trade and treasury were able, with the Bank's help, to weather the storm without excessive damage.

Bonaparte's prestige did not suffer. Since England had torn up the Treaty of Amiens, and had begun hostilities without bothering to declare war (as was her custom), he had every opportunity to place all of the blame on her without any fear of being contradicted. The French nation, under attack, was left with no alternative but to gather around its leader, and its determination was strengthened in the face of new royalist plots, which were now being encouraged and subsidised by the British government. Thus the first consequence of the renewed war was that it yielded Bonaparte the imperial title and the hereditary succession.

Cadoudal had never ceased to keep his co-conspirators at the highest pitch; two of his agents had been imprisoned since the beginning of 1803. On 21 August he landed at Biville in Seine-Inférieure, and made his way to Paris where he was kept in hiding by numerous accomplices. By his own account he wanted to kidnap Bonaparte, not assassinate him; but having decided to kill him in case of resistance, his attempt would certainly have ended in murder. The arrival of the comte d'Artois was to be the signal, but he never came. In the meantime, royalist unrest revived everywhere, and bands of marauders reappeared in the west. In another quarter, General Lajolais was trying to bring Pichegru and Moreau together. Relations between these two had already been established by a certain Abbé David, who had been arrested late in 1802. Lajolais left for

London at the end of August 1803, and returned in December, followed shortly by Pichegru. Moreau agreed to a meeting, but did not commit himself to joining the conspiracy, seeing that the old *Chouan* leader, Cadoudal, had a hand in the affair. Finally, a third branch of the conspiracy was being uncovered by Méhée de La Touche, an ex-Jacobin turned *agent provocateur*; having contacted certain émigré circles in England, he proposed that they join hands with the republican conspirators. He then managed to make his way to Munich, where the English agent Drake informed him of his own schemes to raise the Rhineland in revolt and to keep open communications with Alsace in order to prepare the entry of the duc d'Enghien at the head of a corps of émigrés.

The First Consul was in fact surrounded by treachery, of which he knew but a fraction. In Dresden, the comte d'Antraigues, Alexander's spy, was being kept fully informed about Bonaparte's private life by *'l'amie de Paris'*, one of Josephine's intimates. Another source, *'l'ami de Paris'* (who seems to have been either Daru, future intendant-general of the Grande Armée, or his father – at any rate, an associate of Talleyrand), furnished d'Antraigues with diplomatic documents and information about Bonaparte's policies. Under the uninspired guidance of Chief Judge Régnier, the police had run up against a blank wall, and even though Fouché had put his intelligence system at the service of the First Consul, Bonaparte was still very much in the dark at the beginning of 1804. In February he decided to take action. Two prisoners revealed under torture the imminent arrival of 'a prince', and they also told of Moreau's treacherous negotiations. Moreau was immediately arrested, and terror became the order of the day: frontiers were closed, homes searched, the jury system suspended, and Murat became governor of Paris. The police were not long in laying hold of Pichegru and Cadoudal. Meanwhile, Méhée de La Touche made it known that the duc d'Enghien was residing at Ettenheim, in Baden, not far from Strasbourg, and that the émigrés were gathering at Offenburg. Bonaparte allowed that the duke was the 'prince' whom the conspirators were awaiting, and on 10 March, after holding a council which included both Fouché and Talleyrand, he decided to kidnap the duc d'Enghien.

The kidnapping operation was entrusted to the former marquis de Caulaincourt with General Ordener as his subordinate. Caulaincourt was unable to find any émigrés at Offenburg, but at Ettenheim Ordener arrested the duc d'Enghien on the night of 14 March. On the twentieth the Privy Council set the fatal machinery in motion. The duke was brought to Vincennes at five o'clock in the evening, dragged before a military commission at eleven, and shot at two in the morning. Although there was nothing in his papers to link him with Cadoudal, there was proof that he was in England's pay and that he yearned to lead an invasion of Alsace. He was condemned not as a conspirator but as an émigré being paid by a foreign nation to invade France. Had he been arrested on French soil or in enemy territory, the law would have prescribed the death penalty. But by kidnapping him on neutral soil, Bonaparte blatantly compromised the interests of France and provided the continental powers with the pretext for which they were searching.

The conspirators were now placed on trial. Twenty were condemned to death on 9 June. Bonaparte pardoned twelve, most of them nobles, and the rest (including Cadoudal) were guillotined. Pichegru was found strangled in his cell. Moreau was acquitted, but a second verdict was ordered; this time the judges imposed a two-year sentence, which was commuted to banishment. During the course of the trial, the bourgeoisie and the salons seethed with ferment. 'The hate and vituperation aimed at the government', wrote Roederer on 14 June, 'have become as violent and pronounced as ever I saw them in the time before the Revolution.' Such sentiments were evidenced in the theatres and at the trial itself. The cause of national solidarity suffered a temporary setback; Chateaubriand, who had accepted a diplomatic post, resigned. But the dissidents did not consider going to the people, the press kept its silence, and the country as a whole either remained indifferent or supported Bonaparte.

Bonaparte's entourage, and Fouché who was anxious to regain favour, urged the First Consul to strike while the iron was hot. They suggested to him that the establishment of a hereditary succession would disarm the assassins: childish argument, for if Bonaparte had been murdered, the regime would surely have collapsed. What really put an end to the attempts on his life was the terror and the perfection of police surveillance. Nevertheless, the assemblies pretended to take the argument seriously, so as to preserve for themselves a place in the future order. The republicans, moreover, were not unsatisfied by the execution of the duc d'Enghien: 'I am delighted,' said the tribune Curée. 'Bonaparte is made of the same stuff as the Convention.' On 23 March the Senate announced that the time had come 'to change the institutions'. The Conseil d'État, when consulted, objected to the principle of hereditary rule, but on 23

April Curée led the Tribunate in a resolution for its adoption. Bonaparte then made his reply to the Senate, saying, 'You have decided on the necessity for hereditary rule.' The Senate, which had done nothing of the kind, acquiesced. Between 16 and 18 May a new constitution was drafted, which was then promulgated by Senate decree on 28 Floréal, Year XII (18 May 1804), and finally ratified by a plebiscite. The 'government of the Republic' was entrusted to a hereditary emperor who was to receive a civil list of twenty-five million francs and the revenues from crown lands, which were distinguished from his personal estate. He was given a free hand in the establishment of an imperial court and in the regulation of the affairs of the royal family.

The main problem was to define the rules for the succession. 'Hereditary' had always been synonymous with primogeniture, but Bonaparte had no male issue and was not even the eldest son of his family. The simplest solution would have been to permit the emperor to designate his own successor, as in the time of the Roman Empire. In fact, Bonaparte reserved the right to adopt an heir, while it was denied to those who would succeed him. Even so, he was much too devoted to his family 'clan' to leave them completely out in the cold. His brothers, however, refused to renounce their rights in favour of Louis Bonaparte's son, Charles, the heir-presumptive. Overladen with riches and honours, they knew no gratitude, and with the support of their mother created a thousand difficulties. Lucien had just married Madame Jouberthon, the widow of a bankrupt speculator – a marriage hardly calculated to enhance the imperial dignity. Jérôme, bound for the Antilles in a man-of-war, proceeded to the United States and married the daughter of a merchant. Maria-Paola, rechristened Pauline, took as her second husband Prince Borghese without consulting her brother. Then there was Maria-Annunziata – now elegantly Caroline, the wife of Murat – and Maria-Anna – transformed into Elisa and married to that hopeless Corsican Bacciochi: both of these sisters raged because Bonaparte had not made them princesses. Finally, it was decided that failing a natural or an adopted heir the succession would fall to Joseph, and after him, Louis. Lucien, having refused to divorce his wife, was excluded and left for Italy.

As in Year X, the Senate found this an opportune moment to express its wish (this time officially) for constitutional guarantees. The Senate wanted to become a hereditary body with a veto power which would enable it to protect the fundamental rights of citizens. As for the Corps

Législatif, Fontanes asked that it be granted the right to discuss laws, and that its presidency, which office he in fact occupied, be given some degree of permanence. The net result, however, was that the Senate alone obtained the right to appoint two permanent committees charged respectively with the maintenance of individual liberty and with the liberty of the press. They were empowered only to hear complaints, and to declare after conducting an investigation that there was a 'presumption' that these liberties had been violated. The police, on the other hand, were reorganised and brought under even greater central control; Fouché became minister again (10 July), and France was divided into four *arrondissements* headed by four councillors of state responsible to him. Apart from this, government institutions underwent little change. Napoleon took advantage of the occasion to assume the right to choose an unlimited number of senators, and he decreed that the princes, his brothers, together with the six grand dignitaries of the Empire, be made members of the Senate *ex officio*.

By instituting the grand dignitaries and the grand officers – the latter comprising eighteen marshals and numerous chamberlains – the Constitution of Year XII marked a stage in the creation of a new aristocracy. The imperial court burgeoned in the splendour of its luxury, and the decree of 24 Messidor, Year XII (13 July 1804), concerning precedence, extended a protocol of etiquette to the entire administration. The cause of national solidarity was not long in resuming its course. Napoleon henceforth openly embraced the idea of creating a new nobility, and he wasted no time turning the Legion of Honour to that purpose: it became simply a decoration, much like the old chivalric orders. When ordaining that the representatives of the electoral colleges be invited to his coronation, he specified that they be chosen from among the ancient families which enjoyed public esteem. On the day of the ceremony he vented his contempt for the masses: 'The presidents of the cantons and the presidents of the electoral colleges, the army – these are the true people of France,' and not, 'twenty or thirty thousand fishmongers and people of that ilk . . . they are only the corrupt and ignorant dregs of society.'

Consequently, Napoleon could not regard the popular mandate as a sufficient foundation for the new legitimacy. Like Pippin the Short, he asked for the pope's consecration so that divine right might be restored and written into the catechism. Negotiations were conducted in Paris between Caprara, the pope's representative, and Talleyrand and Bernier;

and in Rome between Cardinal Consalvi and Cardinal Fesch, the emperor's uncle, who as a former constitutional priest had been appointed archbishop of Lyon, cardinal and ambassador to the Vatican. In view of the recent execution of the duc d'Enghien, Pius VII had reason enough to hesitate, fearing as he did to offend the great powers; but since he hoped to obtain modifications of the Organic Articles, and perhaps even the restoration of the Legations, he ended by giving his consent. The royalists broke out in furious uproar, and Joseph de Maistre wrote that the pope had 'lowered himself to the point of being an inconsequential punchinello'. For all his trouble, Pius received nothing except the submission of the remaining constitutional bishops who had persisted in their recalcitrance; even so, Bishop Saurine of Strasbourg continued to refuse to disavow the civil constitution of the clergy. Pius was not even spared a final humiliation. At Notre-Dame on 2 December 1804 Napoleon took the crown from the altar and placed it on his own head. Then, after the pope had retired, the new emperor took an oath to liberty and equality. Josephine, too, was crowned by her husband, but on the eve of the coronation she had played the nasty trick of informing the pope that her marriage had been only a civil one; and so Napoleon had to consent to a religious ceremony which would make divorce more difficult.

If the theatricality of the coronation ritual, which David was to depict, gave Napoleon the reassurance he wanted, it in no way added to his prestige. The French people watched with a sceptical eye the strange procession and the many celebrations that followed in the month of December. No one believed that Napoleon's power had been consolidated by all this. Having re-established the monarchy and heightened the aristocratic nature of the regime, he only served to widen still further the gulf between his own cause and the nation's. 'In those days', said Chaptal, 'the history of the Revolution was as remote for us as the history of the Greeks and Romans.' Maybe so for Chaptal and his like, but among the people its spirit had not been extinguished! Napoleon had seduced the French nation with the promise of peace – he had finished by installing himself, while fanning the flames of war. Now there was nothing to restrain him from fulfilling his real desires. Imperial conquest, despotism and the aristocratic principle would have their day, while the nation, stunned and troubled, was compelled to follow, lest it perish, the chariot of Caesar triumphant.

## PROJECTS FOR AN INVASION OF ENGLAND.
### TRAFALGAR (1805)

The war between France and England dragged on for more than two years without any decisive result being achieved. Both sides had to endure more difficulties than they had anticipated. In 1803 England had fifty-five ships of the line, as against France's forty-two, of which only thirteen were ready for battle. This enormous advantage assured England's maritime dominance from the very start. French ports were once again blockaded and their commerce suppressed, whereas British merchantmen had scarcely anything to fear except corsairs, against which they were protected now that the use of escort convoys had been resumed. England wasted no time reoccupying St Lucia, Tobago and Dutch Guiana. Nevertheless, Addington was accused of waging the war feebly. Many of the ships were old, and few new ones were being built because St Vincent was unable to reorganise the timber supply. Although indirect taxes had been raised, there were still financial difficulties. The Addington ministry continued to be on chilly terms with Russia ever since the affair of the Maltese mediation, and its role in the royalist plots of Year XII had weakened its reputation.

Napoleon pressed for armaments, but he lacked money. In Year XII the government began again to operate at a deficit. Confident of his power, Napoleon finally heeded the advice of Gaudin, his minister of finance, and restored indirect taxes. 'Do I not have my gendarmes, my prefects and my priests?' he thundered. 'If anyone should revolt, I will have five or six rebels hanged, and everyone else will pay.' On 5 Ventôse, Year XII (25 February 1804), he founded the Excise Bureau (Administration des Droits Réunis) and appointed Français de Nantes as its director, but only a modest tax on liquor was imposed. As for the treasury, Barbé-Marbois was unable to keep its coffers filled, and so was forced to seek the assistance of bankers and contractors. In 1804 Desprez, a director of the Bank of France, and two financiers, Michel and Séguin, formed the 'Company of United Merchants'. To some extent this company was affiliated with Vanlerberghe's provisioning enterprise, but its leading spirit was none other than Gabriel-Julien Ouvrard.* In 1805 it bought

---

* Being an association of purveyors and speculators, the company undertook, *inter alia*, to advance money to the French treasury and to supply the army with provisions. TRANSLATOR.

up all of the outstanding rescriptions. In April of that year, Ouvrard offered to advance the government fifty million francs at nine per cent on condition that it would count as part of the loan the twenty million francs that it already owed him and had refused to pay, thus in effect bringing the interest to fifteen per cent. In June Ouvrard lent 150 million francs, of which forty-two million were to count towards the bad debt. In return, Barbé-Marbois pledged assignments of taxes and treasury obligations. Desprez saw to it that all of this paper was discounted at the Bank of France, which thus acquiesced in a disguised inflation. The allies were made to contribute. Beginning in April 1803 Flushing and Dutch Brabant were garrisoned, and Holland, while wishing to remain neutral, had to agree on 25 June to furnish sixteen thousand men and all the ships that might be required of her. It took an ultimatum to bring Godoy to heel, but on 19 October he promised to contribute six million francs every month; on 19 December the government in Lisbon also agreed to disburse sixteen million francs. Nevertheless, neither Spain nor Portugal declared war. Elsewhere the French reoccupied the Neapolitan ports, and in May 1803 Mortier invaded Hanover from Holland, disarmed its army, and then seized Cuxhaven at the mouth of the Elbe and Meppen on the Ems. But all of this could not suffice to make England capitulate; and even if the naval war could have been waged successfully it would have offered only distant prospects. Therefore Napoleon decided to threaten the enemy with an invasion.

Napoleon did not discount certain possibilities in Ireland: in 1803 there had been an insurrection, but it was crushed, and Emmett and Russell were hanged without France being able to intervene. It was to the project of 1801, however, that he devoted his greatest attention. The army was concentrated at the camp of Boulogne; on 2 December 1803 it was named 'The Army of England'. By thus massing his forces, Napoleon was able to separate the army from the nation and gain its personal loyalty through the promise of a grand enterprise. He was also keeping open the possibility of eventually swooping down on the Continent and striking a major blow. In January 1805 he maintained that this in fact was the army's only purpose, while in reality he was trying to conceal an obstacle which was all too apparent – the inescapable fact of seapower. There is no doubt that Napoleon on many occasions had been determined to cross the Channel – quite understandably in view of the military situation in the United Kingdom. Early in 1804 the English army numbered less than one hundred thousand regulars. The militia numbered seventy-two thousand men, on paper, and volunteers again were pouring in to escape the draft, perhaps more than three hundred thousand. On 27 July 1803 Parliament voted a mass levy compelling all men between the ages of seventeen and fifty-five to drill; finally, on 6 July it was decided to create an 'additional force', recruited by lot. But all of these forces were worthless: it seems that the government, in case of a landing, planned to retire into the Welsh countryside to conduct guerrilla warfare. There can be no question that the French could have occupied London without firing a shot. This alone was enough to tempt Napoleon.

The English were well attuned to the danger. The nation became caught up in a movement more vibrant even than that of 1797, and about which Wordsworth left posterity a stirring account. In February 1804 Pitt set out to attack the ministry; the majority crumbled, and by the end of April Addington resigned. Pitt wanted a coalition government, but the king refused to accept Fox, whereupon Grenville, who had reconciled his differences with Fox, declined to take part in the new ministry. Pitt was thus forced to form his cabinet with Addington's colleagues, and he even had to bring in Addington himself in 1805. Pitt never recaptured the strong parliamentary position he had formerly enjoyed. He was further weakened by an inquiry into the Admiralty, which compromised certain speculators, including his intimate Dundas, now Lord Melville, and which forced the latter to resign. But Pitt nonetheless brought a firmness to English policy which it had previously lacked. He wove a new coalition in such a way that Russia, driven into the arms of England by Napoleon's policies, herself ended by proposing it. At the same time he organised the volunteers, putting them at last under state control, and he united the militia and the 'additional force' into a kind of reserve, from which ten thousand men were allocated as reinforcements to the regular army. In order to secure the co-operation of naval purveyors, he allowed them a free hand in provisioning the fleet, which was gradually brought to 115 ships of the line. He also took pains to assure that the coasts were defended, and he placed finances on a sound basis by restoring the income tax. His most felicitous act was the appointment of Sir Charles Middleton, Lord Barham, to succeed Dundas as First Lord of the Admiralty in April 1805. It was Middleton's masterly command of the naval operations of the squadrons that culminated in the Battle of Trafalgar. Until this victory, English public opinion was in no way confident, but

Pitt and Barham never lost their sang-froid. Now it was of little moment that Napoleon had an army: the great obstacle remained the crossing of the Channel.

On the one hand, Napoleon was evidently always willing to leave much to chance: had he not made it to Egypt and back, despite the English squadrons? On the other hand, he was so thoroughly Mediterranean that he failed to consider, initially, the problems posed by the Straits of Dover: the surging tides, turbulent currents and treacherous winds. At first he had planned to clear the way by means of gunboats and flat boats, similar to the barges of the Flemish canals, which would be loaded with cannon and propelled by oars. The army was to be transported on merchant vessels; but the fact had to be faced that these were not in adequate supply, and in September 1803 it was decided that the troops would also be embarked on flat boats. Napoleon had them constructed everywhere along the length of the Channel, but the English squadrons never allowed them to be concentrated in one place. Nevertheless, in 1804 more than seventeen hundred flat boats were gathered at Boulogne and neighbouring ports, and facilities were constructed to enable them to load equipment. Decrès, the minister of marine, and Admiral Bruix, the chief of the flotilla, observed that no more than a hundred ships could leave Boulogne harbour in a single tide: they would have been at the mercy of the enemy squadrons. While a tempest or winds might prevent the enemy from intercepting them, these flat boats could not be risked at sea except in fair weather. And so Napoleon was brought to the necessity of scouring the Channel with his warships; in short, he was forced to return to a war of naval engagement.

Here Napoleon's inferiority was all too obvious. The English possessed not only a superiority of numbers, but boasted a great many more three-deckers, which towered over the classical seventy-four-gun ship and carried carronades on the spar deck which enhanced their firepower even more. Sir Home Popham had introduced a new and effective system of signalling. English ships were in better condition, their crews more battle-hardened, and their admirals, like Nelson, were selected from the ranks of fighting captains. French sailors and warships, shut up in their ports, could not be of the same quality. Nor could their admirals, who proved themselves capable only when commanding their own units. Notwithstanding this superiority, the English squadrons, divided as they were, risked being destroyed piecemeal. Brest was the only port they guarded closely; Rochefort, being situated on the Bay of Biscay, was hard to contain; and Toulon was under the distant vigil of Nelson. The French, then, were not being prevented from sailing. Had they done so, the British Admiralty had planned to rally the fleet at Ushant; as long as the British blocked the entrance to the Channel, they had nothing to fear. Still, the possibility of surprise could not be entirely discounted, however improbable the idea might have seemed to some.

In May 1804 Napoleon decided that his squadrons, running the blockade, would rescue Ganteaume at Brest and then sweep the Channel. He arrived at Boulogne in August, where on the sixteenth he distributed medals of the Legion of Honour. The preparations, however, turned out to be insufficient. First Bruix, and then Latouche-Tréville died. From September 1804 to March 1805 Austria seemed to be poised for an attack, as a result of Napoleon's involvement in Italy, and the project for an invasion of England appeared to be scrapped. Napoleon ordered his squadrons to sail for the West Indies, where they were to attack the English colonies. But only Admiral Missiessy at Rochefort was able to effect a successful sortie (11 January 1805); his expedition to the West Indies proved uneventful, and failing to meet the other French squadrons, he returned to France.

To all appearances, the danger of war on the Continent had now abated: it was not until 15 July 1805 that Napoleon realised the real intentions of the Coalition. Meanwhile, England, after having threatened Spain for a long time, seized several of her treasure galleons on 5 October 1804. In December Spain finally declared war on England, and Godoy placed his fleet at the disposal of the French emperor. Since his position at home was being menaced by the princess of Asturias, Godoy sent his agent, Izquierdo, to propose to Napoleon a partition of Portugal, all in the hopes of carving out a kingdom for himself. Thus encouraged, Napoleon returned to his grand design. The colonial expedition to the West Indies was now made part of a greater strategy: the various French squadrons were to effect a junction in the Antilles, and then, having sown confusion among the enemy, were to return to the Channel and if necessary give battle. In theory this plan may have been ingenious, but it presupposed a *matériel* and a leadership which simply did not exist. Moreover, Napoleon himself did not provide a consistent plan: having finally resolved on combat, he now forbade Ganteaume to break the blockade, thus reducing the latter to inactivity and throwing the whole crushing responsibility on the unenterprising commander of the fleet at Toulon, Admiral Villeneuve.

Sailing on 30 March 1805 with eleven ships (to which the Spaniards added six at Cadiz), Villeneuve first neglected to destroy Admiral Orde's force, which guarded the Straits of Gibraltar. He then set out for Martinique, which he reached only on 14 May. Meanwhile, the English squadrons rallied at Ushant, with the exception of Nelson, who disobeyed orders. Until 15 April Nelson scoured the Mediterranean looking for Villeneuve, who he believed was on his way to Egypt; receiving information at last, he hastened to Gibraltar, where he learned that Villeneuve had sailed west. On 11 May he left for the Antilles under full sail. It was a huge gamble, for the enemy could have veered for the Channel or could have effected a juncture with other squadrons in the West Indies, and thus gained sufficient strength to defeat Nelson. The Admiralty, swayed by the public's alarm over Jamaica's safety, approved the audacious action. But however much Nelson may have been admired for his boldness, the fact remains that the outcome might have been disastrous. He gambled and won. In the Antilles, Villeneuve awaited the arrival of other French ships, but nothing came. He did however receive a despatch from Napoleon in which the emperor at last revealed the grand design and which instructed him to wait yet a month before proceeding back to rally the Ferrol and Rochefort squadrons in a concerted effort to break the blockade at Brest.

Arriving in Barbados on 4 June, Nelson began searching for the French. Upon being apprised of this, Villeneuve decided to return to Ferrol immediately, hoping in vain to throw Nelson off his track. Nelson steered for Europe on 13 June, after having sent off a fast brig to warn the Admiralty. But he was still obsessed by the danger to Egypt, and so went to Gibraltar; since Barham had ordered Admiral Calder to bar Villeneuve's passage off Cape Finisterre, the British once again found themselves dispersed. On 22 July Villeneuve met Calder's fleet. A battle ensued in which Calder captured two ships and then retreated, permitting the French to make port at Ferrol. In another quarter, Allemand, who had replaced Missiessy, put to sea from Rochefort and cruised for several months without encountering either friend or foe. From 12 to 15 August the English once again concentrated their forces near the isle of Ushant, but were immediately dispersed by Admiral Cornwallis who feared for the Convoy of the Indies and for General Craig, holed up in

Lisbon with troops destined for Naples. Calder was sent back to Ferrol, and Nelson returned to England. Villeneuve knew nothing of this favourable opportunity, and so was unable to derive any profit from it. Sailing from Ferrol and Corunna on 14 August, Villeneuve let himself be disheartened by the condition of his ships and by a false report that the enemy was coming up in full force. His instructions, dated 16 July, were to head for Cadiz in the event that he encountered insurmountable difficulties; this he did, anchoring there on 18 August. Had he broken the blockade at Brest and beaten Cornwallis, he would still have arrived too late. On 24 August Napoleon set the Grande Armée on its march towards Germany and ordered the flotilla demobilised.

Villeneuve committed the mistake of not sailing immediately for Toulon and of allowing himself to be blockaded by Cornwallis and Calder, who were reinforced successively by other squadrons. On 28 September Nelson finally took command of the fleet off Cadiz. Nevertheless, the Franco-Spanish fleet was safe enough, sheltered in the harbour, and it was holding down thirty-three English vessels. Napoleon, however, played right into Nelson's hands by ordering the fleet to sail at all costs for an attack on Naples. Learning on 19 October that six enemy ships had departed for Tetuan to revictual, Villeneuve set sail with thirty-three vessels. On the twenty-first, off Cape Trafalgar, as they were sailing in a line six kilometres long, Nelson arrived to attack them. In a memorandum of 9 October he had indicated that he would take on the enemy perpendicularly, not side to side as was the custom. This was to be done by forming two columns which were to sever the enemy line in two places and break his centre, one column cutting off the van, the other destroying the rear. In actuality, the English ships did not preserve the intended formation. The attack was carried out rather confusedly since Nelson thought the allies were headed back to Cadiz. Nevertheless, his plan succeeded: the centre and rear were annihilated. Rear-Admiral Dumanoir le Pelley, commanding the van with ten ships, was late in coming into the fray; four of his ships managed to elude the British, but were captured several days later. During the night, a storm crowned the disaster. Only nine ships of the line returned to port. The allies lost 4,398 killed, as against the British 449. Nelson, however, was mortally wounded. Villeneuve, taken prisoner and heaped with insults by the emperor, committed suicide on his return to France.

England could breathe at last! True, the Coalition had made a landing impossible; but a victorious Napoleon could always return to his grand design. Nelson's triumph, however, postponed this indefinitely. It also put an end to the naval war. Eventually, this victory would make it possible for the English to carry the war on to the Continent with the help of the Spanish rebellion. But, for the time being, they were less inclined than ever to intervene on the Continent, so that the only positive effect of Trafalgar was to save Naples. Thus it seemed that the battle merely confirmed England's dominance of the seas, and one can readily understand Napoleon's view of Trafalgar as no more than a painful incident: as long as he remained victorious on land, England would never beat him.

## THE CONTINENTAL BLOCKADE

The least that can be said of Napoleon's enterprises is that they guaranteed him the initiative. England, forced to defend herself, could no longer undertake fresh colonial conquests. The sole exception was Wellesley, the governor-general in India. He had annexed part of Oudh, taken control of the Carnatic, and had established a protectorate over Surat and Tanjore. Taking advantage of civil strife among the Marathas, he undertook action there, too. Jaswant Rao Holkar, a Marathan prince, had expelled the peshwa Baji Rao from Poona; Wellesley restored the latter to Poona in May 1803, thus making him a puppet of the East India Company. He then began to wage war against Daulat Rao Sindhia whose father, Madhoji Rao, had been on the verge of creating a vast empire when he conquered Delhi in 1788. He also attacked Raghuji Bhonsla, the raja of Berar. He defeated Daulat Sindhia at the Battle of Assaye on 23 September 1803, and Raghuji Bhonsla at Argaon, as a result of which both rulers surrendered a part of their territories. In 1804 Holkar took up the sword and succeeded in cutting Colonel Monson's column to pieces, but he in turn ended by being defeated. The following year, the grand moghul Shah Alam submitted to a British protectorate. These gains notwithstanding, Wellesley's independence and audacity irritated the East India Company and alarmed the English government, which had enough headaches without this one. Faced with dismissal, Wellesley resigned and sailed home on 15 August 1805.

Britain's main concern, as always, was to profit commercially from her maritime supremacy by laying claim to a monopoly of trade. She restored

*Le 18 Brumaire*, in which Napoleon addresses the Council of Five Hundred at Saint-Cloud, threatening to overthrow the Directory. *Below*, Prud'hon's *Apotheosis of Napoleon Bonaparte*, a glorification of Napoleon as the First Consul of the Republic. Napoleon is portrayed as a conquering Roman emperor in a chariot accompanied by winged figures

Napoleon's fellow protagonists. *Above left*, Charles de Talleyrand-Périgord, his minister for foreign affairs, and, *above right*, Joseph Fouché, the minister of police. *Below*, Bonaparte, Cambacérès and Lebrun being appointed the three consuls

The murder of General Desaix during the Battle of Marengo, 14 June 1800. *Below*, General Moreau victorious at the Battle of Hohenlinden, 3 December 1800

*The First Kiss this Ten Years!* – a satire by James Gillray on the Peace of Amiens. A tall, thin, French officer kisses a fat, richly dressed, seated Britannia, while the portraits of Napoleon and King George on the wall behind appear to be shaking hands, but with bad grace. *Below*, a meeting of the deputies of the Cisalpine Republic, on 26 January 1802, in the Collège de la Trinité, Lyon, attended by Napoleon who, days previously, had elected himself president of the Italian Republic

Georges Cadoudal was a fervent Royalist who conspired against Napoleon. *Above*, an attempt to assassinate Napoleon by bomb in the rue Saint-Nicaise, 24 December 1800. *Below left*, co-conspirators of Cadoudal, and, *below right*, his eventual execution by guillotine in June 1804

Emperor Napoleon in his study at the Tuileries, portrayed by David as both a military leader and a powerful statesman

Empress Josephine in the grounds of Malmaison, by Prud'hon

An allegory of the Concordat of 1801, with Pope Pius VII on the left and Napoleon, portrayed as the Greek legendary hero Hercules, on the right. *Below*, Napoleon visiting a silk factory in Rouen. Passionate about encouraging French industry, Napoleon visited factories, showing an interest in their products and techniques, giving prizes and purchasing goods for his palaces

the terms of the blockade in full vigour. From 1803 to 1805 a sham block-ade was enforced even against French-occupied Hanover. At the same time England began reissuing licences on 18 May 1803, and granted them even for the importation of enemy goods on neutral vessels. The 'Rule of 1756'* was applied once again to the enemy's colonial trade, but it was not strictly enforced against favoured neutrals. In Europe, circum-stances created a certain amount of flexibility, but in the case of the United States, difficulties quickly came to the fore. The progress of American shipping was looked upon with increasing jealousy by Eng-land; James Stephen, in his book *War in Disguise* (1805), argued that the 'circuit'† lent itself to fraud and that so-called 'neutralised' enemy goods were not even unloaded or subjected to American tariffs. Since the British Admiralty never precisely defined the conditions under which neutralisation would become effective, prize courts began to confiscate without restraint. On 18 April 1806 the United States Congress retaliated by declaring that the importation of British articles would be prohibited after 15 November. But Napoleon launched his continental blockade at this time, and the entire situation was changed.

Since the Baltic and the Adriatic remained open, England was able to reorganise her commerce as she had in the previous war and she suffered little. Her exports fell from £25,500,000 to £20,400,000 in 1803, but rose to £23,300,000 in 1805. Re-exports suffered more, falling from £12,700,000 in 1802 to £7,600,000 in 1805. The production of sugar con-tinued to increase in the English Antilles, the world's chief supplier, and the price continued to fall, for the market was glutted despite rising Eng-lish consumption. The price of sugar declined from fifty-five shillings a quintal in 1805 to thirty-two in 1807. A series of good harvests, and the opening of new lands, made possible by the Enclosure Act of 1801, resulted in a decline in the price of bread to twopence a pound, which led to the landed proprietors demanding and receiving in 1804 a strengthen-ing of the Corn Laws. Thus, England, relieved from the nightmare of a

---

* This regulation of the British Admiralty Courts declared, in effect, that colonial trade illegal in time of peace would also be illegal in time of war. The continental powers whose ports were blockaded, viz., France, Spain, Holland, sought to relieve their situ-ation by authorising neutrals to trade in the exclusive fields to which these mother countries otherwise claimed a monopoly of trade in time of peace. The 'Rule of 1756' was simply designed to thwart neutrals, e.g., the United States, from doing this, by declaring such cargoes lawful prize. TRANSLATOR.

† For an explanation of this term, see p. 39.

French invasion, fell into a state of apathy, and, until Tilsit, showed only a fitful interest in the affairs of the Continent.

Napoleon's economic policy during this period did not cause the British much concern. On 20 June 1803 he resumed the prohibitions on English goods; but hoping first to invade England and then absorbed by his continental campaigns, he never considered the prohibition as of more than secondary importance, despite what historians have often maintained. He did not even take the regulation very seriously. He remained faithful, in fact, to the moderate policy which he had substituted for that of the Directory ever since his rise to power. He did not put any restraint on neutral trade, which consequently continued to carry goods between the belligerents behind a façade of perfunctory neutralisations of cargoes. The continental blockade fell right in with the protectionism which formed part of Napoleon's mercantilistic thought. Moreover, the blockade was conceived to meet the desires of the industrialists; it excluded foreign competition without, however, excluding indispensable raw materials or hampering exports. The customs tariff indicates that England was not the sole target of this policy. In Year XI refined sugar and molasses were prohibited without distinction of origin. On 13 March 1804 and on 6 February 1805 the rates on cotton fabrics and colonial goods were raised. The latter were again surtaxed on 4 March 1806. Since these items were primarily of English origin, the very existence of a duty on them was an implicit admission that the continental blockade was not being strictly enforced and that Napoleon's policy was not basically military in intent but mercantilistic and protectionist.

As always, the most rabid protectionists were to be found in the cotton industries, especially the spinners, since imports of English yarn rose from 310,000 kilograms in 1804 to 1,368,000 in 1806. Likewise, the manufacturers of Lyon pressed desperately for the exclusion of Italian competition, and they demanded that Piedmontese silk be supplied to them exclusively. It can be concluded from the constantly rising tariff rates that the influence of manufacturers was decisive, and that they gradually extracted measures from Napoleon which he had not originally intended to grant. Chaptal disapproved, and so did the Paris merchants who, speaking through the Chamber of Commerce in 1803, condemned all prohibitions on trade and all measures directed against neutrals. Finally, on 22 February 1806, Napoleon banned the importation of bleached or printed calico, muslin, wick cotton and hardware. But he continued to

permit the importation of other yarns, notions and ribbons, while surtax-
ing them. Cotton-spinning, which had already surpassed a million spindles by 1805, made yet greater progress, and the production of spindles
rose from two million kilograms in 1806 to more than 4½ million in 1808.
The manufacturers of Lyon also were given concessions. Although the
laws of 1803 and 1806 authorised the exportation of Piedmontese silks
from Genoa and Nice, as well as from Lyon itself, the closing of the sea
assured the Lyonnais a monopoly. They also sought advantages in the
kingdom of Italy, and in 1808 imposed a commercial treaty which lowered
the duty on imported French goods and which, by a preferential adjust-
ment of tariff rates, guaranteed Lyon the trade in Italian silks.

There were certain indications, however, that Napoleon, sliding down
the same path as the Directory, was annoyed by the feeling that the blockade was not working as it should. On 13 March 1804 he prohibited the
importation of goods 'coming directly from England', and decreed that
neutrals should produce certificates of origin. His martial spirit blended
perfectly with his instinct for economic nationalism: witness the sudden
appearance of a tax on bale cotton on 22 February 1806 – a measure
which no doubt greatly displeased industrialists and which led to the
increased use of flax and hemp. Finally, the anti-English policy was gradually imposed on the allies – on Holland, Spain, Italy and even, in 1806,
on Switzerland, where only yarn was excepted from the ban. As for
British trade with Germany, it was impeded by the French occupation of
Hanover and Cuxhaven, something the Directory had not been able to
accomplish. The belief continued to be widely held that England could be
defeated by stifling her export trade, and the writings of Montgaillard
only served to express it once again.

All in all, however, no measures were taken against the English blockade, which overstepped the bounds of traditional mercantilist practice
and the restrictive policies usually adopted in time of war. Napoleon
patiently tolerated the authority which England claimed over neutrals. It
can even be shown from his speech delivered to the Conseil d'État on 4
March 1806 that, surprisingly enough, far from wishing to tighten the
blockade at this time, he was waiting until peace was concluded before
bringing his system of embargoes to perfection. 'Forty-eight hours after
peace with England, I shall ban all foreign goods, and I shall promulgate a
navigation act which will close our ports to all but French ships.' But all
this was to change abruptly when Napoleon's continental successes, with

his lightning victories and with the foundation of the Grand Empire, impassioned his lust for power.

### THE ORIGINS OF THE THIRD COALITION

It cannot therefore be said that Napoleon's continental policy was the consequence of his war against England, and that finding it impossible to defeat England on the sea or by invasion he undertook to ruin her economically by shutting off her European market. He could not, of course, have been unaware of this possibility, but when it took shape it was because prior conquests had made such a policy workable. Nor can it explain the rash acts and encroachments which excited the hostility of the continental powers. It would be closer to the truth to say that although the European monarchs, no less than England, were aroused by Bonaparte's aggrandisements, and although they were still infused with an inner hatred for the leader of the revolutionary nation – whom they habitually referred to as 'the Corsican' and 'the usurper' or, like Maria Carolina, 'the successor of Robespierre', not to mention other sobriquets – they were unable to take arms, disunited and impoverished as they were, without the assistance of Great Britain. The rupture of the Peace of Amiens opened the possibility of obtaining that assistance, since England could finance a coalition and had the greatest reasons for doing so. In 1803, however, a spirit of belligerency was markedly lacking, at least in the Germanies, and Austria had even recognised on 26 December 1802 the changes which had taken place in Italy since the Treaty of Lunéville. If a coalition was possible, or even probable, it was not inevitable. To work to delay it, to wait patiently until England should be beset (as in 1801) by difficulties which were bound to come, and not just from France – this was what the national interest dictated. But such an inglorious and prosaic policy never even crossed Napoleon's mind. To spurn diplomacy for brute force was to precipitate a coalition and to run terrifying risks. It meant a commitment to hostilities whose end could only be the conquest of all Europe. No prospect could better have suited Napoleon's temperament.

Until 1803 the accord with Russia had been the keystone of Napoleon's foreign policy. It had been broken by the tsar, so that he might take the initiative in the formation of a coalition. Alexander I, aged twenty-six, the grandson of a profligate queen and the son of a madman, carried within himself the seeds of a morbid instability which the circumstances of his upbringing and a premature marriage had accentuated even more. Entrusted by Catherine to the care of the Swiss La Harpe, who ranted of liberalism without imparting the spirit of it to his pupil, drilled by Paul in the tradition of Prussian authoritarianism, and exposed to the pitfalls of a heinous court – Alexander had become a tissue of contradictions: plain, yet refined; timid, yet obstinate; excitable, yet indolent; moralising, yet corrupt; the 'Talma of the North', a seducer, a Byzantine to whom treachery was second nature. Once in power, he acquired the reputation of a liberal without doing much to deserve it. After promptly disgracing his father's murderers, Pahlen and Panin, he surrounded himself with men who had developed a certain taste for Western civilisation, either at Geneva and London like Kochubei and Novosiltsev, or at Paris like Stroganov, the pupil of the French mathematician and revolutionary Gilbert Romme. To these he added his companion in pleasure, Adam Czartoryski, a Polish turncoat, clever and without character. These men constituted the 'committee of friends' or 'unofficial committee' (*neglasnyi komitet*) in which were bruited projects of constitutional reform, while the senatorial aristocracy clamoured for an important place in the government.

At the same time, Alexander counselled closely with partisans of the *ancien régime* – his aide-de-camp Prince Dolgoruki, Arakcheev, the director of artillery, and Prince Galitsin, the procurator of the Holy Synod who gradually won him over to mysticism. Since the liberal 'friends' did not deem Russia ripe for liberty, and had good reasons not to insist on the emancipation of the serfs, Alexander could with impunity shift his favour from one to the other group during the course of his reign, depending upon whether he leaned towards France or the Coalition, without ever ceasing to be an autocrat. On 20 September 1802 the Russian Senate saw itself established as the highest organ of judicial control, and it acquired in legislative matters a power of remonstrance which no sooner used was overridden. Eight ministries were instituted, but the ministers simply took their place at the head of the already existing administrative colleges. Nothing of consequence was done for the serfs, except in Livonia where Sievers granted them certain reforms by the *ukase* of 21 February 1804. The only real step forward was the creation by the new Ministry of Public Education of universities in Dorpat [Tartu], Kharkov and Kazan.

Conceited, not ambitious so much as vain, Alexander injected into his foreign policy a preference for liberal and humanitarian verbiage, and above all, a desire for showy popularity. He therefore regarded Bonaparte as a rival from the very beginning. He early surrounded himself with Germans who idolised him as the protector of their country and the future liberator of Europe. These were usually former admirers of the Revolution, who had been disillusioned by Bonaparte's restoration of monarchy. Notable among them was Klinger, author of *Sturm und Drang*, who had gone to Russia and been appointed to the staff of Paul I. 'The protector of humanity, justice and enlightenment against the threats of impudent obscurantists and tyrants shall be none other than a prince arising from brutalised Europe . . . and it shall be he!' wrote Klinger. To the extent that he fell under the spell of mysticism, Alexander was persuaded that he was the new Messiah. He had no trouble reconciling this divine calling with the desire to preserve and to expand the Russian Empire. By the terms of the Treaty of Teschen, and as the guarantor of the Imperial Recess of 1803, he saw himself as the protector of the German states, with whose rulers he had many family ties. Czartoryski, following a family tradition of Russophilism, advised the tsar to restore Poland and proclaim himself king. But Alexander's ambitions coincided with Russia's historic mission against the Turks, and so Czartoryski, when he became foreign minister in 1804, drew up a plan to partition the Ottoman Empire. This he combined with a project for restoring Poland which would have involved a complete redrawing of the map of Europe. For the time being, Alexander compelled the sultan to recognise a kind of Russian protectorate in the Danubian principalities: in 1802 a *firman* excluded all Turks except garrisons from these territories; it was stipulated that all public officials would be Greek or Romanian and that the *hospodars* could not be removed from office except with Russian consent. After the death of Heraclius in 1803, Georgia, whose prince had been under Russian protection for twenty years, was annexed outright, and so Russian rule bridged the Caucasus. Alexander's aggressive ambitions thus turned him against Bonaparte, conqueror of Egypt. He reasoned that Constantinople might well be endangered if Bonaparte were allowed to establish himself in Germany. If Alexander envisaged a partition of Europe with Napoleon, it was only with the intention of eventually taking it away from him.

The tsar, worried by Bonaparte's Eastern policy, made overtures to England and indirectly encouraged her to break the peace. But when

France requested Russia's mediation, he cooled towards Britain: the offer was more than he could have wished for; not only could he play Solomon, but here was a chance to acquire Malta. Despite the fact that his ambassadors to Paris and London, Markov and Vorontsov, were pursuing a pro-English policy, he officially accepted the French offer on 5 June 1803. On 19 July he made his recommendations: Malta would receive a Russian garrison; England would occupy the small neighbouring island of Lampedusa; France would keep Piedmont on condition that its king were indemnified; and the neutrality of the Italian states, Holland, Switzerland, Germany and Turkey would be guaranteed by the European powers. In short, he presumed to arbitrate for the whole Continent under colour of mediating between France and England. France had nothing to lose, since her natural frontiers were not being jeopardised, nor even her domination of Northern Italy. From the standpoint of Bonaparte, who did not want to have his hands tied by such conditions, agreement to these terms would have cost him nothing, for on 27 June England had announced that she would not surrender Malta. But Bonaparte had already occupied Hanover and the Neapolitan ports, a move which the tsar took as an affront, and on 29 August Bonaparte finally rejected the Russian proposal as being outrageously partial to England. He treated Markov very badly and demanded his recall. Alexander complied on 28 October, leaving only Oubril in Paris as chargé d'affaires. Now that he realised that Bonaparte would never recognise him as the sovereign judge of Europe, he was profoundly irritated. The abduction of the duc d'Enghien completed the rupture. As Germany's guardian, Alexander protested in the Diet against this violation of German neutrality. Bonaparte withdrew his ambassador from St Petersburg and asked with insulting sarcasm whether Alexander, supposing that the English-paid assassins of his father had settled near the Russian frontier, 'would not have hastened to have them seized'. Oubril in turn requested his passport, and left for Russia at the end of September 1804.

At loggerheads with Bonaparte, Alexander turned of necessity to England. But since he still held a grudge against Addington, he did not make a firm approach until Pitt's return to power. And still it was not easy to come to an agreement. Consistent with the role he had assumed, the tsar wished to form a general alliance which would impose peace and completely redraw the map of Europe; he even suggested restoring freedom of the seas! On 29 June 1804 Pitt proposed simply an Anglo-Russian coalition for the purpose of taking Belgium and the Rhineland away from France. On 11 September Novosiltsev was sent to London with instructions for the negotiation of an alliance which were modelled on a memorandum of his assistant, Abbot Piatoli. The proposals were still ambitious, but in order to make them palatable to Pitt they provided for a France reduced to her former frontiers. Leveson-Gower was despatched to St Petersburg in November, and the terms of the alliance began to take shape. Gustav IV of Sweden signed a secret convention with England on 3 December, and a treaty of alliance with Russia in January 1805. Alexander demanded that England, in co-operation with the Russian troops at Corfu, rescue Naples, and in April 1805 General Craig embarked for the Mediterranean. The treaty was not signed until 11 April, however. England promised to pay Russia an annual subsidy of £1,250,000 for every hundred thousand men contributed by the continental powers to the struggle against France. The division of conquests was to be settled at a later time, but it was understood that Holland would acquire Belgium and Prussia would get the northern stretch of the left bank of the Rhine. An effort would be made, short of outright imposition, to restore the French monarchy. Immediately Alexander sought to alter the agreement. Through Novosiltsev he made one last attempt to come to terms with Napoleon at the expense of the English, who totally failed to see the necessity for it.

And so negotiations went on while hostilities were being prepared. It was agreed that Russia and England would reinforce Gustavus's army in Pomerania, which was to invade Hanover and Holland. In Naples an understanding was reached with Maria Carolina, who had taken control of the government after Napoleon had demanded the dismissal of her prime minister, Sir John Acton, in May 1804. An agreement was signed in November, and an émigré, Baron Damas, took command of the Neapolitan army; meanwhile, Nelson was in control of Sicily. Pressure was also applied at Constantinople, where the Turkish sultan refused to recognise Napoleon as emperor. However, it was not enough to threaten France from the north and the south: to secure victory, Russia had to have an assured route either through Germany or through Austria.

In Germany, the allies made no progress. The working out of the Imperial Recess of 1803 continued to align the German princes against Austria, which was attempting to redress the balance between Catholics and Protestants in the Diet. Austria defended the interests of the Imperial

Knights; these comprised 350 seigneurs, many of them counts and barons, who ruled over fifteen hundred estates, a total area of over 110,000 hectares. Grouped into three circles – the Swabian, Franconian and Rhenish – they owed their allegiance directly to the Holy Roman emperor and were self-governing. Usually impoverished, their sons entered the Church or state service, preferably in Austria. This in fact was the origin of the Metternichs, Stadions, Dalbergs and Steins. Already hurt by the secularisations, they now saw themselves the target of the greedy princes who were attempting to 'mediatise' them, that is to say, make subjects of them. Prussia set the example in Franconia, and the other princes followed; on 13 January 1804 Stein protested against the annexation of two of his villages by the duke of Nassau. Austria, acting perhaps on some knowledge of the conspiracy of Year XII, annulled these mediatisations as violations of the Imperial Recess and threatened Bavaria, which turned to France for help. On 3 March 1804, one week before ordering the arrest of the duc d'Enghien, Bonaparte presented Vienna with an ultimatum; the Austrians disarmed immediately. The result of this crisis was that the Swedish and Russian protests against the violation of German territory were received with silence by the South German princes. In the autumn of 1804 Napoleon visited the Rhineland, and some of the princes came to curry his favour at Mainz. There was an exchange of views on a confederation of the Rhine; Napoleon conceived the idea of marrying Eugène de Beauharnais to Princess Augusta of Bavaria, who was however already affianced to the hereditary prince Charles of Baden; Dalberg came with a proposal for an Imperial Concordat with the papacy, but the German states refused, preferring to strengthen their independence by treating separately with the pope. In any case, the South German states now aligned themselves with France.

Things might have been different had Prussia clearly supported the South German states against Austria, but Frederick William III was pursuing a policy of pure self-interest. Moreover, a pro-French faction, whose leading light was the Cabinet secretary Lombard, continued to exert considerable influence in the king's immediate entourage; this group would gladly have accepted Bonaparte's offer of an alliance. The foreign minister Haugwitz was less decided and at times counselled firmness towards France, but he valued his position too much to press his views. Hardenberg, who replaced him at the beginning of April 1804, boasted a more energetic policy; in reality he was no more firm than his predecessor. The war between France and England placed Frederick William in a terrible predicament: in his capacity as elector of Hanover, George III had declared his neutrality and, if worst came to worst, would have preferred a Prussian occupation to French conquest. This was indeed a magnificent opportunity for Prussia to revive the League of Neutrality of 1795, which had gained her supremacy in North Germany, and also to reoccupy Hanover, as in 1801. The Prussian government cautiously decided to sound out the Russian tsar before taking any steps in that direction. Alexander, suspecting a secret agreement with France, protested. Haugwitz advised mobilisation, coupled with a demand that France limit herself to a pecuniary levy in Hanover; this the king refused to do. The minister returned to the charge on 28 June 1803, pointing to the damage caused to Prussian commerce by the French occupation of Hanover and Cuxhaven. Frederick William chose instead to send Lombard to interview Bonaparte, then in Belgium, with a renewed proposal to enter into a three-cornered alliance with Russia on condition that French forces in Hanover be limited to their present level and that commerce be restored. The attempt failed. Haugwitz then proposed a Prussian guarantee of the neutrality of all Germany providing the French evacuate Hanover. Bonaparte consented only to reopen the ports, and even that only if Prussia became his ally. The king had no sooner resigned himself to this when Bonaparte asserted that the Prussian guarantee should cover the status quo in Italy and Turkey as well, which in effect would have enlisted Prussia against Austria and Russia, leaving her with only the hope of acquiring Hanover. In April 1804 the negotiations with France were abandoned: Prussia coveted Hanover passionately, but was willing to offer only her own neutrality in return.

At this point, the abduction of the duc d'Enghien rekindled Frederick William's fears about the closeness of the French troops in Hanover, and he at last gave up trying to walk a tightrope between France and Russia. A defensive alliance, which Alexander had proffered as early as 1803, was finally signed on 24 May 1804, Russia promising to supply fifty thousand men in the event that Napoleon should strengthen his forces in Hanover or engage in any fresh aggressions east of the Weser. Such a *casus belli* did in fact occur in October when Sir George Rumbold, the English envoy in Cuxhaven, was arrested on Fouché's orders who had hoped to find in his papers evidence linking him to the conspiracy of Year XII. Hardenberg wished to profit from this occasion by mobilising and demanding the evacuation of Hanover, but Frederick William was content to insist upon the release of the prisoner, and when Napoleon did so, the whole affair blew over.

For a long time Austria offered no more hope than Prussia. After Lunéville, she had great difficulty in recovering. Archduke Charles attempted to persuade his brother to reform the government machinery by allowing his ministers to make decisions on their own responsibility, and to deliberate in council. On 12 September 1801 a *Staatsministerium*, consisting of three departments, was created. It was to no purpose, for Francis still wished to exercise personal control over everything. At least he permitted the archduke, who was appointed president of the *Hofkriegsrath* on 9 January 1801, to reform the army with the help of his chief of staff Duka, and his adviser Fassbender. But funds were wanting: between 1801 and 1804 the public debt rose from 613 to 645 million guldens, and the paper *Bancozettel* (treasury notes) in circulation increased from 201 million to 337 million. An injurious inflation resulted; paper money, discounted at sixteen per cent of its face value in 1801, was now discounted at thirty-five per cent. Prices rose, and it became necessary to increase wages and salaries. Speculation enriched a few and ruined the fixed-income classes. In 1804 a famine affecting all of Germany contributed to the general misery. Meanwhile, the privileged classes continued to enjoy tax exemptions which, had they been abolished, would have easily permitted the restoration of sound finances. Under such conditions, Austria, as Charles observed, needed peace above all else. The foreign minister Cobenzl and the influential Count Colloredo were of the same opinion; the former, who held great hopes of an alliance with France, worked hand in glove with the French ambassador Champagny and gave way every time Bonaparte raised his voice.

Nevertheless, there existed in Vienna a war party. Some Austrians like Count Starhemberg and Graf von Stadion belonged to it, but the chief role was played by the ambassadors of the powers already in coalition – the Russian Razumovski, the Englishman Paget and the Swede Armfelt – and it was in the salons of a few Russian *grandes dames* that the intrigue took its course. Through the offices of Johann von Müller, then court librarian, they kept in touch with the comte d'Antraigues, the tsar's agent in Dresden, who was not above taking Austrian money as well. Through Stadion and Metternich, then ambassador to Saxony, they had won Friedrich von Gentz over to their cause. Ruined by his debts at Berlin,

Gentz accepted the post of counsellor to the chancellery in September 1802, without, however, ceasing to receive British subsidies. Although these men were compensated for their services, they truly hated the Revolution – particularly Armfelt, a fiery aristocrat whom Gentz would call 'the last of the Romans'. Gentz himself, having failed to enlist Frederick William in this crusade, still hoped to convert Francis. The Austrian ministers mistrusted him, and used him only as a publicist; thus treated as an inferior, he zealously attacked Cobenzl and Colloredo and exaggerated their feebleness.

In fact, Cobenzl was anything but inactive. He was uneasy about the Anglo-French conflict since he feared that Bonaparte, unable to win at sea, would seek revenge on the Continent at Austria's expense. At the same time he realised that this conflict placed him in a bargaining position, and in 1803 he began demanding subsidies in London, which were eventually received. The Franco-Russian break provided him with new opportunities. On 1 September 1803 Dolgoruki arrived in Vienna; he was given a warm reception and was invited to make proposals. In January 1804 Russia offered to supply one hundred thousand men to force France to return to the terms of the Treaty of Lunéville. Cobenzl rejected the offer as insufficient; besides, he had no desire to undertake the offensive, and the emperor even less so: 'France has done nothing to me,' declared Francis.

The proclamation of the French Empire changed everything. The counter-revolutionaries screamed out their protests: 'The Revolution has been sanctioned, and very nearly solemnised by the incredible outcome of the bitter tragedy of our times,' wrote Gentz. The court in Vienna was also aroused by this event, but primarily because of the implied significance to the Holy Roman Empire and to Habsburg interests. When Napoleon assumed the title of emperor and not that of king, he was not just placing himself at the forefront of the revolutionary tradition; his choice of title implied something of European dimension, for until now there had been only one emperor, the lawful heir of the Roman Empire and the theoretical head of Christendom. In the eyes of legal scholars, the Empire was not necessarily German, and coronation by the pope (which the Habsburgs had allowed to fall into desuetude) appeared as valid in Paris as in Rome. It did not make any difference that Napoleon had nationalised the dignity, calling himself emperor of the French and denying all pretensions to universal dominion; everyone understood that the

German Holy Roman Empire would not survive the birth of a new one. Therefore Francis II, although he consented to recognise Napoleon, demanded that he be accorded the same recognition in return when, on 11 August 1804, he took the title of emperor of Austria. For the time being, he was still Holy Roman Emperor as well, but he evidently expected to be driven from Germany. Moreover, since tradition linked the kingdom of Italy to the Holy Roman Empire, he also feared a fresh extension of French power in that quarter, and in this he was not mistaken. This being so, the creation of the French Empire hastened the formation of the Third Coalition.

Cobenzl's first move was to sound out Prussia, but since he offered her nothing, the attempt proved fruitless. When, in October, he learned that Novosiltsev was on his way to London, he reasoned that Russia, allied to England, would perhaps abandon Austria to her fate, and so he resolved on an agreement with Alexander. Although the convention, signed on 6 November 1804, was in the nature of a defensive pact, it nevertheless provided for joint action in the event that 'circumstances should be such as to require the use of mutual force in other ways'. Then in January 1805 news came that the Italian Republic was to become a hereditary kingdom. To free his own hands, Cobenzl determined to oust from power Archduke Charles, who disapproved of the Russian alliance. Charles's independent ways had long ago earned him the emperor Francis's displeasure, and the latter increased his chicaneries to such a point that the archduke resigned his offices. Duka and Fassbender were pushed aside, and General Mack, of whom the English had a high opinion, was recalled to head the general staff. Even so, Francis still refused to start an offensive, and Cobenzl himself hesitated, with the result that Russia impatiently threatened to renounce the agreement. It took new encroachments on the part of Napoleon to drive Austria into the arms of the Coalition.

None of the vassal and allied states behaved in accordance with Napoleon's expectations. Holland permitted smuggling to go on freely, and the Dutch deputies refused to vote either taxes or loans for armaments. In September 1804 Napoleon had indicated the necessity for a constitutional change. On 22 March 1805 Rutger Jan Schimmelpenninck received the title of grand pensionary along with complete executive power; legislative authority was bestowed upon an assembly of 'Their Eminent Powers' (*Leurs Hautes Puissances*), whose members were to be elected by the citizens from a slate proposed by the government; initially,

Schimmelpenninck chose the candidates. This done, the minister of finance, Gogel, was able to undertake fiscal reforms.

Of much greater consequence was the death of the Italian Republic. As the Republic's vice-president, Melzi had organised the administration and judicial system on the French model, negotiated a concordat, founded an Institute and reopened the universities. In order to suppress brigandage, he abolished the jury system, created a prefect of police and a *gendarmerie*, and set up special tribunals. Public works were increased, and the Simplon road completed. Prina, the energetic and able minister of finance, introduced indirect taxes, liquidated the debt, purged the personnel of his department and improved the supervision of accounts. Finally, a native army was formed, conscription having at last been introduced in 1803 with success. But these reforms irritated much more than they pleased, and the population remained very hostile to the French. Although Melzi favoured the nobility, he received very little support; the Corps Législatif proved recalcitrant, and rejected measures which would have introduced registry offices and a tax on inheritances. Melzi himself hoped for independence and for the evacuation of the French troops. In May 1803 he submitted to the Austrian government a strange proposal which would have placed all of northern Italy, including Venice, under the rule of the former grand duke of Tuscany. Knowledge of this aroused Bonaparte's suspicions and brought him to the conclusion that the affairs of the Italian Republic had to be taken into his own hands.

The proclamation of the French Empire imparted a most dangerous cast to Napoleon's designs on Italy. Ever since Charlemagne, all of the Roman emperors had been either kings of Lombardy or kings of Italy: so Napoleon must needs be, too. As early as May 1804 he notified Melzi of his intentions. A constitution was worked out by an Italian council, but the emperor was irritated to find that some limits had been placed on his authority; he therefore summoned the council to Paris and dictated his own terms. He seems to have been aware of the risk he was taking in assuming the crown himself, for he offered it first to his brother Joseph, and on 1 January 1805 he wrote to the Austrian emperor to assure him that the new kingdom would for ever be kept distinct from the French Empire. But Joseph, who was counting on eventually becoming ruler of France, refused the crown of Italy, and so did Louis, on behalf of his son. Consequently, Napoleon arranged for a *senatus consultum* which was issued on 18 March and which summoned him to the throne of Italy. On

18 May he crowned himself at Milan, and nominated his stepson Eugène de Beauharnais as viceroy. With regard to Austria he simply promised that he would step down in favour of a relative when, with the coming of peace, Malta and Corfu would be evacuated. Thus the coronation in Milan constituted a breach of the Treaty of Lunéville. The treaty was again violated when, on 6 June, Napoleon annexed the Ligurian Republic and created from it three new French départements after Saliceti, his representative in Genoa, prompted a vote for its incorporation with the French Empire. In addition, Napoleon bestowed the principality of Piombino upon his sister Elisa on 18 March, and made his brother-in-law Bacciochi prince of Lucca on 23 June. These two domains were imperial fiefs, and by making such gifts, Napoleon made it evident that he regarded himself as the heir to the Roman emperors.

Austria hesitated no longer. On 17 June the Aulic Council decided to join the Anglo-Russian alliance. At this very moment Novosiltsev was in Berlin *en route* to Paris with the authority to offer France the Rhineland and Belgium (except for Antwerp); on 25 June Alexander cancelled his mission. On 16 July General Winzingerode, then in Vienna, conferred with Mack and decided on a plan of operations. The Anglo-Russian treaty, which had been signed in St Petersburg on 11 April, was finally ratified on 28 July without Pitt and Alexander coming to any agreement on the fate of Malta. Austria added her signature on 9 August. Still, she made some final attempts in Paris to gain concessions which might have kept her out of the conflict. There being nothing forthcoming, Austria invaded Bavaria on 11 September.

In the meantime, both sides exerted great efforts to persuade the German states. Frederick William remained obstinately deaf to the objurgations of the tsar, and on 15 July he refused passage to the troops massed in Pomerania, thus rendering an invaluable service to Napoleon. Alexander demanded in vain to see the king, and threatened to cut his way through Silesia. Czartoryski's hopes soared: on 23 September the tsar arrived at Pulawy, the Czartoryski family château; there he spoke of seizing Prussia's share of the Polish partitions and of restoring Poland. But Alexander was in reality deceiving his friend, for he only meant to frighten the king of Prussia and counted on winning him over.

Napoleon, after displaying some anxiety during the course of the winter over a concentration of troops in Venetia, suspected nothing more until the end of July and did not recognise the danger until 23 August.

Nevertheless, he tried once again to win Prussia to his side by offering Hanover on 8 August and by sending Duroc to Berlin on 22 August. The king replied that he would only conclude an alliance to sustain the terms of the Treaty of Lunéville. In the Prussian court and in the army, a war party began to take shape; Queen Louise never flagged in her sympathy for Alexander nor in her hatred for Napoleon. The majority of Prussians, however, including the military, continued to favour a policy of neutrality. The emperor, needing Bernadotte's corps elsewhere, decided to evacuate Hanover and to permit its occupation by the troops of Frederick William should the king wish to profit from the opportunity, which did not fail to arise. Napoleon foresaw that the king would be so satisfied, at least for a time, that he would abandon all warlike intentions: it was a sound calculation. Napoleon was even more successful in his dealings with the South German states, which were being menaced by Austria. On 25 August Bavaria allied herself with France, and on 5 September Württemberg adhered in principle. The disunion of Germany, which could have been foreseen since 1803, was thus accomplished.

Napoleon manoeuvred with similar dexterity in Italy. On 10 September Maria Carolina, queen of Naples, concluded an alliance with Russia; eleven days later, the emperor signed a treaty of neutrality with the Neapolitan ambassador, the marquis de Gallo, providing for the evacuation of French troops which were needed on the Adige. He also occupied the kingdom of Etruria, and even the port of Ancona over the protests of the pope. Fearing an attack by Villeneuve, Ferdinand IV of Naples ratified the treaty. After Trafalgar, Maria Carolina threw off her mask and on 19 November an Anglo-Russian fleet landed nineteen thousand men at Naples. It was too late; Napoleon had won the game.

The Third Coalition has been called a deliberate attempt to deprive France of her natural frontiers. It goes without saying that if the allies had won, they would have taken back all or part of the French gains. But what remains to be shown is that England in 1803, and Russia and Austria in 1805, took up arms for that end alone – and this has never been demonstrated, not even in the case of England. In the first place, the spirit of aggression, while undeniable, was fostered by passions and interests which have been entirely ignored: England's economic interests and policy of maritime imperialism; Alexander's megalomania and personal jealousy; and the hostility of the European aristocracy, so influential in Vienna – a hostility whose roots lay in the very social order. Secondly, it is even clearer that Napoleon, as if daring the powers, had inflamed this smouldering hostility, had alarmed them all, and had driven even the feeble Austrian monarchy to desperation. Aside from the interests of France, and speaking only of his personal policy, it was not indispensable to his authority to kidnap the duc d'Enghien and to establish the Empire, to provoke England prematurely, to challenge Russia's Eastern ambitions, and above all, to create a hereditary kingdom out of the Italian Republic and to annex Genoa. Although he did not share the revolutionary ardour of the Girondins, he hurled defiance against kings and aristocrats in the same fashion for which they are blamed, and he pursued the turbulent policy of aggression which has earned the Directory so much contemptuous criticism.

Be that as it may, the formation of the Third Coalition after the rupture of the Treaty of Amiens pointed the way to Napoleon's final destiny. Not that his ultimate downfall was determined, as some have argued: it would yet require many more errors and unforeseeable accidents to checkmate him. But from now on, there was no choice other than the pursuit of world conquest.

# CHAPTER EIGHT

# Napoleon's Army

A FTER THE TREATY OF LUNÉVILLE, Bonaparte undertook to purge the army of its war-weary and untrustworthy elements. He discharged many officers, and released soldiers who had participated in at least four campaigns, a total of one-eighth of the effective force. Then between 1801 and 1805 he devoted more than four years to reorganising his troops and to perfecting a system of warfare which would startle the world in 1805 and 1806. Bonaparte's inventive genius showed itself primarily in the elaboration of his principles of strategy and in the formation of a unified body of tactics essential to it. Otherwise, he remained substantially faithful to the methods of the French Revolution: the *amalgame* and promotion through the ranks were the most constant and important characteristics of his army. Although he displayed great executive ability and a meticulous care for detail in his preparations for war, Bonaparte still remained an incorrigible improviser.

## RECRUITMENT AND PROMOTION

Recruitment was based on the law of Year VI, complemented by a great many administrative regulations, all of which were finally codified in 1811. This law subjected all Frenchmen between the ages of twenty and twenty-five to military service, but numerous exemptions were granted in order to save the government the expense of providing relief to wives and children. The first to be exempted were men who had been married, and men who had been widowed or divorced providing they had children, on or before 12 January 1798. Public opinion ignored the limiting date and took it for granted that the exemptions were permanent. But the text of the law was explicit, and until 1808 the levies, even retroactive ones, did not spare married men and widowed fathers. Nevertheless, recruiting officers were inclined to invalidate these categories or to register them in the *dépôt*, that is to say, among the conscripts who had drawn a lucky number and who would be called only as replacements for regularly drafted men. Men in these categories were finally accorded dispensation by a *senatus consultum* of 10 September 1808. Thus the number of hasty marriages became ever more frequent towards the close of the Empire. There was also a feeling of relative tolerance for breadwinners, and even more for seminarists after the Concordat. Lastly, the replacement of recruits by substitutes, which had constituted a mere privilege in Year VIII, became an established right by the law of 28 Floréal, Year X (18 May 1802).

For financial and economic reasons stemming from a desire to conserve the labour force, the law of Year VI did not conscript all the men in each age group except in case of danger to the *patrie*. Instead, a fixed number of recruits was determined annually by the councils, and was called up beginning with the lowest age group. Under the Consulate, recruiting operations were conducted much the same as during the French Revolution, although the quotas were much smaller. The annual contingent was voted by the Corps Législatif, which then apportioned it among the départements. The general and district councils were to distribute the quota among the municipalities; these in turn examined the recruits with a doctor of their choosing, designated those who were to be discharged, admitted replacements into the ranks, and left appeals to the prefect.

This system evolved in the same direction as other institutions. From the very start the practice of 'replacement' favoured the wealthy middle class. On 24 September 1805 Napoleon fixed the quota by decree of the Senate, and henceforth the Corps Législatif was stripped of its powers in this area. Moreover, there was much to complain about in the way of wilful negligence, incompetence and scandalous abuses in many municipalities. And so the municipalities were deprived of their functions in the recruiting system, as they had already been deprived of their financial powers. Local recruitment was confided to a staff of professional civil servants, much to the benefit of the common people. Municipalities were prohibited from choosing recruits by vote, and were encouraged to resort to the drawing of lots. Prefects and subprefects intervened with increasing frequency in the operation of the system. On 18 Thermidor, Year X (6 August 1802), there was established in every département an itinerant recruiting board, composed of the prefect and military officers, for the purpose of re-examining all exemptions based on physical disqualifications. The campaign of 1805 brought a new and decisive change:

according to a decree of 26 August local councils were deprived of their
distributory functions. From now on, the distribution of the quota de-
volved upon the prefect and the subprefects; the latter drew up the list of
eligible recruits, chose them by lot and presided over the medical exami-
nations, which were still subject to review by the itinerant recruiting
council, however. Having been selected, the recruits still retained the
right to be replaced by a volunteer: this was called *substitution*; in addition, one could furnish a paid substitute: this was called *remplacement*.
Even after joining his regiment, a recruit might be allowed to bring forward a paid substitute.

Assignment to regiments was determined by the emperor or by his
minister. Each regiment sent one of its officers as a consultant in the
recruitment operations; accompanied by an escort detail, the officer
brought his regiment's recruits to a military depot. Aside from the
Bureau of Conscription, which was placed in the charge of Hargenvilliers
in 1800 and subordinated to a director, Lacuée de Cessac, in 1807, the system of recruitment did not become a specialised institution. It made great
progress nonetheless. As to corruption and the abuses of the wealthy
middle class, Napoleon unquestionably reduced their importance but he
did not succeed in suppressing them entirely.

Although this system made it possible to harness manpower in a
rational way, it also introduced the drawback of altering the traditional
character of French military service by doing away with equality and by
transferring most of the burden to the poor. Between 1805 and 1811 the
price of a substitute did not rise very much, but in the Côte-d'Or it fluctuated from nineteen hundred to 3,600 francs, so that only five per cent of
the contingent was able to meet the cost of a paid substitute. Yet, if military enrolment became odious to the people, the reason can be found in
the absence of peace after 1805. Drafted contingents were never destined
for the barracks, but were rushed to battle with the briefest possible
delay. Interminable warfare did not permit their discharge: a recruit
returned home only when crippled. In 1803 the army still retained
174,000 men who had been called up between 1792 and 1799; their service was far from over. In addition, the numbers drafted kept increasing
as the enterprises of the emperor multiplied, and after 1806 the quotas
were called in advance, even though the law contained no such provision.
True enough, until 1813 no category was called up in its entirety, but
those who drew lucky numbers and even those who had been replaced

entertained no security in respect of their position. There was nothing to prevent an order for additional recruits to be obtained by way of recall of categories which had not yet been exhausted. As early as 1805 Napoleon called for thirty thousand men from each age group of the classes of 1800–4.

To contemporaries these demands seemed unbearable because they had been unknown during the *ancien régime*. It must be noted, however, that from 1800 to 1812 Napoleon levied only a total of 1,300,000 men, of whom slightly more than three-quarters were drawn from the old French territories. Even taking into consideration the enormous levies of 1812 and 1813 (over a million men), the proportion of those actually drafted to the eligible male population did not exceed forty-one per cent. The Côte-d'Or supplied a total of only eleven thousand soldiers out of 350,000 inhabitants, or 3.15 per cent; the Côtes-du-Nord nineteen thousand out of five hundred thousand, or 3.80 per cent. Just as during the Revolution, Napoleon had to hunt down defaulters and deserters; as early as Year VIII their parents were fined, and after 1807 they were subjected to new penalties. Both the *gendarmerie* and flying columns of the National Guard scoured the country. These measures were indeed effective, since the number of defaulters continued to be moderate until 1812: in the Côte-d'Or, for example, they amounted to less than three per cent from 1806 to 1810. Three times – in Years VIII and X, and in 1810 – Napoleon offered them amnesty. Thus the nation submitted to compulsory military service much more agreeably than has generally been maintained; it became restive only towards the end when mass levies were engendered by military defeats.

Incessantly waging war, the Napoleonic army obtained its recruits by a steady process of amalgamation, a principle derived from the Revolution. At the beginning of every campaign a contingent of raw recruits, dressed and armed for better or for worse, departed for the front in small groups. 'Conscripts need not spend more than eight days in training camp,' wrote the emperor on 16 November 1806. They learned the essentials on the way to the battlefield if they were lucky. Once poured into the regiments, they mingled with the veterans and picked up whatever knowledge they could during the actual fighting. Drilling was regarded as useless and was consequently neglected during periods of respite. The Napoleonic soldier bore no resemblance to the soldier of the garrison: he was a warrior who improvised in the revolutionary tradition, and he retained that same quality of independence. Since the officers, risen from the ranks, were his comrades of yesterday, and since he might himself be promoted tomorrow, he took little notice of rank; for him, formal and mechanical discipline was unbearable; he would come and go as he pleased, and he obeyed only under fire. Few armies have ever tolerated insubordination to such a degree, where mass demonstrations, isolated rebellions and mutinies were common currency. Napoleon thundered, but always proved more indulgent than the government; he regarded the soldier basically as a fighting man, and his great concern was that his men be eager for battle and plunge themselves into it desperately.

One of the legacies of the Revolution was this very fervour in the face of the enemy which inspired initiative, daring and self-confidence in the individual, and which also gave the army its collective spirit. The passions of the Sansculottes, love of equality, hatred of aristocracy and ardent anti-clericalism were undoubtedly dulled by the passage of time, but these feelings were not extinguished, and in 1805 they were very much alive. In the opinion of the Old Guard, 'le Tondu', as Napoleon was familiarly called, had never been a king, but the leader in a war against kings. From the French Revolution there also came a feeling of exalted nationalism, the pride of belonging to *La Grande Nation*. Bonaparte carefully nurtured these sentiments by issuing proclamations in the spirit of the Committee of Public Safety, which had made the war a democratic cause.

Like the armies of the Convention and Directory, the Napoleonic army drew its main strength from the social revolution which had opened careers to talent. In the world of the military, *égalité* meant promotion through the ranks. The Constitution of Year VIII allowed the commander-in-chief to choose his officers at his discretion. Napoleon, although he showed signs of wishing to reinstate a military aristocracy, was essentially guided by merit in making his appointments. Seniority was of no account, and intellect alone got little notice; success did not depend on education, but on daring and courage almost entirely. After every battle, the colonel, who was the officer in charge of promotions, filled the places of the fallen by drawing on men who had distinguished themselves in his regiment, and the regiment was the best judge of his fairness. Napoleon's appointments to the general staff were made on the same basis. In a society where hierarchy was tending to solidify everywhere else, it was the army which offered the greatest opportunity to merit, and it exerted, consequently, a passionate attraction to ambitious young men. Its finest elements instinctively sprang to battle and rushed to the front lines, carrying along the others or at least making up for their shortcomings. Napoleon never ceased to stimulate this craving for glory, at first by distributing ceremonial muskets and sabres, *armes d'honneur* and, later, medals of the Legion of Honour. At the same time, he greatly increased the number of elite companies and corps, of which the most exalted was the Imperial Guard, conspicuous by its glittering and multicoloured dress uniforms.

A consequence of this system was that the officers turned out to be as unschooled in war as the ranks. The disadvantage was minimal, since Napoleon never shared with anyone the responsibility for formulating strategic conceptions and issuing general orders; apart from this, it was sufficient to have daring generals, well trained in the art of manoeuvre. The general staff was not an autonomous body, capable of exerting an influence over the course of operations; those who worked in the bureaux discharged only matter-of-fact tasks: the emperor 'spoke' his instructions, and they relayed them. Their chief, Berthier, an irresolute and mediocre general, yet punctual and compliant, was in effect nothing but a major 'despatching the orders of his majesty'. 'Adhere strictly to the commands which I give you,' wrote Napoleon in 1806. 'I alone know what I have to do.' Berthier himself instructed a marshal: 'No one knows his thoughts, and your duty is to obey.' Napoleon's orderlies, like Marbot, Fesenzac, Castellane, Gourgaud, and his aides-de-camp like Duroc, Mouton, Rapp, Drouet, Savary and Bertrand, were drawn from the regiments because of their qualities of rapid judgement and zeal. They possessed absolutely no authority over the corps commanders; they were simply so many eyes of their master. Always on mission, they surveyed the scene at a glance and reported back. If, however, Napoleon, who was unable to be everywhere at once, deemed it necessary to appoint persons to fill his place, he delegated his authority to men who had his confidence. Such were Murat, Lannes, Davout and Masséna. Real lieutenant-generals, or temporary commanders of the army, they alone were empowered to take strategic initiatives. And so, there existed no necessity for an abundance of truly capable men.

Clearly then, the Napoleonic army was not institutionalised, and it continually underwent impromptu changes. Its strength lay in the importance it gave to individual valour and in the genius of its leader. Innovations in the organisation of the various arms were negligible. The infantry remained divided into line and light infantry (or *voltigeurs*), and their tactics underwent no substantial change. On 1 Vendémiaire, Year XII (24 September 1803), the cavalry received what was to be its classic division into light cavalry (hussars and *chasseurs*), line cavalry (dragoons) and heavy cavalry (*cuirassiers*). Thanks to the efforts of the Convention and the Directory, it was better trained than the infantry. Led by Murat and a host of intrepid horsemen, it had nothing to fear from its Austrian counterpart. The artillery was grouped according to horse and foot regiments, and infantry cannon was abolished. The engineers were organised into separate, independent battalions, to which were attached *pontonniers*. The Imperial Guard was formed on 10 Thermidor, Year XII (29 July 1804), at which time two-thirds of the Guard were veterans; it comprised five thousand foot soldiers and 2,800 cavalry, both of which were divided into grenadiers, *chasseurs* and light-armed skirmishers (*vélites*). Added to these were more than one hundred Mamelukes, a unit of light artillery, marines, *gendarmes* and even a supply train, the only one in the French army.

Armaments underwent no change. The musket of 1777 was accurate up to two hundred yards and at best fired four balls every three minutes. The Gribeauval cannons discharged solid balls of four, eight or twelve pounds at the rate of two a minute, and were excellent at a range of six hundred yards. Shells and canisters, good at four hundred yards, were infrequently employed. A six-inch howitzer was also used. Napoleon attached much importance to firepower, and hence to the artillery. Yet his own artillery was quite small: until 1806 there were twelve pieces per division, and only in that year did there appear a general park of artillery consisting of about fifty-nine pieces. In 1808 field guns numbered less than two per thousand men. Marmont was partly responsible for this lag; in 1803 he had undertaken the work of recasting the entire ordnance, and he was forced to abandon the project when the war resumed in 1805. But there were also deeper causes: a shortage of tools, and above all, an insufficiency of transport; even so, it would have been impossible to procure enough gun carriages or to bring forward a sufficiency of munitions.

The energies of the Napoleonic army were gradually dissipated by war, extended conquests and Napoleon's ever-increasing aristocratic bent. As the veterans of the republican armies diminished in number, and as the draft increased, the *amalgame* became proportionately less and less effective, and in 1809 the army began to form entire divisions of raw recruits.

For its efficacy, advancement through the ranks depended on a sufficient number of deaths in each campaign to open the way to new men: until 1812 at least, this did not happen. The higher ranks especially were becoming overcrowded. Once having attained their grade, the marshals sought only to preserve the money and honours which had been lavished upon them, and so aspired to peace and comfort. Had it been left solely to the emperor, this evil might have progressed more rapidly, for it corresponded to his political designs and to his social ideal of a military elite of nobles, men of wealth and officers' sons. He established a military academy (*prytanée*) for the sons of officers, a school of cavalry at Saint-Germain and a school for cadets at Fontainebleau which was transferred to Saint-Cyr in 1808. Napoleon also contemplated re-establishing the *Gardes du corps* which had been dissolved in 1791: along these lines he created the Volontaires de la Réserve in 1800 and the Gendarmes d'Ordonnance in 1806. He encouraged the formation of local 'guards of honour' recruited from among the well-born members of the National Guard, and on 30 September 1805 he mobilised these parade corps as military units. Although officers enrolled their sons willingly in the military schools, the nobility and the upper stratum of the bourgeoisie were reluctant to follow suit. Napoleon, moreover, appreciated the danger of incurring the discontent of the army, and above all of the Imperial Guard. The Gendarmes d'Ordonnance and the guards of honour were abolished in 1807, and only in 1813 were the latter revived. In the kingdom of Italy alone, where their institution dated from 26 June 1805, the guards of honour formed a nursery for officers, thus revealing Napoleon's true intentions.

The national character of the army grew weaker as well. After 1800 a significant proportion of the French troops came from areas recently annexed, and this proportion increased with every new conquest. In addition, Napoleon revived a custom dating from the *ancien régime* of enrolling the greatest possible number of foreigners into the army. He had Swiss and Polish regiments, Hanoverian and Irish legions organised in 1803, and two 'foreign' regiments created in 1805. These also increased with time. Finally, the Imperial Army comprised soldiers from both subject and allied states: Italians, Dutch and South Germans after 1805. So great was their increase that in 1812 Frenchmen were but a minority in the Imperial Army.

The very success of the system exposed certain concomitant weaknesses. Frequently, as the theatres of war increased, Napoleon's absence betrayed the fact that few of his lieutenants were fit to command in chief. Left to themselves, Ney, Oudinot and Soult proved to be mediocre. Napoleon has been held responsible for this mediocrity because he deprived his commanders of all initiative. This accusation is baseless. Although like all great captains he retained complete control over the direction of the whole, he nonetheless left to his deputies considerable latitude in the choice of means. What he failed to do in forming his high command was to provide his officers with an intellectual indoctrination to grand strategy. Apart from this, every new conquest extended the lines of communications and the territories to be occupied, and this constituted yet another weakness. Devised as it was to end the war by a single decisive blow, the army lacked reserves. No recourse other than a levy in anticipation – summoning the yearly classes in advance of their turn – could bring it up to strength. Appeals were made to allies and to the most untrustworthy of vassals to help defend the occupied territories; at the front the proportion of effective combatants continuously declined. The National Guard, which the Constitution of Year VIII maintained on the basis of the law of 28 Prairial, Year III (16 June 1795), could have supplied the elements of a territorial army. In 1805 it existed only on paper; on 24 September Napoleon decreed its reorganisation and reserved to himself the right to choose its officers; but, in fact, he did no more than form elite companies and guards of honour. Later he partially mobilised the National Guard, as for example in the defence of the coasts: until 1812, however, he did not connect it closely with his military system.

In 1805 there appeared as yet no disquieting symptom. 'La Grande Armée', so baptised by Napoleon at the camp at Boulogne, began to march on Germany on 26 August. It was the best army in the world. Nearly a fourth of its soldiers had fought in all the wars of the Revolution, another fourth, or thereabouts, had fought in the campaign of 1800, and the remainder, brought in during the Consulate, had gained time enough to fuse themselves solidly with the veterans. Almost all of the commissioned and non-commissioned officers had seen action, and if anything, they were too old: ninety lieutenants were over fifty years of age, some were over sixty. The higher-ranking officers, on the other hand, were very young, and full of spirit. It took only three years for this army to extend the frontiers of the Empire to the banks of the Niemen.

## THE PREPARATION FOR WAR

Under the *ancien régime*, war had been a continual improvisation. Every time it broke out, officers and men had to be recruited. Army contractors, turned entrepreneurs, bought goods with which to fill their storehouses and stock supplies at any price. They sucked the king dry and fleeced his soldiers. Although efforts were made to organise a system of accounting, the army commissaries did not possess enough professional conscience to resist corruption. On the surface, these evils resulted from a lack of money; but the real explanation was rooted in the national economy, which was still too weak to supply the requirements of modern warfare and maintain an honest and competent bureaucracy. Thus the policies of the monarchy always overstepped the means with which to execute them. The Mountain, which was also committed to a policy of improvisation, made a superhuman effort to dispense with private contractors, to nationalise supply services and to demand of civil servants devotion and honesty. After 9 Thermidor the Republic found itself in the same position as the monarchy, and this situation became even more critical under Napoleon, as a result of the inordinate growth of the army and the permanence of hostilities.

Like the Jacobins, Napoleon harboured an intense dislike for the contractors, and, like them, he was compelled to make haste while lacking adequate funds and personnel. Since he relied on the notables, he could not resort to Jacobin methods. Just as he had been forced to seek the help of financiers to keep his treasury filled, he now found them indispensable in supplying his army. In 1805 Vanlerberghe and others guaranteed to furnish the home army with food and fodder. When the war broke out, certain companies took charge of monopolies of bread, meat, fodder, hospitals and all transport services, including that of the artillery, all of which was operated at a guaranteed profit. A single battalion of artillery transport had been created in Year IX, and the Imperial Guard alone possessed its own baggage train.

Napoleon made great efforts to enforce the verification of accounts. In Year X the administrative services of the army were organised as the Ministry for Military Affairs, headed by Dejean. The treasury of the army became an independent office. As early as Year VIII the task of verifying the number of troops had been taken away from the commissaries and conferred upon special officials called *inspecteurs aux revues*.

The former, as well as the latter, were responsible to Villemanzy, the intendant-general of the Grande Armée, who was replaced by Daru in 1806. The emperor himself took great pleasure in subjecting the profuse mass of accounts to his personal scrutiny and in uncovering errors. But he was unable to detect by these methods unregistered transactions or undue payments; these could come to his attention only by chance, never by a mere balancing of debits and credits. The commissaries of war, recruited at random, remained dishonest and odious. 'They make me pay all the dead soldiers,' wrote Napoleon on 18 May 1808. Moreover, he was never able to prevent his generals from levying contributions for their personal gain.

In 1805 Napoleon had amassed an army of nearly four hundred thousand foot, but it was beyond his capacity to maintain such a force properly in time of peace. The rank-and-file soldier received five *sous* per day, but the state merely allotted him bread and ammunition, and, in time of war, a ration of meat. Even this meagre pay was not disbursed regularly. On the very eve of departure, in 1805, Napoleon remarked that the soldiers' pay was lacking, and late in 1806 it was five months overdue. This shortage of funds made it impossible to accumulate food supplies, shoes, clothing and the means of transport which were necessary to begin the campaign. Napoleon had to settle for weapons and munitions. In 1800 he had stated his need for a reserve stock of three million muskets, a total which he never received and which, in any event, would have been well beyond the nation's capacity to produce. In 1805 he was provided with 146,000 muskets, and it was estimated that a corresponding number would be lost during the course of a single campaign. Still less attention was given to the artillery, whose losses were made good only by ravaging enemy arsenals. If the supply of ammunition evoked no serious concern, the fact is it was used sparingly: at Jena, the Fourth Corps fired only fourteen hundred cannon shots. Remounts, despite Napoleon's considerable pains, never became fully adequate. Since France was unable to guarantee enough horses, the shortage was made up from the conquered lands.

As for the remainder – food, shoes, clothing – it was expected that the army would live off the land. 'In a war of energetic offensives, such as the emperor wages, storehouses do not exist,' wrote Berthier to Marmont on 11 October 1805. 'It is up to the commanders-in-chief of the army corps to obtain for themselves the means of subsistence in the countries they overrun.' It will be argued that on the eve of the campaign, Napoleon

made a determined effort to supply his soldiers with bread, hard tack and
shoes; but time was too short, and these orders were only partially executed. Many soldiers crossed the Rhine in 1805 with only a single pair of
shoes, and many left for Jena without overcoats in 1806; as for bread, they
carried what they could. That Napoleonic warfare was, in part, based on
the rapidity of forced marches, was in keeping with the general state of
financial penury: given the available transport, supplies, even if they had
existed, could not have kept up with the army. Soldiers departed ill
equipped, because in undertaking each campaign, Napoleon counted on
an immediate and lightning-like victory. This victory became a question
of life and death: nothing was organised in support of the war in the rear;
if the army were forced to fight a retreating action, or even if a tenacious
enemy were given time to ravage the land before surrendering it, the
army would perish from sheer exhaustion.

When war is improvised, it is always at the expense of the soldier. Rare
were the generals like Davout who took the trouble to supply their ceaselessly marching troops with regular requisitions. Usually the soldiers
seized what they could from the population; but following each other in
waves, they would end by finding nothing. Starved, often soaked to the
skin, the soldier slept little. Alternating between total privation on the one
hand and feasting and drunkenness on the other, he was condemned to a
life of disease. No one cared about his health. The medical service continued to be utterly neglected. Although doctors and surgeons had been
summoned to the colours as officers by the Convention, the Directory, for
reasons of economy, decided that they could be dismissed outright in time
of peace, and Napoleon allowed matters to stand unchanged. Apart from
such eminent heads of the service as Larrey, Percy and Coste, the medical
staff was worse than mediocre. Having at their disposal only the most contemptible equipment, they set up ambulances and makeshift hospitals by
requisitioning necessities from the local inhabitants and enlisting them as
nurses. It was a hell whose gallery of horrors was depicted in Percy's
diary: ghastly cannon-ball wounds, amputations without anaesthesia,
gangrene and putrefaction, unspeakable filth, scabs, lice and typhus.
Napoleon absolutely forbade the shipment of the wounded far to the rear,
and especially to France; they would have died *en route* anyway owing to a
lack of sanitary facilities. Understandably, the mortality rate for this
epoch was for long time pictured in terrifying terms. Taine still repeats
that 1,700,000 men died under the Consulate and the Empire, and this

number was confined to those from the boundaries of 1789. Since, however, the total number of soldiers from these territories never exceeded this figure, such an estimate would have precluded any survivors, let alone prisoners. The actual losses between 1800 and 1815 can in fact be estimated at less than one million, perhaps forty per cent of the total, of whom a third were missing and surely not all of these dead. To this must be added about two hundred thousand French from the post-1789 boundaries, and approximately as many others from allied and vassal territories. Above all, one must keep in mind that the number of men killed in action constituted only a small part of the total dead: two per cent at Austerlitz, and, the maximum, 8½ per cent at Waterloo. The remainder died either from wounds and diseases in hospitals or from exhaustion and exposure to the cold.

The manner in which Napoleon treated the problem of supply gave rise to many dire consequences. The French occupation grew increasingly unpopular. The widespread habit of pillaging and marauding led to a marked decline in soldierly discipline and morale. Forced marches left in their rear a gathering mob of cripples and stragglers who indulged in all kinds of excesses. Misery often bred mutinies. Worst of all, Napoleon's military strategy was predicated on the existence of fertile and populous lands, chiefly Lombardy, where he had waged his first two European campaigns. When he invaded North Germany, Poland, Spain and Russia, geographical conditions made his system unworkable, and the army was imperilled.

## THE CONDUCT OF WAR

In the closing years of the *ancien régime*, French writers on military affairs had demonstrated the disadvantages of the classical methods of warfare brought to perfection by Frederick II. An inflexible army, deploying slowly in file along a single road, was incapable of encompassing the entire theatre of operations, and so could not compel the foe to fight or force him to abandon a strong defensive position. Nevertheless, it took the French Revolution to bring about a departure from the former practices. With the advent of mass warfare, involving very large numbers of troops, generals were forced to split their armies into divisions in order to render them manageable. Soon, however, these new groupings were found inadequate, for as they grew in number it became more difficult to co-ordinate their movements. Because the cavalry and artillery were attached to the separate divisions, it was impossible to concentrate their force. A higher organisation, the army corps, had been haltingly attempted during the Directory, and in 1800 Moreau had commanded three corps of four divisions each, but without reserves. Napoleon derived his ideas of strategy from the teachings of Guibert and Bourcet, as well as from the practical experience of the Revolution; but it was at Marengo that he decided upon his final formula: two or three divisions per corps, with a minimum of cavalry; most of the cavalry organised separately, and a reserve of artillery directly under the commanding general. This organisation was applied to the whole army under the Consulate.

The strength of these divisions and corps remained extremely variable. In 1805 the latter consisted of two to four divisions, totalling from fourteen to forty thousand men. The divisions were made up of six to eleven battalions ranging from 5,600 to nine thousand men; regiments comprised one to three battalions. In the following year, the army achieved a more regular definition – divisions numbered six to eight thousand, and every regiment was composed of two battalions.

Napoleon's military genius was best revealed in his ability to combine the movements of several army corps. The art lay in deploying and directing them so that the entire area of operations might be encompassed, making it impossible for the enemy to slip away. At the same time, the various army corps had to remain close enough together to be able to mass their forces for battle. The disposition of the corps generally took the shape of a flexible quincunx. Marching upon the enemy, the front progressively tightened as one or another of the corps found itself open to sudden attack. Sometimes, as at Eylau, they massed together on the battlefield itself, the corps having been aimed towards a distant point in such a way as to flank and envelop the enemy by their very advance. The arrangement of a campaign called for two different plans of action, depending upon whether Napoleon intended to fight a single army or occupy a central position in the midst of several adversaries, as in 1796–7 around Mantua, or as in 1813. In any event, the pattern varied according to circumstances, and was never confined to one formula. Napoleonic strategy was an art which, while possessing certain principles, allowed neither tradition nor calculation ever to impoverish its inventiveness.

Victory was contingent upon the speed and daring of Napoleon's decisions, followed by a precipitate execution of troop movements. Surprise was an important element, and demanded the utmost secrecy. Always covered by cavalry, the army used rivers and mountains as a natural screen for its marches, whenever possible. But while cloaking its own movements, it was quite as essential to discover the enemy's: this was a function of the cavalry cover, as well as the intelligence service, which made use of diplomats, agents of all types (including in all probability the mysterious Countess Kielmannsegg) and, above all, spies, who like the notorious Schulmeister were always ready to play a double game. Once the army was under way, Napoleon placed no great importance on lines of communication with France, since he invariably expected a short campaign. The lines of operations, on the other hand, were a matter of grave concern, and were to be protected at all costs. These were the roads connecting the army with the fortress where the headquarters was located, and whose location was shifted as the army advanced. Heavily travelled highways, dotted by postal relay stations guarded by a few soldiers, linked the army with France. Hence, fortifications had their place in the Napoleonic system. They served as a base of operations and could, by blocking rivers and passes, serve as a bridgehead and supporting cover for the army. They did not, however, play as important a role as in pre-revolutionary strategy. In campaigns aimed solely at forcing a decisive encounter and destroying the enemy, fortified places were never in themselves military objectives.

On the battlefield, Napoleon sought to compel the foe to exhaust his reserves by engaging him along the entire front. This was to be accomplished with a minimum of strength, so as to keep intact a concentrated striking force. Next, he would break the enemy's spirit with infantry and artillery fire, sustained by threats along his flank and line of retreat. Finally, when Napoleon felt that the enemy was sufficiently weakened, he would hurl forward his fresh troops, break all resistance and pursue the beaten foe without mercy. This pursuit, which Frederick II with his small army never dared to order, was the most original feature of Napoleonic warfare. The battle plan, carried out with unparalleled precision, did not alter tactics at the unit level, a subject which Napoleon rarely touched upon. As a rule, the units adhered to the drill manual of 1791: the division was drawn up into brigades on two lines, one regiment deployed to the front, the other massed in columns. But, in fact, the methods of the revolutionary armies persisted: the infantry sent ahead a swarm of skirmishers, all picked men, who advanced under cover of the terrain. The first line of infantry gradually followed, often deployed in the same way. It was this kind of mobile shooting at will which so unsettled the enemy, who was accustomed to facing linear formations where soldiers, ranged elbow to elbow in three rows (the last two rows standing), offered perfect targets. At the signal to attack, the second line of infantry advanced in deep columns. They rarely had to use the bayonet; by this time the adversary was usually in flight.

Still, tactics underwent certain changes. Brimming with confidence, the French tended to replace much of the preliminary skirmishing by massed charges with naked weapons; officers became more partial to the use of columns as the number of untried recruits increased. But once the English, and even the Germans, adjusted to these new methods, the results were disastrous. Perhaps one of the weaknesses of Napoleonic warfare was the lack of attention to unit-level tactics and the failure to revise them in view of the improvements and advantages of the Coalition armies.

Owing to financial limitations, Napoleonic wars tended to be brief. This ensured the emperor enormous prestige. The overpowering vigour of the campaigns, and the faultless dexterity with which they were brought to a swift finish, evoke our romantic admiration to this day. Their speed and daring bore the unmistakable imprint of Napoleon's fiery temperament. As in the case of provisioning the army, his ideas about the conduct of war were conceived in terms of the arena where he fought his first campaigns. The valley of the Po, hemmed in by a ring of mountains, allowed the enemy no chance of escape. It was small enough in area to be easily controlled by the army, cleverly deployed so that it might overrun the territory without taxing its strength. It was fertile enough to provide ample means of recovery. Already in South Germany the distances became greater and the army suffered accordingly. Yet this land, parcelled as it was, could still fit the original strategy. But once the army broached the limitless plains of North Germany, Poland and Russia, things went differently. The enemy could now make his escape, vast distances required exhausting marches, and victualling became an insoluble problem. Soldiers were dropped off to act as occupation forces all along the way, and the army dissolved before it had even begun to fight. The economy failed to provide the required means of transport, and the organisation of the military being what it was, reserves were lacking. Napoleon's strategy, which by its origin was totally Mediterranean, did not anticipate these new geographic conditions, and so never fully succeeded in adapting itself to them.

# CHAPTER NINE

# The Formation of the Grand Empire
## (1805–1807)

T HE CAMPAIGN OF 1805, undertaken within a year of Napoleon's coronation and in the midst of a grave financial crisis, exposed the emperor to mortal danger. Saved by the victory at Austerlitz, he took control of Germany and began to organise the Grand Empire. This in turn provoked the formation of a new Coalition, whose defeat placed all of Central Europe in his hands and, by the Treaties of Tilsit, cemented the 'Continental System'.

## THE FINANCIAL CRISIS OF 1805

Having set the Grande Armée on the road to Germany, Napoleon returned to Paris to improvise his campaign. He found businessmen greatly perturbed, the public panic-stricken at the doors of the Bank of France and the treasury in utter ruin. The royalists were filled with hope. For a long time the minister of the treasury, Barbé-Marbois, had been desperately hard-pressed, and the Bank was rapidly succumbing to inflation. Besides the twenty-seven million francs in rescriptions which the Bank had already directly discounted for the treasury, Desprez, one of the directors, had added twenty million more – these from the Company of United Merchants, who had received them from the treasury. This is not to mention paper accepted by the Bank representing other delegations of taxes. But the evil reached unparalleled proportions as the result of Ouvrard's financial operations in Spain, the most grandiose speculative adventure of that time.

Charles IV's finances were in a pitiable state. Spain had been suffering from a serious shortage of food since 1804, and the flow of piastres from her treasury in Mexico had stopped. The annual subsidy promised to Napoleon was in arrears by thirty-two million francs as early as June 1804. Ouvrard advanced this sum to the French treasury, which handed

over to him new obligations of the tax collectors as security. Having previously provisioned the Spanish fleet, Ouvrard held drafts on the Mexico
treasury to the amount of four million piastres; his brother, who had
founded a firm in Philadelphia, had personally verified that seventy-one
million piastres lay in the vaults of the Mexico treasury and were only
waiting to be shipped to Spain at the first available opportunity. Ouvrard
now came forward with the assurance that he would find the means to
have this treasure transferred to Europe for his own and France's benefit.
Napoleon was naturally delighted with this prospect, and Ouvrard departed for Spain with the emperor's approval in September 1804.

Arriving in Madrid, he proceeded to dazzle the court with his ostenta-
tion, eloquence and presents. Godoy eagerly agreed to pay the arrears of
the Spanish subsidy to Ouvrard, and accepted his bid to supply Spain
with two million quintals of grain at twenty-six francs. Owing to a surplus of grain in France, particularly in the west, the cost to Ouvrard was
eighteen francs. Napoleon, who was always anxious to please the peasants
and to divert the flow of specie into France, willingly granted export
licences on condition that the French government receive half the gross
profit. Ouvrard's next venture involved the Caja de Consolidación, a fund
whose task it was to keep the rate of the *vales reales* from falling. He
granted the Caja an immediate loan and arranged for additional credits
over a period of five months. In return, he secured claims on the contemplated future sale of Church properties, for which the pope would have to
grant his permission. In addition, Ouvrard was made the sole supplier of
the government's tobacco monopoly and given the concession of the mer-
cury mines, both of which had been in the hands of the Caja. When Spain
declared war on England, Ouvrard provisioned the French and Spanish
vessels harboured in the peninsular ports; to cover the cost, he negotiated
a loan of ten million florins from his friend P. C. Labouchère of the House
of Hope in Amsterdam.

Having rendered so many services, Ouvrard was in a good position to
tackle the problem of transferring the Mexican silver. To accomplish this,
he exerted every effort to obtain a safe passage for the treasure from Pitt,
who needed silver for commercial operations in India. On 18 December
1804 Ouvrard received from the Spanish government drafts on the Mexico treasury to the amount of 52½ million piastres; some of these he sent
to Barbé-Marbois, who helplessly turned over to him more of the tax
collectors' obligations. Charles IV, who had been completely won over,

formed a partnership with Ouvrard covering all future shipments of specie from America. But Ouvrard was doing too well to stop there: he also secured the exclusive right to handle all of the trade for Spanish America and to undertake all shipments which the king might require, in return for which he was to receive a commission and the right to a third of the freight space on each ship while Charles would assume all the expenses and all the risks. Ouvrard obtained open licences in which the destinations of the ships were left blank; these he planned to sell to Americans. He then left for Amsterdam with the object of gaining the collaboration of the House of Hope. Labouchère was at first stupefied, but at last consented, on 6 May 1805, to undertake the transfer of the Mexican treasure and to take over the traffic in the licences. Ouvrard, however, was forced to agree to give the House of Hope complete discretion, whatever the outcome, in the final settlement of accounts.

The whole affair consequently took on international proportions since Ouvrard counted on Labouchère – who was the son-in-law of Baring, the most influential London banker and a close friend of Pitt – to secure Great Britain's collaboration. Pitt, in fact, granted his approval, and even sent four English frigates to embark the initial cargo of silver, the value of which was then paid by the Bank of England to Labouchère. But in order to transfer the rest of the treasure and to take advantage of the valuable trade licences, Labouchère despatched David Parish (a son of the famous Hamburg banking house) to Philadelphia, as well as two more agents, one to New Orleans and the other to Vera Cruz. They arranged for the Mexican piastres to be brought on American vessels to the United States, where they were advanced to merchants in exchange for bills drawn upon their European factors. Also, the trade licences were sold to American firms for a percentage of their net profit. This traffic could not get under way until 1806, and it was suspended by Jefferson's embargo in 1807. The entire transaction would have brought the House of Hope and Labouchère £900,000 or 225 million French francs; Ouvrard's share would have been only twenty-four million francs. In the meantime, Labouchère had to come to terms with Napoleon. Consequently, those who would defend Ouvrard's far-reaching plans have grounds to argue that they could have brought results; but they forget that the emperor could hardly approve a scheme that enriched a foreign and, in fact, hostile banking house. Above all, they fail to recognise that it was France that was paying the bill.

It would take a long time for the transfer of the silver piastres and the trade in licences to bear fruit. Meanwhile, money was needed to pay for the grain which had been shipped to Spain and to provide the Caja with the credits and funds which it had been promised. The Bank of France now advanced the money by discounting some of the notes which had been issued by the Caja and the tax collectors' obligations which Barbé-Marbois had pledged, but only as security. Thus while Napoleon was congratulating himself on having concluded a good stroke of business, he was in effect financing the entire operation. Now Barbé-Marbois, for his part, had the Bank discount the Spanish bills which represented the silver reserves he had received from Ouvrard. To crown it all, Desprez and Vanlerberghe had not been paid by the treasury for their purveying services and, being short of funds, they resorted to the expedient of accepting accommodation bills enabling them to raise money and obtain additional credit. All of the members of the Company of United Merchants began drawing bills on each other, or even on themselves using fictitious entities, and the whole 'pack' converged on the Bank, which honoured all these bills without batting an eyelash. By September 1805 the Bank's note issue reached the staggering sum of ninety-two million francs. Such a pyramiding would have been inconceivable had Desprez not been a director of the Bank, and had Roger, Barbé-Marbois's secretary, not been bribed with over a million francs.

Ouvrard remained unshaken, believing that Spain would fulfil her obligations and that the credit situation in France would remain normal. In reality, Spain was very slow in paying for the grain shipments, and the Caja failed to honour any of its obligations since it was unable to carry through the sale of ecclesiastical properties in so short a time. In the summer of 1805 Barbé-Marbois demanded the money which Ouvrard had promised. To pacify him, Ouvrard began buying piastres with what little in the way of *vales reales* he was receiving; shortly thereafter, the *vales reales* lost fifty-eight per cent of their face value, and Ouvrard stopped sending the money, considering the transfer impossible: his Spanish credits were frozen. On top of that, the bears on the Paris stock exchange were making money from the circumstance that war was imminent, and the public began a run on the Bank. Towards the end of September the Bank's cash reserves fell to a mere 1½ million francs. At first the Bank tried to play for time by resorting to various subterfuges, but it was finally forced to announce a partial suspension of payments. The panic quietened down a little after Ulm, but it resumed after Trafalgar and with the prospects of a prolonged war. In November several private banks failed – the Banque Récamier and the Banque d'Hervas among others.

Ever since the end of August, the condition of the French treasury was causing Napoleon serious worry. The paymaster of the Pas-de-Calais département had been unable to meet the pay, and in Strasbourg it was necessary to borrow twelve million francs for which special guarantees had to be given. It is hardly surprising that a great many soldiers crossed the Rhine with only a single pair of shoes. They were the ones who ultimately paid, with their sufferings and even with their lives, the price of their master's improvisations and of the financiers' schemes. Before long, Vanlerberghe found himself unable to continue supplying the marching army and the garrisons with the necessary provisions; on 23 September he had to appeal for advances from the treasury, which was itself forced to turn to the Bank. To make matters worse, Vanlerberghe was given authorisation to take directly from the tax collectors' tills by issuing a simple receipt, whatever cash he might find; consequently, as the tax collectors' obligations fell due, the Bank got back the receipts only. On 1 January 1806 Vanlerberghe was 147 million francs in the red and had to terminate his contract. Under the circumstances, one can well understand Napoleon's summary judgement of Barbé-Marbois: 'Had I been beaten, he would have been the best ally of the Coalition.' But the minister's only sin had been his incapacity. The emperor was making an allusion to a plot, supposedly hatched with Pitt's concurrence, whose purpose it was to place the former émigré Talon at the head of the Bank of France: unfortunately, we do not know any more about it. But in any event, we do have an indication of the fearful danger which the victory at Austerlitz averted.

If the crisis of 1805 was essentially a financial and banking one, it must not be forgotten that the whole economy suffered during this year of Austerlitz, in the agricultural as well as in the industrial sector. In the département of Meurthe, more or less the same old causes contributed to the crisis, but above all it harked back to the cyclical decline in agricultural prices which, as always in the past, adversely affected the purchasing power of the majority of the people. This resulted in a tightening of credit and in the growing importance of money lending. As usual, the most significant social consequence of all this was a corresponding increase in human misery.

## THE CAMPAIGN OF 1805

Fortunately for Napoleon, Austria was not ready for war. The reforms which had been introduced by Archduke Charles had hardly begun to take root. In 1802 he had substituted long-term military enrolment for life service, but this was not scheduled to take effect until 1805. Although he drew up rules governing exemptions, the annual contingent of recruits was still only eighty-three thousand out of a population of twenty-five million. The Hungarian Diet had refused in 1802 to adopt compulsory service and conscription; it agreed to supply a mere six thousand men yearly, plus twelve thousand (granted only once) in case of war. Technically speaking, the Austrians were unable to create more than one regiment of Tyrolean *chasseurs*. When Mack took over the direction of the army, he enacted new regulations to increase the number of infantry and light cavalry and he instituted changes in the training manual, but he only succeeded in spreading confusion. Besides, the condition of Austrian finances reduced all of these efforts to naught. The peacetime establishment was short by eighty-three thousand men, ninety-seven thousand were on leave, and thirty-seven thousand cavalry and the entire artillery were without horses. The degree of improvisation was even greater than in France, and so the Austrian army marched to battle in a state of unpreparedness which was worse than that of its adversary.

Mack, moreover, was badly misled by the Russian general Winzingerode. Kutuzov, who was in command of the First Russian Army, brought with him a force of only thirty-eight thousand men instead of the promised fifty thousand; Buxhöwden, who was to have followed hard by, did not arrive until November. Lastly, as in 1799, Austria's primary concern lay with Italy, and it was there that she sent her main concentration, Archduke Charles with a force of sixty-five thousand men, not counting the twenty-five thousand in the Tyrol under the command of Archduke John. Archduke Ferdinand, who was rapidly subordinated to General Mack, was positioned in Germany with a force of only sixty thousand men, plus eleven thousand in the Vorarlberg, on the understanding that he would be reinforced by the advancing Russians. Ferdinand wanted to await them behind the River Lech, but Mack assured the emperor Francis that Napoleon could not possibly cross the Rhine with more than seventy thousand men. Having decided to push forward to the edge of the Black Forest, Mack crossed the Inn on 11 September and occupied Bavaria, whose army retreated behind the Main.

It was in Germany that the campaign would be decided after all. Napoleon's strategy consisted in moving his forces from Boulogne to Germany in such a way as to defeat the Coalition armies separately. On the Adige, Masséna kept to a holding action with only forty-two thousand men, for Italy was becoming restless and insurrections had broken out around Piacenza and in Piedmont. Napoleon had originally decided to mass the Grande Armée in Alsace: 176,000 men divided into six army corps, a cavalry reserve and the Imperial Guard; a seventh corps, coming from Brest, did not arrive until the end of October. Then, on 24–8 August, he decided that this plan would cause the advancing columns to lose time and that it would make it difficult for them to effect a juncture with Marmont and Bernadotte who were rushing in from Holland and Hanover. He therefore ordered them to veer towards the Palatinate where they crossed the Rhine on and after 25 September. The corps, covered by Murat's cavalry, then headed south-east towards various points on the Danube, downstream from Ulm. Having learned that the enemy was concentrated at Ulm, Napoleon ordered his men on 7 October to begin crossing the Danube near Donauwörth. He then lost contact with the enemy, and fearful lest Mack escape south into the Tyrol, he ordered his corps to deploy in fan order, sending Bernadotte towards Munich to cover the Russians, keeping Davout in the centre, and commanding the main body of his army to march on Ulm and the Iller. Actually, Mack, taken by surprise, was having great difficulty massing his troops, and two of his corps were badly beaten near Wertingen and Günzburg on 8 and 9 October. Mack then decided to strike northward in the hope of cutting the French communications. Ney, who had been sent to cover that side and whose main force was closing in on Ulm along the southern courses of the Danube, ordered only one division, commanded by Dupont, to cross the river. Dupont's division was severely tried at Haslach on the eleventh, and Werneck's Austrian corps, together with Archduke Ferdinand, managed to escape along the northern road. But Mack learned on the fourteenth that the French were marching westward towards the Iller, and thinking that they were beating a retreat to the Rhine, he returned to Ulm to intercept them. Napoleon rushed to envelop the enemy and ordered Ney to force a crossing of the Danube at Elchingen. The Austrian army, surrounded on all sides, capitulated on the fifteenth. Werneck's corps, pursued by Murat, surrendered on the eighteenth, Archduke Ferdinand fleeing into Bohemia with only a handful of cavalry. A total of forty-nine thousand Austrians fell prisoner to the French; Kienmayer's corps alone escaped. Nevertheless, the campaign did not come off as smoothly as some have maintained, and the army experienced more than one tactical reverse. The incessant rains and snows made the advance terribly difficult. 'At no other time, save in the Russian campaign,' wrote Fezensac, 'have I suffered as much, or seen the army in such a state of disorder.'

Ney now entered the Tyrol in pursuit of Archduke John, and reached the valley of the River Drava; meanwhile, Augereau occupied the Vorarlberg. In Italy, Masséna fought an indecisive battle with Archduke Charles at Caldiero, and Charles then withdrew his army in the direction of Laibach [Ljubljana]. Napoleon, wasting no time, drove straight for the Russian army, sending Kutuzov, who had reached the Inn, on a headlong retreat. The pursuit was delayed, however, owing to the sudden narrowing of the Danubian plain east of Enns. Marmont and Davout were forced to head into the mountains, while Mortier was shifted to the north bank to cut the Russian army's communications; but Kutuzov managed to dodge Murat at Krems, and on 11 November he all but destroyed Mortier's leading division at Dürnstein. Pushing on to Vienna, Murat seized the Danube bridges by trickery, enabling the French army to advance beyond Brünn [Brno] in Moravia. However, Kutuzov had already effected a junction in these parts with Buxhöwden's army and an Austrian corps; a third Russian army was in the offing.

Napoleon's position was rapidly becoming precarious. Already he knew that he was outnumbered. To the south there was always the possibility that the archdukes would succeed in combining their forces; to the north there was the threat of Prussian intervention. Hungary refused to budge, annoyed that Francis should have denied her once again in October the use of the Magyar language in official life and the cession of Fiume; the Diet did not possess the means to equip a feudal levy – the traditional 'insurrection' of the Hungarian nation. The Hungarians were not hostile to Napoleon, and when Davout occupied Pressburg [Bratislava], Pälffy declared his neutrality; Archduke Joseph was so hesitant in disavowing him that he was suspected of wanting to proclaim himself king. The Prussian threat was more dangerous. To save time, Bernadotte, on Napoleon's orders, had marched his troops through the neutral Prussian principality of Ansbach; it was a liberty which had been taken in previous campaigns. This time, Frederick William, who had not even been fore-warned, reacted with great indignation. He immediately retaliated by giv-ing the Russians permission to cross Silesia, and he then occupied Hanover without consulting Napoleon. Alexander, deeming the moment propitious, appeared on 25 October in Berlin where he was given an effu-sive reception. The war party began to gather momentum: Müller, now in the service of Prussia, and Hardenberg joined its ranks; Perthes, the Hamburg bookseller and publisher, appealed to Prussia not to abandon Austria to her fate; even Dalberg proclaimed in the Diet on 9 November the necessity of preserving the integrity of the Empire. On 3 November Alexander and Frederick William signed a convention at Potsdam wherein the Prussian king agreed to present Napoleon with an offer to mediate a peace along the lines of the Treaty of Lunéville. In addition, Frederick William promised, should the French reject this offer, to enter the conflict with an army of 180,000 men, not counting the Saxons, who had promised their assistance, or the Hessians, who were still hesitating but whose troops were already under Blücher's command. Meanwhile, Stein was finding the necessary resources to field this army: on 15 October he began resorting to paper money, and he paid the suppliers by means of treasury bills. Nevertheless, the king insisted on giving Napoleon until 15 December to declare his intentions. Haugwitz, the bearer of the ultima-tum, travelled by short stages and did not reach Brünn until 28 Novem-ber; he was then sent on to Vienna where Talleyrand had been told to put him off. Actually, Frederick William had begun to waver again and had ordered Haugwitz to make every effort to preserve peace, as was his inten-tion, no matter what the cost. Fearing lest Napoleon come to terms with Austria and turn against Prussia, he decided to await developments.

If Napoleon was unaware of the Potsdam Convention, he nevertheless felt the danger. Unable to pursue the enemy to Olmütz, he prayed that they would attack him: he simulated fear, drew back his outposts, re-treated his troops, and attempted to negotiate with the tsar. Kutuzov smelled out the ruse, but Dolgoruki and other close advisers persuaded Alexander to launch an offensive. At daybreak on 2 December the French army, massed behind the Goldbach Brook west of Austerlitz, saw through the early morning mist the Austro-Russian forces advancing to the attack. The allies numbered eighty-seven thousand as against seventy-three thousand French, but they were deployed along a wide eleven-kilometre front aiming to sweep around the French right wing and sever its supposed retreat to Vienna. In accordance with their plan, the allies began to descend the heights of Pratzen, thus weakening the centre of their position. The French left under Lannes, and, above all, the French right under Davout held fast against the enemy onslaught. Suddenly Napoleon, in the centre, ordered Soult to storm the heights. The French cut the enemy in two, turned their left, and put the army to flight. The combined Austro-Russian losses totalled twenty-six thousand men; those of the French, eight to nine thousand. Alexander, furious and humiliated, announced that he was returning to Russia, and Austria signed a truce on 6 December.

Now that the Coalition had broken up without waiting for Prussia's decision, Napoleon had no trouble isolating Austria. From 10 to 12 December he strengthened his alliances with Bavaria, Württemberg and Baden. On the seventh he dealt harshly with Haugwitz; then on the fourteenth he again summoned the Prussian envoy, told him that Austria was asking that Hanover be given to the ex-grand duke of Tuscany, and offered him a last chance to accept a French alliance. Thus cowed, Haugwitz gave in and signed the Treaty of Schönbrunn on 15 December. According to the terms of the treaty Prussia finally annexed Hanover, but was forced to cede the principality of Neuchâtel as well as the margravate of Ansbach which, the next day, Napoleon awarded to Bavaria in exchange for the duchy of Berg. On 24 December Francis dismissed Cobenzl and Colloredo; on the twenty-sixth he acceded to the Treaty of Pressburg. Austria yielded all of the Venetian territory she had acquired at Campoformio (including Venetian Istria and Dalmatia) and all of her possessions in South Germany, as well as the Tyrol and the Vorarlberg; in return, Austria received Salzburg, which Ferdinand of Tuscany exchanged for Würzburg, taken from Bavaria. The Imperial Knights were thus delivered into the hands of their enemies. Bavaria and Württemberg, elevated to the status of sovereign kingdoms, were released (as was Baden) from all feudal ties with the Holy Roman Empire. As a consequence of the treaty, Austria was completely excluded from Italy, and aside from an empty title, she kept none of her possessions in Germany.

### THE GRAND EMPIRE

Returning to Paris on 26 January 1806, Napoleon first tackled the problem of restoring the nation's finances. This was done with the help of

Mollien, who replaced Barbé-Marbois as minister of the treasury. On 22 April Napoleon passed a law placing the Bank under the direction of a governor appointed by the emperor, thereby bringing it under state control. Mollien reformed the system of accountancy, forced the *receveurs* to make their rescriptions payable four months after date, and established on 14 July the Caisse de Service to regulate the flow of money; henceforth, the funds collected by the *receveurs* were not to earn interest unless they were actually deposited with the Caisse.

The settlement of the crisis itself proved considerably more arduous. The merchants, summoned before the emperor on 27 January and threatened with their lives during the course of a memorable scene, were compelled to hand over all of their assets to Mollien; Ouvrard, who had been forewarned by Berthier, was nevertheless able to conceal some of his possessions. An accounting of the merchants' securities, credits and warehouse stocks was drawn up, and they were forced to continue their provisioning services for which they were to be paid only half their due up to eighteen million francs. Still, a balance of sixty million francs was found owing, a debt which Spain was made to bear despite the fact that she had only received thirty-four million francs. Charles IV was forced to seek an additional loan from Hope and Labouchère to pay France, and he obtained the pope's permission to expropriate more Church properties. Labouchère himself had to abandon ten million piastres for which he had not yet secured drafts. The whole affair dragged on for years. In the end, Vanlerberghe and Ouvrard, unable to make the Spanish debt good, declared themselves bankrupt; Ouvrard was thrown into prison for debt in 1809. But this enormous task of restoring the nation's finances did not prevent the emperor from undertaking the work of domestic reorganisation: there were still various codes to be prepared, and it was in 1806 that the Imperial University was established.

All of these things were mere trifles, however, compared with the new flights of Napoleon's imagination which the victory at Austerlitz had occasioned. In the South German states, upheavals followed each other in rapid succession. The Austrian possessions were distributed among the king of Bavaria who received the bishopric of Eichstädt, the Tyrol, and the Vorarlberg, the king of Württemberg who took Ulm, in addition to other territories, and the margrave of Baden who annexed the Breisgau, the Ortenau and Constance. In November 1805 Württemberg began mediatising the domains of the Imperial Knights, thus giving the signal for other German princes who also hastened to absorb them. Now that they enjoyed full sovereign power, they strove to fashion their institutions on the Napoleonic model, and the king of Württemberg finally succeeded in getting rid of his Landtag [parliament]. But Napoleon had no intention of allowing Germany to crumble into dust. In January 1806 he proposed the formation of a new confederation of states which would recognise him as their protector. The rights and obligations of the member states were to be set forth in a constitution and enforced by a Diet with the necessary power. Napoleon had already compelled his German allies to grant the mediatised territories a privileged position in their states – an excellent pretext for intervening in their affairs – and he expressed the keen desire that they adopt the *Code Civil*. The new monarchs were indignant that he would thus wish to mutilate their recently acquired sovereignty. 'This is a fatal blow to my political existence,' cried out Frederick I of Württemberg; Montgelas, the Bavarian minister, did not want to go beyond a temporary alliance. Not daring to break away, the states gave in. On 12 July 1806 sixteen princes announced their separation from the Holy Roman Empire and formed the Confederation of the Rhine, promising to supply their protector with a military contingent of sixty-three thousand men.

Napoleon could not dispose of the German princes just as he liked, for he could not rely on Prussia. While the act of union provided for a constitution and a Diet, they were postponed indefinitely and never saw the light of day. Moreover, the submission of the princes was compensated by a fresh distribution of territories: the free cities of Augsburg and Nuremberg were annexed by Bavaria; Frankfurt was allotted to Dalberg. Several minor sovereigns entered the confederation by virtue of their personal connections only in order to escape being mediatised. Such, for instance, was the count of Leyen who became a prince because he was Dalberg's nephew and who was made to contribute a contingent of only twenty-nine men out of a population of four thousand subjects; also in this category was Princess Hohenzollern-Sigmaringen whose husband was a friend of the Beauharnais and whose son, married to the niece of Murat, was the ancestor of the kings of Romania. All of the other petty rulers lost their sovereign rights: the houses of Schwarzenberg, Kaunitz, Ligne, and Thurn and Taxis, to name a few. There were also promotions: Baden, Berg and Hesse-Darmstadt were elevated to the rank of grand duchies; Nassau became a duchy; and Dalberg received the title of prince primate of the Confederation of the Rhine.

All that remained was to abolish the last vestiges of the Holy Roman Empire. For Austria, resistance was unthinkable because Napoleon had used the Russian seizure of the Dalmatian harbour of Cattaro [Kotor] as a pretext for keeping his troops in Braunau. The Grande Armée remained in Germany, living at the expense of the allied states. While this provided Napoleon with a singular opportunity to alleviate the condition of French finances, the army of occupation generated a great deal of resentment. 'I was fond of the French who drove out our enemies and who returned our legitimate rulers,' wrote Madame de Montgelas to Talleyrand, 'but I detest those who live like leeches at the expense of my poor country.' A sense of national consciousness was beginning to pervade the German states; Palm, a Bavarian bookseller, began circulating anti-French pamphlets and Napoleon had him shot. On 1 August 1806 the Diet at Ratisbon announced its separation from the Empire. Given formal notice, Francis II renounced his title and prerogatives as Holy Roman Emperor on 6 August. Thus ended the final act of the drama begun by the Treaty of Basle.

Bringing Holland into harmony with the new political conditions was child's play by comparison. On 6 February Talleyrand pointed out the necessity for a change to Schimmelpenninck, and on 14 March Napoleon revealed his intentions to Admiral Verhuell: his brother Louis would be king of Holland, otherwise he would annex the country. An extraordinary session of the executive council was summoned ('The Great Task') and bowed its acceptance on 3 May, Schimmelpenninck alone dissenting. A treaty guaranteed the integrity of the kingdom and its separation from France, and Louis took the throne on 5 June 1806.

In Italy, Venetia was annexed to the kingdom; Massa and Carrara were given to Elisa; Guastalla was conferred upon Pauline, who then sold it to the kingdom of Italy. Of novel significance was the downfall of the Neapolitan Bourbons, whose fate was decided on 27 December 1805 by a celebrated military decree proclaiming that 'The dynasty of Naples has ceased to reign'. The sentence was easily carried out by Masséna: the Russian force abandoned Naples and returned to Corfu; the English were content to hold on to Sicily, which they used as a place for military exercises; and the royal family sought refuge in Palermo. Gaeta held out until 18 July. In Calabria, bands of native insurgents rose up at once. Napoleon nevertheless believed, at least until July, that everything had been settled, and on 30 March he handed the crown of Naples to his brother Joseph. And yet he readied himself for a guerrilla warfare, as in the later Peninsular War. Maria Carolina had not given up the fight. Commanding but six thousand men, she fomented an insurrection. Its ranks were filled with leaders of all types, from the nobleman Rodio to the highwayman Pezza (styled Fra Diavolo), most of whom had led the revolt in 1799. Many priests aided them. The Calabrians lacked a sense of national self-consciousness and were almost indifferent to the fate of the Bourbon dynasty, but the French occupation overburdened them and they were angry that they had been disarmed. The population was accustomed to brigandage fostered by the economic conditions of the country, by smuggling and by a powerful mafia. The herdsmen and peasants held the bourgeoisie and the nobility as the ones most favourable to the French and to modern ideas, and so they regarded the queen's appeal as a licence to pillage the towns and the property of the upper classes.

The English looked disapprovingly upon this appeal to popular insurrection, which they believed to be of doubtful military value; but having seized Capri and the Pontine Islands, they decided to risk a landing, and by so doing, unleashed the uprising. On 1 July a British force of 5,200 men under Sir John Stuart landed in the Gulf of Santa Eufemia. They were met at Maida on 4 July by a division of more than six thousand men under General Reynier who, without preparation, ordered a charge with naked swords. The English infantry stood firm, waiting for their approach, and routed them by means of successive volleys. This was the first example of a tactic that Wellington would demonstrate from Talavera to Waterloo, and which Napoleon, unfortunately for him, completely ignored. The French defeat became a signal for a widespread uprising marked by unspeakable horrors. Masséna and Reynier reconquered Calabria inch by inch, and were merciless in their reprisals. The town of Lauria was completely destroyed, Fra Diavolo was hanged, and prisons and galleys were filled beyond capacity. Nevertheless, the insurrection had its effects: it proved to be very costly to the French, the British remained in possession of Reggio until 1808 and forty thousand French soldiers were kept immobilised. Meanwhile, Napoleon occupied the port of Leghorn, closing it to the English, and he placed a division of Spaniards in the kingdom of Etruria. Now the only remaining independent territories in Italy were the Papal States.

Long before the coronation, Pius VII had been apprehensive about the progress of France in Italy. He had been forced to consent to the application of the Concordat in Piedmont, annexed to France in September 1802, and then he had to sign yet another Concordat with the Italian Republic. The latter convention was not devoid of advantages, however: it recognised Catholicism as the state religion, treated the clergy favourably and referred undecided questions to the Church. But in January 1804 Melzi issued a decree maintaining the former laws which the Concordat did not expressly forbid. Pius VII protested against the imposition of these new organic articles; the emperor replied with vague promises. In the meantime, a month after being crowned at Milan by Caprara (26 May 1805), Napoleon issued two decrees which, without the prior approval of Rome, reorganised the life of the clergy. While increasing their revenues, he reduced the number of parishes, suppressed monasteries and set a limit to their numbers. Much worse, he extended the *Code Civil* to Italy on 1 January 1806. Except in the kingdom of Etruria where the sovereign was under the sway of Rome, everywhere in Italy – in Lucca, Parma, Piacenza and Naples – the Church became the object of offensive encroachments. Having tolerated secularising trends in France as the lesser evil, Pius VII feared lest they be introduced by the *Code Civil* in Italy, which he regarded as his preserve, at least in a spiritual sense.

Conditions in Germany were no less disconcerting to the pope. The Imperial Recess of 1803 had aggravated the situation, since rulers were secularising Church properties and extending their control over the clergy without consulting Rome. Caesaro-papism was even winning in Bavaria. Now that they ruled over peoples of diverse religions, the princes renounced the principle of *cuius regio, eius religio*, and openly espoused tolerance, thus making rapid strides in the direction of the secular state. At first the papal court thought to negotiate a German concordat with Vienna, but it finally rejected the idea because there was no way to force the German sovereigns to accept it except under pressure from France. Particularly after Austerlitz, there was always the fear that the Grand Empire, the symbol of a claim to universal domination, might some day challenge the priesthood, and this deterred Pius VII from implicitly recognising Napoleon as the temporal head of the Roman Church.

And yet despite these trials and tribulations, the Church derived so great a benefit from Napoleon's protection that Pius VII would never have broken with the emperor had he not himself been a temporal ruler. But such he was, and Napoleon could not permit the pope to imperil his earthly domination. In vain did the pontiff invoke his neutrality: the fact remained that his dominions stood between the French and the kingdom of Naples, an accomplice of the Coalition. When the English and Russians landed there in 1805, they were in a position to invade the kingdom of Italy, and Pius VII would have been powerless to bar their passage across his territories, an eventuality which his court would have welcomed.

Consequently, the French occupied Ancona, and later Civita Vecchia. In answer to the protests of Pius VII, Napoleon replied on 13 February 1806 by summoning him to enter into his 'system', expel the English and close his territories to them. When the pope refused, the emperor recalled Fesch, the French ambassador at Rome. Consalvi's policy was wrecked, and he resigned. The rupture was final, and Napoleon never again wrote to Pius VII.

In April Marmont entered Dalmatia, and Dandolo was appointed commissioner there. However, a Russian force from Corfu seized the harbour of Cattaro with Austrian complicity, and at Ragusa [Dubrovnik] the French general Molitor was attacked by Montenegrins. Napoleon availed himself of the occasion to compel Vienna to grant him a right of way across Austrian Istria. No sooner had he thus reached the threshold of the Ottoman Empire when he decided to interfere in its affairs, and the year 1806 marked the reawakening of his Eastern ambitions. Pouqueville, the consul at Janina, was already busy with intrigues; Reinhard was sent to Moldavia; David was charged with a mission to the pasha of Bosnia, who was in the midst of a conflict with the Serbs. The victory at Austerlitz had strengthened French influence with the sultan, who finally recognised the emperor and sent him an embassy; in return, Sébastiani was despatched to Constantinople, where he arrived on 9 August. At the same time, relations between Turkey and Russia, supported by England, became strained. Nevertheless, the fact remained that like the army in Italy, Marmont's Second Corps was immobilised in Dalmatia.

The war of 1805 inordinately extended the range of Napoleon's enterprises, and so made the French Empire merely the core of the 'Grand Empire' which itself began to evolve through legislative acts. The emperor regarded his new creatures as constituting 'federated states or a veritable French Empire'. Although he made free reference to historical examples, the organisation he adopted was original. At the top were the kings and princes, hereditary and sovereign in their domains: Joseph, Louis and Murat, who was made grand duke of Berg on 15 March. Next came the vassal princes, also sovereign and even entailed, but whose domains, held in 'fief', were subject to a fresh investiture at each change of ownership: such were Elisa in Piombino, and Berthier who became prince of Neuchâtel. Below them were princes with neither an army nor money: Talleyrand, prince of Benevento, and Bernadotte, prince of Ponte Corvo – two domains which had hitherto been disputed by the pope and the king of Naples. At the bottom were the simple fiefs, which carried with them no sovereign powers: six duchies which Napoleon reserved to himself in the kingdom of Naples, and twelve which were created in Venetia, all of which were destined for deserving Frenchmen.

Nor was this all. The princes and kings, while theoretically independent, were vassal to Napoleon as persons, even though their states were not fiefs. In effect, they formed part of the imperial family which the Constitution of Year XII had made subject to a special law promulgated on 31 March 1806. The statute created a special civil status for the family; it conferred upon the head of the Empire wardship over its minors and patriarchal power over its adults, including the power to allow or disallow their marriages and the power to imprison them. Moreover, the princes, even the sovereign ones, remained grand dignitaries of the Empire. Thus the edifice was founded, in good part, on the notion of a family pact, at once recalling the traditional network of Bourbon alliances and reflecting Napoleon's attachment to his clan. Family ties were for him the strongest ones. He also extended this policy to the allied states. On 15 January Eugène de Beauharnais finally married Augusta, princess of Bavaria, and was at the same time adopted by the emperor, although he was excluded from all rights to the French succession. Stéphanie de Beauharnais, Josephine's niece, was also adopted, and given in marriage to the heir of the grand duke of Baden. Berthier had to abandon his liaison with Madame de Visconti and marry a widowed Bavarian princess. The following year, Jérôme married into the house of Württemberg. This same motif, added to Napoleon's anxiety to provide a direct heir for the Empire, now suggested the feasibility of a second marriage for the emperor.

The Grand Empire, tailored to fit the occasion, was nonetheless a first manifestation of the Roman imperial idea which was implicit in the title which Napoleon assumed in 1804. He now no longer hesitated to pose publicly as the restorer of the Western Roman Empire and to lay claim to the prerogatives of Charlemagne, his 'illustrious predecessor'. It stands to reason that these historically rooted pretensions seriously undermined the position of the papacy. Napoleon's letter of 13 February 1806 reminded Pius that although Charlemagne had been consecrated Roman emperor by the pope, he had nevertheless regarded the latter as his protégé, and that he had established the temporal dominions of the Church only as an integral part of his own empire. So too Napoleon: 'Your holiness is sovereign of Rome, but I am its emperor,' he wrote to Pius VII. This admirable formula, truly imperial in its brevity, already indicated that the Grand Empire, even before it had been established, would be but the beginning of a world domination.

## THE BREAK WITH PRUSSIA (1806)

Such a policy could scarcely be expected to bring about a general peace. However, circumstances left room for discussion with the two Coalition powers who remained in the field. In England, Pitt died heartbroken on 23 January 1806, immediately after the disastrous failure of his policy and the sharp attacks of the opposition. The Whigs once again demanded that the Continent be left to its own fate, and they argued that peace was the only means of putting an end to French expansion. 'If we cannot cut down her enormous power,' Fox would say, 'it would at least be something to arrest her progress.'* In other words, he proposed to try Addington's experiment again, even though nothing about the present situation recalled the crisis of 1801. While not all of his friends may have shared his illusions, they were disposed to negotiate, if only to justify their accession to power. To form a ministry, the king called upon Grenville, who insisted on Fox's participation: this time he succeeded in bringing Fox in, giving him the Foreign Office. The Whig administration – Grenville, Lord Petty, the son of Shelburne, Lord Howick, the son of Lord Grey, and Erskine – was joined by Addington, now Lord Sidmouth, to form the 'Ministry of All the Talents'.

The domestic policy of the Whigs inflamed the British public: martial law in Ireland was lifted and Catholic emancipation was once again brought under consideration. No one, however, objected to an attempt to make peace. The war party was frustrated by the attitude of Prussia, who had accepted a French alliance in order to acquire Hanover. When England declared war on 11 May and placed the German North Sea coast

* Here again, the translator was unable to locate the source for this quotation in order to render it in its original (English) version. TRANSLATOR.

under blockade, Prussia closed her Baltic ports to British trade to the alarm of the mercantile establishment. As early as the end of February Fox had reopened channels with Paris by warning of a plot on the emperor's life; Talleyrand in turn communicated to him Napoleon's desire to explore negotiations for peace. Lord Yarmouth, who had been interned in France and who was the intimate of several highly placed persons, set out for London and returned to France on 17 June with full power to act as intermediary. Fox refused to negotiate any agreement unless Russia were made a party to it, nor would he accept the Treaty of Amiens as the basis for a settlement. He insisted on the rule of *uti possidetis* with the reservation that Hanover would have to be restored to England. Napoleon did not object in principle, thinking that some compensation could be found for Prussia; nevertheless, he kept Prussia ignorant of these developments, knowing she would certainly protest.

Meanwhile, Alexander also decided to negotiate. The defection of Prussia had increased the influence of Czartoryski, who in January advised the tsar to abandon his vast projects of arbitration for Europe and to concentrate instead on the interests of Russia, that is to say, on the East. He regarded the situation in the Ottoman Empire as very promising. There, the Janissaries had been restless ever since March 1805 when Selim III had officially established his new standing army (the Nizam Djedid). At the same time, the Rumelian pashas, fearing for their authority, had taken up arms with the connivance of Ypsilanti and the other *hospodars* who were in league with Russia. The Serbs were in open revolt. In March 1804 Nenadovich, who had been negotiating with Austria, was put to death, and his compatriots rose up under the leadership of Karageorge. Supported by the tsar, they demanded independence. In the summer of 1805 they elected a popular assembly (*Skupshtina*) which created a senate and petitioned the sultan. The Turks were unable to subdue them. Czartoryski realised that a victorious Napoleon would be sure to thwart Russia's foreign ambitions, and the proof was not long in coming. Selim refused to renew his treaty of 1798 with Russia, and he also refused to negotiate a trade agreement. In June he revoked the *berats*, by which the powers were authorised to grant the immunities and privileges of their own citizenship to Ottoman subjects. Ever since May 1806 a Russian army had been concentrating on the Dniester, and the English ambassador to Constantinople, Arbuthnot, urged that a squadron be sent. Czartoryski counselled keeping on the defensive in the West and entering into talks with Napoleon: if the latter were willing to give Russia a free hand in the East, a deal could be concluded and Russia could proceed to dismember Turkey. He broached the subject with Lesseps, the French consul, and on 12 May informed him of the departure for Paris of the Russian ambassador, Oubril, who journeyed by way of Vienna. After all, Napoleon's policy in Italy and Germany portended the renewal of a war against Austria in which she might disappear altogether: Oubril always maintained afterwards that he had received instructions to negotiate peace at any price in order to save Austria.

When Napoleon learned of this mission, he changed his attitude. He had been treating with Fox in the hope of isolating Russia; but the opposite alternative interested him much more, since of the two England was the more difficult to defeat. He immediately demanded that Sicily be surrendered to Joseph, adding that Ferdinand IV could be compensated elsewhere. Yarmouth expostulated and the talks were broken off. When Oubril arrived on 6 July, he was at once cajoled, menaced and subjected to unremitting pressure: Russia, he was told, could keep the Ionian Islands and enjoy free passage of the Straits; Albania and Dalmatia might even be given to Ferdinand to create a buffer state friendly to Russia between France and Turkey. Yarmouth did not reject this proposal when he was informed of it, although he had hitherto refused to discuss the question of Sicily. The creation of the Confederation of the Rhine brought Oubril to a decision; convinced that Austria would otherwise be lost, he signed a treaty of peace on 20 July. At the last minute, Napoleon substituted the Balearic Islands for the Balkan provinces which had been destined for Ferdinand. Russia obtained at least a consolidation of her position: although she lost Cattaro, she held on to the Ionian Islands, saved Ragusa and placed Turkey under the mutual protection of herself and France; in addition, Napoleon undertook to evacuate Germany. Alexander would not obtain so much at Tilsit!

For a moment the English were staggered. 'A mortifying agreement,' admitted Fox, finding England abandoned once again. Yarmouth, following in Oubril's steps, submitted a peace proposal which Napoleon returned on 6 August without making any essential changes: England would keep Malta and the Cape, regain Hanover, accept the Balearics for Ferdinand and recognise Joseph, thereby implicitly giving up Sicily. It seemed that Napoleon's game at separate negotiations was about to succeed. Writing to Joseph, he already saw himself as master of the

Mediterranean, 'the chief and constant objective of my policy' – at least for the time being, for he had many other plans in mind.

Suddenly the wind changed. There were many reasons to doubt that Alexander would ratify the treaty for he had just dismissed Czartoryski, whose policies exasperated the anglophile nobility of Russia which was passionately hostile to Napoleon. On 9 July the tsar appointed a new foreign minister, Baron Budberg, a Baltic German who was interested only in continental affairs and who was very sympathetic to Prussia. England could only expect to profit from this. Moreover, Fox had changed his attitude, and his colleagues condemned the Yarmouth agreement even more severely than he. Lauderdale, a new negotiator but one still quite friendly to France, was sent to Paris to demand once again the principle of *uti possidetis*, while nevertheless allowing for the surrender of Sicily provided that a less contemptible compensation could be found for Ferdinand. Napoleon refused to reopen the discussion, counting on Russian ratification to make the English back down. But now the attitude of Frederick William III caused the tsar to refuse to ratify the treaty. Perhaps his only reason for having negotiated with France had been to lure Prussia.

There can be no doubt that the emperor was far from wanting a break with Prussia; when it came he was profoundly disappointed and vexed. The Prussian alliance, which had long been sought by the revolutionary governments and by himself, rendered Austria and Russia powerless and kept Germany closed to the English. Therefore his attitude towards Prussia was entirely benevolent, provided that she, like Spain, entered into his 'system', that is to say, became a vassal state, and Napoleon made this perfectly clear to her. The king had stuck to the unfortunate idea, despite the warnings of Haugwitz, of not accepting the Treaty of Schönbrunn on its original terms; he did not want to annex Hanover before a general peace had been concluded, but only wished to occupy it in order to avoid a break with England. As his appetite grew, he claimed that it was his right to keep Ansbach and to obtain the Hanseatic towns as well. When Napoleon received these handsome proposals on 1 February 1806, he had just been apprised of Pitt's death. He declared that Prussia's counter-proposition annulled the Treaty of Schönbrunn, and on 15 February he made Haugwitz sign a substitute treaty which compelled Prussia to annex Hanover immediately and close its ports to the English, surrender not only Ansbach and Neuchâtel but also that part of the duchy of Cleves which lay east of the Rhine and which now was joined to the duchy of Berg, and permit the French to install a garrison at Wesel. Frederick William III capitulated; it was a terrible chastisement which he never forgave.

The Prussian war party would prove even more vindictive. Momentarily disheartened after Austerlitz, it soon grew in strength. Still, there remained in Prussia admirers of Napoleon up to the very end: Bülow, brother of the future hero of the war of liberation, who wrote a book on the campaign of 1805 in which he treated Prussia very harshly; Buchholtz, who, in his *New Leviathan*, turned Hobbes's philosophy into a eulogy of imperial despotism; and in the army there was Massenbach, a Württemberger. The court, on the other hand, was in favour of war. Queen Louise, comparing Napoleon to her dear Alexander, was full of proposals against the 'monster', the 'scum from hell'. These sentiments were echoed by the king's first cousin Louis Ferdinand, by his sister, who was married to Prince Radziwill, by Countess Voss, and by her sister, Madame Berg. Schleiermacher, Alexander Humboldt, Johann Müller and Merkel had all turned against France. In the military there were many like Phüll, Scharnhorst and Blücher who pressed for action. Hardenberg supported them, and in April Stein asked the king to dismiss Lombard and Beyme, his favourite advisers; this request was again put forward by the royal princes on the eve of the war. Frederick William took offence; however, he was so concerned that he made secret efforts to win back the friendship of the tsar. He despatched Brunswick to assure Alexander that despite Prussia's alliance with Napoleon she would never make war on Russia; when, on 23 June, he learned of Oubril's mission, he repeated these assurances in writing. Hardenberg, for his part, negotiated secretly with the Russian ambassador Alopeus, and concluded an agreement along those lines, which the tsar signed on 24 July.

The creation of the Confederation of the Rhine added to the discontent. True, the emperor maintained that nothing prevented Prussia from forming that Confederation of the North which had been her great dream between 1795 and 1801. But he forbade the Hanseatic towns to become members and he told Saxony that she was entirely free to refuse her adherence. The elector of Hesse, too, did not dare to join. To make matters worse, early in August Yarmouth disclosed to the Prussian ambassador in Paris, Lucchesini, that Hanover would be taken away from Prussia. A false rumour finally brought Frederick William to a decision: Blücher reported a concentration of French troops on the Rhine, and a similar alarm was heard from Franconia. The king believed that Hanover was in danger, and without verifying the facts, mobilised on 9 August after notifying the tsar. During the whole month of August he was in agony, not knowing what the result of Oubril's treaty would be. Actually, Frederick William's own resolution had rendered the Oubril treaty nugatory, and the tsar refused to ratify it. Informed of this fact, the king wrote to Alexander on 6 September, 'I have no other choice but to go to war.'

Just as in 1805, Napoleon would not believe what was happening up to the very last moment. On 17 August he even gave the order to prepare the return of the Grande Armée to France now that the German question had been settled with the abdication of Francis. As late as 26 August he called the Prussian mobilisation 'ridiculous', but when it was shortly followed by Alexander's refusal to ratify the Oubril treaty, he saw the light. Now he was convinced that a new Coalition was being formed. On 5 September he issued his first orders; general instructions did not appear until the nineteenth. After Fox's death on 13 September, his colleagues, confident of Russia and Prussia and much heartened by the fall of Buenos Aires, increased their demands. On 26 September they insisted on obtaining Dalmatia for Ferdinand IV; Napoleon put an end to the negotiations by his refusal on 5 October. He was by then already at Bamberg, *en route* to annihilate Prussia. He improvised this campaign as airily as the preceding one. When he arrived in Franconia, his orders had not even been carried out, and he dismissed the intendant-general Villemanzy, replacing him with Daru. The soldiers set out lacking greatcoats, most of them without a second pair of shoes, and with only a few days' supply of bread and biscuit. Nevertheless, the campaign was so lightning-like that this time they suffered much less. The Prussian ultimatum demanding the retreat of the French troops to the west bank of the Rhine was submitted on 1 October; Napoleon received it in Bamberg on the seventh; by the fourteenth the Prussian army no longer existed.

### JENA AND AUERSTÄDT. THE WINTER CAMPAIGN (1806–1807)

Prussia had full confidence in her army, and all Europe shared it. Even in France, there were many who did not consider Napoleon's fame enduring until after the destruction of the army of Frederick the Great. It did not appear to have changed since its days of glory. Although recruitment of foreigners had become nearly impossible ever since the Low Countries and Germany had dried up as sources of manpower, there were still at least eighty thousand of them in the ranks. The rest of the army was made up of 'cantonists' drafted from the peasantry; the nobility and the bourgeoisie were exempt from service, while the Junkers furnished most of the officers. This army, which had no national character, was admirably prepared by drill for combat in linear formation and in the open field. The infantry was made up of battalions of fusiliers, but they were not trained to fight as skirmishers. The cavalry was still adequate, but the artillery's equipment was worthless. The engineers and medical services were almost non-existent, and notions of conducting a war had made scarcely any progress at all. The regiments did not have divisions. Marches were planned according to the location of military storehouses, and the army was always encumbered by an enormous baggage train. No one realised that this army, when faced with the soldiers of the Revolution, would be singularly outdated, or that its greatest shortcoming was that it was no longer used to fighting. The captains in charge of the companies earned money in peacetime, thanks to extended leaves, and they regarded a campaign as a calamity. The generals were too old and lacked resolution. So the troops, although brave and well trained, were defeated by want of good leadership.

If the Prussians had not been urged on by their own vainglory to cross the Elbe, they would have been able to avoid disaster by remaining behind the river and waiting for the Russians. For his part, Alexander was much more tardy than he had been in 1805 because he was keeping an eye on Turkey. On 24 August Selim had unilaterally deposed the *hospodars*; frightened by an ultimatum, he restored them on 15 October. At the same time, Michelson's army was ordered to occupy the principalities. Consequently, not only were the preparations for war against Napoleon slackened; the Russians would also be fighting on two fronts.

The Prussians converged on Thuringia in three main columns: the duke of Brunswick and the king, with sixty thousand men; Hohenlohe's army of fifty thousand, which went through Dresden in order to mobilise the Saxons; and Rüchel with thirty thousand Hanoverians who passed through Hesse. Brunswick, who had been defeated at Valmy, had little authority over his subordinates and was unable to effect a concentration, screen his army or even impose a plan of campaign. He wanted to advance on the Main in order to threaten the French line of operations, whereas

Hohenlohe advised meeting the French head on by marching through the Franconian Forest. Ultimately, Hohenlohe, leaving two corps at the River Saale, moved towards Jena thus drawing closer to Brunswick's army, but he never did reach him. The Prussians were attacked before they could unite their forces.

Napoleon left Louis and Mortier to guard the Rhine; his German allies held the rear. Around 25 September his main army was concentrated in the vicinity of Nuremberg behind a cover consisting of the length of the Main and the Franconian Forest. There were six corps in all plus the cavalry reserve and the Guard, about 130,000 men. It was imperative for Napoleon to defeat the Prussians before the arrival of the Russian army, and he feared lest they were holding themselves behind the Elbe. When he heard that they were on the march, he assumed that they were heading for Mainz or Würzburg: in that case, he would have engaged them on the Main, and turning their left would have rolled them back towards the Rhine. Seeing that they remained stationary, he crossed the Franconian Forest in three columns between 7–9 October in order to cut them off from the Elbe. Ney and Soult debouched into the village of Hof without encountering resistance; Murat, Bernadotte, Davout and the Guard hustled Tauenzien's division out of Schleiz; and on the left, Lannes and Augereau fell on Saalfeld, where Prince Louis Ferdinand was defeated and killed on the tenth. Next the army advanced north, then wheeled westward, while Murat dashed towards Leipzig where he had heard the Prussians were beating a retreat. The Saale was fordable at two main points: Kösen and Kahla. Davout took possession of the first; Lannes and Augereau seized the second and then, moving up the left bank of the river, reached Jena and occupied the Landgrafenberg, a height overlooking the plain where Hohenlohe was camped. Thinking that the bulk of the Prussian army was there, Napoleon ordered Ney, Soult, the Guard and part of the cavalry to mass on the height; the rest of the army, under Bernadotte, was summoned back from Naumburg to Dornburg with the order to march towards the roar of the cannon fire, in case of need.

In fact, Brunswick and the king were advancing on Kösen with seventy thousand men, and Hohenlohe had but fifty thousand men who were not even concentrated. Against the latter, Napoleon engaged fifty-six thousand on 14 October. Lannes and Soult, rushing down from the Landgrafenberg, crumpled the enemy's first line, attacked the second and turned its left flank. Augereau, delayed by bad terrain, finally succeeded in threatening the Prussian right which, after a sharp resistance, took flight. Rüchel, who hastened with reinforcements, reached the battlefield only to suffer the same fate. All this time, Davout, with twenty-six thousand men, was taking the weight of the main Prussian army near Auerstädt; Brunswick was mortally wounded, and his troops, retreating in disorder, collided with the streams of fugitives from Jena who engulfed them in the rout. As for Bernadotte, although he did indeed cross the Saale at Dornburg, his customary ill will kept him at a distance from the two battlefields. The Prussians lost twenty-seven thousand killed and wounded, eighteen thousand prisoners and nearly all their field guns.

Murat, Ney and Soult pursued the remnants of the enemy through the Harz country, capturing twenty thousand prisoners, but letting several corps escape. The main body of the French army marched from Leipzig straight to Berlin, which Davout was the first to enter on the twenty-fifth; from there, he and Augereau crossed the Oder, where they forced the capitulation of the fortress of Küstrin. The pursuit now became more methodical, and Hohenlohe, cut off from Stettin, surrendered at Prenzlau on the twenty-eighth. Blücher managed to reach Lübeck where he was captured on 6 November. All that remained now of the Prussian army was Lestocq's corps in East Prussia. Fortresses as far as the Vistula opened their gates, all except the Silesian towns, and Colberg, defended by Gneisenau. The populace made no resistance, and the civil functionaries took an oath to Napoleon. The conquered territory was rapidly organised and subjected to war contributions amounting to 160 million francs, not to mention requisitions which were imposed to procure supplies of all kinds which the army utterly lacked.

Napoleon immediately began to pluck the fruits of his victory. As early as 27 September the grand duke of Würzburg had become a member of the Confederation of the Rhine; on 11 December the elector Frederick of Saxony also joined and received the title of king; on the fifteenth the Saxon dukes, and ultimately the other princes of central Germany followed suit. Hesse-Cassel and the duchy of Brunswick were forfeited, along with Fulda, whose ruler, the prince of Orange, had fought on the Prussian side. Frederick William III himself seemed willing to accept vassalage in order to save his throne. Lucchesini and Zastrow negotiated a peace treaty with Duroc, which ceded all Prussian territories west of the Elbe except Altmark and closed the Baltic ports to the English.

Signed on 30 October, the treaty was ratified by the king on 6 November.

But the situation had already changed. When Napoleon entered Berlin on 25 October, he had discovered in the archives the evidence of an entente between Prussia and Russia, and he spread the scandal about the relations between the Prussian queen and the Russian tsar. It was soon clear that Russia would come to the aid of Prussia: an outburst of military wrath roused the Petersburg nobility, and the Orthodox Church excommunicated Napoleon. On 9 November the emperor decided to postpone the signing of the peace treaty, and he substituted an armistice in which he demanded the Vistula–Bug line; the king's troops were to be quartered in East Prussia, whence they would drive out the Russians if necessary. In addition, he declared that he would not evacuate the realm until a general peace had been concluded, including restitution of the French colonies and a guarantee of Turkey's integrity. On 21 November these intentions were publicly announced in a message to the Senate. In effect, Prussia was made a hostage, and it seemed likely that her captivity would endure for some time.

As the army advanced it sequestered English goods systematically; with the occupation of the Hanseatic towns, Germany was now closed to British trade. In the famous Berlin decree of 21 November, Napoleon declared the British Isles 'in a state of blockade', that is, he turned against them their own weapon, the paper blockade. Consequently, no vessel whose voyage originated in Great Britain or her colonies would any longer be admitted to the ports of the Empire.

The continental blockade has been called 'the *raison d'être* of the Grand Empire'. This is simply not so; it spread naturally as a result of imperial conquest. Since Napoleon did not control the sea, the resounding Berlin decree in itself added nothing to the already existing prohibitions on English goods. The new and significant circumstance was that since the neutrals were implicitly affected the blockade would lose that essentially protectionist character which Napoleon had given it when he came to power. Henceforth, it became an offensive weapon. By an abrupt and decisive turnabout, victory led Napoleon back to the policy of the Directory in 1798. The desire to unite the Continent against England had been formulated, thereby giving the 'imperial' and 'Roman' idea a real meaning in contemporary politics. 'I intend to conquer the seas with my land armies,' wrote Napoleon. This is why the Berlin decree marks an important turning point.

The Prussian negotiators, not seeing so far, accepted the armistice on 16 November, but the king rejected it and found himself bound to the Coalition against his will. Not waiting to hear the king's decision, Napoleon advanced his army to the Vistula: it reached Warsaw on 27 November. The emperor was obliged, however, to stay in Berlin for a month to see to the reinforcement and re-equipment of his soldiers. Mortier was sent to occupy Swedish Pomerania and to blockade Stralsund. Jérôme, who had shown repentance and had allowed his American marriage to be annulled, went with his South German contingents to besiege the Silesian fortresses. The class of 1806 conscripts departed for the front. Meanwhile, the march to the Vistula had opened the Polish question. As the French advanced, the Poles rose and drove out the Prussian administrators. The movement principally attracted the bourgeoisie and the nobility, yet they were not of one mind: there was a Prussian party headed by Prince Radziwill – for more than one nobleman made use of the mortgage banks founded on the Prussian example – and above all, there was a Russian party. Czartoryski had once again advised Alexander to forestall Napoleon by proclaiming himself king of Poland, and he was supported by Niemcewicz and by Archbishop Siestrzencewicz who inveighed against 'the perjured conscience of Bonaparte'. Poniatowski himself hesitated until the end of December. The Polish grandees feared reprisals in case of defeat; scarcely less did they fear a French victory which would emancipate their serfs.

Napoleon, in any event, compelled to fight the Russians, could not refuse the help offered. As early as 20 September he had authorised General Zajonczek to form a legion from the Poles who would desert the Prussian ranks. After Jena, Generals Dombrowski and Wybicki were entrusted with the formation of three legions in the insurgent territories. Kosciuszko, also summoned, demanded guarantees. Napoleon had no intention of undertaking a restoration of Poland, a project which would have enraged the tsar and incited Austrian intervention. Kosciuszko blamed the emperor's silence on his egoism: 'He thinks of nothing but himself. He detests every great nation, and he detests even more the spirit of independence. He is a tyrant.' A deeply penetrating judgement, but a misinterpretation of the emperor's reserve: he was not averse to reviving the Polish state in order to make a vassal of it if such a project were possible. Would the Poles be capable of governing themselves? He doubted it, and some of his marshals denied it outright. Moreover, it was too soon now. Nor did he make any promises, despite the persistent demands of Countess Walewska, who passed the winter with him and whom he loved passionately. All he did was create a temporary administration at Posen [Poznań] for Dombrowski, then, in Warsaw on 14 January 1807, a temporary commission which elected Malachowski president. Under the supervision of Talleyrand and Maret, the commission entrusted the administration to five directors, undertook the supplying of Napoleon's army and the formation of a national Polish army, and began to reorganise the judicial system on the French model.

Bennigsen and his thirty-five thousand men had retreated before the Grande Armée to a position between the Narew and Wkra Rivers to await the arrival of Buxhöwden's forty thousand reinforcements. At the end of December Napoleon began an offensive against Bennigsen. With Davout, he forced a crossing of the Wkra at Czarnowo on the twenty-third, and he ordered Lannes to advance on Pultusk. The rest of the army, coming from Thorn and Plock, were to roll up the enemy centre and right and envelop them. But the weather was dreadful and the broken roads slowed up the advance. Bernadotte fell behind, and Ney strayed in pursuit of the Prussians. Napoleon strove to re-establish order, but in vain. On 26 December the French, in Napoleon's absence, launched a disorderly attack at Pultusk and Golymin; the Russians held firmly and were able to withdraw. The emperor decided that it would be impossible to pursue them into the forests and swamps with soldiers who lacked greatcoats, shoes and food, and he established his winter quarters from the banks of the Passarge to Warsaw.

A line so far extended invited surprise. Bennigsen, who was situated behind the forests, now moved northward. At the end of January he crossed the Passarge, intending an offensive against Bernadotte, who retreated on Thorn. Meanwhile, Lestocq advanced as far as Graudenz. But Napoleon was already gathering his other forces, and marched north to cut the enemy's line of retreat. Bennigsen, informed of Napoleon's plans by the capture of a courier, was able to hold out on the Passarge long enough to make his escape. Hotly pursued, he accepted battle at Preussisch-Eylau in order to save Königsberg. On 8 February 1807 Napoleon attacked him, even though he had only sixty thousand men against the enemy's eighty thousand. First he turned the Russian left, and then attacked the centre, but Augereau's corps strayed in the midst of a blinding snowstorm and suffered very heavy losses. Bennigsen then took the initiative, and was repulsed only with great difficulty by repeated cavalry charges. The arrival of Lestocq made matters worse, but at last Ney, who was pursuing him, reached the battlefield at seven o'clock in the evening and turned Bennigsen's right; Bennigsen then ordered a retreat. Twenty-five thousand Russians and eighteen thousand French had fallen. Napoleon called off any attempt at pursuit and led his army back behind the Passarge. He set up his own headquarters at Osterode, then, on 1 April, at the castle of Finckenstein.

He had won a bloody battle, but his plans had again proved abortive and he would be compelled to fight a summer campaign. Once again he was in a precarious situation, so very far from France where the war was causing an industrial crisis which, in turn, necessitated large increases in government orders and loans in order to avoid the spread of unemployment. Meanwhile, Austria might enter the fray, and England could contemplate undertaking action on the Continent. Eylau caused a sensation throughout Europe, and reinforced the impression already left by the Polish campaign. It was said that Napoleon's strategy and the resources of the Grande Armée were ill adapted to the topography and climate of East-Central Europe. The Breidt company had to confess its inability to guarantee transports; the countryside could not provide the needed supplies; and the troops melted away. Of those who remained only a quarter could be brought into battle – the rest were needed to guard the rear. A prodigious effort, both military and political, would be necessary to triumph over Russia.

## THE SUMMER CAMPAIGN AND THE TREATIES OF TILSIT (1807)

The easiest task was to procure soldiers. From September to November 1806 the reserves and half of that year's draft contingent were brought to the Rhine, whence Kellermann sent them to the front, unit by unit. The rest of the contingent was used up in the same way between October and December. Just as he departed for war, Napoleon called up the contingent of 1807 ahead of its time; it too was sent to the front during the course of the winter. Finally, in April 1807, the class of 1808 was summoned, and scarcely had it arrived in camp when it was sped off, half-outfitted and totally lacking in military instruction. The behaviour of the new conscripts becoming difficult, they were for the first time mingled with soldiers of fortune in 'provisional regiments'. Altogether, the Empire called up 110,000 men; the allies – Germans, Dutch, Poles, Spaniards under the marquis de La Romana, and the Army of Italy – furnished 112,000, an increase of seventy-two thousand over the previous year. On 15 July 1807 the Grande Armée in Germany numbered 410,000 men twice as many as in September 1806. Around one hundred thousand men fought in the Friedland campaign. In addition, the emperor kept a force of 120,000 in Italy to watch over Austria and Sicily, and another 110,000 (some of them National Guardsmen) for coastal defence.

The organisation of transport and supply proved considerably more difficult. The failure of the private companies led the emperor to militarise these services, in principle at least. The artillery train was expanded, baggage wagon battalions were created, and the general victualling of the army was placed under state control and entrusted to Maret's brother. Thus the war of 1807 resulted in an extension of the government's activities. But it would be wrong to conclude that the features of Napoleonic warfare were much changed by all this. The new organisations were never adequate, and most of the wagons were still procured along the line of march. The director of the food supply was scarcely ever concerned with the army while it was fighting, otherwise the army would have ceased to live off the land and campaigning would have been even more expensive. During the campaign of 1807 Napoleon took only thirty thousand horses from France to replenish his remount depots at Potsdam and Kulm; it was much more economical and expedient to requisition everything on the spot. Workshops were set up in Germany, and arrangements were made with local bargemen and carters. For the most part, the difficulties remained insurmountable. It did little good to keep production in high gear when the goods could not be transported. The combatants, crammed in the area east of the Vistula – the bleakest spot in Europe – obtained just enough supplies to keep from starving. Up to July the French received only twenty-six thousand greatcoats, fifty-two thousand jackets and as many trousers; an enormous stock of shoes remained unused in the rear. The Russians as usual suffered cruelly, and for the same reasons. Nor did their allies fare any better, even though they fought on native soil: wretched East Prussia was ravaged and despoiled from end to end.

On the diplomatic front, Napoleon conducted negotiations while attempting to sow discord among the Coalition powers and to keep Austria neutral. Frederick William's resolute posture was short-lived. On 16 December he offered the portfolio of foreign affairs to Stein, but the latter refused (to the king's great displeasure) because Frederick William would not dismiss his intimate non-ministerial advisers and appoint a responsible cabinet. Zastrow, who was left in charge of foreign affairs, was very eager to treat with France, for he feared the loss of his estates. Since Napoleon had declared after the failure of the armistice of 16 November that he would not negotiate except on the issue of a general peace, the king let himself be persuaded to ask for the consent of Russia and England, which they granted, provided that France first be obliged to state her conditions. During this time Napoleon, because of his difficulties, was once again entertaining the possibility of that separate peace with Prussia whose breakdown he had previously provoked. He made overtures at the end of January, and after Eylau sent Bertrand to Königsberg to confirm them. In return, the king despatched Colonel Kleist to Finckenstein. While insisting upon his own terms, Napoleon admitted the possibility of a congress, and when in April Prussia submitted an official proposal for one,* he accepted it. On 9 June the king informed England; by that time, the campaign was almost over.

Napoleon rejoiced at the annoyance these negotiations caused Alexander. On 2 April the tsar journeyed to Memel and persuaded the king to replace Zastrow with Hardenberg; on 23 April he induced him to sign the Convention of Bartenstein, strengthening their alliance. Up until then, the Prussians had not lost hope, for the Russians were making great efforts to save Danzig. However, the fall of that fortified town and the plaints of the Junkers against the excesses of the allied troops led to cooler relations. And so Alexander began to formulate ever so dimly the ideas which would ultimately lead him to Tilsit.

Austria could favour only peace. Stadion, the new chancellor, burned with desire to attack Napoleon, but he judged the French still too formidable, and he was apprehensive about Prussian and Russian ambitions. So Austria armed herself and awaited events. Ever since October Napoleon had been cajoling and menacing by turns, proposing an alliance without offering anything but an exchange of Galicia for Silesia, and insisting that Austria cease arming. Stadion was studiously evasive; however, in January he sent Baron Vincent to Warsaw to talk with Talleyrand, who easily caught the baron in his nets. It was more difficult to resist, and still not

* The author probably meant *Austria*, not *Prussia*. See below. TRANSLATOR.

annoy, the other negotiators; the Russian ambassador Razumovski, joined by Pozzo di Borgo, an émigré in the service of the tsar, and the English representative Adair. The project of a peace conference deftly rescued Austria from her embarrassment. On 18 March Stadion made an offer to mediate which upon Talleyrand's approval became official on 7 April.* When all sides had accepted the mediation, Napoleon suddenly fell silent, summoned Talleyrand to his side and left Vincent without any word for the whole month of May. In this manner he was able to reopen the campaign before Austria had taken a position in the mediation.

Alexander found Austria's action unforgivable, but even more exasperating to him was England's attitude. After Fox's death, his colleagues had remained in power, Lord Howick moving to the Foreign Office. English policy became more and more insular. After the fall of Buenos Aires, the public's only concern was with South America; the forces sent there, and the expeditions to the Levant, tied up the available regiments, so that the tsar called in vain for a continental diversion. Sicily would have offered an excellent base against Italy, but General Fox, who was the butt of Maria Carolina's hostility and who received no reinforcements, declared himself unable to undertake any action. Nor was the British government any the less sparing of money, and it refused to guarantee a Russian loan.

England had lost her touch in the field of diplomacy. She demanded the evacuation of Hanover as a condition of peace with Prussia, which was concluded only on 28 January; even afterwards she snubbed Prussia. Her ambassadors at Königsberg and St Petersburg, Hely-Hutchinson and Douglas, lacked both amiability and adroitness, and revealed themselves as warm admirers of Napoleon. Finally, the 'Ministry of All the Talents' became seriously compromised in February over the Catholic question; the king at last consented to the abolition of the Test Act, but he still refused to admit papists to higher ranks, especially in the Navy. On 7 March the cabinet resigned; the Tories returned to power and called for a general election with the slogan of 'No Popery'. The government was only nominally headed by the duke of Portland; the principal ministries fell to Pitt's disciples who would resume their dead leader's continental policy and display the same dauntless determination in its pursuit: Perceval, son of Lord Egmont, who became chancellor of the exchequer; Bathurst, who took over the Board of Trade; and above all Canning, the

* See previous note. TRANSLATOR.

foreign secretary, and Castlereagh, the secretary for war. However, since little was known about these men, their rise made hardly any impression. Canning delayed naming a new ambassador to Russia, Leveson-Gower, until 16 May. He remained distrustful of Prussia, suspecting her of wanting to recover Hanover in order to dominate North Germany; moreover, he felt that there was nothing to be gained by substituting Prussian militarism there for that of Napoleon. His principal activity was to badger Gustavus IV of Sweden into breaking the armistice he had concluded with France on 18 April. Among the Coalition powers, irritation with England stood at its peak as the summer campaign began.

While Alexander was waiting in vain for the English to intervene, he found himself obliged to divert part of his army to continue the struggle against Persia and to maintain the war inopportunely begun against Turkey. Napoleon seized this chance to reach an understanding with the tsar's enemies, and so the European conflict was extended to the Levant, just as in the days of the Directory. Russia's General Michelson had occupied Moldavia and taken Bucharest without firing a shot, but part of his army was recalled and he had to come to a halt. Although Selim III had been encouraged by Napoleon to declare war on Russia, the pasha of Ruschuk, Mustapha Bairakdar ('the flag-bearer'), who commanded the Danubian army, remained inactive until the end of May. The uprising of the Serbs thus took on great significance, especially since they captured Belgrade on 12 December. The Turks granted the Serbs all their demands, but now the influence of the Russian agents prevailed. In March the pasha Suleiman and his troops were massacred while retreating, and the Serbian popular assembly voted an alliance with the tsar. Napoleon did his best to help the sultan; he made peace with Ali Pasha of Janina, and induced him to attack the Ionian Islands of Corfu and Santa Maura [Levkas]; Marmont sent cannons and artillery instructors to the pasha of Bosnia; one officer went to Bairakdar at Ruschuk, another to the successor of the just deceased Pasvan Oglu at Vidin. The emperor even offered to send the Army of Dalmatia to the Danube. But Muslim opinion was affronted by this news, and Selim himself refused to tie himself too closely to France; the embassy which reached Napoleon in March concluded no alliance. At the end of May Russia invaded Little Wallachia in order to aid the Serbs, who were advancing towards the Danube by way of the Krajina; they had to retreat precipitately, for Bairakdar at last crossed the river. He did not get far, however. On 25 May the Janissaries revolted in

Constantinople, massacred the ministers, abolished the Nizam Djedid and deposed Selim in favour of his cousin Mustapha IV. Bairakdar retreated, and the Russians were able to join up with the Serbs under the walls of Negotino on 17 July.

The English came to the rescue of the Russians in the East, intending, however, to work for their own interests. After a fruitless appeal to the sultan to renew the alliance of 1798 and to declare war on France, a squadron under Admiral Duckworth forced the passage of the Dardanelles on 19 February and appeared the next day at Constantinople. Selim's envoys played for time in order to allow Sébastiani to organise the defence of the city; then, on the twenty-sixth, the mask was thrown off. Duckworth had to beat a hasty retreat through the Straits on 3 March, with considerable losses. England did not pursue the matter, not caring in the last analysis to insist on a policy which was of advantage primarily to Russia; instead, the British government decided that it would be preferable to reoccupy Egypt. There, ever since the departure of the French, the sultan had not succeeded in re-establishing his authority. The Mamelukes had defeated Khosrev Pasha, and the Albanian troops, led by their chief Mehemet Ali, had asserted their independence. The initiative passed to Mehemet Ali because the Mamelukes were divided: Osman Bey Bardisi came over to his side; Mohammed Bey el-Elfi allied himself with the English; and both Mameluke chiefs conspired with the French consul Drovetti. Finally, in 1804 Mehemet Ali drove Bardisi out of Cairo, broke with the Turks and compelled the sultan to recognise him as lieutenant of the country (Kaimakam) and, in 1805, as pasha. English intervention at Constantinople brought about his replacement by el-Elfi, but Mehemet Ali held his ground; the two Mameluke chieftains then died, leaving him a free hand. To counter this failure, Duckworth landed a detachment of soldiers from Sicily at Alexandria; they occupied Rosetta where they were soon defeated in a surprise attack by Mehemet Ali. On 22 April 1807 the pasha laid siege to Alexandria, and on 15 September the English agreed to evacuate their forces.

For the moment, they were also checked in Persia. The shah had been fighting the Georgians and Russians since 1804, and a defeat had cost him Baku and Daghestan in 1806. Simultaneously he asked for help both from Napoleon and from the viceroy of India. French agents were sent to negotiate for an alliance, and a Persian embassy visited the emperor at Finckenstein, where a treaty was signed on 4 May. France agreed to take

Persia under her protection and to send weapons and instructors; Persia, in return, promised to help in a proposed expedition to India. On 10 May instructions were drafted for General Gardane who was despatched on mission to Teheran.

In short, everything had turned in Napoleon's favour, but the fact remained that only a decisive victory over Russia could destroy the Coalition. It was Bennigsen who made such a victory possible. Now that Danzig and all of the Silesian fortresses except Kosel had fallen, it was expected that Königsberg would succumb to the first French offensive. Early in June Bennigsen tried to save the city by a surprise manoeuvre, suddenly advancing to the Passarge in the hopes of crushing Ney who was encamped on the right bank of the river. Ney extricated himself and withdrew across the river where he was joined by Davout, while the rest of the French army advanced on 9 June against the Russian right in order to cut it off from Lestocq's twenty-four thousand Prussians. Bennigsen then fell back on Heilsberg, a fortified position on the Alle. Murat, who should have fixed him there while the army emerged on the only available road, rashly ordered a full-scale attack on 10 June which needlessly lost about ten thousand men and enabled Bennigsen to retreat down the right bank of the Alle. Napoleon now threw himself against the Prussians who were retreating towards Königsberg. On 13 June Bennigsen, crossing the Alle at Friedland, attempted to create a diversion on their behalf. He probably intended no more than that, for when he encountered Lannes's corps on the following morning, he made no attempt to take advantage of his superior forces. Thus he gave the emperor enough time to rush to the field with three army corps. The Russian left, after repulsing two of Ney's assaults, was finally totally battered by artillery fire. The bridges were burned, and Bennigsen's army, driven to the river, lost twenty-five thousand men. Its fragments retreated to Tilsit, pursued by the French. Dazed by this blow, the Russian generals deemed an armistice absolutely necessary, and envoys from Alexander were sent to ask for one on 19 June. They were favourably received, and a truce was signed on 21 June. More than that, Duroc had already offered them a final peace on the nineteenth.

Napoleon needed peace: if Russia continued to resist, he would have to cross the Niemen; once again enormous preparations would be necessary, and Austria might take advantage of the delay. Alexander, for his part, was unhappy with his allies, and was in no humour to stake everything. He conferred with his brother Constantine, a devoted partisan of peace, and was undoubtedly convinced by him that in case of an invasion, anything might happen: a revolt of the military, a conspiracy of the nobles, an insurrection of the Polish provinces, perhaps even a serf rebellion. Alexander then met with Frederick William, and on 22 June Hardenberg seized the opportunity to submit a truly startling proposal: Prussia, which no longer existed, advised the tsar to change his entire policy and to offer Napoleon a three-cornered alliance whose purpose it would be to fight England and to redraw the map of Europe; Russia and Austria would divide Turkey and would abandon, together with Prussia, their Polish territories; the king of Saxony would be installed at Warsaw and give up his kingdom to Prussia. Thus it was Prussia who guided the tsar towards an alliance with France and a rupture with England. Alexander, who was infuriated with England, was very receptive to such advice. Moreover, Hardenberg's plan would again set him up as Europe's mediator, jointly with Napoleon as in 1801; for in her present condition, Prussia could scarcely count at all. This coincided exactly with Napoleon's mood; renouncing for the time being all ideas of conquering Russia, he now contemplated taking her as an ally in the place of Prussia. The offer, transmitted to Alexander on 23 June, touched the tsar's vanity. He probably also thought that he would win over Napoleon, as he had so many others, and so Alexander proposed a personal interview which took place on 25 June, on a raft moored in the middle of the Niemen River. There the two emperors held prolonged discussions in the solitude of their own privacy. We shall never know what they said to each other: it is the 'mystery of Tilsit'.

The peace and the alliance presented no difficulty; what remained was to settle the fate of Prussia. Napoleon had never for a moment considered admitting her as a third party. He treated Frederick William with disdain and kept him at a distance. Queen Louise came to see him on 6 July; she was heard out politely and went away empty-handed. Having agreed in principle to Hardenberg's plan, Alexander did his best to defend his ally, but ended by signing the alliance without him. For this he would be accused of treachery. He probably found that Napoleon was immovable, and yielded to his reasons: the emperor argued that he held Prussia by right of conquest and could, if he wished, keep her; nevertheless, out of regard for the tsar, he would grant her an armistice and restore a part of her territory. It is likely that Napoleon also dazzled his new ally with the prospects which would open up in the East once they had brought England to her senses, if not sooner. In short, he swept the tsar off his feet.

The instruments signed at Tilsit on 7 July 1807 consisted of a peace treaty, certain secret articles and an alliance pact. A separate treaty with Prussia was added on 9 July. Russia emerged unscathed; Prussia, on the other hand, lost all of her possessions west of the Elbe, except that she might recover three to four hundred thousand souls should England cede Hanover to Napoleon. East Frisia had already been reunited with Holland, and the Westphalian lands were taken over by the grand duchy of Berg. The rest – Minden, Hildesheim, Halberstadt, Magdeburg – were incorporated with Brunswick, Hesse-Cassel and a part of Hanover, Osnabrück and Göttingen to form the kingdom of Westphalia which was to be ruled by Jérôme. Napoleon kept under his own hand the rest of Hanover, together with Erfurt, Hanau and Fulda. Prussia also lost all of her Polish territories except for a small stretch of West Prussia, an isthmus thirty kilometres wide connecting Brandenburg and Pomerania with East Prussia. Thus mutilated and reduced to four provinces, the Prussian realm was to be handed back to Frederick William; but a convention signed on 12 July made the evacuation of Prussia conditional upon the payment of a war indemnity. Since the tsar was not made a party to this agreement, he had no right to any say in its execution. For the time being, Napoleon held on to all of Prussia.

The key to the future of the Franco-Russian alliance lay in the disposition of the Polish provinces (apart from Danzig which, now isolated in Prussian territory, was made a Free City, but continued to be under the occupation of the French general Rapp). Unfortunately, it is precisely on this point that the Tilsit talks remain shrouded in the deepest obscurity. There is no doubt that Napoleon freely invited Alexander to take part in the dismemberment of Prussia; in fact, he had already proposed that Russia expand to the Niemen. The tsar, it appears, was offered the Polish provinces overrun by Napoleon in exchange for the French acquisition of Silesia. As the offer was phrased it was turned down, and of the Polish provinces formerly held by Prussia, Russia annexed only Bialystok. Perhaps Alexander would have accepted it if Napoleon had renounced Silesia and permitted Prussia to keep her territories in central Germany. Instead, Prussia's Polish provinces were converted into the grand duchy of Warsaw. This solution may have been suggested by the tsar himself as a temporary compromise; or again, it may have been Napoleon's idea. In any event, the grand duchy of Warsaw, with a population of two million inhabitants, was given to the king of Saxony to rule. While passing through Dresden on 22 July, the emperor granted the Poles a constitution. Like Westphalia, the new grand duchy became a member of the Confederation of the Rhine, and thirty thousand French soldiers were garrisoned there. Thus Poland was resurrected in all but name. In reality, she was no more than a military march against Russia, and so contributed from the very beginning to the eventual failure of the Franco-Russian alliance.

While Napoleon was extending the French Empire to the banks of the Niemen, Alexander was renouncing the gains which Paul I had amassed in the Mediterranean. He ceded Cattaro and the Ionian Islands to France, and he even evacuated the Danubian principalities which he had just occupied on the sole condition that the Turks should not reoccupy them until peace had been concluded. In this matter, Napoleon was to act as mediator; if the sultan refused to make peace within three months, France would make common cause with Russia to deprive the Porte of all her European possessions, with the exception of Rumelia. As for England, it was Alexander who undertook to mediate by summoning her to restore her colonial conquests and to recognise the freedom of the seas. If he failed in this attempt, measures would be taken to compel Sweden, Denmark and Portugal to enter into the Continental System. Thus the agreement of 1801 was both renewed and expanded. The tsar could look forward to the conquest of Finland and Turkey; for Napoleon, there was Portugal and a confederated continent closed to English trade. Prussia had adhered to the blockade; Austria, isolated, could hardly refuse to do as much. Caught in the crossfire of the Franco-Russian alliance, these two German powers were reduced to helplessness, effectively ruling out any possibility of a coalition.

For Napoleon, Tilsit was thus a brilliant success, albeit a temporary one. While Alexander appears to have been spellbound by Napoleon, whom he thought under his sway, his vanity and inconstancy stood guarantee that such a state of affairs could not long endure. He would make no honest effort to share the management of Europe's affairs with a man whose temperament brooked no equal partnership. Surely Alexander, artful deceiver that he was, concealed his intentions. He extricated himself from a nasty situation without loss and he calculated that France, more readily than England, would allow him to despoil Sweden and Turkey. Meanwhile he remained absolutely free to take up arms again at his own convenience. Therefore it has been said that it was he who duped Napoleon.

This is simply not so. Napoleon, at the time of Tilsit, remarked to Méneval that he had resolved never to turn Constantinople over to the Russians: 'It is the centre of world empire.' As far as he was concerned, the alliance had not been concluded on an equal basis. Russia was entering into his system, and was thereby becoming a vassal. It could not have escaped him that the war might some day be resumed, but he lived for the present, not the future; he knew that peace was necessary in order for him to rebuild his army, disarm Austria and complete the submission of Western Europe. The alliance made this possible, for the moment at least; perhaps it would even permit him to conquer England. Time alone would tell. If Russia went to war before England succumbed, then he would conquer Russia. But as long as he had Alexander's support, if only temporarily, Napoleon was gaining time to amass the force he would need to defeat him.

# BOOK TWO

From Tilsit to Waterloo
1807-1815

# I

# The Imperial
# Conquests after Tilsit
# (1807–1812)

# CHAPTER ONE

# The Continental System (1807–1809)

ALTHOUGH ENGLAND contrived to put a good face on it, it seemed for some months that the Treaty of Tilsit would bear fruit. The Continent submitted to Napoleon, and the blockade, reinforced by the decrees of Milan, appeared to close it to British commerce.

But the Continental System had scarcely come into being before it was jeopardised by the defection of the East, and more especially by the rising in Spain, which Napoleon had provoked but was then unable to put down.

## ENGLAND AWAKENS

When she heard about the interview at Tilsit, England realised that the Franco-Russian entente of 1801 had been restored and saw the danger confronting her. After losing Germany, she now risked having the Baltic closed to her once more. But thanks to Canning's prompt decision, she stole a march on her enemies. True, Gustavus IV seemed in a secure position: he had just resumed hostilities on 3 July and Cathcart had led ten thousand men into Pomerania. But Denmark was an uncertain quantity, and there was erroneous news that she was mobilising her fleet; besides, Bernadotte could occupy the country from Hamburg in a very few days. Canning was hot-blooded, and had the temperament of a fighter: he did not lose a single moment. Though he knew of the interview of 16 July, he did not begin to get the details – and then in very incomplete form – till the twenty-first; and he only learned of the treaty's signature on 8 August through a French newspaper. On 18 July Admiral Gambier was ordered to proceed to Copenhagen with a huge squadron, and arrived there on 3 August, while Cathcart, who had evacuated Pomerania and received reinforcements, was approaching with thirty thousand men. The Prince Royal at Kiel was notified that he must enter into alliance with England and supply her with ships. When he refused, his capital was blockaded and then bombarded on 2 September. He capitulated on the seventh. Canning then tried in vain to win over the Danes, attempted to induce the Swedes to occupy the Danish archipelago, and in despair of success was even inclined to leave the English troops there, though his colleagues were in favour of evacuation. But the Danish fleet was taken in possession, and the following year Moore landed in southern Sweden, so that Admiral Saumarez was able to move freely into the Baltic and escort merchant shipping, which was the essential thing.

On the eve of the Berlin decree, the big export industries already constituted an element of prime importance in the English economy. It could not fail to be affected by any crisis involving these industries. They depended largely on European trade with the United States for their markets, and in certain cases for the provision of their raw materials; and they were therefore particularly vulnerable to the threat of blockade, especially if accompanied by a closing of the United States to English commerce. Nor must we forget the dependence of England on Northern Europe for her naval supplies and cereals, or the weaknesses of her banking system and her balance of payments. But there is no denying the power and elasticity of the British economy. The technical progress already achieved and her capitalist system gave her an assured superiority over France. England had undergone a veritable demographic revolution, in the course of which the population of Great Britain had risen from 10,943,000 in 1801 to 12,597,000 in 1811. This acted as a stimulus to the whole economy, and in particular supplied industry with a decisively expanding home market and an abundant and cheap supply of labour. English agriculture had become the best in Europe as far as technique was concerned; and although the agricultural revolution had upset traditional rural society, it ensured that a rapidly expanding population need only depend on imports for a smaller portion of its foodstuffs. The oligarchy constituted by the great landowners who governed England were confident of their own destiny, and gave evidence of an almost unshakeable will to win. The most powerful section of the middle classes – the London bankers and merchants and big businessmen – had long been firmly linked with the aristocracy, and were as doggedly opposed to France, seeing how she threatened their commercial and colonial interests. The industrialists, however, enjoyed a much lower social status in general, and their role in politics was as yet a very minor one. The workers were the people who had most to fear from the blockade, for it might well lead to unemployment and high prices, thus making their living conditions even worse – though they were already wretched enough in all conscience. But the social framework of the country, buttressed still further by the Combination Acts of 1799 and 1800, was, as has been emphasised, 'reassuringly strong'. Nothing less than an intense and prolonged crisis had any chance of setting the middle class against the oligarchy and driving the proletariat into revolt.

Far from allowing itself to be intimidated by the Berlin decree, the Tory government reinforced the mercantile character of the British blockade at the expense of the neutral countries. Persons of importance had long been insisting on measures against them under the Navigation Acts. The builders and shipowners were indignant that neutral flags covered forty-four per cent of the ships leaving British ports in 1807, instead of the twenty-eight per cent which had been the figure for 1802. The trade of the United States was more prosperous than ever, their exports in 1807 rising to 108 million dollars, almost sixty million of which consisted of colonial goods, partly from the colonies of England's enemies. The planters in the Antilles were full of complaints about the fall in the price of sugar, but the Whigs had shown little readiness to listen to these grievances. On 7 January 1807 they did no more than extend the 1756 regulations about coastal shipping between enemy ports that excluded English ships. From February Perceval proposed to compel neutrals trading with France to pass through a British port, a measure of retaliation that seemed to be demanded for the honour of the country. Once in office,* Perceval proceeded to act. Although all trading with the enemy was again forbidden, it was made clear that there would be no change in the licence system, which allowed traders to infringe these regulations wherever the national interest required. They were solely aimed at the neutrals, and their purpose was 'to subordinate the trade of the whole world to the development of the navy and the shipping of Great Britain'. By Orders in Council on 11, 15 and 25 November and 18 December 1807, any neutral vessel sailing to or from an enemy port would be obliged to unload its cargo in one of a number of specially designated British ports, and be subject to customs duties – which were now notably increased – and would have to take out a licence. In addition, there was a ban on importing certain goods, such as quinine and cotton, into France. In theory at any rate, neutrals were still allowed to transport direct to their own countries goods

* [As chancellor of the exchequer, March 1807.]

from enemy colonies and even to export grain and raw materials from their place of origin to ports under Napoleon's control. With these exceptions, it looked as though maritime trade would become a British monopoly. In taxing neutral cargoes, the English reckoned to prevent them from carrying the produce of foreign colonies whose competition reduced the profits of the British colonists; and by refusing licences they could, if need be, bring neutral shipping to a standstill. This was precisely what the shipowners and the planters would have liked to happen.

The English were delighted at Canning's enterprise and at all these measures. They did not question the burdens which the government, foreseeing that England was likely to be isolated, imposed upon the country in order to enable it to face its enemies single-handed. Taxes were increased, and Castlereagh set about strengthening the army, which had been somewhat neglected by the Whigs. On 13 April 1806 Windham had repealed Pitt's Act, suspended the militia ballot system and given up the recruitment of regulars from among the militia, to return to the system of ordinary enlistment. He had shown his dislike for reliance upon volunteers. Life service had been abolished, and replaced by service contracts of from seven to twelve years. Castlereagh re-established the militia ballot and encouraged volunteers, but transformed them into a local militia under government control. He returned to Pitt's system for recruiting regiments of the line, and drew twenty-one thousand regulars from the militia. In 1807 and 1808 he added forty-five thousand recruits, while the army lost only fifteen thousand men. At the beginning of 1809 there were two hundred thousand soldiers available in Great Britain, thirty thousand being held in readiness for expeditions on the Continent. It was thus possible to resume Pitt's policy with more ample means, though the cost was heavy. By 1807 the yield of direct taxation had risen from £3 million in 1804, and £6 million in 1806, to £10 million. Expenditure rose from £76 million in 1804, and £106 million in 1806, to more than £120 million in 1808. The burden was all the heavier because exports went down markedly in 1807 and 1808, though bread remained cheap. Yet England kept a stout heart as she watched the Continent rallying to Napoleon, for she was persuaded that his success would be short-lived.

## EUROPE CLOSED TO ENGLAND (1807–1808)

Napoleon had come back to Paris on 27 July 1807. He was officially given the title of *Grand*, like Louis XIV after the Peace of Nijmegen, and on 15 August there were brilliant festivities in honour of *la Gloire* and the Grande Armée. It looked for a short while as if there would certainly be peace on the Continent, and general peace would surely follow before long. Napoleon himself had remarked that the achievements of Tilsit would settle the destinies of the whole world. And so these festivities were genuinely popular, and Napoleon once more became for a time the national leader. The creation of the kingdom of Westphalia was officially announced on 18 August, and soon afterwards Jérôme's marriage to Catherine of Württemberg was celebrated. Then in September and October Napoleon held court at Fontainebleau. As he had done after Austerlitz, he now resumed the work of administration, carrying out a purge of the judiciary in 1807, and organising the Université in 1808.

Particularly striking was his increasingly marked taste for personal despotism and his preference for the aristocracy. On 19 August 1807 he abolished the Tribunate, and on the ninth he had in effect dismissed Talleyrand by decorating him with the title of vice-grand-elector, condemning his venality, and probably being unable to forgive his tacit disapproval. In October 1805 Talleyrand had presumed to advise a conciliatory line towards Austria, wishing to console her for the loss of Italy and Germany at the expense of Turkey. This policy has often since been praised, but was in fact chimerical, for Austria would have taken anything offered to her without for a moment forgetting her deeply felt losses. At Warsaw, Talleyrand had shown contempt for the Poles, and after Friedland he said – in complimenting the victor – that he was particularly delighted with this triumph because he was certain that it would be his last. Napoleon could no longer put up with a servant who showed such independence, and replaced him by Champagny, who was never more than a good clerk, though – most unfortunately, as it turned out – he continued constantly to consult his ex-minister. At the same time he continued to organise the new aristocracy, distributing eleven million in *rentes* to the military chiefs, re-establishing entails and finally constituting in 1808 a fully fledged imperial nobility.

At the same time he began to adopt a sharper attitude towards foreigners. In October 1807 there was scene after scene at Fontainebleau as he stormed at the envoys of Etruria, Bremen and Portugal: 'If Portugal does not do what I want, the House of Braganza will no longer be on the throne in two months' time.' There was no need for these threats, for his plans were already drawn up; but he was showing himself less and less capable of self-control. 'Napoleon has not only ceased to recognise any limits,' wrote Metternich; 'he has completely thrown off the mask.' 'Now that he has made an agreement with Russia,' Champagny admitted, 'he is no longer afraid of anyone.' The world had now become a keyboard on which he could play whatever tune fancy brought into his head.

To begin with, the alliance lived up to expectations. True, Alexander was in no hurry to break with England, and allowed Budberg to receive Wilson, an amateur diplomat who came in as an intermediary. Canning did not positively turn down the possibility of mediation, reckoning that the tsar had only entered into alliance with France to get himself out of an awkward position. In fact, Alexander wanted to seek shelter for Senyavin's squadron which had remained in the Mediterranean, and was afraid of exposing Kronstadt to a sudden attack. The bombardment of Copenhagen cut the knot: Budberg was replaced by Rumiantsev and on 31 October Russia declared war. Prussia was forced to follow her example on 1 December, while privately making excuses and getting her ambassador Jacobi to agree with Canning to maintain communications through François d'Ivernois. As far as Austria was concerned, Napoleon did just condescend to express his satisfaction at her behaviour during the recent war, but he no longer offered her an alliance, and on 16 October put her under an obligation to range herself against England. Starhemberg in London and Merfeldt in St Petersburg protested in vain. The swift *dénouement* of Tilsit had terrified the authorities in Vienna, and there were suspicions of a projected partitioning of Turkey in which the Austrians wanted to have a share. In Paris, Metternich expressed agreement with Stadion and sketched out the line of action he was to follow later on when chancellor. The only possible course was to wait for 'the great day when Europe will be able to put an end to a state of affairs that is essentially precarious, because it is contrary to nature and to civilisation'. On 1 January 1808 Starhemberg, acting under peremptory orders, was forced to hand Canning a note that was badly received, and Austria duly declared war, though privately expressing her regrets. Denmark had signed an alliance with France on 30 October, but Sweden proved obstinate till Stralsund and Rügen fell. On 16 January 1808 Alexander sent her an ultimatum and on 21 February invaded Finland, while Denmark also opened hostilities.

Meanwhile, Napoleon had gone to Milan and Venice on 16 November in order to arrange his Italian affairs. He was displeased with the behaviour of the queen of Etruria, who had been regent since Louis I's death in 1803. She, like her husband, had shown entire submission to the Church, to which she had given complete liberty, declaring the property of the clergy inalienable, and handing over the censorship to the bishops. In addition she had turned a blind eye to English dealings in contraband. By agreement with Spain she was dethroned, and given the northern part of Portugal. Napoleon annexed Tuscany to the Empire and on 24 May 1808 turned it into a grand duchy, as a *gouvernement général*, for the benefit of Elisa. At the same time he annexed Parma and Piacenza. With Eugène as his intermediary, he tried in vain to force the pope to submit. In November 1807 he occupied the Marches and on 2 April 1808 joined them to the kingdom of Italy. Miollis had entered Rome on 2 February. As Turkey was still friendly and Junot had taken Lisbon on 30 November 1807, the continental federation seemed on the point of complete success.

As it progressed, the blockade became more and more of a real threat. Up to the end of the war, the Berlin decree had scarcely modified its range in any way. There had previously been confiscations of English merchandise in Germany and in the Hanseatic cities, but when he was short of money Napoleon would give it back for an appropriate payment and it would return to circulation, so that the act of seizure became a kind of fiscal expedient. As the troops advanced in Poland contraband dealings had grown, and Holstein – and in particular the port of Tönning – provided English depots instead of Hamburg. It soon became known that a little money would procure the connivance of a good many French officers, consuls and even customs officials since Bourrienne and Brune had set a bad example in Hamburg. Moreover, French businessmen were alarmed to see the blockade turning into a weapon of war to the extent of closing Germany, Poland and Russia to trade and provoking a severe industrial crisis. In order to be able to import and export at their convenience, they would have liked to go on leaving neutral ships completely free. The Berlin decree declared that they would no longer be received if they came directly from England or her colonies. But they could always claim that they had merely called in there, and as there was no threat of confiscation, they ran no risk in continuing to come to France as before. In that case, the Berlin decree would lose all meaning. Its ambiguous terms proved that Napoleon, when he made it, was still hesitating between the needs of national production and the requirements of war. The uncertainty continued for more than a year. In order to spare the Americans, he assured them that the blockade did not apply to the high seas, and as late as 26 August 1807 the Danes were dispensed from observing it. In July he had considered whether there might not be a case for granting neutrals a licence to trade with French ports as previously, on condition that they re-exported an amount equivalent in value to their imports. This solution – which was to be taken up again in 1809 – would once more have emphasised the mercantile character of the blockade.

Although the alliance of Tilsit had some effect, the course of events proved contrary. The plan was abandoned. The decree of Fontainebleau (13 October 1807) and the first decree of Milan which renewed its terms on 23 November, reinforced the Berlin decree. They declared that colonial goods and a number of products were to be considered by their nature English, unless they could show a certificate of origin, and in particular that any ships having touched in at England must be confiscated, together with the entire cargo. The Orders in Council, which had increased the subservience of the neutrals for the benefit of England, decided the emperor to take this decisive step. The second decree of Milan (17 December 1807) laid down that any neutral vessel submitting to the English requirements would be considered denationalised, and would be deemed British property. It would therefore be a lawful prize, not only in the ports, but also on the high seas. There was thus a reversion to the position in 1798. As the neutrals could not escape the English, the Empire became closed to them, and the blockade changed from a mercantile device to an instrument of war. Since the Continent rallied to the French cause, the blockade had a considerable effect. The troops had been sent back to Germany and the seizure of ships had been handed over to the customs officers who could call for armed assistance when necessary. Austria moreover was closing the Adriatic.

Although the Baltic remained open, it could only be for contraband traffic, except in Sweden. English exports underwent a serious decline. Their customs value fell from £33.5 million in 1806 to £30.4 in 1808, and the declared value from £40.8 to £35.2. This success had a tonic effect on Napoleon's spirits. From this moment onwards his desire to perfect the blockade began to urge him to further annexations, until it finally became merged with the spirit of conquest in 1811.

Peace on the Continent being now assured, Napoleon was thinking of resuming the war at sea. In Italy, he directed Joseph to prepare to attack Sicily, and told Ganteaume to leave Toulon and join this operation, after having replenished the food supplies of the Ionian Islands, which the French had seized together with Cattaro in August 1807. Reynier drove out the English from Reggio, but Ganteaume was only able to carry out the second part of his assignment. More and more orders went out to Decrès. Naval construction forged ahead on every hand, and on 28 May 1808 Napoleon calculated that he would soon be at the head of seventy-seven French ships, fifty-four foreign ones and three hundred thousand men grouped at various places along the coast, from Texel to Taranto. 'It seems to me', he wrote, 'that this represents a chessboard which, without asking too much of fortune or too great skill from our sailors, ought to lead to great results.' But he did not have time enough to threaten England at sea or at home, for the continental federation began to crumble before it had even received the finishing touches.

The first miscalculations came from the East. Napoleon's policy was bound to go wrong from the moment of his alliance with Russia, since Turkey and Persia had only made advances to him in order to keep in line with her. Mustapha IV having agreed to French mediation, Guilleminot arranged an armistice at Slobodzie on 24 August 1807; on 21 October Alexander rejected it on a variety of pretexts, but in reality he wanted to keep the principalities, and the sultan thought that Napoleon was in agreement. For the present, however, war did not break out again in Europe, but fighting continued in Asia, where the Russians defeated the pasha of Erzerum. The English used this to increase their influence in Constantinople to such good effect that Napoleon finally recalled Sébastiani in April 1808. Before long, new revolutions in Turkey completed the estrangement from France. The Bairakdar undertook to restore Sultan Selim to power, but Mustapha IV just had time to put the latter to death before he himself was overthrown on 28 July 1808 in favour of his brother, Mahmud II. In November the Janissaries rose once again and massacred the Bairakdar. Mahmud, who had caused Mustapha to be strangled, was the last representative of the dynasty, and, as such, his life was spared. On 5 January 1809 he made peace with England.

Events followed much the same course in Persia. Gardane contrived an armistice, while Colonel Fabvier set about organising an army. But here too Alexander refused to relinquish his conquests and was soon besieging Erevan. The shah deserted France and Malcolm reappeared in Teheran. The tsar's attitude, moreover, showed that he intended to be left a free hand in the East, and this was a serious symptom, for Napoleon had already determined to allow nothing of the kind. All the same, there was worse to follow. He had taken it into his head to annex the Iberian peninsula to the Grand Empire, and it proceeded to put up an unexpected resistance whose endless repercussions brought disaster to the achievement of Tilsit.

## AFFAIRS IN PORTUGAL AND SPAIN (1807–1808)

Napoleon had been watching Portugal since the establishment of the Consulate. Almost all its trading was done with England, which had predominant business interests and large capital investments in it, especially in the vineyards. Portugal was one of the chief bases for contraband and an outpost for the British fleet and she could not break with London without being completely ruined, for more than a third of her income was from the customs, and her corn had to come to her by sea. In short, she was in effect an English colony – as British imperialism fully appreciated – which brought in a great deal and cost nothing. Even at Tilsit, Napoleon had decided to conquer her, and on 29 July, as soon as he got back to Paris, he took steps to form an expeditionary corps at Bordeaux. Aranjo refused to stop the English ships and confiscate their goods; the most he would do was to close his ports and declare war, reckoning no doubt that he would only have to make a pretence of hostilities. But Canning refused to join in this farce, and the rupture took place. On 12 October Napoleon set Junot's forces in motion.

But to reach Portugal, it was necessary to cross Spain. So from the very beginning the schemes concerning this country had been dovetailed with Napoleon's Spanish policy. In 1805 Godoy had insinuated that he would gladly carve out a principality for himself in Portugal, and on 24 May 1806 he put his request into writing. But on each occasion war broke off negotiations, and he became so disillusioned that he turned against the French alliance. The loss of Buenos Aires on 27 June 1806 seemed to be a prelude to the loss of the whole of South America, and roused strong feelings in Spain. It induced Godoy to offer to make peace with England, but the English required him to join the coalition, as the Russians and Prussians also advised. Godoy hesitated. If he did not enter into a tacit agreement with Prussia (as he has been accused of doing), he at any rate addressed a proclamation to Spaniards on 5 October 1806 announcing that they would arm. The statement was ambiguously worded, and Napoleon pretended to believe that it was a question of coming to his help; but it was certainly something he did not forget. After Jena, Godoy hastened to break with Russia, joined the blockade on 19 February 1807 and sent the marquis de La Romana to Germany with eight thousand men, who reached Hamburg at the beginning of August. And now at last he was eager to join in the plan for a war against Portugal. By the Treaty of Fontainebleau, 27 October 1807, this country was to be divided into three parts: the north for the queen of Etruria, the south for Godoy, the centre – with Lisbon – being reserved by Napoleon, either because he wanted to hold this port until the peace, or because it formed part of his Spanish schemes.

Spain appeared to Napoleon to be badly governed, and did not provide him with all he considered she should be able to supply. For a long time he had thought Spain needed 'regeneration' – an opinion widely held in his entourage where, with Murat in the fore, there was no lack of candidates for this task, who hoped to find Spain a land even more richly 'flowing with milk and honey' than Portugal. Talleyrand, for his part, was strongly in favour of extreme measures. There was, however, no urgency about acquiring Spain, since it was already part of the Continental System; and there can be little doubt that it was his recent triumphs that impelled Napoleon to action and stimulated still further his urge for power. Nevertheless we can only conjecture how his mind worked, and it is only possible to suggest in a tentative manner the two solutions between which he seems to have hesitated.

It was in fact the divisions in the royal family that came to his assistance. Even as he was signing the Treaty of Fontainebleau he already held in his hands the threads of an intrigue that gave a glimpse of one possible solution. The prince of Asturias was a persistent enemy of Godoy, for he suspected him of intending to usurp the crown on the death of Charles IV. His friends, the duke del Infantado and Canon Escoïquiz, his former tutor, conceived the plan of marrying him to a French princess and so making certain of the emperor's support. Napoleon's ambassador, who was a Beauharnais, probably saw the chance of advancing the family fortunes by putting forward a cousin of Josephine's as a suitor for the Spanish throne, and took it upon himself to get in touch with Escoïquiz. Champagny, learning of this possibility, and clearly acting on his master's orders, asked for a letter from Ferdinand, who produced it on 11 October. As Napoleon's protégé, he could be used as a tool, and would perhaps have had to cede Spanish provinces as far as the Ebro in exchange for Lisbon. At all events, a scheme put forward by the Spanish agent Izquierdo on 29 February 1808 mentioned the possibility of this annexation.

Meanwhile, Junot was advancing by forced marches over appalling roads, in terrible weather. As usual, he had set out with no provisions or transport. Spain was expected to provide everything, but in fact provided very little, and the army soon began to straggle. Fortunately Portugal offered no resistance, and three Spanish columns joined in the invasion along the Douro, south of the Tagus and in the Algarve. On 22 October the regent made an agreement with the English authorising them to occupy Madeira and arranging for the transport of the royal family to Brazil. The vast contents of the British depots were shipped to safety; Senyavin's fleet, which had put in to Lisbon, was escorted to England; and on 29 November the Portuguese court sailed overseas. On the thirtieth Junot entered Lisbon. He imposed on the country an indemnity of one hundred million francs, and despatched to France the remnants of the Portuguese army, some eight to nine thousand men. The peculiarly risky situation occupied by Junot had given Napoleon an excuse for his progressive occupation of Spain. On 12 October he had ordered a new corps to be formed, and in November Dupont brought it along to occupy Old Castile. In January it was followed by another under Moncey at Burgos, and eventually by a third, organised by Mouton.

At this point a second solution of the Spanish question had become possible. At the end of October Godoy had discovered and denounced Ferdinand's intrigue, and had put him in prison. The prince complained to Napoleon, who swore vociferously and barefacedly denied all complicity. Charles IV and Godoy were appalled, and hastened to withdraw. They released Ferdinand, his friends being acquitted and sent into exile; but from that point onwards the emperor seems to have admitted that the heir presumptive might be declared incapable of coming to the throne. On 2 December he spoke to Joseph at Venice, and though he asked Lucien to send his daughter Charlotte to Paris, there is nothing to prove that it was to marry her to Ferdinand. On 12 January he ordered some leaflets to be drawn up on the subject of the Escurial plot and the indignity suffered by Ferdinand, but they were never distributed. Meanwhile the French troops were steadily advancing. In February they seized Pamplona and San Sebastian. Duhesme was now bringing up a corps from the eastern Pyrenees to enter Catalonia and take possession of Barcelona and Figueras. At the beginning of March Bessières came and took command at Burgos, and Murat, now put in command of the army of Spain, proceeded to march upon Madrid, which he entered on the twenty-third.

It would seem that in March Napoleon was again inclining towards the first solution. But once more events in Spain cut short the debate. Godoy was uneasy, and had recalled to Andalusia the corps operating in Portugal south of the Tagus. There was widespread alarm at the progress of the French armies, and it was suggested that the king's favourite meant to escape to Cadiz with the royal family and there embark with them to America. In the night of 17 March 1808 an insurrection broke out at Aranjuez. The troops deserted; Godoy was thrown into prison; and on the nineteenth the king abdicated. Napoleon learned of the rising on the twenty-sixth and decided at once to leave for Bayonne. On the twenty-seventh he heard that Charles IV had abdicated, and he mentally saw the throne as good as vacant. That same day he offered it to Louis, which is the first positive indication we have about his views. He left Paris on 2 April and reached Bayonne by the fifteenth.

Charles IV, however, had complained to Murat of the violence done to him, and Napoleon had invited him to come and see him. He also gave directions that Ferdinand should be sent to him, and the latter did not dare resist. On 2 May Madrid, stirred up by these departures, rose against the French. Murat suppressed the rebellion harshly, and Napoleon paid no heed to this ominous sign for the future. 'The Spaniards are just like the other nations,' he said; 'they will be only too pleased to accept the imperial constitutions.'

Charles IV claimed the throne for his son, and then on 5 May handed it over to the emperor. The prince of Asturias was thoroughly frightened, and capitulated; and the whole royal family were sent to Talleyrand's château at Valençay. When Louis and Jérôme refused the offer of this crown, Napoleon conferred it authoritatively on Joseph, while the kingdom of Naples went to Murat, who was thoroughly disappointed. He had passed on to the emperor the desire expressed by some liberals for a

constitution, but it seems that Napoleon showed no interest, being preoccupied particularly with administrative reforms; all the same, he
complied with the request. A junta elected by three groups of electors
sorted into three classes sat at Bayonne from 15 June to 7 July – though
only ninety-one members out of 150 had responded to the appeal. Spain
was given a constitution like that of the vassal states, except that all
attempts to secularise the state were abandoned. Roman Catholicism
remained the only lawful faith, and the Inquisition was not abolished. In
deference to the susceptibilities of public opinion, there was nothing to
indicate that Spain was becoming a vassal state, and her financial contributions were not increased. On 20 July Joseph made his solemn entry
into Madrid. But he only resided there for eleven days, for his kingdom
was already in revolt.

## THE SPANISH INSURRECTION (1808)

Certain elements of the Neapolitan insurrection crop up again in the
affairs of Spain. Yet the subjects of Charles IV had a more dynamic loyalty to the dynasty, and although the particularist spirit had a different
kind of strength from its counterpart in France, there was no lack of a
strong national spirit as well. Among the common people, however, there
was as yet nothing to distinguish it from hatred of the foreigner and religious fanaticism, which had such strong roots in the struggle against the
Moors. This spirit was encouraged by the physical nature of the country
and by the backwardness of its economy, and was deliberately fostered by
the clergy who had prevented the minds of Spaniards from making contact with European thought. Hatred of foreigners was at this time
particularly directed against the heretical English and against the French
– so long enemies and now oppressive allies – denounced ever since 1789
as instruments of the devil. But in order to provide a popular incentive to
insurrection, foreigners must be sufficiently numerous to be an obvious
menace to everyone; and it is clearly in this sense that the French invasion
proved decisive. Yet the revolt began more especially in the provinces
untouched by French influence – Asturias, Galicia and Andalusia. There
was thus a need to explain to the people what was happening elsewhere,
and call them to arms; and this was done, not by the authorities, who generally adopted a submissive or hesitant attitude, but by the nobles and the
clergy.

The nobles displayed a more refined and passionate national sentiment than the common people. As a class, they were cut off from power, and despised Godoy as a mannerless parvenu. They were therefore only too delighted to seize the chance of resuming authority. Distrustful of any reforms the French might suggest, some of them dreamed of a monarchy after the English pattern, while others had no intention of renouncing their social supremacy. If the middle classes had been powerful and imbued with the new ideas, the movement might perhaps have been opposed, for except in Cadiz it had little strength and was ill informed. Apart from the maritime provinces and Catalonia, where the economic and social structure was democratic, Spain remained a country of large properties where the great ones had only to lift a finger in order to call out the peasants who were in bondage to them. Moreover, the Spanish ascribed all their country's misfortunes to Godoy. This was the reason for Ferdinand's brief moment of popularity, and if only Napoleon had used him as a screen in order to get rid of the favourite, he would have met with little resistance. But when it was possible to represent the invader as in league with the hated minister, it was not difficult to carry the common folk in the towns along with the peasants. It is only surprising that the revolt should have been directed in the first place against the representatives of the central power, several of whom were massacred.

In Napoleon's eyes, the clergy was responsible for playing a leading part in the uprising – 'an insurrection of monks', he called it. This verdict has been disputed because a certain number of bishops and priests figured among the junta at Bayonne, men like Cardinal de Bourbon, archbishop of Toledo. Yet a few exceptions among the higher clergy prove nothing: for there were sixty thousand secular and one hundred thousand regular clergy in Spain, and it was they, in close touch with the people, and not their leaders, who instilled the spirit of revolt. As in the Vendée and elsewhere, preaching and the confessional served to produce a mood of overwrought fanaticism which showed itself in miracles; and it is not hard to understand the exasperation of the clergy at the thought of a secularised state and at Napoleon's rupture with the pope. There are, however, certain indications that some at least of the leaders directed the propaganda and were not slow to work out a plan of organised resistance. Cardinal Desping y Dasseto, formerly archbishop of Seville, wrote from Rome on 30 June 1808 to the archbishop of Granada: 'You must be well aware that we cannot recognise as our king someone who is a Freemason, a heretic and a Lutheran, as are all the Bonapartes and all the French nation.' Foreseeing that he might be forced to leave the Holy City, he added: 'I shall try to come to Spain, so as to carry out our plan.' What was this plan? We can get some inkling of it when we see the same archbishop of Granada, the assistant bishop of Seville and the bishop of Santander taking a leading part in the insurrectionary juntas, and when we note that circulars were sent to the bishops with a request to distribute them as widely as possible. Some of them were intercepted, such as the following:

> Once they have mastered our country, they will introduce all kinds of strange cults and abolish the true one . . . They will force you all to become soldiers in order to carry out their plan of conquering Europe and the whole world . . . To arms, then! Go forward in the name of God, his Immaculate Mother and St Joseph her blessed spouse, and you will certainly win the victory.

The insurrection did not break out at once: there was almost a month between the departure of Charles IV and the first rising. It began at Oviedo, where the Asturias Estates, urged on by the marquis of Santa Cruz, declared war against Napoleon. On 6 June the Seville junta did likewise. The movement then spread like a train of gunpowder. Often enough the risings were accompanied by murder and pillage. At Valencia, for example, Canon Calvo directed the massacre of 338 French subjects. Soon there were seventeen revolutionary juntas in existence, principally in the north-west, the south and Aragon. These were completely inexperienced committees, consumed by personal rivalries, and jealous of their independence. The bands of men were without any military value, and in the provinces possessing militias – such as Asturias and Catalonia – there was nothing like a unanimous response to the appeal or willingness to fight a regular war. But the insurrection was nonetheless formidable on two particular counts. First, because Spain, unlike Portugal, had an army of some importance, concentrated more especially in Galicia and Andalusia, so that these two provinces naturally took the lead. The Galician junta assumed command over its counterparts in Asturias, and more still in León and Old Castile; the Seville junta claimed central power as 'the supreme junta of Spain and the Indies' and as early as 15 June laid hands upon the French fleet in Cadiz. In the second place, Canning avoided the mistake made by Pitt in the Vendée. By

30 May the Asturian representatives were in London, and by 12 June he had promised them help. True, he gave a less warm welcome to the other juntas who immediately flocked to see him, because he was mistrustful of their sectional interests and wanted to unite them into one single authority. He knew that the Spanish would not welcome an English army, but, having a free hand in Portugal, and knowing that Junot was cut off from France by the insurrection, he decided to make the most of these advantages. An expedition was sent to Spain, and there was nothing to stop them in the last resort from marching on Madrid. It was then that the command of the seas secured by the English victory at Trafalgar showed its full worth. England accordingly decided to take advantage of it and carry the struggle on to the Continent, where it would eventually have to be decided.

On 1 June 1808 the French army numbered 117,000 men, and it took in a further forty-four thousand up till 14 August. This was too small a force for the conquest of Spain. Besides, it was far from being the equal of the Grande Armée, which had remained in Germany, seeing that it had been improvised with the help of 'temporary regiments', conscripts, together with miscellaneous elements such as seamen, Paris National Guards and more especially foreigners – Hanoverians and other Germans, Swiss, Italians and Poles, who for the first time constituted an important part of the effective strength. The command was also distinctly second-rate, and material preparations – as always – more or less non-existent, and that in a country incapable of providing the resources usually presumed to be available on the spot. The geographical conditions, moreover, were once again unfavourable to Napoleon's methods. Nevertheless, this army was conveniently massed and had nothing to fear in set battle. It was the emperor who brought disaster upon it by despising the rebels and so dispersing it in order to occupy all the provinces at the same time.

In the north-west, the French took possession of Santander, Valladolid and Bilbao. The Galician army, commanded by Blake, thirty thousand strong, advanced against them, but was routed by Bessières on 14 July at Medina del Rio Seco. In Aragon, Palafox, who was famous as a leader but in fact very second-rate, was hurled back beyond Tudela, and Verdier besieged Saragossa, carrying part of it by assault at the beginning of August. But in Catalonia Duhesme had to raise the siege of Gerona and found himself hemmed into Barcelona, while Moncey, reaching Valencia without any siege equipment, had to retire towards the Tagus. The war at once assumed a fearful character, the Spanish torturing or massacring their prisoners; the French, wild with rage and hunger, burning the villages by way of reprisal and putting the inhabitants to the sword. But these were minor difficulties compared with the terrible reverses which began to show up the hazards of the whole adventure.

Dupont had been told to move to Toledo, and on the emperor's order left it on 24 May with a single division to go and occupy Cadiz. Arriving in Andalusia, he forced the passage of the Guadalquivir at Alcolea on 7 June and took Cordova, which was plundered and sacked. He soon found out, however, that Castaños had thirty thousand regulars lined up against him, reinforced by at least ten thousand insurgents, so he withdrew on the nineteenth to Andujar to wait for reinforcements. Vedel's division debouched from the Despeña-Perros pass and covered it by taking up a position at Baylen, and then – after being replaced by Gobert's division – joined up with Dupont. Andujar – some twenty-seven kilometres from Baylen – was a bad defensive position, and there was a risk of Dupont's being attacked and surrounded; but his only thought was to resume the offensive. He probably despised his adversary, and was longing to bring off a great success that would earn him the marshal's baton he had deserved at Friedland, but which had gone instead to Victor.

Castaños carried out a clever manoeuvre. He pinned down Dupont by a feigned attack and despatched Reding against Mengibar. Gobert was killed, and his division fell back towards the pass. Nevertheless Reding, considering his position too risky, recrossed the river and Vedel, leaving Dupont, came and reoccupied Baylen on 17 July. So far nothing had proved disastrous; but then Vedel also fell back upon the pass, and Dupont, who was to have followed him closely, delayed his departure till the evening of the eighteenth. Reding and Coupigny were able to re-enter Baylen with eighteen thousand men, so that when Dupont attempted to force the passage with not many more than nine thousand soldiers on the morning of the nineteenth, he was unsuccessful and, being wounded, began to sue for terms. Meanwhile Vedel, who had retraced his steps at the sound of gunfire, was on the point of taking the enemy in the rear; but his commander-in-chief having once given his word, refused to renew the fight, and ordered Vedel to cease fire. On the twenty-second Dupont signed an agreement which included Vedel, who was weak enough to come and surrender his forces, though he had in fact managed

David's ambitious composition of the coronation of Emperor Napoleon I and Empress Josephine at Notre-Dame Cathedral by Pope Pius VII on 2 December 1804. After the proclamation of the Empire in May 1804, David became the official court painter. *Below*, the imperial procession crossing the Pont-Neuf, returning to Notre-Dame for the sacred ceremony, by Bertaux

Napoleon had grand plans to invade Britain and built up a huge naval fleet mainly based at Boulogne, although his fleet of flatboats (*above*) would only be suitable for calm seas. In the counter-plan *below*, the British squadron, comprising Admiral Lord Keith's flagship in the centre, the two-decker *Monarch*, 74 guns, with frigates and sloops around it and a line of smaller British sloops and brigs, is poised ready to attack Boulogne on 2–3 October 1804

Napoleon as king of Italy, by Appiani the Elder

*The Battle of Trafalgar, as Seen from the Mizen Starboard Shrouds the Victory*, by Turner. The British victory at Trafalgar on 21 October 1805 confirmed their maritime supremacy and removed the threat of Napoleonic invasion, but saw the death of Admiral Nelson (*left*), killed by a French sniper as he strode the quarterdeck of his flagship, *Victory*

Napoleon's first distribution of medals of the Legion of Honour in the church of the Invalides, 14 July 1804. *Below*, the scene of victory at the Battle of Austerlitz, 2 December 1804, in which French General Rapp presents Napoleon with the standards taken from the enemy

A meeting between Napoleon and Archduke Charles of Austria at a hunting lodge in Stammersdorf, before the Treaty of Pressburg was signed on 26 December 1805. *Below*, Napoleon, victorious at the Battle of Jena, 14 October 1806, is shown turning to acknowledge the salutation by a grenadier of the Imperial Guard

*A Rosey Picture of the Times*: a satirical impression of trade relations between Britain and Europe as a result of Napoleon's 1806 Berlin decree, questioning who would be most adversely affected. *Below*, Napoleon visiting the battlefield of Eylau. Although painted in celebration of France's victory, it records a bloody battle with some fifty thousand French and Russian victims, so Gros emphasises the cruel reality of victory, with the leaden sky, the field littered with corpses and Napoleon's ashen face, marked with pity

A meeting between Napoleon and T[?]
Alexander I of Russia on the Nieme[n]
River, 25 June 1807, which resulted [in]
the signing of the Treaty of Tilsit o[n]
7 July. *Left*, an alliance of the three
monarchs, Emperor Francis II of
Austria, Tsar Alexander I and King
Frederick William III of Prussia

to withdraw them. There was no question of capitulation: the Andalusian army was to be repatriated by sea, and Dupont's decision was in itself no more blameworthy than the one taken by Junot shortly afterwards, without ever incurring any reproaches from Napoleon. But the Seville junta refused to recognise the agreement, and the unfortunate prisoners were interned in the small island of Cabrera, where they were deliberately allowed to die of hunger. The emperor dealt very hardly with their commander. He overwhelmed him with insults, as he did Villeneuve, cashiered him and kept him in prison till 1814. Attempts have sometimes been made to minimise Dupont's responsibility to an excessive degree. Undoubtedly, he made mistakes; yet it remains true that the disaster was primarily due to Napoleon's rashness. The hard treatment meted out to the defeated general would be bound to call forth sympathy if he had pleaded his cause with dignity, instead of seeking revenge by violently espousing the cause of the Bourbons in 1814.

Meanwhile, Junot was confronted with a rising of the Portuguese, who followed their neighbour's example. The Spanish division at Oporto rallied the forces of Galicia, and the French were obliged to concentrate in the neighbourhood of Lisbon. Nevertheless, they retained Almeida and Elvas, and the guerrilla bands proved no match for them. And then suddenly, on 1 August, Wellesley, the brother of the marquess and the future Lord Wellington, landed at the mouth of the Mondego with more than thirteen thousand men, who were then joined by seven thousand Portuguese. As Delaborde had not succeeded in stopping him at Roliça, Junot decided to attack at Vimeiro on 21 August with no more than 9,500 men. He too was unsuccessful, and on 30 August he signed the Convention of Cintra with Sir Hew Dalrymple, who had just taken command of the allied army. It was agreed that the French army in Portugal – more than twenty-five thousand men – should be transported back to France, together with the Portuguese who had become involved on its side. This arrangement has been defended from the English point of view, for it surrendered Lisbon without a blow and opened the way for a march on Madrid; but it was severely criticised at the time, for Junot's corps returned and took part in the 1808 campaign.

The Cintra affair made less commotion than Baylen because it was said that the victory in the former case had been won by a regular army. On the other hand, the disaster to Dupont caused a sensation in Europe. It was seen as proof that the French were not invincible, and came as an encouragement to all their enemies. Forgetting that the victors had also been regular troops, people celebrated the event as a triumph for the popular movement of insurrection. On 15 June Sheridan, speaking in the name of the Whigs who had long been supporters of the French Revolution, greeted the Spanish revolt as a movement inspired by the genuine principles of the French Revolution, principles which they had later violated in order to give themselves over to oppression, but which they now saw being used against themselves. But the aristocracy of Europe was not fooled: no doubt, the Spanish insurrection was popular, and as such even filled the nobles with a secret distrust; but it had in fact been instigated and managed by them and the clergy, and was actually defending the *ancien régime* along with the nation, showing how the ruling classes can use popular patriotism to further their own private interests. Since they had not so far succeeded in achieving victory for their own cause, the aristocrats of every country took good care not to point out the ambiguity, but were delighted to welcome this heaven-sent help.

Napoleon felt the shock, and to make good the damage and re-establish his own prestige, he decided to take the Grande Armée to Spain. But from now onwards, who would there be to hold back Prussia and Austria? Under the arrangements made at Tilsit, the task fell upon the tsar; and this was going to be his testing-time.

### THE BEGINNINGS OF THE FRANCO-RUSSIAN ALLIANCE AND THE INTERVIEW AT ERFURT (1808)

When he returned to St Petersburg, Alexander had found the aristocracy solidly opposed to the French alliance. Savary had been appointed ambassador, and the part he had played in the affair of the duc d'Enghien was used as a pretext to bar all doors against him. The nobility did not wish to rub shoulders with the Revolution, and were afraid of the blockade, which might well leave them with corn and timber on their hands. Caulaincourt, who succeeded Savary in December, mollified them somewhat by his luxury, but did nothing to disarm their suspicions. The Russian ambassadors were of the same opinion. In Vienna, Razumovski was entirely Austrian in sympathy; Alopeus had been altogether on the Prussian side in Berlin, and was all for England in London. Count Tolstoi, who had been sent to Paris, was among the sworn enemies of France, and set about organising treason and espionage. He joined forces with

Metternich, finding his worldly connections and love affairs with Pauline and the duchesse d'Abrantès highly useful as sources of secret information. But Alexander appeared to be quite unmoved. He was affable to Savary and more than affable to Caulaincourt; his internal policy became liberal once again – in speech, at any rate – as though French influence were bringing him back to the plans he had announced in former years. Since 1805 the 'committee of friends' had dispersed, but Speranski was clearly gaining influence with the tsar and putting one plan after another before him. Nevertheless, if he seemed well disposed towards the French alliance, it was only because he hoped to reap advantages from it. In Paris, Tolstoi was relentlessly demanding the evacuation of Russia in order to deprive France of a military base against his country. Rumiantsev at St Petersburg, though he was well disposed to Napoleon, was nonetheless insistent on retaining the principalities. Not without some regret did Alexander feel himself to be in the same shoes as Prussia, and wished that he had not weakened his position in the East by giving up the Adriatic. He let his agents go their own way, each one pursuing his particular personal policy.

The evacuation of Prussia had been fixed in principle for 1 October 1808, and on 22 July Napoleon, being in need of money, commissioned Daru to arrange for the payment of the indemnity as soon as possible. First of all a reckoning had to be made of the sums paid by the different provinces, as well as of the requisitions. It was agreed to deduct forty-four million and pay a balance in cash of 154 million. In actual fact, the Prussians had provided for more – fifty million was their claim. But Napoleon would only take into account the regular requisitions carried out through the stewards and refused to allow the king to count the mortgage credits he had arranged for him in Poland, some four million *taler* or more. How was Prussia to manage payment? Her budget showed a deficit; her paper money had lost twenty per cent in value and was left to take its course, being no longer exchangeable except at a market rate; and Niebuhr had negotiated an unsuccessful loan in Holland. The simplest course seemed to sell the royal lands in the territories left to Frederick William, which were said to bring in about 3⅓ million *taler*. In spite of Daru's objections, Napoleon appeared disposed to accept the property; but that would have amounted to creating a kind of French state within the kingdom of Prussia, which the king could not make up his mind to allow. When 1 October arrived, the emperor declared that in the meanwhile he would continue to take the proceeds of taxation, and Daru gave notice on 7 November that Prussia would have to pay over one hundred million as the first year's instalment. Then the affair proceeded to drag on because Russia was still occupying the Danube principalities, and Napoleon from this time onwards preferred to hold on to Prussia as a kind of security. Prince William, the king's brother, came to Paris in January 1808 to offer an alliance in return for a reduction in the indemnity and immediate evacuation of Prussia, and Alexander and Tolstoi hastened to give him their support. But their intervention was declined on the ground that they had not signed the convention of 12 July 1807, and were not in a position to take over Prussia's debts. In August 1808 the question still awaited a solution.

The Eastern question was thornier still. As the memory of Friedland gradually faded, Alexander became increasingly convinced that he had given far more than he had received in return; and since he had broken with England he thought he had a right to some compensation. After rejecting the armistice of Slobodzie, he asked on 18 November to be allowed to keep the principalities. But he little knew Napoleon if he imagined that this was how he viewed their alliance, more especially as the emperor's case was legally speaking quite unassailable. According to the terms of Tilsit, the tsar was bound to evacuate the principalities unconditionally; but it was a question of 'the old familiar tune'. Napoleon was not unwilling to let Alexander have what he wanted on a give-and-take basis; in that case, he would help himself to Silesia. But for Alexander a fresh dismemberment of Prussia was out of the question, and he felt thoroughly disappointed. The emperor sensed the danger, and it was to gain time that he wrote him the famous letter of 2 February 1808, suggesting the possibility of dividing up the Ottoman Empire and sending an expedition to India by way of Persia and Afghanistan. Alexander once again came under the spell of Tilsit, and from 2 March to 12 March Rumiantsev and Caulaincourt discussed the dismemberment of Turkey. Russia would advance as far as the Balkans; Austria would take Serbia and Bosnia; and France Egypt and Syria. But when they came to discuss Constantinople and the Straits, they could not agree. If Russia took the Bosporus, Caulaincourt claimed the Dardanelles, to which Rumiantsev replied that that would be giving with one hand and taking away with the other. In the end, they sent all the papers to Napoleon, and on 31 May he proposed to the tsar that they should meet in order to settle the whole question. Alexander accepted, but the meeting had to wait till Napoleon came back from Bayonne.

Meanwhile the Russians, having occupied Finland, were not at all satisfied with the French attitude in that direction. Bernadotte, La Romana and the Danes could easily have brought Sweden to heel by landing in Scania [southern Sweden], yet they made no move. The Swedes resumed the offensive, repulsed their enemies, and reoccupied Gotland and the Aland Islands. To crown it all, Alopeus transmitted to Paris, on behalf of Canning, an offer to negotiate under the tsar's mediation on the basis of *uti possidetis*. Napoleon did not refuse, and this attempt, although it was not followed up, no doubt produced the effect Canning had intended: Alexander suspected his ally of possible desertion, and took offence.

Thus by July 1808 Napoleon had extracted from the alliance all the advantages he had counted on, and had given nothing in exchange, though he had not asked for anything beyond the terms of the treaty. But Napoleon now needed Alexander to restrain the German powers in the absence of the Grande Armée, and therefore grew more demanding. Almost overnight he granted what he had hitherto been obstinately refusing, and announced to the tsar that he was going to evacuate Prussia and leave him the principalities. Alexander agreed to an interview at Erfurt on 27 September, but he did not come to it as one seeking favours, for the Grande Armée could not depart for Spain without leaving Prussia. He was well aware that he was in a position where he could dictate his own terms. The concessions being now granted to him were ones he had already claimed as his due: they could neither dispel the bitterness of the past nor justify new obligations. Besides, the evacuation of Prussia came about in a manner quite different from what he had hoped for. Napoleon kept the taxes levied since 1 October and fixed a lump sum of 140 million. Needing liquid assets for his Spanish expedition, he accepted the bills drawn up by Prussian merchants and the *Pfandbriefe*, bonds secured on the royal lands and endorsed by the mortgage banks of the different provinces, hoping to be able to discount both of them. Though he recalled his army, he kept three fortresses on the Oder and subjected Prussia to new humiliations. She had to agree to limit her effective forces to forty-two thousand men and enter into an alliance against Austria. Champagny only succeeded in getting the agreement signed on 8 September by showing some intercepted letters indicating that Stein, who had become the head of the Prussian government, was preparing to attack France.

Napoleon was the first to arrive at Erfurt on 27 September. He had brought all his court with him, and assembled all his vassals. Alexander was received with great magnificence, and there was a performance by Talma before 'an audience of kings'. His guest was perhaps less flattered than envious at seeing so much splendour; at all events, he did not allow himself to be dazzled. If we are to believe Metternich, Talleyrand boasted that he had put Alexander on his guard, suggesting to him that Russia had no interest in supporting Napoleon against Austria and in helping him to increase his power. Russia should, on the contrary, seek to restrain him, and this would pay France, as well as the rest of Europe: 'France is civilised, but her sovereign is not.' When the emperor sounded his ally as to the possibility of a marriage with his sister, Grand Duchess Anne, Talleyrand advised Alexander to steer clear of such a course. Moreover, he persuaded his friend Caulaincourt to represent himself to Alexander as a kind of mediator between the two sovereigns, which could only harm his own sovereign's cause. Talleyrand's perfidy is beyond doubt, and he was not long in reaping his reward, thanks to the good offices of Caulaincourt, in the shape of a marriage between his nephew and the duchesse de Dino, a daughter of the duchess of Courland. But if he did actually use the language attributed to him by Metternich, he exaggerated her merits in order to raise her in Austrian esteem. Alexander, pressed by Caulaincourt to intervene with Vienna and persuade Stadion to suspend his rearmament, had already declared that he would restrict himself to giving advice. Napoleon was not only prepared to allow Alexander to annex the principalities: he offered as a further concession to evacuate the grand duchy of Warsaw. But the tsar still refused to threaten Austria; in fact Metternich, acting on Talleyrand's information, became convinced that Russia was no longer capable of being turned against her.

Once again, we must not jump to the conclusion that Napoleon had allowed himself to be duped. Erfurt, like Tilsit, was only a means to an end. It was a matter of gaining enough time to crush the Spaniards and bring the Grande Armée back on to the Danube. He might reasonably believe that the agreement on 12 October would assure peace till the following summer, and that was all he asked. That same day the Grande Armée was brought back behind the Elbe and for the moment dissolved. Davout remained alone in Germany with two corps constituting the new Rhine Army. On 1 November Prussia, whose debt had been reduced at the tsar's instance to 120 million, paid off fifty million of this in the form of commercial bills payable at the rate of four million a month, and covered the rest by state bonds until such time as those of the mortgage banks should be issued. In accordance with the recent Franco-Russian agreement, Rumiantsev went to Paris to try to renew the discussion with England. This effort was bound to fail. Canning could not possibly admit that on the basis of *uti possidetis* Portugal and Spain should belong to Napoleon. It would at least be necessary for him to have conquered them!

## NAPOLEON IN SPAIN (NOVEMBER 1808–JANUARY 1809)

In spite of his brother's orders to hold on firmly to Burgos and Tudela, Joseph had fallen back behind the Ebro. Moreover he had scattered the sixty-five thousand men he possessed (apart from those in Catalonia) from the Bay of Biscay to Aragon. It had not taken him long to see himself as another Charles V or Philip II. He signed himself 'I, the king', and refused to award Bessières the Order of the Golden Fleece. 'He considers himself every inch a king,' said Napoleon when he came to see him. When Jourdan had been sent to assist him on 22 August, he began to work out strategic schemes. 'The army', Napoleon wrote to him, 'looks as though it was being run by post-office inspectors.'

But the Spaniards failed to take advantage of these favourable circumstances. They did not reach Madrid from Valencia till 13 August, and Castaños not till the twenty-third, and then only with a single division. This was because the juntas, who were thoroughly ineffective and commanded little obedience, were primarily interested in their own provinces and wrangled among themselves. Galicia watched Asturias reasserting its independence and Cuesta, the general in command of Old Castile, defying their authority. In Seville, Count de Tilly proposed that the army should not leave Andalusia, and others that the junta of Granada should be forcibly subjugated. Pretenders to the regency were plentiful. From Sicily there came a son of Ferdinand IV, accompanied by the duc d'Orléans, who had made it up with the legitimate princes; but the English refused to let him land. At the suggestion of the junta of Murcia, whose leading spirit was Florida Blanca, a central junta was in the end set up, composed of thirty-five delegates from the provincial juntas, mostly nobles and priests. They met at Aranjuez on 25 September but were soon lost in discussions about protocol or constitutional matters. A majority gathered round Jovellanos showed sympathy for the English system, while Florida Blanca remained faithful to an enlightened despotism. A ministry was formed, but in order not to offend the generals, no commander-in-chief was appointed, and as they were under a minister of war whose hands were tied by a council, they did very much what they pleased. Recruiting was not given much attention, and the regions directly administered by the central junta, León and Old Castile, raised the smallest number of men – less than twelve thousand by October. England had sent 120,000 rifles, cargoes of equipment and five million in coin; but a large part of these supplies was left unused in the ports. In Lisbon, Dalrymple had re-established the regency nominated by Prince John, but it was almost completely inactive. The regular troops were recalled to the colours; yet out of thirty-two thousand, only thirteen thousand had rifles by the end of November and none of them saw fighting before 1809. The *ordinanza* (general *levée*) was only armed with pikes and did not do anything but spread disorder. The only organised force was the English army of twenty thousand men commanded by Sir John Moore. But it only got under way in October, and it was not till the end of this month that Baird landed another body of thirteen thousand men at Corunna.

When Napoleon reached Vitoria on 5 November he found himself confronted by two chief Spanish forces spread out from the Bay of Biscay to Saragossa. These were the army of Galicia, under Blake, near the sources of the Ebro, and the army of the centre, under Castaños, towards Tudela. Between them, Galuzzo was approaching from Estramadura and making for the Douro with some twelve thousand men. Moore's army was advancing in two widely separated columns, and was only just reaching the frontier; Baird had scarcely got under way at all. Confronted with Napoleon's army of infinitely superior quality, the allies seemed doomed to disaster. All the same, the emperor had to manoeuvre with caution, since he only had 120,000 men at hand, Mortier's and Junot's corps being well in the rear. In the centre, Soult overthrew Galuzzo and took Burgos and Valladolid, from which points Napoleon counted on being able to sweep down on the two wings, one after the other. But before he arrived Lefebvre and Victor had become prematurely engaged with Blake and had driven him back far enough to put him out of reach. Yet through failure to keep in touch with one another – owing to their mutual jealousy – they only partially checked him at Espinosa on 10 and 11 November.

Operations were therefore directed against Castaños, who was beaten by Lannes coming down the Ebro – at Tudela on the twenty-ninth, while Ney worked his way up the Douro in order to cut off his retreat. But these movements were badly synchronised, Ney being unable to arrive in time to fit in with Lannes's premature attack. Castaños's very experienced army succeeded in escaping towards Cuenca by way of Calatayud. Napoleon marched on Madrid, and on the thirtieth, at the Somosierra pass, an enemy division, under fire from sharp-shooters and charged by a mere squadron of Polish light horse, fled in panic. The capital was occupied on 4 December and its approaches cleared. Lefebvre thrust Galuzzo back beyond the Tagus and Victor routed the central army at Uclés. Taking up his quarters at Chamartin, on the outskirts of Madrid, Napoleon issued a whole series of decrees for the reorganisation of Spain without consulting Joseph. He abolished the Inquisition, reduced the number of convents and seized their property.

Meanwhile, however, Sir John Moore was completing his concentration north of Salamanca and joining up with La Romana, who had escaped from Denmark, come back to Asturias and taken over command. Suddenly adopting a very bold policy, the English general was marching towards Soult, who was covering Burgos, in order to cut the French communications. Napoleon was late in getting information of this move, but despatched Ney's corps towards Salamanca and Astorga on 20 December through the snowstorms of the Sierra de Guadarrama to take him in the rear. On the twenty-fourth Moore hurriedly began to retreat, and managed to escape because he was so feebly pursued by Soult. On 3 January 1809, at Astorga, Napoleon relinquished command. Soult gave battle at Lugo on the seventh, then at Corunna on the fifteenth and sixteenth, but not incisively enough to prevent the English from re-embarking. Lannes meanwhile had gone to join Moncey in front of Saragossa, which was heroically defended by Palafox. It took a whole month to break through the fortifications and another month to take the houses by assault. When the struggle came to an end in February 1809, 108,000 Spaniards had lost their lives, forty-eight thousand of them from disease.

In a country where the distances, the winter and the difficulty of communications all told against him, and where the inhabitants only gave information to his enemies, Napoleon was very far from having disposed of them. If only he had succeeded in destroying Sir John Moore's army, the English government would have had considerable difficulty in getting parliamentary support for another one; and in any case it would have taken a long time to get a fresh force ready. Moore, being mortally wounded himself, had to blow up his magazines and sacrifice a great many men, but the bulk of the army escaped, and was soon to be back in Portugal. Nevertheless if Napoleon had been able to stay longer in Spain he would soon have reached Lisbon and Cadiz. But on 17 January 1809 he left Valladolid for Paris. It was now certain that Austria would attack in the spring.

So Spain still remained to be conquered, and Napoleon never ceased to feel the load of this task which he had so unnecessarily assumed in a spirit of pure display. After bringing about an English intervention it produced the same result in Austria and led to the rupture of the Franco-Russian alliance. From now onwards, Napoleon needed two armies. The proportion of recruits rose, and spoiled the army's cohesion. Not daring to ask France for an adequate number of conscripts, he fell back upon an increasing proportion of foreigners, and the quality of both armies began to suffer.

# CHAPTER TWO

# The War of 1809

THE WAR OF 1809 was the natural result of the rising in Spain. The departure of the Grande Armée awakened new hopes in Austria, and spurred her on to new adventures. The example of Spain roused the Germans to a state of romantic excitement which hastened the crisis. Napoleon was taken by surprise and was compelled to raise a new army that won its victories with difficulty. The victory of Wagram seemed for the moment to restore the Continental System; but the Franco-Russian alliance, proving unequal to this new attack on the Empire, stood inexorably condemned.

## THE AWAKENING OF GERMANY

Since the early years of the century, German thought had been more and more given over to a Romantic mysticism. Goethe, serene and impassive as ever, remained true to himself, although Schiller's death in 1805 had left him cruelly isolated. With the Jena and Berlin friends scattered, and Novalis dead, Heidelberg now became the centre where Grenzer, the expounder of mythologies, gathered round him the chief leaders of the second generation in the Romantic movement – men like Clemens Brentano, the son of a Rhineland merchant of Italian origin, Achim von Arnim, a Prussian Junker, and Bettina, sister of the former and wife of the latter, together with La Motte-Fouqué, who was descended from French refugees. After teaching at Coblenz, Görres finally joined them, and they were in touch with Tieck, with the brothers Boisserée, who were trying to revive the study of medieval art in Cologne, and with Jacob and Wilhelm Grimm, librarians at Cassel. The vogue of this school was of advantage to Schelling, who was increasingly absorbed in a mystical symbolism against which Fichte was having some difficulty in defending his reputation. Not till 1806 did Hegel approach the completion of his *Phenomenology of Mind*.

The Romantics were rapidly being impelled by a return to the past – and sometimes by their own interests – towards the traditional religions and the counter-revolution. Schleiermacher had taken up his duties as a pastor once again; Adam Müller and Friedrich Schlegel became Catholics, in 1805 and 1808 respectively. There was general praise of the good old days – which they painted in quite imaginary colours – when the people lived happy lives under the fatherly authority of the aristocracy. Even Fichte, whom they despised for his intellectualism, and who had broken off relations with them, did not escape their influence. As early as 1804, in the third edition of the *Science of Knowing*, he brought back, above the level of the *ego*, an absolute which demanded effort, thus withdrawing the unconditional autonomy of the self. In his *Characteristics of the Present Age*, he distinguished certain periods in human history which he called, in sermon-like fashion, the 'age of innocence', 'the beginning of sin' and 'the age of total sinfulness' – this last characterising man's present condition, given over to an unrestrained individualism from which it was necessary to rescue him in order to secure his 'salvation'. True, he was still a democrat and a republican; but having studied Machiavelli, he was temperamentally inclined to admire the heroic and conquering state and turn away in distaste from the merely utilitarian ideals of the Enlightenment. With an increasingly pessimistic and authoritarian outlook, he was more and more looking to the state to compel men – who were decidedly evil by nature – to conform to reason and to the *Science of Knowing*.

In itself, German Romanticism as defined by August Schlegel in his Berlin lectures from 1801 to 1804, gave a powerful stimulus to a cultural patriotism. He denounced classical art as the apotheosis of the artificial, while Romanticism, the natural expression of the Germanic genius, was entirely spontaneous; from which he drew the conclusion that German civilisation led the world. But the Heidelberg Romantics, making a concrete study of their country's past literary history, exercised a far more rapid influence. Poets as they were, they cared little for strict method, but applied themselves to an enthusiastic and inquisitive examination of legends and popular tales which they translated and adapted. Tieck had led the way in 1803; and in 1805 and 1808, Brentano and Arnim published their famous collection, *Des Knaben Wunderhorn*. Görres followed in their footsteps, and in 1807 collected a certain number of tales taken from the *Teutschen Volksbücher*. The *Minnesinger* was rescued from oblivion, the *Nibelungenlied* was translated, and *Sigard* was discovered by La

Motte-Fouqué. It was in this sense that Stein could write: 'It was Heidelberg that chiefly kindled the German flame which later swept the French
out of our country.'

At this deeper level, national feeling thus remained cultural rather
than political; but there was more than one latent sign of a hidden development at work. The re-establishment of despotism in France filled the
liberals with irritation and despair. Posselt committed suicide not long
after Moreau's condemnation; Schlabrendorf and Reichardt began to
write against Napoleon, and Beethoven removed the name of Bonaparte
from the score of the *Eroica* Symphony. All these men had a grudge
against France for having, as they thought, disavowed the principles of
1789, and they declared the French nation to be vicious and frivolous. In
1804 Herder's cosmopolitan outlook was for the moment obscured by a fit
of nationalism, causing him to dedicate an ode to 'Germania'. Nor were
the Prussians alone in being stirred by the Austrian defeats and the disappearance of the Holy Roman Empire. In 1805 Arndt, in the first part of his
*Geist der Zeit*, adopted a tone of undisguised hostility to France. The state,
which had so far been distasteful to German thinkers as an organ of
restraint, now began to take on a certain value in their eyes as a protector
of the community and an educator of the individual. In 1802, in another of
his books – *Germanien und Europa* – Arndt had declared that natural frontiers and access to the sea were necessary for the free development of a
people; and as early as 1800 Fichte, describing a socialist society which
would assure freedom and equality to all, thought this would only be possible in 'a closed state' that was self-supporting – a state to which he consequently gave the right to a sufficiently large and varied extent of territory
to provide for all its needs. In 1805 he was also inclined to look to the state
to rescue man from a condition of sin.

Nevertheless it needed the catastrophe of 1806 and the French occupation to precipitate and generalise this development. Not that this was
any sudden or universal movement: after Jena, as well as before it, there
were still admirers of Napoleon, like Buchholtz in Berlin. Johannes von
Müller became Jérôme's minister; the University of Leipzig named a
constellation after the victor; Goethe had an interview with him at the
same time as the Erfurt conversations; Hegel, who had caught a glimpse
of him at Jena, called him 'the soul of the world', and even in 1809, when
he was professor at Nuremberg, he advised the Bavarians to adopt the
Civil Code. Nonetheless, it is clear that certain of the intellectual leaders

in the German nation began to change their tone as from 1807, either in
aggressive praise of the superiority of German culture, or in proclaiming
their loyalty to local rulers; and there were certain symptoms to show that
among the mass of the people, particularly in Prussia, apathy was being
succeeded by irritation and hostility. Some of these manifestations are
well known, such as Schleiermacher's sermons at Halle and Berlin,
which ended by rousing distrust of the French authorities, or the publication by Arnim of the *Zeitung für Einsiedler* in 1808; and, above all, the
*Addresses to the German Nation* given by Fichte in Berlin in the year 1807.
It was natural enough for Prussia's misfortunes to find a special echo in
the outlook of men who were specially linked to it by birth or career.
Simultaneously, however, Germans in the north, in Dresden and in
Vienna, began implanting a Romanticism and a national pride that were
fast becoming inseparable. In the spring of 1806 Adam Müller, who was
Prussian in origin, a convert to Catholicism and a friend of Gentz, who
had successfully managed to find him a place in the Austrian administration, began a series of lectures on the principles that ensure the life
and the continuity of states. Together with Kleist, he published in 1807 a
review entitled *Phoebus*, intended to 'foster German art and science'; and
in Vienna, August Schlegel, after a long spell at Coppet as the tutor of
Madame de Staël's son, followed her in her wanderings through Germany,
and was authorised to begin a course in literature in which he took an
even more incisive line than in Berlin. Soon Romanticism found a home
in Caroline Pichler's salon, and a centre from which it could spread.

Everywhere these literary figures now began to enter into close relations with the champions of warlike action. Obliged as they were to tread
delicately where foreigners were concerned and beware of governmental
suspicions, they could not exactly summon their audience to take up
arms, but had to go on stressing more particularly the original characteristics and the superiority of Germanic culture. Fichte more especially
took up and developed Schlegel's theme – that each people shows its
inner soul through an art that is its own particular and specific expression; but that of all nations, the Germans were privileged to possess a
language which had developed by a continuous progress from its earliest
beginnings, an *Ursprache*, which had never undergone any serious con-
tamination. Thus its essential character and the forms expressing it
constituted a harmonious whole. The Romance languages, on the other
hand, were the mere debris of a dead language, and English nothing but a

hybrid dialect, while the genres and the rules of classical French literature had been borrowed from antiquity. The Latin and Anglo-Saxon
peoples, Fichte maintained, not having created their means of expression, therefore had to translate their thought by artificial methods which
stifled its life and spontaneity; whereas German literature, being the only
truly original one, was supreme in the spiritual realm, and its culture was
a message from God to the human race. The pretensions of the Holy
Roman Empire to universal dominion and more especially the oppression
suffered by millions among the Baltic and Slavonic peoples were already
making Germans look upon themselves as a master race; and Fichte's
*Addresses*, with the mystical justification of national pride which had
intoxicated their spirits since the time of Luther, were to become part of
the gospel of pan-Germanism. As far as the conception of the state was
concerned, Adam Müller, though less emotional, was perhaps more
novel in outlook. For Fichte still considered the state as a fitting instrument for ensuring individual progress. Once the French were expelled,
his nation would have the same right to bring about a democratic and
republican revolution. Müller, on the other hand, as a true Romantic,
regarded the state as a being in its own right, pursuing specific ends to
which the individual destiny must be subordinated. Speaking to an aristocratic audience, he would defend both the independence of Germany
and feudal society against any newfangled ideas.

Expressed by word of mouth these doctrines must, to start with, have
exercised a fairly limited influence; and even in print, their spread can
only have been gradual. Yet it is possible that they proved a stimulus to
masonic lodges and secret societies, and so spread more rapidly than
might have been expected at first sight. In any case their immediate importance has been exaggerated through a failure to take sufficient account
of the economic and social consequences of the French conquest which
imbued all classes with a direct hatred of the foreigner, without there
being necessarily any assistance of an ideological kind. Among writers
themselves, there was still the steady fear of seeing French supplant German once again as the language of literature and so reducing the field of
professional activity. 'Who knows', wrote Kleist, 'whether in a hundred
years' time there will still be anyone in the country who speaks German?'

Except in East Prussia, the war damage had not been very great; but
the contributions and requisitionings seemed a crushing load, and military occupation, with all its excesses, abuses and manifold burdens – such

as billeting, transport and work on fortifications – was an even greater source of annoyance. In this respect, Napoleon's methods of warfare had unexpected repercussions from the moment when hostilities seemed in danger of lasting for ever, as in 1807. All the same, his financial policy and the political upheavals were probably even more important in their consequences. In the countries under his authority he levied war contributions just as he did in enemy countries, and neither Jérôme nor Murat was spared. In order to put them in a position to provide troops he restored their finances by cutting down debt, suspending the payment of dividends and pensions, and dismissing a number of officials and officers without any compensation. Prussia, face to face with bankruptcy, had to do likewise, and at any rate in her case, with the army being reduced and so many provinces taken away from her, there seemed to be little prospect for the future. The wretched state of the people was partly the reason for the rising in Hesse in December 1806 and for the sporadic attacks on French troops in Pomerania and Prussia. But more widespread causes were to be found in the impoverishment of the nobles and the middle classes, the exasperation felt by officers and officials who had lost their posts and the unrest among the youth of the universities who were seeking employment. All these sufferings and passionate feelings became focused in a national sentiment that seemed both to justify and to ennoble them. These then were the social elements most likely to provide leaders for resistance, and it was among them that the Tugendbund, for instance, came into being. Founded at Königsberg in April 1808, it had twenty-five lodges by 1809 and more than seven hundred members. Its authority was not confined to Prussia, for we know that Karl Müller made contact with the patriots in Leipzig. It was in fact a 'society for the promotion of civic virtues', and aimed at keeping a watch upon the agents of the state and its citizens, and at punishing any who should co-operate with the enemy. Despite the approval given to it by the king, his ministers looked upon it as a rival authority, and Stein deplored the reappearance of a Holy Vehme.*

There is every reason to believe that this society was eventually destined to become the nucleus of a popular uprising against Napoleon. The idea of a mass insurrection had its roots in the ferment of Romanticism; in the literary idealisation of the primitive German warrior under the command of Hermann in the middle of primeval forests, defying the

* [Medieval secret society which administered summary justice, including torture and execution, for heresy, crime and immorality.]

Roman legions who were the instruments of despotism; and in the revolt of William Tell and the German Swiss, which Schiller's masterpiece had added to the national heritage in 1805. It drew sustenance too from the recent history of France, recalling on the one hand the example of the Vendée, and on the other the volunteers of the Committee of Public Safety. But it was the revolt in Spain that was principally responsible for raising excitement to fever pitch. From July 1808 onwards newspapers, pamphlets and speeches vied with one another in its praise, with the tacit approval of the various governments. Its complex origins enabled it to win the approval of all parties: the aristocrats saw the Spaniards as faithful subjects, the democrats as free men rising up against their oppressors, and the statesmen as good citizens who had hastened to the assistance of the regular army.

Nevertheless, a mass uprising was inevitably associated with the ideas spread by the Revolution. In appealing to the people to take part in public life, it was also an inducement to claim in return for their military services to their country the civil and political rights that properly belonged to them. It seemed to be the symbol of the new power that would be acquired by the state if it abolished privilege and set free the energies of the individual man. It borrowed from Napoleon, the revolutionary leader, some of his own weapons and used them back against him. This was why in the end the aristocracy and the governments of the *ancien régime* refused to make an open appeal to the masses. And so in the history of the German national movement, Austria and Prussia would once again be found in opposing camps. From the very beginning, patriots turned to one or to the other, according to their origin, their career and their religion, but also according to their political leanings. Austria, with its Catholic tradition, stifled all intellectual life, and obscurantism stood in the way of any hopes of reform or popular movement. Prussia, on the other hand, had always prided herself on allowing a certain freedom of thought and had recently raised to power a certain number of men drawn from all parts of Germany who were open to Western influences and determined to modernise both government and society. Yet it was Austria that provided the Romantic ferment with its man of action in the person of Stadion, while in Prussia the leaders of the patriotic party were in the end disowned by the king. The eminently dramatic crisis of 1809 is thus a proof of the demoralising effect of this dual and contradictory strain in the German outlook.

## PRUSSIA

The old Prussia was led by a bureaucracy, and its army by the nobility. In any other country, the catastrophe of 1806, which was thought to be impossible in Prussia, might have produced a revolution. True, Napoleon would not have permitted it, for he knew the simplest way to exploit a conquered country was to preserve its traditional framework. Because they lacked a powerful middle class, the Prussians were unable to rebel. The reforming party was recruited from the higher bureaucracy itself, and had the assistance of a small number of nobles and cultivated bourgeois. But the unique feature was that these aristocrats, who were both conservative and liberal in outlook, were intelligent enough to realise the need for revitalising the state, and had the necessary moral strength to impose their views. Although the creation of modern Prussia took a long time, extending right through the nineteenth century, these men did at least make a beginning.

Immediately after Tilsit, Frederick William III was reinstated in Königsberg. A commission was appointed to purge the army command under Scharnhorst and Gneisenau, who gradually enlisted the help of Grolman, Götzen and Boyen. Another commission was appointed to carry out a special reorganisation of East Prussia in collaboration with Schrötter, its president; it included Schön, Niebuhr and Altenstein. By 10 July Stein had been recalled on Napoleon's own advice – probably because he had been told of the good impression he had made on the French in passing through Berlin on his withdrawal to the Rhine provinces after his dismissal. He reached Königsberg on 30 September, armed with a scheme for reform drawn up by him in the course of the summer, the famous Nassau memorandum. A certain number of these reformers, such as Schön, Schrötter, Clausewitz and Boyen, were Prussian-born, but the most famous of them came from other parts of Germany – men like Grolman, the son of a Westphalian magistrate; Götzen, a Franconian count; Scharnhorst, a native of Hanover; Gneisenau, from Saxony; Stein, who belonged to the Rhineland *Ritterschaft*. Some of them were of humble origin. Scharnhorst's father was a non-commissioned officer and Gneisenau, though the son of an officer, had had a haphazard upbringing. Prussia, which was less set in its ways, and had been disorganised by the shocks of 1806, began to act as a focus for the national energies of Germany.

These men differed greatly in origin and in temperament, and it is not surprising that there is not complete agreement about the spirit that inspired them and their work. Some would see in them no more than men who carried on the traditions of enlightened despotism in Prussia; but their will to create a nation by associating the common people with their schemes of regeneration clearly shows that such a classification is far too narrow for them. It must not be forgotten that the Junkers were strongly opposed to them, and that the king himself was not at all in their favour. Others have seen them rather as the representatives of Germany's moral and religious culture, intent on linking up their reforms with the nation's past; but though they clearly betray the influence of philosophical Idealism and Romanticism, it is nonetheless true that some features of their schemes are more naturally explained by Western influences. No one, it is true, would deny the influence of England, which has already been discussed; nor can it be questioned that Stein had read Montesquieu and had probably known the Physiocrats, as well as the projects of Turgot and Dupont de Nemours. On the other hand, the influence of the Revolution is a debatable point. This at any rate must be conceded – that there were men in Prussia who were fairly familiar with it. Frey, director of police at Königsberg, who prepared the municipal regulations in 1808, had certainly studied the laws of the Constituent Assembly, and Rehdiger, the Silesian noble who submitted to Stein a scheme for a constitution, was well versed in Sieyès's writings. Gneisenau seems to have had the best grasp of the use that might be made of French experience:

What infinite powers lie dormant at the heart of the nation, quite undeveloped and unused! While an empire lies mouldering in powerless shame, there is perhaps some Caesar guiding the plough in a wretched village, and some Epaminondas who is eking out a living from the work of his hands.

It is, however, generally agreed that however much attention they paid to England and France, they never dreamed of borrowing the English parliamentary system or the French spirit of equality which was the essence of the Revolution. In a modern Prussia as they conceived it, the middle classes and the peasants were to be associated with the life of the state, but power was to remain with the king. Castes were to disappear, but the social authority of the Junkers would remain. This was an original scheme of things, half-way between the Western countries and the monarchies of the *ancien régime*, though much more akin to the latter than to the former.

The task confronting the government in Königsberg was not an enviable one. While the discussions with Daru were going on concerning the indemnity, attention was being given to the restoration of the devastated villages, and the question of agrarian reform necessarily came to the fore. The cost of rebuilding the farms fell upon the seigneurs. It was they who had to reconstitute the livestock, provide the peasants with seed and even supply them with food in hard times like these. The seigneurs themselves were extremely hard-pressed, and it had been necessary to grant them an *indult* or moratorium on their mortgage debts. In their eyes, the simplest course was to join the devastated peasant holdings on to their own *Gut*, their own property, and reduce the holders to the state of day labourers. The law forbade eviction and demanded the abolition of the *Bauernschutz*;* but it offered nothing in exchange, and left the peasant as a mere *Untertan* (subject). But the government officials did not view the matter in this light. Steeped in the lessons learnt from Smith and Young, they declared themselves – Schön in particular – in favour of large-scale cultivation, and had no objection to the abolition of the *Bauernschutz*; but it was a first principle of liberal economy to abolish the feudal system. Although the monarchy had allowed individual bourgeois to acquire land and had gone a long way to abolishing serfdom on its own crown lands, together with the transformation of tenant into owner, it had never yet dared question the Junkers' monopoly of the landed property, or interfere in the internal affairs of the manor.

But now it seized the opportunity – and this is the cardinal importance of the 1807 reforms. On the one hand, the government abolished *Untertänigkeit* in exchange for the suppression of *Bauernschutz*; on the other, it authorised the middle classes and the peasants to acquire land. The nobles were freed from their caste restrictions, and allowed in return to enter professions that had hitherto been reserved for the middle classes, and also gave the peasants the same rights. A start was made in replacing the various castes by *Stände*, classes based upon wealth and profession. The East Prussian Landtag gave way, and the reforms were decided upon in principle in August 1807. Altenstein's advice was to extend it throughout the royal dominions, without waiting for the approval of the other

* [Protection of the peasantry by the state.]

*Landtage*. Napoleon reorganised society on French principles in the grand duchy of Warsaw and in the kingdom of Westphalia; and this example was not without its influence, for it was likely to provoke discontent and lead to emigration.

Stein only arrived on 30 September and was thus not the initiator of the reforms. They were not even mentioned in his Nassau memorandum. He did not favour capitalism, and it should be noted that as far as the peasants were concerned, he had not set them free on his own lands. His role was to support Altenstein and make certain reservations about the outright abolition of the *Bauernschutz*, the regulation of it being postponed till later. The order was signed on 9 October 1807. Instead of a general law to regulate the *Bauernschutz*, provincial edicts were substituted. These appeared between 1808 and 1810, and represented in effect a compromise. The new holdings – that is to say, those established between 1752 and 1774 according to the respective regions – were given over to eviction; the old ones could only be joined to the *Gut* if the new units constituted farms whose total extent was equivalent to all the holdings that had disappeared, but of course much larger than any single one of them. The royal lands kept their more advanced position as compared with the private manors. On 28 October 1807 Frederick William III abolished *Untertänigkeit* in them, which was hardly of any importance except in Silesia, and on 27 July 1808 he extended to East Prussia the arrangements previously promulgated by edict in the other provinces concerning the making over of properties to tenants, in return for compensation payment and the compulsory redemption of the feudal dues. There are good grounds for believing that some thirty thousand peasants in this province thus became landowners.

The order of 1807 and those which completed it produced a chorus of praise in Germany and England, some of which can be rightly discounted. The motives behind these measures were primarily fiscal and economic, and the essential results told in favour of the state and the Junkers. The terms of the settlement ensured the treasury a considerable gain. By conceding ownership of property to the peasants, the king got rid of his customary obligations to them and abolished their common rights on his own lands, chiefly in the forests, which profited greatly by this step. In the private manors, the concessions made to the peasants were chiefly of a legal kind. As from 1810 *Untertänigkeit* was to be abolished – though it was never really defined. Henceforward it would appear that peasants might leave the glebe, have freedom to marry and withdraw their children from the *Gesindedienst*;* but a measure of uncertainty hung over many of the other obligations, which worked to their disadvantage. The feudal dues and forced labour rights continued in their entirety, and tenure remained just as precarious as before. The seigneur kept the right to administer justice, which made him the administrator of the village and gave him power over all police arrangements and the infliction of penalties, even of corporal punishment. In so far as there was real progress, it was more than offset for a good many peasants by the evictions which turned them into mere daily wage earners. On the royal lands, the cost of redemption and the wretched conditions of those times obliged many of them to sell their land, and allow the concentration of land in the hands of big owners to go forward. No one even thought of allowing them to benefit by mortgage loans, though these were readily available to the middle classes. Apart from the monopoly in landownership, the nobles retained all their other privileges.

These reforms worked out in favour of the regrouping of land, the disappearance of the customary rights, and so the dissolution of the rural community. Economic liberty would likewise have called for big reforms in industry and commerce. In East Prussia, Stein did carry out a few such reforms. He abolished several corporations and the lords' milling dues, and proclaimed equality of status as between town and country, thus making it possible for peasants to buy and sell on the spot. This last reform had a very serious effect on the receipts from the excise, which was chiefly levied in the towns, and made a reform of taxation seem probable. Stein did in fact show a marked preference for taxation of income. As East Prussia had contracted a debt in order to pay a war contribution, he induced the Landtag to vote an income tax, the first of its kind; but it remained exceptional, and was not extended to the rest of the kingdom.

Stein's personal efforts were chiefly directed to reorganising the bureaucracy, whose power he wished to reduce by linking representatives of the nation with it. He was authoritarian, quick, and sometimes surly in manner, and had insisted upon dismissing two favourites – Lombard and Beyme – and placing Scharnhorst at the head of the military cabinet which became part of the Ministry of War in 1809. Moreover, he planned a reorganisation of the central government under five strictly specialised ministries, and the creation of a council of ministers. In fact, however, he

* [Obligatory domestic service.]

could not get the better of the clique: the king of Prussia's civil and military cabinets still held the real power. He also planned to set up a national consultative Landtag. When he had to get approval in East Prussia for the *Einkommensteuer* [income tax] and for mortgage bonds on behalf of Napoleon, he changed the constitution of the Landtag by increasing the number of middle-class representatives, admitting representatives of the peasants elected on a property-qualification basis, and introducing individual voting. His national Landtag would have been constituted by 'orders', with individual voting at any rate in financial matters, and there would have been popular representation, to the advantage of the rich. But in the other provinces, there was no reform of the Landtag, and the national Landtag never came into existence.

The administrative reforms were promulgated after his fall, on 26 December 1808. They did not do more than join together in the provincial subdivisions the powers of the old *Kammer* [courts] on the royal lands and the *Regierung* [administration], which remained collegiate in structure, while taking away from the latter all that remained of its judicial functions. At the head of the province was the *Oberpräsident* [governor], formerly a customary office, but now made an official appointment. In the *Regierung*, there were representatives of the nobles associated with the officials, but it was soon obvious that they would not be able to work together. Stein's purpose had been to keep the bureaucracy and at the same time imitate the English justices of the peace; but he met with no success. In order not to have to borrow the Napoleonic *préfet*, he kept the collegiate principle, without seeing that this was against his plan of giving more drive and initiative to the administration. Only in the towns did his order of 19 November 1808 produce significant and enduring results. Without excluding local features, he laid down the broad lines to be followed by all the cities. They were given an elective municipal assembly and a magistrature whose members were appointed by the latter, thus restricting – though not altogether abolishing – the supervision exercised by the state. The really new feature was to withdraw elective rights for the assembly from the corporations, and to transfer them to all householders with certain property qualifications, for Germany had never before had anything but a corporative franchise. Even in the English towns, an individual franchise was rare, and in any case the Germans were not very well acquainted with their organisation. In spite of all that has been said to the contrary, it remains beyond a doubt that Stein's chief reform was inspired by French models and this was certainly due in part to his adviser Frey.

Stein was only in power a little over a year, and it is therefore not surprising that his ministry should have been more noted for its promise than for its performance. It must even be admitted that the results were not such as to arouse much enthusiasm, and that the reformers' military achievements made a much more substantial contribution to the resurrection of Prussia. These military reforms carried out by Scharnhorst and his assistants had already advanced some way in 1809. The purging and reorganisation of the command had already been carried through, the independent company had disappeared, and the infantry was under new regulations which took account of French tactical methods. Yet in spite of all this, the Prussian army was not in a condition to beat Napoleon, as the reformers were well aware. Up to July 1808 they had no thought of anything but an evacuation. In January Scharnhorst was working in concert with Stein on a scheme by which Prince William should, with this end in view, offer a Prussian alliance, or entry into the Confederation of the Rhine. Gneisenau's only objection was that 'once in the Cyclops' cave, the only favour we could hope for would be the privilege of being the last to be devoured'. But at the news of the Spanish insurrection and even before learning of the Baylen disaster, they completely changed their attitude. As early as 23 July Götzen was sent to Silesia to get secretly in touch with the Austrians. On 6 August it was decided to call up for one month the conscripts whom financial stringency would not allow them to take on a permanent footing, so that it would at any rate be possible to mobilise them in an emergency. These were the famous *Krümper*, the cavalry reinforcements. In the course of the month, further details of the plan were embodied in a number of memoranda. The idea was to call the whole German nation to arms in order to fight a war to the death. The women and children would be evacuated, the countryside laid waste, and the enemy harassed and encircled by guerrilla bands. Clearly, this was a revolutionary spirit: the princes and nobles who refused to lead the national uprising would be deprived of their rights and dignities, and the king would give his people a constitution.

For the first time Germany, as she was to be in the nineteenth century, began to shape herself in men's thoughts as a political entity over against the foreigner. Austria, no doubt, figured as a possible ally, but also as a separate and distinct power: it was Prussia who would appeal to the German people and take the lead. But there was as yet no idea of Prussia's being more than an instrument, nor of the risks to which her dynasty would be exposed. Nothing shows more vividly the effects of the Spanish rising and the state of romantic exaltation it produced. As a prudent precaution, Stein consented to hoodwinking Napoleon by means of an alliance till all was in readiness for the decisive move. 'Is Napoleon the only one who should be allowed to replace law by caprice, and the truth by lies?' His secret organisations were not extensive enough to prepare for insurrection, nor did he possess, like Spain, a docile clergy largely made up of monks. Too many people had to be let into the secret, and he was not sufficiently on his guard against French espionage. Two of his letters, one of them to Wittgenstein who was taking the waters in Mecklenburg, fell into the hands of Napoleon.

The Prussian aristocracy was thoroughly indignant. Oh yes, they wanted to drive out the French, but under the leadership of the king and with the help of the regular army, in concert with the allied princes, while keeping the common people in their traditionally subservient position. They were jealous of the threat to their privileges, and hated the parvenu immigrants, whom they treated as Jacobins. There was a positive chorus of attacks from Vienna, and Frederick William was by no means insensitive to them. He held fast to the *ancien régime* and to his autocratic power and made a more prudent estimate of the risks involved, so that he would take no action without the tsar. In a council held on 23 August he rejected the conspirators' proposals. Alexander, then on his way to Erfurt, had advised him to play for time, and he therefore ratified on 29 September the agreement signed in Paris on the eighth. The patriots had done all they could to dissuade him from this course, and Boyen suggested calling together a national assembly, but his decision was not communicated to them till October. After offering to resign, Stein returned to the attack. On the twenty-eighth he outlined a new plan for insurrection, and on 6 November he put before the king a proclamation announcing sweeping reforms in order to rouse public opinion. Meanwhile a third party was forming: men who favoured the reforms, such as Hardenberg and Altenstein, but who were concerned to spare the nobility as the state's only bulwark, and who wished, in common with the king, to gain time and avoid any unfortunate adventures. As Stein was against his sovereigns' proposed visit to their beloved Alexander, the queen threw him over; he was dismissed on 24 November, and on 15 December declared an outlaw of the Empire by Napoleon.

Altenstein and Dohna took over the reins of power, and the movement for reform began to lose its impetus. Scharnhorst, who stayed in office, was the only one to continue the work. But work on a national scale was postponed to an indefinite future, and the Junkers were triumphant. On 26 November Yorck wrote:

There's one of those madcaps' heads broken, at any rate; the rest of the viper's brood will succumb to its own poison. The safest and wisest course is to wait quietly for the outcome of political events. It would be pure folly to provoke and attack the enemy at one's own peril. Germany will never lend itself to any Sicilian Vespers or Vendéan uprising. The Prussian peasant will do nothing unless he is ordered to by his king and has the support of the big battalions . . . Our situation begins to look distinctly better, both at home and abroad.

This optimism enraged the patriots and plunged them into despair. Götzen, when negotiating with the Austrians, had spoken angrily of the resistance they were meeting with, and announced that the national movement, when it got under way, would soon see some heads falling. Grolman had followed Stein into exile – and he was not the only one to do so. The dynasty lost prestige, and so did Prussia. For a moment, the attention of Germans was once more concentrated upon Austria, which had awoken to the world of political thought, and Kleist voiced their hopes in uttering the watchword 'Austria and Freedom'.

## AUSTRIA

After Austerlitz, the emperor Francis had changed his ministers and military staff. Archduke Charles once again became commander-in-chief, and on 10 February 1806 resumed the presidency of the *Kriegsgerath* [general staff]. The office of chancellor was taken by Philip de Stadion, a former ambassador, whose elder brother, Canon Frederick, was representing Austria at Munich. Archdukes Charles and Regnier also urged a change in the system of government, but without success. Francis continued to want to be in control of everything. In his cabinet, Baldacci enjoyed the same ascendancy as his predecessor Colloredo. He was intelligent, hard-working and honest, though he was supposed to be the son of a Corsican mercenary, while others said he was a noble's bastard. Stadion, who came from the mediatised *Ritterschaft*, was authoritarian, and ambitious to play an important part in affairs. Though well educated and liberal-minded, he was too much attached to his noble birth to lay a hand on the nobles' privileges. He played the enlightened despot, setting up factories, founding schools and constructing roads, but without making any changes in the structure of the state or society. As a charming, witty and worldly man who enjoyed life to the full and was extravagant in his ways, he was too light-minded to conceive of great reforms – in fact another Choiseul, rather than a Stein. He did not even succeed in obtaining from Hungary the appropriate subsidies, or the military modifications required. In the 1807 Diet Nagy condemned any idea of intervention in the war and repeated the usual complaints. Acting in his customary way, the emperor postponed any examination of them, and was satisfied with a contingent of twelve thousand men and a moderate level of taxation. The only fruitful piece of work, carried out by Archduke Charles, was hindered by a lack of resources, and the chronic deficit meant that the debt rose from 438 million guldens in 1805 to 572 million in 1809, and paper money from 337 to 518 million, till the loss in face value at Augsburg rose from twenty-six per cent to sixty-seven. In 1806 Count Zichy tried to reduce the issue of money by a forced loan, but the 1807 armaments annulled the effect of this measure, and in August 1808 he was replaced by O'Donnell, who had come to no decision when war suddenly supervened. Inflation had warm champions among the speculators and exporters, and more especially among the partisans of war, who saw no other means of financing a campaign.

Stadion had from the start been thinking of another war as a means of building up a reputation, but the lesson of 1805 had been such a stern one that for a long time the war party was powerless. From Paris, Metternich encouraged an attitude of caution, and Stadion was obliged to acquiesce and let the winter of 1807 pass without intervention. The Peace of Tilsit then forced him to join the blockade and break with England. During this lull, some were inclined, under the influence of the Romantic movement which was spreading in Vienna, to point back to the past history of the monarchy and use it to justify the existence of Austria as a European state, a Christian bulwark against the infidel and a missionary of Western civilisation among the Magyars and the Slavs. The same arguments were used to support its primacy among the German-speaking peoples. A distinguished protagonist of the movement was the historian Baron Hormayr, director of the state archives. He had close links with Archduke John, and longed to become a man of action.

Another factor in rousing Austria from her torpor was the insurrection in Spain. Stadion kept the public well informed about the tragedy of Bayonne and sang the praises of Ferdinand's faithful subjects. This propaganda at once had an effect on the Magyar nobility. On 28 August 1808 the Diet gave an enthusiastic welcome to the new empress Maria-Luisa d'Este, Francis's third wife, who was crowned queen of Hungary. The strength of the contingent was raised to twenty thousand recruits by abolishing the right of substitution, and the king was granted in advance absolute powers for three years in case of war, which would allow him on his own authority to call for an insurrection. Hungarian authors began to attack France. Verseghy, who had formerly translated 'La Marseillaise', published in 1809 a *Magyar Loyalty*, and Kisfaludy a 'Patriotic Address to the Magyar Nobles'. The Spanish example immediately suggested that the lost provinces – especially the Tyrol, which was discontented under Bavarian administration – might possibly form a valuable rallying point. The departure of the Grande Armée and Talleyrand's speeches at Erfurt finally brought Stadion to a decision. Moreover Metternich himself thought that the moment had come, for he noted that Napoleon only had one army, and it had just left Germany. Stadion took Talleyrand's word for it that the emperor's position in France was thoroughly shaken.

It did not take long to build up a war party again. It was supported by all the archdukes except Charles, and likewise by all the imperial ambassadors. Vienna once more became the headquarters of the European aristocracy. Razumovski reappeared, along with Pozzo di Borgo, and Madame de Staël had just arrived, accompanied by August Schlegel, who was joined by Frederick, now secretary to Archduke Charles. The emperor was urged on to war by his new wife and by his mother-in-law, who could not reconcile herself to the loss of her duchy of Modena. He finally gave way in 1808. Charles held out for longer, but in the end had to yield. Another centre of action was growing up at Prague, where Stein had taken refuge and where there were plenty of links with the German patriots. The movement won over the middle classes, and the students and the populace in the large towns, thanks to propaganda organised on the advice of Metternich by Stadion and Hormayr according to the French model. They poured out gazettes and pamphlets, and made use of the theatres and concerts. Gleich wrote patriotic plays and Collin

patriotic songs. There were also great ceremonies to celebrate the establishment of the *Landwehr* [militia]. Among the students too a certain
number of volunteers came forward including Grillparzer – though he very
quickly changed his tune. These appeals to the people could not be
allowed to mislead as to the true nature of Stadion's policy. Though he
sought to rouse men's spirits, it was strictly within the limits and for
the advantage of the Austrian state of the *ancien régime*; and it was the
Junkers', and not Stein's, approval that he deserved. Nor must we be
deceived by Hormayr's tactics when he received delegations from the
Tyrolese, at the beginning of 1809, one of them led by Hofer, who had
come to plan a peasant rising with him; it was only a question of carrying
through a legitimist movement. If Austria probably reckoned that disturbances would break out in Germany, she was nonetheless opposed to a
German nationalist movement, and made no secret of it. The patriots
who had looked to her were labouring under an illusion: while she welcomed their good wishes for victory and would have willingly accepted
their services, she had no intention of consulting them, reckoning that
she would conquer Napoleon in her own strength and then re-establish
her own sovereignty as of old in Germany and in Italy.

The Austrian army had made undeniable progress under the leadership of Archduke Charles. In the first place, it had built up some reserves
by forming in each recruiting zone for the respective regiments two battalions who were obliged to put in three weeks' training every year. On 10
June 1806 the *Landwehr* had been established, composed of ex-soldiers
and volunteers grouped together in battalions in each district, and
commanded by retired officers and notables. At the beginning of 1809 it
numbered 152,000 men in Austria and Bohemia, Galicia having been
kept on a separate footing. On the other hand efforts were made to
introduce the French methods. The 1807 regulations adopted a battle
array with the use of skirmishers, but the infantry did not in fact use it.
On 1 September 1808 it was decided to form nine divisions of Tyrolese
*chasseurs* – twenty-three thousand skirmishers – who proved extremely
useful. As the Austrian cavalry had a tendency to scatter its forces,
Charles grouped part of them together in independent corps. He also
grouped the artillery in regiments – up till then they had been divided
between the infantry battalions – organised a pioneer corps, and improved the services behind the lines by setting up a medical corps, a
remount corps and an army post. He reduced by half the regimental

baggage trains and lightened the convoys by establishing on-the-spot
requisitioning. Finally, in July 1808 the army was in principle divided
into corps and given a general headquarters.

These improvements, however, needed time and money to produce
results. No army corps were created because it would have needed too
costly a reconstruction of the garrisons. The troop movements remained
unwieldy, because the magazine and convoy arrangements had not been
completely given up. Tactics, too, were little improved, because the superior officers were too old and promotion was blocked by incompetence and
corruption. But in spite of everything, the Austrians showed up much
better in 1809 than in 1805, which was a warning that Napoleon would
have done well to heed. Yet what they most decidedly lacked was a real
war leader. Archduke Charles had great qualities, such as diligence, prudence and coolness; but he was more effective in defence than in attack,
and too much wedded to traditional strategy which treated war as, in
Niebuhr's phrase, 'a game of chess', and aimed not at destroying the
enemy but merely at conquering a geographical objective, as Clausewitz
remarked. And worst of all, he was hesitant. These faults were a matter of
temperament. Although he was only thirty-eight, his health was not
good, and he therefore lacked keenness and initiative. Niebuhr observed
that he went to war in a joyless manner.

But the Austrians were so confident in themselves that they were not
concerned to find allies. They could in fact only count on the English, for
Stadion's overtures had not borne any fruit. Even in London, there was a
certain reticence. In October Metternich had promised to place four
hundred thousand men in the line in return for £5 million, plus half as
much again for the expenses of mobilisation. But the English replied –
though not till 24 December – that this was asking too much. Then King
George insisted that Austria should first of all make peace – which
she could not do without breaking with Napoleon. Canning conveyed
£25,000 in notes to Trieste; but on 10 April he was still demurring and
quoting the cost of the war in Spain. The truth of the matter is that the
English government was deeply divided. It was no longer a question of
debating whether they should act on the Continent; on this point there
was no objection raised by any minister. The only difficulty was to decide
where. Canning wanted to concentrate all available forces in the Iberian
peninsula, while Castlereagh advanced the claims of Holland, and there
had even been some talk of Pomerania. These last two diversions would

have had the widest possible repercussions, particularly the latter, which might well have produced an extensive rising in Germany and brought Prussia in as well. Castlereagh opted for the Low Countries, the central objective of his European policy. A well-conducted expedition, he held, might take Antwerp by surprise. Through lack of preparation it did in fact prove useless to the Austrians. But like Mack in 1805, Stadion did not wait for support, and this time he could give good reasons for his decision. Napoleon was unprepared, and there were hopes of taking him by surprise. Yet there can scarcely be any doubt that the romantic excitement let loose by Stadion finally swept even him off his feet.

## THE CAMPAIGN OF 1809

For Napoleon, this war, coming at a point when he had not yet finished with the Spanish campaign, was a disaster. The only man who could have prevented it with a single word was Alexander: but the word was not spoken. His experience at Erfurt had taught him that in order to extract advantages from Napoleon you must catch him at a disadvantage, and the Austrian aggression came at precisely the right moment. War was still going on in Finland, and was about to be resumed in Turkey, where Russia would be able to enjoy a free hand. Moreover, Alexander was reverting to his Polish schemes of 1805. In spite of the disgrace of Czartoryski, who had retired to Palavy, there was still agitation going on from the Russian party in the grand duchy. In the spring of 1809 the Warsaw and Galician nobles came to the tsar to offer their support if he would promise to re-establish the kingdom. On 27 June he replied that he would never abandon the provinces that had become Russian; if circumstances allowed, he would gladly re-create a Poland by joining the grand duchy to Galicia. Clearly, this was to be through his agency and to his advantage, for soon afterwards he was to forbid Napoleon to carry out the same measures. Sentiment, too, may have played its part, for in January 1809 the king and queen of Prussia had come to St Petersburg, and that had revived old memories. While advising the ambassador Schwarzenberg to play for time, Alexander is said to have added: 'The moment for vengeance will come a little later.' It must therefore be concluded that from then onwards a new war between Russia and France was only a matter of time. From Valladolid the emperor sent him one of his officers to suggest that their respective ambassadors should send Stadion identical notes ordering diplomatic relations to be broken off unless the reply was satisfactory. Alexander accepted the notes, but would not agree to breaking off rela- tions, insisting moreover that this step should be the object of special diplomatic missions, which postponed it *sine die* [indefinitely]. Napoleon was no longer under any illusions. Though he proposed to the tsar that they should join in guaranteeing the integrity of Austria provided she would disarm, it was only in the vain hope of gaining time and finishing the concentration of his new army before the archduke should take the offensive.

Returning to Paris, he had to confess that the country's morale was not good. He was not seriously troubled by the royalists; but they were not disarming. On 23 August 1806 the bishop of Vannes had been kid- napped by Lahaie-Saint-Hilaire, who was not apprehended until 1807. The following year saw the end of the Normandy exploits of Lechevalier, an accomplice of the vicomte d'Aché. The royalist agency in Jersey kept sending agents to the West, and in 1808 Prigent and six others were shot, followed by Armand de Chateaubriand, a cousin of the vicomte, on 20 February 1809. The Jacobins were still less of a threat, for they were being relentlessly harried by the police. At the end of 1807 they arrested Didier, formerly a juror of the Revolutionary Court; in 1808 a republican plot – the first since 1801 – was denounced to Dubois, the prefect of police, in which Demailot, formerly an agent of the Committee of Public Safety, General Malet, the Convention members Florent-Guiot and Ricord, and the ex-tribune Jacquemont were implicated. Fouché suc- ceeded, with Cambacérès's agreement, in persuading the emperor that it would be best to hush the matter up.

These various attempts had no further repercussions. What alarmed the nation was rather the policy of Napoleon himself. His triumphs never reassured anybody, for they always involved a further instalment. 'This war must be our last,' he had been careful to say on entering the struggle against Russia in 1807. Then he had represented Tilsit as the pledge of peace; yet less than a year later there was the Spanish affair – and this time it was not possible to place the responsibility on Charles IV. 'France is sick with anxiety,' wrote Fiévée to the emperor. And there was no less uneasiness among the emperor's servants. Fontanes, as president of the Corps Législatif, dared to express their feelings on the eve of the 1808 campaign: 'You have only to speak, and your hearers are overcome with nameless fears that are compounded of love and hope.' In private, Decrès used much more direct terms: 'The emperor is mad, completely mad: he'll bring ruin upon himself and upon us all.' Since he was running so light-heartedly to perdition, some thought it prudent henceforward to betray him in order to save their own skins, dressing up their villainy as the interest of their country, which it was only right to distinguish from the tyrant's cause. Moreover, if he should be killed or meet with a disaster, a successor would have to be found; but as nothing could be done without foreign approval, the safest course was to offer the powers certain guarantees – and this was Talleyrand's secret.

One cannot fail to see the significance of the fact that attempts were made to find a successor to Napoleon during the Spanish expedition and on the eve of the Austrian attack, as at the time of Marengo. In December 1808 Talleyrand became reconciled with Fouché, and it appears that they came to an agreement on the subject of Murat. Rumours spread abroad to this effect. Eugène was said to have intercepted a letter to the king of Naples, and a secretary of Fouché's was thought to have let the matter leak out, so that Madame Mère was able to warn her son. It is certain at any rate that Napoleon thought he had been betrayed. He made a terrible scene with Talleyrand and removed him from the office of grand chamberlain. Fouché was spared – perhaps in order not to disorganise the police at a dangerous moment, perhaps because after Tilsit he had taken the initiative in proposing a divorce, and had even spoken of it to Josephine. After such an outburst, Napoleon's tolerant attitude seems as surprising as it was ill advised. Probably he was afraid that if he struck down one of his old accomplices he would alarm others and provoke new plots. But he had either said too much, or not enough. Talleyrand's disgrace, as Mollien says, roused 'a kind of anxiety, all the more widespread because most people did not know its origins, and so no one could therefore feel safe'. Yet surrounded as he was by the *ci-devant*, and dreaming of an alliance with a royal family, how could Napoleon have shot another prince on the score of high treason?

With Napoleon absent at the front, his enemies kept on the alert. It was quite possible that there might be an English landing on the French coast, for in April they had damaged the Rochefort squadron in the Île d'Aix roadstead. In Provence, there was unrest among the royalists and republicans. Barras was in touch with Generals Guidal and Monnier, with the former corsair Charabot and with a merchant who advanced funds. There were suggestions of arranging the escape of Charles IV and

Godoy, who were then interned at Marseille. In July Charabot tried to link up with Collingwood, who was cruising off the coast. Napoleon's conflict with the pope was rousing a seething unrest in Catholic circles; and in the course of the summer, the West gave new cause for anxiety, while there were disturbances in the Saar and the Ourthe districts. Even the army contained some doubtful elements. We have no information about the Philadelphes* said to have been under the orders of Colonel Oudet, who was killed at Wagram; but in Soult's army in Portugal, an officer named d'Argenton formed a conspiracy and tried to get Wellington's support. We must not exaggerate the danger, but a comparison between the public mood of 1809 and the ovations of August 1807 reveals a striking contrast. The whole Empire was built on victory, and the reverses in Spain had struck a blow at its prestige which was all the more powerful because it was the cause of a new war in Germany, which – as the nation was well aware – was starting at an awkward moment. Facing Napoleon there was an armed Austria, a Spain that had risen in revolt, Portugal invaded by the English, and Germany trembling with excitement: behind him lurked an agonising anxiety and treason; never had he played for such tremendous stakes.

Yet he proceeded to prepare for the contest with his usual coolness and calm. He had some ninety thousand men immediately available, the remnants of the Grande Armée left behind in Germany and labelled the Army of the Rhine. To this could be added one hundred thousand allied men – Germans, Dutch and Polish. The 1809 class, who had been called up in January 1808, were not yet fit for service. In order to take their place in the depots, the emperor had called up in September 1808 the 1810 class as from 1 January 1809. Almost at the same time he raised the contingent numbers from sixty to eighty thousand, to take effect retrospectively as from 1806, resulting in a total call-up of 140,000 conscripts. Existing regiments had a fourth battalion added to them, and new divisions were constituted in the Boulogne and Alsace camps, and then sent beyond the Rhine. Finally, the Guard was brought back with all speed from Spain. In March 1809 Napoleon had three hundred thousand fighting men at his disposal in Germany, of whom he left some one hundred thousand in Italy, sixty thousand of them in Venetia; and Marmont kept a further fifteen thousand in Dalmatia. To have created this new army at all was a marvel; but there could be no illusions about its value. Almost half of it consisted

---

* [Secret masonic society with extensive army membership.]

of foreigners who were a great disappointment in the front line. The French effectives were more than half recruits, and their formations were incomplete and largely improvised.

The deficiencies of the material preparations – as usual, of a rather perfunctory kind – were particularly apparent to these young troops. Even the superior command had lost some of its glamour. With Ney and Soult still in Spain, three army corps had to be entrusted to Lefebvre, Vandamme and Jérôme, and the Italian army to Eugène. The 1809 army, though much inferior to that of 1805, contained more than one hundred thousand French who had fought the 1807 campaign, and they were enough to ensure victory; but they were a makeshift collection, a foretaste of the army of 1812. For the moment, however, the danger did not lie in its composition, but in the fact that Napoleon, for all his activity, could not create it quickly enough to get it assembled in time. At the end of March Bernadotte was still in Saxony with fifty thousand Polish and Saxon troops; Jérôme was in central Germany with the Dutch and West-phalians; Davout's corps – sixty thousand picked men – were in Bavaria, north of the Danube; Oudinot, the Bavarians and other Germans on the Lech; Masséna further in the rear, and the Guard still on their way from Spain. The bulk of these forces was therefore spread over a front of 150 kilometres, within a single day's march of the enemy. The archduke took up the offensive on 10 April, and Napoleon did not arrive at Donauwörth till the seventeenth. If the Austrians had made a massed attack there is no knowing what might have happened.

The allied forces were more judiciously arranged than in 1805. Archduke John had only fifty thousand men available for the invasion of Venetia, and only ten thousand of them were stationed on the Tyrol side, under Chasteler, and six thousand in Croatia. However, it was necessary to give thirty-five thousand of the total to Archduke Ferdinand for the protection of Galicia against the Poles. In Germany, Archduke Charles had two hundred thousand men at his disposal. His first plan was to debouch from Bohemia in order to crush Davout and cut the French forces into two halves – a piece of strategy that would have been worthy of Napoleon. But he was uneasy at the thought of leaving Vienna un-defended, and he decided to move along the right bank of the Danube and occupy the Bavarian plateau. In so doing, he lost precious time and tired out his troops; nevertheless, this revised plan would have likewise pro-duced decisive results if only it had been carried out speedily and with all his strength. As it was, he left two corps in front of Davout; and having crossed the Inn, he advanced slowly towards the Isar, his left supported by Hiller, in numerous columns whose movements were badly co-ordinated. Davout was able to fall back southwards, and would have joined up with the other corps near Ingolstadt if Berthier, through a misinterpretation of the emperor's orders, had not kept him at Ratisbon.

Napoleon had no sooner arrived on the seventeenth than he hastened to summon him to join up with him, and on the nineteenth the marshal set out by the right bank of the river, thus passing in front of the enemy and giving him a last chance of striking a crushing blow. But the archduke failed to seize the opportunity, and Davout was able to resist the feeble pressure of the Austrians at Tengen. Meanwhile, Napoleon had mistaken Hiller's corps for the main body and was preparing to cut the Inn and force him back on the Danube. In the centre and under Lannes's command he massed a force that attacked the Austrian columns on the left towards Abensberg on 20 April and pushed them back on Landshut, while Masséna was marching on this town to take them in the rear. But he arrived too late, and on the twenty-first Hiller, thrust out of Landshut, was able to fall back upon the Inn. The archduke took advantage of the delay to join up with his forces that had remained to the north of the Danube – the Ratisbon garrison having meanwhile capitulated; and on the twenty-second he at last decided to launch a vigorous attack on Davout. But before his right wing had been able to come into action to cut him off from the river, Davout himself attacked his left wing at Eckmühl, and soon after, Napoleon, hastening up from Landshut, took him in the rear. He accordingly retreated, and managed to cross the Danube without difficulty; but his army had lost about thirty thousand men, and was cut into two parts, though both of them were still free to move downstream towards Vienna and effect a meeting, and still comprised more than one hundred thousand men. On the twentieth the French recaptured Ratisbon, but Hiller inflicted a reverse on Bessières. The archduke had not suffered the same fate as Mack.

The emperor did not pursue him into Bohemia, but marched on Vienna. Not that he was drawn aside by this political objective: it was rather in order to interpose between the main Austrian army and those in Italy and the Tyrol. While Davout – now supported by Bernadotte – was keeping an eye on the archduke's movements, Masséna rolled back Hiller's forces, and Lannes simultaneously tried to outflank them through the mountains. Meanwhile Lefebvre, seizing Salzburg, threw Jellachich back towards the Drave and could keep a watch on the Tyrol. After a bloody affray at Ebersberg, near the crossing of the Traun, Hiller managed to get across the Danube to link up with his chief, and the French entered Vienna on 12 May. But this time they found the bridges cut, and an enemy force of 115,000 on the left bank of the river. Napoleon made for the islands which divide the river into several branches below the city, set up improvised bridges, and on the night of the twentieth risked a crossing, in spite of an already dangerous flood level. On the twenty-first thirty thousand French were attacked by the whole Austrian army; yet fortunately for them the attack was not concentrated at one point, but spread over a half-circle between Aspern and Essling, so that they were unable to effect a breach. On the twenty-second Napoleon, with sixty thousand men, took the offensive in order to drive in the enemy centre. He would moreover have succeeded if the chief bridges had not been swept away, so holding up the supply of reinforcements. A halt had to be made, then he had to fall back and stand on the defensive, against a counter-attack, though short of munitions. But somehow or other they made shift to hold on, and from the twenty-third to the twenty-fifth were able to evacuate the left bank of the river. Twenty thousand French and twenty-three thousand Austrians had fallen: Lannes and a number of generals had lost their lives. The archduke had not been able to seize his opportunity, but his opponents had also failed in their objective. The Battle of Essling caused an even more profound sensation than Baylen. This time, a blow had been struck at Napoleon's personal prestige.

A dangerous situation was again beginning to develop. In the rear of the army the Tyrol had risen as one man at the news that Chasteler was entering it by way of the Pustertal on 9 April. Bavaria had spread popular discontent by abolishing the Landtag and doing away with its independence. Nevertheless it was above all the economic situation that produced the feeling of exasperation. Taxes were considerably on the increase; trade was being ruined by the blockade and the closing of the Italian and Austrian frontiers; and everyone was being hard hit by the invalidation of Austrian paper money and the suppression of the convents, which acted as banks and benevolent institutes. Finally, conscription threatened to spark off a conflagration, and had to be suspended to stop the trouble spreading further. Besides, Montgelas's enlightened despotism was Josephist in pattern; and the Catholic clergy, seeing their ascendancy and privileges

threatened, had taken up the gauntlet. As in the Vendée and in Spain, they
wielded tremendous influence, particularly as the chief insurgent leader,
Andreas Höfer, had for his spiritual adviser the Capuchin monk Hasp-
inger. Hormayr and Archduke John had had a good chance to prepare the
insurrection. It was essentially peasant in origin, and did not spare the
middle classes, who were pillaged and roughly handled just like the Bavarian officials. There were only five thousand soldiers to hold down the
country, and they were soon surrounded and forced to capitulate. All the
same, Chasteler did not succeed in organising the insurgents, who went
back to their homes after the rising, and Höfer, although his bravery and
piety inspired them with confidence, was a limited and rather undecided
character. Lefebvre did not have much difficulty in advancing along the
Inn and entering Innsbruck on 19 May. Chasteler evacuated it, and with
the revolt apparently over, it was decided to leave only Deroy's division in
the Tyrol. Yet when the news of Essling became known, a fresh insurrection broke out. Napoleon, needing all his forces, recalled Deroy and left
the country to itself. The peasants had no intentions of leaving it to fight a
campaign. They made forays into Bavaria and in July their example was
followed by Italy, where an extensive insurrection broke out in the Adige
region and in the Romagna.

If only Archduke John had concentrated all his forces scattered in the
south of the kingdom, he would have found most valuable support. But
he took a very different course. On 10 April he had taken the offensive by
way of the Natisone valley and Caporetto. Eugène's forces, still scattered
over a wide area, were surprised and fell back to the Mincio, thus surrendering the whole of Venetia. But when Vienna was threatened the
archduke retreated without any attempt to concentrate the Austrian
forces. He himself reached the Semmering, with Eugène in pursuit, and
then withdrew behind the Raab; Giulay drew away towards Laibach,
whence he went upstream again via Marburg [Maribor] to Graz, hard
pressed by Macdonald. Chasteler, who had come from the Tyrol, did
not contrive to join him. In Croatia, Marmont had fallen back in order
to concentrate his forces, but then drove them back again via Fiume,
Laibach and Graz. In the end all the French army corps rejoined the
Grande Armée, whereas Archduke John found his strength reduced to
some twenty thousand men. Davout proceeded to threaten Pressburg,
and Eugène defeated the archduke on the Raab on 14 June. Then both of
them pressed on towards Vienna to take part in the battle, and John did

likewise, crossing to the left bank of the Danube, but arrived some few hours late.

The most serious consequence the defeat at Essling might have had would have been to invite intervention by the king of Prussia. Several of his officers had already taken it upon themselves to compromise the situation. Katte made an attempt against Magdeburg and on 28 April Schill made a sortie from Berlin with his hussars, but was easily overcome by General Marchand. Central Germany was also astir. On 22 April Dörnberg, an ex-colonel, marched on Cassel at the head of some hundreds of peasants; and in June another retired officer tried to produce an insurrection in Marburg, while there was a rising of the countryside near the Tauber. The Austrians, for their part, entered Saxony and the king fled; and the duke of Brunswick-Oels, at the head of Hessians transferred by their elector to Bohemia, occupied Leipzig. Finally, the English were working on Hanover and Holland and on 8 July made an attempt against Cuxhaven. If the Prussians had got under way, Jérôme would have had considerable difficulty in defending his kingdom. To start with, Frederick William seemed disposed to take action; but on second thoughts he confined himself to stopping payment of the indemnity. Though he did in the end send an agent to Vienna, he did not arrive till 21 July.

As things turned out, then, Napoleon was able to reassemble all his forces, and did not have much difficulty in exploiting the occupied countries or bringing up the reinforcements and supplies that were available in France – twenty thousand foot, ten thousand cavalry, six thousand men for the Guard and a large amount of artillery so as to make up for the doubtful reliability of his troops. The island of Lobau was meticulously fortified and the number of solid bridges extended. In the midst of danger the emperor himself remained imperturbable. He even went ahead with a measure that was of all things the most likely to sow disaffection among his own subjects: on 17 May he decided to annex Rome. On hearing that Pius VII was about to excommunicate him, the emperor gave orders that he should be taken prisoner and deported, and on 6 July, the day on which the Battle of Wagram was fought, the pope was in fact removed by the *gendarmerie*, and a *senatus consultum* of 17 February 1810 subsequently regularised the annexation. It was thoroughly typical of the man that he should give an order like this at such a moment of crisis. He continued with untroubled brow to play double or quits with fortune. And once again he forced destiny to take his side.

At his disposal there were now 187,000 men and 488 guns, against the enemy's 136,000 – though their artillery was almost of equal strength. The crossing of the Danube began on 4 July, a stormy night, downstream from Essling, and was completed by the following afternoon. By this move the emperor reckoned to turn the archduke's flank; but when his forces fanned out over the plain, they failed to find him. The French preparations had not escaped his notice, and realising that he could not stop this crossing, he had fallen back a short distance, with his left behind the Russbach and parallel to the Danube, and his right perpendicular to it, the top of the angle being marked by the villages of Aderklaa and Wagram. This position, supported on the left by fortified heights, possessed distinct advantages, but it was too extended, and left the archduke with no reserves. Napoleon, disappointed of his prey, had to improvise a manoeuvre and could not attack the Russbach front till seven in the evening, and then without success, for the Saxon forces yielded ground at Aderklaa. He renewed the assault at dawn on the sixth with all his available strength: Davout turned the position and forced Rosenberg to retreat. But at Aderklaa, Carra-de Saint-Cyr was overwhelmed and Bernadotte's troops from Saxony once again disintegrated. Meanwhile the Austrian right was vigorously hammering at Boudet's division, which alone stood in their way, capturing Aspern and Essling and threatening the French communications with the rear. The emperor was forced to alter his dispositions in the midst of battle. Masséna moved down towards the river and stopped the Austrian right by a flanking manoeuvre, and the gap was filled with a huge battery of one hundred guns, behind which the reserves advanced in massed column under the command of Macdonald. At two o'clock, there was a resumption of the general attack on the Russbach. The enemy left wing was in the end completely overrun and the centre forced to fall back. The archduke gave the order to retreat, but there was hardly any pursuit from the exhausted French. He had lost fifty thousand men to the enemy's thirty-four thousand. Tacticians have been full of admiration for the military genius displayed by Napoleon in the course of that day; but judged by results, it cannot compare with Austerlitz or Jena. For the enemy forces – still more than eighty thousand men strong – withdrew through Moravia in good order, and battle was renewed at Znaim on the eleventh. Yet the archduke was no Blücher, and he had no hope of a successful issue. He requested an armistice, and his request was granted on the twelfth.

The final crisis, however, was long-drawn-out. Excitement in Germany remained intense, and there was an attempt to assassinate the emperor by a student named Stabs, though order was quickly re-established. The king of Prussia adopted an attitude of increasing reserve, the Austrians evacuated Saxony, and Brunswick made a daring transit of Jérôme's kingdom to reach the coast where the English were waiting to pick him up. The Tyrol, on the other hand, though attacked in July by forty thousand men coming up from Salzburg, the Vorarlberg and the Adige, continued to hold out, exterminating a division from Saxony and again forcing Lefebvre to retreat. Not till after peace was signed did Drouet d'Erlon and Eugène succeed in breaking down their resistance. Höfer had submitted, and then taken up arms again, only to be betrayed by one of his compatriots and shot on 20 February 1810. Yet the English gave still more trouble. Their expedition at last appeared off Walcheren, and on 13 August captured Flushing. This was the largest contingent they had sent to the Continent – forty thousand men escorted by thirty-five vessels and twenty-three frigates – but their commander, Lord Chatham, a great courtier but totally incompetent, kept his men doing nothing when a straight march on Antwerp would probably have captured it. As it was, his troops were rapidly laid low by epidemics, and he re-embarked on 30 September with a loss of 106 killed and four thousand who had died from disease.

Nevertheless, the expedition had meanwhile spread alarm throughout the Empire, for which Fouché had been largely responsible. On 29 June Napoleon had left him for the time being in charge of the Ministry of the Interior, since Crétet was unwell. Finding himself in charge of the two political ministries, he displayed extraordinary activity, suppressing the *congrégations* [Jesuits], arresting Noailles, who was acting as intermediary between the pope and the Catholics, putting down disturbances in the West and in the Rhineland, and supporting government stock by purchases on the stock exchange without any reference at all to Mollien. On learning that the English expedition had landed, he proposed to his colleagues that the National Guards should be mobilised in the fifteen northern départements and brushed aside all objections. Bernadotte had quarrelled with Napoleon because he had gone to the defence of Saxony after Wagram, and had just returned to France. He now accepted an offer from Fouché, who put him in charge of the defence of Antwerp. The *préfets* were then instructed to hold themselves in readiness for a mass levy of the National Guards in view of the fear of other coastal attacks, particularly in Provence. In Paris, the National Guard was reconstituted. Fouché dealt out ranks to the citizens, who eagerly accepted them, and himself reviewed the force. The military authorities grew alarmed: were they back again in 1793? Clarke was loud in fury, and Fiévée wrote to the emperor. There seems to be little doubt that Fouché, overjoyed at once again finding himself in a commanding position, had allowed himself to be carried away by memories of his days as representative of the people. Yet there may also have been certain other thoughts at the back of his mind, for he probably knew of the plot in Provence and was most likely in touch with the English through Montrond, an agent of Talleyrand, whom he had sent to Antwerp. One can well imagine what suspicions must have run through Napoleon's mind after all the intrigues of 1808. In August he was supporting Fouché's first measures; but by September, with the English showing no signs of action, he was beginning to listen to the critics. He did away with the Paris National Guards, replaced Bernadotte by Bessières, and peremptorily requested Fouché to stop turning the Empire upside down in this fashion. When he returned he gave him a sharp dressing down on 27 October, but did not dismiss him, because he was on Napoleon's side in the coming divorce, and had even been promoted to be duke of Otranto on 15 August.

These harassments in the rear only made the emperor the more anxious about Alexander's attitude. At Caulaincourt's request the tsar had massed sixty thousand men on the Galician frontier, but had postponed the question of hostilities. Naturally enough, he was primarily occupied with his own affairs, which had taken a favourable turn. In March Baron Adelspare, in command on the Norwegian frontier, pronounced against Gustavus IV, and the king had to abdicate on the twenty-ninth in favour of his uncle, the venerable duke of Sudermania, who took the name of Charles XIII. Sweden immediately entered into peace negotiations and ceded Finland on 17 September. War with Turkey had begun again in April. In December 1808 Karageorge, who had been proclaimed hereditary prince of the Serbians, invaded Herzegovina; and in August the Ottomans entered Serbia from their side, but had to evacuate it in September, when Bagration captured Ismailia. As Galicia had been left without defending forces, Alexander could – in spite of these preoccupations – have occupied it very easily, and thus secured its possession when peace was signed. But his objections to Napoleon got the better of his own interests, and so became obvious to all. Archduke Ferdinand was therefore able to invade the grand duchy and occupy Warsaw. Poniatowski let him proceed without interference, but himself invaded Austrian territory, occupying Lublin, Zamosc and even Lemberg [Lviv]. At this point – on 3 June – Alexander made up his mind to enter Galicia in order to take the province from the Poles. Meanwhile, however, Ferdinand was hastening to the scene and succeeded in recapturing Sandomir. Galitsin refused to help Poniatowski to save this place, and entered into a secret agreement with the enemy, by which he promised not to proceed beyond the Wisloka, and the archduke withdrew without firing a single shot. But better still, when Poniatowski approached Cracow, he called in the Russians and handed the town over to them. Alexander was showing increased feeling against the grand duchy, and Rumiantsev, now that he had got rid of the Swedes, could think of nothing else. On 26 July Napoleon was invited to give an assurance that he would never reconstitute Poland. 'At all costs I want to be left quietly at peace,' said Alexander to Caulaincourt on 3 August. Such a declaration was intended to separate the Poles from France and at the same time imply a veto against all increase of territory for the grand duchy – for the name was basically irrelevant. The tsar's attitude filled Napoleon with a growing irritation. 'This is not the behaviour of an ally,' he said. He had for some time been straining at the leash, and now he was still forced to manoeuvre for position.

Austria meanwhile was taking good note of the difficulties that confronted him on all sides. Francis had sought refuge in the castle at Dotis [Tata], near Pressburg, where he was surrounded by a war party who were loud in their protests. The empress, Stadion and Baldacci all blamed the archduke for having suspended hostilities and abandoned the Tyrol and Saxony. They reduced his command to that of a single army, which led to his resignation on 23 July. There was hope of support from Russia, and this was why the peace negotiations, opened between Metternich and Champagny at Altenburg in the middle of August, were allowed to drag on. These tactics suited Napoleon; for on 12 August he had offered the tsar to partition Galicia between him and the grand duchy, the latter to receive four-fifths. In return, he promised to start official negotiations on Poland; and while waiting for a reply he claimed the right to keep all the Austrian territory he had occupied. Finally, on 1 September Chernyshev arrived to warn the Austrians that for the moment Russia would not break with France. And so the vanquished had to resign themselves to giving up whatever was required in Galicia, while defending inch by inch all their western provinces. The game was only too obvious: like Napoleon they now knew that Alexander was laying claim to almost everything they might give up. Not wishing either to benefit the man who had betrayed him or to drive him to extremes, the emperor now took the line of reducing what there was to be shared. Austria's last resistance was broken by an ultimatum, and on 14 October peace was signed at Schönbrunn. Bavaria was given the Inn district and Salzburg; Napoleon took maritime Croatia with Fiume, Istria and Trieste, together with part of Carinthia and Carniola. The grand duchy of Warsaw increased its population by 1,500,000, including Lublin and Cracow; and Russia, with Tarnopol, by four hundred thousand. Austria lost 3½ million inhabitants along with all access to the sea; and she had to pay an indemnity of seventy-five million.

The most outstanding characteristic of the treaty was that Napoleon had ignored Alexander's claims by maintaining the proportions fixed at the outset for the partition of Galicia. He thus reminded Russia of her vassal status. She had failed to give her master due and proper service, so her wages were reduced. Alexander expressed his dissatisfaction to Caulaincourt, but the emperor was not alarmed. He kept making a parade of his intentions to satisfy the tsar by giving up all claim to reconstitute Poland. But the Russian demands were never more than a screen. Alexander had really hoped to be offered the grand duchy, not to mention Galicia, as the price of his help against Austria; but in his disappointment he had tacitly refused his aid, though he nevertheless clung to his own ambitions. As autumn went on a rupture with France seemed inevitable to him, and when Czartoryski returned to St Petersburg he began to talk to him in covert terms about his 1805 plans, and the use that could be made of the Poles against Napoleon. The emperor, on the other hand, refused to believe the evidence, for in his eyes the Continental System remained firmly based upon the agreement of Tilsit. The fact is that he had now made up his mind to get rid of Josephine, and had been thinking since Erfurt of replacing her by Alexander's sister. As usual, the plan of the moment held the entire field; and as the Russian alliance might help it, he refused to see that it was no longer more than a name. The unexpected turn taken in the choice of a new empress was to convert this alliance into a relationship of avowed hostility.

## THE AUSTRIAN MARRIAGE

Napoleon's second marriage was destined to upset the balance of the Continental System which had not been fully restored, and hasten the outbreak of a war in which he himself would perish. It was far less inspired by external policy than by the development of Napoleon's personal power. As soon as there were suggestions of making him a hereditary sovereign in 1800, the possibility of divorce came into the picture because Josephine was not giving him an heir. Once monarchy had been brought back, this became a much more urgent question. It is possible, however, that Napoleon may have doubted for a time whether he could become a father. Although several illegitimate children have been attributed to him, it would seem that there was still some uncertainty in the matter until the birth of Count Léon* on 13 December 1806. Nor is it unlikely that the separation from Josephine caused him a good deal of suffering, for the passionate love she had inspired – even though unfaithful – was one of his loveliest memories; and even after he had deserted her, he could never bear to hear that she was unhappy. 'I don't want her to cry,' he would say. When Hortense had given birth to a son he had him baptised with great ceremony, and it was thought that Napoleon might adopt him, but the child died on 5 May 1807. Up till then, moreover, Napoleon could not see any possible substitute for Josephine. Being an emperor, he was bound to marry a princess of a reigning royal family. As his power grew more aristocratic and more despotic, the papal anointing began to seem more and more insufficient to him. It was no good his boasting, even before kings, that he had built his own fortunes, for he suffered from a constant itch for legitimacy.

Tilsit, however, had suddenly seemed to make the hope of entering into a royal family belonging to a traditional dynasty something more than an idle dream. By the end of the year, the possibility of a divorce became more definite through the efforts of Fouché; and although Napoleon disavowed his help, he nevertheless made up his mind before going to Erfurt, since he then made overtures to Alexander for the hand of his sister. Returning to Paris on 15 November 1809, his only thought was to proceed to action. On the twenty-second Caulaincourt was ordered to present an official request. Since Alexander had insisted that the promise concerning Poland should be embodied in a treaty, the ambassador was at

* [Napoleon's first certain illegitimate child.]

the same time authorised to sign the document. But the tsar had reached a point where there could no longer be any question of this marriage. Nevertheless, this approach was just as much of a windfall, because it might perhaps make it possible, before saying no, to get the treaty rectified, which would then be a step towards winning Poland over to the Russian side. It is strange that Caulaincourt should have been taken in by this manoeuvre. He began by negotiating the agreement, which was signed on 4 January 1810, laying down that the kingdom of Poland should never be reconstituted, and that the very name of Poland should disappear from all public documents. He waited till 28 December to come on to the subject of the marriage. Yet he knew that the tsar was likely to put the matter off, since Talleyrand had suggested a pretext for doing so at Erfurt. He would explain the necessity for consulting the dowager empress, who wanted to consult her daughter Catherine then residing at Tver. The daughter had no objection to the marriage, but her mother, while not making an outright refusal, produced objections concerning the young girl's age – she was only sixteen – and the difference in religion. Inwardly she was deeply opposed to this union. Yet the final decision rested with Alexander in his autocratic position of head of the family; and he took good care to delay his answer.

But the matter was urgent. On 30 November, in a celebrated scene with Josephine, the emperor told her his will. On 15 December she declared her consent to the divorce before an assembly of princes and high dignitaries, and it was confirmed on the sixteenth by a *senatus consultum*, though this was not in accordance with the Civil Code, nor with the spirit – if not the letter – of the statute regulating the imperial family. Josephine kept the title of empress, and was given Malmaison and a dowry. The annulment of the religious marriage was rather more difficult. It was not possible to approach the pope, because he was a prisoner; moreover, in Abbé Émery's opinion, precedent did not positively indicate that his intervention would be required. Fesch accordingly held up proceedings, while the ecclesiastical officials in Paris – at diocesan and at metropolitan level – took the responsibility of declaring the marriage null. The diocesan authorities alleged that the union had been celebrated secretly, without the parish priest and witnesses. This was something that could not be authorised – according to the Gallican Church – by any dispensation, even from the pope. The metropolitan authorities preferred the grounds put forward by the emperor, namely that the ceremony of

1804 had been imposed by circumstances and was therefore invalid in default of a positively expressed consent.

Once this point had been settled on 12 January 1810, Napoleon waited impatiently for the tsar's reply. When he realised that it was being delayed, although the treaty of 4 January was submitted to him, he suspected a trap and held up the ratification. Alexander's refusal, which now seemed probable, was no doubt mortifying, but he could have his revenge, for Austria offered him an alternative bride.

Since the signing of peace, Metternich had been at the chancery. There were some obvious resemblances between him and Stadion. Metternich, too, had been sobered by the French conquest. He was a worldly aristocrat, and a libertine who was capable of endless infatuations. He too had a double motive for hating France and the Revolution. Yet he possessed more experience of diplomacy and especially more cool deliberation, for there was never any trace of romantic enthusiasm about him. He was a man of the eighteenth century, a disciple and son-in-law of Kaunitz, and attached to the old idea of a European balance of power to be restored by bringing down Napoleon. Moreover, he remained faithful to enlightened despotism, and certainly felt no hostility in principle to reforms calculated to strengthen the state, provided that the social preponderance of the aristocracy was more respected than under Joseph II. Attempts have been made to attribute to him an original political philosophy inspired by Burke and characterised by an experimental rationalism. Having made a disciple of Gentz, whom he could get to justify any thesis, Metternich did in fact possess a whole arsenal of principles, but to explain his policy as the outcome of disinterested reflection gives the man too great a stature.

Delighting in the exercise of power, and determined to keep it, Metternich was a most able manager of the Habsburgs' affairs. Though the faults of the regime did not escape his notice, he took good care not to antagonise the emperor and the nobility by making efforts to correct them. The European crusade which Gentz expected the dynasty to undertake only really interested him in so far as it could bring advantage to Austria in Italy and Germany. His unflinching realism was his greatest quality. By 1809 he had come to the conclusion that Napoleon had done all he could; and this mistaken opinion was responsible for the extreme caution with which he acted during the following years. His only thought was to survive till the moment came when he could safely join in the rush for the spoils. Already the shock to the Franco-Russian alliance was working in his favour; it was only a question of helping to turn it into positive antagonism. The safety of Austria would be better served by coming to terms with the victor, and this new Tilsit might be turned to positively good account. Napoleon's desire to take a wife was thus an unlooked-for opportunity: by marrying Archduchess Marie-Louise he would bring about a final breach with Alexander, and would then look upon Austria as a natural ally.

No one knew better than Metternich that the Habsburgs were bound to regard such a union as a blot on their reputation. But by suggesting that Napoleon should put forward a request and by presenting it to Francis as an ultimatum, it would be made clear to him that he must give way for reasons of state. The chancellor seems to have first alluded to the matter on 29 November in a conversation with Alexandre de Laborde, an *auditeur* (assistant to the Conseil d'État) on a mission to Vienna; and chevalier de Floret, chargé d'affaires in Paris, talking to Sémonville in the course of an official dinner, was explicit enough to send his table-partner in haste to report to Maret. On 16 December Napoleon gave orders to make a tentative approach to the Austrian ambassador, Schwarzenberg, who was then seen by Alexandre de Laborde when he returned at the end of the month. There is no reason to believe that from now onwards Napoleon preferred an Austrian bride, but he must at all events have felt flattered. When he heard that the tsar was playing for time, the solution seemed to lie in Austria. There was a division of opinion among the imperial entourage. The smart counter-revolutionary circles were in favour of Austria, fondly imagining that the court of Vienna would demand the disgrace of the regicides, and that this would be a big step towards reaction. The revolutionaries, led by Fouché, were accordingly of the opposite opinion. The Beauharnais and Josephine herself were for Marie-Louise; the Bonapartes – headed by Murat – were for the grand duchess. Napoleon gave a hearing to both sides in a Privy Council on 29 January 1810, but reserved his decision. Finally, on 5 February a despatch from Caulaincourt announcing that the tsar was asking for further delay suggested to Napoleon that there would be a humiliation in store for him, and made him decide to forestall it. In the evening of the sixth, Eugène presented the official request to Schwarzenberg, requiring immediate consent to an engagement; and this was agreed to on the following day. It was the right moment, for on the fourth Alexander had just signified his refusal to Caulaincourt. He was annoyed to find himself outmanoeuvred but – diplomatically speaking – he came off best, for he was able to accuse Napoleon of playing a double game. Metternich had been right in his calculations: the breach between France and Russia began to widen.

Marie-Louise arrived at Compiègne on 27 March, Napoleon went to meet her, and with his usual impatience took possession of her in defiance of all etiquette; he then led her away to Saint-Cloud. The marriage was celebrated at the Louvre on 2 April and was followed at the end of the month by a journey to the north. On 20 March 1811 a son was born who had been given as early as 17 February 1810 the name of 'king of Rome'. His baptism on 9 June was the last great celebration of the regime.

The Austrian marriage hastened the development that was removing Napoleon further and further from the Revolution. For her personal attendant, Marie-Louise was given Madame de Montesquiou, formerly governess to the Bourbon royal children; Fiévée became master of requests, and those who had come over to Napoleon took the upper hand in the court of one who had now become by this new alliance the nephew of Marie-Antoinette and Louis XVI. Fouché, on the other hand, was dismissed on 3 June and replaced by Savary. The *ci-devant* were right in reckoning that there would be other measures to follow. A rumour went round that there was a secret article in the marriage contract stipulating that the regicides should be exiled, and that there would be a solemn rehabilitation of the memory of Louis XVI, who was constantly being whitewashed in the royalist brochures. Those who had come into possession of nationalised property also began to receive threatening letters. Institutions, too, moved further in the direction of the *ancien régime*. In 1810 the state prisons and arbitrary imprisonment were officially re-established and the censorship of books was openly reorganised.

Then again, Napoleon, in starting a new family, offended his own kith and kin, whom he constantly loaded with honours, but who never seemed satisfied. Their backbitings, discords and escapades had for some time disturbed his private life and damaged the new dynasty's prestige. Marie-Louise, with all her eighteen-year-old freshness, roused him to a second youth and to pleasures which she seems fully to have shared, for she was of a rather soft and sensual nature. But his critical sense did not desert him with respect to his son. He realised – as we know from his words – that the king of Rome would only keep the Empire if he too was a man of genius; he had a father's pride and did not despair of his son. His lively sense of the family bond, which has been attributed to the Latin tradition, but goes back more probably to Corsican custom, naturally led him from now onwards to show preference for his own posterity. When arranging the dowry for the new empress on 30 January 1810, the apanages of his future children and the possible division of the crown possessions between them, he had made no reference at all to his brothers. Some have therefore been disposed to attribute to the Austrian marriage a deep influence on the change in the structure of the Grand Empire that begins to be evident from this time onwards. It has been said that its federative – if not Carolingian – structure tended now to become dynastic or Roman, with all conquests reserved for the king of Rome and so annexed to France. In any case they could only be distributed among his possible future brothers. In this way the kingdom of Italy was assigned in advance to his second son, so that Eugène de Beauharnais saw his title of heir presumptive taken away, and was made instead the heir to Dalberg in the grand duchy of Frankfurt. Yet there has been some exaggeration of the influence which the marriage exercised in this respect, for the emperor had long been exasperated at the refractoriness or incompetence of the vassal princes, and had long been threatening to annex their states. When Louis lost his kingdom, or when Murat and even Joseph and Jérôme thought that a similar fate was in store for them, they may perhaps have accused Napoleon of sacrificing them to his new family; but the truth is that the federative Empire was evolving spontaneously towards a unified structure.

The essential consequence of the Austrian marriage lay elsewhere. In crowning the triumph of Wagram, it restored the Continental System in Napoleon's eyes, and raised his will to power to an even higher level through his feelings of personal euphoria. In entering into a closer relationship with Austria, it never occurred to him to treat her as an equal or to make a new Tilsit with her, as Metternich hoped. In Paris, the Austrian statesman had expressed his anxiety about the Russian advances in the East, and insinuated that they might agree to set limits to it. Napoleon admitted that France and Austria had common interests in this direction, and promised to intervene if Alexander claimed the right to expand south to the Danube; but he would not sign any document. Austria was still at his mercy, and imagining probably that the Habsburg ruler would not be willing to do anything against the interests of his son-in-law, he continued to treat him as a vassal. His refusal to contest the

Danube principalities with Russia in conformity with the agreement of
Erfurt made him continue to delude himself for several months that the
pact of Tilsit was still in existence.

Once again, then, the only enemy was England. Metternich cherished
the hope of re-establishing peace on the seas so as to avoid the dangerous
obligation of coming out against her. In March 1810 he drew up an
astonishing memoir in which Gentz solemnly proceeded to show the
English that France was invincible, and that in her own interests she
should leave her the whole continent, including Spain. About the same
time Fouché was making efforts in the same direction. He had sent to
Marquess Wellesley, then at the Foreign Office, a former émigré called
Fagan whose father lived in London. Louis too considered a general reconciliation to be the only way of saving his kingdom; and it seemed likely
that England would like to prevent the annexation of Holland, which
remained an important outlet for her produce and so was of prime value
to the bankers, Labouchère in particular. He also saw Wellesley in February 1810. Finally Ouvrard was employed by Fouché, who never ceased to
protect him, no doubt in recollection of their common speculations. This
financier was always involved in transactions with Labouchère, and did
not forget the piastres of Mexico. This led him to suggest a political combination by which Charles IV would be transported to Mexico, England
would hand Sicily over to Napoleon, who would give her Malta and help
her to reconquer the United States! When set free from prison in Sainte-
Pélagie, he came to an agreement with Labouchère, who let Baring into
the secret. After discussing this plan with the latter and with Canning,
Wellesley refused to give up Spain and Naples. At this point Louis,
thinking that his brother was in the secret, spoke to him about it on 27
April when he was passing through Antwerp. Ouvrard was arrested, and
a pretext found for dismissing Fouché. The talks were broken off. The
emperor had no more intention of giving way than the English.

In the course of this year he set himself to perfect the blockade. On 5
August the famous Trianon decrees were published, and on 18 October
the Fontainebleau decree. In order to keep a close eye on their application, Napoleon pushed on more vigorously than ever with annexation, so
much so that the blockade could now truly be said to have given a new
impetus to the spirit of conquest. At the beginning of 1810 Holland had
had to cede Zeeland and its southern provinces as far as the Rhine; on 2
July Louis fled to Bohemia; and on the ninth his kingdom was annexed, a

step legitimised by a *senatus consultum* of 13 December. In order to put a solid padlock on all the North Sea ports and the frontiers of Holstein, Napoleon called together on 22 January 1811 all the German countries lying north of a line between the Lippe and the Trave – namely the Hanseatic ports, a part of the grand duchy of Berg and the kingdom of Westphalia, the principalities of Arenberg and Salm, and the grand duchy of Oldenburg. In order to shut off Italy definitely against Swiss contraband he took possession of the Valais and occupied the canton of the Ticino with troops.

Meanwhile, however, the Iberian peninsula was still under arms. It seemed likely then that after Wagram Napoleon would prepare a big expedition to destroy the English army or force it to re-embark, after which the surrender of the whole country would only have been a matter of time. He did to be sure send 140,000 men by way of reinforcement, but this was not enough to strike a decisive blow, nor did he supply them with the indispensable material support. Most important of all, he did not follow them in person. Absorbed in his dynastic plans, and giving himself entirely to his new wife, he let this crucial year slip by, till at the end of 1810 there could no longer be any question of his being able to go to Spain with all his available forces, because the attitude of Alexander was giving cause for anxiety. Thus his dreams of personal grandeur and his new marriage prevented him from restoring the unity of the Grande Armée and condemned him to a struggle with Russia in the absence of an important part of his fighting force.

The Austrian marriage was not the root cause of this supreme contest, but it precipitated the crisis, although Napoleon would not admit it to himself, by exciting the jealousy of the Russians, who saw the Austrians being given special favours at Napoleon's court, and more still by ensuring the failure of the Polish negotiations. At the same time that he addressed his official request to Schwarzenberg the emperor had rejected the treaty signed by Caulaincourt. He drew up another, which he then sent to Caulaincourt already endorsed with his ratification, indicating that he would give no one any help in re-establishing Poland and would agree to removing the very name from all official documents. In return, Russia and Saxony would agree not to take for themselves any of the Polish provinces outside the grand duchy, and the treaty was to remain secret. This did not suit Alexander at all. On 13 July Nesselrode refused to make any modifications in the January agreement, and Napoleon at once broke off the negotiations. He refused moreover to authorise a Russian loan. In the summer of 1810 he did not yet regard war as inevitable, yet he was well aware that Alexander, cut loose from France, might make it up with England, in which case he would have to take up arms.

At the same time events in Sweden served to irritate the tsar. Charles XIII had signed a peace treaty with France on 6 January 1810, and joined the blockade. But he did not really possess enough authority to be able to obey its requirements to the full, especially as Saumarez's fleet was in command of the Baltic. The emperor was soon furious, and threatened to reoccupy Pomerania. Sweden promised to do all he demanded, all the more readily because she was in the throes of a crisis about the succession. The brother-in-law of Frederick VI, king of Denmark, Charles Augustus of Augustenburg, whom Charles XIII had accepted as his heir, had died on 28 May 1810. The opponents of the 1809 revolution were accused of having poisoned him, and on the day of his funeral Fersen was massacred in the course of a riot. The government wanted to replace the dead man by his brother, but Napoleon would give no explicit answer, and an intrigue – of doubtful origins – took advantage of this ambiguous situation. There was a party in Stockholm who favoured the French and would have preferred a relation or lieutenant of Napoleon's as a means of winning his protection against Russia. At the end of June Lieutenant Mörner came to sound Bernadotte in his name and won the support of Count Wrede, who had been sent to Paris on the occasion of the marriage. Bernadotte informed the emperor, who hesitated. It was perfectly clear that Alexander would not take at all kindly to the election of a French marshal; on the other hand, if war broke out, Sweden would be a great help. Bernadotte, it is true, was not a very reliable man: Eugène would have been a better choice. But the emperor reckoned that the French party, who wanted to reconquer Finland, would hold him to his duty. He therefore did not forbid him to accept, though he would make no official pronouncement, in order to spare the feelings of the tsar. The Swedish Diet, meeting at Örebro, seemed to be in favour of Augustenburg, until a man called Fournier came on the scene. He had been formerly consul at Göteborg, a merchant who had failed in business, and was now sent by Champagny to act as an observer, but was really Bernadotte's agent. Giving himself out to be the emperor's official agent, he recommended the election of the marshal; whereupon one of the king's inner circle, Count Suremain, an émigré, brought his consent and the Diet followed suit on

21 August. Napoleon was surprised at such a rapid result, and was doubtful whether he should endorse it; but the thought that it would be particularly mortifying to England finally carried the day. Sweden, moreover, seemed to be confirmed in its francophile policy and on 17 November declared war against England. But there was a reverse side to the medal. Alexander was furious. Yet Napoleon did not know that Bernadotte was losing no time in reassuring the tsar by declaring to Chernyshev, who was passing through Stockholm, that he would by no means be merely the emperor's man, and would never attempt to resume possession of Finland. Thus Alexander was very soon filled with hope that the new king's disloyalty would guarantee him the neutrality, if not the positive assistance, of Sweden.

Though the emperor was unaware of the fact, Russia's preparations were steadily taking shape. The tsar's first preoccupation was to induce Czartoryski to come forward with some offers. Then, in April 1810, he made up his mind to speak out. War would begin in nine months' time: would it not be possible to have the help of the grand duchy, and so be able to transport Russian troops in one move to the Oder, thus involving the Prussians? Czartoryski showed considerable reserve, for Napoleon had been very successful in hoodwinking him. Nevertheless, Alexander proceeded to steal a march on him. He appointed Alopeus and Pozzo di Borgo as ambassadors to Naples and Constantinople respectively, but sent them by way of Vienna, where they found opinion in the salons very favourable to their master, and still infatuated with Razumovski and Princess Bagration. They managed to obtain an audience with Metternich's father who was holding the fort while the chancellor was away in Paris. The suggestion was that Austria might take Serbia, particularly in order to settle the Eastern disagreement. But when Metternich reappeared he put an end to negotiations. Nevertheless, the Russian army began during the last months of the year to move quietly westwards. It would seem probable then that, failing Austria, Alexander was building some hopes upon Poland; perhaps Czartoryski had after all made up his mind.

By the end of the year the alliance had been officially broken by a double violation of the agreement made at Erfurt. Like all the purely agricultural countries, Russia suffered from the blockade, but without any kind of compensation. Alexander now lent an ear to the aristocracy's complaints, and came to the conclusion that the sluggishness of trade was harming the finances. Having now taken sides against Napoleon, he was inclined to make an approach to England. Though he had decided to go to war, he nevertheless wanted to put himself in the right by provoking his enemy to take the offensive. Already, he had taken good care not to adopt the edicts of Trianon and Fontainebleau; and on 31 December 1810 he went one better. Goods imported over land were now made subject to very heavy duties, while favoured treatment was given to seaborne trade in neutral vessels, together with the English trade, which was officially forbidden by Napoleon. Meanwhile Napoleon was annexing the grand duchy of Oldenburg, whose integrity had been guaranteed at Erfurt, after offering in vain to compensate the grand duke, Alexander's brother-in-law, in Thuringia. From that moment onwards, another war was inevitable.

# CHAPTER THREE

# England's Successes (1807–1811)

WHILE NAPOLEON was strengthening his continental hegemony, England was achieving the mastery of the seas as the outcome of her quiet and dogged efforts. Up till 1808 there did not appear to be any very decisive results. Squadrons were still coming and going from the French ports, and there were still some colonies that had not succumbed. It was the Spanish insurrection that brought decisive aid to British policy, on sea no less than on land, by finalising her command of the seas and at the same time inducing her to set foot once more on the Continent in order to give direct help to the coalitions which were the only means of defeating the conqueror.

## THE COMMAND OF THE SEAS AND ITS CONSEQUENCES

After Trafalgar, the British fleet had resumed the blockade of the enemy ports. Ships kept a close watch on the ports while the squadrons out at sea stood ready to pursue any vessels that might contrive to escape. This monotonous and humdrum watch was not without its hazards. Between 1806 and 1815 the English lost eighteen vessels, without a single one of them being captured or sunk by the enemy. The convoys also required a large supply of vessels. Naval construction was therefore unceasing: the budget – which was less than £9 million in 1803 – rose to more than £20 million in 1811; and by 1814 the English had 240 vessels, plus 317 frigates and 611 minor craft. Gradually all the warships that might have reinforced the French had fallen into their hands, Dutch, Danish, Neapolitan and Portuguese. In 1808 and 1809 the Spanish and Turks also joined the English side; and after those of Senyavin, the Russian ships blockaded at Kronstadt were escorted to England in 1812.

Napoleon was also engaged in constant construction – eighty-three vessels and sixty-five frigates between 1800 and 1814, at the end of which period he possessed 103 vessels and fifty-four frigates. But he could only have restored the balance by making himself master of the whole Continent, which would have needed years of effort. Up till 1809, however, he did not give up squadron action, but limited it to raids on the enemy lines of communication or against their colonies. There were some successful attempts to slip between the meshes of the blockade – by Leyssègues and Willaumez in 1805, Leduc and Soleil in 1806, Allemand and Ganteaume in 1808, Willaumez, Jurien, Troude and Baudouin in 1809. But they were immediately pursued, and almost all of them suffered enormous losses or complete disaster. The English destroyed Leyssègues's squadron at San Domingo; Willaumez lost two ships out of six; and in 1806 Linois, returning from the Île-de-France [Mauritius], was roughly handled in the Canaries. In 1809 Willaumez and Jurien, having effected a junction in the Île d'Aix roadstead on the way to the Antilles, had fire-ships sent in among them by Gambier. Their ships foundered, and none of them would have escaped if Gambier had supported the intrepid Cochrane. Troude's squadron succeeded in reaching Les Saintes,* only to disintegrate. Allemand and Ganteaume were allowed to get through with new supplies for Corfu, but this was due to the age of Collingwood, who died at sea in 1809. The Spanish insurrection put an end to these attempts, because the juntas took possession of the French ships in Cadiz and Ferrol, and the English – who had previously been forced by the alliance between Charles IV and the Directory to abandon the Mediterranean – now found the peninsular ports a most valuable help. In more distant waters, there were even more important results. The Spanish colonies ceased to serve as French bases and now became available to the other side, thus bringing about a complete reversal of conditions in the war at sea and the course of the colonial struggle.

Between 1806 and 1815 France and her allies lost 124 vessels, 157 frigates and 288 smaller craft. In 1806 there were thirty-six thousand French prisoners in England and 120,000 in 1815 – a large part of them captured by the British sea forces. The war between squadrons came to an end, and all the French could now do was to attempt random attacks. The English suffered some damage from these, the maximum losses being 619 in 1810. Between 1803 and 1814 the total rose to 5,244, or 2½ per cent of all comings and goings. Added to the losses at sea, this meant a five per cent reduction in the merchant navy. Although construction had fallen from 1,402 ships drawing 135,000 tons in 1803 to 596 drawing

* [South-west of Guadeloupe.]

sixty-one thousand tons in 1809, this gap was subsequently more than filled, so that the merchant fleet rose from twenty-two thousand ships in 1805 to twenty-four thousand in 1810. These results were a clear proof that corsairs, unsupported by squadrons, were unable to strike an effective blow at the enemy shipping, which mostly moved in escorted convoys. The measure of safety is attested by the insurance rates. They varied a good deal according to the region, and were always higher for the Baltic; but they came down at once for more distant waters, and fell on the average from twelve per cent in 1806 to six per cent in 1810, whereas they had risen to twenty-five per cent in the Revolution and fifty per cent during the American War. Now that they commanded the seas the English were able to destroy the merchant navy of France and her allies. In 1801 France possessed fifteen hundred ocean-going vessels; in 1810 she still had 343; but in 1812 only 179 remained. The fishing industry had dwindled to nothing. Her naval supremacy therefore assured Great Britain control of the maritime trade and enabled her to extend it significantly, thus allowing her to cope with the continental blockade, cover her constantly increasing expenses and provide finance for the coalitions.

This commercial exploitation of the successes achieved by her warships was what occupied her chief attention. Contrary to what might have been expected, colonial conquests only came second. In the eyes of the mercantile world, the essential thing was to prevent the neutrals from trading with enemy colonies and to monopolise this trade for Great Britain. Up to Trafalgar, moreover, the British government had to concentrate all its forces in European waters. After the seizure in 1803 of St Lucia, Tobago and a part of Dutch Guiana, there was a pause till 1806 before Surinam could be captured. In 1807 Britain took possession of Curaçao, and the Danish Antilles, St Thomas and Santa Cruz; in 1808, of Marie-Galante and La Désirade. Attention was also given to the African ports of call along the route to India. In January 1806 Popham, Baird and Beresford landed at the Cape and forced Janssens to surrender. In 1807 Madeira was occupied, then the other Portuguese colonies; in 1808 Gorée succumbed, and in 1809 St Louis. In America, the face of things was changed by the Spanish insurrection. Up till then the English had felt obliged to go warily because the coasts of Latin America might be used as bases for hostile expeditions. Then the situation completely changed. In 1809 Guiana and Martinique were conquered; in 1810 Guadeloupe, St Martin, St Eustatius and Saba.

In the Indian Ocean, the change of sides by Spain also deprived Decaen, who was in command of the Île-de-France, of the support provided by the Philippines, but the final decision was dependent in the main on the policy of the governors of India.

After Wellesley's departure, his successors – Cornwallis, Barlow and Minto – adopted an attitude exactly the opposite of his own and came to terms with the native princes in order to re-establish peace. Sindhia was the first to treat, and he was given Rajputana; Holkar then recovered the greater part of his states; Ranjit Singh, who ruled over the Sikhs of the Punjab, and who had momentarily reoccupied it, finally sided with the English and in 1809 signed an agreement fixing the frontier at the Sutlej and giving him Jaipur. Having secured this frontier, he took possession of Multan, Peshawar and Kashmir and entered into alliance with Afghanistan, which reoccupied Baluchistan and Sind. All this took time and opened up considerable problems for the future. Moreover, central India, left to itself, soon relapsed into anarchy. Roving bands of ex-soldiers and brigands, known as the Pindaris, committed appalling ravages in these parts. Nor were the fortunes of the missions without their hazards. The London Missionary Society opened work in India in 1804; and the Baptists entered Burma in 1807 and Ceylon in 1812. In 1813 India had its first bishop. There was, however, an element of frenzied fanaticism in the revolt of the sepoys at Vellore in 1807. At any rate the abandonment of Warren Hastings' and Wellesley's aggressive schemes had the advantage of allowing Lord Minto to pursue a vigorous external policy.

In the Mascarenes, Decaen had succeeded in imposing Napoleon's views. He suppressed the colonial assemblies, reintroduced centralisation and reorganised the old militias under the name of National Guards. The colonists missed the autonomy they had in fact enjoyed during the Revolution, but gave in to authority because slavery was reintroduced. To supply the slave trade, Decaen entered into contact with Madagascar and created a trading centre at Tamatave. But his thoughts were never far from India, and in 1804 he asked for reinforcements to support the Mahrattas. After Tilsit, he proposed a maritime diversion to support the projected Franco-Russian expedition. In January 1808 his brother came and spoke about it to the emperor, who promised a squadron and fifteen thousand men. Although the English never had real cause for alarm, they hated this 'nest of pirates', for Surcouf had given them a hard time. In 1810 Lord Minto resolved to have done with it. In July he seized the Île

Bonaparte (formerly the Île Bourbon or Réunion). In August Duperré and Bouvet destroyed a squadron of four frigates in the Port Louis roadstead; but at the end of November sixteen thousand men landed in the north of the Île-de-France, and Decaen, who had only 1,846 men, was defeated. He surrendered on 3 December. The following year the English occupied Tamatave. The Seychelles had entered into an agreement of neutrality from the start. Then Lord Minto turned his attention to the Dutch Indies, where Java and the Moluccas fell into his hands.

The French and Dutch colonial empires counted very little, however, in comparison with the Spanish. As soon as the Spaniards had declared war in 1804, Windham and Grenville sponsored the schemes of Popham and Miranda. After offering his services to Napoleon, who had had him extradited in 1801, when he was immersed in his negotiations with Spain and well aware that he was in the pay of the English, Miranda had returned to London. In October 1804 he proposed – with Popham's agreement – to attack simultaneously Caracas, Buenos Aires and Valparaiso. Grenville wanted to get at Mexico, by way of the Gulf on the one hand and the Pacific on the other. At the same time there was to be an expedition from India which would land at Acapulco, having taken Manila on the way. But Pitt, busy with negotiations for the Third Coalition, confined himself to sending Miranda to the United States to attack Florida. Jefferson, however, refused permission, and only allowed him to organise a small expedition against Venezuela, which came to grief in February 1806. Cochrane, who was cruising off the Antilles, assembled a new squadron which left Grenada in July, but was no more successful than the first. In 1807 Miranda came back to England.

Thanks to Popham, the matter had now a more serious complexion. Acting on his own responsibility, he took Beresford's troops from the Cape and landed them south of Buenos Aires in June 1806, where the viceroy was defeated and lost possession of the city. A French émigré, Jacques Liniers by name, who had a district command, hastened to Montevideo and collected a small body of men who forced Beresford to capitulate on 12 August. But the English government had not been able to resist the temptation to hold on to this acquisition, and Auchmuty's expedition was already on the way. But finding Buenos Aires in Liniers's hands, they took possession of Montevideo on 3 February 1807. They were followed by Craufurd, who had originally been meant for Valparaiso, and then by Whitelocke, who took over the command. On 5 July he gained a footing in Buenos Aires, but was surrounded after some street fighting, and on the next day signed an evacuation agreement. In recognition of his services Liniers was made a count and a grandee of Spain, and appointed viceroy.

Once more Spain provided the means of revenge for England. In May 1808 Napoleon had the idea of using Liniers to procure recognition for Joseph – Liniers having written to him as to the ally of Charles IV – and sent him the marquis de Sassenay, while he sent another noble to Caracas. But the result was deplorable. At Montevideo, Sassenay found a Spaniard called Elio who was jealous of Liniers and passed on the word to warn his fellow countrymen in Buenos Aires. When Sassenay arrived, they forced Liniers to send him back to Montevideo, where there was a rising that forced the governor to expel the French ship, which was then captured by the English. Everywhere Ferdinand VII was proclaimed king, and Spanish America slipped from Napoleon's hands. But Spain too was in danger of losing it, for the half-castes, knowing that Spain was powerless to intervene, and regarding a captive king as a ruler only in name, intended to take advantage of this chance of securing their independence. At Buenos Aires, they were satisfied merely to support Liniers against the Spaniards who attempted to overthrow him, but at Caracas Bolivar and his friends seized power in July 1808, and did the same the following year at Quito, Charcas and La Paz. But it was a premature effort, for the Seville junta sent out fresh officials who generally speaking asserted their authority without much difficulty. Emparan re-established the *ancien régime* at Caracas, and Cisneros took Liniers's place. The troops from Lima subjugated Quito and the towns of high Peru. Now that they were in alliance with Spain, the English did not dare to support the rebels; nevertheless, they reaped the expected benefits from these events. As early as 1807 Popham had addressed a circular to British merchants, inviting them to send all the cargoes they could to Buenos Aires, which had resulted in an amazing rush. The half-castes then began to trade freely with the defenders of their sovereign; and on 6 November 1809 the government of Buenos Aires officially allowed England to trade with the colony. In 1810 customs produced more than 2½ million piastres as compared with less than one million before the war. Brazil too had opened her ports to the English. At a time when Europe was threatening to close its doors to British exports, the acquisition of such valuable markets elsewhere aroused much enthusiasm in England. But the fresh half-caste rebellions and the resulting civil war were soon to prove an impediment to the progress of British trade.

The European advantages of the command of the seas in the commercial world soon became equally evident. The process of tightening the blockade of the Empire, and the bases incidentally utilised, served to develop contraband and outwit the continental blockade. In the North Sea, Heligoland became an English depot, and a number of islands along the French coast were put to the same use – Saint-Marcouf, Les Chausey, Les Molènes, Les Glenans, Houat and Hoëdic, L'Île Verte opposite La Ciotat, and the islands off Hyères; and the English anchored buoys in Quiberon roads and in Douarnenez Bay. Furthermore, the English fleet remained in command of the Sound and the Baltic. Progress, however, was particularly remarkable in the Mediterranean and the Levant, with the result that the chain of alliances contrived by Napoleon in order to extend his influence as far as Persia began to recoil against him. With Gibraltar and Malta in her possession, England could close the western Mediterranean. She had been in command of Sicily since 1798, and in 1806 she occupied its north-east tip. The alliance signed on 30 March 1808 granted Ferdinand IV a subsidy of £300,000, later raised to £400,000 expressly earmarked for armaments, so that the government in London could insist on accounts being rendered, and before long on the right to inspect the Neapolitan troops. In spite of this, there were always some lingering doubts about the intentions of the court, Maria Carolina in particular. The English supervision seemed oppressive and the subsidy meagre. In 1810, having failed to induce the assembled Estates to vote new taxes, the king authorised them himself and broke all resistance by arresting and deporting five of the most recalcitrant barons on 19 July 1811.

On the twenty-fourth Lord William Bentinck landed in Sicily, invested both with diplomatic powers and with the rank of commander-in-chief. He had formerly been governor of Madras, and was a colonial of the authoritarian and peremptory type. Moreover, he was a convinced Whig, to whom the introduction of the British constitutional system in foreign parts seemed to be a matter of conscience and essential for the welfare of the human race. Besides, in supporting the opposition he reckoned that he would have a means of making the court see reason. But as they would not listen to him, he re-embarked on 27 August, and went back to London to seek full powers and the suspension of the subsidy. On his return he concentrated his forces round Palermo, demanded the control of the Sicilian army, the recall of those who had been banished and the dismissal of the existing ministers. The king saved face by delegating his powers – at least nominally – to his son as vicar-general on 14 January 1812. Bentinck subsequently forced the queen to leave Palermo; and in March the prince was obliged to hand over the reins of government to those who had been banished, and Bentinck made them call Parliament to approve a constitution worked out by himself. At this juncture the western Mediterranean – thanks to the Spanish insurrection which had brought about the surrender of the Balearic Islands – had become something very like an English lake. Even the Berbers, while not giving up piracy, adjusted themselves to the new situation and the sultan of Morocco kept on good terms with the rulers of the sea. Malta and Sicily provided an easy gateway into the Adriatic, and in 1809 the British cruisers succeeded in finally gaining control of the Ionian Islands – all except Corfu. They then proceeded to attack the Dalmatian Islands and occupied several, winning a naval victory at Liasa in March 1811. Control over the Adriatic gave them the upper hand in Albania and Epirus; and Ali Tebelen once more changed his allegiance.

In the eastern Mediterranean action was likewise taken in 1807 from Malta and Sicily against Constantinople and Egypt. Although it was not successful, the Turkish coasts were nevertheless soon at the mercy of the English, and the sultan, alarmed and exasperated by the Franco-Russian alliance, made peace and undertook once more to close the Straits to foreign warships. From now on the British agents – and in particular Stratford Canning, a cousin of the minister, who began a famous career at Constantinople in 1809 – worked to bring about a reconciliation between the Turks and the Russians. England monopolised the markets of the Levant, which soon developed tremendously. Persia too changed sides, while in spite of Gardane's efforts, war broke out again in Armenia. After a victory at Nakhichevan, the Russians besieged Erevan. The English, however, having made peace with the Turks, entered the Persian Gulf from India, and in May 1808 Malcolm landed at Bender-Abbas. The shah, who was not obtaining any benefits from France, decided to receive the British envoy, Sir Harford Jones, whereupon Gardane left Teheran on 1 February 1809. By a treaty signed on 12 March the country was closed to the French; and in 1814 a further treaty aimed at guaranteeing its integrity against Russia. In 1809 a mission to the emir of Afghanistan obtained an assurance that he would not assist any expedition directed against India.

The independence of the pashas in Egypt, Syria and Baghdad was another constant source of concern. The English therefore entered into relations with the Wahabis, who were hostile to all of them. Saud, the son of Abdul Aziz, having captured Medina in 1804, threatened Damascus and Aleppo, and in 1808 and 1811 attacked the pasha of Baghdad. When the latter was being attacked in the north by the pasha of Suleimania and by the Kurds, he saw the English effecting a landing at Bassorah [Basra] and decided to make friends with them. Saud performed the further service of defeating the imam of Muscat and harassing the French throughout Arabia. As for Mehemet Ali, he was engaged for a long while and subjugated the last of the Mamelukes, who had taken up arms again in 1808. On 1 March 1811, however, he got the better of them by means of a trap. He invited them all to a meal in the course of which he had them massacred. He then undertook to subdue the Wahabis, and after an unfortunate attempt in 1811 his son Tussun reconquered the holy cities in 1812. Mehemet's campaign in the following year was unsuccessful; but in 1814 Tussun seized Taïf, and in 1815, after Saud's death, Mehemet was able to take Ras, the capital of the Nejd, and sign a treaty of peace. These arduous undertakings did not allow him to cross swords with the English. Thus the whole of the East eluded the clutches of Napoleon and from Gibraltar to India, by sea and by land, the English had succeeded in isolating the Empire.

### WELLINGTON'S CAMPAIGNS

The Napoleonic Empire had the appearance of an island from which there was no means of escape, while its enemies could enjoy free movement all around and anywhere they liked in the world. But it was also a fortress which could neither be reduced by famine nor taken by assault as long as the French army was intact. All the British fleet could do was to land troops at suitable spots to help the continental allies. But this threat, though useful in itself, because it forced Napoleon to guard every coast and kept the inhabitants' nerves on edge, was not enough to be decisive. England's allies were well aware of this, and though very ready to pocket English money, were not satisfied with this alone. As long as English ships did not bring redcoats, they were criticised with the suggestion that the command of the seas was exercised solely for England's benefit. Yet most English ministers and the vast majority of their fellow citizens were nonetheless averse to fighting on the Continent. Their insular feelings – strongly reinforced by the experiences of 1793 and 1799 and then by the threatened landings in Great Britain – were increased by the fact that manpower was not overabundant. Though the English were willing to enlist in defence of their own country, the army was only recruited by dint of offering bonuses among the poorer classes, and even then there was a dearth of recruits. Her overseas possessions were continually extending, and it was not practicable to denude England entirely of troops, let alone Ireland, which was still under martial law. There were thus very few troops available, and there was all the greater reluctance to risk an expeditionary force, seeing that it would be extremely difficult to replace.

It was also necessary to take expenses and monetary difficulties into account. The English troops were accustomed to pay for what they took from the country, even in Portugal and Spain, and in France in 1814, and they consequently needed coin or means of exchange. And lastly, there was the difficulty in Parliament, where any continental undertaking provided the opposition with a means of stirring up strong feeling. They had no hesitation in declaring that Napoleon was invincible on land, which was an indirect argument for peace. For all these reasons, Fox and his successors refrained from any interventions on the Continent – apart from the reinforcements sent to the Swedes in Pomerania; and this was an attitude that contributed not a little to the alienation of Russia. Canning and Castlereagh were in favour of an exactly opposite policy; but Tilsit had dissolved the Coalition, and it was not till Copenhagen that Canning was able to show his abilities.

Here too the Spanish insurrection was of capital importance. Canning did not hesitate to promise the juntas his support and, not content merely to promise them money and supplies, he arranged for the reconquest of Portugal, which up till then had been denied any military aid, and despatched Baird to Galicia. His path was smoothed by the initial support of the Whigs, who first of all greeted the insurrection with enthusiasm. But after the emperor's campaign they changed their tune. The opposition came to life again and proceeded to criticise the Convention of Cintra, and to maintain that Portugal was not defensible. Sir John Moore had also been of this opinion, and the government began to wonder whether they should recall Cradock, who had remained in Lisbon with ten thousand men, or transfer to Portugal the army that had returned from Galicia in a deplorable state. This time, it was Castlereagh who made the decision. After consulting Arthur Wellesley, he made up his mind on 2 April 1809 to despatch this army to Portugal, acting on the assurance that thirty thousand men would be enough to save the country. At this juncture, however, Austria was just entering the war, and Castlereagh, like a good disciple of Pitt, keeping his eyes firmly fixed upon the Netherlands, could not resist the temptation to send an expedition to Holland under the pretext that it would help Austria. And so England, having neglected to take action between 1805 and 1807, now intervened simultaneously in two places, but the reinforcements sent to Portugal hardly raised the strength to more than twenty-six thousand men. On the other hand, in the spring of 1809, if England had sent all available forces to the German coast, she might have struck a decisive blow. But the Walcheren expedition was a failure, and from this time onwards England's activities abroad were to be confined to the Spanish peninsula.

Even then, English policy was not pursued without considerable hesitation and debate. In 1809 the Portland Cabinet was disintegrating, for Canning and Castlereagh were so different in background and character that they found it hard to work together. The former aspired to becoming the head of the government and to direct the war effort as well as diplomacy, and in April he called upon his colleagues to choose between his rival and himself. They put off making a decision until the end of the war, but the Walcheren expedition was followed by a crisis. Canning resigned, and was wounded in a duel by Castlereagh on 21 September. And then Portland died, enabling Perceval, who had remained at the Exchequer, to reconstitute his government and call Marquess Wellesley to the Foreign Office. He had formerly been governor of India, and did his best to provide reinforcements for his brother's army. Nevertheless, this continued to be a weak government. The defeat of Austria and Napoleon's marriage had produced a division in public opinion. Grenville, Grey [formerly Lord Howick] and Ponsonby were strongly in favour of evacuating Spain, they criticised the general and were unwilling to admit his successes. The government had been obliged to hold an inquiry into the Zeeland expedition, and the throne came in for a good deal of mud-slinging because of the scandal involving the duke of York's mistress, who was convicted of having sold officers' commissions. To crown everything, the king once again went out of his mind. The prince of Wales had a bad reputation because of his quarrels with Caroline of Brunswick, whom he publicly accused of adultery; but he nevertheless found himself being made regent, under the same conditions as in 1788, up till 1 February 1812. As he had always enjoyed intimate relations with the Whigs, it was to be expected that he would call them to office now that he was invested with full power. Finally, in 1811, the country was hit by a severe economic crisis which upset the finances and produced a number of disturbances. It is thus not surprising that the Perceval government showed some reserve in their attitude to Arthur Wellesley, who had meanwhile become Viscount Wellington. It was made clear to him that if he were to meet with a serious reverse, evacuation would be bound to follow. When Masséna's offensive was announced in 1810, Wellington was warned that he would be excused if he withdrew his forces earlier rather than later. There was extreme parsimony in the supply of reinforcements, and the general was left to grapple with the most harassing financial difficulties.

But Masséna's retreat brought a renewal of confidence. Reinforcements were notably increased, and made the victorious campaign of 1812 possible. For three years, however, Wellington had only himself to rely on: he had not only to fight a war but also to raise the morale of the government. This fact explains the cautiousness of his strategy up to well on in 1812, and the care with which he reorganised the Portuguese army. One of his outstanding qualities was his ability to persist in spite of all difficulties in carrying on the war within the framework of the general British policy, which he understood to perfection. He showed that the Spanish undertaking as such possessed immense possibilities and lent a real effectiveness to the command of the seas. It was thanks to him, as well as to Canning and Castlereagh, that England was able to come to close grips with the Napoleonic giant.

In 1809 Arthur Wellesley, soon to-be Viscount Wellington, was forty years old, the same age as Napoleon. He had served under his brother for a long period in India – from 1798 to 1805 – and was only just beginning his European career. He was a sober character and blessed with an iron constitution. Like the emperor, he could work long hours and do with little sleep. He had a clear and precise mind of a positive cast, with good organising ability. He was a man of cool and tenacious will-power, though this did not exclude an ability to take bold and calculated risks. As a young man, he had shown himself very independent, but when he came to command he proved extremely authoritarian, never allowing his officers – who were incidentally of rather mediocre calibre – any initiative whatsoever.

His expression was marked by an aristocratic pride, hardened still further by his long years among the Indians. He treated his officers with a haughty disdain, and had an unlimited contempt for the common people, and for his own soldiers who were of the people, calling them 'the scum of the earth', 'a pack of rascals', 'a crowd who only enlist for drink, and can only be managed with the whip'. At any rate his pride of country bound him closely to his own social caste and to the land of which they were, in his view, the lawful owners, and his only thought was to serve them. With a hard and dry character in which imagination and affection were equally wanting, he was at any rate preserved from the romantic individualism that was the ruin of Napoleon, but his talent lacked the unending fascination exercised by the genius of the emperor.

Wellington's mind and character were perfectly suited to the life he was leading as a warrior in command of a professional army of only moderate effectiveness, slowly and monotonously campaigning with defensive battles whose object was to wear out the enemy. Considered from the technical point of view, he was essentially an infantry leader, hardly making use of the cavalry, and very rarely pursuing the enemy. His artillery, whether mounted or unmounted, was excellent but not very plentiful. There were no sappers, engineers or siege equipment: his foot soldiers had to suffice for all tasks, and suffered enormous losses in taking fortified places by assault. Yet of all the emperor's enemies he was the one who enjoyed the pre-eminent advantage of having given mature thought to the tactics to be adopted in his encounters with the French. He preserved the line formation, while giving greater elasticity to the method of combat. For defence against sharp-shooters, he would shelter his lines behind hedges, ruins or houses with loopholes, or conceal them on a counter-slope, and did not despise dispersed fire or individual random fire. Each battalion had a company strung out ahead of it, and from 1809 onwards he used a regiment of 'rifles' and foreign troops deployed in the same way. He did not fail to realise that the enemy, whose triumphs had turned their heads, tended to cut short the sharp-shooting preparation for battle and advance more and more promptly with their battalions in deep column. At Maida, they had attacked without preliminary firing. Wellington concealed his troops, reckoning that the French were incapable of appreciating the results of fire, or would be impatient at the slow progress made by their skirmishers, and that they would then be all the more eager to charge with the bayonet. In that case, troops who were arranged in shallow order, were cool-headed and almost intact, would be at a great advantage. The professional English foot soldier was well drilled in firing volleys, and his weapon fired heavier bullets than the French. Furthermore, Wellington adopted a line two-deep instead of three-deep, so that a battalion of eight hundred men could fire eight hundred rounds in one salvo. The French battalion, however, was arranged in column by companies, forty wide and eighteen deep, or in double companies, eighty wide and nine deep, so that the first two ranks could only reply with eighty or 160 rounds. If they attempted to deploy, they would lose a good many men in the process, and as a rule got out of formation, so bringing the attack to a halt. When he had proved the effectiveness of these tactics, the English general did not hesitate to use them now and again – as at Salamanca – to attack in the same order, the line advancing at walking pace, and stopping deliberately every so often to fire. But Wellington's tactics were above all marvellously effective in a defensive battle, and so fitted with the conditions generally prevailing in his campaigns. They demanded, moreover, a professional army, implacably disciplined to an automatic obedience by the use of corporal punishment, like the army of Frederick II. Napoleon's lieutenants failed to learn their lesson through the reverses that Wellington inflicted upon them; and because he never came to observe these tactics in action, Napoleon was only able to appreciate their value on the field of Waterloo.

Yet for all his talent, Wellington would probably not have succeeded in maintaining his forces in the peninsula without having Portugal at his disposal. He used it as a base that could be freely replenished by the British fleet, and reorganised a national Portuguese army which provided him with important contingents. The regency was never able to treat with England on level terms, and in 1810 it co-opted the assistance of Charles Stuart, who became the head of the administration. But Wellington never ceased to complain of the nepotism and ineffectiveness of the aristocracy, and their obstinacy in maintaining their own fiscal privileges. He wanted the subsidy – £1½ million and then £2 million – to be put at his disposal for feeding the army, but London would never agree, in deference to the feelings of the Portuguese. As the country subsisted solely on goods imported from the United States, and was selling half as much wine as before the war, the regency could only make both ends meet by feeding the soldiers on requisitions paid for by a depreciated paper money, with the result that they were badly fed, and fell ill or deserted in large numbers. In February 1809 the regency asked the English to appoint a commander-in-chief. They chose Beresford, who was not outstanding as a general, but was a good organiser. He introduced a certain number of British officers and instructors into the Portuguese regiments, and, with two exceptions, the generals were also British. In September 1809 there were forty-two thousand men available, and by 1810 they had more or less reached an effective strength of fifty-six thousand, which was the target. All the same, there were great difficulties in providing them with weapons, and the cavalry was always short of mounts. The militia was also used for garrison duties, reconnaissance and guerrilla warfare, and in 1810 they had to fall back upon the *ordenanza* or *levée en masse*.

The Spaniards did not procure the same degree of help. They had no intention of letting themselves be governed, and up to 1812 refused to put their forces under the command of the English. The central junta, however, had only a limited authority. It had to flee to Seville in December 1808, and then in January 1810 took refuge in Cadiz, where it abdicated in favour of a council of regency. In September the Cortes met and set up an executive council which was replaced in 1812 by a new regency. All these governments showed indecision, and were suspected of nepotism and corruption. The old council of Castile and the former junta of Seville disputed one another's powers, and certain persons such as the count of Montijo, the duke of Infantado, the brother of Palafox, conspired to overthrow them. The provincial juntas too were unstable, generally moving from one town to another, and only obeying orders when they felt inclined. Co-operation between the juntas and the military leaders was always precarious, and the guerrillas were a law unto themselves. Moreover, though the population hated the invaders, it by no means followed that most of the men were disposed to fight; and in any case they disliked the conscription that was imposed by the central junta in 1811. Although the aim had been an army of eight hundred thousand men, the regulars never in fact rose to one hundred thousand men. There were difficulties too in organising them and supplying them, in spite of the funds sent from America, which rose to nearly three million in the first year. Conscription was followed by a mass insurrection, which was a customary institution in several of the northern provinces, and was made general by the central junta on 17 April 1809; but here again the results were disappointing. In Asturias, for example, the peasants were successfully mobilised in 1809, but in 1810 they stayed at home. Moreover, as they could be provided with neither officers nor arms, they could hardly be used for anything but auxiliary services.

Guerrilla warfare was what suited the Spaniards best of all, because in it the soldier could remain his own master. The central junta legalised partisan warfare on 28 December 1808, and there was an abundance of guerrilla bands, some of which became famous, such as those of the Castile farm-hand El Empecinado, and the two Minas in Navarre. They embarrassed the French by attacking forage parties, convoys and isolated posts, and wore down their strength by small daily losses, or by forcing them to detach a significant number of fighting men to guard their communications, while in the north the emperor had to increase the number of *gendarmerie* squadrons. But the effectiveness of these bands has been exaggerated: whenever the French could occupy a province in sufficient strength, the guerrillas, far from being able to prevent them, were not even able to be a serious threat to their security. This was so in Asturias under Bonnet's command, though the country was ideal for guerrilla warfare. Besides, these bands were a motley collection, and not always clearly to be distinguished from highwaymen. Even when they consisted of peasants loyally serving the cause of religion, they were nonetheless a terror to the rich by reason of their extortionate demands and their plundering, so that sympathies sometimes lay with the French. Bonnet was able to organise a counter-guerrilla force, and in Andalusia Soult succeeded in creating companies of *escoperelas*, a genuine national guard consisting of *afrancesados*. With their resistance decisively broken in this open country, the *guerrilleros* would soon have disappeared. Now without the English help, the regulars would never have been able to hold on. Nevertheless the central junta was highly mistrustful, and refused to allow them into Cadiz; and in spite of the efforts of Henry Wellesley – the future Lord Cowley – they would not consent to recognise Wellington as commander-in-chief, even after the Battle of Talavera, and the Spanish commanders only co-operated with him in a grudging manner. The disturbances in South America and the opening up of the Spanish colonies to British trade merely made the misunderstandings worse.

If Napoleon had come back to Spain after the Battle of Wagram, there would have been no doubt about the triumph of the French forces. This might even have been ensured if he had left someone like Davout in command, armed with full powers. But Joseph, even with Jourdan by his side, was incapable of managing a war like this. He did not even wield civil authority, though he had behind him Urquijo, Azanza, Cabarrus, Canon Llorente and others – enough to form a court, a ministry and a council of state. But there was a lack of money, and the king only subsisted with difficulty on municipal tolls, forced loans and paper money backed merely by the doubtful security of a possible sale of clerical property. Napoleon reserved for himself the confiscated property of the rebels. In the provinces the generals were left to their own resources, and did not even receive their pay. They laid their hands on anything that was available, and acquired the habit of thinking only of their own sector. When Napoleon gave supreme authority to a particular marshal, the others ruined all the plans by ill will or negligence. Ney went so far as positively to refuse obedience to Masséna. This anarchy was made worse by Napoleon's habit of sending direct orders to the army chiefs, quite apart from the fact that he was often imperfectly informed or unable to judge properly at such a distance, so that he sometimes sent out instructions which were impossible to carry out or out of date. Though Wellington had reason to complain of the Spanish generals, the enemy operations were equally disjointed, and he was usually able to beat them or hold them up one at a time.

As regards the physical and economic conditions in which the war was fought – the mountainous nature of the country, the climate, the absence of roads, the scantiness of foodstuffs – it has usually been said, and rightly enough, that they were greatly to the disadvantage of the French. But it should be added that their enemies also suffered a good deal from the same conditions. The English were decimated by disease, and they had great difficulties over transport. One is particularly struck by the central importance of food supplies, which was equally vital and difficult for all the combatants. The Spanish and Portuguese were no doubt used to living on very little; but the English found themselves badly in need of supplies. The cavalry had more than once to be partly dismounted through shortage of fodder. The regulars were thus reduced, one way or another, to the habit of living like the guerrillas, so that the peninsula might well seem to have reverted to the days of the *grandes compagnies*.* The inhabitants were despoiled by friend and foe alike, and marauding encouraged desertion. As there were many foreigners in the English ranks, and as Napoleon sent a number of regiments to Spain from vassal or allied countries, deserters commonly passed from one camp to the

* [Mercenary bands of looters in the Hundred Years War.]

other, or fraternised among themselves, and bands were formed operating solely on their own behalf. The French, who were used to making shift with living on the country, ended up by becoming demoralised in this country where one was perpetually hungry and where nothing was to be had but by stealth and force of arms. Too often their commanders set them a bad example of extortion – for example, Sébastiani, Kellermann, Soult, Duhesme in Barcelona, and Godinot, who, when his conduct was subject to an official inquiry, committed suicide in 1811. The English compensated for their sufferings by appalling orgies of drunkenness, and by the systematic plunder of all towns taken by assault. From the strategic point of view, Wellington's unwillingness to stray too far from his base and to return to it after each campaign is clearly to be explained by the scarcity of provisions and the difficulties of transport. Hence also his justifiable confidence in face of the French offensives. He reckoned he would be able to hold them up by laying waste the intervening country-side, calculating that if they had achieved the impossible in the way of supplies, mules and wagons would certainly be lacking. Things would have been very different if Napoleon had come over in person to prepare the campaign with the same care that he displayed in Russia. Since he decided not to do so, the advantage – taken all round – lay with Welling-ton. As he paid cash, the peasants – who were on the whole friendly – brought him what they could. Thanks to the British fleet, he received outside help and built up stores, while the French were sent no supplies by their own country. When Wellington opened his winter campaign of 1812, he took the enemy by surprise, for they were barely in a position to begin operations before harvest-time.

These general conditions gave the fighting in Spain a character that was entirely different from the other Napoleonic campaigns. A consider-able part of the Spanish and Portuguese forces remained in scattered units, who engaged in a whole series of random engagements, without having the means to impose a decisive result, so that they alternately advanced and retreated with monotonous regularity. When he left the peninsula, Napoleon little imagined that things would turn out like this. In January 1809 there only remained Cradock with ten thousand English at Lisbon, and it looked as though they would have to withdraw, after which the Spaniards could not hold out for long. Wellington's arrival completely upset the emperor's plans. Of the 193,000 men he left in Spain, slightly over one-third were in the west. Ney was keeping watch

over Galicia, while Soult, leaving this province with twenty-three thousand men, was marching on Lisbon, where he would link up with Victor,
who was coming down the Tagus with a force of twenty-two thousand.
Lapine, who had set out from Salamanca, was to be responsible for liaison. With considerable difficulty Soult reached Oporto, and took it on 29
March 1809. Once there, he refused to move. He had dreams of becoming
king of Portugal, and spent his time organising petitions in his favour.
The army, moreover, did not take at all kindly to the prospect of a King
Nicholas – for that was Soult's Christian name – and the discontent grew
to such proportions that it culminated in a plot and Argenton got in
touch with the English. Meanwhile Victor was driving Cuesta back
beyond the Guadiuna. Having beaten him on 28 March at Medellin,
though without destroying his forces, he called for reinforcements from
Lapine; but they allowed the Alcantara bridge to be cut – the only one
available for crossing the Tagus and entering Portugal. Wellington was
therefore able to land unmolested on 22 April, concentrate twenty-five
thousand men at Coïmbra, and attack the two French armies one at a time.

In the first place he turned his attention to Soult, who was off his
guard and lost Oporto on 12 May. As Beresford had crossed the Douro
upstream, Soult could only escape via the mountains, which meant abandoning his artillery. Instead of planning joint operations to save, at least,
Galicia, Ney and Soult proceeded to go their separate ways, and finally
evacuated the province and retired on León and Zamorra respectively.
Wellington had turned back on Victor, but having experienced a great
deal of difficulty in getting ready and coming to an agreement with
Cuesta, he did not resume action till 27 June. Victor fell back towards
Madrid so as to link up with Sébastiani. They were also counting on help
from Mortier; but Napoleon had placed him, together with Ney, under
Soult's orders, with instructions to cut off Wellington's line of retreat by
crossing the Sierra de Gredos. Nevertheless Victor and Sébastiani –
nominally under Joseph's command – took the offensive and on 28 July
attacked the allies, who had slightly superior numbers and held a strong
position at Talavera. But they were thrown back. Wellington, under
threat from Soult, recrossed the Tagus and withdrew towards Badajoz;
nevertheless, his success made a great stir and he was raised to the peerage as Viscount Wellington. Although there were five French corps
grouped together and the road to Lisbon lay open, no one dared take the
initiative and boldly seize this chance: the armies simply went their sev-

eral ways, and Sébastiani hastened to repulse Venegas's army at Almonacid, which had come from the direction of La Mancha.

Wellington, however, was not at all satisfied with this Spanish commander or with Cuesta, or with the junta's refusal to make him commander-in-chief; from now on he therefore went his own way. He had a feeling, moreover, that after his defeat of Austria Napoleon would launch a great effort against him in Spain, and thought it wise to reserve his strength and organise a fortified base in Portugal. The junta disregarded this plan and ordered a general offensive. Areizaga advanced towards the Tagus at the head of the Andalusian army and was routed by Soult at Ocaña on 29 November. Del Parque made a momentary entry into Salamanca; but Kellermann came on the scene and on 28 November overwhelmed the Estremadura army, led by Albuquerque, at Alba de Tormes. Joseph and Soult then suggested the conquest of Andalusia and Napoleon gave way, lured on by the prospect of the resources to be found there. The French occupied Seville on 1 February 1810, and Malaga on the fifth, meeting with hardly any resistance. However, they made the mistake of not marching straight upon Cadiz where the junta had taken refuge, so that Albuquerque arrived in time to shut himself in there on 3 February, and the French had to undertake a siege which proved unsuccessful. Three army corps were thus immobilised in Andalusia.

This was all the more vexatious because Napoleon, as Wellington had foreseen, was preparing a new expedition to Portugal. In 1811 he had more than 360,000 men in the peninsula. In theory, Masséna's army should have numbered 130,000. But as he had had to commission Bonnet to reoccupy Asturias and make solid provision for Navarre, Biscay and Old Castile, he in fact had only sixty thousand men left – an altogether insufficient fighting force. He did not set up any powder magazines or transport depots; and he waited till the end of the harvest to take Ciudad Rodrigo and Almeida. Not till September was he ready to move. He found the countryside more or less empty after the summoning of the *ordenanza*, which involved the evacuation of the inhabitants and the destruction of all food that could not be carried away. Wellington only offered battle at the gates of Coïmbra. Entrenched on the heights of Busaco, he was able to throw back Masséna on 27 September; but as the French general was manoeuvring to turn the position, Wellington withdrew. In the course of pursuit, Masséna soon came up against the lines of Torres Vedras, three of them, one behind the other. The first, forty kilometres long, contained 126 fortifications armed with 247 guns. Wellington had thirty-three thousand English, thirty thousand Portuguese and six thousand Spaniards, not to mention the partisans; and there was no question of being able to reduce the position by famine, since its supplies were replenished by sea. Masséna had no siege equipment, and only thirty-five thousand men. In spite of urgent requests, Drouet only brought him ten thousand. There was an appalling dearth of food. On 5 March 1811 he gave orders to retreat, and did not halt till Salamanca was reached. Wellington followed in pursuit and at once laid siege to Almeida. In order to free it, Masséna came in to attack on 5 May at Fuentes de Onoro, on the Coa, and was driven back. Just at this moment, Napoleon was beginning preparations for the war against Russia; and for the time being, at any rate, this reverse could not be remedied. Only Soult had received orders to support Masséna. He did not dare refuse, but only went so far as to capture Badajoz on 11 March. Wellington thought his own position strong enough to send out Beresford against him, who forced him back, besieged Badajoz once again and repulsed the attacks on Albuera on 16 May. Wellington, who was now rid of Masséna, then joined up with him; but Marmont, who had taken command at Salamanca, likewise went and joined forces with Soult. Here was one last chance to fight a major battle in favourable conditions against the Anglo-Portuguese forces. But this does not appear to have occurred to the two marshals; they separated, and went their separate ways. Wellington made for Ciudad Rodrigo; but as Marmont was approaching, he did not persist, and instead retired to Portugal.

This, however, was only a short breathing-space. When he had been reinforced he knew that – contrary to the emperor's belief – he was now stronger than Marmont, who had a bare thirty-four thousand men; besides, he was reckoning on the surprise value of a winter campaign. This time he acted with a boldness that proved completely successful. Setting out on 7 January 1812, he took Ciudad Rodrigo by assault on the nineteenth and straight away marched on Badajoz, which he captured on 6 April. Soult had been slow to move, and Marmont did not dare to undertake any major diversion. Wellington gave orders, moreover, to multiply attacks on every hand so as to give no chance of coming to their assistance. The Galicians besieged Astorga; Popham appeared on the Biscay coast and kept Caffarelli busy, while Bentinck sent Maitland to the coast of Valencia to look after Suchet. Since Napoleon had recalled twenty-five

thousand men to send to Russia, Joseph besought Soult to evacuate
Andalusia, but in vain. On 14 June Wellington resumed the offensive and
Marmont was forced to withdraw behind the Douro. Recalling Bonnet
from Asturias, he made a clever crossing of the river and turned the
enemy's flank, so that they fell back towards Salamanca. On 22 July he
crossed the Tormes and attacked the Arapiles position, but so clumsily
that he was set upon in mid-manoeuvre and routed. The French lost
fourteen thousand men and Clausel was able only with great difficulty to
get them back to Burgos. Wellington marched on Madrid, Joseph evacuating it in order to join up with Suchet. Soult finally left Andalusia,
linked forces with them and retook the capital in October. Wellington, on
his way to occupy Burgos, now fell back upon the Tormes, and Soult
seemed in no hurry to attack him, but withdrew to Portugal, having taken
twenty thousand prisoners, captured or destroyed three thousand guns
and freed Andalusia.

In the east of Spain, operations pursued an independent course. In
Catalonia, Rosas fell in 1808 and Gerona in 1809. Figueras was lost and
recaptured in 1811, and it seemed impossible to bring peace to this province. In Aragon, Suchet at first withstood Blake, who was threatening
Saragossa; but when he had been reinforced he took Lerida and Mequin-
enza in 1810, and in 1811 Tortosa and Tarragona. After he had been
proclaimed marshal he discomfited Blake outside the fortress of Sagunto,
then before Valencia, which he entered on 9 January 1812. As part of his
troops had been taken away from him, he did not venture further forward, and Maitland was able to occupy Alicante.

Wellington had thus more than lived up to his promises. Not only had
he saved Portugal, but he was holding down a considerable French force
in the peninsula. It should be noted, however, that England's continental
diversion had not up till then been decisive, for it had prevented neither
the defeat of Austria nor the invasion of Russia. If Russia had been defeated, Wellington would have stood no chance of maintaining his
footing, even in Portugal. Not till 1813, when the old army of Spain had
ensured Napoleon's victory in Germany, was he able to give decisive help
to the Coalition – and even then, not until winter had destroyed the
Grande Armée.

# CHAPTER FOUR

## The Continental Blockade

ALTHOUGH ENGLAND COMMANDED THE SEAS, she could not – in spite of the Spanish diversion – wrest the Continent from the French army. On the other hand Napoleon, by concentrating on a federated Europe under his own control, was depriving himself – at any rate for a considerable period – of the ability to attack his enemy at home. This is why the economic war played such an important part after the Peace of Tilsit. The British blockade was more or less of a purely mercantile character. Far from attempting to starve out her adversary and to disrupt her manufacturing war potential – which the state of the continental economy would have made useless – England's effort was bent upon selling her, through neutral channels, all the goods she could possibly desire. The maritime blockade aimed at enriching England herself, and not at destroying the military power of France – a goal that would in any case have been beyond her capacity.

During his early years Napoleon had followed a similar policy. But subsequently he had returned by way of the Berlin and Milan decrees to the policy of the Convention and the Directory, with the avowed intention of hermetically sealing the Continent against English goods, thus condemning her to live as an enclosed economy purely on her own resources. Such a decisive resolve, involving so many risks, could only be based upon a relentless determination to transform the continental blockade into a weapon of war. As long as he did not possess the command of the seas, he had no illusions about the possibility of starving England out and depriving her of raw materials. While not appreciating to the full the solid basis of England's capitalism or its up-to-date structure, he realised that it depended on credit and export, and was therefore vulnerable. He thought that if he could severely shake this edifice, he could bring about bankruptcy, mass unemployment, possibly even a revolution: at all events, force England to give in. But was this a realistic threat? This has been generally denied by the economists, and others have been disposed to follow their verdict; yet it remains an open question. Moreover, did Napoleon ever put the policy into force with maximum rigour? And did he ever completely free himself from the mercantile and fiscal considerations which were bound to weaken its impact? This is a subsidiary question which is also worth examining.

## ENGLISH COMMERCE DURING THE EARLY YEARS OF THE BLOCKADE

Up to the time of the Berlin and Milan decrees, England had the advantage of attack in the economic war. Once she had eliminated enemy shipping and obtained complete control over the neutrals, she could interfere with French exports and deprive her of markets, while continuing to sell to her and even buy from her when convenient. But the Napoleonic conquests and the continental blockade reversed the positions. Now the French intention was to prevent her from supplying the Continent – much her best customer. She was now reduced to the defensive, and it was up to her to make the enemy take her goods.

In order to get the better of these awkward circumstances, she had no need to modify her policies, and in fact she did not make any change at all in them. It was rather the opposite: her economic pragmatism was if anything intensified. In April 1808 the government even obtained parliamentary powers to grant licences as it liked, in violation of the principles recently laid down by itself in the regulations of 1807. It thus gave permission for the import and export of forbidden goods, for sailing to ports that were effectively blockaded, for proceeding in ballast-trim from one enemy port to another, and even allowed the French flag to appear on sufferance in its own harbours. Though as a result of the Franco–Austrian war, licences for ships proceeding to the Empire were abruptly discontinued on 26 April 1809, they continued to be issued for Germany and the Baltic, and in fact soon began to be granted for Holland and Italy. With the harvest giving cause for anxiety, the government even went so far on 28 September as to authorise ships to ply between any ports from Holland to Bayonne, in ballast-trim, which was quite unprecedented. This toleration was withdrawn in November, re-established in May 1810, suspended in October, and then reinstituted once again, according to the prevalent view as to the state of supplies. In 1811 trade with the enemy was once again prohibited; but it was reopened in 1812, even with the

United States, which had already declared war. From 1807 to 1812, 44,346 licences were granted, nearly twenty-six thousand of them in 1809 and 1810. The neutrals received their share, and it would seem that there was a traffic in these documents even on the Continent. This was in fact the channel through which all the maritime commerce flowed, and even when the government did not insist on licences, they were nevertheless in request because the war fleet made hardly any distinctions in practice between friend and foe. The distribution of licences came in the end to be regulated not by any real rules, but solely by judging each case on its merits. This encouraged arbitrary dealings, corruption, slow procedure and mistakes; and protests were raised against a regime that perpetuated the suspension of the Navigation Acts and for practical purposes abolished the regulations of 1807. Nevertheless, this system helped England to defend herself, for in most cases, the licences only allowed imports with a view to re-export. It could when convenient be used to exert diplomatic pressure; and as the licences cost £13 or £14, they were a not inconsiderable source of revenue.

In Europe, success depended primarily on the effective strength of the Continental System. In 1807 and 1808, after the Peace of Tilsit, it was for a while extensive enough to make a perceptible reduction in imports coming from Great Britain. But its strength soon diminished. Spain and Portugal were lost to Napoleon, and in 1809 Turkey made peace with England and threw the Levant open to her; Austria was once more accessible; the requirements of war drew the French forces away from the German coasts, and trade again became very nearly free there. This was what they called the second Tönning period in Holstein. Moreover, there was a more or less open government connivance among Napoleon's allies or vassal states. Up to 1810 Holland continued to be an important market for Britain. Louis had promulgated the Berlin decree, but did not manage to secure respect for it; and from 1806 onwards he too began to allow licences, and exports to England went steadily ahead, involving, of course, return journeys and cargoes. More than 237,000 quarters of grain arrived from the Low Countries in 1807. In addition, ships became accustomed to providing themselves with two sorts of papers, one to show to the English and the other to the French; and a Liverpool house sent out circulars offering to provide such documents. Finally, the English made full use of the dealers in contraband. In order to encourage the blockade-runner, the French methods of packing and labelling were adopted. All kinds of subterfuges came into play, such as lowering nets full of goods at agreed spots, which would then be picked up at night by fishermen. Most important of all were the depots set up as close as possible to the Empire coasts. In 1808 Heligoland was chosen as a North Sea base. Extensive works were carried out there, and two hundred merchants took up permanent residence there – among them one of the Parish brothers of Hamburg – so much so that it became known as 'Little London'. Between August and November 1808, 120 ships called in there, and arrivals were valued at eight million a year. From this point goods went on to Holstein for Hamburg via Altona, or were landed by night with the help of coastal fishermen; after which there were all sorts of devices for despatching them to Frankfurt, Leipzig, Basle and Strasbourg. In the Baltic, Göteborg became the principal centre. By 1808 this port was already exporting 1,300,000 pounds of coffee and nearly three million pounds of sugar, and these figures rose respectively to 4½ and 7½ million in 1809, and doubled the following year. These consignments found their way via Pomerania and Prussia partly to Leipzig, and also to Poland and Russia. In the Mediterranean the requisite bases were provided by Gibraltar, Sardinia and Sicily, Malta, the Balearic Islands (after 1808), and the Dalmatian and Ionian Islands after 1809, Malta being undoubtedly the essential depot above all others. There was access to Austria via Trieste and Vienna, and thence by another route to Leipzig. When the English gained a footing in Turkey a new route was opened up from Salonica and Constantinople to Belgrade and Hungary, all the profits from which went to Vienna.

According to the English statistics, exports to Northern Europe, including France, were only perceptibly diminished in 1808; they recovered in 1809, and by 1810 had risen to a level very close to the value of 1805. Taking the latter as one hundred, then the index figure for 1808 would have been 20.9 for goods of English origin and 51.6 for re-exports, essentially colonial produce. In 1809 they rose to 55.2 and 140 respectively; in 1810 to 74.6 and 97.3. For the total of exports to the same region, the index figures in comparison with 1805 were 32.6 in 1808, 87.5 in 1809, and 83.2 in 1810, the 1809 rise being due to the Austrian War, and the 1810 fall to the first effects of tightening up the Continental System and the Trianon and Fontainebleau decrees. In 1810 British exports to Northern Europe and France were thus not notably diminished; but the devastating drop in 1808 proves that the continental blockade was in itself effective, though it all depended on the length of time and the completeness with which it was applied, that is to say, on the power of the French armies.

All the same, even if the Napoleonic blockade had been extended over the whole of Europe, and even if it had been perfectly observed, British exports would not have been killed, for the Continent only took three-quarters of them as far as colonial produce was concerned, while the proportion of goods coming directly from England was not more than one-third – thirty-seven per cent in 1805, twenty-five per cent in 1808 and thirty-four per cent in 1810. The emperor could therefore only have been certain of attaining his goal by conquering the East as well, and if overseas countries, or at any rate the United States, whether they were in concert with him or no, had adopted the same policy. In fact, the real difficulties encountered by England were due to the American rebellion against the ordinances of 1807, in which respect they reacted differently from the Swedes and Norwegians, the Greeks and the Berbers. To be sure, the Americans did not like the Napoleonic decrees either, but they had other grievances as well against the English, leaving the question of the 'press gangs' and the nationality of crews for the time being in suspense. On 27 May 1807 the English captured a ship of theirs and took several of its crew to London. Those who had taken these steps were reprimanded, but England refused to give way on the basic issue, and a breach between the two countries took place. On 22 December Jefferson declared an embargo, closing his ports to belligerents who had taken measures against neutrals, and forbidding his own ships to leave these ports. Only the English stood to suffer by this ruling. In actual fact, the embargo was not scrupulously enforced, in spite of the passing of an Enforcement Act in 1808. All the same, the import of grain that year from the United States was only a twentieth of the amount imported in 1807, and Liverpool received only twenty-three thousand sacks of cotton instead of 143,000. The price of bread rose, and there was a manufacturing crisis, while a fall in wages led to a general strike in Manchester and a series of disturbances. On the other hand on the Continent, though colonial imports fell off considerably, this was due only to the withdrawal of the American ships. According to Gogel, the Dutch minister of finance, Holland received from America in 1807 nearly thirty million pounds of coffee and forty-one million pounds of sugar; in 1808 she obtained only a million pounds of coffee and four million of sugar. These goods came of course mostly from the English colonies. And lastly, the sale of English goods to the United States fell by more than half, though in the ordinary way they formed a third of her exports.

But thanks to the acquisition of new markets, England was able to guard against this situation, which was becoming serious. Portugal and Spain were only a moderate help. Though the amount of goods sent to them rose greatly, the increase was chiefly devoted to feeding Wellington's troops. On the other hand, the Levant markets proved a most valuable acquisition. The total figure for peninsular and Mediterranean exports rose from £4 million in 1805 to more than £16 million in 1811. But the really crucial event was the opening up of markets in Brazil and the Spanish colonies. We have no exact information about their trade; yet this development is the most likely explanation of the sudden rise of English sales in America – excluding the United States – which increased from £8 million in 1805 to £11 million in 1806 and 1807, and to nearly £20 million in 1808 and 1809. One of the permanent results of the crisis was therefore to reduce the importance of the continental market in British eyes and to turn attention to outlets overseas. Apart from the Levant, Asia and Africa did not for the moment play any part in this development. If anything, British exports to those parts fell off during this period. The importance of Napoleon's Spanish adventure stands out all the more clearly against the facts that have just been reviewed.

Thus renewed in strength, England could afford to wait till the United States came to a better mind, which they were not long in doing. They could not live without exporting their corn, wood, cotton and tobacco: on this point New England and the South were agreed. Moreover, there had been protests from the shipowners, and the agitation soon threatened to lead to civil war. At all events, the embargo provided an excellent platform for the Federalists, who accused Jefferson of siding with the French. Nevertheless, Madison was elected in 1808; but it had been agreed that the embargo should be withdrawn. On 4 March 1809 a Non-intercourse Act was substituted, forbidding all trade with the belligerents; but it did not apply to Spain or Portugal, Denmark or Sweden, and once on the way, American ships contrived to go where they liked, particularly to Holland and to England. Girard, for example, was arranging food supplies for Portugal, and from there his ships went on with wine for England, from which they returned with fresh cargoes. Moreover, the English ambassador promised that the Orders in Council would soon be repealed, and although the government issued a disclaimer,

Madison had meanwhile been elected, the Non-intercourse Act had been repealed and there was an enormous rush for Europe. In 1809 English exports to the United States rose to nearly £7½ million, and the American fleet was once more put at the disposal of the British. In 1809 the percentage of ships leaving British ports under foreign flags rose from forty-five to seventy.

Making allowance for the variations in price, and so in profit, and for the hazards of payment, which were apt to be very much a matter of chance in these new countries – as was soon to be discovered – the result of the English entry into Latin America and the Levant was that Napoleon's designs were effectively foiled. To be sure, the export index went down a little in 1808 to ninety-one; but thanks to the shock administered to the Continental System, and to the reconciliation with the United States, it was remarkably buoyant in 1809, when it rose to 125, and even to more than 126 in 1810. These customs figures are confirmed by estimates of imports by weight in the cotton industry. From 1801 to 1805 England imported on the average 56.5 million pounds of cotton bales; from 1807 to 1812 the figures were 79.7 million, or an increase of 40.7 per cent. The sale of cotton goods rose from £8,600,000 in 1805 to £12,500,000 in 1808 and £14.4 million in 1809. There was an equal growth in the production of coal and iron, and continued technical progress. The population rose from 10,943,000 in 1801 to 12,597,000 in 1811. All this evidence goes to prove that Britain's economic structure during the early years of the century emerged victorious from the tests it had undergone. Success was primarily due to its unrivalled use of machinery and the monopoly of goods from the colonies. And so the publicists employed by the government were able to snap their fingers at Napoleon, in particular d'Ivernois, whose book *Les Effets du blocus continental* came out in July 1809:

> *Votre blocus ne bloque point*
> *Et grâce à notre heureuse adresse*
> *Ceux que vous aVamez sans cesse*
> *Ne périront que d'embonpoint.\**

> \* Your blockade doesn't block,
>   And thanks to our nautical skill
>   The folk you think you're starving
>   Can more than eat their fill.

Yet it was too early to imagine that the day was won. After the defeat of Austria, there was a tightening up of the Continental System, and there seemed to be nothing to prevent Napoleon from making an end of Spain. It looked as though with Alexander's support – or when he had been defeated – Napoleon would contrive to expel England from the Levant. Besides, the continental blockade could well go hand in hand with closing the American market. Just then Latin America was proving a disappointment in the matter of payments, and by plunging into civil war was narrowing down the markets; and it was not long before there was a renewal of the conflict with the United States. Even during the years of prosperity, certain imports gave cause for grave anxiety. It was no good Saumarez commanding the Baltic, because as its ports were gradually sealed, it became increasingly difficult to export the wood, grain, hemp and flax that had previously come from those parts – and these were goods that did not lend themselves to contraband dealings. For textiles, England now turned to Ireland. But wood supplies were a very different matter. In 1808 the consumption rose to sixty thousand loads, each load being roughly equivalent to a cubic metre and a tenth. Although the British forests were denuded and a great deal of wood was imported from Canada from 1804 onwards, England had in that year to buy twenty thousand loads abroad. The House of Solly always managed to send some from Danzig; but from now on, the supply dwindled – not more than 3,319 poles and 2,500 loads in 1811, while Canada sent twenty-three thousand poles, twenty-four thousand loads of oak and 145,000 of pine. Previously, more had come from Sweden, and especially from the United States; but in 1810 there was nothing at all from this quarter. There was a search for new sources of supply; but the wood trade was not organised anywhere else as it was in the Baltic, and freights often proved prohibitive. There was particular difficulty in obtaining supplies for the Malta docks, in spite of the treaties signed with Adamitsch of Fiume and after 1809 with Ali Tebelen. Once again it proved necessary to infringe the Navigation Acts by arranging for the construction of ships – even warships – at Halifax and in India. The merchant navy suffered in consequence. Instead of the ninety-five thousand tons delivered in 1804, it received only fifty-four thousand in 1810. The year 1810 was a very hard one, and only forty-seven thousand loads were used in construction, ten thousand of them coming from abroad.

Grain supplies required even more careful consideration. High prices had led to a large increase in home production. Something like three hundred thousand hectares were cleared for cultivation at this time, chiefly in the common lands. Ireland also provided important supplies. In her struggle with Napoleon England's trump card was the progress made by the capitalist system, which gave her industry an invincible superiority, though not to the extent of making home-grown foodstuffs superfluous. Nevertheless, according to Young's estimate imported food supplied a sixth of the total consumption. Although prices never reached the 1801 level, corn remained more expensive than on the Continent. A quarter rose to one hundred shillings in 1805, then fell to sixty-six in 1807, and rose again to ninety-four in 1808–9. For these two reasons, opinion was always nervous about anything that might hold up consignments. Three-quarters of the imported corn came from the Baltic, the other quarter from the United States and Canada. Now the Baltic ports were in Napoleon's hands, and in spite of contraband, England managed to get only sixty-five thousand quarters from the Continent in 1808 as against 514,000 in 1807. On the other hand the United States only contributed six per cent to grain imports in 1808, instead of the fourteen per cent of the previous year. Since the harvest was not a bad one, no great harm was done; but in a poor season the result would have been very different. Besides, there were Portugal and Spain to feed; and here America came to the rescue and so indirectly gave help to England. But supposing they were to declare war? Finally, there were the Antilles to consider. In 1808 the home country had to be responsible for feeding them too. If the Baltic and the United States had failed simultaneously, there would have been at least a two months' deficit, and even more in a bad harvest season. It has been said that England could have managed by introducing rationing, by raising the extraction rate for milling and so on. Nonetheless, the psychological effect would have been tremendous.

In 1809, then, prospects for the Napoleonic blockade were uncertain; but there was a tendency to be too complacent and to minimise its chances of success. By itself, it would not have brought England to her knees. Nevertheless, if applied rigorously and to the whole of Europe, it might have so weakened her that at some moment or other she would have felt unable to endure such stress, quite independently of Napoleon's specific endeavours, but decisively enough to give him certain victory. Thus the essential point for him was to extend his domination of the Continent and at the same time maintain an unrelenting blockade. But he did just the opposite – he relaxed its rigours.

## THE DEVELOPMENT OF THE CONTINENTAL BLOCKADE

If strictly applied, the continental blockade, representing the Mercantile Theory at its extreme, would have required Europe to live entirely on its own resources. But as the vast majority of Europeans were still engaged in agriculture, there was no need to be uneasy about food supplies. For the same reason she was self-sufficient in fatty products and in textiles, apart from cotton; nor was it impossible for her to supply her own needs in fuel and mining products. On the other hand she was very hard hit by the disappearance of colonial goods. Attempts were made to find substitutes – chicory for coffee, honey and grape syrup for sugar, two thousand tons of which were manufactured in France about 1811. More important still – at least for the future – was the attention now paid to sugar-beet, which was isolated by Margraf in 1757 and had been produced commercially in Silesia by a German called Achard since the beginning of the century. For lack of indigo and cochineal, recourse was had to woad and madder. Attempts were also made to cultivate salt-wort – in the Papal States, for instance – and the chemical industry quickly popularised the product Nicolas Leblanc had produced by breaking down sea salt. There were efforts also to acclimatise cotton round Naples and Malaga, and they proved quite successful, since France ended by obtaining a sixth of her whole consumption from these sources, and managed to gain access to cotton from the Levant by way of Illyria. Nevertheless, this remained a permanent difficulty where cotton supplies were concerned, and but for contraband imports, the looms would have had to shut down, especially in Switzerland and Saxony. Napoleon's attitude to this industry shows most clearly of all his desire to reduce the Continent to a position of economic self-sufficiency. He had never liked the cotton industry just because it was dependent on supplies from abroad, and quite early on he gave protection to Douglas in setting up in France the manufacture of machinery for spinning wool. Moreover, he agreed to grant loans to cotton manufacturers wishing to change over their machinery to a different raw material, and offered a prize of a million francs to anyone who could invent a machine for spinning flax. In 1811 all cotton materials were barred from the imperial palaces.

Even if Europe had been well supplied with raw materials, her troubles would not have been at an end, for her manufacturing capacity was very much smaller than her needs. It could only be hoped that as the blockade became a more perfect instrument for establishing protection, production would achieve the requisite advances. But time would be needed, for up till then both machinery and skilled mechanics had come from England. Moreover, there was nowhere an adequate amount of capital, and the situation was not such as to attract it. Industrial centres being few and the seas closed to commerce, self-sufficiency required amongst other things a general rearrangement of distribution and methods of transport. And so the blockade upset people's habits, interfered with the usual routines, and damaged an untold number of interests. The shipowners, merchants and industrialists in the seaports knew that their interests were disregarded out of hand. Consumers – that is to say, everybody, alas! – felt that they were expected to stand the racket. They did not like chicory and grape syrup, and woollens and linens were much dearer than cottons. In a general way, leading industrialists and even Napoleon himself were concerned to supply the market without much concern for costs. The ideal of self-sufficiency clashed at too many points with the producer's and the consumer's independence, which was founded on individual liberty and free employment, everywhere proclaimed by Napoleon to be one of the cardinal principles of the new society. A conspiracy was bound to develop of its own accord against the blockade, and nothing but the controls and pressures exercised by a military and police state would have succeeded in enforcing obedience to the system.

The allied countries prevented by the blockade from exporting their agricultural produce often lacked the industries that would have compensated for this loss. Others again – like the Hanseatic towns – were nearly killed by the veto on all sea trade, but they more or less openly contrived to get round the regulations in proportion as they still enjoyed some measure of independence. All they had to do was not to apply the measures relating to neutrals. And so the blockade relaxed or tightened up according as Napoleon's military ascendancy decreased or increased. It had started by being a symbol of the Grand Empire, but in the end became a reason for its extension, and had an effect upon its structure, for the vassal states scarcely behaved any more obediently than the allies of Napoleon.

Holland provides the most instructive example. In response to threats from his brother, Louis closed the Dutch ports on 4 September 1807. But as early as 1808 La Rochefoucauld, the French ambassador, pointing out the importance of contraband, particularly in East Frisia, which had recently been annexed, and in Walcheren, which gave access to Antwerp, was advising the annexation of the country at least as far as the Meuse. A royal decree authorised the export of butter and cheese; but Napoleon decided to close his frontier to the Dutch on 16 September. Then on 23 October Louis forbade all exports, and closed his ports to all ships. In French eyes, such excessive measures showed the absurdity of the blockade; besides, these regulations had no sooner been made than they were undermined by a series of exceptions. In June 1809 Louis once more opened his ports to American vessels on condition that they should consign their cargoes to the state warehouses until peace was signed – from which place it was mere child's play to remove them. On 18 July Napoleon replied by setting up a customs cordon from the Rhine to the Trave, and Louis had once again to give way. A dogged repetition of these efforts finally provoked Napoleon into annexing his kingdom in 1810.

Murat was already pursuing the same tactics. Sovereigns like the king of Saxony and the grand duke of Frankfurt, who had no contact with the sea, were in an even better position to ignore vetoes on contraband. Since Western Germany had been at peace, Frankfurt had recovered its prosperity by acting as a clearinghouse on the French frontier, and in 1810 the Prussian representative stated that there had never been so many colonial goods in transit. Leipzig continued to be a big English market providing goods for Central and Eastern Europe. At the Michaelmas fair of 1810 there were more than 65½ million *talers*' worth of colonial goods on sale; and Switzerland was a regular buyer of all the yarn she needed – 190,000 pounds in 1807–8, 430,000 in 1808–9, 950,000 in 1809–10; and it was through her territory that British exports reached Italy. The blockade thus became one of the factors pointing to the superiority of an Empire organised on a unitary, rather than on a federative, basis.

Even where Napoleon was in sole command, it was not easy to get the better of contraband traffic. At no period had it been so flourishing, thanks to the enormous profits reaped from it and the universal connivance at the system. In 1810 the emperor himself gave some idea of the excellence of his arrangements in detailing his various agents, such as the *entrepreneurs*, the *assureurs*, the *intéressés*, the *chefs de bande*, the *porteurs*. For goods intended for France, Basle and Strasbourg were the busiest centres, and fortunes were made there by this trade. Customs officials were not sufficient for keeping watch over such an extent of coastline and more particularly of land frontiers; military occupation alone could be effective. When Napoleon needed to withdraw troops, as in 1809, there were breaches in the system everywhere. In 1811 he had to exclude Dalmatia and Croatia from the imperial customs domain because he could not keep an adequate watch on them. Nor could the emperor rely completely upon his officials. Consuls became corrupt – like Bourrienne at Hamburg and Clérambault at Königsberg: Masséna had put up licences for sale in Italy. Customs officials could be bribed too, including their chiefs, as we learn from what took place at Strasbourg. These disadvantages would have been best overcome by reducing the size of the sectors controlled from each centre; from which it seemed obvious – as always – that the whole of Europe should be annexed to the Empire – an argument that was by no means displeasing to Napoleon.

There would thus have been no inducement to modify his policy if the blockade had not involved consequences that seemed to be dangerous to him personally. Decrès was not long in complaining that the navy could not get its vital supplies, which usually came from the Baltic. The cotton manufacturers, who had at first rejoiced in the exclusion of English cotton goods and had extended their factories, began to change their tune because raw material was running short: if this was to be the result of the blockade, then they had no use for it. However impatient the emperor might be at their complaints, he was forced to take note of them because there was nothing he so much dreaded as unemployment. Moreover, the Empire's exports were going down. In spite of the war, they had steadily risen up to 1806, when they were valued at 456 million francs; in 1807 they dropped to 376 million; in 1808 and 1809 they were hardly more than 330 million. Certain industries showed a decline, particularly silk manufacture, and in the West, textiles, so that there was a further threat of unemployment from this direction too. The salt refiners on the coasts, the vine-growers, and the peasants in the provinces adjacent to the Channel and the North Sea were equally loud in complaint. There were difficulties in disposing of butter and cheese, fruit and vegetables, and – what was more important – wines and brandy. When there was a glut in the corn market the situation grew even worse. Under the Consulate, corn had been dear, which had had no small part in making Bonaparte popular with the landowners and large-scale farmers. In Year X and Year XI the average price had been more than twenty-four francs a hectolitre. Since 1804 a series of good harvests had brought the price down below twenty francs; in 1809 it even went as low as fifteen francs, and in the Paris Basin and in Brittany it actually fell to eleven or twelve francs, and in the Vendée to less than ten. Napoleon became disturbed: though he did not want bread to be dear, neither did he wish slumps to spread discontent among the growers and make it difficult to collect the tax. In such cases he would give previous authorisation for corn export on a provisional basis, as was the custom under the *ancien régime*. On 23 November 1808 a trader in Le Havre had asked for permission to export, and England would have been delighted to be able once more to buy from France.

Again, the question of export had more general implications, for it also affected the balance of trade. Napoleon would have made a distinction between this and the balance of account which Colbert would hardly have allowed, for though France in his time did not possess the resources derived from freightage and tourism, her capitalists did at least conduct certain speculative operations in the conquered countries, and war provided significant quantities of specie. Nevertheless, his ideas were too traditional not to insist at all costs on giving the precedence to export. Up to 1808 he did not succeed, although the deficit fell from eighty-three million francs in 1803 to seventeen million in 1807. Among its other advantages, the continental blockade seemed to Napoleon to have the merit of redressing this whole situation. Imports went down from 477 million francs in 1806 to 289 million in 1809. From 1808 onwards, there was a favourable balance of trade, leaving a cash balance of forty-three million francs in 1809. In the emperor's eyes, this was the essential thing; but the result would have been even more satisfactory if exports, instead of going down, had also maintained their level. Since the war blockade as he saw it was aimed at England's currency, it did not contradict his mercantile theories: the essential point was to go on selling to the English, while not buying from them, so as to rob them of their coin. When he heard in 1808 that Louis was issuing export licences for Great Britain, he forgave him on condition that nothing should be bought from her in exchange: 'They must pay in cash, but never in goods – never, do you understand?'

For him, however, there was no relaxing the rigorous attitude to neutrals. When he heard of Jefferson's embargo, he announced in the Bayonne decree of 17 April 1808 that it must now be assumed in principle that American navigation had ceased to exist, and that any vessels claiming United States allegiance must be deemed fraudulent, and might therefore be taken as lawful prize. Napoleon had them sequestrated, and by the Rambouillet decree of 23 March 1810 ordered them to be sold together with their cargoes. When neutral vessels were excluded, French exporters ran short of shipping, and there was bound to be a fall in the quantity of goods despatched. It is possible that to begin with, Napoleon may not have noticed this contradictory state of affairs, seeing that his gaze was fixed above all on France, and that he was quite indifferent to the fate of the agricultural countries' export trade – the Baltic states, for example. Even if he had conquered the whole of Europe, France would nevertheless have remained the essential port of the Empire, the centre to which money must flow. Since the blockade gave her the continental market (he argued), she had only to seize it to maintain, and even to increase, her sales. But were French resources really sufficient to replace the goods from England? And could overland porterage and canal traffic be so greatly increased that transport by sea would become unnecessary? Events were to prove that these hopes could not be realised, and even if they had been, there would still have been the problem of what to do with the superfluous corn.

Most of the men who served Napoleon did not really approve of the new character he was giving to the blockade and wanted to return to the system in force before 1806. Chaptal made no secret of his opinion; Crétet and Montalivet at the Ministry of the Interior were in touch with the cotton manufacturers and seaport traders, and would have liked to meet their interests. They could not go so far as to ask that the Berlin and Milan decrees should be repealed, but they insinuated that it would be profitable to follow the English example and issue export licences, and that it would be as well to allow the neutrals to have them too, though without giving them back complete freedom. In order to meet the needs of the army and navy, certain goods would be delivered in return; all other outgoings would be only against payment in money, which would ensure a comfortable cash balance. Did not Coquebert de Montbret recommend in 1802 that there should be exchanges on a compensatory basis? And in 1807 did not Napoleon himself consider at a certain point issuing import licences on condition that an equivalent amount of goods was exported to keep the balance? Contrary to what he relates in his memoirs, Mollien opposed this plan, pointing out that exporters, even if refused authority to exact payment in kind, would nevertheless not fail to take on a return cargo – even if fraudulently – and that they would moreover be compelled by the English to do so; and in this way, Mollien reckoned, the exchange with Britain would be equalised. Coquebert de

Montbret likewise pointed out that if corn was sent to the English, this would spoil the chance of starving them out. These results could not be reconciled with the theory of an offensive blockade.

They were right: but another argument advanced by Gaudin and Collin de Sussy, the head of the customs, won Napoleon over. By reducing imports, they argued, he would curtail the customs revenue, which went down from sixty million francs in 1808 to 11½ million in 1809. On the eve of the campaign against Austria, it was important to restore the level of receipts; moreover, the export of corn would enable the peasants to pay the land tax. In March 1809 Napoleon did in fact dictate a plan for licensing. A confidential circular from Crétet announced on 14 April that it was a question of an exceptional and temporary expedient which would not be publicised. These licences – later called 'the old-type licences' – would allow the export of wines and brandies, fruit and vegetables, grain and salt against the import of wood, hemp, iron and cinchona or against payment in coin, plus the customs dues and a tax of from thirty to forty *louis* for each licence. Crétet issued forty of these; but Fouché, who succeeded him as the intermediate authority, was much more generous, for by 5 October he had issued two hundred. However, Gaudin and Montalivet insisted on the needs of industry being also considered, and so a second type of licence was brought out on 4 December 1809, incorporated subsequently in a decree of 14 February 1810. This measure reserved three-quarters of each cargo exported for agricultural produce – to which were now added oils and textile raw materials; the rest of the cargo could be taken up by manufactured products.

As was to be expected, the conditions governing re-import and payment in coin clashed with the English requirements, and there was not as great a demand for licences as might be imagined. In June 1810 it was reported to the emperor that 351 had been issued, exports being valued at ten million francs against six million of imports. Nevertheless, the export of grain is still shrouded in obscurity. According to the English figures, the Empire and its allies sent Great Britain in 1809 and 1810 nearly 1,500,000 quarters, and this was said to have been paid for in gold, involving a transfer of £1,400,000 sterling. The value of English imports did in fact rise in 1809 to £75.5 million, and in 1810 to £89.7 million, whereas the famine of 1801 had only made the figure go up to £73.7. It therefore seems likely that corn was exported not only under imperial licence. Since the end of September 1809 England had been issuing licences to go and fetch corn from the Continent, even as ballast; and it looks as though Napoleon closed his eyes and allowed the enemy ships to load as freely as they liked, until it came to the poor harvest of 1810, when he stopped exports at the end of the summer. The glut in corn had been cleared; but the vine-growers, the industrialists and the treasury had little cause for satisfaction. During the first half of 1810 the emperor became convinced that this first attempt was not enough. In the course of his northern journey, the manufacturers' grievances were more and more loudly voiced, and on 12 January he gave permission for selling prize goods, in spite of the veto against them – except for certain cottons – subject to a duty of forty per cent. These were called products 'of permitted origin'. In other words, he authorised certain imports. Where exports were concerned, he organised official relationships with the English smugglers at Dunkirk, and in 1811 their base was moved to Gravelines. On 6 June a traders' and manufacturers' council was set up, and at the end of the month the emperor began to work out with them a general rearrangement of the blockade.

A new motive was also urging him in that direction. On 1 May 1810 the American Congress authorised the president in the Macon Bill to forbid imports by belligerents who had not repealed the measures directed against the neutrals before 3 March 1811. If England persisted in maintaining them, Napoleon would, while giving the United States favoured treatment, urge them to break off relations with her. By the decree of Milan, neutrals who stood up for their rights would be exempt from these provisions. Through a diplomatic device it was arranged to advance the date of their coming into force, an event of considerable importance, since it would reinforce the effectiveness of the blockade.

On 3 July 1810 the decree of Saint-Cloud made licences an official institution. They were subsequently granted to Italy, and the Hanseatic cities; and to Danzig out of consideration for the Poles. By a further decree of 25 July the French Empire's maritime trade was put under state control. It was now forbidden to enter or leave Empire ports without a licence signed by the emperor in person. These licences were called 'normal licences', and were only issued to French subjects. Thus Napoleon had in effect promulgated a navigation act, like the one passed by the Convention. But as his ships could not sail, it was inoperative. And so an exception studied by the Trade Council in an important session on 25 June was made in favour of the Americans. On 5 July they were granted by decree permission to import, provided that they re-exported the equivalent. But as Madison had forbidden his countrymen to ask for licences, which in his view implied an authorisation contrary to the freedom of the seas and his country's sovereignty, his veto was evaded by calling them 'permits' when they applied to seamen of the United States. The truth was that France could not do without them; but – diplomatically – this concession was much publicised, and on 6 August Champagny gave notice that the emperor would repeal the Berlin and Milan decrees in November, if the English on their side would revoke the Orders in Council. Montalivet at once proposed that these permits should be granted to all allied or neutral vessels; but the emperor refused, and even impounded some Danish ships. It must therefore be realised that he had most adroitly turned his absolute need for neutral vessels into a diplomatic manoeuvre likely to put the United States at loggerheads with Great Britain.

The decree of 25 July stipulated that all imports must be balanced by an equivalent export of certain designated goods, which varied from port to port, but always contained from a third to a half in silks. If the general prohibitions and those relating to English manufactures had been observed, imports ought only to have consisted of foodstuffs and raw materials from the United States or the Continent; but in actual fact, colonial goods were once more admitted, although known to be of enemy origin. Thus the method put forward by Coquebert de Montbret in 1802 had in effect been adopted – state regulation of all maritime trade, and a compulsory minimum export to balance the imports. Napoleon gave up demanding that the former must be paid for in money in order to revive the export trade and especially to provide industry with the necessary raw materials, and consumers with their sugar and coffee. He had had the same inspiration as the Committee of Public Safety; yet in Year II France, though obliged to import at all costs, agreed if need be to pay in coin. Now, in Napoleon's time, the position was reversed, and France expected the foreigner to pay her in cash. Nonetheless, it was clear that the emperor, by consenting to purchases which would partly be to the enemy's advantage, was in fact diminishing the rigour of the continental blockade.

The treasury also took its share, for each licence cost a thousand francs. The customs tariff had been revised, and on 1 August the Trianon decree was published, increasing the tax on colonial goods to a formidable degree. The American colonist, who had paid one franc per quintal in

1804 and sixty francs since 1806, would in future have to pay eight hundred. The duty on indigo was raised from fifteen to nine hundred, and on coffee from 150 to four hundred. There seemed to be a flat contradiction between the policy of obtaining raw materials for the manufacturers and the imposition of this overwhelming level of duty. But in thus striking a blow at cotton Napoleon was aiming at giving an advantage to the national textile industry; he also imagined that the English would lower their prices to make up for the duty and thus no longer show a profit, while the regular imports would discourage buyers from turning to contraband sources. But he was over-optimistic. The English ruled the market and could hold to their prices; and exorbitant taxation was not likely either to discourage fraudulent dealing. And so there was soon a tightening up of repressive measures. By the Fontainebleau decree of 18 October the contrabandist could be sentenced to ten years' penal servitude, not to mention branding, and put under the jurisdiction of a new court, the Cours Douanières, which followed the same procedure as a special court. In 1812 the Hamburg court pronounced 127 sentences in a fortnight, several of them death sentences in view of aggravating circumstances. Contraband colonial goods were to be confiscated and sold, and manufactured products destroyed. But there remained the goods that had already been brought in despite the blockade in order to improve the market and bring in some money. To deal with this situation, the Trianon decree set a huge police operation on foot. Throughout the Empire, house-to-house searches were the order of the day; and as the vassal states showed some reluctance to comply, Napoleon decided to make an example of Frankfurt. In the night of 17 October the city was surrounded by a division and occupied the next day, and 234 merchants – including Bethmann and Rothschild – had everything confiscated that they had not managed to hide. The princes of the Rhine Confederation, Prussia and Switzerland were threatened with invasion, and had their German frontiers closed – after which they decided to obey the emperor's orders.

The decrees of 1810 did not, however, yield all the results that had been hoped for, and constantly involved serious drawbacks. The new licences were not much more popular than the old had been. According to the report produced by Montalivet, the emperor had signed 1,153 by 25 November 1811, but only 494 were issued. They covered exports estimated at forty-five million francs and imports of nearly twenty-eight million. The Americans had only taken out some hundred permits, brought

In October 1807 Napoleon turned his attentions to invading Portugal and Spain. Manuel de Godoy (*above*, by Goya) was the then Spanish prime minister. He signed the Treaty of Fontainebleau expecting to be given the south of the country, but when the promises proved empty and French troops invaded Spain in December, Godoy fled. On 7 July 1808 Napoleon appointed his brother Joseph king of Spain (*right*)

The surrender of Baylen, 19 July 1808, in which the Grande Armée led by General Dupont was defeated by General Castaños' Spanish force. It was the first major defeat of Napoleon's Grande Armée. *Below*, Napoleon receiving the Austrian ambassador Baron Vincent at the Congress of Erfurt, 1808. Talleyrand stands behind the table, while Tsar Alexander watches from the right

The brutal assault on the monastery of San Engracio by the French during the second siege of Saragossa, 8 February 1809. *Below*, Marshal Lannes mortally wounded at the Battle of Essling, 22 May 1809. Napoleon himself had led an army attempting to cross the Danube, but they were forced back by the Austrians – 'a blow had been struck at Napoleon's personal prestige'

In the first Battle of Oporto on 29 March 1809 the French army led by Marshal Soult were victorious against the Portuguese and captured the city. However, a few months' later, on 12 May, the city was reclaimed by the British and Portuguese

In 1807–9 England faced blockades on her exports from both Napoleon and Jefferson. *Right*, a despairing English manufacturer is unable to shift his goods. *Below*, 'The happy effects of that grand system of shutting ports against the English' – Jefferson is addressing a group of disgruntled citizens trying to defend his trade embargo against the English

In December 1809 Napoleon divorced Josephine (*above*), and in the following April he married Marie-Louise of Austria. *Below*, the marriage procession through the Tuileries gardens

On 20 March 1810 Napoleon's son, the 'King of Rome', was born, shown here by Rouget being presented to dignitaries of the Empire

Napoleon on a hunt in the forest of Compiègne – hunting was one of his favourite pastimes. *Below*, Napoleon surrounded by his nephews and nieces on the terrace at Saint-Cloud

in rather less than three million in goods, and purchased about 3½ millions' worth. This favourable balance appeared in Napoleon's eyes to justify the experiment. In actual fact, it is doubtful whether there was any gain. In the ministry's figures, the estimated value of exports was increased by fifty per cent to allow for the French merchants' profits, and imports were reduced by one-quarter; moreover, the English refused to purchase, and in Illyria the emperor had to make an exception because when re-exports were demanded they simply refused to deliver any salt. The result was that the exports were often artificial, their only purpose being to justify the corresponding imports. The customs were cheated by arranging for consignments of cheap goods which were subsequently thrown overboard. In any case, though industry experienced a certain relief, it was not enough to disarm the hostility of the business community. Savary has passed on to us Lafitte's strictures; and the Chamber of Commerce at Geneva, through the pen of its secretary Sismondi, was loud in its criticisms of the blockade, to the consternation of government departments. As soon as Napoleon was not willing to grant licences with the same degree of opportunism that was shown by the English – which would not have been consistent with the Berlin and Milan decrees – he might as well not have issued any at all.

Moreover there was still a long way to go in cleaning up the market. People succeeded in hiding a great deal of the illicit goods, or in declaring them legal, by bribing the French agents or obtaining the connivance of the local authorities. For colonial goods, the emperor was willing to make a variety of concessions. He authorised the payment of dues in kind, allowed the Dutch seizures to come into the Empire at a reduction of fifty per cent, permitted the Danes extra time to import the stocks for Holstein at Hamburg, and subsequently accepted the sequestrations in Prussia by way of payment to be deducted from the war indemnity. All that was already in circulation was remitted so that it again became impossible to exercise any kind of check on it. Moreover, this whole procedure had produced the most violent reactions. The destruction of the confiscated manufactured goods brought their holders face to face with bankruptcy, for it required an enormous sum of money to enter into possession of the colonial goods – more than nine million at Frankfurt – which many were quite unable to advance. Each state claimed the right to apply the Trianon decree to its own advantage, with the result that the whole movement of goods came to a standstill until it was agreed only to require the dues to be paid once; and even then, because Prussia accepted payment in its own depreciated paper money, its certificates ended by being refused. This shock led to the great economic crisis of 1811; and so the customs extortion and red tape only served to aggravate the evils which the licences had been intended to cure.

Nor was the effect on morale at all healthy. The licences and the Trianon decree confused public opinion by suggesting that the emperor had seen his mistake and was now going to give up the continental blockade; and in August, after the assurances given to the United States, even Montalivet was for a while under the same illusion. The Fontainebleau decree and the ruthless manner in which it was applied were a bitter disappointment to the peoples concerned, who considered they had been more hardly treated than the English, and thought it a scandal that the produce they so badly needed should be burnt in the public squares or thrown into the rivers. It was possible at a pinch to persuade the French that this procedure was in the national interest, but not so the other nations. The American envoy at St Petersburg had called it 'a policy of vandalism', and this was the generally voiced opinion. And then again, by reserving licences for the French, Napoleon justified the view of those who proclaimed the blockade to be solely in the interests of the dominant nation; and by making an exception for the Americans, he called forth the indignation of the allied and vassal states. From the end of 1809 onwards Murat was in league with Fouché, Ouvrard and Labouchère to issue licences himself; and Russia, seeing corn going out of the Empire, began to demand an explanation. She did not apply the Trianon decree, nor did Austria. Finally, Alexander resumed his freedom of action. Since France was trafficking with the enemy and admitting American ships to her ports, he decided to reopen his to the neutrals on 31 December 1810. The new arrangements therefore compromised the blockade and at the same time shook the Continental System. The break with Russia had other underlying causes as well; but it would have been possible to avoid giving it a further pretext if – in keeping with the spirit of the continental federation – licences had been issued to the vassal states and allies, as well as to the French, for trade with Empire ports; and this would likewise have been profitable to the Americans. The Navigation Act of 1810 was in such circumstances completely useless. It was a most untimely and dangerous demonstration of the obstinacy of Napoleon's mercantilist outlook.

Apart from this mistake, contemporary recriminations do not conceal the plain fact that his policy was remarkably astute. Not for one moment did he intend to give up the continental blockade, and his reorganisation of it still gave only a secondary place to the difficulties of industry. The purpose had been essentially fiscal: the emperor needed money for the war against Austria, and by allowing the peasants to sell their corn he could pocket the tax – a point that did not escape the English. In 1810 he foresaw that he would need still more money to get ready to fight against Russia; and at the end of 1810 the Trianon and Fontainebleau decrees brought him in an estimated 150 million, not to mention the proceeds from the sale of confiscated goods. As always, he bent his policy to meet present needs, and he got what he wanted. At the same time he combined this financial policy with a diplomatic move calculated to win over the United States, and was equally successful in this as well. Taking the emperor's promises seriously, Madison re-established free trade with the Empire on 2 November 1810, whereas English imports were still forbidden.

The Berlin and Milan decrees, however, remained in full force, and there is no doubt that if licences had seemed to Napoleon likely to impair their effectiveness, he would have brought the system to an end; for as in 1809 licences were only a temporary expedient. Nor would he have continued the American permits unless the United States had been destined (in his view) to declare war against England. There was a peremptory note about his announcement of 24 March 1811 to the merchants of Paris:

I regard the neutral flags as a territorial extension. But the power that allows them to be violated cannot be looked upon as neutral. The fate of American trade will soon be decided. I will give it my help if the United States obey these decrees. If not, their ships will be turned away from my imperial ports. The Continent will be closed to all imports from England. I shall be prepared to use armed force, if need be, to carry out my decrees.

To be sure, in 1811 England was back in the bad days of 1808. Sweden had just joined the blockade, and the English fleet had no port left in the Baltic to which they could have free access. But in September 1810 they encountered a severe reverse. When six hundred ships which had had to shelter from gales in the straits tried to make land on the southern coasts, 140 of them were seized, with an estimated cargo of a million and a half

sterling; and Sweden herself had to put up with the confiscation of a further hundred, worth half a million. Holland and the German North Sea
coast were now annexed and the Grande Armée poured over Germany
on its way to Russia, and made the watch more strict. Never before had
English exports been so seriously affected. In 1810 they were still rising,
and reached £7,700,000 for Northern Europe inclusive of France, plus
£9,160,000 for re-exports. In 1811 these figures fell respectively to
£1,500,000 and £1,960,000: in other words, to only 14.5 per cent and
32.2 per cent of the 1805 values. That same year England sold the United
States only £1,870,000 worth of goods, instead of the £11,300,000 of
1810. At the same time the disturbances that had begun in Spanish
America brought down the figure for exports to the New World – excluding the United States – to less than thirteen million, against more than
17½ million in 1810. The total of British exports fell to £39½ million in
1811, or eighty-two per cent as compared to 1805, and sixty-five per cent
as compared with 1810.

It may perhaps be alleged that in 1811 England was suffering from a
severe industrial crisis; but this was responsible for a startling drop in
prices and the building up of enormous stocks of goods. Though England
sold less, it was only because no one would buy her wares, and not
because there was any shortage of them. Thus the blockade was working
satisfactorily: certain factors outside Napoleon's control, which had previously worked against him, were now running in his favour; and as was
shown by the 1811 crisis, there were other favourable factors as well. It is
therefore easy to understand his confidence: 'I know that my measures
have been severely censured,' he was still saying on 24 March 1811;
'those however who have recently come from England and have seen the
effects now beginning to be felt in the interruption of their trade with the
Continent cannot but say that the emperor may possibly be right, and
that his plans will very likely succeed.'

He had failed, however, to take advantage of some of the favourable
factors. It annoyed him to see England continuing to sell on the Continent and pocketing the returns in cash or passing them on to her allies in
the form of subsidies; but he ought to have laid the blame at his own door.
For he continued to respect the international banking framework which
acted as a support for the British trade and managed the transfer of
specie, which played an important part in payment, as well as the circulation of commercial paper money – a vital necessity for exchange, at least

in Western Europe. As the Dutch minister Valckenaer wrote to King Louis on 25 January 1808,

> Of all the English manufactured goods circulating on the Continent, none is more profitable or more important to the English than bank paper money . . . Its magic power sustains the vast fabric of English trade in the four quarters of the world . . . Such is the powerful effect of the system of bills and letters of exchange drawn either directly on England, or indirectly on English accounts, in all the commercial centres of the European continent.

Again, the banks served as intermediaries for the elector of Hesse and Dutch capitalists to subscribe to the English loans, and for Nathan Rothschild to send funds to Wellington by procuring French bills! The key centres were Amsterdam, Hamburg and Frankfurt. The Houses of Hope–Labouchère and Parish kept in touch with them, as well as with the Baring Bank and the financial houses of Paris. The continental Rothschilds kept in touch with their brother Nathan in London, and in 1811 three of them – James, Charles and Solomon – came to do business in Paris, where James remained to found the French branch of the family. The big banks on the Continent were under the emperor's control. However, if the export of coin was still forbidden in the Empire, this was not so elsewhere; it does not even seem to have ceased in Holland after the annexation. Again, commercial discounting went on uninterruptedly everywhere, though the *Moniteur* had stopped quoting the London exchange rate in 1807. No one had failed to realise that this was in fact the Gordian knot. Commercial paper credit, according to Valckenaer, was the only kind of merchandise that was not forbidden, and, he said, 'that is where we must strike.' He therefore proposed to reckon as high treason any creation, acceptance, endorsement, discount, despatch or payment of any bill to the benefit or credit or account of any English subject. No doubt Louis took good care not to let this suggestion come to his brother's notice; but the cleavage in policy could not escape Mollien or Napoleon, and in 1811 he fulminated against 'the discounters of English commerce'. Nevertheless, he did not take measures against them – an omission that can only be explained by his mercantilist outlook. Although he wished to stop the English from selling, he did not give up exporting to them and drawing on their coin. Holland, too, continued to obtain important revenue from her investments abroad, and the emperor had no intention of giving these up: to have taken steps against the international bank would have been a blow to his own interests. The warlike ardour which had inspired the Berlin and Milan decrees did not contain any such mitigations; and so he was prepared to curb it – though perhaps without quite admitting to himself that he was doing so.

The lure of gold and certain fiscal considerations also made him turn down the chance of starving England out and led him to deliver her the corn she badly needed. It would seem that in the first flush of warlike ardour he had argued otherwise, for the export of foodstuffs had come to a complete halt in France in 1807, had been forbidden in Holland and had ceased in Germany in 1808. But in 1809 he authorised it again, in spite of Coquebert de Montbret's observations, and it was by this means that his new policy showed a substantial profit. Out of the total imports of 1,567,000 quarters in 1810, Great Britain received 1,306,000 from the Empire and its allies. As Napoleon had hoped, her rate of exchange went down and her gold left the country; but she kept some reserves, which is proved by the fact that in spite of the disastrous famine of 1810, she imported in 1811 only 336,130 quarters of corn, a third of which still came from Prussia; and that nevertheless the quarter, which averaged 103 shillings in 1810 (about forty-four francs a hectolitre), went down to ninety-two shillings (33½ francs a hectolitre). There is no doubt that without French help England would have gone short over several weeks; and even if she had managed to come through by one expedient or another, prices would certainly have soared. Now at this particular juncture England was going through an unprecedented economic crisis; and by tying his hands in advance Napoleon missed what was perhaps a unique opportunity of achieving his purposes.

## THE CRISIS OF 1811

An important part in this crisis was played by the Trianon and Fontainebleau decrees, but they were not an indispensable element in bringing it about. Here, too, it must be realised that Napoleon was helped by circumstances that were not under his control. Capitalist production is by its nature subject to periodical disturbances, and the war and blockade simply created unhealthy conditions which precipitated the crisis. They did not altogether spare the Continent; yet the English economy, just because of its more advanced development, suffered infinitely more serious damage.

Prices since 1807 had been artificially inflated. In England, for example, supplies from the Baltic, silks and cotton had more than doubled by 1808. Freights from Canada were twice as much, from Riga, three times or more. In 1810 it was calculated that the voyage of a hundred-ton vessel from Calais to London and back needed £50,000, and from Bordeaux to London and back, £80,000, with the result that there was more and more capital locked up in maritime trade. At the same time risks were on the increase, not only because of captures and confiscations, but also in proportion to the exorbitant and unforeseeable variations in prices. Thus in Paris Pernambuco cotton was worth seven francs a pound in 1806, fifteen in 1807 and twenty-four in 1808; and in 1810 the price stayed between twelve and fourteen. At Hamburg, a sack was quoted at seventy-five guldens at the beginning of 1808, 260 in the middle of the year and 175 at the end. In London, the fluctuations were smaller, though large enough to provide huge possibilities for speculation. In Hamburg, the father of the Parish family was already deploring in 1800 that short-term speculation was getting such a grip on the business world. And in the end it became a ruling passion. In England, there was gambling on every kind of goods, and societies were even formed with this one and only purpose.

On the Continent, the chief interest was in the colonial products, and opportunities for speculation were found in the larger towns. All the same, there were not such constant arrivals of shipping, and the activity was much greater in Amsterdam and in the Hanseatic cities, where French banks invested large sums, either on their own account, or for their clients. In 1810, for example, there was mention of the tenant of the Café du Caveau as a strong investor in colonial goods at Antwerp. The bulls took the lead, and there was plenty of scheming, especially by circulating false rumours. In April 1807, in order to force the price of cotton up, the news was spread abroad that the English were blockading Lisbon. In Holland, the big firms bought up stocks in the warehouse, so as to control the market. In England, where government borrowing was continuous, there was also much interest shown in stocks and shares. In this department, the bears were in control of the situation. The brokers were all the more insistent on bringing down the Consolidated Funds because the bankers, with one exception, would not lend on forward dealings; they themselves advanced it at the rate of five per cent (the legal maximum), by borrowing on much more favourable terms, while the Bank of England countered their operations through the Goldsmith Bank. In Paris, speculation on stocks and shares did not become nearly as important, though it was by no means neglected. The uncertain political situation made it a very unstable business. As long as Talleyrand was at the Foreign Office, he took advantage of the information reaching him in his official capacity to make highly profitable deals on the Stock Exchange. Mollien kept up the price of government stock to the best of his ability; but the bears never ceased to justify the invectives launched by Napoleon. The spirit of speculation spread into business and industry. There were two big booms in England – one in 1807 and 1808, when Popham announced the capture of Buenos Aires, and when the news came through that the Spanish possessions had proclaimed Ferdinand VII and would henceforward look upon the English as their allies; and the other in 1810, when the last French colonies had fallen and when the Americans reappeared in Europe. In order to cope with all the orders, factories were extended, and the artisans working in their homes were given better equipment in the shape of looms, either on hire or sold to them on credit. In France, Saxony and Switzerland, the veto on English cotton goods had similar effects. Considerable capital sums were likewise invested, the service of which was a heavy burden on these firms, and put them at the mercy of any crisis.

Although circumstances provide an explanation for this feverish excitement, it would not have been able to develop in this way without the existence of inflation, both in money and in credit. In this respect England's position was very different from that of France. After freeing the banknote from gold, the British government had bent its efforts to maintaining a healthy financial state of affairs in order to avoid having to fall back on paper money. In general, their efforts had been successful, no doubt thanks to the increase in taxation, for from 1804 to 1811 taxation nearly always covered more than half the national expenditure; but also thanks to the plentiful supply of capital and the confidence they were at pains to maintain by supporting the consols through the sinking fund and by intervention on the Stock Exchange, so that they were always able to borrow both on a short- and on a long-term basis. In spite of all these efforts, however, the government had to compel the Bank of England to keep a considerable quantity of exchequer bills on hand – more than forty millions' worth from 1808 onwards – with a resulting increase in the money circulation. The actual rate of increase is not known; but it rose from seventeen million in 1805 to 23½ in 1811. In that year a committee of inquiry gave the assurance that there had recently been issued to the public £2 million in banknotes. In addition to this, local banks – of which there were now eight hundred – were thought to have issued some four or five millions' worth of notes. And lastly, banking methods were steadily improving. Forty banking firms were affiliated to the clearing house, and the result was a more rapid circulation of money. The rise in prices, moreover, was continuous: in relation to 1790, the index figure was 176 in 1809. The rise was gradual, and as wages always lagged behind, while the plentiful supply of money lowered the rate for borrowing, there can be little doubt that inflation was a contributory factor in encouraging the spirit of enterprise. Nevertheless, some of the contemporary critics were positive that the private banks – if not the Bank of England – gave excessive credit, and we can well believe them. And lastly, merchants themselves offered long credit for payments in order to attract customers – often twelve to fifteen months – and in Latin America and the Levant, it was credit without adequate guarantees.

On the Continent, most of the states also issued paper money; but as the economies were not usually very advanced, production does not seem to have been much stimulated by it. Napoleon, on the other hand, had ruled out paper money once and for all; but he was nonetheless keen to increase the stock of metallic money by all possible means, and war provided him with substantial indemnities, a good part of which came back into the Empire, and the money in circulation was therefore correspondingly increased. All the same it is clear that credit was chiefly inflated by unsound procedures, as happened under the Consulate. Since banks were still rather rare, especially in the provinces, traders, industrialists and speculators continued to obtain money by mortgaging their real estate or by accommodation bills. In spite of the reforms in the Bank of France, it is not certain that these did not go on being accepted; for we know that Martin's son, a Genevan who was one of the Bank's auditors, went bankrupt in 1811 as a result of speculation and having been involved in some contraband business.

It did not require the decrees of 1810, then, to produce a crisis, and in England at any rate the crisis preceded the decrees. Although there was greater activity than ever, the economy began to show signs of weakness from 1809 onwards through a sagging of the money market. The price of gold and silver had not increased since 1806; but the Bank of England's cash reserves, which were more than £6 million in 1808, suddenly fell to £4 million. The pound, which had been worth twenty-three francs in Paris and thirty-five shillings in Hamburg the previous year, suddenly dropped to twenty francs and twenty-eight shillings respectively. By August 1809 Ricardo was sounding a note of alarm, thus opening up a controversy which has remained famous in the history of monetary theories. He blamed inflation for the crisis, and laid the responsibility at the door of the Bank of England. At this point Huskisson intervened to defend the Bank; and in February 1810 the Commons appointed a committee of inquiry which reported in 1811 in favour of Ricardo. Even today, the debate is by no means closed. The premium on precious metals must have encouraged a certain degree of hoarding, but capital did not leave the country because there was easy government borrowing: besides, where else could the capital have gone? The fall in the rate of exchange and the disappearance of gold must therefore have been due to external payments by the state, and not to internal inflation. These payments had been considerably increased by the Peninsular War, by subsidies to the Portuguese, the Spaniards and the Austrians, and finally by grain purchases, which were responsible for almost an additional £6 million in 1809. In short, England paid out an annual average of about £3 million on the Continent in the years between 1805 and 1807. The total was more than 6½ million in 1808, eight in 1809 and fourteen in 1810. It should be added that she was always having to pay out sums in other parts of the world for the upkeep of her garrisons, her ships and her agencies, as well as finding the interest on the funds invested by foreigners in Great Britain. On this last account, Holland by herself took thirty-two million florins from London. Finally, the commercial balance showed a deficit of £15.5 million sterling in 1809, 8.9 million in 1810 and 11.1 million in 1811.

Even if we admit that the budget was balanced, it is nonetheless certain that the Ministry found itself compelled to send large quantities of specie abroad, part of which they sought from the Bank of England. The prime reason for this drain on money was the carelessness and incompetence of the treasury. Nathan Rothschild has related that one day, learning that the East India Company wished to dispose of a large sum of silver, he quickly acquired it and sold it again at once to the paymaster, who could not manage to find any ready money. He then undertook to send it to Wellington, and despatched it with this end in view to France, where he bought bills drawn on Sicily, Malta and even Spain. All the same, the accounts could not be balanced in the ordinary way, for the conditions imposed on trade by warfare, the blockade and the opening up of new and distant markets made payments from abroad slow and irregular, while the government could not delay paying its own debts without serious trouble. For the same reasons, credit transfers were often not possible: Wellington could not be satisfied, for instance, by paper credits drawn on Germany. Advances and the transfer of precious metals were therefore unavoidable. It was not only the exchange rate that suffered, for it was not possible to ensure that these transfers were scrupulously carried out. At the end of April 1812 Wellington found that he was short of five million piastres. By striking at exports from England, Napoleon was thus also able to make things difficult for him in the military sphere.

If Ricardo's view had won the day, the emperor's success would have been greater, for his solution was to go back to the gold standard. If this had happened, the Bank of England would not have been able to advance cash any longer, and it would have been difficult to maintain Wellington in the Spanish Peninsula. Moreover, there would have been a deflationary crisis which would have restricted productivity and restricted the market for capital. It would then have become difficult for the treasury to obtain funds, and so to finance the war. It is strange that the Bank's opponents did not envisage any of these consequences. No doubt there were private interests lurking behind the theoretical arguments, for the re-establishment of the gold standard would have prevented the Bank from supporting consols, in which case the bears would have triumphed. It is probable, too, that Ricardo's supporters had a shrewd insight into the situation, and realised that his scheme would be bound to force the country to make peace. The government denounced this dangerous course. 'I am bound to regard the proposed measure', wrote Perceval, 'as a declaration by Parliament that we must submit to no matter what conditions of peace rather than continue the war.' And so a return to the gold standard was rejected on 10 May 1811, and depreciation continued. In 1811 the cash reserves fell to three million, and the gold premium was only a quarter. The French franc was at thirty-nine per cent and the Hamburg shilling forty-four per cent. Inside the country those living on investments began at last to protest, and Lord King claimed from his tenants a bonus equal to the loss in the value of the banknotes. As a result, Parliament had to decide to make the note legal tender at its nominal value, and England found herself firmly saddled with an artificial exchange rate, which meant – as it always does – considerable hardship for those on fixed incomes.

But neither the monetary crisis nor the blockade seriously worried the industrialists and merchants during the first six months of 1810. It was rather the reverse, for the fall in the pound was an advantage for exports. But when they had exhausted their credit or completely immobilised their liquid pounds, the shortage of money coming in from abroad finally brought them hard up against reality. Latin America was generally held to be the villain of the piece. At the beginning of August 1810 five Manchester firms went bankrupt, with liabilities amounting to £2 million, and a veritable cyclone was unleashed. The banks, hit by bankruptcies, re-stricted credit and by so doing brought about further bankruptcies, or forced manufacturers to slow down production and finally come to a halt. There was a landslide in prices: the 1811 index figure was 158 instead of the 176 of 1810. Colonial goods fell in value by fifty per cent, and coffee by nearly two-thirds. Napoleon could not have chosen a better moment for tightening up the blockade. His draconian measures, the Baltic seizures, the staggering fall in British exports which resulted – all these aggravated the crisis and made it last longer. The year 1811 was marked by a profound stagnation in the business world, accompanied by a fall in prices in manufactured articles, a slowing down of production and widespread unemployment. The index figure for business activity as a whole in Great Britain was sixty-four, as compared with 74.8 in 1810. In the big exporting industries, the slowing down was no doubt even more marked, and seems to have been to something like only twenty-five per cent of the 1809–10 level. Production would have fallen off still further and brought even severer unemployment if the firms working for the American market had not continued to produce, gambling on a rapid repeal of the Orders in Council, and the reopening of the United States market. The depression went on into 1812, up to 23 June, when the Orders in Council were repealed. This step enabled the exporting industries to clear their stocks, which were despatched with all speed to the United States. There was an undoubted recovery, but it was short-lived. At the news that America had declared war stagnation once again descended upon industry, and lasted till the news of the Russian disaster. For the year as a whole, the index figure of general business activity was scarcely higher than for 1811 – 65.3 as against sixty-four. It would no doubt be an exaggeration to say that British industry was paralysed by the blockade and Madison's policy combined; but it is quite clear that the effects were most serious.

There were violent social repercussions. In May 1811 the cotton mills were only working three days a week, and at Bolton the weekly wage was down to five shillings. Two-thirds of the looms were out of action. As the workers had long considered their wretched condition to be due to the introduction of machinery, it was the machines that they attacked. The trouble started in March in the Nottingham district, and had become extremely serious by November; by 1812 it had spread to Yorkshire, Derbyshire and Leicestershire. Lancashire and Cheshire also rose in revolt, and in these parts there were not only attacks on machinery but also market riots, for bread was still dear. These 1812 disturbances were the longest, most widespread and most serious that had taken place in England since the seventeenth century. For several weeks certain districts were practically in the hands of the rebels, and twelve thousand regular troops were needed to put down the disturbances. This outbreak showed up in glaring fashion the faults, not to say vices, of the social and economic system in Great Britain, and the inadequacy of its antiquated system of local government.

Clearly, this was where Napoleon made his mistake in delivering corn to England. No one can say what the turn of events might have been if famine had come in to make the crisis still worse. Grave though the crisis was, it did not produce panic. In spite of their misgivings, neither the aristocracy nor the middle classes lost their heads. The finances, too, stood up to the squall, in spite of the rise in the country's expenditure from £128 million in 1810 to 147 million in 1812, and a slight fall in revenue, where there was a two-million drop in 1811 and 1812 from a falling off in customs. The government had borrowed £22½ million in 1809; in 1810 it had to be content with a million less, but managed to collect £23½ million in 1811, and in 1812 nearly thirty-five million. But as that was not enough, the government also borrowed an additional thirty-seven million on short term in 1810, forty-one million in 1811 and forty-five million in 1812. A longer ordeal would have been needed to exhaust Great Britain's reserves.

Although the emperor's confidence was increased by these difficulties in England, he did not escape the counter-effects of the measures he had adopted in 1810. In March of that year, some misgivings had been produced in Paris by the bankruptcies in Brittany; but it was definitely the Trianon decree that let loose the continental crisis. It began in the Hanseatic cities and in Holland, where speculation in colonial goods had been rasher than elsewhere, so that the effects of the decree were more damaging. In September the House of Rodda of Lübeck went bankrupt to the extent of 2½ million marks; and a little later on, the Desmedt Bank at Amsterdam stopped all payments. Since the Paris banks were closely linked to both of them, businessmen expressed their fears in no uncertain terms in November at a Trade Council meeting; and the following month the Fould Bank collapsed, as well as the Simons, whose chief was the husband of Mademoiselle Lange [the actress], and thirty-seven other firms. This was the signal for the spread of panic, and Talleyrand even went so far as to recommend a moratorium. In January 1811 Bidermann, who had been a constant speculator ever since the end of the *ancien régime*, went bankrupt along with sixty others. Little by little all districts were affected, and manufacturers were hard hit, with consequent severe unemployment. Since Napoleon had cleared out all stocks of corn, the average price of corn again rose above twenty francs in 1810, and a poorish harvest added to the rise, which continued in the following year. There were not any disturbances like the English ones; but it is well known how nervous Napoleon was of such outbreaks in similar circumstances.

Neither in London nor in Paris was there any liking for government interference. The British cabinet and Parliament showed a growing inclination to adopt a laissez-faire policy. Though Napoleon was inclined to pursue an opposite course, he had no tender feelings towards industrialists, and towards bankers and merchants more particularly, but rather reproached them bitterly for having run into these troubles through their own wild speculations. But both countries were forced to seek a remedy for the unemployment. Parliament provided a credit of two million for loans on the security of goods, as in 1793. In France, the emperor at first tried to get more commercial discount by buying up a certain number of shares from the Bank of France, and by compelling it to open branches in the provinces. He also considered forming a loan fund on the security of goods; but in the end he did not do more than give local or individual help, as in 1807. The Amiens Chamber of Commerce obtained an advance for setting up an emergency loan fund, and others were granted to large banks like Tourton-Ravel or the House of Doyen in Rouen, as well as to important manufacturers like Richard-Lenoir in Paris and Gros-Davillier in Alsace. Mollien estimated these at a total of twelve or thirteen million. Besides this help, the state greatly increased its purchases. Napoleon bought two millions' worth of silks and six of other goods, which he put in the hands of the exporters in return for the necessary licences.

Without advertising his own hand in the affair, he arranged a two-million credit with the Hottinger Bank in various places, especially at Rouen, for the financing of orders.

The crisis was a severe test of both the belligerents, and its most curious result was to make them more accommodating to one another, and to lead them to harmonise their respective licensing system so as to make exchanges easier. In England, business people could make their voices heard, and put vigorous pressure on the Board of Trade. But it would appear that they received offers or encouragement from the Continent – probably from Holland – in the course of negotiations with Fouché, Ouvrard and Labouchère, and also from Belgium, for van Acken, a merchant and adviser to the *préfecture* at Ghent, passed on to Montalivet letters that had been sent to him from England relating to these efforts. In 1810 the Board of Trade showed a readiness to accept goods that Napoleon had agreed to export under licence, on condition that he would take British products and colonial goods in exchange; but in November he went back on his promise. As the crisis was growing worse, the merchants returned to the attack. For example, on 14 April 1811 the Glasgow Chamber of Commerce demanded that there should be an agreement with the enemy. On 15 November the English newspapers announced that trade with France would once more be allowed on a reciprocal basis; and a circular of 14 April had in fact admitted wines to England. In February 1812 Mollien announced that England was going to allow them warehouse facilities: 'Such an event seemed a miracle at the time.'

The Board of Trade did not go as far as that; but it granted facilities to French ships, lifted the embargo on cinchona and baled cotton, allowed enemy subjects to take up quarters in England to organise trading under licence and expressed its view that insurers could safely quote on cargoes intended for France. Napoleon seems to have been surprised, but Montalivet kept things moving by advising on 25 November that the licences should be adapted to comply with the English conditions. The proposed exchange was between wine and silks on the one side and sugar on the other. Montalivet would appear to have won the day, for in December numerous licences were issued to this effect. On the thirty-first it was decided also to accept coffee, dyestuffs, skins and medicaments; and on 13 January 1812 Napoleon spoke in council of importing 450,000 quintals of sugar. Up till February he was still signing licences; from March to July these became few and far between; but as Mollien's records were lost in the retreat from Russia, it is difficult to know exactly what happened. In any case, from July to October 299 licences were issued, more particularly for bringing cotton to Rouen. Napoleon is thought to have signed in all 799 in the course of 1812. The English were more and more conciliatory, and as from 25 March 1812 they issued licences along the same lines as the French.

This unspoken agreement was a great help to international finance, which alone was in a position to make adjustments between the two regimes. It was in this context that the Rothschilds took up their abode in Paris and succeeded in rendering the services to the British treasury which have been referred to above. According to a report by Montalivet on 6 January 1813, the Empire exported fifty-eight millions' worth and imported to the value of twenty-two million. It was recognised in England that the balance was in favour of France; but the vital task was to sell at all costs. There is no need, moreover, to exaggerate the importance of this deal. If English exports rose in 1812, this was more particularly due to the reopening of the Russian and Swedish markets, and to the resumption of contraband traffic after the Grande Armée had cleared out of Germany. The Empire, which had been much less badly affected, seems to have recovered fairly quickly. At Ghent during the last three months of 1812, there were about as many spindles and rather more looms in action than in 1810; and in the kingdom of Italy, the export of silk and silk-stuffs was greater than in 1809, and the total trade almost equal to that of 1810. Production also started up again in Lyon and Rouen. During the winter a pronounced shortage made itself felt, but Napoleon looked upon this as merely a passing trouble. Come what might, he was confident that the continental economy would stand up to the inevitable inconveniences produced by the blockade. He was less than ever inclined to give it up: the licences issued in 1812 were of the same kind as before, and were viewed by him as a temporary expedient which harmed the English rather than France, since the balance of trade was unfavourable to them. Because he had given way in the matter of corn exports, he had not made all the capital he could have out of the crisis; but if he had come back victorious from Russia he would surely have applied his decrees with new vigour and new effectiveness, seeing that his dominion would have been even more far-reaching than before.

But for the French economy, circumstances would not have been so favourable. Since the crisis had produced a healthier market and kept

down prices, business was beginning to revive. The number of bankruptcies was diminishing, though the figures were still as high as for 1810; and
exports to Britain rose to fifty million, an increase of twenty-eight per
cent over the 1811 value, though seventeen per cent below the figure for
1810. Although imports generally were recovering, coffee and sugar had
dropped again, showing that the market for colonial goods was still suffering from the glut. In the same way baled cotton sank to sixty-three thousand pounds against ninety-one thousand in 1811 and 132,000 in 1810 – a
sign of weakness, suggesting that exports were drawing more particularly
on liquidated stocks at rock-bottom prices. The Bank's gold continued to
drain away, and there was no significant improvement in the exchange
rate. Corn kept going up in price, reaching 154 shillings in 1812. Disturbances among the working classes broke out more violently than ever. On
the other hand if the emperor had been victorious, he would no doubt
have closed the Levant to English trade; and the American market was
already lost. On 2 February 1811 Madison, relying on Napoleon's promises, had called on England to repeal the Orders in Council. Under the
pressure of public opinion the Cabinet in London agreed to do so on 21
April 1812, provided it could be shown that the emperor had repealed his
decrees. Maret then took a decision in line with this policy, antedating it
for 28 April 1811, and the English – quite taken aback – complied on 23
June. But it was too late: on 19 June Madison, maintaining that the question of the press gangs had still not been settled, decided to declare war.

A blockade can always be used for several purposes. In the eighteenth
century, the English had used it more particularly as a source of enrich-
ment; but nowadays its main aim is to destroy the military power of the
enemy. The Napoleonic blockade was a kind of half-way stage. It was
forward-looking, in the sense that it sought to break down England's
resistance. But it was also tied to the past, in that it aimed at reaching its
goal by a roundabout and thoroughly mercantilist route designed to rob
the enemy of his gold, but not to starve him out. In this watered-down
form, its effects could not be rapid; moreover, the British fleet had command of the seas, and the blockade, to be successful, needed the help of
circumstances more or less outside Napoleon's control. Nevertheless, the
experiment had been worthwhile, though in the ultimate analysis its success depended on the Grande Armée, whose ruin in so short a space of
time no one could have prophesied. It was not the natural laws of a liberal
economy, but the Russian winter, that saved England.

# CHAPTER FIVE

# The Preliminaries of the Russian
# Campaign (1811–1812)

LEXANDER HAD BEEN WELL AWARE that his attitude since Tilsit,
and especially since the 1809 campaign, was bound sooner or later
to provoke a conflict with Napoleon. He was itching to cross
swords with his rival, to determine which of them should be master of the
Continent, or at any rate of the East. It took some time for the emperor to
become convinced that anyone was actually bold enough to defy him; but
after the *ukase* of 31 December 1810 he decided to make an end of this
presumption. The tsar should be reduced to the rank of vassal; and if he
resisted, he should be hurled back into Asia, and the fairest of his European provinces incorporated in the Grand Empire.

Napoleon has been blamed for having compromised the real national
interests of France by indulging in such an adventure; but since 1803 at
least, these interests had ceased to count: the only thing that mattered to
him was to rule the Continent and the world. The Continental System
could contain allies, but without allowing them real independence or
tolerating any rebellions. Once Rome had been conquered, the emperor's
dreams turned inevitably to Constantinople; and to take possession of
this, the power of the tsar must first be broken. The blockade provided a
concrete justification for the new undertaking; and Alexander's infringe-
ment of it made this fresh enterprise seem absolutely necessary, for his
defeat would then enable Napoleon to recapture the Levant market from
England. Napoleon did not in any way conceal from himself the fact that
this was the most dangerous campaign he had ever conceived. He could
hardly fail to remember that Charles XII had taken this risk and that it
had been his undoing. It is said that he spent three sleepless months
before finally making up his mind. Yet as there was no other court of
appeal but his own will, he could hardly draw back. He expressed the
matter very simply when he left Paris, saying that he owed it to himself to
'finish what he had begun'.

## THE SCARE OF 1811

For several months Napoleon's attention was absorbed by the difficulties involved in transferring half a million men to the Russian frontier, a task which involved immense transport facilities, huge supplies and proportionately vast expense. The 1811 class had been called up and was already in the depots, and from the end of January he began to reinforce the troops in Germany, doubling the units one by one, forming new corps, bringing up arms and munitions and laying down supplies and depots. But in spite of the precautions he took, these measures did not escape the notice of Chernyshev and Nesselrode through their espionage service. By getting in the first blow, Alexander might surprise the emperor in the midst of his preparations and by carrying the war into Germany give Russia a protective cover. But would he dare to do so?

At the beginning of 1811 this was what he intended to do. But his finances were in a pitiful state, with a deficit running up to one hundred million roubles and paper money losing up to five-sixths of its value. Russia under the tsars, however, had never been deterred by difficulties of this kind. There were 240,000 Russians grouped in two armies, who confronted on the other side of the border fifty-six thousand men from Warsaw and forty-six thousand Frenchmen, though the latter were at some distance, and widely scattered. In March five divisions out of nine were recalled from the army on the Danube, and everywhere the troops went steadily marching on day by day towards the grand duchy frontier. Yet although Poniatowski was giving Napoleon time to move his forces forward, Alexander did not feel sure of his ground. Accordingly, on 8 January, he returned to the charge with Czartoryski, the need for money finally brought home to him, cap in hand, proposing that he should win over the support of Poland, so that her army, by moving in as far as the Oder without striking a blow, would induce the Prussians to enter the lists. Once again the prince observed that in order to gain his country's support it would at least be necessary for the tsar to enter into a formal engagement to reconstitute the kingdom of Poland, fix its boundaries and accept the constitution of 1791. Alexander promised to hand over his Polish provinces, and Galicia if possible; as to internal government, he conceded that there should be autonomy, but said nothing about a constitution.

Meanwhile, he did not inform Rumiantsev of his plans, for he was always against war and disposed to come to terms with Napoleon; but he put out secret diplomatic feelers in the direction of Sweden, Prussia and more particularly Austria, and on 13 February Metternich was offered the Danubian principalities. But these tentative approaches met with no success. Czartoryski had to admit that the Poles were not willing to betray the emperor, and Metternich refused to accept the proffered gift. Frederick William, who had bought a faked memorandum from Champagny, composed by Esménard, which announced the intention to eliminate Prussia, became so worked up that in May Hardenberg proposed an alliance with France. Bernadotte, who had become regent and was looking out for subsidies, hoped to get some from his motherland. He offered Alquier, the new French ambassador, a contingent of fifty thousand men against Russia, provided he was allowed to take over Norway. The offensive policy continued to have its partisans, notably Armfelt; yet among the tsar's cosmopolitan entourage, where there were beginning to be many enemies of the emperor, it also had its opponents. A Prussian named Phüll proposed that they entrench between the Dvina and the Dnieper in order to make a flank attack on the Grande Armée as it marched on Moscow. Alexander was not yet resigned to a policy of methodical retreat; but an offensive policy was definitely rejected, and the troops were brought to a halt.

Caulaincourt remained quite unaware of what was happening. The Poles, on the other hand, became alarmed. Poniatowski sent an aide-de-camp to Napoleon; and then, on his way to be present at the baptism of the king of Rome, he put the government at Dresden on the alert. Davout, who was at first incredulous, became convinced by the evidence. During the month of April the emperor remained constantly on the alert, and from the fifteenth to the seventeenth, in the midst of the festivities following the birth of the king of Rome, he redoubled his military preparations. The Poles, when mobilised, were to evacuate the duchy at the first signal and move to join up with Davout and the Saxon contingent on the Oder. Champagny, who was probably blamed for not having been aware of what was afoot, was replaced by Maret, and Napoleon gave orders for negotiations with Prussia, Sweden and Turkey, while he himself spoke to Schwarzenberg of a possible alliance. In May there was more reassuring news. Rumiantsev had in fact managed to arrange for negotiations to be opened for compensating the duke of Oldenburg, hoping that part of the duchy of Warsaw could be made over to him. Neither he nor his master said so in explicit terms; but the emperor understood, and refused point blank. The discussions went on, however, the duke receiving another offer of Erfurt, and Russia an offer of the treaty proposed the previous year relating to Poland; but the tsar replied with various complaints, though without advancing his claims. Caulaincourt, who had returned to Paris on 5 June, was at once received by Napoleon and vouched for Alexander's loyalty. He asked for reasonable proposals to be put before the tsar. Lauriston, who succeeded him, assured the emperor that the Russian sovereign was still peaceful in his intentions. Caulaincourt, however, made it clear that in case of attack Alexander would decide to retreat and lure the Grande Armée on into the unending plains, where winter would bring destruction. 'One good battle will get the better of your friend Alexander,' was Napoleon's reply. The two protagonists seemed at one in playing for time, the emperor in order to complete his preparations, the tsar to contrive the alliances which at present seemed to elude him; but each was equally determined to force his rival to give in. Napoleon did not exclude the possibility of a bloodless surrender, but he was growing impatient. On 15 August there was a scene with Kurakin; and shortly afterwards, he decided to go to war in June 1812.

Alexander was better informed. Nesselrode and Chernyshev had long ago corrupted various employees in the Ministry of War, and Talleyrand – who was constantly asking Alexander for payment – was lavish in advice. He it was who had suggested the offer of the principalities to Austria; and he continually insisted on the necessity of peace with Turkey and an accommodation with Bernadotte. Caulaincourt himself was disposed to listen to him, and Nesselrode wrote that his behaviour was 'in keeping with the confidence that Louise (that is, Alexander) has in him'. Talleyrand also advised the Russians to remain on the defensive and to refrain from carrying the war into Germany, so that he could pose as the defender of an oppressed Europe. Alexander's duplicity was perfectly suited to such a part; and Napoleon – whether out of infatuation or negligence – let him win several hands in the diplomatic game.

### THE DIPLOMATIC CAMPAIGN AND THE MARCH
### OF THE GRANDE ARMÉE

To start with, Russia had considerable hopes of Prussia. Since Napoleon had not responded to his offer, the king decided on 16 July to seek the support of the tsar, and sent him Scharnhorst, who signed a military

convention with him on 17 October. The army, meanwhile, was being
organised as best it could, and the war party began to look up. Gneisenau,
who was temporarily head of the general staff, was writing a memorandum to advocate a new national rising. In Prague, Stein and Grüner, a
former Berlin prefect of police, were in touch with representatives of the
Tugendbund, which had nevertheless been dissolved by the king. In
Berlin, they also worked through the agency of Ompteda and other representatives of Count Münster and Baron Hardenberg, a relation of the
Prussian minister in English service at Vienna as the representative of
Hanover.

Once again, however, the king disappointed them. The agreement
brought back by Scharnhorst stipulated that the Prussians would retreat
before the French if they invaded their kingdom, and would link up with
the Russians on the Vistula or shut themselves up in their strongholds.
But Alexander would not even allow his generals to enter East Prussia if
plainly requested by Berlin to do so. Frederick William decided that the
risk involved would be too great; but by way of consolation he allowed
Scharnhorst to go and try his hand in Vienna. As was to be expected,
Metternich roundly rejected his approaches on 26 December. From this
moment onwards, there was no other course open but to submit to
Napoleon. He, too, was kept very badly informed in this quarter by the
ambassador, Saint-Marsan, who was Piedmontese by birth. In Prussia,
at any rate, his police gave him due warning, and on 4 September he
ordered Hardenberg to disarm. As he was just then awaiting a reply from
the tsar, the minister made promises that he failed to keep, and in October he had to submit to French inspection. At last, on 29 December, he
was forced to obey orders and resign himself to declaring that he was prepared for an alliance. The emperor was in no hurry; but finally, on 23
February, the Prussian ambassador Krusemark was suddenly called upon
to sign, and complied immediately. It was just as well he did, for all preparations had been made to occupy his country; and on 2 March Gudin
crossed the frontier while the king was still unaware that a treaty had
been signed. On the fifth he ratified it. Prussia thereby agreed to let the
Grande Armée take up quarters in Prussia, promised to supply it with
provisions of every sort, to be set against the war indemnity, which was
still far from being paid off, and to send to Russia a contingent of twenty
thousand men. In the end, Victor, commander of the Ninth Corps,
assumed complete control of Berlin and compelled the Prussian forces to

evacuate it. This was a terrible blow for Stein's friends, and it seemed likely that the prestige of the dynasty would not survive it. Scharnhorst was sent on leave; Gneisenau went on a mission to London; Boyen, Clausewitz and many others emigrated to Russia; and in May Stein accepted an invitation from Alexander and left Prague.

Meanwhile, Austria was also siding with France, and without much hesitation, though Metternich was prodigal of advice to the tsar to avoid a war which he feared would lead to disaster, whichever way it went, for it would put him at the mercy of the victor. On 17 December Schwarzenberg was summoned to decide, and the two parties promptly came to an agreement. Napoleon would exchange the Illyrian provinces for Galicia, and would guarantee the integrity of Turkey; Austria on her side promised to contribute an army of thirty thousand men. The treaty was signed on 14 March 1812. Nevertheless the war party was taking shape again in Vienna, and Gentz, Metternich's friend and secretary, distrusted by England since he had come down on the side of peace in September 1809, was trying his best to reopen negotiations with the British treasury by drawing up memoranda against the continental blockade, one of them intended for the tsar in person. But the chancellor did not intend to have his hand forced. He even took advantage of the circumstances to complete the rout of the Prussian National Party, whom he looked upon as the harbinger of revolution. Although Hardenberg was being lenient towards his enemies, he gave him support when he saw him in Dresden at the end of May; in August Grüner was arrested at Prague.

Alexander, then, could not congratulate himself upon his efforts with the Germans. But as he had himself at times bowed to necessity not long before, he did not bear them any grudge. He knew, moreover, that they would desert Napoleon at the first opportunity. Besides, Metternich, who was the most suspect in Alexander's eyes, was certain that the principalities would not remain Russian, and lost no time in recovering his self-assurance; for in the army of the Danube, Chichagov was talking of an alliance with the Turks and the possibility of taking Austria in the rear by engineering a rising of the Slavs and Hungarians. The Count Saint-Julien came to warn the tsar that they would only fight him as a matter of form and that their contingent would not be reinforced; and a secret agreement was signed on 2 June. Behind the screen of a dynastic alliance, Metternich was playing a double game that would at any rate guarantee the safety of Austria, while waiting for better days.

With the Swedes and the Ottomans, Alexander was more successful through Napoleon's own fault. The emperor seems to have believed that both of them could not fail to come to him of their own accord. Perhaps he was also unwilling to treat with them until the last possible moment, as he had with Prussia and Austria, in order not to drive the Russians into taking the offensive; but his opponents outpaced him. In 1811 his relations with Bernadotte had become strained, and the ambassador, Alquier, had something to do with this. Knowing that the blockade was being openly violated in spite of his protests, he decided to break off diplomatic relations, and there was a violent scene between him and the regent on 25 August. The emperor recalled him, but made no effort to win over Bernadotte, who from now onwards swung decidedly towards Russia. In January 1812 Davout was ordered to occupy Swedish Pomerania in order to seal it off from English trade, and this was the finishing touch. On 18 February Count Loewenhielm came to St Petersburg to propose an alliance. Bernadotte offered to disembark troops in Germany in the rear of Napoleon, on condition that Russian troops should first help him to conquer Norway. Alexander accepted, but stipulated that he must first make an agreement with Frederick VI, king of Denmark, who might be indemnified – say by the duchy of Oldenburg. He sent Suchtelen to Stockholm, and the details were discussed in both capitals, each of the plenipotentiaries making it a point of honour to steal a march on his opposite number. They signed at almost the same time, on 5 and 9 April respectively.

With the sultan, Alexander had been negotiating since 1811. After Bagration's successes in 1809 the war had dragged on. The Turks evacuated Serbia, which had for a moment shown French leanings, but returned to the Russian alliance after Karageorge's *coup d'état* eliminating the influence of Austria, as well as that of his rival Miloš Obrenović. In 1810 Kamenski conducted a successful campaign to bring about the surrender of the Danubian strongholds, and advanced in the direction of Chumla. In the Caucasus, Imeretia and Mingrelia both fell, and Sukhum-Kale and Akkalkalaki were conquered. Finally, in 1811 Kutuzov won a decisive victory. When the Turkish army had crossed the Danube in the direction of Ruschuk, he cut it in two, surrounded thirty-six thousand of the enemy, and only allowed an armistice on condition that peace should be negotiated on the basis of annexing Bessarabia as far as Sereth. The talks opened at Giurgiu on 25 October, but produced no agreement, the Turks being unwilling to concede more than the line of the Pruth, and refusing to give Serbia her independence. Another attempt was made on 12 January 1812, at Bucharest, Stratford Canning doing his best to persuade Mahmud to treat, but in vain. Finally, just as the French invasion was about to begin, Alexander ordered his representative to give in, and peace was signed on 28 May. Chichagov, Kutuzov's successor, could set out for the north, while the troops in Asia could turn their attention to Persia. Since the summer of 1811 Napoleon's forces had taken possession of Germany, and by the beginning of 1812 it only remained to concentrate them and move on the Niemen. Danzig was transformed into a base stocked with an abundance of supplies and guarded by Rapp with twenty-five thousand men. Poniatowski covered the Vistula with sixty thousand more; and Davout was in command of one hundred thousand on the Oder and had pushed forward beyond it with vanguards; while Oudinot was crossing Westphalia and entering Berlin on 28 March. Ney was just reaching Mainz with troops from the camp at Boulogne; the Germans were working their way towards the Elbe; and the Guards, who had been in cantonments in the east of France, were getting ready to follow. There was still the difficulty of managing to get the army in Italy back across the Alps. Napoleon gave final orders at the beginning of February, and on the twenty-third Eugène got under way and the whole army began to move at the same time. In order to foil the Russian espionage, Savary managed to harass Chernyshev so thoroughly that he secured his departure on 26 February; and the police discovered in his apartment a note that enabled them to shoot a certain traitor in the Ministry of War and to compromise the Russians in the eyes of the French public.

The army could not be assembled on the Niemen before the end of May. Now, on 8 April, Alexander, who knew that he could safely count on Bernadotte, finally decided to put forward his demands. In the first place Napoleon would have to evacuate Prussia and Swedish Pomerania and bring his troops back behind the Elbe. Then a commercial treaty would be negotiated, along with the indemnity promised to the duke of Oldenburg; but in any case neutral trade was to remain free. Meanwhile, Napoleon kept Kurakin on a string until 7 May, trying meanwhile to wind up affairs in Spain, and proposing to Canning on 18 April that peace should be signed on a basis of *uti possidetis*; except for Portugal, which would go back to its ruling house. Sicily would remain Ferdinand's, and

Spain continue to belong to Joseph. All three countries would be evacuated by France and England. But England refused to leave Joseph in Madrid. When Kurakin finally demanded an answer, the emperor left Saint-Cloud on 9 May without a word and the next day Maret followed, also without giving any answer. Narbonne had already left in order to negotiate with Alexander. He found him at Vilna, and was dismissed without a chance to enter into discussion. On 25 May the emperor reached Dresden where he received the emperor of Austria, the king of Prussia and a number of vassal princes. On the twenty-eighth he set out for the Niemen.

The great adventure had begun. Napoleon could only return from it master of the whole of Europe, or fallen from glory. Once again he was playing double or quits.

# II
## The World in 1812

# CHAPTER SIX

# Imperial France

I N 1812 the French Empire covered about 750,000 square kilometres. It had, in all probability, forty-four million inhabitants, and was divided into 130 départements. Gradually Napoleon had added to his legacy of 102 départements bounded by natural frontiers, lands which constituted two antennae pointing towards the north-east and south-east. One of these was made up of Holland with its nine départements together with the German territories bordering the North Sea, which constituted four others – here, in fact, the Empire, with the Bouches-de-la-Trave, whose capital was Lübeck, reached as far as the Baltic. The other was made up of the Valais, Piedmont, Liguria, Parma, Tuscany and the western part of the Papal States, fifteen départements in all. The majority of these recent annexations were by no means completely assimilated. They were more in the nature of vassal states. So it was that Holland had a governor-general, as had Tuscany. The German départements, forming the twenty-second military division, remained subject to the orders of a special commission, while Illyria, although annexed to the Empire, had always had a separate administration and its territorial divisions were not counted among the 130 départements. In short, the Napoleonic system of government functioned normally only within the framework of the natural frontiers – if we except Piedmont and Liguria, incorporated quite early on.

This system was never absolutely rigid. From 1804 to 1811 Napoleon was constantly remoulding his institutions. From the experiments he continued to make in the vassal states, we may conclude that the era of perfecting was not yet ended; and in particular the social order in France had not yet assumed the form he desired. Nonetheless, though his work remained unfinished, it was sufficiently advanced in 1812 for its spirit to be discernible.

## AUTHORITARIAN GOVERNMENT

Success had, little by little, transformed the person and way of life of the emperor. After Tilsit, it is hardly possible to recognise the man of Brumaire, angular, sombre, the absolutely Roman cast of the countenance. The complexion had become softer, serenity had made the features less rigid. His activity was no less intense, but was more subject to order. At eight o'clock at the latest he started to work at his desk, and only broke off for lunch which he normally took alone and, once or twice a week, he would go for a walk or go hunting. At six, he dined with his family and, after a few minutes' conversation, returned to his work and went to bed between nine and ten. Sunday was a day of ceremony. After Mass and the parade, he reviewed his court which waited in silence in the salons, drawn up in precise order of rank and elaborately attired in accordance with the strictest etiquette. In the evening there was a great family dinner, after which the sovereigns provided a concert or play and held a reception.

Round about 1810, slight signs of ageing began to show. His face grew fat, his complexion dulled, his body slumped and thickened; there were indications that the Empire, with its vast extent, overtaxed his energies. 'Did I not give such and such an order?' he would write. This, however, was not so important; to the end his mind remained astonishingly vigorous and lucid. What is more evident is the effect of omnipotence on his moral attitude: 'My people of Italy know me well enough to stop them ever forgetting that I know more in my little finger than they do in all their heads put together.' Pessimism made him brutal: 'I have always observed that the respectable are good for nothing.' The worship of force and success became cynical: 'There is only one secret of managing the world and that is to be strong, because in strength there is no error or illusion; that's the naked truth.' 'You have to succeed; I only judge men by the results of their actions.' As a natural consequence, he felt himself more and more solitary; he showed himself increasingly disillusioned about the permanence of his work. 'Both within and without', he said to Chaptal, 'I only reign by the fear I inspire'; and, later, to Mollien, 'They joined up with me to enjoy security; they would abandon me tomorrow if disorder returned.' How would men feel when his end came? – 'All they would say is "*Ouf!*" '

The fewer obstacles he met, the more jealous and irritable he became.

Like Frederick II, he continually emphasised the personal character of his government. Judging by the constitutions he gave to the realms of Naples and Westphalia, his intention was to eliminate finally the elective principle. However, neither the electorate nor the assembly did anything to hinder him. The district assemblies, embodying universal suffrage, were not consulted until 1813 and then only in certain départements. The choices of the colleges were settled in advance by personal relationships and few members took part. In 1810 in the Côte-d'Or the list of candidates for the general council could not be completed and the *sous-préfet* of Châtillon-sur-Seine himself proceeded to designate the council of the *arrondissement*. For legislative functions all proposals favoured officials and soldiers, except one position which fell to Berlier's father-in-law. Little by little the assemblies became dominated by these people. The Tribunate disappeared in 1807 and the sessions of the Corps Législatif became gradually shorter, Napoleon legislating either by *senatus consulta*, for such things as conscription levies and annexations, or by decree, as for the re-establishment of the tobacco monopoly. As long as the Codes were still unfinished, the Conseil d'État was still to some extent active; after their completion, it was hardly left with anything but legal points, whereas the administrative councils, dealing only with the technique of execution, preserved their importance.

The part played by ministers became more and more reduced, and their powers continued to be whittled down. The Grande Armée and the foreign territories had their supervisors; conscription and the commissariat had their two directors. One after the other the regime's great administrators saw themselves thrust aside – first Chaptal, then Talleyrand and finally Fouché. The emperor preferred to have in their stead second-rate men whom he treated as clerks, like Crétet, Champagny, Bigot de Préameneu, Savary and Maret. A growing share of the places fell to survivors from the *ancien régime*. Napoleon believed that they had a prior loyalty to the new legitimate line, and thought they would be easy to manipulate: 'It is only people like that who know how to be servants.' Many of them were lacking in ability or experience, and so those he noticed received rapid promotion. Molé, for example, *maître des requêtes* in 1806, became *préfet* in 1807, councillor of state and director of roads and highways in 1809, and a minister in 1813; and this accounts for the holding together of a number of posts. In 1806, in order to set up a reserve of officials distinguished by birth and fortune (and so very poorly paid), but shaped by himself, Napoleon reintroduced the *maîtres des requêtes* in the Conseil d'État, appointing in all seventy-two, and multiplied the assistants in the councils and in the administration, in the provinces no less than in Paris. In 1811 there were 360 of them in the ordinary service. As far as the Conseil d'État was concerned, he cannot be said to have made any radical changes in the nature of its composition; indeed in 1813 he even appointed the former convention member Zangiacomi (though not a regicide) and Coffinhal-Dunoyer, the brother of Coffinhal.* He only got rid of a dozen councillors, and carried out two dismissals – incidentally, for reasons that had nothing to do with the work of the council. Nonetheless, one can clearly see the direction in which things were moving; and there is no doubt what the outcome would have been if the Empire had lasted. Moreover, the men of Brumaire were beginning to feel at home: they were awarded the Legion of Honour, and took their place among the new nobility; some of them even set up entails.

The recruitment of *préfets* underwent a much more perceptible change. The Côte-d'Or, previously in the hands of a former member of the Constituent Assembly, then in those of a tribune, subsequently passed to Molé, and finally in 1812 to the duc de Cossé-Brissac. Survivors of the Revolution were few and far between – such men as Jeanbon, who continued to be loyal to the past. In Marseille, Thibaudeau, influenced by his wife and out of prudence and vanity, became a promoter of the movement for reaction. Such *préfets* were following their master's example. To begin with, the Conseils d'État contested particular items of expenditure, audited the accounts and passed resolutions; but they lost heart when they found that the credits they had refused were officially reinstated, supporting documents were withheld and their wishes scornfully disregarded. Purges were made from time to time and when vacancies occurred. In 1809, in the Bouches-du-Rhône, six out of seven nobles and officials were got rid of in one sweep; in the Pas-de-Calais, the Artois nobility began to get an entry. The same procedure took place for the councillors in the *préfectures* and *sous-préfectures*. The evidence from the Côtes-du-Nord suggests that the revolutionaries put up a better resistance in the west, where the *Chouans* offered stubborn opposition. As for the municipalities, there continued to be the problem of finding capable men to fill the places. It often proved impossible to complete the councils or ensure their meeting;

* [J.-B. Coffinhal, prominent judge on the Revolutionary Tribunal, 1793–4.]

but a mayor at least was necessary, and for this the *préfets* fell back upon the big proprietors, even if they were hostile to the regime. The difficulty was still greater for the minor offices, such as secretaries and rural police; and the same was true in all administrative departments. The people could not yet provide the material for a lower middle class from which to draw officials well enough educated to have a sense of professional integrity. Some *préfets* attempted to govern directly through itinerant secretaries or inspectors – for example in the Bas-Rhin, Pas-de-Calais and Meurthe; but they were obliged to extract their salaries from the already heavily indebted *communes*. There can thus be no illusions about the imperfections of local administration, which only time could improve. But such as it was, it gave Napoleon what he wanted – money, men and the preservation of order.

It is not easy to say how far centralisation was in practice carried out. From Year XI onwards, the *préfets* were regretting that they were not allowed more initiative, and pointing out that the necessity of corresponding with each of the ministers meant that they often received contradictory orders; and those they governed complained that constant reference to Paris delayed decisive action. Some of them, all the same, made free use of their authority, including summary arrests. For example, in the Doubs in 1805, de Bry put through a forced loan. The emperor accused them of playing the despot – a rather amusing touch – and the ministers sometimes expressed dissatisfaction with them. 'In general,' wrote Montalivet in 1812, 'the *préfets* say what they like to me; but I see more clearly than ever that we do not know anything about what is really going on.' When Napoleon really wanted to know where he stood or wished to 'repair the machinery', as the Committee of Public Safety had tried to do, he would send down special commissioners, as he did in 1812. Moreover, in the départements the central power was in collision with the covert power of the important civil and military figures, whether they were natives of the district or no; especially the bishop, who contrived – without defying the central power – to intervene in the choice of persons and the details of administration. Taken as a whole, centralisation may be said to have been more thoroughgoing than before 1789; but the slowness of communications tended to safeguard the *préfets*' independence, so that it varied in accordance with the distance, the circumstances and the character of the men concerned. In proportion as the Consulate *préfets* disappeared and the country grew more peaceful, centralisation progressed.

The reorganisation of justice was doggedly pursued. There were soon complaints of the people who had been chosen somewhat at random in Year VIII. Napoleon took steps to improve the methods of recruiting. In Year XII he established the law schools, and in 1808 judges who would hear cases in a consultative capacity. From 1807 onwards he thought it possible to undertake a purge, which was handed over by a *senatus consultum* to a special commission. Of the 194 magistrates denounced, 170 were proposed for dismissal; and in actual fact, the decree of 24 March 1808 deprived sixty-eight of office and accepted the resignation of ninety-four. At the same time the codification of the law was nearing completion. The code for civil procedure was finished in 1806; the commercial code in 1807; the criminal code in 1808; the penal code in 1810. The rural code, which had also been drawn up, was not promulgated. The spirit of 1789 did not altogether disappear from it. The Conseil d'État preserved unimpaired the social work of the Revolution. It was at pains to separate the administrative from the judicial machinery, took care to assure the judges' independence and obstinately defended the jury system. But, in parallel with these provisions, the property and authority of the middle classes could reckon on its support provided they did not trespass on the authority of the state, which was regarded as in the general public interest. Whether revolutionaries or men of the *ancien régime*, all its members would unhesitatingly sacrifice their principles out of class interest or political opportunism. Necessity knows no law, said Portalis; there is no theory that must not give way to necessity, Berlier confirmed. These traits were already apparent in the Civil Code; and subsequent codes were to mark the reaction even more clearly.

The first two codes are very close to Colbert's ordinances. The second in particular did not prove well adapted to the conditions of economic progress, for example as regards insurance and companies; at least, although continuing to subordinate the limited liability company to the extent of authorising only those under a collective name or in limited partnership, it made the concession that the responsibility of the shareholders should be restricted to their holdings. Previously, the law had been doubtful on this point, some judgements obliging them to support the company with the whole of their possessions. But there was nothing as striking as the discussion relating to promissory notes. Well aware that the expansion of the economy depended on that of credit, and so on the trustworthiness of the banks, some were in favour of treating the single private individual, in any case of protest, like the businessman, and so making him liable to bodily constraint. But Molé spoke up loudly for the opposing view, pointing out that such conduct was a departure from common law, entailing the sacrifice of personal liberty in favour of business interests and bankers, who were a selfish minority – as had happened in England. France, he maintained, should no doubt foster trade, but above all remain essentially agricultural. The opposition party went on to point out that if the methods of trade and finance were to be adopted, citizens would be inclined to entrust their savings to these agencies and invest them in life interests, giving pride of place to personal estate, which is always unstable. It would mean the end of the great families and classes, and would undermine the monarchy – considerations that were well calculated to appeal to Napoleon, particularly at that period. But his broad intelligence won the day, and he came down in favour of a compromise: it was decided that the private person should be treated as a businessman if he had subscribed his share as a result of commercial transactions.

The last two codes in particular marked an important date. They came into force in 1810, when the law of 28 April once more refashioned the judiciary organisation, giving it the form that it still preserves, though it gave the mayor – except in the cantonal capital – powers of simple police which he has since then lost. This law regulated the manner and conditions for nominating judges, as well as their discipline; and the occasion served as an opportunity to carry out a fresh purge: the Paris court of appeal lost eight councillors out of thirty-one. These changes do not seem to have been inspired by political motives; but nonetheless, the composition of the staff moved in the same direction as in the other cases. At Besançon, for example, two presidents and five councillors from the former *parlement* became members of the court. All the same, the revolutionaries kept their power more successfully here because – apart from the purges – they were appointed to their posts for life.

But now there was a further increase of repression. The standing magistracy (*parquet*) was at this time given its definitive organisation. Instruction was made a matter of complete secrecy. The *magistrat de sûreté* disappeared, and the business of accusation became centralised in the hands of public prosecutors, advocates general and examining magistrates. The *préfet* regained the power to appoint juries to try cases; and when the grand jury was suppressed, its functions passed to one of the courts of appeal. The special tribunals were retained under the title of 'ordinary special courts', but they were now manned entirely by soldiers. Provision was also made for 'extraordinary special courts' where the jury had been suspended, or for combating certain crimes; and the same year saw the appearance of the 'special customs courts'. Moreover, the Senate could by virtue of the constitution quash a jury's verdict as detrimental to the safety of the state. For example, in 1813 it brought the mayor of Antwerp before a special court on the charge of indulging in contraband, a charge of which he had been acquitted in the assize court. As for the penal code, while not restoring torture, it re-established branding, the iron collar, the loss of a hand for parricide and the loss of all civil rights.

In spite of the strengthening of penal justice, the Empire did not rely solely upon this, any more than the Consulate had done: it placed more reliance upon administrative repression, that is to say, on the police. Under the minister – first Fouché, then in 1810 Savary – there were councillors of state in charge of the *arrondissements*; then, from 1808 onwards, directors-general in Turin, Florence, Rome and Amsterdam. Centralisation was not pushed to an extreme: the *préfets*, who were not solely dependent on Fouché, kept their own powers. Councillors and directors corresponded direct with the emperor, and so did Dubois, the prefect of police, who was replaced by Pasquier in 1811.

The *gendarmerie* had its own chiefs, and was in competition with them. They claimed, as the *préfet* of the Loire-Inférieure observed in 1808, 'to be armed magistrates, with the duty of keeping an eye on all civilian officials'. In the emperor's view, the ideal system would have been to keep an up-to-date file of all persons who had any influence whatsoever. Fouché had already compiled a comprehensive list of the *Chouans*; Napoleon wanted to draw up 'personal and moral statistics' for the whole Empire. His knowledge was extensive, but did not cover everything; and the *préfets*, who would have been in the best position to give him information about people's private lives, usually preserved their discretion. Secret informers and Lavalette's postal censorship remained the chief means of information.

The police were all the more feared because they themselves sanctioned enquiry by means of arbitrary detention, for which mental asylums were used in addition to the prisons. The poet Desorgues, who had taken the liberty of perpetrating a famous epigram in 1804 ('Yes – Napoleon is great – a great chameleon'), and Faure, a medical student of Saint-Louis, who had cried out on 5 December 1804, when the eagles were distributed,

'Death or freedom!' were both confined as lunatics. Nobody felt safe; and the provision merchant Lassalle, whose deals had been interfered with by the emperor, was in addition imprisoned without trial. And even release did not end the matter: a large number of individuals were told where they must live and kept under supervision. Finally, on 3 March 1810, a decree reintroduced the state prisons, in which internment could be decreed *in camera* by the *grand juge*, the minister of justice and the minister of police, though in practice he was rarely consulted. In Napoleon's eyes, administrative detention was not only calculated to stifle opposition, but also to eliminate offences under common law where the jury allowed themselves to be intimidated, or legal proof was lacking. It was, however, convenient to use the expression 'prisoners of state' so as to present the public with 'a terrifying image', while not being under any illusions about the abuses deriving from a police who were under no control. The *gendarmes* were held in such fear that 'it would be difficult to collect evidence against them', as the *préfet* of the Loire-Inférieure remarked, although he accused them of fraud, extortion and even assassination. Even the *préfets* were swayed by the importunities of influential persons. In 1808, for example, the camp-commandant Despinoy de Saint-Luc was arrested in the Somme district, on the *ordre verbal* of the mayor, who owed him money. The decree of 1810 therefore directed that prisons should be annually inspected. But they were not all examined, and the emperor only looked at some of the reports. In 1811 he released 145 individuals out of the 810 mentioned; in 1812 twenty-nine out of 314. By 1814 it was estimated that there were 2,500 of these prisoners. As for the senatorial commission entrusted with the protection of individual freedom, it did not even ask for a list of those in detention, and only intervened when petitioned. In 1804 it managed to get forty-four people set free out of the 116 petitioners; but Fouché's passive resistance soon discouraged its efforts. In short, France from 1800 to 1814 lived under a regime where the law could condemn on suspicion; but Napoleon took good care not to apply the system too rigorously, realising that a reign of terror would only be tolerated if it was confined to a small number of victims, and that this would in no way detract from its success.

Speakers and writers were particularly liable to attract attention. The Institute, which had relied so much upon Napoleon, did not escape his scrutiny either. As early as 1803 the classes in moral and political science had disappeared; in 1805, when Lalande had suppressed Maréchal's

*Dictionnaire des athées*, the emperor denounced him as 'in his second childhood' and forbade him to publish anything at all. Again, when annoyed by the speech of welcome which Chateaubriand found he was not allowed to deliver, Napoleon threatened to suppress the class in language and literature, formerly belonging to the French Academy, calling it 'an undesirable club'. There were police informers in every salon, one of whom was the academician Esménard. As far as the lawyers were concerned, Napoleon positively hated them. 'They stir up trouble and are the authors of crime and treason . . . I should like to cut out the tongues of barristers who use them against the government.' In 1804 he had obliged them to apply to the courts for registration in the list of authorised barristers, and he did not give them back the right to a president and a disciplinary commission until 14 December 1810; and even then, they were only allowed to bring candidates before the public prosecutor, the court itself retaining the right to inflict penalties on them.

His hatred of 'the printed word' was almost as vehement, by the very fact that 'it appeals to public opinion instead of to authority'. 'You must print very little,' he wrote to Eugène, 'the less, the better.' From 1805 onwards newspapers had to submit their accounts to the police and hand over up to a third of their profits to pay those who were given authority to keep an eye on them. In 1807 an article by Chateaubriand caused the *Mercure* to be suppressed; in 1810 it was decided that each département should only have one paper, and more than a hundred disappeared; in October Savary reduced the Paris press to four gazettes, the *Moniteur Officiel* being one of them. In February 1811 a paper formerly called *Les Débats* and now renamed the *Journal de l'Empire*, was taken out of the hands of the Bertin brothers, who were suspected of having relations with the English, and split up into shares, a third going to the police; and in September the *Journal de Paris* and the *Gazette de France* suffered the same fate. In order to control the publication of books, new restrictions had been placed upon the printers in 1805, compelling them to have a personal licence that could be revoked, and to take an oath of loyalty; and the police would seize their productions whenever they thought fit. Fouché added to his Press Office a consultative office comprising Lemontey, Lacretelle and Esménard.

An official censorship would have been better than arbitrary police action; and on 10 February 1810 the emperor finally made up his mind to establish it. He created a directorship of the press, entrusting it in the first

place to Portalis's son, then to the former *préfet* Pommereul, as well as
'imperial censors', one of whom was a theologian; but in the provinces,
power remained in the hands of the *préfets*. At the same time, ninety-seven
out of the 157 Paris printing presses were shut down; and in the end book-
sellers also had to be licensed and take the oath. As might have been foreseen, the censorship used its authority to cover its tracks, and abused its
powers at its own sweet will. Not only did it prove absurdly Gallican,
anglophobe and suspicious, but extremely prudish and hostile to genres
such as the historical novel. In December 1811 Napoleon showed his displeasure: the censorship was to confine its efforts to suppressing libels and
'on other subjects allow freedom of expression'. The lesson went home: in
1811 nearly twelve per cent of manuscripts had been refused publication;
in 1812 the proportion sank to less than four per cent. Here too he showed
more liberality than his agents, which indeed was not difficult, and up to a
certain point he remained faithful to the best traditions of enlightened
despotism. But the administration remained nonetheless hostile to reading rooms and lending libraries, and especially to pedlars. It realised the
importance of almanacs and popular coloured prints, and even school
primers were not forgotten. The Senate also possessed a commission for
the protection of freedom, but it achieved nothing. As for the theatres,
where political parties easily clashed, they too were not spared. In 1805
Napoleon asked Fouché's opinion about Mozart's *Don Giovanni* 'from the
point of view of public morale'; and Brifaut, who had written a play entitled *Don Sanche*, had to transform it into *Ninus d'Assyrie* on account of
the Spanish war.

To sum up, it may be said that the imperial administration perfected
the work of the Consulate, and accentuated its arbitrary features. Nothing
remained of liberty but freedom of conscience, because intolerance at this
point would have been harmful to the state by depriving it of good servants. Even so, it was not permissible to attack the recognised religions, to
profess atheism or adhere to the schismatic *Petite Église*. Frenchmen were
not much surprised by the Napoleonic despotism, just emerging as they
were from the *ancien régime* and the turmoil of revolution; moreover, they
knew that other countries were very much in the same boat. The original
feature of Napoleon's despotism was its simplicity, and the nice adjust-
ment of its machinery; and this it owed to the Revolution, which by its
destruction of the chaotic institutions and privileges of the *ancien régime*
had made it possible to build anew.

## FINANCES AND THE NATIONAL ECONOMY

Money provides the very sinews of war, and the example of Louis XVI had proved that a crisis in the national finances can be fatal to authority. Frederick II, who served as a model for enlightened despots, had always been very careful about finance. He had given preference to indirect taxation as easier to collect, providing a more regular yield and more popular with the ruling classes. And Napoleon followed suit. From 1804 to 1812 he reduced taxation on land and personal estate, which had the advantage of making the consent of the Corps Législatif a pure formality. Moreover, he carried out a rational reassessment of the former class of property, and finally in 1807 undertook a register of landed property, thus meeting one of the essential requests made in the *cahiers* of 1789. He spent fifty-five million francs on it, but never succeeded in completing it in more than five to six thousand communes.

From the very start, Gaudin had suggested the re-establishment of the duties on consumption; but they were so unpopular that Napoleon did not dare take the risk before 1804. On 5 Ventôse, Year XII (25 February 1804), there came into force the 'combined duties', which were put under the management of Français de Nantes. The first tax to be instituted was one on drinks, at a low rate, but nevertheless requiring inventories. Under the authority of the state, the 'cellar rats' of the former excise department once more came into action. The method of collection was modified and the rate raised in 1806 and 1808. In 1806 an additional tax was imposed on salt in compensation for the abolition of the transit duty on the roads. After an increase on the tax on tobacco, a monopoly was finally re-established in 1810. In that year, the yield of the 'combined duties' seems to have been considerably greater than that of the direct taxes, not to mention the customs. There was active public discontent, and more than one disturbance. Property owners, for their part, noted that the relief in direct taxation was no more than apparent, for a share of state expenses had been transferred to local finance – for example, a proportion of the Church expenses, the property register, canals and casual wards; and, in 1810, half the *préfets'* salaries. When the extra centimes were taken into account, the Côtes-du-Nord, which had paid out 2,489,000 francs in Year IX, paid 3,423,000 in 1813. Moreover, in order to make existence possible for the municipalities, the local tolls had to be increased in number. Besides, there was much coming and going of troops, who had to be billeted, and more than one of the *préfets* – Molé, for example – reinstituted forced labour on the roads. Although Napoleon was very economical, the situation – taken all round – was that he increased the financial load on the French nation. Civil expenses did not figure largely in this increase. In the départements, the various services were so poorly provided with money that there was little progress in the roads, schools and public assistance. In the Côtes-du-Nord, much paperwork was necessary in order to restrict the various plans, through shortage of funds. From 1807 onwards some thirty-seven million were allotted to public works; but not many regions benefited. The increase came chiefly from the civil list, Church dues, the national debt and above all the war, which still absorbed fifty to sixty per cent of all receipts, if not more, in spite of the large contribution made by the enemy.

If the treasury escaped the foregoing risks thanks to the reforms of 1806, it was nonetheless never in a comfortable position through lack of borrowing powers. This constituted the essential difference between English and French finance, even more than before 1789. The sinking fund was the only department to succeed in issuing some millions of bonds. Although it managed to find the interest, and although Napoleon bought some on behalf of the Legion of Honour, senatorships and inalienable endowments that he dispensed – to such an extent that in 1809 only thirty-three out of the fifty-eight million were in private hands, and that the market was becoming more and more restricted – the market rate remained low and the position weak. And so various expedients were tried: there was an increase in premiums; a little money was minted; and in 1807 and 1810 the war fund provided eighty-four, and subsequently forty-five, million. But the favourite method continued to be to assign the payment of contractors to particular funds, and to make them wait for their proceeds to be realised, an old *ancien régime* device that led to speculative interest rates and misappropriation; or to postpone auditing on the pretext of checking the figures. From time to time part of the arrears would be liquidated by distributing sinking-fund bonds or interest-bearing securities – a disguised form of forced loan. Thus, in 1813 there was a million-franc issue to cover the balances dating from 1801 to 1808. By the end of the reign, the permanent debt had risen to sixty-three million and the floating debt, arising particularly from ecclesiastical pensions, had reached fifty-seven million. In spite of all this, contractors continued to hold great power because their advances were indispensable.

In the circumstances, Napoleon's finances seem to have been as successful as could have been expected; but to all appearances, they were never in balance. What harmed them particularly in the eyes of the public was that no one knew (or ever will know) the true position, for the indefinite postponement of payments due is the negation of a genuine budget. Moreover, the public audit department, which had been re-established in 1807, was not given the right to examine the legality of expenditure. If the emperor was unable to borrow, it was because investors remained distrustful after so many bankruptcies, and because his policies did not inspire confidence in anyone that his regime would last; but it was also because his financial operations remained mysterious. Rather than put himself under the control of the middle classes, Napoleon preferred to do without their help.

Besides, there was a better way open to him. Like Frederick II, who had earmarked for himself the revenues from Silesia, and had reconstituted the *roi-sergent*'s war fund, Napoleon possessed cash resources under his sole management, namely the civil list, the crown lands and his private estates. He aimed at making certain of a freely disposable fund of at least one hundred million, saying that with such resources a sovereign could be prepared for all eventualities. Moreover, to avoid exhausting the peoples of the Empire or stirring up unrest, he needed financial machinery in the conquered territories as well if he was to avoid financing warfare from the pockets of the Empire alone; and of such machinery he became the sole master. On 28 October 1805 he set up the army fund, which levied war contributions from Austria and Prussia. We learn from his receiver, La Bouillerie, that it was supposed to have produced 743 million between 1805 and 1810, 311 million of which were used to supply his forces. On 30 January 1810 the emperor instituted the *domaine extraordinaire*, and put it under the management of Defermon; and to him was handed over any surplus from the army fund, as well as the lands and revenues the emperor had reserved for himself in the vassal states, then estimated at two thousand million, with an income between thirty and forty million. Napoleon used it to control the circulation of money by buying investments or shares in the Bank of France and other large undertakings, and to make advances to industry in 1811, and above all to reward his servants or give them pensions. Warfare therefore provided him with large resources. On the eve of the Russian campaign he is reported to have said: 'It will help my finances too; for haven't I rehabilitated them by warfare? And wasn't this how Rome acquired the whole world's wealth?'

For the nation, however, the advantage was more doubtful. A certain number of individuals enriched themselves from these spoils; the stock of metal was usefully augmented; and the budget was momentarily eased. But the war fell no less heavily upon the tax-payer. Although Spain was said to have contributed 350 million, it was still necessary to despatch just as many supplies to it, apart from twenty-four to thirty million of monthly instalments and the pensions for the fallen princes, all at French expense, for the army treasury and the foreign estates did not contribute a half-penny. And finally it must be noted that if Napoleon increased his personal authority in these ways, his liquid reserves never rose to the figure he had set himself, for he had to spend a large part of the revenue from his domains under the pressure of circumstance.

Whatever profit he made from war, it accordingly remained essential to develop the country's contributory capacity. To this end the enlightened despots had encouraged production by obeying the principles of the Mercantile Theory; and Napoleon did the same. Regimentation was natural to an authoritarian government; and on various sides pleas were made for a return to guilds and to trade marks. The upper middle classes remained in a general way faithful to freedom of employment; and Napoleon showed more respect for them than he has usually been credited with. At Lyon, he confined himself to imposing on the home workers a certificate of book-keeping. Trade marks were re-established for brocades and velvets in Year XII; in 1807 for cloths for the Levant; in 1810 for Louviers cloth; in 1811 for soaps; in 1812 for the whole cloth trade, though they remained optional. The monopoly in weapons of war, powder, minting and tobacco can be explained for reasons of public order or fiscal considerations. The same is true of the laws governing expropriation for reasons of public utility, those relating to unhealthy premises, and to the mines. Here, the law of 1810 attributed ownership of such property to the state, but allowed it to be exploited by private individuals, with the exception of the Saar mines. The same also applies to the control of the baking and butchery trades, where the return to the *ancien régime* was most marked of all. The corporative constitution of the bakers, which had been re-established under the Consulate, was extended to several provincial towns; and in 1811 the syndical savings bank of the Paris butchers became once again the Caisse de Poissy, its duty being to advance on behalf of the town the necessary sums for paying the graziers. At the request of the wine merchants, their numbers in the capital were limited and they had to be authorised by the police; the professions of wine-dealer and wine-taster were made into official posts under government nomination.

As far as agriculture was concerned, it was more or less left to itself. The forests were once more put under guards, but nothing was done to disrupt the collective customs, nor were the land registers used so as to favour or compel regrouping – a process which nearly all the peasants would have opposed. The blockade simply made the emperor insist that certain crops should be grown, in particular that thirty-two thousand and then one hundred thousand hectares should be allotted to sugar-beet. Concern for public order obliged him to do as the *ancien régime* had done, and act to some extent as arbiter in fixing the price of corn as between peasant and consumer, either by raising it by authorising its export, or by imposing a maximum price – as he did in 1812.

But it was the working classes who particularly felt the hand of the law. This was no novelty, for the law of 1791 had re-enacted the prohibition of strikes and workers' associations, and the law of Year XI and the penal code did no more than confirm it. But apprenticeship was also re-established, and the expression 'master and workman' was reintroduced. Certain administrators went further still. For example in Paris, in 1806, the *préfet* of police fixed the hours of work for the building trade, and in the Yonne, the *préfet* regrouped the craftsmen and fixed a tariff for them. But the Conseil d'État rejected schemes for apprenticeship and the regulation of workshops; and the minister refused to intervene to sanction disciplinary action against the Maine-et-Loire slaters, the paper-makers in the Paris region and the Bauwens spinning-mills in Ghent. The setting up of 'conciliation boards' on 18 March 1806, for settling differences between employers and workmen, without any representation for the latter, was solely due to the technical incompetence of the ordinary judges. With certain reservations, the nascent forces of capitalism were a law to themselves, quite independently of the regime. They maintained the various regulations against the workers and prevented all attempts to act in combination, which would have been contrary to their own freedom of action.

Thus of the two principles of the Mercantile System, protection occupied the foremost place. Yet war and the blockade were much more powerful than any specific measures in closing down national markets and handing over allied or vassal countries to the power of France. This hardly produced any advantage for agriculture, since Napoleon insisted on controlling the price of corn. On the contrary, it proved more difficult to sell its wines and brandies. Industry was what Napoleon – like Colbert – chiefly encouraged, using exhibitions, special orders, honours for inventors and sometimes even concessions in the form of buildings or advances. But he gave no privileges, and, taking good care of the pence, was only willing to grant loans in times of crisis, and then rather in order to avoid unemployment than to benefit the industries concerned. In his opinion, the greatest service he could render them was to lower the money rate by increasing the Bank of France's discount. He was less interested in profits than in the amounts produced; but because machinery was giving England an advantage, he did much for technical progress, helping Douglas to set up a factory in Paris to produce machinery for the woollen industry, and invited open competition for several inventions, such as a light steam-engine in 1807 and a flax-spinning loom in 1810. He added a school of arts and crafts at Angers to the one at Châlons, opened mining schools, resurrected the Gobelins dyeing school, added a practical course to the Conservatoire des Arts et Métiers, and recommended new procedures and tools by means of official propaganda, as the Committee of Public Safety had also done. Roads and canals would have been of great service in knitting together the national markets and linking them to the vassal countries. Napoleon accordingly set work in train on the Burgundy, Rhône and Rhine, Ille-et-Rance and Nantes to Brest canals, finished the Central canal and Saint-Quentin canal, repaired a big proportion of the *routes nationales*, and opened the Alpine routes, which were vital for trade with Italy and the Levant. He would have done more still if there had been the time and the money.

All the same in the plans for these various works the economy was of less importance than military considerations and questions of prestige, the first predominating for the Alpine routes, those to the Rhine and the West, the extension of the Cherbourg dyke and the Antwerp undertakings; and the second in the attractions and improvements carried out in Paris, where he lengthened the quays, constructed new bridges, cleared the surroundings of Notre-Dame, the Place du Châtelet and the Carrousel, opened up the rue de Rivoli, rue de la Paix, rue de Castiglione, built the Bourse and the Vendôme column, undertook the construction of the Arc de Triomphe and planned a Temple de la Gloire. In connection with the provisioning of the capital, there was the Commarket and the Grande Halle, the Grand Reserve, the slaughterhouses and the Ourcq canal. Great builder that the emperor was, his motive was partly to give employment; for one of the essentials in the policy of all Caesars has always been to provide the people with work and cheap bread.

In agriculture, progress followed the same lines as under the Directory, but was extremely slow. There was far more perceptible advance in industry. The production of luxury goods was resumed, especially in the silk trade; and the blockade gave an impetus to metallurgy, ironmongery, cutlery and the manufacture of machines and tools, sheet iron, tin and brass, pins and needles. It was also favourable to chemical products and textiles; cotton-spinning and printed materials continued to show the greatest activity and the newest improvements, so much so that in 1812 the former had a million spindles in action and produced ten million kilograms of thread. At the end of the Empire, there was a flourishing new industry with a great future, for in the year 1811 the factories at Lille and Auby produced the first lumps of sugar from sugar-beet. Allart at Chaillot and Delessert in Paris set up refineries, and Napoleon established four technical schools and a sugar-works on his own property at Rambouillet. By 1813 the estimated production was 3½ million kilograms in 334 factories; the amount actually realised seems to have been about a third of this figure.

But there was another and tragic side to these beneficial effects of the blockade, namely the total ruin of the maritime ports. In 1807 Marseille still had 330 ocean-going ships, but by 1811 only nine were left; and the product of her manufactures fell from fifty million in 1789 to twelve million, while her population fell in the same period from 120,000 to ninety thousand. Bordeaux, which was reckoned to have the same number in 1789, only had seventy thousand with the result that these two towns became the citadels of royalism. On the other hand Strasbourg and Lyon, taking advantage of their rivals' misfortunes to acquire the monopoly of the German and Italian trade, were bitterly to regret the fall of Napoleon. It is not surprising that in spite of the annexations external trade remained below the figure reached in 1789, seeing that France had lost her colonies. It goes without saying that peace and a commercial treaty with England would have been of more benefit to the national production than the blockade. Napoleon's policy being what it was, it is nonetheless true that the Empire succeeded in keeping alive, and even enjoyed a certain measure of prosperity.

To sum up, it might be said that the emperor behaved much less despotically over the control of things than he did over persons; his state despotism in the economic sphere has been exaggerated. On the other hand, although he did not introduce many innovations in this department, he was successful in conciliating a wide variety of motives and interests. Finally, he maintained sufficient activity in his various states to enable them to support the war; and it must not be forgotten that as far as he was concerned, this was the cardinal point.

## THE CONTROL OF MEN'S MINDS

His system did not consist simply and solely in prohibiting all criticism and placating as many interests as possible. Although Napoleon usually affected to despise ideas, he would sometimes admit their influence. 'There are only two powers in the world,' he said, 'the sword and the spirit; and in the long run, the sword is always conquered by the spirit.' What was needed then was to rally the spirit to the dominance of the sword, so that there might be willing obedience, and as far as possible, joyful and devoted obedience. It was in order to make the churches teach this along with morality that the enlightened despots had gained control over the churches; and when the Concordat had been concluded, this was one of the advantages Bonaparte derived from it. He filled the ranks of the Catholic clergy with a view to holding their allegiance out of self-interest and getting them to produce loyal subjects. Fearful of priests who were not his own officials, he introduced his own supporters everywhere, especially in the state schools; and this he did as a precaution, and to avoid worse possibilities. There were always covert struggles going on around him between the friends and enemies of the Roman Church; of the former Portalis and Fontanes finally won the victory over Fouché, and Cardinal Fesch, who had a good deal to be forgiven, showed himself full of zeal. The emperor more than once rebuffed him, ascribing his fears to 'a delirious imagination' and advising him 'to take cold baths'; but it suited his ends to give way to him on many occasions.

The first requisite was to make certain of the clergy stipends and the conduct of worship, for the pressure that had been put upon the municipalities to stimulate their generosity was only a moderate success. 'The peasants', wrote one priest, 'are well disposed to their religion and their priests, provided they do not cost them anything.' Napoleon decided to take a part of the expense upon himself. From 1803 he granted stipends to the canons; then in 1804, as the plebiscite and the coronation drew near, five hundred francs a year to twenty-four thousand officials, raising the number in 1807 to thirty thousand. In 1804 he had handed over a monopoly in funerals to the Church councils, and had guaranteed to support a large seminary in each diocese, allotting six hundred thousand francs in 1807 for the provision of scholarships. The rest of the expenses fell on the local finances – such as the salaries of those officiants who were not paid by the state (26 December 1804), the parochial clergy's board and lodging and the expenses of worship (2 February 1805). In order to manage the Church services subsidy, an 'external' council was set up in 1807. In 1809 the administration of parish funds was all handed over to the parochial church councils, who were now appointed for the first time by the *préfet*, then added to by co-optation, and who had to elect a body of churchwardens. The *préfets* continued to require them to vote supplementary stipends and to support the curates. Finally, the law of 14 February 1810 definitely settled the charges falling on the commune. The curates' salaries, and the upkeep and repair of buildings, also became a compulsory charge in cases where the church councils had insufficient resources; but the supplementary payments remained optional. This organisation of church finances continued in being for nearly a century. In 1811 it cost the communes of the Bouches-du-Rhône one hundred thousand francs; and the state spent sixteen million, over and above the thirty-one million for pensions.

The Church was very much aware of the respect shown to it, which gave it good standing in the eyes of the people, and of the favours which helped recruitment to the ministry and the extension of its influence. The members of seminaries were exempted from military service; Church dignitaries were favourably placed in the decree of Year XII fixing the order of precedence; processions were revived almost everywhere; 'home missions' were subsidised, and Cardinal Fesch set up a society to organise them. Some *préfets* closed the taverns on Sundays during the hours of divine service; and Portalis gave them his approval, and even an assurance that the Conseil d'État would be responsible for punishing those who remained standing, or kept their hats on, while processions were passing by. As early as 1803 the *lycées* and colleges had acquired almoners, and religious observance had become compulsory. Portalis expected the bishops to keep him informed about their staff. When the bishop of Versailles, in 1805, claimed the right to appoint the schoolmasters, he signified his agreement; and in 1807 they were authorised by decree to take charge of religious instruction in the schools. In 1809 a circular from Fontanes advised them to get the curates to supervise the masters, promising to replace with their own nominees any on whom there should be an unfavourable report. Besides this, the bishops organised confessional teaching, being authorised to found smaller seminaries as preparatory for the main ones; and these became the equivalent of colleges. The clergy were also admitted to the commission for hospices and the office for charitable aid; and the sisters reoccupied the hospitals. And lastly, the unity of the Church was defended in face of the 'little Church', and its discipline supported in at least one point, the marriage of priests being forbidden by administrative action. It was due to Napoleon that the secularising of the state did not run into further difficulties, for he refused to give way to Portalis over the observance of Sunday, the respect to be shown for processions and the nomination of schoolmasters. He blamed Fontanes for having handed over control of the latter to the bishops.

It was owing to him moreover that the progress of the regular Orders was kept within bounds. In principle, he disapproved of masculine Orders. 'There are to be no monks,' he said, 'for monastic discipline destroys all virtue, energy and initiative.' But under the Consulate, he had allowed the re-establishment of some Orders, notably the Pères de la Foi or Paccanaristes, whom the police quite rightly held to be the heirs of the Society of Jesus. In the end, Fouché won the day, and the decree of 3 Messidor, Year XII (22 June 1804), made the existence of the regular Orders subject to authorisation. The Lazarists, the Fathers of the Holy Spirit and those of foreign missions, although in principle amalgamated, continued nevertheless to exist because of the services they were able to render to French influence in the outside world. The Frères de la Doctrine Chrétienne and those of Saint-Sulpice were treated with equal favour; and toleration was extended to certain Trappist houses because they looked after the Alpine hospices. The other Orders were suppressed, including the Pères de la Foi, their superior, Paccanari, being a foreigner. But this Order, claiming that they had been given back their autonomy, nevertheless managed to be left in peace, Fesch even putting them in charge of the Largentière seminary; and they were not definitely condemned till 15 December 1807. Nuns received better treatment from Napoleon, because he reckoned that it paid to put them in charge of the hospitals. He authorised a number of communities and tolerated the existence of others as well. To keep a more effective eye upon them, he would have liked to group them together, and would gladly have united them. At any rate in 1807 he called together 'a chapter general of the hospital sisterhoods and the daughters of charity', presided over by Madame Mère, who had been made their protectress; and in 1808 a decree gave them a certain status. In fact, these hospital sisters often ran a school, like the new Order, the Sisters of Mercy of the Reverend Mother Postel, or the Ladies of the Sacred Heart of the Reverend Mother Barat, who were by profession contemplatives. There was moreover no lack of teaching Orders. The inquiry in 1808 noted a total of more than two thousand houses and ten thousand nuns. As for the non-conventual groups and communities, Portalis decided that the Year XII decree did not refer to them. The Penitents, for instance, reappeared everywhere in the south; the Congrégation de la Vierge grew in numbers in Paris, and added branches in the provinces; and the same thing happened at Bordeaux and Lyon, where Ampère became an enthusiastic proselyte.

Taken as a whole, the bishops showed their gratitude. In 1806 they even resigned themselves to accepting the catechism drawn up by Bernier and Abbé d'Astros, Portalis's secretary, in which Napoleon himself had a hand. It contained a long chapter detailing amongst a Christian's duties obedience to the emperor, payment of taxes and the acceptance of conscription. Some of them – Bernier, for example – were zealous to the point of becoming auxiliaries of the police when Fouché wrote to them: 'There are a number of links between your functions and my own.' Others, however, such as the brother of Cambacérès at Rouen and Caffarelli at Saint-Brieuc, made themselves intolerable by their demands. But most of them reaped an advantage from their prudent compliance and increased their influence. Knowing that in the end they would be sacrificed, the *préfets* gave up the struggle: in Marseille, Thibaudeau consulted Champion de Cicé before choosing his officials. The power of the bishops, protected by the official Gallicanism against the papacy, also put them into a position of strength over against the lower clergy, since the latter had been unreservedly subordinated to them by the Concordat, with the sole exception of the parish priests as such. All the same, the position was far from being one of moral unity, and the conforming bishops remained in bad odour. At Besançon, Archbishop Le Coz was constantly at odds with his priests and seminarists, who were egged on by rebellious spirits from revolutionary days. Nor did the parish priests resign themselves at the outset to lay control, and there were numerous incidents; but in the end the majority of the clergy remained attached to royalty, as the sequel clearly showed. As for their influence on the people, this must not be measured by the material progress of the Church. In many regions, there remained a large measure of indifference, and in the towns, there was always a public ready to applaud a performance of *Oedipus* or *Tartuffe*. Moreover, there is reason to believe that Napoleon was not anxious for a complete re-Christianising of France; he was content with an arrangement which gave him control of those whose first loyalty was to their priests; and this was all he needed.

But the conflict with the papacy prevented this policy from being entirely successful. It was not religious in origin; and although Pius VII rebuked the emperor for the Organic Articles, and much more so for his policy towards the clergy in the kingdom of Italy, there would never have been a rupture if Napoleon had not been a temporal sovereign. But this rupture led Napoleon to revive the claims of the Roman emperor to rule over the clergy, and to treat the bishop of Rome as his vassal. As it was, the *senatus consultum* of 7 February 1810 made the declaration of the four articles into an imperial law; and in the Conseil d'État Napoleon declared that he was about to 're-establish the right, always possessed by the emperors, of confirming the papal nomination' and demanding that 'before his enthronement, the pope should place his hands in those of the emperor of the French and swear that he submits to the four articles'. Popes can no longer make the monstrous claims which in former times were so calamitous to the nations, and so shameful to the Church; yet fundamentally, they have renounced none of their pretensions, and even today they look upon themselves as masters of the world.

Pius VII was a prisoner at Savona. The cardinals had been taken to Paris, and when thirteen out of twenty-seven had refused to be present at the emperor's marriage, he exiled the 'black-leg' cardinals. It then became impossible to implement the Concordat. From 1808 onwards the papal bulls granting investiture to the bishops had departed from the formula laid down by the Concordat to such an extent that the Conseil d'État refused to accept them. It then became impossible to fill the vacancies: the emperor directed the nominated bishops to take up the administration of their dioceses, and Cardinal Maury accepted the see of Paris, and d'Osmond that of Florence. But this could only be a temporary expedient. In 1809 an ecclesiastical committee gave the opinion that if

for temporal reasons the pope delayed a bishop's investiture, the metropolitan could make provision; but it refused to come to a decision, and
advised the convening of a national council. In 1811 a second committee
tendered the same advice. The only man to stand up for the authority of
the Holy See – and that with great boldness, in the very presence of the
emperor – was Abbé Émery, whose Gallicanism grew less and less pronounced as the temporal power became more and more burdensome
to the clergy. But he died before the opening of the national council,
which had been fixed for 17 June 1811. Up till now the bishops had
been cowed into silence, and were too frightened to utter a word. As in
the days of Louis XIV and the Constituent Assembly, they felt that the
Church of France, hard pressed on the one side by the head of the nation
and on the other by the head of the Catholic Church, was in danger of
having to bear the whole brunt of the dispute. Napoleon was obliged to
get round them one at a time in order to press them to agree to his plan;
but even then, they would only agree subject to the pope's approval. If
after six months the pope had not conferred investiture, it was agreed
that it could be given by the metropolitan or the senior suffragan; and this
amounted to a return to the civil constitution of the clergy. Pius VII consented, provided that the investiture was conferred 'expressly in the name
of the sovereign pontiff', which allowed him to forbid it if he thought fit.
On 23 February 1812 Napoleon declared that this brief was unacceptable,
and that he regarded the Concordat as annulled.

This rupture with the pope changed the clergy's feelings with regard
to the regime. A section of the priests gradually went back into open
opposition. The bishops were forced to resign, or sent into exile; priests
had their stipends or pensions suspended; refractory seminarists lost
their scholarships and had to join the army; the men's Orders were disbanded. The Pères de la Foi came under the decree in 1807; the Lazarists,
the Fathers of the Holy Spirit and of Foreign Missions were suppressed
and their superior, Hanon by name, arrested; and in 1810 it was the turn
of Saint-Sulpice. The Congrégation de la Vierge were struck down as
early as 1809, but their members spread the bull of excommunication
throughout France and kept up a secret correspondence with Pius VII.
Next came a number of brotherhoods; and finally the reform of the University in 1811 involved the closure of most of the episcopal schools
or minor seminaries. The Concordat had robbed the royalist cause and
the counter-revolution of the clergy's support: the breach with the pope

meant that this support was regained; it also revived hostility to France in the countries that had been annexed. Nevertheless the years gained by Napoleon bore their fruit. Most churchmen hesitated to press their opposition once again to an extreme and thus lose the benefit of the advantages already won. As long as worship was not suspended or parish priests removed from office, the people were not inclined to protest overmuch. The conflict revived royalist hopes and helped their intrigues; but it was not in itself enough to shake the regime.

The Protestants did not cause him any difficulty; but it was a very different matter with the Jews. If it had been a purely religious question, there would have been no difficulties, for the rabbis themselves asked for comprehensive articles of agreement. The difficulty was to know whether they thought the law of Moses compatible with the civil law and the duties of a French citizen. The Sephardim in the south and in Italy were thought to have long been well adapted to the customs of the country, while the Ashkenazim of the east were reckoned to be attached to ritualism; and in 1805 Bonald threw doubts upon the possibility of assimilating the Jews. And finally, certain Jews in Alsace and Lorraine had aroused fierce hatred by lending at high rates of interest, which often led to peasant expropriation. The emperor had a prejudice against usury and on 30 May 1806, in spite of the Conseil d'État, he granted their debtors a moratorium. There was thus a threefold problem. An assembly of Jews, the seventy members being appointed by the *préfets*, met in Paris on 20 July 1806, and came to an agreement with the imperial commissioners. It was then decided to resurrect in theatrical fashion the Great Sanhedrin, consisting of twenty-six laymen and forty-five rabbis, which addressed a proclamation to all European Jews, and on 9 February 1807 admitted the abolition of polygamy, allowed civil marriage and military service without the right to send a substitute, and such economic measures as might seem necessary. The emperor's decision was not made known till 18 March 1808. Worship was organised in synagogues, with not more than one consistorial synagogue in each département and a central consistory in Paris, supported by compulsory subscriptions from the faithful. By another decree, valid for ten years only, which excluded the Gironde and in fact only applied to Alsace and Lorraine, the debts of minors, women and soldiers were cancelled. The Jewish creditor had to prove that he had provided the whole of the capital, unless the debtor was a businessman; and the courts were authorised to reduce or cancel interest in arrears and to grant a moratorium for payment. A special licence was imposed on the Jews, and their pawnbroking was regulated. They were forbidden to settle in Alsace, and made subject elsewhere to the purchase of a property in the country. Finally, in 1810 they were compelled to choose a family name. One can well understand Napoleon's anxiety to put an end to extortionate interest, which might give rise to disturbances and force peasants to emigrate; but it is doubtful whether his measures were conducive to assimilation, and the free choice of a patronymic actually worked against it. In spite of everything, his contemporaries did not think his policy unfavourable to the Jews. It had repercussions in Europe, by comparison with which it earned him the favour of Jewish communities and the abuse of their enemies.

The emperor also involved himself in Freemasonry, which had been revived under the Directory and more particularly the Consulate. In 1805 Joseph became grand master of the Grand Lodge of France; and when the 'Scottish' branch, organised in 1804, finally seceded, Kellermann and Cambacérès undertook its management. The emperor's protection worked in favour of unity and the hierarchical principle in Freemasonry, and led to the multiplication of lodges. The Grand Lodge, under the effective management of Roëttiers de Montaleau, had control over three hundred lodges in 1804 and a thousand in 1814. There were many Freemasons among high-ranking civilians and soldiers, and the order proved thoroughly loyal. But its ideas remained those of the eighteenth century, and some of the *préfets* finally came to the opinion that the lodges were a bad influence. 'It is always a question of equality, our brothers, philosophy and republican notions,' wrote Capelle in the département of Léman. But Napoleon never took offence at these views.

The shaping of youth proved a more anxious task. Although wishing to give religion a place, he had no intention of simply handing it over to the churches: his aim was to produce good subjects rather than good Christians, men of the age and not theologians. All the enlightened despots had aimed at this. The spirit of the regime tended towards a state monopoly; and as state education would have cost a great deal of money, Napoleon's scholastic policy was dominated by the question of finance. First and foremost he provided for the recruitment of officers, officials, jurists and health officers by setting up *lycées*, national scholarships, a military academy in Year XI and schools of law and medicine in Year XII. Even so, he had to leave the recognised secondary schools to the municipalities, and admit the existence of numerous private institutions, as well as confessional teaching in the minor seminaries. Yet the *lycées* were slow in opening, owing to the lack of funds: by 1808 only thirty-seven of the forty-five planned had come into being. Nor did they flourish as Napoleon had hoped; for he had reckoned that with their fee-paying pupils they ought to cost him nothing at all. The order of Year XI had introduced military discipline, which the middle classes did not like; and the clergy saw the *lycées* as sinks of iniquity, since their staff included ex-priests and independents. Lastly, there was the objection that the independent schools gave their education on the cheap. There were thus two possible courses: to close the *lycées* and so cut down costs, or to suppress the private establishments. This latter solution would doubtless have been preferred by Fourcroy as head of the educational department, and by the party of the *philosophes*; but Portalis was against it, upholding the parents' right to freedom of choice – an argument that benefited the Church. The emperor ended by adopting a compromise solution, for he had neither the money nor the staff to set up a state monopoly. The law of 10 May 1806 announced that a corporation would be formed called the Université, with the sole right of teaching; nevertheless private institutions could continue to exist under its supervision, subject to the payment of a tax which would relieve the budget and limit the competition. The organisation, though adopted on 4 July, was postponed because of the war, and did not come into force until 17 September 1808. Meanwhile, thanks to Fesch and Fontanes, the Church consolidated its position; and the decree, and more especially the way it was applied, were regarded as a defeat for the party of the *philosophes*. Fourcroy, who expected to be made head of the Université, was superseded by Fontanes.

Fontanes was now given the title of grand master, and though not ranking as a minister, he was in direct correspondence with the emperor, and was given the help of a chancellor, a treasurer, a council of thirty members and a body of inspectors-general. The Empire was divided up into academies under the control of rectors assisted by inspectors and academic councils. Education was split up into three grades: primary, secondary and higher. For the first time the state took control of the primary school. The municipal council, which had up till then appointed the schoolmaster, now had to rest content with proposing its own candidate; and the grand master awarded teaching certificates. The *lycées* remained as before, but the secondary schools were now called colleges. It was at last decided to organise science and arts faculties – the masters, however, remaining attached to the *lycées*; and theological faculties were also added. The Collège de France and the great revolutionary institutions continued as they were and did not become part of the Université. The staff were all appointed by the emperor or the grand master. The teaching staff in the *lycées* and faculties came under regulations which laid down their grades, titles, dress and salary, with deductions for retirement pensions, and disciplinary measures. The masters in the *lycées* were the only ones allowed to marry.

The private schools could only open with the authorisation of the Université (which could always be withdrawn), and had to be staffed by persons holding its degrees, as well as coming under its inspectors and disciplinary control. Thus there was no absolute monopoly for public education: private and competing establishments continued and even increased in number. Moreover, the sovereignty of the Université was only nominal, for its degrees were not to become compulsory until 1815, and freelance masters with ten years' service could be exempted; nor were there enough inspectors to exercise effective control. And finally the seminaries were simply exempted from these measures of authority. On the other hand, the Catholic Church was given a share of influence in the state schools. Its doctrine was made one of the express bases of the teaching given, and Fontanes's loyalty to the Church was such that he wrote to his friend Gaillard: 'I advise you to send your son to Juilly' (the famous Oratorian college). A bishop was appointed chancellor of the Université; and Abbé Émery, as well as Bonald and Ambroise Rendu – both keen Catholics – were members of the council. Joubert, and the Protestant Cuvier, who played an important part in reorganising public bodies, were both inspectors who approved of religious instruction. Abbé Frayssinous, a member of the Congrégation de la Vierge, became an inspector in the Paris academy. Priests were headmasters of *lycées* and colleges, or members of the teaching staff. Nonetheless, it was the emperor who had undertaken to organise public education on these definite lines, which was why the Church could not forgive this self-styled monopoly exercised by the Université, for it had counted on setting up its own.

For the moment, moreover, the grievances of the private boarding schools, whether secular or Church schools, were of a more matter-of-fact kind, since the decree controlling their organisation compelled their heads to take out a certificate for a consideration and for each of their pupils – even day-boys – to pay over a twentieth of the whole boarding fee. But this was a system which proved difficult to check. It was not possible to exact complete payment of this deduction; moreover, the seminaries were exempt. Savary was accordingly told to hold an inquiry in 1810, especially as Napoleon, having fallen out with the pope, now viewed the seminaries with suspicion. On 15 November 1811 the monopoly was strengthened by a new decree. The new measures prescribed that in every town possessing a *lycée* or college, the pupils of private schools must now join their classes, and permission was given for only one minor seminary or episcopal school in each département. The result was clear enough: by 1813 the *lycées* and colleges with thirty-eight thousand pupils in 1810 had risen in numbers to forty-four thousand; and since 1811 the private schools had lost five thousand. Nevertheless the application of the decree remained incomplete, and the mitigations contrived by Fontanes and his colleague contributed towards easing its harshness. In 1814, when talking to Louis XVIII, the grand master boasted that he had been able to 'prevent a certain amount of harm'.

The emperor achieved his immediate aim of drawing from the secondary schools and high schools a succession of capable administrators. The curriculum of the central schools was considerably pruned in favour of Latin and Greek, and philosophy was reduced to the study of logic; history, modern languages and the experimental sciences were neglected. But the national literature and mathematics kept the importance given to them by the Revolution; and in higher education, the original character it had imparted to French science was maintained, and scholars continued to concern themselves with research as well as teaching. Yet Napoleon's dream of a complete control over the moulding of French youth was far from being realised. He cared little for the common people, and did nothing for primary education, which he was content to leave in the hands of the municipalities. Apart from a few regions such as Alsace, the smaller schools showed no improvement; at the most, they were restored to their condition at the end of the *ancien régime*. Still less was Napoleon interested in the education of women. But it was important that he should mould the sons of the middle classes; and here he was hardly successful, for a large number of them were educated outside his schools, and at the university he did not manage to put before the rising generation any fitting ideal that would have won them over to his support.

The same may be said of his intellectual and artistic activities. He

wanted to play the part of a Maecenas, for it was universally agreed that no
sovereign was truly great unless he had had his *siècle*. In 1804 he established the decennial prizes which were to be awarded for the first time in
1810. He claimed to control literary production through the censorship,
the academies and the French Academy in Rome. He exercised a strange
form of control over the theatres, forcing them to take Rémusat as their
superintendent. In 1807 he limited their number to four big and four
secondary ones in Paris. Five other towns were authorised to form two
companies, and fourteen were only allowed a single one. The rest of the
Empire comprised twenty-five districts, each with one or two travelling
companies. In Paris, each theatre was given a particular style of play to
perform, and all of them had to pay a contribution to the Opéra. The
decree establishing the Théâtre Français was signed at Moscow in 1812.
Napoleon felt particularly at ease in protecting the arts, more especially
architecture, since he himself was a great buyer and builder.* It would be
an exaggeration to say that he left his mark upon works of art, for the
Empire style is not derived from him; but he managed to gather great
artists round him. In literature, on the other hand, he was completely
unsuccessful: only the second-rate rallied to his side, the first-class writers
all giving him a wide berth. He does not seem to have had the same idea as
the Committee of Public Safety, namely to use writers and artists to
mould the public mind; at the most, he thought of having the history of
his campaigns taught in the schools, using the *Bulletins de la Grande
Armée* and the articles in the *Moniteur* to build up the Napoleonic legend,
and commissioning the painter David to execute some topical pictures. To
be sure, he had neither the financial resources nor the technical means of
subsequent dictatorships for organising propaganda. Moreover, claiming
as he did to be the founder of a universal empire and dynasty, he had no
particular message for his compatriots as such. Those who followed him
to the end, with utter loyalty and no thought of self, were defending in his
person both the nation and the Revolution; but others could not seriously
accept the legitimacy of this Vendémiaire general,† even though he had
been anointed by the pope. Though he managed to lull and constrain the
public mind and spirit, he did not succeed in becoming its master: the two
poles of thought remained Tradition and the Revolution.

* See page 415.
† [Napoleon's early promotion was in reward for his defence of the Directory against the
insurrection of Vendémiaire (October 1795).]

## SOCIAL DEVELOPMENT AND PUBLIC OPINION

Napoleon was well aware that the mind of the nation would never be fully brought under control. He therefore continued to work as he had done under the Consulate for the re-establishment of a social hierarchy. His aim was to win over, either out of personal advantage or vanity, all who wielded authority, and strengthen this authority in order to subject it to himself. He continued to bring influential people into his orbit, those who controlled an immense number of farmers and smallholders, of workmen and contractors, by drawing them into the circle of councils and administration, ministerial office and public institutions. In multiplying officials, he was not only extending the powers of the state; he did so because he saw the advantages of building up a social group whose dignities and livelihood depended on him, and who would therefore be set on maintaining the established order, not to mention the additional influence exercised by their family relationships and their personal connections. Moreover his wars, with the resulting increase in offices, also provided him with a large number of devoted servants.

He kept up between these two groups a corporate and personal rivalry which divided them, made them assiduous in their duties, and caused them to look to him as the source of money and distinctions. This was why he attached great importance to decorations, for which he realised there was a keen desire. In 1805 he had completely transformed the Legion of Honour, so that the whole value now lay in the insignia. In the kingdom of Italy, he created the Ordre de la Couronne de Fer, which was received by many Frenchmen. In 1809 he created the Trois Toisons d'Or, and in 1811 the Réunion. There was an endless distribution of rewards, pensions, gifts in the form of income or land. The army received the lion's share; but true to his promise, he did not refuse to decorate civilians, and even gave Talma the Legion of Honour, though more than nine-tenths of the crosses went to soldiers. Frenchmen fell in with this policy, to which they had been accustomed in the *ancien régime*, because these distinctions, carrying no privileges, being open to all, and not being hereditary, did not seem contrary to a civil equality which reserved reward for merit. It remained possible to rise in the social scale, along lines sanctioned by the Revolution; war and promotion were in favour of it; and the extension of public functions and scholarships gradually built up from among the people a lower middle class.

With his dreams of establishing a legitimate dynasty and his desire to complete the attachment of the ancient aristocracy, whose titles he was nonetheless unwilling to recognise, Napoleon took a further step and re-created a nobility. It was to be one of office, held directly from himself, but hereditary and linked to a degree of wealth that would allow the holder to preserve his rank. The organisation of the imperial court, and the creation of the vassal states and the great fiefs, served as a prelude. A *senatus consultum* of 14 August 1806 authorised Napoleon to extend the system of great hereditary fiefs over the whole Empire, with entail to the eldest son. Finally, on 1 March 1808 the imperial *noblesse* came into being. It belonged as of right to great dignitaries who had been made princes, to ministers, senators, archbishops, councillors of state for life, and the president of the Corps Législatif, who became counts. Other officials, such as the mayors of the large towns, were made barons, and the members of the Legion of Honour, knights. The emperor could also confer nobility by commission. The title became hereditary, provided that it constituted an entail for the benefit of the heir, to which Napoleon often made a contribution. In parallel with this development, the numbers at court constantly increased, and after the Austrian marriage it once more became an institution, as it had been under the *ancien régime*. In 1812 there were sixteen equerries and eighty-five chamberlains. Precedence had been re-established in 1811, and was marked by the chair, the stool and the number of carriage-horses, court dress and presentation at court. At this point, the return to the old ways was even more marked. M. de Ségur was master of ceremonies: the ladies-in-waiting and the chamberlains came for the most part from the old nobility. The Revolution seemed no more than a bad dream. Napoleon was soon to say to Molé: 'The doctrines that are called the principles of 1789 will always remain a threatening weapon in the hands of the malcontents, the ambitious and the ideologues of every age.' He also spoke of the knitting-women who hated the new empress. His violent dislike for any opposition to his authority grew so great that he no longer made any distinction between these Sansculotte women and the royalist citizens who had risen against the Convention: 'As long as I am here, these dregs of society shall never again be given a chance to stir, because they saw what stuff I am made of on 13 Vendémiaire; and they know that I shall always be ready to crush them if I find them up to any tricks.' And his supporters joined in the chorus: Réal, the former deputy to Chaumette, was to exclaim in 1812:

'The common people have never been properly put in their place!'

If Napoleon had been given the time, he would perhaps have gone still further. There are certain indications suggesting that he would have liked to group his subjects in social categories, in such a way that the constitution of the vassal states would have carried a corporate suffrage, seats being distributed between landed proprietors, businessmen and the liberal professions, for they all were clearly property holders. In this respect, it was tempting for him to reconstitute the corporations. If re-created under state control, equipped with auxiliary institutions and technical instructors, and forbidden to strike or enter into combinations, they would have provided a framework for subjecting the workers to the patriarchal authority of the leaders in industry and commerce. The emperor was also in favour of granting perpetual leaseholds as a suitable means of setting up patronage for the landed proprietors.

Of all his schemes, the ones aiming at a reconstruction of society were the most uncertain. The fact is that they were contrary to the course of evolution, which swept away the few that were realised, leaving no permanent effect on the national life. In the first place, Chaptal was wrong in imagining that the Revolution had been forgotten. Even at court, there was only a superficial fusion between the old and the new aristocracies; and the imperial setting often did no more than produce a surface impression. 'Another chamber-pot on the head of these nobles' – as Pommereul was heard to mutter at each new chamberlain's nomination, although he himself belonged to the *ancien régime*. 'Have you seen Sieyès?' said Doulcet de Pontécoulant after the ceremony for the Order of the Réunion in which Sieyès, like the others, had appeared in robes covered with gold and spangled with stars. 'Have you seen Sieyès? *What is the Third Estate?*'

Deep down, Napoleon himself did not feel at ease in the midst of the nobles of the *ancien régime* who were in a position to make so many comparisons, and for whom he never ceased to express contempt. 'I opened my antechambers to them,' he said, 'and they rushed in.' Witness again the evidence of this note on a letter from the prince-bishop of Basle, in 1805, who was concerned about his financial interests: 'Oh! you cowardly nobles: what would your ancestors say if they saw you – your ancestors, who were so proud of their virtues!'* But things were very different in the country. The people of privilege under the *ancien régime* never ceased

* *Fürstenbriefe an Napoléon I*, published by F. Kircheisen (Stuttgart and Berlin, 1929), vol. ii, p. 336.

bemoaning what they had lost; and the imperial nobility, like the middle classes, remained determined not to give any of it back to them. Those who had accepted the new regime put up with conditions as they were. Those who were irreconcilable dreamed of the *ancien régime*, some of them even attempting to form groups to prepare for possible action in favour of the legitimate monarchy. For this purpose Ferdinand de Bertier and Mathieu de Montmorency, both members of the Congrégation de la Vierge that was to become famous under the Restoration, organised a secret society of the Knights of the Faith, which seems to have revived in Bordeaux memories of the Institut Philanthropique that had been so active under the Directory. The rest of the nobility, as they waited for better days, rebuilt their fortunes and resumed their rank as far as that was possible. The returning émigrés bought back their land on good terms (half of it situated in the Côtes-du-Nord) or had it given back to them. They remained in secret agreement with a large section of the clergy; and once again they had friends in all the administrative bodies and in the lawcourts. They were in no way grateful to Bonaparte, but were waiting for his downfall. If only he had taken over the national possessions to hand them back to themselves! For their part, the new owners began to grow uneasy. In 1807 the estates department had undertaken, for a very small profit, to revise the deductions allowed; it also went into the question of the nationalised revenues, and sought to demand proof from debtors of their feudal status. Some courts – at Dijon, for example – claimed the power to restore the feudal revenues themselves when the creditor could prove that they corresponded to a concession in land; and the General Council of the Côte-d'Or expressed the same desire. Nothing could fill the gulf created by the social revolution: the old and the new nobilities were long to remain at enmity, and in spite of anything that Napoleon could say or do, democracy would take advantage of their discords to gain a further triumph.

On the other hand Napoleon had only become the most powerful of the enlightened despots because when he rose to fame the French aristocracy had been annihilated. Any real re-establishment of it was something of a contradiction. Firmly based upon big landed properties and supported by a body of tenants in perpetuity, the nobility would have recovered an independent power which he – or at any rate his successors – would, like Louis XV and Louis XVI before them, soon have confronted as a rising force ranged against themselves. The nobility that he had created and intended to keep under control only amounted to a clique of courtiers and officials who gave him no support; and once he had gone, they melted away. Finally, it was just as contradictory to pose as the representative of a revolution carried out in the name of equality and yet to wish to restore an aristocracy worthy of the name. At the time, a personal nobility may well have seemed generally acceptable. It was just a decoration, much the same as any other; and the common people were quite disposed to have their dukes and counts after they had set up kings. It was a new way of humiliating the *ci-devant*. But to revive the rights of primogeniture was going too far; and in immobilising a part of property by the principle of entail, Napoleon came into conflict with one of the essential principles of the capitalist economy.

The action of Napoleon upon society was only really effective to the extent that it strengthened and increased the predominance of the bourgeoisie, because at this point it was in line with the national evolution. By giving the nobles an essential part in the regime he unconsciously prepared the way for their assumption of political power. But he also greatly increased their influence, their prestige and their wealth by reconstituting the administrative posts and making them virtually an invitation to corrupt practices through the misappropriation of securities; by reestablishing in the financial system treasurers and receivers personally interested in the manipulation of funds by their right to a percentage on them; and by multiplying public offices of every description. The Bank of France, the formation of certain large companies and the restoration of investment in stocks began to develop moneyed estate. Industrial expansion and the prosperity of various big business chiefs were a sign of a developing capitalism, though the middle classes continued to draw their wealth from the traditional sources, namely the purchase of land and the supply of the sinews of war. And lastly, the imperial legislation kept the workers in a state of subjection. Nevertheless, the more power the middle classes acquired, the more they turned away from the Napoleonic regime.

True, the government under Napoleon was far from meeting his interests at every point. It is hardly possible to approve of his financial management, his arbitrary control over the contractors, the adventurer's attitude to war and the excesses of the blockade. But none of this was perhaps the heart of the matter. The middle classes had only helped him on that day in Brumaire in order to install themselves in power under his wing; but he seized the whole power and deprived the middle classes of all freedom.

Thus constitutional monarchy came to be regarded with nostalgic longings, and the English parliamentary system came back into fashion. Royer-Collard even went as far as to blame those who accepted the new regime, although he ended by accepting a chair at the Sorbonne. In the Corps Législatif, Laîné waited for an opportunity of posing as an opponent; and Guizot, who had been appointed to the Sorbonne, refused to slip into his first lesson a passage in praise of the tyrant. There was talk in the salons, particularly in Madame Récamier's circle; in the theatres, there was applause for any passages that could be taken as topical allusions; books and articles passed in all innocence by the censorship were eagerly devoured; pamphlets were circulated in manuscript, and people let themselves go – not without some risk – in personal correspondence. The more startling incidents were connected especially with the history of literature. In 1807 Chateaubriand, who had only just come back from his travels in the East, was ordered to leave Paris because of an article in the *Mercure*; and although he was elected to the Academy in 1811, he was unable to deliver his inaugural speech. Madame de Staël was even worse treated. Returning to France after the publication of *Delphine*, in which she gave a picture of 'silent France', she was asked to leave the country again; and in 1806 she was not allowed to come within thirty-two kilometres of Paris. At Coppet, she gathered a circle of admirers around her – Benjamin Constant (though he was now a married man), Sismondi, Bonstetten, the Barantes and August Schlegel – a court that rivalled the official court. From 1808 onwards it was hardly possible to risk being seen there without the chance of official disfavour or worse; and in 1810 the impression made by her *L'Allemagne* was the last straw. Barante, who was *préfet* of the Léman département, was dismissed and Madame Récamier exiled. The heroine herself fled on 23 May 1812 and made for St Petersburg.

But these events were only of episodic importance, concerning no one but so-called 'society' or 'the fashionable world', that is to say, an infinitesimal number of people. It is more important to note the hundred and one less well known signs that everyone was living in a state of doubt and expectancy; for who could consider the Empire as finally consolidated when each new campaign threw it into the melting pot? The Lyon Chamber of Commerce boldly expressed in a memorandum what everyone was thinking: 'France cannot stand up to the all-out effort required by an indefinitely prolonged state of war. The extreme tension resulting from this effort exhausts the energies of the whole of society.' The stock exchanges unwearingly reflected the universal pessimism by steadily remaining at the lowest level. It was this uncertainty that continually fanned the current fears and discontent.

Yet neither of these was reflected among the lower classes. They were scarcely affected by the Napoleonic despotism. Only taxation, conscription and poverty would have stirred them to action. Up to 1812 military service did not provoke as much resistance as has been supposed. The privations and high prices due to the blockade scarcely affected the poor, as long as bread was not too expensive and unemployment not too bad. The combined duties were very unpopular, but they were not nearly as oppressive as before 1789. As long as he remained victorious, Napoleon's demands do not seem to have been greater than the people could bear provided they had their daily bread, which was as far as possible the case from 1803 to 1811, thanks to good harvests and the emperor's measures to ensure the supply of work.

The condition of the rural population was tending to become more settled. During the whole of the Empire, the nationalised lands continued to be sold, but not much of them remained, apart from the forests, which the state kept under its own control. The lands mostly went to the middle classes, and the peasants who bought them were already fairly well off. In Year XII, the sharing out of the common lands had been confirmed, provided the legal requirements had been respected; but as this was not often the case, many transfers were annulled. On the other hand, though the law of 10 June 1793 was not revoked, it ceased to be applied.

Nevertheless, it seems that peasant property-owning continued to spread because the marked drop in the price of land was in favour of private purchase. Moreover, the laws of succession ensured that it quickly became subdivided. The working units seem likewise to have become smaller and more numerous. The 1814 inquiry noted that in the Mantes district and in the Seine-Inférieure, large farms had been split up, and that small-scale cultivation was on the increase in Alsace, in the Ille-et-Vilaine, in the Doubs and in the Tarn. All the same, although the original features of the country's social structure were growing fainter in this process, they remained easily recognisable. The great majority of peasant proprietors still owned too little land; the cost of farming was on the increase, and the expenses of those who paid rent-in-kind were rising. There was a rapidly growing population, and the daily wage proletariat had hardly gone down in number. The rural community only managed to subsist by virtue of the customary rights, such as free access and pasture on the commons, gleaning, and common lands, so that the closing of the forests was often a cause of suffering to them. As under the *ancien régime*, they sought to add to their livelihood by means of industry, by temporary migrations and by begging. In Alsace, Lorraine and the Rhinelands the peasants, making poverty the ostensible reason, emigrated to Russia in fairly large numbers, especially in 1808 and 1809; and severe measures had to be taken to put a stop to this movement.

There was still less change in the situation of the workers. Not till 1813 did Napoleon intervene – and then solely on behalf of the miners – to prevent accidents, forbid the employment underground of children less than ten years of age and approve the formation of an optional provident society in the coal mines of the Ourthe département. He announced his intention – which had been expressed so often before – of abolishing all mendicancy, but his efforts were no more successful than those of his predecessors, although in 1808 he seriously undertook to set up institutions for interning beggars. But with the exception of a few towns, public assistance made little progress: the machinery set up by the Directory was kept going, but there was a lack of funds. Only by private initiative were a few improvements obtained. In Paris, La Rochefoucauld-Liancourt and his friends had in Year IX revived the Philanthropic Society, which opened the first dispensaries, and others were founded in the provinces. They supported the savings banks and mutual assistance societies, of which there were more than a hundred in 1815; the Société Maternelle was also revived. The essential point was that wages remained steady or increased, in both town and country. In Paris about 1811, they rose from two francs 50 to four francs 20; but as prices were rising to an equal degree, people were not much better off, though with bread not too dear, life was just possible. The rapid increase in the population proves that this was so. Early marriages were more than ever a contributory factor, because this was a possible way of avoiding conscription. In 1812 there were 220,000 marriages, and 387,000 in 1813, resulting in 122,000 more births in 1814 than in 1813. From 1801 to 1810 the birth rate exceeded thirty-two per thousand, and the nation never showed greater vitality. Some administrative efforts were made to reduce the death rate, especially by extending the use of vaccine. In the Bas-Rhin, Lezay-Marnésia organised a free medical service. From 1801 to 1810 this venerable France, in spite of her wars, added 1,700,000 souls to her population. Many there were who deplored the fact, believing that it would only lead to an increase in poverty and begging.

The industrial crisis of 1811 interrupted the succession of good years; but there was a rapid recovery in 1812, which was fortunate, for there had been a bad harvest in 1811, and as export had meant the disappearance of all old grain stocks, the dearth of that winter was as severe as in Year X. The crisis came in the spring of 1812, when the average price of a hectolitre rose from fifteen francs in 1809 to thirty-three francs, and bread in certain regions from two *sous* a pound to twelve. The usual disturbances recurred. Beggars multiplied and formed bands, farms were raided and set on fire, grain supplies were seized, and there were market riots, such as those at Caen at the beginning of March. The formidable repressive machinery of the regime went into pitiless action. Caen was occupied by a detachment of the Imperial Guard and a military commission ordered six executions. At the same time efforts were made to import grain. As early as 28 August 1811 Napoleon set up a food council, and the director of supplies undertook considerable purchases. As always, Paris was the chief consideration, the state selling 450,000 sacks of grain there, at a loss of 14½ million, in order to keep the price of bread at 4½ *sous* a pound. On the eve of his departure for Russia, the emperor nevertheless felt overloaded with stocks, and had no compunction in following the example of the Convention. By a law passed on 4 May it was made compulsory to sell in the markets; their regulation was authorised, and the grain merchants were compelled to declare their stocks. On 8 May a maximum price was again fixed. Corn was fixed at thirty-three francs in the Paris district, and the *préfets* were ordered to fix prices in each département. The results were the same as those that followed the law of 4 May 1793, because the authorities did not go as far as to requisition supplies: the open markets were deserted, and a secret 'black-market' trade grew up. As soon as the harvest began the maximum price was abandoned. In spite of these trials, the Empire does not seem to have gone down in popular esteem. The reports issued by Las Cases, one of the commissioners who was sent on a tour of enquiry, do not anywhere leave the impression that Napoleon had lost popularity; in any case, it did not even cross the minds of peasants and workers that he could be replaced by a Bourbon.

In the countries annexed before 1804 – Belgium, the Rhineland, Geneva, Piedmont and Liguria – the revolutionary changes had been thoroughly carried through and the Napoleonic system was in regular operation. The inhabitants appreciated its merits, particularly the zeal and firmness of *préfets* like Jeanbon in Mont-Tonnerre and Lezay-Marnésia in Rhin-et-Moselle. Moreover, there were signs of economic progress. This was when large-scale industry began in Belgium, thanks to the opening of the French market, and capital and orders from Paris. The same was true of the Rhineland plain between Aachen and Cologne, and of the Saar region. Belgian and Piedmontese agriculture do not seem to have shown great improvement; but a great deal of fallow land was brought under cultivation in the Rhineland. Although Belgium (apart from Antwerp) could not show any large public works, Piedmont took full advantage of the great Alpine roads. The Rhineland saw the opening of a road along its river, the Moselle, and another from Paris to Hamburg via Wesel; and the Saar was linked up with Lorraine by canal. Circumstances prevented all interests from being satisfied: Genoa, Antwerp and the Rhineland ports were condemned to stagnation; and the Palatinate failed to find in the Empire the agricultural market it had lost east of the Rhine. As in France, there seemed to be heavy burdens. Taxation was better spread, but it more than made up for the dues that had been abolished; the consumer suffered under the blockade; and conscription was even more unpopular. Nevertheless, the population increased everywhere; and although there was not much advance in the standard of living, the inhabitants were certainly not weighed down by poverty.

In all regions it was the middle classes who reaped the greatest gains from the regime and were most solidly attached to it. The sale of the national lands, together with industry and public enterprise, led to the appearance of *nouveaux riches* and a lower middle class who stood to lose everything by a return to the *ancien régime*. But the Concordat had also allayed the fears of the Catholic clergy; and even the aristocracy were partly won round when they saw Napoleon getting rid of the Jacobins and the patriots. The Piedmontese Saint-Marsan became an ambassador; the duc de Mérode-Westerloo and the duc d'Ursel were mayors of Brussels. What the notables especially complained of to the emperor was his failure to show them enough confidence. The *préfets*, bishops and principal heads of the services were French; only a few from the annexed countries obtained similar posts in the rest of the Empire; in their homelands they became *préfets*' councillors, judges, mayors, professors, not to mention various more humble posts. There could be no question of giving them a monopoly of employment in their home countries; and seeing that they had only been recently united with France, the emperor may be considered to have given them a fair share. The essential difference between the old and the new départements was that in the latter the inhabitants did not reap nearly as much benefit from the laws of the Revolution. The abolition of feudal rights had not caused much of a sensation in Belgium and the north of Italy, where not many of them existed, it would seem, when the French regime was set up. But it was a different matter in the Rhineland, though the popularity of the measure was compromised for a long time by the claim to make those who owed rent prove their feudal status. The suppression of tithe had a great effect everywhere; yet the peasants only reaped the full benefit if they were owners of the land. Now in Belgium the alienation of the national lands had only begun at the end of the Directory; in the Rhineland and in Piedmont, the religious Orders were not suppressed till 1802 and 1803, and the land was not sold till 1804. By this time the laws of 1793 were no more than a memory, and as in France, the methods operated against the poor and in favour of the middle classes, in spite of the *préfets'* opinion that the surest way of winning over the country people would be to divide the lots before putting them up for sale. 'The people are avid for land,' said one of them in Year XI. Jeanbon prided himself on having carried out this division, so creating ten thousand proprietors. The property-dealers split up their purchases in order to resell them. Nevertheless, it cannot be denied that the operation disappointed the peasants of the annexed countries even more than in France.

It is equally clear that the break with the pope made more impression in these territories than in France, especially in Belgium and the Rhineland, which had never been national states and so were strongly Ultramontane. At Mainz, for example, Bishop Colmar was training a generation of priests for Alsace and Germany who were devoted to Rome. French influence was also cancelled out to a large extent in Piedmont by the memories of its own dynasty, in Genoa by the ruin of the port, and at Geneva by the regrets of the local aristocracy, who could not forgive their loss of power. But in spite of all the reservations that can be made, it remains true that no one in the occupied countries raised a finger against Napoleon's sovereign sway.

# CHAPTER SEVEN

# The Continental System

GREAT AS IT HAD NOW BECOME, the French Empire was only the kernel of the Grand Empire, which had come into being in 1806, and was completed by the vassal states allotted by Napoleon to his relations or servants, or taken under his protection, as was the case for Switzerland and most members of the Rhine Confederation. After the Peace of Tilsit, this Grand Empire became in itself the predominant element in the Continental System, in which still independent states ranged themselves as friends or allies. This system never became as stable as the Grand Empire. At the beginning of 1808 only Sweden was lacking; but it soon began to disintegrate, and from then onwards the history of Napoleon is the story of a perpetual effort to piece it together again. Portugal and Spain were the first to escape from it, the former never rejoining, and the latter being only nominally reintegrated. Austria left it in her turn, only to seek readmission almost immediately. In 1810 Sweden submitted; soon after, Russia broke free and took her neighbour along with her. Besides, these states remained unequal and variable in their dependence. Up to 1808 Spain remained France's benevolent ally; Russia and Denmark were forced by circumstances into apparently willing acceptance of the same position. Without being admitted as equals, Prussia in 1807, Austria in 1808 and again in 1809, Sweden in 1810, were all obliged to join the system, and the first two were transformed into allies by an authoritative edict in 1812. And lastly Turkey, coming in in 1807 and 1808, was never more than a friend.

This European federation, which was in a perpetual state of formation, had as its immediate and avowed aim to fight against England. In this sense, the reverses of the war at sea and the plans for invasion were its logical antecedents; but historically speaking, it was only after the war of 1805 that the idea took shape in the form of the Grand Empire and the blockade, and only at Tilsit that it expanded into the Continental System. Circumstances thus helped in its birth, while being heavily loaded against its realisation, and imposing France as both its manager and its model. All the same, arising themselves from Napoleon's policy, these circumstances only had the effect of multiplying tenfold the impetus behind this policy from the time of Lunéville onwards, the first sign of which was the foundation of the Cisalpine League in 1796. There was no need to have broken the Peace of Amiens; and even if one takes the opposite point of view, there were other possible methods of carrying on the battle against England. Napoleon deliberately assumed the title of emperor; he made constant reference to Charlemagne and the Roman Empire; he chose Rome as his second capital; he refused along with Constantinople to allow Alexander 'the empire of the world': in all these ways Napoleon showed the profound unity given to his work by his energetic temperament and the thirst for power which is its psychological expression, an energy which spontaneously tended to refashion the Western world as a political unity and at the same time to renew its civilisation. This was abundantly proved by his systematic efforts to instil new life into the administrative and social structure of the Continent: there was no positive necessity for the imposition of the Civil Code in order to defeat England. Beneath the flux of events there lay concealed a plan which gradually became conscious – the intention to restore an *orbis Romanus*.

## THE POLITICAL ORGANISATION OF THE SYSTEM

We must not, however, allow ourselves to be misled by this reference to the Roman Empire: the constitution of the Grand Empire was not based upon a historical memory or on any abstract conception. Geographically, it comprised three domains corresponding to the possible directions of French conquest. The Italian domain deserves the first place, by virtue of its seniority, the advances made in concentration of territory and the perfection of its institutions; and within it was included the extension to Illyria and the Ionian Islands. It was grouped round four great centres of unity: French Italy, the kingdom of Italy, the Illyrian provinces and the kingdom of Naples, the first three in the hands of the emperor, the fourth handed over to a protégé. The peninsula provided a base against England, for possible landings in Sicily and threats to Malta, and then for launching an expedition to the East. Meanwhile, it was less important than Northern Italy and Illyria, which would make it possible to take Austria in the rear and break into the plains of Hungary. The same route would lead to Salonica and Constantinople; and on this side economic relationships with the Levant had already been established. The Confederation of the Rhine constituted an even more valuable domain covering the most exposed of the French frontiers, holding Austria and Prussia to ransom, and serving as a parade ground from which to attack the heart of Russia. The possession of Germany closed Central Europe to English trade and opened the chief continental market to the trade of France. The third domain was the Spanish peninsula, mastery over which would have opened up interesting prospects for taking up the struggle again in the Mediterranean and in the Atlantic Ocean, and would have been of even wider scope if it had brought with it the submission of the Spanish and Portuguese colonies; but in actual fact it turned out to be nothing but a very serious burden.

The influence of circumstances is very perceptible too in the organisation of the Grand Empire. It was important for Napoleon to group his territories in huge units, both in order to raise strong auxiliary forces from the conquered lands and to hasten the unification of their social and administrative services. In Italy, this work was reasonably far advanced; in Germany – bearing in mind its fragmentary character – there had also been a tremendous advance in concentration; but as long as Prussia and Austria continued to exist, and Russia was still independent, the loyal princes had to be humoured, and the work of unification remained incomplete.

Moreover, it was necessary to conciliate the peoples who were accustomed to autonomy or who possessed a strong national tradition. As a preparation for the unity of France the Capetian kings, instead of at once uniting newly acquired provinces to their kingdom, had made them into apanages for the benefit of their relatives. In the Girondin idea of surrounding France by a girdle of protected states Napoleon saw an analogous method of compromise; besides, his strong attachment to his own family and his desire to reward faithful servants made it convenient to multiply the number of vassal countries. Hence he first of all envisaged the Grand Empire as a federative system. While remaining sovereign over the kingdom of Italy, he gave it an independent status under his viceroy Prince Eugène. Later on, countries annexed to the French Empire enjoyed an apparent autonomy under governor-generals, Borghese in Piedmont and Liguria, Elisa in Tuscany, Marmont in Illyria, Lebrun in Holland. Outside the Empire, certain territories such as Hanover,

Bayreuth, Fulda and Hanau were for several years under the rule of imperial administrators; and Erfurt never had any other status. An apparently more real sovereignty was enjoyed under a hereditary title by the emperor's brothers and brother-in-law, Joseph, first in Naples and then in Spain; Louis in Holland; Murat in the grand duchy of Berg and then at Naples; and Jérôme in Westphalia; but although they were members of the family and dignitaries of the Empire, they remained subject to the authority of their head. If the pope had been willing, he would have constituted a unique and special category among these vassal princes. Along with them, but on a lower level, were Elisa at Piombino, Bacciochi at Lucca and Berthier at Neuchâtel, all of them hereditary sovereigns, but only able to transmit their heritage subject to a fresh investiture. Next came Talleyrand, prince of Benevento, and Bernadotte, prince of Ponte Corvo, who were invested with a purely administrative authority. And finally, within the sphere of sovereignty, Napoleon left his direct mark by distributing a number of useful fiefs, such as the Italian duchies, and various gifts of land.

Among the federated princes, Napoleon met with the same difficulties and dangers as the Capetian kings had done with the holders of appanages, or the German emperors in the Middle Ages with the ducal dynasties. To start with, he was under an illusion about their talents, and imagined they would be as active and able in administration as himself. In practice, they proved very mediocre; and he would have been still more disillusioned if he had not shouldered part of the work himself – in Westphalia, for example – or provided them with able administrators, as he did at Naples. He at least had a right to hope they would remain his loyal lieutenants. 'Never give up being French,' was his advice to Louis. 'Remember,' he said to Murat, 'I've only made you king to further my system'; and Berthier passed this on to the king of Naples in equally expressive terms: 'Do as king what you did as a soldier.' And to Caroline he wrote: 'Above all, my wish is that people should do what suits France; for I have only conquered kingdoms in order that France should reap the benefits.' It was not for his protégés to reason why – and some of them were well aware of this. Prince Eugène always remained loyal: so did Elisa, who was not without ambition, but was fairly talented, and in whom Napoleon – rather grudgingly – saw something of himself. Jérôme, too, did his best, though, truth to tell, this was nothing very great. On the other hand, some of them proved refractory. True, they had no easy task:

they had to remodel institutions, create an army, apply the blockade and find money at a time when Napoleon burdened their budgets with various gifts and war contributions, and reserved for himself a part of their domains. In his attitude to them, Napoleon proved touchy and impossible. 'If you were to ask his majesty for orders or advice in altering the ceiling of your room,' said Duroc to Eugène, 'you would have to wait till they arrived; and if Milan were on fire and you asked for the wherewithal to put the fire out, you would have to let Milan go up in flames and await his orders.' And it was not advisable to go ahead without asking for orders. To his stepson he wrote: 'On no pretext whatsoever, even if the moon threatened to fall on Milan, are you to do anything that falls outside your authority.'

Nevertheless, the root of the trouble went deeper. As nearly always happens in such cases, the emperor's puppet rulers considered themselves the owners of their fiefs and founders of independent dynasties. 'I have not been made a king in order to obey!' exclaimed Murat. They instinctively tried to take on their subjects' nationality in order to get their support against France. 'If they want me to govern Spain for the sole benefit of France,' said Joseph, 'well – they needn't expect me to oblige!' They showed the naïve and comic vanity of the parvenu, surrounding themselves with favourites, living in exaggerated luxury, creating court duties and marshals, and instituting decorations. Furthermore, they shared their mother's uncertainty about Napoleon's future, and attributed his success to chance. They did not intend to be dragged down in his fall, and so tried to make themselves popular. Caroline noted this fact when she wrote to her husband with an unconscious frankness:

> The whole of Europe is bowed down beneath the yoke of France. What is your aim? It is to contrive to stay where we are and keep our kingdoms. We are therefore bound to do what he [Napoleon] wants and not cross him when he makes a request, for he is stronger, and you can do nothing against him. And if in the end you are reduced to leaving the kingdom, let it only be when you cannot hold out any longer, and your children will then have nothing to reproach you with.

That was also Talleyrand's outlook: and it was to lead Murat to commit treason. In the end, his family's rivalries were equally upsetting to the emperor. His sisters had lovers, and Pauline's escapades in particular were notorious. Louis and Hortense were an ill-assorted couple, he quite incurable and suffering from megalomania even more than his brothers, and with persecution on the brain; she, orthodox and steeped in improving advice, yet laying herself open to suspicion. They had separated after the birth of their second son, and only came together again for a short while in 1807. The future Napoleon III was born at Paris in 1808, but Louis never believed himself the father of his youngest son, nor of the one before him. In 1811 Hortense gave birth secretly to a child, the son of the comte de Flahaut, and the future duc de Morny. Napoleon sided with his stepdaughter rather than his brother. When in 1809 he handed over the duchy of Berg to their son Charles, he took guardianship of the child himself, and then immediately handed it over to Hortense. There were also strained relations between Murat and Caroline. The treaty that had given them Naples offended Murat, for the present was in fact meant for Caroline. She was to survive her husband and wear the crown to the detriment of her eldest son, though she lived quite apart from public life and in semi-seclusion. As for Lucien, he ended by embarking for the United States on 7 August 1810, but was captured and taken to England. Napoleon's mother took the part of her other children against Napoleon. He waited till she disavowed Jérôme's first marriage and then gave her an official title, with the style 'Son Altesse Impériale, Madame, mère de l'empereur'; but she was not satisfied and clamoured in vain for a dowry and 'some political status'.

Thus from 1806 to 1810 we see the emperor growing more and more annoyed with his vassals and threatening to annex their states. In this way the evolution of the federated Empire, destined for final unity by the introduction of Napoleonic institutions, was given more rapid development. The Austrian marriage, the desire to increase the heritage of the king of Rome and the prospect of having to find places for the future younger sons of the family, made the Bonapartes' position more and more precarious, though they had known long before that it was already compromised. The annexation of Holland is almost contemporary with the marriage. It seemed to be imminent as early as 1809; but early in 1810 Louis delayed it by ceding Zeeland and the southern provinces as far as the Rhine, and on 2 July 1810 he fled and succeeded in reaching Austria. In April Murat in Paris was equally certain that his cause was lost; but Caroline, having accepted the position of chaperone to Marie-Louise, patched up a reconciliation which only lasted for a very brief space. The emperor forbade the king to appoint ambassadors. Murat was surrounding himself with suspect Italians, such as Gallo and Maghella, whom he appointed minister of police. This man was in touch with the secret anti-French societies, and may have been one of the first to conceive the idea of a united Italy under his master's rule. Caroline was once again sent into retirement and threatened with divorce. Murat took various customs measures against France, dismissed several high French officials, and finally made those who continued to live there take an oath of loyalty. Then matters came to a head. On 2 July 1811 Napoleon forbade his subjects to take the oath, and a rumour went round that he was going to annex the kingdom of Naples. But tempers were cooled by the threat from Russia. Murat was present at the baptism and left for Russia with the Grande Armée. But no one believed that matters would rest there. At the same moment, Jérôme saw a part of Hanover taken away from him and was afraid it would be made over to Poland; and Joseph complained that he was no more than a nominal king. And finally, since Murat's departure for Naples, the grand duchy of Berg had been administered by the emperor.

In contradistinction to the vassal states, the protected federations, which were linked to the Empire by a permanent alliance, continued to exist as before. There was no reason for Napoleon to alter the Act of Mediation which he had drawn up. Switzerland, now encircled by territories subject to Napoleon, was no longer of any immediate strategic importance; and there was no need to occupy it in order to reduce it to obedience. Swiss neutrality was only violated by the use of the bridge at Basle in 1809 and by the occupation of the Ticino. On the other hand, the Confederation of the Rhine demanded reorganisation, for its territory still remained too fragmentary. There was no equality even in the legal status of its members. The grand duke of Berg and the king of Westphalia were vassal princes, while the grand duke of Frankfurt, a puppet of Napoleon's, did not belong either to the family of the French Empire or to its great dignitaries, as long as Eugène did not take the place of Dalberg. The existence of the grand duchy of Würzburg was guaranteed by the treaty of 1809 with Austria, which secretly considered itself invested with the right of being next in succession that it had possessed over Ferdinand's former domains, Tuscany and Salzburg. The other sovereigns' rights were based upon legitimacy, although the most important of them held their new titles under agreements signed with the emperor. But above all the Confederation still had no constitution, and was without a central authority able to push on with unification in administrative affairs, in the Church, in social life and even in military matters.

In its further extensions, the Continental System was completed by alliances that depended upon the ups and downs of policy, alliances that future efforts would have to convert into permanent bonds. For Prussia and Austria, resistance was impossible; and Prussia was in fact reduced to vassal status by the treaty of 1812. Only Alexander, firmly persuaded that he had negotiated as one equal with another, although he had been conquered, figured as a genuine ally. He was resolved to consult nothing but his own interests and to exact payment for his support, whenever this was required, by demanding appropriate gratuities. This perpetual blackmail was a strong inducement to undertake the campaign against Russia. As long as Alexander remained independent, the political constitution of the Continental System would remain incomplete. Once this last obstacle had been removed, Russia could be absorbed into the Grand Empire; and with allies transformed into vassals, the Grand Empire itself would in time have been absorbed into the French Empire.

Up till 1811 French supremacy was only represented legally by the status of the vassal princes. Murat's resistance led Napoleon to define the position of Frenchmen in their service. While forbidding his subjects to take an oath of allegiance to his brother-in-law, he decreed that they were legally citizens of the kingdom of Naples. This decision was all the more remarkable in that he had done his utmost to break the links which allowed the great families under the *ancien régime* not to take on a particular nationality, holding possessions as they did here and there across the frontiers, as vassals of several sovereigns and serving whom they pleased, and forming a small cosmopolitan society outside the national states. The law of 21 Floréal, Year XIII (11 May 1805), confiscated the possessions of the imperial princes in France and only restored those of the other German lords subject to alienation unless their owners opted for French sovereignty. In the vassal countries – Westphalia, for instance – he forbade the subjects of the new princes to remain in foreign service. Schulenburg could only keep his lands by leaving the king of Prussia's service; and the other members of the Confederation of the Rhine had been invited to recall those of their dependants who had made their careers in Austria. The principle laid down for the kingdom of Naples was therefore a privilege for the French, for without losing their French nationality they were to become citizens of the states in the Grand Empire to which they might happen to be sent. If this system had lasted, it might have been the beginning of something like Roman citizenship. This would have worked all the more conveniently in that the Grand Empire was not simply a political unity, for Napoleon's intention was to give it the same institutions and social structure as those of imperial France.

## THE NAPOLEONIC REFORMS

In implanting his system of government, the first idea in the emperor's mind was to give a certain sacrosanctity to his power, for it was important that he, his vassals and his allies should all hold undisputed sovereignty. Any intermediate bodies, privileges or feudal rights must therefore be swept away, so that all men should become directly subject to the state. It was also advisable for the laws of succession to reduce the size of the great fortunes, so making the aristocracy subordinate to the sovereign, and the priests his officials. Another primary obligation fell upon all the members of the Grand Empire, namely to provide money and men. The *ancien régime*, with its slow and chaotic administration, could not mobilise the country's resources quickly enough: a clean break had to be made, and the Napoleonic bureaucracy put in its place. In this respect the emperor was even urged on to further conquests by the desire to prove the superiority of the methods which an ally like Charles IV seemed unable to appreciate.

These preoccupations did not prevent him from seeing that a renewal of the administration and of society would give him a chance to conciliate the peasants and the middle classes. He wrote to Jérôme:

> What the peoples of Germany long for is that those who are not nobles and have some abilities should have an equal right to your consideration, and to employment. This means that all kinds of servitude, and all intermediate links between the sovereign and the lowest classes, should be entirely abolished . . . To be quite frank with you, I place more reliance on their efforts for extending and strengthening this monarchy than on the results of the greatest victories in the field.

Civil equality, religious liberty, the abolition of tithe and feudal rights, the sale of Church property, the suppression of the corporations, the increase in officials, 'wise and liberal' administration, a constitution carrying the right to vote taxes and make laws on the part of the people who really counted – all those were intended to weave a network of interests closely bound up with maintaining French ascendancy; and the control of public opinion, as in the French Empire, would see to the rest. The Civil Code embodied the essentials of this policy, and that is why the emperor made such vigorous efforts to introduce it everywhere. As early as 1807 he wanted to impose it on the Hanseatic towns, on Danzig, on his German protégés and of course on Holland and Westphalia. In 1808 he was thinking of applying it to Portugal, and in 1809 to Spain.

A realist attitude could not justify the jealous passion with which he set about its propagation, for he made this an all-out effort. The cast of mind which he inherited from the eighteenth century gave him a sincere aversion to feudalism, intolerance and the chaotic hand-to-mouth methods of the old administrations. He resumed the work of the benevolent despots, and although his task was made considerably easier by the tradition they had left behind, he surpassed them all in speed and boldness. On the other hand, his authoritarian spirit invested his work with a kind of perfection: 'If you retouch the *Code Napoléon*,' he said to Louis, 'it will no longer be the *Code Napoléon*.' And to Murat, who wanted to cut out divorce: 'I would rather have Naples in the hands of the ex-king of Sicily than emasculate the *Code Napoléon* in this fashion.' In the same way, the system became invested with an eternal and universal value; he saw it as the framework for a European civilisation which would consolidate the Continent's political unity and be in harmony with it. The idea that the peoples might protest struck his mind as absurd: in the first place, what was good enough for the French must be suitable for everyone, for – as he wrote to Eugène – 'There is very little difference between one people and another.' In any case, if particular differences existed, they must be removed. When he reproached Louis for his behaviour, on 20 May 1810, and remarked that if only he had been loyal it would have meant adding north-western Germany and Hamburg to his Dutch kingdom, Napoleon added: 'This would have formed a nucleus of peoples to banish the German spirit, which is the foremost aim of my policy.' In the end, any objection was seen as rebellion against his despotic power. 'I think it is ridiculous for you to tell me that the people of Westphalia do not agree,' he informed Jérôme. 'If you listen to what the people think, you won't do anything at all. If the people refuse what makes for their own welfare they are guilty of anarchism, and the first duty of the prince is to punish them.' The expansion of French institutions was one of the expressions of his love of power.

But the supreme goal of his endeavours never made him lose sight of the need for taking circumstances into account. His mania for assimilation and unity has been much criticised; yet this is what he wrote in the margin of a letter dated 9 September 1807:

> What interest can France have in her forms of administration being adopted in Holland? What is there in common between French interests and the imposition of a unified system in Holland and a hundred and one other things connected with the various views that may be held about the administration of the country?

In the vassal and allied states he did in fact put up with more than one alteration to his plans, and even more than one pruning of his codes; but in the countries where he was completely master – particularly in the kingdom of Italy – his system reached a perfection even greater than in the French Empire. On the other hand continual warfare, the need for dealing tactfully with sovereign allies, the constant changes of frontier, the fragmentation which was allowed to continue in Italy and Germany, all these worked against the complete spread of his system, which remained very unequally applied. For example, the grand duchy of Berg, although governed by the emperor after Murat's departure, was less thoroughly transformed than Jérôme's kingdom. When one considers how short was the period of Napoleon's ascendancy, the results achieved were really tremendous; but they nevertheless remained uneven.

But there were even worse hindrances from a social point of view, for opportunism was often in conflict with the 'system'. Being in need of money and wishing to provide for the foreign territories, Napoleon saw in the property of the dispossessed monarchs, émigrés and clergy a ready source of help. Now tithes and feudal dues formed a substantial part of this wealth: should they be given up? Then he needed a government and administrative staff to raise taxes and conscripts; and for this he had to fall back not only on the middle classes but on the aristocracy, because outside France the former were insufficient. Moreover, how was he to draw upon the kings' courts without the help of the nobility? Once this was admitted, the agrarian reforms could not take the radical shape that would have been needed to win over the peasants to the Revolution, as they had in France. Besides, Napoleon was everywhere getting rid of the Jacobins who would have warmly approved of this course; in France, he was courting the old nobility and looking for a dynastic alliance; there the Revolution was an accomplished fact for which he could decline responsibility; but in the Grand Empire, the responsibility was his, and this contradiction crept into the very heart of the system. In the end, the peasants were sacrificed: the personal dues and sometimes even the tithes were declared redeemable, and this constituted a stumbling-block both for French influence and for the Napoleonic reforms.

But it is not enough to analyse the components of Napoleon's European work and direct attention to his imaginative picture of a unified Europe. More than this is needed in order to set the part he played in historical perspective, for the Continental System was never fully formed, and however inspired it may appear as a human dream, it proved to have no lasting legacy in the long run.

On the other hand the creative side of his work comes out in what he managed to infuse of the spirit of the Revolution into his conquered territories. At the head of the Grande Armée for which the Revolution had prepared the way, Napoleon destroyed the *ancien régime* which the popular uprising of 1789 had uprooted in France, replacing it by an organisation which the middle classes helped him to work out more fully under the Consulate. Seeing that some at least of his principles – such as equality before the law and a secular state – agreed with those of the Freemasons, it is not surprising that everywhere in the lodges a large number of its members made common cause with the upholders of the French regime, to such an extent that several of his opponents spoke with horror of his Masonic Empire.

To remain a soldier of the Revolution was inconsistent with the plan of reviving a legitimate dynasty and a hierarchical corporative society. But his intellectual make-up, his career and the needs of his policy of conquest would not allow him to escape from the clutches of an evolution that was working towards the downfall of the aristocracy and the rise of the middle classes. Whatever he might say, his genius hastened on its course. One of the permanent features of his work was that wherever his arms were triumphant, his progress was marked as it were by the emancipating forces like a night of 4 August.*

* [In 1789, when the National Assembly abolished feudal privileges.]

### THE MEDITERRANEAN COUNTRIES: ITALY, THE ILLYRIAN PROVINCES AND CATALONIA

Italy was the country where the system left its deepest mark, which is not surprising, seeing that the intervention of the revolutionaries and Bonaparte himself had opened the way. Piedmont, Liguria and Parma were entirely assimilated to France by annexation. The kingdom of Italy was increased by the addition of Venetia and Guastalla in the Marches in 1808, and the Trentino in 1810. He could use it as a field for experiment, not having to take account – as in France – of the traditions of monarchy and the memories of the Revolution. He paid no attention to the constitutional statute of 1805. When the Corps Législatif took upon itself to discuss and even reject certain of his plans, he wrote to Eugène: 'I shall not convene it any more,' and proceeded to legislate by decree. He continued methodically with centralisation. As from 1806 justice was organised on the French model. Public works and education, hitherto left to the local authorities, were now taken over by the state; so was the Public Health Department, and then in 1807 public assistance.

Having extended his powers, Napoleon proceeded to increase the number of officials. In 1805 he had created a general superintendent of police; the Bridges and Highways Department was set up in 1806; the magistrates in charge of dykes and canals were put under the authority of the *préfecture* councils. Central and departmental councils were established for public health, a superintendent and departmental committees for assistance, and a managing body for education under the Ministry of the Interior. *Lycées* were opened, and at Milan a girls' college, which had no equivalent in France; a school for the Highways Department, a veterinary school, a music conservatoire and three academies for the fine arts; and the theatres were put under the control of a general director. In 1806 one of the Caffarelli brothers replaced Pino at the head of the army, which steadily improved and added to its effective strength. Prima, the minister for finance, met his growing commitments by a special war tax, imposed in 1806 and then continued as a personal tax, by extending indirect taxation, and by introducing registration. He was a remarkable administrator, both assiduous and inventive; but his zeal aroused formidable hatred, and he lost his life in a riot in 1814. The kingdom was systematically encircled by a ring of customs barriers and put closely under the control of the French economy by the opening of the Alpine roads; but it reaped certain advantages from some other public works.

The statute of 1805 envisaged the introduction of the Civil Code on 1 January 1806, but it had first to be translated and printed; and in spite of work at high pressure, the date for the adoption of the code in civil procedure had to be postponed till 1 April. The creation of facilities for mortgages and the organisation of civil status then followed in due course. This was in fact no more than a crowning of the work of the Republic, which had abolished privilege and the feudal system. The effort of the code was nonetheless sensational because it set up civil status, introduced divorce and made revolutionary changes in the customary habits of succession. Nor were the clergy at all pleased with the reforms that had followed the Concordat. On 8 June 1805 the parishes had been reduced in number, the establishments of the seminaries strictly limited and the convents suppressed, except for a few in which they grouped those religious who wished to continue a monastic life; and in 1807 the brotherhoods were also dissolved. Yet the secular clergy were more favourably treated than in the Empire, for the bishoprics were given an endowment in land or state funds, and so were the chapters and seminaries; and the clergy's property had not been nationalised. Moreover, by the terms of the Concordat the priests came under the authority of Napoleon, and on the whole they showed themselves compliant. The imperial catechism was imposed on them in 1807, and the pulpit used to preach submission to the payment of taxes and to conscription. It proved much more difficult to win over the landed aristocracy, though the emperor saw this as an essential. A few nobles succumbed to the allurements of Eugène's luxurious court, or accepted sinecures and gifts because they were in need; but the majority boycotted all public office, and their sons could not be attracted into either the *lycées* or the armed forces. Only the middle classes – including the officials who came from them – showed a certain attachment to the regime. The 'Royal Italian Freemasons', which was organised on uniform lines by the Grand Orient of Milan, played an important part in bringing all Napoleon's supporters together under the leadership of its high officials. As in France, Napoleon made the maximum use of decorations, giving the kingdom its own particular award – the Ordre de la Couronne de Fer. But he attached supreme importance to the guards of honour which became one of the most characteristic institutions of the country, though he had hesitated to organise them in the Empire.

He needed officers, and was intent upon choosing them from among the aristocracy and the middle classes, to some extent as hostages, but still more because he considered the army to be a school for developing the civic and dynastic feeling that had so far been completely unknown among Italians. The coronation gave an opportunity for mounting some guards of honour; then on 20 June 1805 a decree ordered the formation of four companies of cavalry mounted for service at the palace. They were to be recruited on a voluntary basis from the midst of the families whose heads figured among the electoral colleges or the most heavily taxed citizens. As the right of finding a substitute was suspended in those départements that had not furnished contingents for guards of honour, the voluntary basis was purely nominal. The relatives had to pay a sum of twelve hundred *lire*, and the young man could become a lieutenant at the end of two years. For the lower middle classes, a dozen companies of light-armed troops were formed, who paid only two hundred *lire* and provided the non-commissioned officers. But recruitment for the guards proved not at all easy: although the obligation had been imposed in 1810, by 1811 there were only 367 of the required 551. They saw service for the first time in Russia. The light-armed troops were easier to find. Though Napoleon's expectations were not completely realised, he cannot be said to have completely failed. The influence of conscription could not but penetrate down to the people, although they had the least to congratulate themselves upon in the imperial regime. Neither the abolition of feudalism nor the sale of the national lands seems to have changed the condition of the peasants, at any rate in the plains, which continued to be a land of large properties cultivated by smallholders and day labourers in wretched conditions. For the small proprietors, the weight of taxation must have made up for the disappearance of the tithe and the dues which the Republic had admittedly abolished without compensation. A comparison between the land registers of fifteen communes in the plains of Bologna drawn up respectively in 1789, 1804 and 1835, shows that the property belonging to the nobles had been reduced from eighty to sixty-seven per cent, and then to fifty-one per cent, while the property in bourgeois possession rose between these same dates from seventeen to thirty per cent, and then to forty-eight per cent. The figures show, however, that the large landed estates had held their ground; they still accounted for 72.01 per cent of the total area in 1835, as compared with 72.77 per cent in 1789.

At the other end of Italy, the French impress on the kingdom of Naples was also very marked. Reforms began as soon as Joseph came to the throne, and were carried out by a group of Frenchmen and Italians whom he had selected – Saliceti, Miot, Dumas, the son of Roederer and the lawyer Ricciardi. They first reorganised the ministries, creating two new ones, a Ministry of the Interior and a Secretary of State; then there was the Conseil d'État and the Sommaria, or Court of Accounts. The provinces continued as such, but were divided into districts, while the parishes were grouped into municipal administrative bodies, on the pattern of the municipalities in the French constitution of Year III. The *préfet* and *sous-préfet* crop up again, but under different names, being now styled *intendant* and *sous-intendant*, and the *Conseil de Préfecture* the *Conseil d'Intendance*. The province and the district both had their councils, and the communal group came under a *décurionat*. But no electoral colleges were set up: the king nominated the *décurions* put forward by the *sous-intendants* and chose the members of councils from among the candidates proposed by the *décurions*. The lawcourts and police were remodelled on the French pattern, and no time was lost in setting up an armed police force. The minister of finance was faced with a particularly tough task. He replaced the countless taxes of the *ancien régime* by a land tax and a tax on industry. Privileges were all abolished. The state resumed control of indirect taxation, which had been farmed out. Steps were taken to liquidate the debt by means of IOUs or *cédules* recorded in the Great Book of the Public Debt; and as these changed hands at a loss, they were quickly extinguished by redemption at the market price. By 1808 the debt had been reduced from one hundred million ducats to fifty-nine million. An important part of the revenue came from the royal domain, which took over the funds of the Jesuits, vacant bishoprics and a good many convents that had been closed. This summary can give only a faint idea of the enormous task of unifying, simplifying and cleaning up the administration undertaken throughout the country by the new order. The suppression of sinecures and corruption, the separation of justice from administration, the creation of public accountancy, the formation of a disciplined body of officials with a respect for the law – all these were much more of a novelty than in Piedmont or Lombardy.

The abolition of the feudal system – here much more oppressive than in Northern Italy – was decreed as from 2 August 1806. The barons kept their titles and their own land; but they lost their right to administer justice, and became subject to the common law, both for their lands and in their personal status. The question of feudal rights and dues was settled according to the principles laid down by the Constituent Assembly. Personal rights, the money payments that represented them, and the seigneurial rights were simply suppressed; property rights were declared redeemable; and a feudal commission including Cuoco among its members was appointed to carry out the law. Furthermore, agricultural reforms were set in train by a decree of 1807. In this region, *maquis* and wasteland turned over to common use and seasonal pasture, covered enormous tracts; and it was decided to divide them up among the communities in proportion to their respective populations. Moreover, it was agreed to split up the cultivable common lands among the inhabitants, giving preference to those who had occupied some part of them, provided they had cultivated and enclosed them, on condition that they paid a reasonable rent. The state itself undertook to tax the Apulian Plain, which had been farmed out each year up till then; and the same was done with the property of religious foundations.

Just as Joseph was about to hand over his kingdom to Murat, Napoleon made an arrangement intended to tie the hands of his successor. Joseph, acting on his orders, promulgated at Bayonne on 20 June 1808 a constitutional statute modelled on the kingdom of Italy, but reducing the part played by election and allowing the clergy and the nobility a special representation – a sign that the emperor's political ideas had undergone some development. The parliament was composed of a hundred members, divided into five benches, the first two – clergy and nobles – being the king's choice. Colleges – likewise set up by him – elected representatives for the owners of property; while the king chose representatives for the businessmen and *dotti* from among the list of candidates put forward by the colleges or bodies of officials. Only Neapolitans were eligible for public employment. Two days later, it was announced that the Civil Code would be introduced the following year.

Although Joseph's work had been by no means negligible, it remained incomplete, and to a large extent nominal; above all, he had hardly begun to organise the army. Murat's reign was accordingly a time of great progress. His minister of finance, Agar, count of Mosbourg, continued Roederer's work. He finished reforming the tax on land, introduced a licence system, set up machinery for collecting indirect taxation and for the waterways and forests department, founded a royal bank, completed the liquidation of the debt either by entries in the Great Book of the Public Debt or by giving national land in its stead, and converted the interest on it from five to three per cent. On the appointed day the Civil Code came into force, but with some important modifications. It was followed by the codes for civil and commercial procedure and the penal codes, as well as the code governing mortgages, registration of births, marriages and deaths, the official body of notaries and the order of barristers.

In 1809 Murat also confirmed the decisions of his feudal commission and gave some attention to economic life. Corporations and internal customs were abolished, a body set up for bridges and highways, and public works undertaken with considerable vigour. If it had rested with him, the kingdom would have put up barriers against French imports; and he was very half-hearted in applying the blockade. All the same, his efforts were mainly directed towards the army, the creation of which was really his work.

In the kingdom of Naples, the ground had not been prepared by the Revolution, and the whole transformation took place in a bare seven years; nevertheless, it was a solid piece of work. When he returned to power, King Ferdinand did not re-establish the feudal system, nor did he abrogate the Civil Code. The middle classes and the few liberal nobles who had welcomed the French in 1799 showed that their feelings had not changed, and formed themselves into lodges, as in Northern Italy. Murat, with his liking for sensation and display, exercised a certain fascination, and roused some sympathy by taking such an independent line with France. But in spite of reviving entails, he did not succeed in conciliating the majority of the nobles or the clergy, for he failed to make a new Concordat and to reorganise the hierarchy of the Church. The people, for their part, were too poor to redeem the dues, and the crown lands passed into the hands of companies, or the nobility, or rich middle-class citizens. The legal arrangements for sharing out the common lands took some time to complete, and had hardly got under way before Murat's fall. The hill people who lived by grazing were very little concerned with these reforms. The only attention General Manhes showed them was to subject them to merciless oppression; besides, the coastlands were continually under threat from the English. The kingdom of Naples, moreover, was not administered – like the kingdom of Italy – by civilians, and according to the ordinary laws of the land; it was kept in a continual state of siege, and was governed on a military basis.

In central Italy, Napoleon's influence was slower in making itself felt. In her principality, at Lucca, Massa and Carrara, Elisa suppressed the feudal system, adopted the Italian concordat, closed the convents and confiscated their property, opened schools and undertook public works. When made responsible for the government of Tuscany, which had been annexed to the French Empire, she was obliged to introduce French institutions, the management of which fell to a junta that included Gérando and Count Balbo, a Piedmontese who was destined to become famous. The two main operations were the suppression of the convents and the liquidation of the ducal debt. In spite of inevitable upsets, this modernisation of the government did not meet with resistance in a country where enlightened despotism had had some of its more advanced representatives.

But the course of things was very different in the part of the Papal States that had been taken over. Here, the *ancien régime* was without doubt at its most backward, and it was completely transformed by an Extraordinary State Council, which was appointed on 9 June 1809 and sat till the close of 1810. Among its members Gérando and Balbo once more took part, along with Miollis. The territory was put under two départements, with Roederer's son and, at Rome, the comte de Tournon – formerly *intendant* at Bayreuth – as *préfets*. The management of the police was taken over by Norvins. Feudalism and the Inquisition both disappeared; and in 1810 the chapters were dissolved and the convents closed. The Civil Code had been promulgated as early as 1809; but the institutions that were indispensable for implementing it – in particular the *état civil* – never came into being. Nevertheless, the religious liberty proclaimed by it caused a sensation. The Jews left their ghettos, and the imperial staff, as they had done everywhere else, formed themselves into masonic lodges. The finances received particular attention from the administration. They introduced the French system of taxation, except for the combined duties, instead of which they kept the tax on milling; they unified the debt at two per cent by repaying the capital at the rate of five times the interest by means of a new issue payable in secularised property. The creditors lost – in theory, at any rate – up to or more than three-quarters of the capital value. The *préfets* proved extremely active. Tournon reorganised the hospitals and prisons, took an interest in culture and set up cotton manufacturing under the management of the Alsatian Bocher. Napoleon also had great ideas for his second capital. He repaired its buildings, tidied up and lit its streets, and made plans for building quays, bridges, roads and imperial residences. A commission for ancient monuments carried out excavations, and Canova was put in charge of a museum; and finally the Pontine Marshes were tackled, a quarter of the area being put back into cultivation. But nowhere did the new regime meet with such great hostility. The people were used to indolent officials, begging and brigandage; discipline, regular taxation, public accountancy and regularity, and more particularly conscription, were altogether against the grain, and there was not enough time to overcome the opposition. In the towns – and especially in Rome – the middle classes lived largely on the clergy and pilgrims; for them the departure of the pope and his court, and the suppression of 519 convents with their 5,852 monks and nuns, were an irreparable disaster. In addition, thousands of inefficient and useless officials had been dismissed. The chief form assumed by the opposition was a refusal to take the oath. It was led by the clergy and followed by many officials and nearly all the lawyers. The emperor replied by dismissals, removal of pensions, imprisonment and exile. It was the nobles who proved to be the most compliant.

In spite of these reservations, the application of the system in Italy made rapid strides, and only a few more years would have been needed to achieve full administrative and juridical unity. But conditions were infinitely less favourable in the Illyrian provinces. Geographically, they were cut up into isolated units; the country was everywhere mountainous and poverty-stricken, and the inhabitants differed from one another in language, religion and cultural level. They were in bondage to officials of the *ancien régime*, the nobility and the clergy, and there was no real middle class, apart from a few strongly Italian coastal towns. From 1806 to 1809 Napoleon only had possession of the former Venetian territory, that is to say, Dalmatia and a part of Istria and the islands, to which was added in 1808 the republic of Ragusa, though it was allowed a degree of autonomy. Marmont held the military command, while the administrative power was in the hands of Dandolo, who had the title of *provéditeur*. He was a rich pharmacist of Jewish extraction who had taken up new ideas in the Venetian states. Although a man of integrity and a hard worker, he was dictatorial and touchy, and did not get on well with the commander of the occupying forces. There was never any question of setting up an electoral system in Illyria; and the result was an enlightened despotism, with the added incubus of military interference. Dandolo gave himself the help of a general council with a membership of his own choice. In actual fact, he made all the decisions in his office at Zara [Zadar]. Having first divided the territory into four départements, subdivided into districts and rural communities, he appointed the various delegates, vice-delegates and *anziani*. He organised the lawcourts and set up a police force by using the *pandours* [local militia] whom the peasants already provided for the Austrian and Venetian administrators. The old taxes remained in force, attention being directed principally to the management of public funds and the administration of the state lands.

The chief reforms were aimed at the clergy. In order to reduce the number of bishoprics, vacancies were not filled; some of the convents and all the brotherhoods were suppressed; and apart from the existing bishops' revenues, all Church property was sequestrated, part of the income being used to provide rather better stipends for the parish priests and the seminaries. In 1807 Dandolo also issued regulations for public education, instituted a *lycée* at Zara and set up some colleges. The work on the roads was undertaken by Marmont. Conscription had to be suspended because of the disturbances it caused, and the authorities had to rest content with partial and more or less voluntary levies. As to the Civil Code, it was considered enough to introduce the sections dealing with the family and succession, which allowed women to inherit and abolished entails and trusts. Nothing was done, it seems, to curtail the rights of the great lords who held sway over a tenant population – in the Poglizza region for example, near Salona [Solin] – but ecclesiastical tithe was abolished. In the interior of Dalmatia, the agrarian problem came up in an unusual form. In 1756 the Grimani law had reserved to the Venetian state all ownership of the land; but the inhabitants – the Morlachs – were given two-thirds of a hectare a head (women being excluded), with the right to farm out their plots and leave them to their male heirs, but without the right of alienation. The beneficiary owed military service and paid tithe to the government. Dandolo repealed this law and conferred possession on the tenant, keeping the state tithe as a land tax. In 1807, realising that speculators were persuading the peasants to sell their holdings, he imposed certain formalities which made alienation almost impossible. In spite of everything, this was one of the most solid land reforms in any of the countries held by Napoleon.

Up till 1809, then, this French possession enjoyed autonomy, and assimilation to France was only carried out with substantial reservations. But after that date there was a radical change in the situation. Carniola, Upper Carinthia, Austrian Istria and Trieste and a good part of Croatia were added to the Venetian lands and the whole was then given the title of the Illyrian Provinces, borrowed from the Roman Empire. Separate treatment was given to that part of military Croatia which fell to Napoleon, preserving its social organisation in *zadrugas* and its state economy under the military authority, keeping it outside the imperial customs system, and letting it still provide a contingent along traditional lines. On 25 December 1809 the rest of Illyria was given a provisional organisation consisting of ten *intendances*, with Laibach as capital; and soon after this Dandolo gave up his position. It was not till 15 April 1811 that the regime assumed its final shape. Power was delegated to a governor – Marmont first of all, then Bertrand and in 1813 Junot, who was succeeded by Fouché. The governor proposed and the emperor nominated the high officials who formed his council, in particular the general supervisor of finance and the general commissioner for justice. Six provinces were created, each under an *intendant* and their delegated officials. From now onwards, Napoleon worked ceaselessly to unify the government and the legislation. The whole Civil Code and all the French laws came into force as from 1 January 1812; lawcourts were organised, along with registration, mortgages and an official body of notaries, but not complete civil status, although civil marriages had become the rule. From 1810 to 1813 the French taxes were introduced, except for the tax on doors and windows. The liquidation of the debt was continued with the help of the nationalised lands; and in 1812 the liquidation of pensions was completed. Conscription too had come into force on 27 November 1810. The bridges and highways department, set up in the same year, used forced labour to push ahead with the road from Karlovac to Fiume and the Route Napoléon from Laibach to Ragusa.

The ecclesiastical tithes had been generally abolished, and on 15 April 1811 the feudal system had been brought to an end. With the disappearance of the nobles' special status and the fief went all the personal seigneurial rights; forced labour and land dues were made redeemable, the latter being reduced by a fifth to compensate for the land tax which fell upon those who were liable for it. This decree was widely welcomed, and the peasants at last began to show some interest in French rule, if only to press for complete freedom. They took the lead and refused to redeem their obligations, till in 1812 Bertrand called upon them to submit and send down bailiffs. Discontent had also been caused by depriving them of their customary rights in the forests. The nobles, likewise irritated by these policies, had continued to emigrate to Austria. The lower clergy, who were used to the regime of Joseph, remained neutral; but the Franciscans, who had formerly been the masters of the country, raised a furious agitation. Unfortunately, it did not prove possible to revive the export and transit trade which provided the country with vital resources and formed the sole livelihood of Trieste, with the result that the middle classes suffered greatly, on top of their previous trials connected with the elimination of Austrian paper money and the liquidation of the debt on disadvantageous terms. The regime thus only succeeded in conciliating a small minority, and its departure was not regretted. No one believed, moreover, that it would last for long; and in fact the 1812 treaty of alliance promised to cede the Illyrian provinces to Austria in return for the relinquishment of Galicia.

In Spain, war conditions did not make it possible to apply the Bayonne constitution to the full, nor to carry out effectively the reforms planned by Napoleon during his residence there in 1808. The only exception was Catalonia. In December 1811 the military government under Macdonald gave way to a civil administration, though this was still subordinate to General Decaen. A decree divided the province into four départements, and in view of Napoleon's decision to annex it, assimilation with France went steadily ahead. This period did not last much more than a year, for Suchet was obliged to recross the Ebro in June 1813, which brought the country back to military occupation. Besides, the changes only affected the part effectively occupied by the French, who could only find a small number of *afrancesados* to help them, who did not show much enthusiasm for the new measures. These did not run to extremes: the Church's property was not sold, and the clauses in the Civil Code dealing with divorce and the prohibition of trusts were removed.


## HOLLAND AND GERMANY

Holland differed from Italy in possessing a strong national tradition. The upper middle classes had long held the reins of power, so that privilege and seigneurial rights had considerably diminished. The Batavian Republic had already achieved unity. Napoleon remodelled the central government by the constitutions of 1801, 1805 and 1806, and Louis carried out certain complementary reforms. Up to 1810 this was as far as the emperor had gone. As in Switzerland, he made no attempt to destroy autonomy in the interests of perfect assimilation. Nevertheless there were still traces of the *ancien régime*. Although corporations had been abolished in principle in 1798, it is to be noted that in December 1806 the Amsterdam municipality were discussing a scheme for the abolition of guilds. The Jews had been granted citizenship in 1796; all the same, the special tax falling upon them was not abolished till 1809. Though feudalism had disappeared, feudal dues and tithes were still in existence. There was a covert resistance to unifying the tax system, and more still to reducing the debt which Napoleon wanted to achieve by declaring a partial bankruptcy. But after union, there was a complete change. Holland was definitely a separate government, in the hands of Lebrun, and was outside the Empire as far as customs were concerned; but assimilation went on as unsparingly as in Illyria. The Civil Code and all the French laws came into force as from 1810. By 9 July the interest on the debt had been reduced by a third. A decree of 15 July 1811 ordered that the French taxes should be levied as from 1813 at the latest. As always, it was the land reforms that produced most resistance and least success. In the end, it was agreed to maintain the tithe under the plea that in a secularised form it could be considered a kind of ground rent; and Louis's Conseil d'État – which had not been dissolved – pronounced against the redemption of dues on real estate.

Unlike Italy, Holland and Switzerland, which had been occupied and partly transformed by revolutionary governments, Germany beyond the Rhine did not lie open to reform until after the war of 1805. Even if Napoleon had been completely in possession, the obstacles would all the same have been greater than elsewhere, for this country was large and diverse. As it turned out, what remained of Austria and Prussia escaped his authority in this respect; for the need to keep on good terms with his allies meant that he had to allow them to adopt only the parts of his system that suited them. Even in the regions ruled by him, circumstances did not always permit him to round off his work.

Parts of the conquered lands were not distributed until 1810. Bayreuth went to Bavaria, Hanau and Fulda to the duchy of Frankfurt, a part of Hanover to Westphalia, the rest being finally annexed to the Empire, which also retained Erfurt. The provisional administrations made no changes in the previous system except for the abolition of serfdom in 1808.

The grand duchy of Berg, formed in 1808 from a part of the duchy of

Cleves, plus Duisburg, and from the whole duchy of Berg plus Düsseldorf, Elberfeld and Barmen, was then increased by certain territories taken from Nassau or mediatised. To this were added in 1808 the Prussian possessions of Westphalia, Mark [north of the Ruhr] and Iserlohn, Münster, Dortmund and Essen, and the counties of Tecklenburg and Langen – nine hundred thousand inhabitants in all, constituting the first Napoleonic state beyond the Rhine. Murat, to whom it was handed over, ceased to summon the local Diets and took on discretionary powers. He abolished collegiate administration, divided the country into *arrondissements*, each under a councillor, and set up municipalities in the towns. Except in the matter of customs, he made no attempt to unify the various lands constituting this state: he left them their own budgets and systems of accountancy, though everywhere he introduced the land tax and the personal tax, and brought in conscription, which the king of Prussia had not dared to introduce. When Murat became king of Naples on 15 July 1808, the grand duchy reverted to Napoleon; and although he had made it over to one of Louis's sons, aged three, he still continued to administer the country himself through special commissioners – first Beugnot, then from 1810 onwards Roederer. In 1808 he unified the administration, and the taxation was progressively remodelled along French lines. In 1811 came the turn of the lawcourts; and Héron de Villefosse set matters in order in the imperial lands that included mines, forests and six hundred thousand francs' worth of feudal rents. Finally, in 1812 the emperor promulgated a constitution containing a Conseil d'État elected by notable people to be chosen by the government, though this did not take place till 1813.

Assimilation was therefore slow and incomplete. Little change was made from the *ancien régime* as far as the Church was concerned. Only the chapters were secularised; there was no concordat, and not till 1810 did the budget contain some provision for paying the clergy. A university was planned for Düsseldorf, but only on paper; the sole institution to take shape in this town was the *lycée*. Legal and social reform were equally slow in coming. On 12 December 1808 Napoleon abolished serfdom and the personal dues and obligations for forced labour, and made real property rights redeemable. On 11 January 1809 he abolished fiefs and feudal customs. Privileges were swept away, and marriages between nobles and commoners were authorised; and finally, on 1 January 1811, the Civil Code was introduced. The peasants protested against the maintenance of the land dues, and refused to pay them to their lords. They were encouraged by a certain bookseller at Dortmund, Mallenkrodt by name; but the lawcourts found against them, and in 1811 two peasants were sent on a deputation to the emperor, and put into prison on their return. Napoleon was told of this and ordered an inquiry; but Beugnot intimated that this matter concerned the imperial lands, and the decree of 13 September 1811 confirmed the preceding ones. Feudal rights properly speaking remained in abeyance without compensation, including the *tailles*, the *banalités*, the *retrait* and the *justices*; but real property rights remained redeemable. The peasants continued their obstinate resistance: nowhere else had they shown themselves so wide awake, which is easily explained by the annexed territory of the Rhineland; and nowhere else did the emperor show such consideration for the local aristocracy – who thought themselves hardly dealt with and had no love for him – although this tenderness on his part was clean contrary to the advancement of French interests.

Taken as a whole, his policy in the duchy was in marked contrast to the abrupt introduction of the new system in countries like Illyria or Poland, though these were in fact much less ready for it. It is hard to say whether this was absent-mindedness or negligence, or uncertainty about the future of the duchy. The inhabitants had been placed within the jurisdiction of the Supreme Court of Appeal in Paris, which seemed to be a prelude to union with France; and they several times demanded this in the expectation of opening up new markets for their products. Their competitors in Aix-la-Chapelle and Mönchengladbach were equally vigorous in their protests, which were partly responsible for the ill success of their requests. It would seem, all the same, that if Napoleon had intended to absorb the duchy, he would have pressed on with assimilation.

In the kingdom of Westphalia, he behaved quite differently. There, the system was introduced in principle from the start, and was applied with unfailing zeal, so that it became the Napoleonic model state in Germany, as the kingdom of Italy was in the peninsula. Yet it was made up of very diverse regions – the duchy of Brunswick, the electorate of Hesse-Cassel, the Prussian territories of Halberstadt and Minden, Osnabrück and Göttingen (split off from Hanover) – not to mention other secularised or mediatised lands; there were two million inhabitants in all. On 14 January 1810 the remainder of Hanover was joined on to it, but it lost the northern part again on 13 December. Even before Jérôme had taken possession, a constitution was proclaimed on 15 November 1807, which had been submitted to a deputation of notables in Paris. They had been chosen by the aristocracy, and put forward requests, several of which were thoroughly characteristic, showing that in this essentially Germanic country, as elsewhere, the social question was a major preoccupation. They made reservations about the abolition of serfdom, insisting on the payment of some compensation, at least as a set-off against their property rights; and they asked for the introduction of the Civil Code to be delayed, and for the continuance of *majorats** and entail. But Napoleon, as was to be expected, did as he pleased. The principles governing the modern state were laid down uncompromisingly: the union of the executive and the administrative, centralisation, the separation of the judiciary from the executive, and a division of labour between these last two; civil equality, religious liberty and finally a constitutional system. This was to include four ministries, a secretariat and a Conseil d'État, with departmental colleges, nominated by the king, which would be authorised to put forward candidates for local councils and for justices of the peace, and to elect a legislative assembly of a hundred members, seventy from the landowners, fifteen from the merchants and manufacturers, and fifteen from the liberal professions. The administrative and judiciary organisation was to be entirely on the French model, and so was conscription; likewise the Civil Code, with its natural corollaries – the abolition of privileges, serfdom and corporations.

The government had been entrusted to a French regency including Beugnot, Siméon and Jollivet. General Lagrange held the Ministry of War, and Jean de Müller the office of secretary of state. But no sooner had Jérôme arrived than he disrupted these appointments to find places for the various adventurers who followed in his train. This young man had a good deal of the light-opera king about him, and ran up a debt of ten million francs, which increased the difficulties of the financial situation. Nevertheless the new system continued to be applied with persevering firmness. The French taxes – the land tax, personal tax, licences, indirect taxes and stamp duty – were all brought in, though not without consultation with the Legislative Assembly; the debt was unified and consolidated; and a system of public notaries and mortgages was organised. The majority of the inhabitants were Protestants, and Jérôme therefore found himself the head of a large part of the clergy, instead of their former sov-

* [Estates inherited by primogeniture.]

ereign. He made no concordat, but he took upon himself the choice of the Catholic bishops. The Jews were declared citizens, and given a consistory; the registration of births, marriages and deaths was brought in, but the work was left to the clergy; and in 1810 the greater part of Catholic Church property, that which belonged to the chapters and the convents, was totally abolished, sequestrated and subsequently sold. There only remained the reform of the land. The constitution had only abolished serfdom and personal services; but even so, several laws were required to define the latter. The redemption of property rights was regulated by a tariff drawn up in 1809. In these regions, forced labour constituted the most oppressive part of these rights. These services were now fixed, so that no new ones could be created, nor could they be altered or sold. Nevertheless, the peasants often refused to fulfil them, and hardly ever consented to their redemption. The obligation to do so had to be repeatedly confirmed; and while waiting for them to make up their minds, the courts seem to have done their best to maintain the indivisibility of tenure, in spite of the Civil Code, in order to guarantee the payment of the dues and compulsory services. On the other hand the *préfets* were encouraged to press on with the partition of the common lands and the abolition of the rights of free pasture, in order to hasten the disappearance of compulsory rotation of crops, which had in theory been abolished.

The nobility suffered bitterly from the loss of their caste privileges; yet they consoled themselves to a certain extent when they were offered superior rank and employment, for not many Frenchmen came to this country, and German was freely used in the government services. King Jérôme employed former Prussian officials – Bülow, a cousin of Hardenberg, Malchus, Schulenburg and Dohm; Baron Wollfradt of Brunswick became minister of the interior; Strombeck was largely responsible for the introduction of the Civil Code; and the electoral colleges and the army were filled with nobles. As for the middle classes, it is at least clear that literature kept its position or accepted new office – men like Leist, Martens, Jacob Grimm – not to mention Jean de Müller.

The annexations of December 1810 brought a third German territory under Napoleon's control, consisting of the northern part of Hanover, the Hanseatic towns and a quarter of the duchy of Berg, plus a few princely possessions which were enclosed within them; and Oldenburg was added on 22 January 1811. The whole was divided into three départements under one common commission. As he did at the same period in Illyria,

Napoleon set about a rapid introduction of the French regime and promulgated the Civil Code on 9 December 1811. The fiefs with their rights of
succession, serfdom, personal rights, the lords' honorific prerogatives,
peonage, seigneurial rights, fishing and hunting rights – all these were
swept away in one fell swoop, and with no compensation, while in Westphalia and especially in the duchy of Berg the process had been several
times reversed. All the same, annexation was too short-lived to have any
deep effect on social relationships; and the advantages seem to have been
less appreciated here than elsewhere, seeing that the strict application of
the blockade involved a military government that was extremely severe in
the suppression of smuggling.

In the other states of the Rhine Federation, Napoleon was not in sovereign control. The princes were very jealous of their own newly acquired
sovereignty, and had only accepted a permanent alliance and protectorate
through fear that Napoleon would keep the lands ceded by Austria,
and so install a French *préfecture* in Southern Germany, as Montgelas
remarked. Napoleon, on his side, had written their sovereignty into the
Act of Confederation, and put off the convening of a Diet until a general
peace should be signed. 'It is not yet time to set up institutions,' he would
say. Meanwhile, he had recourse to persuasion. At Milan in 1807 and at
Erfurt in 1808 he made more or less definite overtures on the adoption of
the Civil Code, and told his diplomats to recommend this step. He would
hardly have been likely to obtain any concessions if the traditions of
enlightened despotism and circumstances had not continued to persuade
the princes to adopt at least a part of his system. His ideals were shared by
Montgelas in Bavaria and Reizenstein in Baden. Besides, the largest of
these states, suddenly increased by additions of varying origin – Austrian
territory, Church possessions, mediatised lands, former free cities – were
a chaos of differing institutions, privileges and religious confessions that
were as a rule mutually exclusive. It was important to fuse them together,
and nothing seemed more suitable for this than the French methods.
Finally, there was a need for the men and money indispensable for the
creation of a strong army. This would satisfy Napoleon, serve to fight
against him if he were conquered, and provide defence against the victors
if they looked like withdrawing the benefits he had conferred. This is why
the new states and those who had acquired most were, as a general rule,
the ones that carried through the greatest changes; and this is also why
constitutional government, which remained largely theoretical in France,

was hardly at all appreciated, since it was repugnant to the sovereign rulers. Finally, the liberation of the peasants was left in the background or completely ignored, for enlightened despotism had never broken the past that linked the monarchy and the aristocracy, and Joseph II had paid dearly for his attempts to infringe it. In this sense, the states of Southern Germany, although they imitated France, continued to be more like Prussia, where the reforms strengthened the state, but dealt lightly with the aristocracy.

One might at least have expected that in the two principalities created from all the separate components on the Main – the grand duchies of Frankfurt and Würzburg – Napoleon's influence would have been triumphant. In the former, it was indeed considerable, but amounted to nothing in the latter, although the former duke of Tuscany, who had now become the grand duke of Würzburg, was favourable to Napoleon and enjoyed his court. There can be no clearer evidence of the carefulness with which he felt bound to handle his German allies. Ferdinand, it is true, knew that he was protected by the treaty with Austria in 1809, and that as a Habsburg he enjoyed some additional influence with the emperor after his second marriage. Dalberg, on the other hand, owed everything to Napoleon. As coadjutor of the archbishop of Mainz, he was the only one of the ecclesiastical electors to receive some compensation in 1803, in the shape of Ratisbon, the principality of Aschaffenburg and the town of Wetzlar. In 1806 he became German primate and was presented with several mediatised lands, Frankfurt being the most important. He did not abolish the autonomy of these ancient free cities, but was content to appoint a commissary and reserve for himself the right to choose their senates from among the lists of candidates drawn up by the inhabitants. In 1810 he had to cede Ratisbon to Bavaria and accept Fulda and Hanau by way of compensation. It was at this point that he became grand duke, with Eugène as his prospective heir. His lands contained three hundred thousand inhabitants and Letters Patent of 16 August 1810 gave them a unified administration and judiciary, and the same system of weights and measures. It proclaimed religious freedom, abolished privilege and serfdom, and established freedom of employment by doing away with the corporations. Dalberg was a *préfet* of the eighteenth-century type, a sincere believer in 'enlightenment' and a supporter of Joseph II; and there is no doubt that these principles seemed to him in accordance with reason. As a good Catholic and loyal German, he had witnessed with some sorrow the secularisations, and finally the end, of the Holy Roman Empire; but this worldly and ingratiating person was not disposed to make sacrifices; and both his tastes and his interests dictated a policy of making himself agreeable to the emperor. He adopted the Civil Code in 1810, and the Penal Code in 1812. Nevertheless, while appreciating the system, he was not passionately attached to it, and took pains to rule his subjects with a light hand, particularly those of his own class, the nobility.

And so in matters of detail the grand duchy of Frankfurt remained a good deal behind the kingdom of Westphalia, though it is true that Dalberg's term of office was still shorter than Jérôme's. The central government included a ministry occupied by Albini and Beust, a Conseil d'État, and Estates nominated by electors chosen for life by the grand duke, and grouped into corporative colleges, as in Italy and Westphalia. The land was divided into four départements and given the same institutions and names as in France. The same was true of the communes, so that Frankfurt lost its senate and the remnants of its independence. But between the département and the commune the *Amt* or *bailliage* continued in existence, combining administrative and judicial functions. Moreover, although new taxes borrowed from France, registration, stamp duty, licences, indirect taxes and the abolition of privileges, brought about a certain fiscal unity, it was left to each of the regions constituting the duchy to continue with its traditional taxes, its budget, accounting system and treasury. The grand duke's exchequer only took over the surpluses.

In 1813 a reform of the judiciary was undertaken. A supreme court was set up, with two courts of appeal and a civil court and a court of summary jurisdiction for each département; but seigneurial justice still continued to preside over courts of the first instance and official positions still kept their jurisdiction – a peculiar proviso that is probably to be explained by Dalberg's ecclesiastical status. In spite of the Civil Code, freedom of conscience was not recognised, for marriage in church remained compulsory, and there was no advance beyond a degree of toleration. In 1807 the Jews had been allowed to become landowners and to carry on certain industries, though they were still confined to a special quarter, liable to a special tax and deprived of any right of citizenship. At Frankfurt, where they were many and wealthy, they managed in 1811 to obtain the right to redeem the tax, and in 1812 to become citizens; and those living at Fulda and Aschaffenburg also contrived to get rid of the tax in 1813. The financial services rendered to the grand duke by the Jew-

ish banks, particularly by the Rothschilds, no doubt helped to hasten
their liberation. Amschel Rothschild and Oppenheimer were appointed
members of the Electoral College at Frankfurt, and Börne became secretary to the superintendent of police.

Social reform remained still more incomplete. In conformity with the
Act of Federation, those who had been mediatised kept their privileges,
the nobility retaining not only their judicial and honorific rights, but also
their fiefs and their private rights. In the principalities of Hanau and
Fulda serfdom had been abolished by the emperor without compensation
in 1808. Everywhere else, its abolition, though decreed under the constitution, remained merely nominal, for the peasants were made to redeem
all the dues connected with serfdom, and only a few communities decided
to do so. As far as land taxes and tithes were concerned, redemption was
permitted on the ducal estates, and the sequestrated Church property,
but no steps were taken for the manors. The Conseil d'État and the
officials entered a formal protest, as a result of which the Civil Code was
given a new twist, and peasant tenure was held to be indivisible as long as
it remained liable to feudal dues.

Passing from Frankfurt to Würzburg, we are met by an equally striking contrast. From 1803 to 1805 the bishopric belonged to Bavaria,
which secularised the property of the clergy and introduced toleration,
but continued to use administrative methods that had as yet been very
little modernised. The grand duke set up a ministry and a Conseil d'État
under the leadership of Seufert. This was the only change he made in the
Bavarian system. Administration and justice both continued to be indiscriminately managed by colleges; the old laws remained in force and the
Civil Code was not adopted. Yet Ferdinand was not hostile to enlightened
despotism: his lethargy is more probably to be explained by the wish to
live at peace after the shocks to which he had been exposed, and to deal
gently with the court of Vienna, whose outlook grew more and more
unenlightened.

On the other hand the large states of Southern Germany were profoundly changed by the inspiration of reforming spirits. In Bavaria,
under the influence of Montgelas, reforms had begun before the electorate became a kingdom, and even before the annexations of 1803. From
1799 onwards the powers of the various ministries were rearranged so as
to unify the services, and a Conseil d'État was set up. In 1802 the judiciary and the administration were separated; in 1805 the bureaucracy was

reorganised, corruption, reversions and bribery being abolished. Recruitment and promotion were thrown open to competition, and discipline
was regulated. The powers of the state were on the increase. In 1800 it
took on responsibility for fire insurance, municipal courts were gradually
reduced or abolished, and in 1804 conscription was introduced. In 1805 a
Public Education Office was added to the Ministry of the Interior. In this
stronghold of the Ultramontane outlook, Montgelas's Josephist policy
was rigorously applied and caused a considerable sensation. Protestants
were allowed into the family circle in 1801, and Maximilian married as
his second wife a Protestant princess from Baden. In 1803 annexation
brought freedom of conscience and worship to Christians of all confessions, with admission to public employment and permission to celebrate
mixed marriages. In 1804 the schools became interconfessional in principle, and the Catholic Church more and more closely subjected to the
secular power. The mendicant Orders were suppressed in 1802, then all
convents in 1803, the state taking over their property. Montgelas showed
interest in the spread of 'enlightenment', making education compulsory
in 1802, and the following year doing away with the censorship of books.
If left to himself, he would also have abolished the corporations; but he
had to be content with reducing their monopoly and abolishing the
hereditary character of the master craftsmanship, except in Munich.

There was then no need for Napoleon to win him over. But he conferred on him the sovereignty of enormous territories, notably the Tyrol,
which was quite untouched by reform; and the very fact of Napoleon's
prestige speeded the course of the new regime. Its principles were summed up in the constitution of 1808, clearly inspired by the example of
Westphalia. Bavaria, up till now the patrimony of the prince, became
judicially a state with a public legal system. Its territory became indivisible,
the royal succession unalterable; the royal lands became distinct from the
sovereign's own personal possessions, and were declared inalienable.
Once the civil list had been fixed, the court's expenses became a private
matter, and could not fall to the charge of the public debt. Central power
was definitely concentrated in the hands of five ministers, the collegiate
system being discarded. Montgelas did in fact manage everything, for he
had three departments under his personal control, and the projected
ministerial conference never came into action. Nevertheless, the *Geheim-
rat* was reorganised and commissioned to prepare laws and be responsible
for administrative justice. The ancient provinces were replaced by *Kreise*

administered by commissaries, assisted by a chief chancellor and councillors. In each *Kreis*, finance was separated from administration and placed under a director. The large towns were given a *Polizeidirektor* nominated by the king, and an elective council and the other communes were allowed to put forward their candidates for the office of Bürgermeister [mayor]; but both groups found themselves kept in administrative leading-strings. The organisation of the judiciary was completed by the creation of courts of appeal and a supreme court, and by making the judges irremovable from office.

The state also turned its attention to public assistance and public health. Vaccination was made compulsory in 1807, thus setting an example for the whole of Germany. The first teachers' training colleges were opened, and in 1808 Niethammer organised a secondary education that included *Gymnasien* and *Realschulen*. The Bavarian Academy was remodelled, and a Department of Fine Arts was added; those universities that were retained were brought up to date. The religious edict of 1809 made the churches even more dependent, so much so that the pope refused to enter into a concordat. Bavaria also made some progress towards economic unity. Internal customs disappeared, the state took possession of the postal services and imposed a single system of weights and measures. The great difficulty was to find money, for the regime's expenses were high. Direct taxation was extended throughout the territory, along French lines; the land tax was reformed on the basis of a new land survey. This was undertaken by a statistical board which took on the mapping of the whole country; new indirect taxes were brought in, as well as a strongly protectionist customs tariff. The army went on steadily growing. In 1812 an end was put to the system of exemptions; meanwhile in 1809 the National Guard had been introduced; and in 1812 the *gendarmerie* was remodelled.

The constitution also strengthened the power of the state by proclaiming civil equality and abolishing the *Stände* or orders, as well as privileges. As early as 1807 fiscal exemptions had been swept away; and with the *Stände* went the assemblies representing them. They had already lost the power to vote taxes in 1807. The constitution did in fact guarantee individual freedom, freedom of conscience and freedom of the press; it also brought in constitutional government and national representation; but in practice, the Corps Législatif was not summoned, and the regime remained a police state with absolute powers, such as arbitrary imprisonment, a secret cabinet, a rigorous censorship of the papers and a complete veto upon all associations. At least there was a strengthening of religious liberty. In 1808 the last restrictions on the Protestants were removed. By the edict of 1809 they were granted an official organisation, the freedom to transfer from one religion to another, and the abolition of the compulsory contribution they had so far been obliged to make to the Catholic parish priest. In 1813 the Jews were granted freedom of worship on a private basis, but did not become full citizens.

Transported to the Tyrol, this ready-made system, with its despotic and centralising features, produced an insurrection. From the Napoleonic point of view, however, it was far from perfect. In the lower stages, justice remained linked to administration, the corporations were allowed to continue, and although the French Penal Code was adopted in 1813, the full Civil Code was not, and each of the regions that made up the kingdom kept its own customary law. Montgelas, afraid that the emperor might interfere, seems to have toned down his reforming zeal from 1806 onwards. Perhaps he also gave up all hope of breaking the resistance of the aristocracy, for whom the *Code Napoléon* would have been the last straw. According to the agreement, those who had been mediatised retained their fiscal, judicial and honorary privileges, as well as their special courts. The nobles also succeeded in preserving a part of their special status. As in France, entails were brought in by royal favour to take the place of the trusts that had been suppressed. Moreover, in 1809 women were once more debarred from succeeding to property held by the nobility. A register of the nobles was compiled, and their prestige strengthened by imposing certain obligations on pain of being struck off the register. Seigneurial courts were regulated, but not abolished. But little was done for the peasants. In 1808 serfdom was abolished, without compensation, and the personal obligations belonging to it. The year before, it had been decreed on principle that compulsory labour could not be altered, but could be redeemed, and likewise the feudal dues, subject to the signing of a contract with the lord, which he could however refuse. From the social point of view, then, Bavaria was behind the times compared with the other Napoleonic states; for though the balance between the aristocracy and the state had been upset to the advantage of the latter, they still remained allies. Peasant property was only set free in the secularised lands, and then only with the payment of compensation and subject to a redeemable tax. There had been more marked changes in the agrarian arrangements of the *ancien régime*, for in 1803 the village community and the compulsory rotation of crops had both been abolished, the common lands were to be divided, and the *Hof* or family tenure was allowed to be split up; but these measures were slow in bearing fruit.

Württemberg seems to have developed in a different and even more characteristic manner. The duke – who had become elector in 1803 – continued till 1805 to quarrel with his Landtag, and could not therefore undertake any reforms. He had to be content with reorganising his ministers, and appointing Wintzingerode as one of them, taking good care not to unite his recent acquisitions to his older lands, and governing them despotically, but introducing religious toleration. The Landtag demanded union, complained to Paris and made common cause with the heir apparent. Frederick replied with a *coup d'état*; but the newly elected Landtag refused to vote the taxes and appealed to Vienna, which gave a verdict in their favour. Passing through Stuttgart on 2 October 1805, Napoleon advised making short work of this opposition: 'Get rid of these bounders,' he said – for the Landtag had incurred his displeasure by refusing the money and the men that France required. On 30 December Frederick, who had now become fully sovereign, abolished the Landtag. From this time onwards, he was able to transform his state. Between 1808 and 1814 he never relaxed his efforts: there were in all 2,342 rescripts and ordinances. Bavaria, on the other hand, which had carried out a good part of the work during the previous period, now gradually slackened the pace.

The new king, like his neighbour, felt the need for strengthening his power. But being of an autocratic character, and furious at having been so long resisted, he was passionately intent on governing in a despotic manner. His ministers were no more than clerks, and although he set up a Conseil d'État, he hardly ever consulted it. Unlike Montgelas, he had no love for 'enlightenment', and so no respect for intellectual freedom or social progress. He therefore retained still more exclusively those elements in the Napoleonic system that were to his personal advantage.

Württemberg was divided into districts administered by *Kreishauptleute*, that is, *préfets*; but the king took it upon himself to nominate and keep control of the municipalities. The higher lawcourts followed the French pattern, and were not responsible for any administration. A *gendarmerie* was set up, and the police force was extended to a most unusual degree. The financial framework was rebuilt, the state took on a monopoly in salt and tobacco, and the land tax was considerably increased. The

state took over the post and the management of the schools, and brought
the churches under its regulations. Frederick was careful not to set up a
constitution or give his subjects the smallest rights. The criminal courts
were not even empowered to pass sentence: they simply gave their opinion, and the king made the decision. Emigration was forbidden, travel
needed a special permit and all meetings were prohibited. A strict censorship prevailed; the University of Tübingen lost its independence and was
given a warden. Permission was needed to apply for entry, and students
were given no choice over the faculties to which they were assigned.
Espionage was shamelessly encouraged, and the population were systematically disarmed. From this time onwards Württemberg was more op-
pressively governed than the French Empire; it was in fact a Metternich
regime.

The only reform to find favour was a certain religious toleration. By
the edict of 15 October 1806, all Christians received some benefit. Jews
were now allowed to own land and carry on a trade. Where the organisation of society was concerned, Frederick was also careful not to commit
himself to any principles, and though he unified the legal system, he did
not adopt the Civil Code. The nobles were kept under strict control and
had to pay taxes. They were partly deprived of their special courts, lost
their trust rights and saw their ranks invaded by a number of upstarts.
Marriage was now authorised between themselves and the middle classes;
and from now on, everyone could own land. The property of the Catholic
clergy was secularised. But the feudal system did not disappear: no
change was made in the tithes, the feudal dues and forced labour, the
king being content merely to abolish personal serfdom. Nor was any hand
laid upon the corporations. Thus unification, centralisation and despotism advanced more notably in Württemberg than in Bavaria, while the
*ancien régime* continued to prevail in the social sphere.

In Baden, reform was still later in beginning. After the annexations of
1803, the property of the Catholic clergy was secularised and the convents
closed (with a few exceptions). The old and the new territories were fused
into three provinces, though the local ministry and administration did not
lose their collegiate form. No resistance was met with: the government
had no difficulty in depriving the mediatised towns of nearly all their
powers, and in 1806 the Estates of Breisgau were abolished. Charles Frederick enjoyed a well-deserved reputation as an enlightened despot; but he
was growing old, and his advisers were deeply divided, for his second wife,

the countess of Hochberg, wanted to make certain that her children would succeed to the throne in case those of the first marriage had no heirs. In the end, Napoleon plainly showed his impatience, particularly as he was very displeased with the grand duke's grandson, who was getting on very badly with Stéphanie de Beauharnais. In 1807 Dalberg's nephew introduced a number of new measures. He replaced the colleges by five ministers, set up a Conseil d'État, and began to reform the finances.

But the radical measures were the work of Reitzenstein, who was of Bavarian origin, and – like Montgelas – a supporter of 'enlightenment' and the entente with France. He divided the country into districts, which amalgamated the annexed principalities, and took the municipalities under the government's wing. All the same, he did not push reorganisation to extremes, perhaps through lack of time, for he was dismissed in 1810. The districts remained subdivided into *bailliages*, in which administration and justice were linked together. Conscription was also adopted, and – most important of all – the Civil Code, as from 1 January 1811, although certain modifications were introduced. Religious toleration had already come to Baden, and was extended to the Jews in 1808. The country was less hardly treated than Württemberg, but no constitution was introduced. Civil equality – a cardinal point – existed only in theory. To begin with, those who had been mediatised kept their privileges, as they did everywhere else, including the private courts, honorary and feudal rights, armed guards and special family status; then the officials remained personally subject only to the superior courts, and the same advantage was accorded to the nobility, who were likewise exempted from personal tax and from conscription. They managed to preserve the right to form trusts and entails; and in addition they contrived to have the land tax on their estates reduced by a third. In the end, moreover, nothing was done to disturb the fief and feudal rights, nor the tithe, the dues or forced labour. As serfdom had disappeared at the end of the eighteenth century, there was not much change in the position of the lower classes.

Among the other members of the Rhine Confederation there was one who closely imitated France – the prince of Anhalt, who ruled over twenty-nine thousand subjects. He gave these a *préfet*, a *préfet*'s council and a departmental council and a court of appeal and district courts, not to mention a Conseil d'État. He adopted the *Code Napoléon*, abolished privilege and seigneurial justice, and did not fail to introduce conscription. Without displaying this amount of zeal, certain other princes made

use of their advantages and showed good will. The most important of
these was Louis I, grand duke of Hesse-Darmstadt, who hastened to
abolish the Landtag and do away with fiscal privilege, except for the
mediatised lands. He also adopted the Civil Code in 1808, though making
some alterations in it, fixed the limits of forced labour and put an end to
serfdom, with due compensation. The duke of Nassau likewise did away
with exemption from taxation, serfdom and a number of strictly feudal
rights. In 1810 the prince of Salm also made all his subjects liable to the
land tax. The other princes of Anhalt in Thuringia and Mecklenburg
were satisfied with a few changes in the fiscal system and the recruitment
of officials, but the Landtag and the social system continued as of old.
Saxony too belongs to this category. Senft would have liked to take the
initiative, but he did not have enough character to carry the day with
the minister of the interior, Hopfgarten, who was firmly opposed to all
innovation, as indeed was the Landtag. The nobility continued to enjoy
exemption from taxation, and Calvinists were still excluded from toleration, which was only granted to the Catholics. The main attention was
given to reorganising the army, to which was added a *gendarmerie*. The
case of King Frederick was somewhat similar to that of the grand duke of
Würzburg. He too was a faithful ally of Napoleon; but he was limited and
apathetic in outlook, and showed no interest in reform, though he would
perhaps have yielded to imperial persuasion. Napoleon did not press matters here any more than in Bavaria or Württemberg, because he was afraid
of losing his good will. Yet in the grand duchy of Warsaw which he had
presented to the emperor, Napoleon saw no need for the same delicate
handling, but proceeded to organise it with the freedom he had shown in
the kingdoms of Italy and Westphalia.

### THE GRAND DUCHY OF WARSAW

On 22 July 1807, at Dresden, Napoleon had given the country constitutional status. The central power, the administration and the judiciary
were all based upon the French model. The prince was to nominate six
ministers and a secretary of state, to be joined later on by superintendents
of public education, waterways and forests, food supplies, war and state
lotteries. At first the Conseil d'État was no more than a council of ministers; but in 1808 it was enlarged by councillors and then by referendaries,
and became considerably more important than in France, for it combined

administrative justice with the powers of a supreme court of appeal. Besides, it came to play an increasingly important part in politics, for its members were the official representatives in the Diet and in the Chamber of Nuncios, and in 1809 it began to take part in governing the country. Nonetheless, it remained true that in Warsaw the executive continued to be in fact of the collegiate type, and lacked effective guidance. The grand duke lived in Dresden, and did not exercise his right to appoint a viceroy. True, there was a president of the Council of Ministers, Stanislas Potocki by name; but he did not wield the influence of a chief of state.

The territory was divided into départements, districts and communes. The collegiate principle was abolished, and administration put in the hands of a *préfet* assisted by a secretary-general and a *préfet*'s council, a *sous-préfet* and a mayor and municipal magistrates. The grand duke chose the *préfet* and *sous-préfet*, while the senior *préfet* chose the municipal members. In each area a council was set up, also nominated by the grand duke from among the candidates put forward by the *diétines*, or assemblies of the nobles in a département or district, or by the communal assemblies. The districts were given a justice of the peace, chosen from those put forward by the *diétine*; and the départements a court of permanent judges. There was a criminal court for each two départements, and a single court of appeal. Commissioners of police were also appointed. The French tax system was brought in forthwith and a court of accounts set up. Education benefited from the serious attention given to it, and it was put into the hands of local committees. The Catholic Church was placed under the authority of the state, for the constitution gave the grand duke the right to nominate the bishops. The command of the army fell to Poniatowski, and in 1808 conscription was brought in. Thus for the first time in history, the Polish state had a centralised administration and a body of professional officials. The latter were destined to provide the material from which the middle classes of the Western states had been formed.

This was an authoritarian government, as in the other Napoleonic states. Individual freedom was guaranteed by the constitution, but the police enjoyed just as extensive discretionary powers as in France. Not a word had been said about the liberty of the press. Nevertheless, the duchy was given a Diet, though without the power of initiating measures, and only meeting for a fortnight at the most every other year; besides, its marshal or president was appointed by the king. At all events it met regularly in 1809 and 1811. There was also a Senate of bishops and nobles appointed for life by the grand duke, whose sole duty was to see that laws were in conformity with the constitution, and a Chamber of Nuncios or deputies comprising, for each district, a noble resident – a landowner or son of a landowner – elected by his peers assembled in Diet, and the representatives of the communal electoral assemblies, in which the peasant proprietors, the parish priests and the curates took part, as well as merchants worth ten thousand florins, officers, and soldiers who had received decorations. This Diet differed in its constitution from the Italian or Westphalian assemblies, and was more like the one in Naples, though it was still more aristocratic in character. Although some part was played by professional and property qualifications, the distinction between the two curias still rested mainly on the preservation of the social orders. True, the deputies each had a vote; but the nobles held three-fifths of the votes, not to mention the fact that the communal assemblies could also elect noblemen. On the other hand the electoral system was more enlightened than in Naples or Westphalia, where the members of the electoral colleges were nominated by the king, and merely elected candidates. In Poland, the electors' rights were guaranteed by the constitution, and their elections were genuine elections.

Thus Napoleon was accustomed to take local conditions into account. Since the middle classes in Lombardy and Westphalia enjoyed a certain stability, he did not give the aristocracy special representation. In Southern Italy, where the aristocracy were much stronger than in the north, the case was very different; but as the Bourbons had stripped them of all political authority, they were only given an upper chamber nominated by the king. In Poland, the power of the nobility as compared with the insignificance of the middle classes was too great to give them anything but a dominant position; moreover, it was not so long since they had been the real masters of the state, and it was advisable, while putting them under the law, to give them a genuine liberty to shape policy, and liberty from which the commoners reaped some incidental advantage. Napoleon's efforts to get the aristocracy on his side were therefore more marked in this country than anywhere else. The result was that the nobility kept its specific identity and became the real controllers of the state.

This was by no means an advantage for the peasants. While maintaining the privileged position of the nobility as a political institution, the constitution had proclaimed civil liberty and abolished serfdom. The Civil Code was promulgated on 15 August 1810, freeing the peasants

from the glebe and giving them the right to go to law; but the land nevertheless continued to belong to the nobles, and the decree of 12 December
1807 pronounced all tenure to be precarious in default of a contract,
which put the tiller of the soil in a worse position, for when his right
of possession was for the most part hereditary or for life, he could not
usually call anything except custom to his assistance. Feudal rights,
land dues, forced labour and tithe all continued to exist; and so did even
arbitrary forced labour. Notaries were appointed and model contracts
published in order to encourage fixed tenure, dues and labour; but very
few written agreements saw the light of day. The lord could use his right
of eviction to maintain the existing burdens, or even increase them; and
there is reason to believe that a good number of peasants cultivating only
small plots took advantage of their new freedom and left the land. But as
the country had no industries, this could only lead to economic and social
unrest. The property of the clergy, however, was left untouched, and
what had been secularised by Prussia was kept as part of the royal lands.
In 1812 Bignon, who represented France in Warsaw, recorded: 'The
condition of the peasants has hardly altered at all.'

In spite of this, the aristocracy were a prey to anxiety lest Napoleon
should not call a halt at this point. The great families were even more
annoyed because the level of equality for all landowning nobles established by the political constitution, and the opening of the Diet to commoners, seemed to strike a mortal blow at the authority that had hitherto
been theirs. They nevertheless continued to hold the major offices of state
or to fill them with their own protégés. The Czartoryskis in particular,
although remaining in the background, kept well informed about the various ministries, for Stanislas Potocki had married a Lubomirska, a niece
of Adam Czartoryski's father, and Matuszewicz, minister of finances, was
regarded as a supporter of the latter; and Niemcewicz, the secretary of the
Senate, and very hostile to France, continued to be his devoted servant.
Nor was the opposition of the Roman Catholic Church by any means to be
ignored, for it was paramount over the peasants. It had been deeply
offended by the proclamation of freedom of conscience and worship,
although it had been allowed to keep its privileged position as the religion
of the state and had been given the management of all civil registration,
divorced persons being handed over to the secular arm. Though there was
little protest from the secular clergy, the reaction of the monks was very
different, especially after the break with the pope. The Benonists – most

of whom were German – were supported in their agitation by the nuncio from Vienna, and had to be expelled. The establishment of masonic lodges – there were a dozen of them by 1810 in the Grand Orient – was a further source of grievance. The Jewish question (which was at the same time a social question) gave the clergy an excellent weapon. There were no exceptions in the constitution, and Jews were therefore given the same rights as Christians. But this caused such feeling that in 1809 their political rights were withdrawn from them for ten years, with certain individual exceptions granted by the prince to those who paid a licence fee. In 1808 they were forbidden to acquire land without authorisation, and in 1812 to lease imperial domain lands or to sell beverages; and in order to keep down their numbers, a system of authorisation for marriage was imposed upon them. It must be admitted that they seemed in no hurry to become assimilated; and in 1812 they were at their own request – we are told – given exemption from military service upon payment of a contribution.

## EUROPEAN CIVILISATION

It is clear then that in the Grand Empire the Napoleonic system showed a significant division. On the one hand, the state reforms went steadily ahead: on the other, social reform dwindled or proved abortive. The increasingly marked favour shown by the emperor towards the aristocracy makes it difficult to say what would have been the future course of his liberating efforts. All the same, he was so bent upon the Civil Code that once peace had been established on the Continent, we can well believe he would have taken the necessary measures to apply it to the full in every place. Thus it may be said that everywhere he strove to add administrative and social unity to political unity, and this was to form the framework for a new European civilisation. This did in fact develop after his time, in the course of the nineteenth century, in spite of the counter-revolutionary reaction; but with a slowness, and with disturbances and distortions, that Napoleon might well have avoided. For the most part, the principles were in alignment with those of 1789, and that was what stamped this civilisation as essentially French.

Outside the French Empire, Napoleon did not take any steps to add an intellectual culture for which the French language would have served as the vehicle. In the kingdoms of Italy, Naples and Westphalia, by far the majority of the staff were locally recruited, and Italian or German remained the languages used for administration and education. But the case was different in the French Empire. Thus in Holland, the decree of 22 October 1811 made it compulsory for the heads of private schools to provide, within a period of three months, instruction in French. As the annexations increased, so would the sphere of the French language have extended. Even at this period, it had come into use at the courts of the vassal kings and in the great Napoleonic administrators' offices. Knowledge of French was becoming indispensable for all who aspired to the highest levels of employment, and teaching was obliged to take this into account. It would not be right to suspect Napoleon of deliberately wishing to uproot the other dialects, any more than he had done in old-world France. But French would have come in alongside them as the language of continental unity. It would have served as a medium for consolidating classical culture all the more so as no other existed in the emperor's eyes. There is no doubt at all that he intended Paris to become the intellectual, artistic and secular capital of the European Empire, as it already was the political capital. He was intent on making it the world's museum by bringing to it the works of art taken from the countries he had conquered. In stark opposition to this conception of a universal civilisation, surviving from the eighteenth-century ideal, looking back to the traditions of Rome, and inspired by the Catholic Church, stood the Romantic idea of national cultures of spontaneous diversity, and irreducible in nature, which were a fundamental denial of the oneness of the human race.

## THE CONTINENTAL ECONOMY

Locked in combat with England, the European federation had as its symbol and its weapon the continental blockade; but the blockade reacted on its economy, because it was reduced to living on its own resources. This way would, if successful, increase its strength by creating interests which would have been damaged by an English victory; and by the same token it might well undermine the economy if there was any failure to organise the continental market so as to provide a livelihood for each of its members.

Wherever it was applied with some rigour, the blockade's effects were similar to those in France. The maritime cities and their industries were ruined. In the Mediterranean, there was first Genoa, then Venice and Leghorn, and finally Trieste. In this last port, the figures dropped from more than five thousand ships and 208,000 barrels in 1807 to 2,600 boats

and sixty thousand barrels in 1812. In the north, the Hanseatic ports were
the first to feel the pinch, followed by the Baltic ports, and lastly by those
of Holland.

The trade of the great German fairs, fed as they were by contraband
goods, became a precarious business, which meant that the blockade provoked the hostility of the shipowners, the big business interests and the
banks. But in industry it was different: although the cotton industry found
it difficult to get raw materials and other branches suffered from the ban
on exports, local production was rather fortunate in being delivered from
English competition; and the veto on exports acted as a stimulus. As in
France, cotton spinning and weaving showed the most marked progress,
although this was lessened by the importance of contraband. In Saxony,
although results were on the whole less good than in 1805, they showed a
twenty-five per cent improvement in 1810, and the production of printed
materials rose sharply, increasing more than fifty per cent during this
period. Switzerland, the southern part of Baden and even Northern Italy
likewise took advantage of these favourable circumstances. Wool prospered too, for instance in Switzerland and Denmark. In Germany, the
Silesian and Westphalian mines extended their markets; so did ironmongery, weapons produced in Thuringia, straw hats and brushes in Baden,
and chemical products. The processing of sugar-beet also developed,
especially in the duchy of Frankfurt and at Magdeburg, and struck root in
Holland and Russia. At a time when the spirit of enterprise was everywhere being stimulated by England's example, the blockade taught (more
effectively than the theory or fragmentary practice of the Mercantile Theory in the *ancien régime*) how much it could be helped in its early stages by
protective customs duties. And after 1815 this lesson was to be well
remembered. In this sense, it was in the interest of all the members of the
Continental System to maintain a common front against British industry.
All the same, not every member reaped the same advantage, for as one
went east and south, agriculture assumed a growing preponderance, so
that the blockade was especially favourable to France, and in the second
place to Germany, Switzerland and Northern Italy. Needless to say, the
consumer did not share the industrialists' satisfaction; and the states
themselves, seeing their customs revenue diminish with the cutting off of
English imports, shared the anxieties felt by the emperor.

Hence it was not enough simply to produce at all costs: it was also a
question of adapting the wheels of commerce to new conditions and

redistributing markets so as to provide for the consumer and find new customers for the manufacturers who had hitherto exported overseas, such as the cloth-makers of Hanover and Silesia. And this was an extremely difficult task. The English market, with its control of the seas, underwent a natural growth, by virtue of the living impetus of productive activity. On the other hand each of the continental regions naturally turned towards its particular coast, and the European market, though in theory unified by the blockade, tended in practice to be split up as it were by a centrifugal force. The proof of this was the persistence of the cross-country trade routes which had come into being across Central Europe since France had been cut off by war. The Frankfurt, and more particularly the Leipzig, fairs continued to be well patronised, and as late as 1809 Trieste was still getting the produce of the Levant through to Bavaria and Saxony. From then onwards, the cross-country traffic tended to stretch still further east, along caravan routes from the Baltic to Leipzig, and from Salonica to Vienna.

On the other hand the really new feature was the advance of essentially continental routes running from west to east. It may be said that the success of the blockade and the consolation of the Continental System depended on the routes running north and south, thus bearing witness to the vitality of the maritime traffic and the dealers in contraband. Strasbourg and Lyon were the chief centres where these trade routes crossed. The former became the French depot for goods destined for Germany, Austria and Russia, which were subsequently sorted at Leipzig. In return, the town also received goods from Frankfurt via the Rhine, and from Vienna, which up to 1810 sent it cotton from the Levant. But the transformation of Lyon's commerce was an even greater novelty, because Napoleon was completely master of Italy and had opened the Alpine routes. His first object was political and military. To begin with he concentrated on the Simplon in order to link up with Milan, and the road was finished in 1805. But as Piedmont had just been annexed, the main effort was switched to the Mont Cenis, which was completed as early as 1806. Work also went ahead on the Genèvre, which was of purely strategic importance.

As French rule spread to central Italy, the Corniche road came into the picture; and in 1810 Napoleon decided to build it and extend it via La Spezia and Florence towards Ancona and Trieste, but he never had time to complete it. Up till 1810 the Simplon, which had difficult approaches and was not easily controlled by the customs, was chiefly used by troops and travellers. On the other hand the Mont Cenis at once assumed great economic importance, and the pre-eminence of Lyon was largely due to it, for nearly all the Italian traffic went that way, amounting in 1810 to almost three thousand travellers' vehicles, fourteen thousand heavy wagons and thirty-seven thousand pack-mules. As Piedmont and the kingdom of Italy had become to some extent colonies of France, buying her manufactures and sending her agricultural and textile goods, the industries of Lyon reaped the advantage, for the Mont Cenis route was used by the silk trade. Illyria became important in another way, for in 1810 the emperor made it the centre for the cotton caravans arriving from the Levant. Lyon then became the gateway for cotton, since Strasbourg had been closed against goods coming from Vienna. The Mont Cenis route proved inadequate for the cotton trade, and when the Valais was annexed, the Simplon grew in commercial importance.

It remained to be seen whether these supply routes would be able to carry enough to replace the coastal traffic, which was becoming more and more difficult. There is no doubt that it proved insufficient. France's system of waterways was still very incomplete, while elsewhere there were hardly any canals, and the rivers were barely usable. Even on the Rhine, the local tolls set up by the ordinance of 1803 had lessened the burden of the tolls payable for navigation, though they had not altogether removed it. Nor had the privileges controlling certain stretches been abolished, where transhipment had to be carried out for the benefit of certain porters' unions. Wheeled transport enjoyed great prosperity at this time, for instance at Chalon-sur-Saône, for goods being sent to the interior of France, and at Lyon, where the House of Bonnafour became one of the largest concerns of the time. But it was no substitute for water transport where heavy goods were involved; and even if enough vehicles had been built, there would not have been enough horses, and the roads would not have stood up to the traffic, for except in France and a few parts of Southern Germany and Italy they had no hard stone surface.

As there were already a good many centres of industrial production outside the Empire, the best plan would have been to give each of them a sphere of activity and divide the continental market into customs zones. The creation of large economic units would even have been an inducement to accept this concentration of territory. The grand duchy of Berg, for example, continued to ask for union with the Empire in order to draw on its custom; and Holland would have taken a kinder view of annexation if the customs barrier had been done away with. Napoleon was in a master position for bringing about commercial unity in Italy; and Beugnot and Bacher repeatedly urged the setting up of a German customs union.

But there were various considerations working against, or at any rate delaying, this solution of the problem. In the first place, the vassal and allied states had to be humoured, for they were inclined to be jealous of their sovereignty, and would not have agreed to give up their autonomy in customs. As Napoleon's institutional reforms and military needs were expensive, it was difficult to cut down their resources, and they even put up their customs tariffs. Territorial arrangements were in a state of constant flux, so that conditions for doing business and exchanging products became worse rather than better. A number of regions naturally belonging together or linked by their histories found themselves cut off from each other: for instance, the kingdom of Italy from Dalmatia and Istria, from Novara and from Piedmont, from Genoa and Leghorn. Switzerland was cut off from Italy, from Genoa and from the Black Forest; the Tyrol from Italy and from Austria, and Illyria from Hungary and Vienna, although Fiume would have seen to the matter of transport, and so would Trieste in 1812. The grand duchy of Berg, strangled between the French Empire on one side and her German neighbours on the other, was in a pitiful plight. Her sales fell from fifty-five million in 1807 to thirty-nine million in 1810. Trade agreements would have provided some relief, but Napoleon did not encourage these, for he wanted to keep all the profits for France.

The reef on which his European policies were wrecked was, to be sure, his failure to see the European market as a thing in itself, and not simply with reference to the French Empire. 'France comes before everything else,' he wrote to Eugène in 1810. Having conceived and planned the Continental System, he would not deviate in his own territory from the mercantilism he had espoused in the days of the Consulate. His frontiers remained strictly closed against allies and vassals, no less than against the English, even for the Swiss or the inhabitants of the duchy of Berg. In order to avoid all rivalry with his own producers, he even refused to annex the duchy and kept Holland and North Germany out of the Empire as far as customs were concerned, although he had joined them to France politically. On the other hand he did his utmost to impose against all nations preferential tariffs that benefited his own subjects, and succeeded as far as the kingdom of Italy and Naples were concerned. This attitude of his can be explained by the position of France. Being the most industrialised of all the continental peoples, she suffered most of all from the blockade and the war. She had lost both the colonial and the English markets, and then Spain in 1808 – Spain, her best remaining customer; and it was from this time onwards that Napoleon made every effort to keep his hold on Italy. France was the heart of the system, and at all costs he felt he must preserve her from economic collapse. Yet political considerations once again saved him from pushing this policy to extremes. He took no steps to prevent the people of Saxony and the Swiss from getting possession of the German market; and at the Leipzig fair, France only sold the highest-quality goods. On the other hand, he kept a close hold on Italy, where he reigned supreme. In this way he contrived to get a share of the chief three industrial regions. Moreover, pressure from the inhabitants of Lyon made him determined to hold on to this private preserve, and he proceeded to erect progressively a series of impassable customs businesses around the kingdom of Italy, except on the French side. In 1808 he forced her to accept a commercial treaty, and in 1810 arrogated to himself the sole right to import cotton goods and cloth; he put a tax on the export of raw silk to Austria and Switzerland so as to give Lyon a monopoly; and he insisted on it giving free passage to cotton from Naples and from the Levant, as well as allowing transit between France and Illyria. The kingdom of Italy bought forty-three million's worth of goods from France in 1810, and eighty-two million in 1812, mostly cereals, flax, hemp and silk – seventy-three million in 1810 and ninety-two million in 1812. But she does not seem to have fared as badly as has sometimes been suggested, for her balance of trade remained favourable. France did not ruin her industries; she simply took the place that had previously been held by England. As she was only in a position to supply her with high-priced goods, local production still provided for the bulk of the population. Nor did Napoleon refuse her all opportunities for improving her own industries. True, he would not send her qualified workers, but he allowed her two hundred thousand francs for buying spinning machinery. But the country's industrialists only had cause to remember this one fact – that a blockade could have been useful to them if France had not pocketed all the profits. And there was a louder chorus of complaint from those who were the chief sufferers.

Although industry was in favour of the blockade, especially where the outlook was progressive, this approval was not without serious reservations, particularly with regard to the hindrances to free trade inside the

Continent, which the emperor was accused of maintaining and even re-
inforcing in the sole interests of France. In agriculture, the problem
seemed insoluble. It concerned especially Prussia, Poland and the Russian provinces bordering on the Baltic, which could find nobody to take
the grain surpluses they formerly exported to England. Norway, with her
constant demand for imports, was the only country that might have provided a market, but she was inaccessible by land. These countries' timber
would have been acceptable in the West, but it was hardly possible to
export it without ships. Napoleon himself found it difficult to dispose of
his wines and brandies, and in good years he also had too much grain on
his hands. The peasants only sold sufficient to provide for local consumption, so this disadvantage must not be exaggerated, for it only applied
to a small number of big proprietors among the nobility and large-scale
farmers; yet these were influential people, and the fact remains that the
blockade tended to depress agricultural prices and rural purchasing power,
thus injuring the industries that in other respects benefited from it. The
imperfections in the continental market, the poor economic tone and the
fiscal deficit that resulted from them finally decided the emperor to reorganise the blockade and to ease it for the time being through a system
of licences. However urgent his motives, the effect of this alleviation was
nevertheless to revive the centrifugal tendencies that were undermining
the system. By closing his ports to the Continent while opening them to
the Americans, Napoleon gave some justification for the accusations levelled against France for her selfishness. Her allies and vassals claimed the
right to follow her example, and Russia gave the lead.

To strengthen the European federation by setting up a single market
that was relatively independent would obviously be a long-term policy
requiring years of constraint. The first obstacle to be overcome arose
from the fragmentation of the lands concerned and the interior customs
that went with it; and it was the business of the Grande Armée to put an
end to these conditions. But in face of world opinion, England had the
advantage of being able to show that the Continental System in all its
forms was based upon a military dictatorship.

## THE CONTINENTAL SYSTEM AND NATIONALITY

The continued existence of the Continental System depended on the
campaign against Russia. As a rule, Napoleon would concentrate his

attention on the next victory. The rest would follow of its own accord, and would largely depend on circumstances. He therefore had no hard and fast plans for the future of a European federation. All that can be said is that from 1810 onwards he laid more emphasis on the Roman character of the Empire. In the Eternal City, which had now become his second capital, his successors would henceforward be anointed before the tenth year of their reign. He wanted to take Marie-Louise there himself and have her crowned, and preparations for this great event were under way. The pope would live in either Paris or Rome. Some time or other, Pius VII would be succeeded by a pontiff who would accept this new Babylonian Captivity. As to what would then follow we can give free range to our imagination. After Alexander's army had been destroyed, we could picture the rebuilding of Poland; the creation on Russian soil of new principalities intended to protect this resurrected state; the expulsion of Bernadotte in favour of some reliable successor; the reorganisation of Germany; the submission of the Iberian peninsula; and the conquest of Constantinople, to become the third capital of the Empire. Peace on the Continent would then seem to have been secured, and European civilisation as Napoleon conceived it would have made a steady advance.

Attempts have been made to reconcile this extrapolation with the nationalism that was so characteristic of the century, suggesting that Napoleon had planned to transform the Continental System into a society of sovereign nations forming a voluntary association. Certainly the cosmopolitan civilisation he envisaged was far from being opposed to such an ideal; but the unity created by conquest was diametrically opposed to the free union of peoples which the Revolution in its early stages looked forward to as the crowning of its endeavours. This illusion can, however, be explained if we note that Napoleon, ever eager to convert to his own use the forces he found at work, took good care not to neglect national feeling whenever it suited him for the moment. It was to this force that he owed his power in France; and although he sacrificed his country's interests to an imperial dream, Frenchmen always looked upon him as a national leader, for their interests could no longer be separated from his. Moreover, he carried on the work of the Revolution in strengthening France's internal unity by centralisation, by military service, by the wars that fostered a sense of unity in face of the foreigner, and by the victories which exalted the feeling of collective pride. Outside the French Empire, he showed much greater reserve. Though the Poles could not

accuse him of treachery – since he never positively promised them anything – he took advantage of their patriotism and there were clearly
certain further considerations behind his actions when he first wrote the
name of Italy into political geography, revived the name of Illyria and
gave official status to the Slovene and Croatian languages.

Moreover, it can be maintained that his system of government and
his policies both tended strongly to advance the cause of nationalism.
Although he did not complete the territorial unity of Italy and Germany,
he enormously simplified the map in both of them; and he brought a part
of the Yugoslavs together – something that had not happened since the
fourteenth century. Nor were his reforms less important. By abolishing
provincial autonomy, privileges and feudalism, and replacing them with a
central administration, civil equality and a unified internal market, he created the essential conditions for the expansion of political nationalism. In
this sense, he must count as one of the creators of several modern states.
But these were consequences he did not intend: a statesman's actions
always involve repercussions that were not foreseen by him, and in this
respect the emperor was not above his fellows. It may be replied that he
intended Italy to go to his second son, and that it would have been imperative to set up large territorial units in order to administer an empire
stretching across the whole Continent. All the same, it is clear that the
linking together and the division of its sections among the members of his
house had no necessary connection with independent nationalities.

The fact is that, having no contact with national aspiration in either its
monarchical or its revolutionary form, Napoleon had no love for it, and
even distrusted it. He realised that patriotism in the home country gave
the nation an awareness of its own permanent interests and a certain dignity over against its leader, however popular he might be, and a certain
impatience with self-centred despotism; and he knew these forces might
one day work against his personal power. So he did his best to replace
them by 'honour', and individual attachment to his own person and
dynasty. It was more important still that this disposition should prevail in
external affairs, and from his point of view he was right: nationalist feelings were still more incompatible with the imperial concept than with
despotism; and it was in these feelings that despotism encountered its
most formidable foe.

# CHAPTER EIGHT

# The Independent Forces

THERE WERE OTHER FORCES – social, spiritual and economic – in action alongside the genius of Napoleon, combining to help or hinder his work. He was creating a method of government and a society where the revolutionary effects of setting free the forces of individualism blended with the traditions of enlightened despotism, the restoration of a social hierarchy inspired by the *ancien régime* and the fashioning of a new legitimacy. The former dynasties and the old aristocracy would not allow themselves to be dispossessed; the middle classes claimed their freedom; and the nations resisted his attempts at a universal monarchy. Intellectual life, too, preserved its autonomy. Lastly, capitalism continued its advance, and tended to hamper Napoleon's enterprises in more than one respect. It is possible that these forces would have been overthrown or at least kept in check if the Grande Armée had not been suddenly destroyed; but the historian can only record that after 1812 they triumphed over the shattered Continental System and continued to dominate the nineteenth century.

## THE CONTINENTAL STATES OF THE ANCIEN RÉGIME

Outside the Empire the Napoleonic system came into collision everywhere with the obstinate resistance of the aristocracy, who saw in it a revival of revolutionary egalitarianism. Napoleon offended them by abolishing seigneurial power and reducing the nobleman to the level of the subject who tilled the soil. In vain did Napoleon spare the nobility in the vassal states at the expense of the peasants: the nobility merely thought that he was waiting for a more favourable moment to strike. In vain did he establish a hereditary nobility: it only resulted in the *parvenu* rubbing shoulders with the *ci-devant* – and that was intolerable. 'These people are forcing us down to a lower level than dirt,' the comtesse de Voss wrote in 1807; and in the eyes of Wellington and other noble lords Napoleon was never anything else but 'Bony', and the king of Rome was his bastard. The kings too were full of the same haughty pride. Deep down in their hearts they could not admit the legitimacy of a man who had unceremoniously unseated so many of royal line. Moreover, they were afraid of the nobles, and when they felt themselves threatened by Napoleon, they were all the more disposed to retain their services. They also feared that any lowering of the nobility's status would encourage a spirit of insubordination. Nevertheless, the power of the state in France was a constant allurement to them, and persuaded them to adopt certain modifications. Their attitude depended on their intelligence and more particularly on their entourage. But whatever novelties were adopted, they had to be consistent with preserving the aristocracy. It was this feature that distinguished the Prussian reform – the only one that succeeded – from the Napoleonic system. Thus the gulf created by the Revolution continued to exist, whatever Napoleon might do: in the eyes of Europe, he was still the soldier of the Revolution.

In Prussia, after the dismissal of Stein, the work of renewal had been concentrated particularly on the army. Scharnhorst had far exceeded the fighting forces that had been contracted for, especially in the country; and additional reserves had been formed with the help of the *Krümper*, and by making use of soldiers given six months' leave, as was customary, in order to train the young generation in the parishes. In 1811, on the pretext of improving the fortifications, he called up the pioneer corps, who in fact spent their time in drilling. It became clear that there had been real technical progress. The army was divided into six corps. Efforts were made – with only relative success, it is true – to accustom the infantry to fighting in skirmishing order; baggage was reduced and tents done away with; the artillery was reconstituted and its equipment renewed, and the necessary requisitioning plans made for the commissariat. All the same, Scharnhorst did not succeed in creating a really national army. Although exemptions were cut down, and corporal punishment abolished in order to make the army appeal to the middle classes, the king refused to decree compulsory service or to set up a militia. Though would-be officers – the *Portepee-Fähnriche* – were obliged to take an examination, and non-commissioned officers were not barred from rising to lieutenant, the nobles' monopoly – apart from certain exceptions made by the king – was in fact confirmed, because officers were authorised to recommend their own candidates for vacancies. Three schools were opened for training the

*Fähnriche*, but the cadet schools reserved for noblemen were still kept in being; moreover, the officers were granted a corporate court of honour, and so remained very much a closed aristocratic caste. At least, Scharnhorst was able to form at the General Staff Headquarters, and at the Military Academy, a High Command that was less notable for its technical ability than for its unity of spirit, readiness to take the offensive and the subordination of all to the common good. As for Wilhelm von Humboldt, who was recalled from his post as ambassador in Rome in December 1808, to take command of education and the control of the churches, he only held this position for a year and a half. His main task was to create the University of Berlin, which had been projected ever since the loss of the University of Halle. He assembled a famous group of professors – Fichte and Schleiermacher, Wolf, Savigny, Niebuhr, Bückh – and so gave it a prestige that brought great advantages to Prussian policy.

The administrative and social reforms were only resumed after Hardenberg's recall on 4 June 1810. He had himself appointed chancellor, thus at last providing a head for the central government. But this dissolute opportunist did not inspire confidence in all the patriots; yet though he mistrusted the hotheads and the secret societies, he was at one with them in his aims, and had a secret interview with Stein in Silesia. He was much more sensitive than the latter to Napoleon's example, and did not have the same respect for the aristocracy. As early as 1807 he was saying that Prussia too needed a revolution, but a revolution from above; and he would gladly have taken the kingdom of Westphalia as his model. And so he aroused much more indignation than Stein, and his reputation today does not stand as high. Finance was his first consideration. Although the Trianon tariff and the seizures that followed procured him twelve million *taler*, he had to find further new resources. He did not even dare to keep the *Einkommensteuer* in Eastern Prussia, but confined himself to increasing the stamp duty on 27 October, as well as the consumption tax on meat, and to extending the milling tax to the lowlands. But he used the occasion to take away the lords' feudal milling, brewing and distilling rights. He also planned to carry through the agrarian reforms, particularly as there were still disturbances in Silesia. In 1807 it had been necessary to call in the French to restrain the peasants, and there was a new insurrection in 1811. Hardenberg wanted to abolish feudal dues and forced labour, proposing in exchange that the lords should be freed from their obligation to provide aid and protection.

The customary rights and the *Bauernschutz* would also disappear, and there would then be nothing to stop a full redistribution of the land, the suppression of compulsory rotation, and a sharing out of the commons. In order to arrange the *Regulierung*, the peasant's obligations would be set against those paid by the lord. If there was a credit balance, the peasant would pay it by giving up a part of his tenure or by paying rent. It was clear that this system, which was in force during the nineteenth century not only in Prussia but in the whole of Eastern Europe, would more or less reduce the peasant to go on working as a day labourer in the service of his lord, and would keep him in a state of subjection. Yet in principle, the state would be the one and only master, and Hardenberg even considered taking the right of policing, if not the right of meting out justice, away from the Junkers. In 1812 he borrowed the French *gendarmerie* system and in each district set up a superintendent of police nominated by the king.

Foreseeing that there would be vigorous opposition from the aristocracy, he sought to get support from public opinion. Moreover, like the patriots, he thought that the nation should have a part in the government. To begin with, he was satisfied with an assembly of notables chosen by himself, sitting from February to September 1811. The Junkers, led by Marwitz, protested vigorously: they did not want popular representation, and demanded a return to the Provincial Estates, where they were the sole representatives – apart from a few from the middle classes. The king had to submit, and arrested Marwitz and Finckenstein. It was a straight social conflict. The king could certainly create nobles, as Marwitz observed, but he could not create noble minds and spirits. And as Yorck was to exclaim in front of Prince William: 'If your highness robs us of our rights, on what then will your own be founded?' The nobles of the Mohrungen district would protest, in 1814, against 'the poisonous influence of French legislation'. Nevertheless, in 1812 an Elective Chamber was called together, comprising two nobles and two deputies representing the towns and the countryside, chosen by the landowners in a two-stage election. This assembly asked for a constitution; but as in the previous one, the nobles were predominant, and their recriminations forced the minister to temporise. The *Regulierungsgesetz* of 1811 tranformed the *Lassits* [leaseholders], who only enjoyed a right of user on the land, into owners, and abolished their dues and forced labour obligations in return for a relinquishment to the lords of a third of the land held, if tenure was hereditary, and of half, if the tenure was for life for a limited period. Seigneurial protection, feudal customs and the *Bauernschutz* were of course still in abeyance, without any compensation for the peasant. The law was so burdensome that it did not affect the obligations of the hereditary tenant proper who could prove a title – the *Erbpachtbauer* or the *Erbzinsbauer* (quit-rent tenant). But the Junkers did not like it any the more; and as early as 1812 they began to discuss possible restrictive amendments. In 1815 the law was suspended, and in 1816 annulled as far as most of the peasants were concerned.

The attempts at restricting the seigneurial rights of policing were equally unsuccessful. On 7 September 1811 Hardenberg had already done away with the milling tax in the countryside, restored their feudal rights to the nobility and fallen back upon direct taxation, capitation fees, taxes on capital and income, and finally licences. This last, which was taken over from France, at any rate involved the abolition of the corporation monopolies. The Junkers' privileges were left intact. They kept their rights of succession and trusts, their powers of justice and patronage, their hunting rights and their fiscal exemptions. Thus Prussia remained very much behind Western Germany, the unity and centralisation of the state having made only a very moderate advance. The aristocracy still kept their privileges, and the emancipation of the peasants was little more than nominal. In several respects there had been more modernisation even in the grand duchy of Warsaw.

Russia, however, had changed still less. After the Peace of Tilsit, Alexander recovered his liking for reform, the war having shown him that the machinery of government called for improvement. From the very outset, the French alliance revived the memories of youth and his taste for liberal catchwords. Although Speranski had been more definite in his plans and more determined in action than the *comité des amis*, nothing much was left of his efforts. This son of an Orthodox priest, who has gone down in history with the surname given him in the seminary, was a distinguished preacher and professor. The Kurakins had introduced him into the Chancery, and he had then become Kochubei's right-hand man in the Ministry of the Interior, entering into direct relationship with the tsar in 1806 and going with him to Erfurt. When they came back Alexander asked him to draw up a constitution, and in 1809 accepted it in principle. The Empire was to be divided into *gouvernements*, *arrondissements* and *cantons*. The *canton* would have a *duma* elected by the landowners, which would in its turn nominate a directory and a delegate to the *arrondissement duma* – and so on in succession, up to an imperial *duma* which would vote the laws and the budget. There would be a ministry responsible to it, with executive power; and each district would have an elective court supervised by the Senate. The tsar would also appoint a consultative Imperial Council.

This scheme owed something to British influence, for Speranski had married an English clergyman's daughter, and showed early signs of great admiration for British institutions. His plan originally involved setting up a parliament with two chambers, one of them representing the landed aristocracy; but he soon realised that the Russian nobility had neither the independence nor the ability of the English lords. All the same it would appear that the territorial divisions he had in mind, the administrative organisation and the election of judges, together with a Conseil d'État and ministries, showed that French influence was also at work. It is therefore all the more remarkable that his social reforms were not even honoured with a trial. There was no question of emancipating the serfs, and although the merchant class were not given the power to buy land, the landowners with the right to elect were nearly all nobles. Alexander decided to adopt this plan by stages. In 1810 he set up the council, and in 1811 the ministries. Speranski became secretary of state, and required all candidates for public service to have university degrees and to pass an examination. This completed the official machinery, and the result – which was far more on the Napoleonic than on the English model, and more in keeping with Russian development – was all that survived of Speranski's plan. Although Speranski had done nothing to impair the nobles' privileges, they viewed him with suspicion, knowing that he was preparing a legal code and a new law for the Jews. He made himself unpopular in his efforts to repair the Empire's decaying finances by increasing taxation and planning an income tax that would not have spared the privileged classes. In Prussia, as in France, the aristocrats put these innovations down to French influence; and when there was a threat of war, he was accused of treason because in obedience to the tsar and in furtherance of his 'secret', he kept up a correspondence with Paris. Alexander needed his nobles in his stand against Napoleon, and therefore sent his friend into exile on 29 March 1812.

When Joseph II came to the throne, his complete change of policy won the admiration of the reactionary aristocracy, for Francis I, who had been equally limited and obstinate in outlook, had refused to contemplate the slightest change in anything at all. All that was left of the Napoleonic regime in Austria was the repression of free thought and speech and indiscriminate power for the police; but these had not been borrowed from outside, and Napoleon, who was not riddled with bigotry and obscurantism, seemed in comparison to be a liberal ruler. The Austrian administration continued to be wholly occupied with finance. In order to pay the war indemnity, it had been necessary to pledge the crown plate and raise forced loans; and even then, there were still seventeen million owing in 1811. His son-in-law granted a further respite, and when the king of Rome was born, he was satisfied with undertakings to pay which were not given him till 4 July 1813, and not one penny of which he ever saw. To cover internal expenses, paper money was printed. On 20 February 1811 Count Wallis, successor to O'Donnell who had died in harness, proclaimed a state of bankruptcy. He exchanged notes for a new issue at a fifth of their value, but the new ones soon went down heavily. The Hungarian Diet protested so vigorously that it had to be dissolved; and – clean contrary to the constitution – a dictatorship was set up.

The struggle against France thus never lost its social character. With Napoleon's so-called allies, the *ancien régime* aristocracy carefully kept its dominant position, knowing that it was doomed for certain if the Continental System was successful; and the emperor's downfall was celebrated as a personal triumph. The Holy Alliance was turned into a kind of insurance against the middle classes and the peasants. From now onwards, Austria was the obvious country to take the lead in it.

### THE ANGLO-SAXONS AND LIBERALISM

Confronted by a despotic continental regime in Europe, the Anglo-Saxons held fast to their own traditions. In England, the Tories no longer protested against the parliamentary system. The suspension of habeas corpus was not renewed – except in Ireland – and the acts of 1799 were applied with some degree of moderation. As the disciples of Pitt, the Tories had borrowed largely from the eighteenth-century Whigs. They took their stand on the Established Church, but they nonetheless gave short shrift to any dissidents. They threw open the peerage to upstarts and distinguished soldiers, were lavish in handing out decorations, and

Imperial France. *Above left*, the new Simplon Pass, a mountain road across the Alps opened by Napoleon for trading between the Rhône valley and Italy. *Above right*, an assembly of the Grand Sanhedrin of Jews reunited by Napoleon on 9 February 1807. *Below*, Napoleon's desire to 'mould the public mind': several generations of a family are reading about his campaigns in the *Eleventh Bulletin of the Grande Armée*

Developments in French intellectual life. *Above*, the famous French zoologist Georges Cuvier. *Below*, *The Adoration of the Kings*, by the Nazarene artist Overbeck

By 1811 Napoleon's relationship with Russia had deteriorated, and in June 1812 he began his invasion campaign. The Battle of Borodino (*above*) fought on 7 September was a long and bloody battle with heavy losses on both sides, but enabled the Grande Armée to enter Moscow on 14 September (*below*)

On 19 October 1812 a disillusioned Napoleon gave orders to retreat from Russia. Charlet's dramatic scene (*above*) shows the Grande Armée as a directionless and anonymous group of soldiers sinking beneath a snow storm. *Left*, Marshal Michel Ney during the retreat from Russia

Marshal Ney defeated at the Battle of Dennewitz, 6 September 1813. *Below*, the Battle of Leipzig, 16–19 October, in which Napoleon was defeated by an alliance including Prussia, Russia and Austria

Napoleon bidding farewell to his troops in the courtyard of the Château de Fontainebleau, 20 April 1814 – 'the only people to remain faithful to the last'. *Below*, Sergeant Ewart of the Royal Scots Greys capturing the French colours at the Battle of Waterloo, where Napoleon was finally defeated, 18 June 1815

On 8 July 1815 King Louis XVIII returned to Paris, restoring the Bourbon monarchy. *Below*, a meeting of the Congress of Vienna to discuss the fate of Napoleon and the French Empire

Turner's romantic image of Napoleon's 'tragic exile in a distant island, lost in the ocean, beneath a tropical sun'

wisely welcomed the upper middle classes into the ranks of the old aristocracy. Their social policy was in fact not unlike Napoleon's, for it aimed
at keeping a hierarchy, though without establishing any position of legal
privilege. But they were nonetheless opposed to the Napoleonic system
because they continued to be attached to their constitutional and liberal
ways; and although not unwilling to open their ranks to a certain number
of newcomers, they were intent on keeping the power in the hands of the
great families of ancient descent.

The continental nobility, for their part, both feudal and military, were
jealous of their own privileges, and reckoned their English counterparts
as too unselective, and too inclined to give wealth precedence over birth.
There were not many men with the insight of Speranski or Stein to take
them as their model. The chief aristocrats envied the English aristocracy
for their skill in keeping their political authority; but they nevertheless
agreed with the absolute monarchs and with Napoleon himself that the
English were a clear example of the weakness of party government. The
Tory party was riddled with personal rivalries, which first brought about
the fall of Castlereagh and Canning and then put Perceval and Wellesley
at loggerheads. When the prince of Wales was invested with full royal
powers as regent in February 1812, he offered the Whigs – as was to be
expected – a place in government (though his own moral authority was at
a low ebb, for public sympathy was entirely on the side of his wife Caroline and his daughter Charlotte). But Grey and Grenville stood out for a
one-party cabinet. Wellesley retired and when Perceval was assassinated
in May, confusion reached its height.

Napoleon was at that moment marching on the Niemen, and a realisation of the great danger won the day over internal strife. Castlereagh was
called to the Foreign Office, and Vansittart joined him at the Exchequer.
Together with Bathurst and under the leadership of Liverpool they
formed a government which was to prepare the way for the destruction of
the Continental System. In September Parliament was dissolved, and the
new House of Commons was solidly behind them; but they had not as yet
won their spurs.

On the other hand there were those on the Continent who wondered
whether Parliament would continue to uphold the *ancien régime*. Certain
symptoms made it doubtful whether the Tories would one day or another
come to grief. For while they continued to support the Corn Laws, the
industrial and trading middle classes were clearly swinging over to free

trade, and the youthful Peel was already showing disquieting signs of taking an independent line on this point. In Parliament, its determined opponents – Whitbread and Burdett – were not much of a danger, for they had little support from the Whig leaders, the Russells, the Hollands and the Greys. But the party was recovering its outside influence thanks to the actions of a growing group in Scotland, centred round Brougham and Sydney Smith. The *Edinburgh Review*, founded by Jeffrey in 1802, and the *Letters of Peter Plymley*, published by Sydney Smith in 1807, were so successful that in 1809 Canning and Southey decided to start the rival *Quarterly Review*. Now that the Tory Party changed its policy and came out in favour of war, the Whigs, taking the opposite line, supported the cause of peace, and found it a highly popular platform. These Whigs did not at any rate style themselves democrats. But political radicalism was beginning to crystallise into a party. Cobbett, who had changed his allegiance, was carrying on an impassioned war of words against the government; Major Cartwright was demanding universal suffrage; Francis Place was resuming his propaganda, and James Mill found a valuable recruit for them in the person of Bentham, who was now won over to political action, and in 1812 drew up his *Catechism for Parliamentary Reform*. But in Europe, those who were intent on preserving or recovering their privileges thought that, all things considered, it was better to put their trust in absolutism.

The influence of England therefore had its chief effect on the middle classes and what remained of the liberal nobility. In itself, Toryism did not hold out any particular attraction for them. Its representatives, like the Whigs before them, seemed to be nothing much more than a venal oligarchy, whose reputation was tarnished by many scandals. True, they had made some slight changes in the penal laws, accepted a few improvements in the administration, and in 1807 abolished the slave trade – though this was just as much in order to raise the price of sugar as to placate the religious abolitionists and the humanitarians; but they were more and more disposed to fall in with Walpole's advice – *quieta non movere*.* Catholic emancipation was still being held up, and in 1810 O'Connell, who had become president of the Irish committee, had given a lively impetus to propaganda. Grattan had come round to the side of reform, and in 1812 the House of Commons decided to vote for it; but the attempt failed, because O'Connell and the clergy refused the requisite

* [Leave well alone.]

guarantees concerning the choice of bishops. The more modern outlook of the Whigs, however, stood them in good stead; and in any case it was hardly of much consequence, for in the eyes of Royer-Collard, Benjamin Constant or even Chateaubriand, who were under an iron despotism, England was the home of constitutional government and freedom, all the more attractive because it eschewed democracy and had kept some reverence for lawful monarchy. England became fashionable once again, as it had been a hundred years before.

France towards the end of the Empire was infatuated with the idea of parliamentary government, though without being very certain what it meant – as the sequel of 1815 would show. But enthusiasm outran knowledge, and anglomania, which was to be all the rage in the Restoration period, was already proving an annoyance to the Napoleonic regime.

The Tories showed no inclination to encourage other nations to adopt their country's political institutions. Probably even Castlereagh was in his heart of hearts not too pleased at having to give account of his actions to Parliament. In any case, there was general agreement that other nations were incapable of governing themselves on their own. Among the Whigs there were at least some men who disagreed with Burke and ascribed universal value to British political customs. They even went so far as to think that they should be reformed according to their ideas before export, so as to give them a certain coherence and uniformity that was quite unknown under the old regime in England. It looked as though the various French constitutions had set them thinking. So it came about that in 1812, when Bentinck found himself master of Sicily, he prided himself on presenting it with a constitution on a logical plan and arranging for the election of a chamber on a suffrage based upon property qualifications and valid for the whole country. This Sicilian parliament abolished the feudal system; but when Bentinck had left for Spain, an opposition party demanded still more radical reforms, and under cover of disturbances provoked by a scarcity of food, the king seized the chance of recovering his authority. On his return, Bentinck demanded the removal of the queen, dissolved the parliament, and in spite of new elections made himself dictator. When he was recalled in 1814 his successor, A'Court by name, used this rather unsatisfactory experiment as an excuse for abandoning the whole project to the vengeance of King Ferdinand.

As far as American democracy was concerned, its calm political life might well have served as an example. Party strife appeared to have

ceased. Under Jefferson's first presidency, the Federalists had disappeared from the scene, and the Republicans seemed gradually to have
adopted the views of their opponents. It is true that Jefferson reduced the
army and the fleet and paid off half the national debt; but nevertheless he
acquired Louisiana, and in order to apply the embargo of 1807, increased
control at the centre. Madison, who succeeded him in 1809, finally
declared war against England, which forced him to progress still further
in the same direction. But in the circumstances of that time, the United
States did not strike Europe as a practical example; their influence had a
greater effect on South America, when combined with that of England
and the French Revolution.

If there were better prospects for liberalism on the Continent and more
especially in France, the causes are to be seen in the growth of the middle
classes and the development of the ideas of 1789. There can be no doubt
that Napoleon only respected religious and economic liberty; but he had
nonetheless kept the sovereignty of the people and the elective principle,
and conquered countries were given a constitution on French lines. The
framework of political life was thus still in existence, and his very despotism reacted to turn men's minds to it. In England, the Whigs appreciated
the liberal quality of his reforms and were quite ready to praise them.
On all sides it was freely recognised that they had been inspired by the
Revolution; and it was constantly natural enough that everything he
had cut away from the revolutionary programme gradually found its way
back again. Even in Russia, Speranski's tentative efforts prepared the way
for Russian officers to catch the infection of French ideas when victory
turned their steps westwards. From 1812 onwards events proved how
great the influence had been in Spain, although it had risen against
France. Jovellanes had managed to induce the central junta to convene the
Cortes in 1809, and they met on 24 September 1810, having been in principle elected by the provincial juntas. But the deputies from the invaded
areas were chosen in Cadiz, even by the refugees, or nominated by the
council of regency, as were the twenty-six American delegates. Now
Cadiz contained the most powerful of the middle classes, and those who
were the most imbued with the new ideas. There was thus a ready-made
liberal majority which certainly did not reflect the opinion of most
Spaniards, for in Napoleon they were not only resisting despotism and
foreign influence, but also the Revolution. Nevertheless, the constitution
of 1812 was an offprint from that of 1791. True, it kept Catholicism as the

state religion and forbade the practice of other faiths; but as the clergy and the *serviles* refused all the same to accept it, the liberals decided in 1813 to abolish the Inquisition, reduce the number of convents and seize the revenues of the monasteries that had been dissolved.

With the fall of the Empire, liberalism would at once resume the battle against the *ancien régime*. On his restoration to the throne, Louis XVIII did not dare to refuse a parliament to the middle classes in France, and Spain was to be the first to rise in 1820 against the Holy Alliance.

## INTELLECTUAL LIFE

During the Napoleonic period, there was a strange slowing down of intellectual life. On the Continent, despotic governments made it their business to stop men's mouths. The English were more interested in detailed reforms than in ideas, and there was no intellectual activity at all in the United States. Besides, discussion seemed futile during these years when each person had taken up his position and was only awaiting the arbitrament of war. Above all, war called forth youthful energies, while the growing political nationalism distracted the attention of a good many minds. Yet in so far as this kind of life went on, it drew no new inspiration from the Napoleonic experiment, and it was between the traditional ideas and the ideas of the eighteenth century that the debate continued in the days to come.

The general state of mental torpor was not favourable to revolutionary thought, and the official papers, the administration and the churches, which were free to express themselves, more or less openly preached in favour of the counter-revolution. Though Napoleon himself defended a certain part of the heritage of 1789, he did it in his own peculiar way, and he had no intention of enlisting the help of the ideologists. Cabanis died in 1808; but Destutt de Tracy, Ginguené and Fauriel all went on with their labours, and their rationalist positivism still had its faithful adherents, such as Stendhal. All the same, it was increasingly eclipsed by a spiritual outlook in harmony with the religious revival, and taught at the Sorbonne by Royer-Collard. Maine de Biran was concerned to bring back to the process of thinking an intuitive awareness that it existed in its own right, and enable it to construct its own metaphysics. Joubert's thought showed the same development, and even an ideologist such as Laromiguière had made some concessions to the intellectual fashion of the moment. In England, there was Bentham, the father of philosophical radicalism, with a markedly more empirical outlook than the French ideologists. He showed an increasing interest in political and economic reform. In Germany, the reigning philosophy was a transcendental idealism, though it had not made many disciples outside the country. It was becoming more and more imbued with mysticism, especially in the thought of Schelling.

The sciences, however, continued their steady advance. In mathematics, Laplace, Monge, Legendre, Poisson, Poinsot and Arago kept France very much in the van. The fame of Gauss in Germany was only in its early stages. French physicists and chemists were equally numerous and distinguished – men such as Malus and Biot, Gay-Lussac and Dulong, Chaptal, Berthollet and Thénard. But England was not behindhand, for she had men like Dalton and Davy; and there was Berzelius in Sweden, while Rumford, although domiciled in France, was Anglo-American in origin. Chemistry had now really come into its own with the formulation of the basic laws of chemical combination. New elements were being constantly isolated, and the new industries based upon these discoveries were rapidly expanding. France enjoyed a striking supremacy in the natural sciences, where such men as Cuvier and Geoffroy Saint-Hilaire now came in to join the already famous Lamarck. Zoology, comparative anatomy and palaeontology were ceasing to be purely descriptive; and the controversy that now arose between Lamarck and Geoffroy Saint-Hilaire, who were working out the first conceptions of the transformation of species, and Cuvier, who championed the principle of fixed species, was one of the most famous in the whole century. Haüy had established the bases of crystallography, and Candolles was carrying on his botanical research. Bichat had thrown light upon the cellular composition of the tissues, and medicine was turning the discoveries of Broussais, de Laënnec, Corvisart and Dupuytren to good account. Alexander von Humboldt, famous for his exploration of South America, was the only man to rival the French naturalists. In history and in linguistics, Germany was once again taking the lead, and England was coming to the fore in the sphere of political economy.

In the eighteenth century, there had been a continuous use of scientific knowledge to break down traditional ideas; and its further extension seemed to augur a revival for rationalist positivism. The emperor smoothed the way for its development by giving science a large place in secondary education and by keeping the great institutions of the Convention period through which the scholars saw to it that their discoveries were made widely known. Moreover, Laplace, Lamarck, Cuvier and Ampère were some of the best writers of the time. Several of these notable men, it is true, were able to reconcile their researches with traditional ideas. Cuvier, for instance, whose training in Stuttgart had accustomed him to think in terms of genera and species like the scholastics, and who saw as the sole purpose of science the discovery in nature of the order that had been established by divine decree, prided himself that his work would form a solid barrier against the positivism of his rivals. But as always, the experts' objective research helped in more or less indirect ways to transform not only men's ideas, but the whole economy, and consequently the structure of society and its habits and morals; with the result that all indirectly helped to bring about the downfall of traditions which were inseparably bound up with it.

The leaders of counter-revolution continued to make use for their own ends of the empirical rationalist movement. In 1802 Bonald had published his *Législation primitive* and in 1810 de Maistre his *Essai sur le principe des constitutions politiques*. In 1808 Charles de Haller, by way of prelude to the *Restauration de la science politique* (the first volume of which did not appear till 1816), had produced his *Abrégé de la politique universelle*. Up till then, he had announced a purely positive doctrine, founded, like Bonald's, on the sovereign rights of the head of a family, which was simply stated as a fact. Nevertheless, while Bonald and de Maistre justified a hierarchy of authority and held modern kingship to be lawful, Haller took the opposite line, defending the political claims of the aristocracy and questioning the power of the state. The head of the government, he held, was simply one owner among others, an owner who had wrongly encroached on the rights of the seigneur; and reason dictated a return to the feudal system.

Bonald and more especially Joseph de Maistre were nonetheless convinced of the necessity for divine sanctions, and even Haller had recourse to it later on and ended by becoming a Catholic. In the same way, the general thought of the counter-revolutionaries inclined towards traditional religious views when in search of a philosophy, a course in which they were encouraged by the secular power. The temporal interests of the Catholic Church had continued to encounter some severe shocks. Secularisation had spread throughout the Empire and through many of the vassal states, even including Bavaria. But these trials had not been without value for the Church's spiritual influence. Pius VII's captivity, following upon his predecessor's, had called forth a sympathy for the papacy which had been unknown shortly before the Revolution. The lower ranks of the clergy, closely subject as they were to the state and so to the bishops, instinctively turned for help to Ultramontanism. The Church had been purified and disciplined by her sufferings, and her ministers were more popularly recruited than in former times. She was now massing her forces for a great offensive, and waiting only for the downfall of the emperor to give the signal. Yet her system of apologetics was very mediocre in quality, and contaminated by the spirit of the age. Everywhere the state was imbued with a spirit of Josephism, which only saw the catechism as a manual of morality and the priest as a political agent. The Romantic influence, with its hostility to the intellect, was bringing into Catholic thought elements that were foreign to Thomism, and dangerous for Catholic doctrine. Bonald and de Maistre were not altogether free from this tendency, and a school of thought had grown up round Chateaubriand's aesthetic and sentimental Catholicism, while Lammenais's attempts to show the common-sense basis of Christianity, which could not but win universal assent, was unconsciously laying the foundations for future schism. The fact remains that by these various ways people of considerable importance were brought back to the fold. Several German Romantics had had violent conversions, and there was a group of German artists at Rome, called the Nazarenes, who were attracted by the primitives, and inclined to the same turbulence of expression. Overbeck, their leader, became a Catholic in 1813. In Germany and in England, a Protestant renaissance was also under way. Schleiermacher was still a reputable pastor; Fichte and Schelling bowed to the conformist spirit. The Methodists, in spite of a fresh internal split in 1811, remained popular; so did the Baptists, who two years later made an opposite move and united in one body. There were now two million Dissenters.

Somewhat on the fringe of traditional religion, mysticism continued to flourish and abound. Saint-Martin had died in 1803, but he had left disciples, and so had Antoine de la Salle – people like Azaïs and Gence, later professor at the École des Chartes. The centres of mysticism were still Lyon and Alsace. In the former, the printer Ballanche was meditating on the successive interpretations of dogma in the light of an intuitive mysticism; and in Alsace, Oberlin (until his death in 1806), Baron de Turkheim, Salzmann and the *préfet* Lezay-Marnésia were all more or less given over to mystical illumination. Some of these speculations had a syncretist and polytheistic tendency, or pursued a cabbalistic line, with research into the magic properties of numbers. Fabre d'Olivet, for instance, had in this way passed from 1805 onwards through ideology to theosophy, and in 1813 had published his *Vers dorés de Pythagore*. In Germany, the oracles of mysticism were Baader and Jung Stilling, who had been professor at Karlsruhe since 1803. Like Bergasse in France, he dabbled in millenarianism, Napoleon providing a very convenient figure for Antichrist. In Alsace, the French and the German streams tended to merge, and it was here that Madame de Krüdener seems to have become initiated into these mysteries. After meeting Jung Stilling she came into touch with Oberlin and at Sainte-Marie-aux-Mines with Pastor Fontaine. A little later on, we hear of her again at Geneva, from which she was expelled in 1813. She passed on her musings to Madame de Staël, who was already getting August Schlegel to read Saint-Martin to her, and was entertaining Zacharias Werner, a literary figure and renegade mystic who ended by becoming a Catholic priest. In a fit of emulation she began to study the *Imitation* and Madame Cuyon. In Russia, as always, there was a whole host of mystical sects. 'Spiritual Christianity' was fashionable at that time among the aristocracy; and Alexander, who had been won over by Galitsin and Kochelev, began to read and study the Bible in 1812, preparing himself in this way for playing the part of Madame de Krüdener's White Angel.

In literature and in art, the Romantic movement was the great source of renewal and excitement. Germany, having worked out a philosophy for it and adopted it wholesale, considered that her own genius had created the movement, though it was in fact widespread throughout the West, and owed too much to Rousseau for there to be any doubt about its parentage. The German Romantics were not concerned to be too precise about their metaphysics. The Heidelberg group were chiefly interested in exploring the past, several of them bending their efforts towards an apology for the *ancien régime* and for Germanism. Before long, a third generation would only be concerned with interpreting the sentiment of nationality. In particular, what remained from the didactic activities of the initiators of the movement was a disdain for aesthetic conventions and an apologia for creative imagination. Goethe had finally condemned the extravagance and arbitrariness of their literary efforts, and had parted company from them, although his *Elective Affinities*, which came out in

1809, had not perhaps gone so far as to disclaim the passionate fatalism which was one of the principal themes of the movement in every country. They did not succeed in producing any great works – unless Kleist is to be numbered among them by reason of his unstable inner life and his inability to fit in with his surroundings, which led him to suicide in 1811; and this remained the permanent central theme of the Romantic movement. But the idealist symbolism expounded by Novalis, with its harmony between the ideal and the visible world as united in the heart of Eternal Being, was very far from answering to his condition, for his own nature and the disasters of the period meant that he could see nothing in this world but insoluble conflicts and universal antagonisms. His dramas are therefore entirely tragic in their genius. In *The Schroffenstein Family*, we have the struggle of the individual against his own kin; in *Robert Guiscard*, the struggle of the hero against hostile forces; in *Penthesilea*, the clash between the sexes and between different races, and between the nations in *Die Hermannsschlacht*; and finally the conflict between conscience and law in *The Prince of Homburg*.

But the German Romantics are to be remembered for something more important than their literary works, namely the impetus they gave to linguistic, historical and juridical studies. Following on from their friends at Heidelberg, the brothers Grimm had produced their *Fairy Tales* and undertaken the study of their languages while Creuzer was publishing his works on the symbolic interpretation of Greek mythology. The new interest shown in literatures that could be contrasted with the classics did not stop short at Shakespeare: it went on to include the *Romancero* and Camoens, as well as the literature of the East and of India. Wilhelm von Humboldt was also devoting himself to linguistic studies. Philological criticism had been brilliantly represented from the end of the eighteenth century onwards by Wolf's *Prolegomena ad Homerum*, published in 1795. His disciple Böckh went on to add historical research, and in 1811 Niebuhr began to bring out his *History of Rome*. Finally, the Romantic spirit had penetrated the conception of law. Savigny and Eichhorn contrasted what they saw as the unconscious creation of the *Volksgeist* age with the *Code Napoléon*. This they considered to be an artificial product of the intellect, and above all a foreign importation having no genuine links with the life of the German nation. This process of exploring the relationship between juridical studies and the general history of societies was to bring new vitality to the whole subject.

In England, famous poets were beginning to be inspired by the Romantic movement. The Lake Poets, Wordsworth and more especially Coleridge, had long been under the influence of a national outlook, and had begun to adopt a preaching tone, while Southey had rallied to the Tory cause. He was in receipt of a pension, and became poet laureate in 1813. But the increasing influence of a certain puritan outlook was temperamentally repugnant to a number of young aristocrats whom position and fortune exempted from the necessity of earning a living; and they set themselves up as the champions of an anarchical individualism. Though he remained classical in form, Byron became a type of antisocial Romantic. He was an authoritarian aristocrat, impatient of all rules and in revolt against a caste solidarity: not at all the kind of revolutionary who dreams of coming to the rescue of the oppressed classes, although he did in the end meet his death in the ranks of the Greek insurgents. He was rather the unique figure, alone against the rest of the world, claiming the right to be his own law-giver and choosing as his model the outlaw, or better still, Lucifer in rebellion against God himself. Byron was also the temperamental Romantic who gives himself over with a mixture of delight and torment to the fatal forces of passion, and who feels predestined to misfortune and to death. Or, fleeing from society, from his own country and from himself, he takes refuge in the contemplation of nature and in solitary exile. It was thus that he discovered the East and in 1812 published *Childe Harold*, in 1813 his *Giaour*, and in 1814 *The Corsair*; and it was these works that were destined in the course of the next few years to have such a powerful effect in making the exotic fashionable, and popularising the cult of local colour.

Shelley too suffered from a want of social discipline and an unhealthy sensitivity. When sent down from Oxford, he defied the religiously minded by his intellectual pantheism and defence of free love. His first essays came out in 1810 and his *Queen Mab* in 1813. De Quincey, who was – like Coleridge – an opium addict, was likewise bent upon breaking away from his country's conventions. But England repudiated these bold spirits; yet at the same time, Walter Scott was introducing a Romanticism not unlike that of the Heidelberg school, at once medieval, conservative and nationalist in outlook, first in his poems, and then in his historical novels, which enjoyed an extraordinary popularity throughout the world, particularly after the publication of his *Waverley* in 1814. In this form, Romanticism could deeply move the common run of men,

without irritating the great; for the virtuous rebel or the knight who
went about righting wrongs was made acceptable by being adorned with
the usual trappings of popular romance, such as mysterious birth, dis-
guises, visions and dark conspiracies.

In France, literature was still honoured by the Institute and sought the
approval of Geoffrey, the doyen of critics, not daring to depart from the
traditional rules. There were a few graceful writers, among the best of
whom was the poet Delille. Benjamin Constant's masterpiece, *Adolphe*,
belongs to the classic line; but official doctrine did not reckon the novel
among the noble literary genres. In spite of his liking for Ossian, Napoleon remained faithful to this aesthetic outlook, for it seemed to him that
French influence was suffering from its decadence, and towards the end
of his reign he was constantly suspicious of the successes won by the
Romantic movement in Germany and England. Yet it was hardly possible
to go on deceiving oneself: the Revolution had put the final touches to the
decay of classical art by breaking up the old aristocracy who had been its
chief patrons, by causing a decline in those studies which alone would
enable the middle classes to appreciate it, and by swelling their ranks with
uneducated *nouveaux riches* who were more interested in Pixérécourt's
dramas, Alexandre Duval's plays and Pigault-Lebrun's novels. This popular literature bore some of the marks of an ingenuous Romanticism,
such as unbridled imagination, a mixture of genres and attempts at realism. Official criticism affected to consider the drama as a kind of debased
tragedy; but Lemercier's *Pinto* (1801) and *Christophe Colomb* (1809), in
which the conventions were isolated, showed – despite their weaknesses –
that there was a real upheaval coming. Moreover, the pre-Romantic
tastes of the eighteenth century were still alive. There was still appreci-
ation for the troubador genre, as was shown by the welcome given to the
so-called Clotilde de Surville, and Ossian was even more popular. Oscar
and Malvina were in favour as Christian names; and Le Sueur, in his
opera *Les Bardes*, drew inspiration from Macpherson's forgeries, as did
the painters Gérard and Girodet.

All the same, it was really contemporary events that were chiefly
responsible for the Romantic climate. Imaginations had been raised to
fever pitch by the disturbances of the Revolution, the rise of Napoleon
and continued warfare. Not everyone could find his niche, and fortune
did not favour every temperament alike. Those who were disappointed
took their revenge – if they could write – by telling their own story. As

early as 1802, in his *Génie du Christianisme*, Chateaubriand laid bare
the boredom of the misfit with a disgust that was a mixture of anger
and pride. Sénancour's *Obermann* exhibited the same disease, though
with an even more mournful despair, while in the work of Millevoye
and Chênedollé, it was softened down into a Lamartinean melancholy.
Besides, although the ideals of liberty and equality had been proclaimed,
the customs of the time and the Civil Code had not by any means embodied all their implications. After portraying Atala as the victim of passion
in conflict with duty, Madame de Staël gave an equally unhappy portrait
of Delphine and Corinne because – in her view – social prejudice refused
to allow woman the right to be happy. Horizons were being broadened by
returning émigrés, full of the memories of strange lands, and by the stor-
ies of the emperor's soldiers and officials; a taste for the exotic was being
developed. Chateaubriand's publication in 1811 of his *Itinéraire de Paris à
Jérusalem* revived the curiosity about the East that had earlier been
aroused by the Egyptian expedition; and his *Martyrs* had an equally
nostalgic effect on those who read it. And lastly, there was a growing
closeness of contact with foreign literatures. The ideologists like Fauriel
and Gérando, faithful to their objective positivism, condemned the
prejudice of Frenchmen and recognised that the works of each nation
had their own particular merits and the right to claim a certain beauty.
Under the Empire, this eclecticism was of special benefit to the southern
nations. Madame de Staël's *Corinne* had already raised the reputation of
Italy in French eyes; and from 1811 onwards Ginguené began publishing
his *Histoire littéraire d'Italie*, while in Geneva Sismondi was giving a
course on the literatures of the South. All the same, Madame de Staël
acted as a kind of spokesman for Germany, and the part played by her was
therefore of the first importance, for it was in Germany that Romanticism
had first come into its own.

Madame de Staël came of German stock on her father's side. She had
married a Swede, and was a Protestant, and with her Genevan connections felt much sympathy for Calvinist England and Lutheran Germany.
Temperamentally, she was more inclined to be passionate than to exercise
the critical spirit, and it was therefore quite natural for her to be taken
with the northern literatures. As early as 1801 she had written an essay on
*La Littérature considérée dans ses rapports avec les institutions sociales* in
which she questioned the universal value of the classics, admitted that
beauty was relative and drew a contrast between the different climates of

the northern and southern countries, taking Ossian as characteristic of the former and Homer of the latter. She could hardly say too much in praise of the northern nations, with their seriousness, their zeal for liberty, their strong moral sense and their religious spirit, which yet avoided superstition. Nevertheless, at this period she was still disposed to consider the classics superior, for she had been brought up on them, and she knew nothing as yet of Germany and the German language. But when Napoleon sent her into exile in 1803, she crossed the Rhine, and on her way back she brought August Schlegel along with her. He stayed with her till 1810, initiating her into the mysteries of German Romanticism. Her circle were likewise won over, for Benjamin Constant wrote *Wallenstein* in 1809, and Madame Necker de Saussure translated Schlegel's *Course of Lectures on Dramatic Art* in 1811. It was this development that was the inspiration of her book *De l'Allemagne*, in which French literature now received far less favourable treatment as compared with Shakespeare and the Germans. Here, Madame de Staël repudiated the classical conventions and the critical attitude, and extolled the virtues of enthusiasm, in a spirit of pure Schlegelism. This famous work was printed in Paris in 1810. It was immediately impounded, and only reappeared after the downfall of the emperor. Nevertheless, during the later years of the Empire criticism came openly face to face with the conflict between classicism and Romanticism, and the question was no longer ignored in Italy, where there had been a tendency to favour Nordic literature, either directly or more often indirectly, through French translations. In 1807 its influence was openly shown in Foscolo's *Sepolcri*.

The plastic arts were also beginning to feel the influence of the Romantic movement, although here the classical tradition put up a much better defence. Napoleon was particularly interested in architecture, and his thirst for prestige was in accord with his personal taste in preferring the majesty of the classical order. 'There is always beauty in grandeur,' as he was accustomed to say. Unconsciously, however, he directed several artists along a new road that led towards the Romantic by suggesting to them – and sometimes ordering – pictures based upon his exploits in contemporary history; but he had little to do with forming the rich and heavy 'Empire style', the roots of which go back to the Etruscan and Egyptian influences of the eighteenth century. Denon, who was the head of his Museums Department, was an artist and a rather eclectic enthusiast. The supporter of classical art as derived from antiquity was Quatremère de

Quincy, whose notion of the beautiful went back to ideal Platonic arche-
types, which must be imitated as closely as possible by eliminating all
individual peculiarities and concentrating on design, so that he held
sculpture to be the essential form of art. Faithful exponents of this doctrine were Percier and Fontaine in the Louvre, and Gondouin, the
designer of the Vendôme Column, together with Chalgrin, who was
responsible for the Arc de Triomphe; and David's favourite style was also
in accordance with Quatremère's doctrine. But the great sculptors of the
period were foreigners such as the Danish Thorwaldsen and particularly
Canova, who was a special favourite of Napoleon.

Art was, however, very far from offering the uniformity that Quatremère desired. Alexandrian influence, which became fashionable in the
eighteenth century after the exploration of Pompeii, produced a reaction
against the firm and somewhat tense lines of David; and there slipped
into Girodet and Prud'hon's work a kind of tired and melancholy volup-
tuousness, while in Canova, the purity of style was marred by a certain
unmanly gracefulness and a taste for the picturesque. In decorative art, the
Alexandrian style continued to hold its own alongside the imperial fash-
ions. On the other hand, a certain realism was necessary in portraiture,
and here there was no one to match Gérard, or better still David. Finally,
the subjects taken by Girodet from Ossian or from Chateaubriand or
from contemporary history, David's *Coronation*, the battle scenes by
Gros, the soldiers painted by Géricault – all those brought back variety of
idea, movement as well as design, and brilliance into the colour scheme,
and were purely Romantic works. There was a still greater freedom
about the paintings of Goya and British painters such as Lawrence, Rom-
ney and Raeburn, while England was at the same time giving birth to the
school of landscape painters, led by Constable and Turner, who were to
bring into the new style of painting one of its most novel and appealing
features.

As far as music was concerned, there was no continuation in France of
the new life brought by the Revolution once the revolutionary ideas had
been condemned. All that remained was a certain preference for melody
and prejudice against 'clever' music, together with some weakness in
technique, and a degree of emphasis no longer justified by any supporting ardour or enthusiasm, though not without links with the art of David.
Among the chief composers were Frenchmen like Méhul or Italians who
had settled in France, like Spontini. *Joseph* and *La Vestale* both appeared

in 1807. Then there was Boïeldieu, who returned from Russia in 1811, and was successful in raising the reputation of comic opera. Cherubini, who was Berlioz's teacher, was already showing a truly Romantic productiveness and power, but his music was not popular.

But all other lights were already being eclipsed by Beethoven in Vienna. While still composing for the piano, he had since the beginning of the century been producing his great instrumental works, his quartets and overtures, and the first eight symphonies. His works often shocked his contemporaries by their daring technique, and by their novel vigour of expression, but they won them over by the richness of their inner life. In many respects, Beethoven was akin to the Romantics. His was a violent and uneven temperament, full of fire and highly sensitive, but cut off from the world by his deafness, and tortured by many a hopeless love affair. He was suspicious and apt to take offence, and condemned by his plebeian background and his poverty to all kinds of painful incidents in the aristocratic circles he was obliged to frequent. Like Novalis, he had created through his music a magic world which cushioned him against reality. All the same, there was nothing weak about him. Many of his songs express joy and grace and vigour, and have the light touch of a healthy human being who was full of purpose and buoyancy; others express an aspiration to heroic greatness and to battle with the hostile forces of the universe. Beethoven never sank into fruitless despair, for he was a son of the eighteenth century, on fire with a restless but dogged optimism. He was a natural republican, with a deep sense of human solidarity and a great confidence in the future of the race. In several respects he was akin to Rousseau, and among the Germans his thought was nearer the classical than the Romantic, and particularly near to Schiller's. Fundamentally, he was a tragic figure like Kleist: the deepest pathos in his works centres round the struggle between the heroic soul and a refractory nature, but also – when seen in the light of the times that gave them birth – the stormy conflicts between the Revolution and the old world, between freedom and despotism, and between the rising new nations and the Napoleonic Empire.

## THE RISE OF NATIONALITY IN EUROPE AND AMERICA

The progressive expansion of intellectual life among the peoples during the eighteenth century had resulted – especially in Germany – in developing a nationalist culture among the writers and in the universities. Classical civilisation was seen as a French creation, which reduced them to a subordinate position. The Napoleonic system reinforced the spiritual influence of France through institutional reform and military conquest, thus strengthening this reaction still further. While not denying the principle of a universal civilisation, which is an essential part of Christianity, the nations instinctively guarded their independence in the field of literature, art and manners, and sought to discover the characteristic features of their original springs of feeling and action – what Jahn in 1810 called *Volkstum* – whether in the past, where there seemed to be no trace of foreign influence, or in the lower classes, whose ignorance kept them apart from all cosmopolitan trends. Herder and Burke had defended this type of nationalism by representing each people as a living being, impossible to assimilate to any other; and the German Romantics crowned this philosophy by endowing each nation with a *Volksgeist*, the most significant expression of which is language. In the Napoleonic period these opinions were shared by Cuoco in Italy and Karamzin in Russia.

The characteristic feature of Italian thought at this period was that it showed much more vigorous resistance to French ascendancy at a time when it seemed that this was likely to be strengthened by Napoleonic rule, and when the writers who had supported the regime, such as Monti and Cesarotti, together with a whole body of official literature, *la littérature des préfets*, had meekly given in to the domination of France. Cesari brought the Tuscan language back to its classic purity, and compiled a dictionary; and without entering into political opposition to France, Cuoco, serving under Melzi and Joseph in Milan and Naples, and Foscolo at Pavia, showed an uncompromising spirit in any questions of linguistic or literary autonomy. In Florence, Niccolini, who was openly hostile to the victors, published nothing, but went back into the past in search of famous works belonging to his country. Canova's art and Italian music were also a source of national pride, a feeling which Napoleon would seem to have taken into account. Although the reintroduction of the indigenous language in the Italian lawcourts in 1809, in those parts that had been annexed by France, was doubtless a necessary concession in the interests of the administration of justice, literary circles were jubilant when the Accademia della Crusca was reconstituted in 1812. In Belgium, there was no resistance to French culture. In the Rhine provinces, it made little progress, though there was no concerted opposition. In

Holland, on the other hand, the literary world gave up all attempts at imitation and simply retreated into itself.

Outside the Empire, Norway obtained a university in 1813. Further east, Russia now had her literary journals, such as the *European Messenger*, founded by Karamzin in 1802, and the *Russian Messenger*, published by Sergei Glinka from 1808 onwards. Karamzin set about producing a literary language and eliminating the classical genres, the ode and the tragedy. After the Peace of Tilsit, Glinka and Rostopchin came out in vigorous opposition against the foreign manners and modes adopted by the court and the nobles, and Glinka was particularly concerned to uphold the conventional Russian past and to combat Western innovations. Karamzin, who had formerly been in sympathy with the Enlightenment, was now won over to the national traditions, and began to write a history of the Muscovite state. Among the Habsburgs, Hungary continued to demand recognition for Magyar as the official language, and the Czechs were also stirring, for there had been a chair in their language at Prague University since 1792. Dobrovski was stabilising its grammar, and Šafáryk and Palacký were preparing to become writers. After Illyria was conquered, Marmont admitted the Slovene and Croatian languages in public documents and in the elementary schools; and under his protection, Abbot Vodnik wrote elementary books in Slovene. Finally, there were stirrings among the Balkan Christians, the Greeks being the most advanced, and multiplying the number of their *hetairia*. Among the Serbs, national tradition, supported by the parish priests, kept them loyal to the Orthodox faith; but there was a revival of Romanian language and history in Transylvania, and in 1813 a Moldavian school was opened at Jassy.

In countries that had long been national states or had kept a lively memory of their former independence – England and Holland, Switzerland, Poland and Hungary, Spain and Portugal – a national culture was a normal part of political nationalism; but in other countries, it was something that helped to bring political consciousness to birth. The Czechs, the Illyrian Slavs, the Romanians and even the Greeks did not as yet, like the Serbs, appear to contemplate fighting for their freedom; but in Italy, the transformation of a cultural into a political patriotism, which had begun in the revolutionary period, was making some progress, while it had actually taken place in Germany. The Revolution had helped this movement by making sovereignty a national matter, and it was only natural that this principle should have been used against the Napoleonic ascendancy. In practice, the French were equally responsible for preparing the way for the expression of national sentiment by forming a framework for government, with a hierarchy of officials and more especially – at least in Italy – armies which recruited the boldest opponents of the Holy Alliance. In Southern Italy, they also established the societies known as the Carbonari, originating in Franche-Comté, which had since the beginning of Murat's reign been apparently won over to some extent to the idea of unity.

The influence of these various factors must not, however, be exaggerated: they were none of them as important as the fact of conquest. Whatever idealism the patriot may aspire to, it will only take political shape for extremely practical motives, even among the upper classes, who are the normal exponents of a national culture. At all events, among the bulk of the lower classes, hatred of the foreigner and all new ideas have always been in the forefront, and the appearance of soldiers and foreign administrators had always produced a prompt reaction. The Napoleonic system had its merits; but its benefits had always to be weighed against its burdens, and the balance was hardly a favourable one. In the first place, the emperor threw the cost of warfare upon the shoulders of the conquered country, which had to bear the demands and depredations of his armies and the requisitions for supply, not to mention the war taxes. Westphalia, for instance, was taxed at twenty-six million. Once these arrangements had been made, Napoleon laid it down as a principle that these conquered countries should be self-supporting, even poverty-stricken Illyria. At the very most – as in the case of Naples and Spain – he would produce the ready money for paying the army of occupation as long as the country was not yet pacified, though he did this with extreme reluctance. In 1807 Joseph set aside forty-four million for the army, only six million of which were repaid. Westphalia had to find ten million for the 12,500 French who constituted half its army. In 1809, out of expenses amounting to 127 million, the kingdom of Italy had to pay thirty million over to France and spent only forty-two million on its own troops. Moreover, the new administrations were expensive. It may be said in general that everywhere taxes rose out of all proportion. The grand duchy of Berg paid six million in 1808, but thirteen million in 1813; and in Venetia the sum was trebled. Moreover, men had to be found as well. The Italian army, for example, was increased from forty-nine thousand in 1810 to ninety-one thousand in 1812; the duchy of Berg had only five thousand men in 1806, but 9,400 in 1811. Finally, it may be said that the blockade exasperated more people than it pleased. Apart from Spain, which was largely laid waste by war, it was Germany, and particularly Prussia in 1812, that had the greatest cause for complaint. It was not a purely spiritual fervour that induced this country to become the heart and soul of the national uprising in 1813; for Germany was on the high road to Russia, and ever since the summer of 1811 she had had to lodge the bulk of the Grande Armée. Prussia, like Poland, was the base for the Russian expedition, and had to hand over all she possessed. As early as 5 December 1811 Jérôme (whose possessions were nevertheless somewhat to the rear of this area) was already sounding a note of alarm:

> Excitement has reached fever pitch . . . Spain is being held up as an example, and if war breaks out, all the countries between the Rhine and the Oder will rise as one man. The cause of unrest is not simply a strong impatience with the foreign yoke; it lies deeper, in the ruin that faces every class of people, the crushing taxation; the war levies, the billeting of troops, all the military coming and going, and a constant series of harassments. There are good reasons to be afraid of a movement of despair on the part of people who have nothing to lose, because all they had has already been taken from them . . . The common people are indifferent to affairs of higher policy: they are only concerned with the present evils that weigh so heavily upon them.

The king of Westphalia might well have added that the aristocracy and the middle classes had long been equally affected, which was even more serious. In the vassal countries, the national debt had been left as it was or only partly reduced, retirement and pension agreements had been repudiated and officials and officers of the old regimes dismissed. The states that had remained independent – in particular Prussia – had been compelled to do the same. And the conquerors were held responsible for all these evils.

On the other hand the Napoleonic system, introduced ruthlessly in the most varied regions, often resulted in a revival of the efforts formerly made by the enlightened despots to improve the lot of their subjects without consulting them; but now they were applied much more decisively, and over a much wider range. All this seemed overcomplicated, formal and much too demanding to countries that were not as rich as

France and accustomed to very indolent – and often half-barbarian – governments, such as existed in Illyria. The Civil Code did even greater harm by upsetting family customs and property arrangements. Its openly lay character, which put all religions on the same footing, introduced a secular state and divorce, gave freedom to the Jews and protected the Freemasons, ensured the solid opposition of the clergy. In the Protestant states, the equality given to Catholics did not always meet with favour. In Holland, for instance, attempts were made to dismiss them from employment – or so the French authorities maintained. In Illyria, Poland and Russia, the Orthodox priests looked upon Napoleon as Antichrist. Catholic opposition was specially pronounced because of the secularisations, the abolition of tithe and the break with the papacy. Even more formidable was the aristocrats' rage at seeing the feudal system abolished and the secular state introduced. The gentry of Berne and Geneva, the patricians in Holland and the Hanseatic cities never forgave the French on this particular point. Nor was there any lack of further grievances for the populace or the middle classes. The artisans were alarmed by the suppression of the corporations; the officials were riled at seeing Frenchmen appointed to the higher posts; and the 'patriots', who had so faithfully supported revolutionary France, were systematically turned down as Jacobins. The peasants complained that agrarian reforms always spared the seigneurs. The only people to keep a certain affection for the Napoleonic regime were a number of powerful middle-class citizens who had greedily bought up national property, attained to important positions and profited by the blockade. In all the countries where Napoleon set up the framework of modern national and social administration, common interests brought the inhabitants together in a strong desire for independence and opposition to France. Poland presents a particularly interesting example, because she owed a great deal to Napoleon and would have owed more still if he had been victorious over Russia. Yet the Polish clergy remained covertly hostile to him, and the nobles were hesitant, fearing the new reforms that a small nucleus of democrats were already demanding. Moreover, they could not forgive the emperor for not having remitted the entire mortgaged debt which Prussia had made over to them, consisting of forty-three million plus four million in arrears of interest, which he reduced to twenty million, payable in three years. The peasants had not gained complete liberty, and were only concerned with the charges that still lay heavy upon them. Like the Prussian peasants, they had suffered from the passage of the Grande Armée, and it was to the French that they attributed all they had had to put up with from it. There was no question of Poland doing what Napoleon hoped for, namely to give him enthusiastic and unquestioning support.

In a variety of unforeseen and roundabout ways, the wars of this period helped on the progress of other nations as well. Finland was separated from Sweden and was given a constitution by Alexander, drawn up by Speranski, which gave her independence. Norway, cut off from Denmark by the English fleet and reduced to starvation, did in fact become independent, although she had not risen in any way against Frederick VI. In America, the Spanish colonies were in process of forming new nations, and Brazil was no longer willing to pay allegiance to Portugal. The year 1812 is a memorable date in the history of the United States, for it marked the beginning of the Second War of Independence against England, to throw off the yoke of economic dependence that the ex-colony had had to bear up to this time, a dependence from which England had reaped considerable advantage. Madison seems to have been advised to break off relations by a group of new men, such as Clay, Calhoun and Webster, who wanted to seize Canada and make certain of their country's autonomy by developing industry under the shelter of a customs barrier. It was a difficult war to fight, for the United States had no army and no money. Funds had to be borrowed for equipping a militia, in spite of protests from the Northern states, which on the very eve of peace threatened to disobey the federal government. The invasion of Canada was a failure: in 1813 and 1814 there were English attacks to be met on Lake Erie and in the direction of Lake Champlain; Baltimore was assailed and Washington burnt down; and again in 1815 Jackson had to repel an attempted assault on New Orleans. At sea, the success of the American frigates and privateers, who captured 2,500 enemy ships, was nevertheless powerless to prevent the ports being blockaded. The losses were reckoned at thirty thousand killed, and two hundred million in dollars. There were no territorial gains, and the damage to trade was considerable. But industry took advantage of the war to capture the home market, and after peace had been signed, the 1816 tariff ensured its preservation. Moreover, the crisis was responsible for a considerable strengthening of national feeling.

The various national resistances made difficulties for Napoleon. In the Tyrol, insurrections were an embarrassment, and in Spain a source of weakness. But there was no desperate danger as long as his armies remained intact, for the people of Prussia made no move before they heard the news of disaster in Russia, and when Napoleon's position began to crumble, no other nation followed their example. But it must also be noted that although the discontent aroused by French domination was an undoubted factor in the development of national individuality, only very small minorities were animated by a spirit of pure and disinterested nationalism. This was only a secondary cause as compared with the sufferings of the lower classes and the various interests that had been damaged. The Tyrolean rising is a perfect case in point, for it was a rising against Bavaria, which had in no way infringed its Germanism. The popular exasperation was in fact due to the war, more especially the preparations for the Russian campaign; and it would have calmed down again if the emperor had won the day and re-established peace on the Continent. All the same, the awakening of nationalism is a hint that the Continental System would not have survived once the emperor who founded it had gone.

As for the social grievances, they were in part contradictory, with the result that in the countries where the economy had already been modernised, there were obstacles in the way of a united social front. This explains why the coalition between the monarchy and the aristocracy held back from the national movements and turned against them after they had won their own triumph. In the spring of 1812 Alexander was already posing as the protector of downtrodden nations, and from 1813 to 1815 he and his allies were lavish in making vague promises. But they certainly did not intend their own convenient territorial arrangements to be in any way upset. They took it as a matter of course that there should be no reduction in their own power, and that the peasants and middle classes to whom they appealed would have to submit, as they had before, to the superior position of the aristocracy. Austria, obstinately loyal to the *ancien régime*, felt very closely threatened by the subjection of so many nations, and was eager to regain her ascendancy over Italy and Germany. Never for one moment did she consent to giving any kind of revolutionary character to the struggle against France. There is thus already revealed in this duplicity of purpose the history of the first half of the nineteenth century, in which the oppressors wreaked a cruel revenge against their subjects who had allowed themselves to be deceived.

## THE PROGRESS OF CAPITALISM, AND THE EXPANSION OF
## EUROPE THROUGHOUT THE WORLD

During the whole of the Napoleonic period, money was abundant. As this book has already several times explained, this was one of the central features of the British economy. From 1809 onwards there was increasing inflation in Great Britain. The Bank of England dealt with an increasing number of exchequer bills, and in 1811 its commercial discount rate stood at a figure five times as high as in 1795, and there were £28½ million in circulation in the form of banknotes. There was not much increase in the number of private banks in London, with their own issue of notes; but in the provinces there were something like eight hundred of them in 1809. As the Bank of England issued £1 and £2 notes, coins gradually disappeared and prices continued to rise. In 1814 the index was 198 as compared with 100 in 1790. The Bank of England's gold and silver reserve fell to two million in 1815, and the exchange rate dropped from fifteen per cent to twenty per cent, though this did not damage the export trade. In France, inflation was less pronounced. There was a continuance of hoarding, and complaints about the scarcity of coin remained frequent; but there can be no doubt that the note issue increased. The Bank of France's issue rose from sixty-three million in 1806 to 111 million in 1812. The rate of circulation increased too. From 1809 to 1812 bills rose from four hundred to five hundred million and reached 747 million in 1810. If it had had the emperor's support it would have been more lively still, and would have extended greatly in the provinces, where the local banks cannot have done much – though nothing is known about their transactions. Paper credit was as yet only used by a small number of business people, and the increase in metallic coin was of greater importance. This was achieved partly by new minting, partly by the positive funding of the trade balance, chiefly through war indemnities and the income from the foreign territories. The gold and silver brought into France from 1799 to 1814 have been calculated at 755 million. In the Empire, although manufactured products grew dearer, the price of agricultural products sometimes fell; but the general indications are that prices remained perceptibly higher than in 1789. Many of the continental countries went over to paper-money systems. But as their coin was hidden, or had passed to France or England, these were the two chief countries where the monetary inflation made for economic advance.

Moreover, the extension of the revolutionary reforms to a large part of Europe – freedom for the worker, the abolition of serfdom and feudal dues, the opening up of the land, the abolition of internal customs and tolls, a uniform system of weights and measures – all these were in favour of the growth of capitalism. They were in accordance with Adam Smith's doctrine as popularised by Gamier and especially by J.-B. Say, who clarified and supplemented it in his *Traité d'économie politique*, which came out in 1803.

Warfare, too, was a constant stimulant. In England, it forced traders to look for new markets, and on the Continent it ensured effective protection for industry. The continental blockade only underlined the consequences of incessant hostilities, which makes it impossible to determine its exact effect on the conditions of production. Nevertheless, the havoc wrought by war certainly outweighed the advantages. Political uncertainty and the interference with commercial relationships were a widespread brake upon enterprise; and as industrial progress on the Continent depended particularly on the popular spread of British machinery, it would have been speedier still if Englishmen had continued to come over and install it.

In the economic sphere, the inventive spirit, stirred up by scientific research, did not lose its impetus as much as elsewhere; but as compared with the inventions of the eighteenth century, the results were slender. The expansive power of steam when condensed, which had been thought out by Hornblower in 1792, was taken up again in 1804 by Woolf, who made use of medium steam pressures to produce a double effect; and this was the origin of the compound steam-engine. In Philadelphia, a workman and mechanic called Evans introduced some remarkable improvements in the construction of boilers. Murdock, who had succeeded in lighting Boulton's workshops in Birmingham by gas in 1798, installed the first lamps in the streets of London – in Pall Mall – in the year 1807. In France, Philippe Lebon had made the same discovery, but died in 1804 without having been able to get it adopted. Towards the end of the Empire, Philippe de Girard also succeeded in producing a machine for spinning flax. Moreover, the problems of transport were claiming increasing attention. In 1811 Mcadam laid before the House of Commons the process which bears his name for providing roads with a hard stone surface – although it was already in use in France. The English coal industry was making increased use of transport by rail, with improvement in the gradients. Finally, efforts were made to construct a steam-engine to run on an 'iron road', and in 1804 Trevithick achieved a primitive locomotive, and Hedley one in 1814, while Stephenson began his researches in the same year. The revolution in water transport was also in its early stages, though only in America. In 1807 Fulton organised a regular steamship service on the River Hudson, but no one dared as yet to venture on the ocean.

The evidence suggests that the war inclined the manufacturers to rely on military success and on contraband for maintaining their markets, rather than on technical improvements or a reduction in the rate of profit, which would help to explain why there was this slowing down in the progress of inventions. Although in England the use of machinery continued to spread, this took place fairly slowly, even in the cotton industry, where the 'mule' had not yet entirely replaced the 'jenny', and where in 1812 there were not more than two thousand mechanical looms at work. In the woollen industry, mechanisation was in its early stages, and was confined to spinning, though it was more used in lace-making. The metal industries were more advanced. Wood-burning furnaces were dying out, and for smelting cast iron, the puddling furnace and the rolling mill had won the day. Hydraulic power and steam power were still rarely used, except in cotton-spinning and in the mines. Moreover, although there was an undoubted tendency to concentrate industry, it was not so far very marked. Cotton factories only numbered fourteen in 1812, and the first factory in Manchester using steam power only opened in 1806. In the lace industry, the oldest dates only from 1810. The production of metals was still widely dispersed, and other industries even more so, except for distilleries. In London, the working classes undoubtedly held the most prominent position. Taken as a whole, capitalist enterprise was still markedly commercial in character. Merchants had piece-workers engaged in making goods in their own homes out of raw materials supplied them, often on hired looms.

In the Empire, there was still greater weight behind the urge to increase production along traditional lines, in spite of the interest shown in new methods, such as the mule, the Jacquard loom, the revolving cylinder for printing calicoes taken over by Mulhouse from Oberkampf in 1805, and Douglas's and Cockerill's machines for wool-spinning. The first reverbatory smelting furnace appeared at Le Creusot in 1810. Progress was sporadic, and chiefly to be seen in Alsace and the North, at

Lyon and Saint-Étienne, in Normandy, and in the state-owned mines of the Saar: it was most marked in Belgium and the Aachen region. It was then that the Belgian mines began to be equipped with machinery; and at Liège, Périer – with Napoleon's help – set up a gun foundry. In 1810 Dony established the factory where he used his special process for treating zinc, the origin of the 'Vieille Montagne'. Ghent underwent a revival through the establishment of cotton manufacture: and at Verviers the beginning of the industrial revolution as far as woollens were concerned was the introduction of English machinery. The town became a very important centre, with eighty-six manufacturers and twenty-five thousand operatives in 1810. Italy, on the other hand, had few improvements to show; and several regions, deprived – like the West of France – of their traditional markets, devoted themselves more and more to agriculture. Taken as a whole, there was only a very limited installation of new machinery. For cotton-spinning, the spinning wheel had not disappeared, and the jenny reached its peak in about 1806. The metal industry remained faithful to charcoal smelting, there were few steam-engines, and Belgian mines did not use them until 1807. In spinning, they were not brought in until the end of the Empire, for instance in Alsace, in 1812. There was only a concentration of industry in cotton-spinning and in wool. On the other hand, there was striking progress in commercial concentration. One of the notable features of the period is the increase in the number of big businessmen. There were Bauwens and Richard-Lenoir, the great cotton magnates, at Oberkampf; then Ternaux, who specialised in wool and was a pioneer in the making of cashmere shawls. Dolffus-Mieg at Mulhouse, Japy at Montbéliard, Peugeot at Audincourt, Cockerill at Liège were all great names. They made no attempt to divide their activities, being at once traders and manufacturers. Though they were the creators of factory products, they still went on employing a whole host of piece-workers in their homes. In comparison with England, the capitalist economy was as behindhand in development as the banking system.

Outside the Empire, the same characteristics recur in Saxony and in Switzerland, the only countries where there were any signs of mechanisation and a beginning of the concentration of industry, which was in cotton-spinning and the printing of calicoes. In the United States, there had likewise been great progress in the former, with a rise from four factories in 1804 to five hundred in 1815. But weaving was well behind: the first mechanised factory was not set up by Lowell till 1813. The outstanding features in the American economy were the progress in cotton-growing, in which production doubled between 1801 and 1811, and the growth in external trade and in navigation, for it was still the period of magnates like Astor and Girard.

Agriculture remained much more wedded to tradition than industry, except in England, where her superiority over the Continent was even more marked. Only the Low Countries had adopted modern methods, and parts of Northern France. In the Baltic countries and in Prussia, the lords much preferred to evict the peasants and multiply forced labour rather than make any change in their customary methods.

On the Continent, capitalism was making too gradual a progress towards concentration for its social consequences to be for the time being very extensive. Agricultural day labourers and operatives at the looms went on living much as they had always done, paying more attention to looking for work and keeping an eye on the price of food than on the conditions of work and the rates of wages. They only came into occasional collision with the employers, in certain localities, and only in matters of strictly professional concern. The only attempts at organising themselves concerned the revival of the trade guilds and the formation of a certain number of mutual-help societies. As in the eighteenth century, their history was chiefly marked by periods of severe unemployment, and high prices caused by bad harvests.

But the case was quite different in England. There, the working classes were growing in numbers and becoming increasingly massed in the Black Country of the West Midlands. The exodus from the countryside brought about by the enclosures, the employment of women and children, endemic unemployment due to the introduction of machinery, and the periodical economic crises all prevented wages from keeping pace with prices. There was a sinister deterioration in the living conditions of these masses, uprooted from the country, crowded together in insanitary slums, undernourished, uneducated and altogether lacking in any amusements. In spite of the Act of 1799, unions continued to be formed. Since they went on appealing to ancient statutory rights, Parliament repealed those which authorised a levy on wages in the year 1813, and in 1814 those which concerned apprenticeship. As in France, all that was left of the ancient laws were the clauses that bore so hardly upon the workers. In 1802, at the instance of Peel's father, Parliament had introduced the first Factory Bill to protect children, but it remained a dead letter. Deprived as they were of all legal redress, it is not surprising that there were peri-odical outbreaks of violence among them, usually directed against the new machines. The most famous of these Luddite riots in 1811 and 1812 were the result of the economic crisis, although attempts were made to ascribe them to conspiracies and to the influence of French ideas. Mait-land, who was entrusted with their suppression, assured the public that 'there was a pernicious spirit abroad', tending 'to subvert the government of the country and destroy all property'. To judge by the speeches made by some men, such as John Baynes of Halifax, there were memories of the democratic agitation that had occurred at the time of the Revolution. He was condemned at the age of sixty-six to transportation for having greeted the recent disturbances as a prelude to revolution:

> Too long have these vampires fed upon our blood . . . They have stirred up wars; they feed on them, nay, they grow fat on them. They have sent us all over the world to fight in order to stamp out freedom in France and maintain despotism over the whole of Europe . . . I have waited a long while for the dawn to break; but old as I am, may I still live to see the glorious triumph of democracy.

But if the masses in Great Britain had been filled with revolutionary fire, they would at least have demanded universal suffrage: as it was, these events can only be seen as the writhings of a tortured people who had lost all political spirit. It is possible – as some have maintained – that there were certain influences at work holding the populace in check, such as the Dissenters, Hannah More's Sunday School movement, and the schools for self-help instruction recommended by a young Quaker called Lan-caster in 1798, and fostered by an organisation from 1810 onwards. Nevertheless, the absence of any general uprising was essentially due to the fact that as yet the working classes were not very closely massed together; and since 1795 wages had been made up to a certain figure in proportion to the price of bread. For the property-owning classes, the Poor Law was an insurance premium.

Some thinkers, however, were beginning to have new ideas in the face of these social developments. Although the British economists found no fault with the existing system on the score of justice, it filled them with a profound pessimism, as already exemplified by Malthus. The banker Ricardo, who began to write in 1810, founded all value upon work; but he noted that in England the cultivation of the less and less profitable land, made necessary by the increasing population, ensured a differential income to the owners of the better land, while he also confirmed the iron law of supply and demand which controlled wages. Man's attempts to ward off famine would become more and more desperate, labour would absorb an increasing proportion of the cost of production, and the capitalist's profits would continually decrease. The final result would be that no new land would be taken into cultivation, and Malthus's law would exercise its inexorable sway over the whole situation. On the Continent, Sismondi, adopting a moral standpoint altogether absent from Ricardo's thought, was working out his *Principes d'économie politique*, which appeared in 1819. It contained a sharp criticism of the new organisation of labour in which the wage earner became a mere chattel whose value was constantly being lowered by the competition of the machine. As early as Year XII, Fourier had denounced the state of social chaos that had arisen from the individualism of the Revolution. Saint-Simon, taking an opposite line, retained the eighteenth-century enthusiasm for the productive capacity of modern industry; but he proposed to organise it in such a way as to increase production still further.

These men were no champions of democracy, and Fourier and Saint-Simon's violent attacks on the effects of the Revolution were quite in keeping with the reaction of contemporary thought. Saint-Simon, for example, claimed that society should be run by 'the really capable people', that is to say, by the experts and the technicians, so that the 'ruling class' should be 'always more enlightened than those whom they ruled'. It was thus his intention to reconstitute an aristocracy invested with absolute power. But he realised that this new aristocracy would, in order to continue to deserve its privileged position, have to be constantly renewed by fresh blood; and he was therefore against the principle of inheritance. Like Saint-Simon, Sismondi and Fourier attacked economic liberty and competition. Their ideal was that all men, regardless of politics, should be concerned solely with creating wealth for the benefit of all mankind. Socialism could afford to disregard the noise and tumult of war, for it was the inevitable outcome of capitalism; and it was about to infuse new life into the democratic movement. By this time, Robert Owen was already planning his experiments in community.

Outside Europe, capitalism pursued its conquering career by the English spirit of commercial progress shown in America; but it continued to be a brake upon white expansion. In the Far East, the agents of the East India Company continued their efforts to establish trading centres. As early as 1802 the Portuguese were asked to admit a British garrison at Macao, and in 1808 a squadron put in an appearance there, though still without success; while in Canton a series of incidents produced continual friction between the Chinese and the English. Gia Long also had to repel attacks on Cochin China in 1804 and against Hanoi in 1808. In Japan, a ship appeared at Nagasaki in 1808 in an attempt to capture the Dutch ships; and later on Raffles, who had established himself in Java, tried to get his authority recognised by the Batavian trade settlement of Deshima. In China, Chia Ch'ing was increasingly threatened by secret societies, and in 1813 a great insurrection broke out in Shantung. Japan could not have put up any serious resistance, and the appearance of Captain Pellew in 1808 had struck terror into the leading spirits. It was only the internal struggles of Europe that gave the Far East more than a quarter of a century of respite.

As far as colonisation was concerned, it did not make more than very modest progress in the British Empire. Emigrants were few, and preferred to go to the United States. None came to the Cape till 1808, and Canada hardly received any. In Australia about the year 1815 there were only some six to seven hundred colonists, four hundred of whom were convicts, cultivating about eighty thousand hectares. Canada showed the most favourable advance. At the end of the period, Lower Canada had about 250,000 inhabitants, twenty to thirty thousand of them English, and Upper Canada seventy thousand. American contraband was very profitable to Halifax, and the needs of the Admiralty gave an advantage to timber export, thus laying the foundation of a prosperous industry. In Java, Stamford Raffles went in for new methods, transforming the native chiefs into officials, renting land to the inhabitants and allowing them freedom to work it and to engage in trade; but he did not have the necessary time or money.

White expansion continued to prosper, particularly in the United States. This was due less to immigration than to the excessive birth rate, which led to a continuous trek from the Atlantic coast to the north-western territories. Ohio had become a state in 1802, and Indiana and Illinois were to be admitted soon after 1815. In the south, on the other hand, the Negroes were increasing in numbers with the growth of the cotton plantations, and were now reckoned at more than 1½ million. Louisiana was admitted to the federation in 1812, and Florida was having greedy eyes cast upon it. Madison occupied the western part of it along with Pensacola, which was disputed territory; and Jackson, at the head of the Tennessee militia, was conducting operations against the Creeks.

The only serious rivals to the Anglo-Saxons were the Russians. They had entered Transcaucasia, defeated the Persians and by the Treaty of Gulistan in 1813 been recognised as the possessors of Daghestan and Baku, with the sole right of having a fleet on the Caspian. They tried unsuccessfully to establish relationships with China; and in 1805 an embassy from Alexander was arrested in Mongolia. The Bering Company, established in 1799, was expanding in Alaska, and in 1803 they sent the cruisers *Razanov* and *Kruzenstern* round Cape Horn. The first appeared at Nagasaki in 1804, but was not admitted to harbour, and in 1806 proceeded from Alaska as far as San Francisco. From Okhotsk, the Russians attempted to seize Sakhalin and attacked the Kurile Islands and Ezo, to the great consternation of the Japanese. A little later on, they were planning to establish a colony in California as a supply base for Alaska, and in 1811 set up a fort north of San Francisco, coming into contact at this point with the Canadian company that was beginning to work in Columbia and Oregon.

The part played by the missions remained a very subordinate one. In China, the apostolic vicar Dufresne had called the first synod together in 1803; but it was not attended by any priest from Europe. In 1805 persecution broke out again, and Dufresne himself was beheaded in 1815. In 1807 a Protestant missionary called Morrison landed at Canton, and Baptists had also begun to work in Burma. The Bible Society was founded in 1804, but conditions did not so far allow it to engage in much activity.

In the minds of Europeans, the colonies were still playing the part assigned to them by the Mercantile Theory; but the old colonial system was already threatened. France had at a particular juncture abolished slavery, thus giving up one of her chief advantages, and she lost San Domingo in an attempt to reintroduce it. In 1807 England abolished the slave trade, which was bound to cut off the supply of Negroes. On the other hand, the United States took a distinctive line, for the colonists and the half-castes had made up their minds to have done with exclusiveness, and to separate from Europe to get rid of it. Spain was in a fair way to lose her colonial possessions. After recognising Ferdinand VII, the colonies

had not been slow to remember that they were only his personal possessions, and that during his captivity they were their own masters. In 1810,
when the news came through that Andalusia had fallen and that the junta
were shut up in Cadiz, they took a further step. Caracas deposed its
viceroy on 19 April, Buenos Aires on 20 May. New Granada rose in July,
Quito in August, Chile and Mexico in September. The colonies offered
to sign a commercial treaty with England, and Bolivar went to London.
Wellesley intervened, but the Cortes refused to abolish the trade monopoly, and declared their American subjects to be rebels. Bolivar returned
home again, followed by Miranda. They called together a congress which
declared Venezuela independent on 7 July 1811, and voted a constitution.
New Granada did the same. In the Argentine, the leaders were already at
odds, and one of them, Moreno by name, had been expelled. The Constituent Assembly did not meet till 1813. Everywhere the rights of man
were proclaimed, while keeping for Catholicism its privileged position as
the religion of the state; but slavery, the *mita* and the *comiendas* were suppressed.

Discord promptly broke out in the new states. The half-castes cold-
shouldered the Spaniards. The moderates took alarm at the appeal to the
Negroes and the half-breeds, while the leaders quarrelled, and the towns,
in their jealousy of one another, changed sides in order to defend their
independence. The mountain-dwellers, led by the clergy, supported the
Spaniards; and in Venezuela, the *llaneros* were prepared to fight for anyone who would pay them. But Spain succeeded in retaining some solid
advantages. In Mexico, they shot the parish priest Hidalgo in 1811; and
his confederate, Morales, who made a new attempt in 1813, suffered the
same fate in 1815. The Spaniards retained possession of Lima, from
which point they could successfully contest Quito with the Granadinos;
and after varying fortunes, they recaptured High Peru from the Argen-
tinians. Paraguay finally slipped from their grasp, but Elio put up a long
resistance at Montevideo and called in the Portuguese to his assistance.
The town was not finally freed until 1814, under Alvear. In Chile, Rosas,
Carrera and O'Higgins were rivals for power; and in 1813 the Spaniards,
concentrating their forces in the south, regained the offensive and
reconquered the whole country. But the struggle took its most dramatic
turn in Venezuela and New Granada. The Spaniards had been able to
hold out in the region of Maracaïbo and in the Orinoco valley; and in
1812 they fairly easily got the better of Miranda, who capitulated on 25

July. He was sent to Cadiz, where he died in 1816. Bolivar managed to escape and reached Cartagena. The following year, the Granadinos authorised him to invade Venezuela, and he entered Caracas on 6 August. His enemies once more retreated eastwards, whence in 1814 they renewed their attack and defeated him, forcing him to retire to New Granada. Just at this moment, Ferdinand VII, restored to power, despatched reinforcements, and in the spring of 1815 his fleet appeared and Bolivar embarked for Jamaica. The Argentine alone remained free; but it was weakened by dissensions, and Alvear, who was elected governor in 1814, and had asked for English protection, was overthrown in April 1815. There was thus still some uncertainty about the eventual destiny of Spanish America; but it was certain that the mother country could never fully re-establish the old colonial regime.

Since the objective of capitalist production was profit, it represented a power that was quite foreign to Napoleon's political and military ideals. It is true that in its most developed forms it is inimical to national barriers, which are a hindrance to the exploitation of natural wealth and prevent a rational division of labour among the different regions of the earth; and in this sense, a universal empire might have been favourable to it. But capitalism was only just beginning, and its champions, who were thoroughly imbued with the Mercantile doctrine, simply viewed their own country as a preserve to be guarded at all costs. Moreover, in their human capacity as patriots, they were devoted to its independence; and the favours Napoleon reserved for France would sooner or later have turned them into partisans of nationality in opposition to the Empire, until such time as national feelings set them at odds with one another. Nevertheless, this was not the worst aspect of things for Napoleon. More serious for him was the fact that England was the country where industrial capitalism had originated, and where it had acquired the greatest resources and power. It alone enabled England to finance the war: in this sense, Great Britain's victory over the emperor was a victory for capitalism.

# III

# The Fall of Napoleon
## (1812–1815)

# CHAPTER NINE

# The Disintegration of the Continental System
## (1812–1814)

T HE CONTINENTAL SYSTEM had been created and upheld by the victories of the Grande Armée. But each new war made its continuance more and more doubtful. The Russian campaign was intended to put the finishing touches to it; instead, its outcome was disaster. After the disintegration of the Grande Armée, all the emperor's efforts were set upon rebuilding it; and although, with the *amalgame*, it had lost the chief secret of its strength, he would again have been victorious if he had only had to fight against one or two of the continental powers, as in the previous struggles.

But on this occasion, remembering the lessons of the last twenty years, the powers united to fall upon him. The Continental System disintegrated, Napoleon vanished from the scene and France was left to pay for his failures.

### THE RUSSIAN CAMPAIGN

To bring against Russia, Napoleon had over seven hundred thousand men, more than 611,000 of whom successively crossed the frontier in the course of the campaign. These forces followed the pattern of the Grand Empire. There were three hundred thousand French, including those from the annexed territories; 180,000 Germans, including thirty thousand Austrians from Schwarzenberg and Yorck's twenty thousand Prussians; nine thousand Swiss; ninety thousand Poles and Lithuanians; thirty-two thousand Italians, Illyrians, Spaniards and Portuguese. These contingents proved to be of very variable loyalty. Never had the Grande Armée been so large, and never of such motley composition and with so little cohesion; Frenchmen of France proper constituted hardly a third of the total.

The shock troops, who had taken up positions beyond the Vistula, consisting of 450,000 men and 1,146 guns, were divided into nine corps, plus the Guards, four cavalry corps and the allies. With this customary division of forces, the army seemed unwieldy enough because of its very size, the length of the front and the difficulties of liaison. Napoleon did in fact group these corps into armies. He was on the Niemen with 227,000 men. Eugène was a little to the rear with eighty thousand. Jérôme was in command of the right wing, with seventy-six thousand; beyond him were Schwarzenberg, and, on the extreme left, Macdonald and Yorck. But really good army commanders were needed, and Jérôme could hardly be reckoned as such. In choosing him, Napoleon had been swayed by dynastic reasons. Never again was there to be the same precision of manoeuvre.

As usual, Napoleon intended this to be a short war. Up to 20 June he hoped that it would be fought in Poland. While he was making for Kovno with the bulk of his forces, he refused to give battle with his right wing towards Warsaw, where Jérôme's mediocre generalship was a positive snare. If the enemy made a massed attack on the grand duchy, he would fall back on his right flank and disperse them, and there would be a quick peace. But the Russians made no move, and it was therefore necessary to attack them on their own ground. His soldiers took a four-day bread ration, and the convoys followed them with a flour supply for three weeks. By the end of this period, a decisive blow would have brought Alexander to his knees.

It is certain that there was no lack of voices advising Alexander to take a conciliatory line, men like Grand Duke Constantine and Rumiantsev. On 28 June Balashov was despatched to Napoleon to offer negotiations if he would evacuate Russian territory. The enemies of France, such as Armfelt and Stein, never ceased to fear that the tsar might give in, and perhaps they had good grounds for their anxiety. At all events, pride won the day. Nevertheless, the Russian army's inferiority seemed quite irremediable. Behind the Niemen, Barclay de Tolly had 120,000 men at his disposal, while, on the Bug, Bagration had less than forty thousand. Further south, Tormasov could bring up rather more; and in the second line of defence, Wittgenstein was advancing to protect the Dvina and Riga. In the interior, there remained three to four hundred thousand recruits, Cossacks and militiamen, and Chichagov was getting under way with the Danube army, but still needed time. Time could be gained by concealment, and those who – like Rostopchin – considered the distances and the winter to be their best allies, saw nothing but advantage in this delay. The majority, however, could not stomach the idea of invasion, or were afraid that it would break their master's resolve. In the end, the plan adopted was that of Phüll, a German émigré, according to which either Barclay or Bagration – whichever of them was attacked by Napoleon – would resist, while the other would fall upon the assailants' flank. Alexander had no thought of the war being carried to the heart of the country. But that could scarcely fail to happen, because his generals knew they were weaker than their enemies, and were very much afraid of them. They were given a good deal of latitude as to their movements, fell back in order to avoid disaster, and thus condemned their opponents to wear themselves out in pursuit.

Napoleon's army crossed the Niemen on 24 and 25 June 1812, and on the twenty-sixth reached Vilna by a forced march of forty kilometres, with the intention of crushing Barclay. But it struck thin air, for Barclay had retreated towards the entrenched camp at Drissa, behind the Dvina. So Bagration remained to be dealt with. Davout set out from Vilna towards Minsk, in order to cut off his retreat, while Jérôme went in pursuit. But Jérôme had a long way to go, and did not hurry. Bagration, seeing that he was not directly pressed, slipped out of Davout's way by turning south, crossed the Dnieper, and then went on upstream. Jérôme, deprived of his objective, turned back towards Westphalia. Davout defeated Bagration at Mogilev, but was unable to stop him. The Vilna manoeuvre had failed.

On 3 July Napoleon set out again for Vitebsk, in order to come between the two Russian armies, but when he arrived on the twenty-fourth it was too late. Barclay had evacuated Drissa and then Vitebsk, and was withdrawing towards Smolensk, where he managed to join forces with Bagration.

The two Russian armies being thus united, Barclay agreed to take the offensive towards Vitebsk. Napoleon immediately put a third plan into action. He slipped away southwards, crossed the Dnieper, and appeared before Smolensk on 16 August. But his attack failed, and Barclay, who had been forewarned and had begun to withdraw on the twelfth, arrived in time to defend the town. On the seventeenth, as the result of a bloody battle, the French only managed to capture the suburbs. Again the Russian army retired, and on the nineteenth its rearguard covered the retreat at Valutina. Would the French follow it to Moscow?

From the start, it was clear that this was to be a new kind of war.

Napoleon's strategy had proved faulty: the enemy were shamelessly withdrawing, and there were no natural obstacles to bring them to bay, nor was
it possible to catch them by surprise, because in these deserted plains the
cavalry wore itself out without collecting any information, and because
the sheer distances deprived the French rapid marches of their usual
effectiveness. And the marches had been more than usually exhausting.
As early as 26 June there had been many stragglers and deserters in
the advance on Vilna, and these had assumed alarming proportions. The
convoys were unable to keep pace, and almost from the start the army had
to live on the country – and the country produced absolutely nothing.
Deprived of their fodder, the horses died by the thousand. Then the
weather took a hand in the game, with storms, rain and cold nights at the
end of June, followed by sweltering heat. At Smolensk, the available
troops were reduced to 160,000 men. How many of these would be left by
the time Moscow was reached? The foreign troops in particular were visibly melting away. The Württemberg division, sixteen thousand strong,
had only 1,456 men left by 4 September. On the flanks and in the rear,
the situation was far from promising. Macdonald had failed to take Riga,
and Gouvion-Saint-Cyr, who had been victorious at Polotsk, saw Wittgenstein's army visibly increasing in size to bar his path. Reynier and
Schwarzenberg were making Tormasov move cautiously; but Chichagov
was moving towards them. Napoleon had counted on the Poles to rise as
one man and invade the Ukraine. But on 28 June the Diet gave way to a
confederation presided over by Czartoryski's father, which immediately
re-established the kingdom of Poland. The emperor gave a cold reception
to this news and remained silent, realising that it was not wise to irritate
Prussia and Austria, nor to drive Alexander to despair before having
beaten him. He did not even join Lithuania on to the duchy, but handed it
over, like Courland, to French officials. The Poles were in a state of disappointment and unrest. Moreover, they were exhausted, and Napoleon's
ambassador, de Pradt, archbishop of Malines, did not arouse much
enthusiasm. They were waiting to show their hand until victory was well
on the way. In these circumstances, would it not be wiser to stop and
organise the country so far conquered, and arrange to provision the army
while it went into winter quarters on the spot? Napoleon had already
asked himself this question at Vitebsk. There was one way of making a
radical change in the whole complexion of the war, and in the chances of
success, and that was to promise the peasants the abolition of serfdom.

The emperor was well aware of this; but the revolutionary tradition was now too much against the grain with him for this expedient to seem anything but hateful. From this time onwards, he decided that the efforts demanded from the Empire could not continue without damage to his own prestige. In Germany more particularly, the consequences might well be incalculable. Moreover, he was convinced that the fall of Moscow would bring Alexander to his knees, and he decided to go forward.

On 5 September he suddenly came up against the Russian army on the outskirts of the River Moskva. Kutuzov had replaced Barclay, and did not intend to give up Moscow without a struggle. His right flank was covered by the river, and was therefore protected: his left, resting on a forest, was only turned at a later stage. Napoleon attacked in the centre on 7 September, and carried the redoubts after a long and bloody battle. The French lost thirty thousand men and the Russians fifty thousand. At the critical moment, Napoleon had refused to throw the Guards into the battle, and Kutuzov was able to withdraw without a breach in his line behind the Nara, south of Moscow, while Napoleon entered the capital on 14 September. From the fifteenth to the eighteenth it was devastated by fires, kindled at least in part on the orders of Rostopchin.

Alexander meanwhile had come back from Drissa to St Petersburg. He made peace with England and handed over his fleet. At the end of August, his alliance with Bernadotte was confirmed in an interview at Abo. But although Bernadotte had now obtained a subsidy from Great Britain, he was in no mind to risk anything in Germany without first conquering Norway, and then only so long as Napoleon remained victorious. It was clear that the tsar must rely simply upon his own efforts. His sister Catherine, and the émigrés, joined by Arndt, d'Ivernois and Madame de Staël, insisted on fighting to the bitter end. If Alexander had capitulated, he would no doubt have been in great danger from the nobility, who were beside themselves with anxiety and rage. But it would appear that what finally prevailed with him was the attraction of striking a heroic attitude. The international circle surrounding him saw in him their last hope and greeted him as the liberator of Europe; and he was secretly sure that victory would make him its master. He had always dreamed of playing this part, which suited his vanity, his lip-service to liberty and his deep-down instinct for domination. With his increasing tendency to mysticism, he was easily persuaded that he was God's chosen vessel in the fight against Antichrist. Having thus put himself at the head of this crusade which

Burke had formerly preached, he remained deaf to all Napoleon's suggestions.

Napoleon did not possess the means to go any further into Russia. In Moscow, the army was in no immediate danger: nevertheless, it only held the ground it occupied, and its lines of communication were far from secure. Official tradition has no doubt exaggerated the national character of this war; but the serfs, like everyone else, could only flee before a starving foe, and, reduced to despair, they could only reply by guerrilla warfare. The Cossacks, with their usual elusiveness, kept a close watch on all the French detachments. If Napoleon allowed winter to hem him in, he might lose Europe and even France in the general uncertainty about his fate. Up to the middle of October he continued hopeful. Kutuzov was keeping Murat happily occupied by negotiating for an armistice; but he suddenly took his enemy by surprise at Vinkovo. The next day Napoleon, thoroughly disillusioned, gave the order to retreat.

Kutuzov could reckon on several days' start from Tarutino to Smolensk. In order to intimidate him, Napoleon advanced southwards and defeated him on the twenty-fourth at Maloyaroslavets, after which he slipped away and continued to make for Smolensk, while Davout – not without some difficulty – covered him against Miloradovich. When he set out, it was still fine weather; but quite abruptly snow began to fall. The countryside had been devastated on the forward march, and now offered no shelter and nothing in the way of resources. The horses fell by the wayside, vehicles and guns were abandoned, the trail of stragglers grew constantly longer under the daily scourge of the frost and the Cossacks. From 9 to 13 November the army entered Smolensk, and from the fourteenth to the eighteenth they left it in successive stages. The Russians went ahead and cut the road to Krasnoi. On the fifteenth Napoleon got by without much resistance; but on the sixteenth Eugène, and on the seventeenth Davout, had to give battle. On the eighteenth, Ney was stopped, and only managed to escape by miraculously crossing the frozen Dnieper. The army regrouped, and reached the Beresina, though now reduced to about thirty thousand men. At this point, a serious danger confronted it. Chichagov, having rejoined Tormasov, had moved northwards, and without being pursued by Schwarzenberg had taken Minsk, and then Borisov. Wittgenstein, for his part, had crossed the Dvina and was driving back Oudinot and Victor. Oudinot hastened back to recapture Borisov, but found the bridge had been destroyed. In the night of the twenty-fifth to twenty-sixth, Eblé's sappers built two new bridges. Napoleon crossed on the twenty-seventh, and the next day there was a furious battle on both sides of the river. On the right, Chichagov was held; but Kutuzov's weakness allowed Victor to escape, though he had to sacrifice his stragglers. At this point the cold, which had up till then been relatively moderate, since the Beresina was not frozen over, grew desperately severe, and finished off what was left of the Grande Armée. Some twelve thousand men reached Vilna on 9 December and retreated by way of Kovno to Königsberg, to be gradually joined by forty thousand stragglers who had been cut off. Macdonald, falling back towards Tilsit, and Reynier and Schwarzenberg towards the Bug, had between them no more than fifty-five thousand men. Napoleon had lost four hundred thousand, plus one hundred thousand prisoners.

The Grande Armée, the shield of Europe, no longer existed, and would take a long time to rebuild. There was no longer any possibility of the binding force that had held the French armies together since 1793, nor could new cavalry be improvised. Nevertheless, Napoleon was not altogether shattered by this catastrophe, and was already giving his whole mind to the problem of rebuilding an army. On 5 December, before Vilna, Napoleon had received the news of General Malet's attempt to seize the government in Paris on 23 October, which all but succeeded; but he and his accomplices had been shot on the twenty-ninth. Yet Napoleon realised it was high time to go and take over the reins again before the terrible news from Russia became generally known. He handed over command to Murat and hastened back to France by sledge, accompanied by Caulaincourt. He was full of illusions, demanding new contingents from Prussia and Austria, and counting on Murat to hold the Russians at a safe distance on the Vistula, while he himself would reappear there in the spring with new legions.

## THE DEFECTION OF PRUSSIA AND THE
## FIRST CAMPAIGN OF 1813

If the Prussians and Austrians had remained faithful, Murat might perhaps have been able to hold on. Kutuzov was exhausted and did not venture across the frontier, thinking that his country had no interest in prolonging the war, an opinion shared by many of his countrymen. It was Alexander who decided to resume the offensive. Dismissing Rumiantsev in disgrace, he appeared at Vilna with Nesselrode on 23 December. He was spurred on by Stein, who had been imploring him since 17 November to set Germany free. The people would be called upon to rise, and the princes would be urged to join the right side on pain of losing their thrones. Overtures had already been made to Yorck by the Italian Paulucci and the German émigrés. Yorck asked for instructions, and it is possible that none reached him. But, separated as he was from Macdonald by the Russians, he made no attempt to force his way through – which he could easily have done – but signed a convention of neutrality at Tauroggen on 30 December. The Russians invaded Prussia, and with Bülow refusing to work with Murat, Macdonald had some difficulty in regaining the Vistula. Frederick William dismissed Yorck; but Yorck pretended to be unaware of the fact and followed the Russians, who had good reason to count upon the Polish aristocracy. In December Czartoryski had asked the tsar to re-establish Poland under the sceptre of one of his sons. Several members of the Warsaw government offered the grand duchy to Russia, asking for reunion with Lithuania and the granting of a constitution. Nesselrode and Stein opposed this plan, the former in his country's interest, the latter on the plea that the coalition would then become impossible. On 13 January 1813 Alexander did not do more than assure the Poles of his good intentions; but they were satisfied with this, and offered no resistance. Schwarzenberg for his part began to enter into discussions and withdrew without a fight. Warsaw was occupied on 9 February.

The French retreated towards Posen, Eugène taking the place of Murat, who had left for Naples. On 30 January Schwarzenberg signed a separate armistice, as a result of which he withdrew towards Warsaw, followed by Poniatowski, thus exposing Reynier, whose army corps was partly destroyed. On 12 February Eugène left Posen, and at the end of the month he prematurely abandoned the line of the Oder. From this time onwards, the desertion of Prussia was more or less an accomplished fact.

Frederick William took time to convince himself that the ruin of the Grande Armée set him free; and if Napoleon had offered him the duchy of Warsaw, he would perhaps have been satisfied. He was afraid of Austria, which he thought to be in league with France, and suspected Russia of wishing to annex the whole of Poland, and even Eastern Prussia. His entourage were very divided. Knesebeck – followed more tentatively by Hardenberg – was in favour of an immediate alliance with Alexander.

Ancillon would have preferred an agreement with Metternich to impose a mediation which should deliver Germany without offering an entry to the Russians. At the end of December the king was inclined to put off a decision till the spring, and then to desert in the rear of the emperor if he made a new entry into Russia. In Vienna, Knesebeck learned that Prussia had nothing to fear from Austria and surreptitiously advised to make an agreement with the tsar. His proposals for an alliance were rejected.

The decision was finally swayed by the revolutionary actions of the patriots. Yorck's desertion set matters in motion. The king at first met the news with consternation. He decided to send the tsar an agent who promised to 'reconstitute' Prussia and follow up his urgent request by threats. Reckoning moreover that he had incurred the wrath of Napoleon, Frederick William allowed himself to be persuaded on 22 January that it was better to leave Berlin and establish himself instead at Breslau. During this time, Yorck had gone ahead into Prussia; Stein appeared at Königsberg as the tsar's commissary and had taken the initiative of calling together the Estates. The officials were frightened and in the end took offence, and he had to give way to Yorck; but basically it was realised that the two parties were in agreement. Subject to royal approval, the Estates set up a *Landwehr* which Yorck was commissioned to organise, without prejudice to ordinary recruiting. In default of volunteers, all men between eighteen and forty-five were compelled to serve in a contingent; but provision was made for substitutes. The Estates were careful to reserve to themselves the choice of officers, in order to deprive this arming of the people of any possible menace to the nobility. The king did not take kindly to this illegal step; but it might have cost him his crown to resist it; besides, the war party at Breslau, led by Scharnhorst, had been considerably strengthened by this measure. For his part, Frederick William sent out on 3 February an invitation to those of his subjects who could equip themselves to form volunteer corps in support of the regular troops; and in order to give this movement some impetus, he abolished on 9 February, for the duration of the war, all rights to exemption for men between the ages of seventeen and twenty-four. On the tenth he sent out a first appeal to his people. At the same time, he sent Knesebeck to the tsar. The talks dragged on because Prussia wanted to be given back her frontiers of 1806, at any rate on the east, while Alexander would only promise to give an equivalent in territory. Stein resolved the difficulty by going with Anstett to Breslau, where the king gave in. The alliance was concluded on 28 February at Kalisch. Alexander joined Frederick William on 15 March; on the sixteenth a declaration of war against France was despatched, and on the seventeenth the king instituted the *Landwehr* through the kingdom for all men between seventeen and forty years of age, with no right of substitution. The officers were to be appointed by district councils, with two nobles and a representative of the peasants. On 21 April there was a further call-up of men over forty to form a *Landsturm*, but it was scarcely put into operation. In order to conquer France Prussia was thus borrowing from her the system of wholesale levies, as Scharnhorst and Gneisenau had long wished to do; and as she had only five million inhabitants, she applied it with a rigour that even the Committee of Public Safety had not thought necessary.

This alliance was of outstanding importance to the Russians. They could hardly produce more than seventy thousand front-line troops. Although the *Landwehr* was not ready for the front before August, and only seven to eight thousand volunteers joined up in May, the regular army – thanks to the recall of thirty to forty thousand *Krümper* and officers who had been commissioned in 1807, as well as to the recruits – was able to send thirty-five thousand men straight away to the front, and to play its part in the sieges. As early as 4 March Eugène had left Berlin and retired behind the Elbe. The enemy immediately crossed this river. Hamburg had risen in revolt on 24 February and the Russians entered it on 18 March. That same day, Davout evacuated Dresden. Saxony was thus immediately overrun and the French pushed back behind the Saale.

This national movement on the part of Prussia also had a great moral effect, for it gave the war the character of a struggle for freedom, which had been Alexander's dream; and in German histories, it still goes down as the *Befreiungskrieg*. There was particularly marked enthusiasm among the university students, the middle classes and the nobility. In Berlin, Fichte interrupted his course of lectures and joined with Steffens and Schleiermacher in giving ardent support to the king's appeal. There was a very uneven response in the different provinces. In Silesia and West Prussia, the Poles refused to obey, or deserted; in East Prussia, there was considerable use of the substitute system. In the country especially, the obedience which the peasants were accustomed to give to the Junkers and officials – for they had barely emerged from serfdom – was responsible for bringing more men to the colours than any patriotic fervour. Moreover, the nobility contrived only to admit the middle classes to the lower grades, and so one of the chief stimulants that had given strength to the revolutionary armies no longer made itself felt. Nevertheless, the results were considerable: from March to April fifteen thousand volunteers enrolled in the free corps, not to mention the *Landwehr*, which finally numbered some 120,000 to 130,000 men. In August it first saw fire, and formed more than half the operational force; it made a real change in the character of the Prussian army. It need hardly be said that the professional soldiers had not much use for the *Landwehr*, for, like the early revolutionary levies, it was somewhat untrained and inclined to panic.

The rising in Prussia had a stirring effect on all Germany. Since the end of 1812 the patriots had been more and more active in their propaganda, for which Paulucci had made use of Merkel, while Arndt wrote leaflet after leaflet, in particular a *Catechism for German Soldiers*, calling upon all Germans to fight against 'the spirit of evil' if need be, even if not supported by their princes. Stein wanted to go further still. He wanted Alexander and Frederick William to decree and organise a national war, which would rally the cautious and the indifferent. Sure enough, on 19 March the sovereigns addressed a proclamation to all Germans, in which they declared the Confederation of the Rhine at an end and summoned the princes to change sides on pain of being unseated from office as unworthy to rule their subjects. They set up a council to administer the territories to be occupied, empowered to organise a *Landwehr* in them, and Stein was made its president. The excitement immediately spread to Hamburg and Saxony; and further afield – for instance at Hanau and in the duchy of Berg – Napoleon's new levies caused disturbances, which assisted the propaganda against the French. Mecklenburg deserted, and the majority of the princes would certainly have done likewise if they had not still been afraid of the emperor. Stein's threats and exhortations to rebellion had the effect of estranging them, and were not at all helpful to the influence of Prussia: the result was rather to make them look to Austria for support.

The national enthusiasm gave rise to a new generation of poets who despised all dreams and speculations, and whose only thought was to celebrate the heroism of the soldier. One of these was Theodor Körner, who fell in action, leaving behind him a famous collection of poems entitled *Lyre and Sword*; others were Rückert, whose *Sonnets in Arms* appeared in 1814, Schenkendorf and Uhland. Nevertheless, although a great change was clearly coming over German patriotism, it was very far from complete. The Germans could not help feeling at one in their desire to get rid of the French who had made life so hard for them; but for the most part, this was the limit of their vision, and they had no clear idea of a political nationalism. Even the patriotic leaders did not always make a clear distinction between this and a purely cultural nationalism. Gneisenau, for example, had no feelings against the idea of England setting up to her own advantage a great state between the Rhine and the Elbe. Those who were all for unity, like Stein, did not always succeed, because of the historical circumstances, in forming a clear conception of it. It mattered little to them whether the leadership fell to Prussia or to Austria; and Stein did not even see any disadvantage in the complete disappearance of Prussia. But this indifference did nothing to solve the problem, and was in fact an expression of their powerlessness to solve it. And what was more, these men realised that the Germans would not manage to achieve freedom without the help of Europe; and they were therefore coming round to the view that Europe should organise the new state and place it under a European guarantee as a protectorate. Moreover, the middle classes' patriotism was blended with more or less advanced liberal ideas, while the nobles associated the thought with the maintenance or restoration of the *ancien régime*, both politically and socially. As for the princes, they were not interested in any unity that would diminish their sovereign rights, nor in any constitution that would put restraint upon their authority.

National union came about in equivocal circumstances, in which each party looked to turn the victory to its own advantage. As long as it was necessary, the common people were left with the hopes that would encourage them to fight; but Austria's intervention was destined to ensure that the princes and the nobles were to reap the advantages.

This intervention was being prepared for by Metternich with an equal degree of circumspection and resolution. The disaster to the Grande Armée having set Austria free, her alliance with France had been virtually dissolved, for she could not willingly help the Grand Empire to remain in being when it had largely grown rich by despoiling Austria. Bubna was sent to Paris at the end of December to inform Napoleon that his master would not increase his contingent; then Schwarzenberg withdrew from the front line. 'This is the first step towards desertion!' Napoleon exclaimed. It was a cruel disappointment for him, when he had built such hopes upon this dynastic alliance. But he calmed down, and did his best to put a good face upon a gloomy situation. He would first deal with the Russians and the Prussians: after that he would settle accounts with Austria. Metternich had no doubts about this. People have wondered whether Napoleon could not have reaffirmed the alliance by offering to strike some sort of bargain. But this was not possible, for if Austria had helped him to defeat Russia and Prussia, she would then have found herself entirely at his mercy. Metternich could accept no terms that had not been agreed at least with the Prussians in order to re-establish a balance of power and a lasting peace by holding both Alexander and Napoleon in check. That is why he sent Bubna to offer his assistance in persuading France to make some concessions. As a statesman, he would have perhaps viewed such a solution with some satisfaction, for he was not anxious to increase the size of Prussia, and he was even more distrustful than Frederick William of the tsar, whom he suspected of having ambitions not only in Poland, but also in Turkey. He mistrusted the effervescent mood of Germany as equally threatening to the *ancien régime* and to Austria. But in order to restore the former powers in Germany, France would have to consent to the limits fixed at the Peace of Lunéville, and Metternich was convinced that Napoleon would never agree to this. It only remained then for Austria to join the Coalition at the opportune moment in order to overthrow it. As an aristocrat and a victim of the Revolution, Metternich personally viewed the prospect with some pleasure, as did the whole Austrian nobility. Lebzeltern, his ambassador to Alexander, boasted that 'he had always acted in agreement' with the Russians and the Prussians 'to crush the Revolution and bring victory to the righteous cause'.

In fact, the emperor did not go further than to make Bubna the generous offer of Illyria. He was also willing to re-establish the throne of Portugal. But he would abandon none of the countries constitutionally united to the Empire, nor the grand duchy of Warsaw. And he publicly reaffirmed this declaration before the Corps Législatif. True, he would agree to negotiate through the Austrians; but by that time Metternich had made up his mind and only entered into discussion in order to gain time and be able to mobilise with perfect safety. This game was not altogether easy, for the aristocracy were growing impatient, and Gentz himself was not happy about these delaying tactics. Meanwhile, Hormayr was again up to his tricks, causing an insurrection in the Tyrol, and had to be arrested in March. In April Schwarzenberg was sent to Paris.

This time, Metternich announced his conditions: Napoleon must relinquish Illyria, the grand duchy and the whole of Germany. In the end,
Napoleon agreed to partition the duchy between Austria, Prussia and the
duke of Oldenburg; but by way of compensation, Saxony was to annex
the Prussian provinces between the Elbe and the Oder. Austria gave
notice that she would now no longer be an ally and intermediary, but
would go over to armed mediation, with the firm resolve to intervene
against the party that refused to accept what she considered to be satisfactory conditions. This attitude was already enough to disturb a good
number of loyalties. In February the king of Saxony had left Dresden and
finally took refuge in Austria, thoroughly frightened by Stein's threats.
On 26 March Metternich offered to guarantee the integrity of his states,
and to see that he was compensated for the loss of the grand duchy. On
26 April the agreement was signed, and the army of Saxony undertook
to join the Austrian forces if the negotiations failed. At this moment,
Metternich was also negotiating with Bavaria, which from now on only
gave very halting support to Napoleon. On arrival in Naples Murat had
sent an envoy to Vienna to offer his co-operation, provided only that he
could retain his kingdom. He was well received, and his act of treachery
was only postponed because Bentinck, who had just occupied the Ponza
Islands and had visions of an Italian national movement under English
protection, reserved the rights of Ferdinand, demanded that he should
have Gaeta and claimed the right to land twenty-five thousand men.
Murat was upset, and once more rejoined the Grande Armée.

   There is no reason to be surprised at Napoleon's refusal to capitulate
without a fight. He had not been defeated, and as in 1807, a devastating
campaign might well put the Russians and the Prussians *hors de combat*
before Austria had made up her mind about her policy. And if he had
capitulated, what would the French have thought of him? They would
willingly have forgiven him if he had agreed simply to become once more
their national leader; but if he had confessed himself beaten he would
no longer have been their master, and rather than compromise, he preferred to risk disappearing from the scene. He has been criticised for his
selfishness; but having for so long lost all sense of his nation's true interests,
he could scarcely reason in any other way. Besides, if he had accepted
Metternich's conditions, there was no guarantee that his opponents
would not have taken advantage of this respite to make increased
demands; and this would certainly have happened. The tsar only

accepted mediation on 11 March, and then with a bad grace, and solely to spare the Austrians, who assured him it would fail, and that their assistance would then follow as a matter of course. At the beginning of April Wessenberg saw Castlereagh in London; but he roundly refused all idea of Austrian mediation, and quoted the declarations made by Napoleon. Metternich was willing to admit that there could be peace on the Continent if nothing but British interests were at stake. But now Castlereagh, who had held his hand since the beginning of the Russian campaign, realising how helpless he was, proceeded to go into action in the new situation that was taking shape, without concerning himself in the least with Metternich. On 3 March he promised Bernadotte Norway and Guadeloupe provided he could bring the tsar thirty thousand men. There was still some hope of enlisting the help of Denmark, which had signed a treaty of neutrality with Alexander.

The Treaty of Kalisch had made England decide to go to the aid of the Coalition. At Alexander's headquarters she was already represented by Lord Cathcart and Wilson; and in April Castlereagh sent the king of Prussia his own brother, Lord Stewart, accompanied by Jackson. He made an offer of subsidies, on condition that Hanover was enlarged and more especially that the Prussians and Russians should undertake not to treat with Napoleon without the English. As to the frontiers to be offered to France, he made no stipulations: it all depended on the military outcome of events. But it is clear that the conditions agreed upon between Metternich and Napoleon would have come up for scrutiny as soon as the treaty proposed by Castlereagh was signed. It was therefore necessary to win a new victory. The only objection was that it might well be no more than a modest one; but this would be enough to ensure peace if it was decided in advance to make certain reasonable sacrifices. In Napoleon's mind, however, no victory must be allowed to call for any concessions on his part.

Austria was not yet ready. Since 1809 her army had been reduced to 150,000 men, and for lack of money she had not at the beginning of 1813 more than sixty thousand in a state to undertake a campaign. On 9 February it had been decided to mobilise a further forty thousand, but there was no equipment for them. On 16 April it was agreed to issue new paper money over and above what had been created in 1811. Not till the beginning of May was it possible to undertake the formation of an army in Bohemia. Napoleon thus had time to defeat the Russians and the Prussians – and it was his last chance.

With his usual energy he set about this attempt. From Moscow, on 22 September 1812, he had called up the 1813 class and raised the contingent from eighty thousand to 137,000 men. He recalled some troops from Spain and sent the Paris municipal guard to Germany. On 11 January he transferred to the regular army the hundred thousand men of the National Guard, the first draft of which he had formed into cohorts in the spring of 1812. At the same time he called up the 1814 class, the effective strength of which was brought up to 150,000 conscripts and one hundred thousand men from the 1809 and 1812 classes. On 3 April he asked for a further ninety thousand men from the 1814 class and eighty thousand from the first draft of the National Guard. There was a reappearance, too, of the guards of honour, and it was intended to get them to provide ten thousand mounted men. The troops in Germany were reorganised, and provided the units for incorporating the recruits in Thuringia and on the Rhine. Napoleon managed without too much difficulty to find the guns, rifles, munitions and vehicles, but not the horses, so that he had to begin the campaign with only a few thousand cavalry. Finance was a great source of worry to him. Gaudin had estimated for 1813 more than a thousand million in expenses against 906 million in receipts. The emperor sacrificed the eighty million reserves he had accumulated from his private treasury; he exchanged property of communes for treasury stock, and against the probable proceeds of the sale was able to issue 131 millions' worth of bonds. He laid more stress on the fiscal character of the blockade by issuing hundreds of licences, and by authorising exporters to import freely once more, subject to a six per cent tax. But confidence had been shaken, and economic enterprise upset. Money was scarce and became very dear. The amount of colonial goods decreased because it looked as though the days of the blockade were numbered. There was a panic on the stock exchange from 20 to 23 May; and by June it had become very difficult to provide funds for the treasury.

Napoleon thought he would both strengthen the dynasty and flatter Austria by organising a regency and entrusting it to Marie-Louise. He also tried to conciliate the Catholics by coming to an arrangement with the pope, whom he had brought to Fontainebleau in the summer of 1812. He went to talk to him and on 25 January persuaded him to sign the preliminaries of a concordat published as a state law on 13 February. There was to be a canonical investiture according to the scheme put forward by the National Council in 1811. But there were representations from several cardinals, and on 24 March the pope withdrew his consent. The conflict broke out once again, and numerous and rigorous steps were taken against the opposition parties. The Corps Législatif met in February, and as usual kept silence. All the same, there was no mistaking the mood of the nation. Never had the emperor called upon it to make such sacrifices. The 1814 class was called to the front in its entirety, and even the conscripts who had already found substitutes were recalled to the colours, and in the cohorts married men were being enrolled. Although Frenchmen remained faithful to Napoleon, they followed him without enthusiasm, as if this war were no longer any concern of theirs.

Napoleon left Paris on 15 April and rejoined the army of the Main which was marching on the Saale, while Eugène was marching up the Elbe with part of his troops. On the evening of the twenty-eighth they joined forces, and on the twenty-ninth and thirtieth the French crossed the Saale at Merseberg and Weissenfels. They had a crushing superiority in numbers – 150,000 men against forty-three thousand Prussians and fifty-eight thousand Russians. But having practically no cavalry, they were unable either to scout ahead or to pursue; and the chief difficulty was that several of their commanders proved to be of poor quality: Bertrand and Lauriston had never commanded an army corps. As far as the allies were concerned, Wittgenstein, their commander-in-chief, had purely nominal authority. On the twenty-seventh they were once more dispersing, Blücher in front of the Mulde, and Miloradovich and Tormasov to the rear, when the former gave the order to concentrate south of Leipzig so as to attack the French at the mouth of the Saale. On the twenty-ninth the tsar, taking Toll's advice, adopted another plan, namely to wait for Napoleon at the foot of the mountains, and if he marched on Leipzig, to attack his flank.

Napoleon's tactic, which he reckoned as one of his most skilful displays, was to bear down towards Leipzig in order to overwhelm the enemy, cunningly arranging his corps in echelon so that they could support one another in case of attack. Once the city had been taken the whole army would swing round to the south in order to drive the enemy back on Bohemia, trap them there and wipe them out. On 2 May he was directing the attack on Leipzig, when Ney's corps, who were not on the look-out, were surprised in front of Lützen and vigorously attacked by Blücher, receiving only weak support from Marmont. The emperor hastened on the scene and redressed the situation while waiting for Bertrand to intervene on the allies' left flank, and more especially for Eugène to come and cut off their retreat to the east. But both of them were late in arriving, and then came with only part of their forces. Thus Wittgenstein was able to get clear and retire towards the Elbe, with the loss of far fewer men than the French – only some twelve thousand against twenty to twenty-two thousand. The plan had failed. There was at least this compensation, that the king of Saxony decided to change sides. He handed over Torgau and his army to Napoleon.

While the Russians were making for the Spree, the Prussians were moving north, pursued by Ney, and finally decided to rejoin their allies, leaving only Bülow to cover Berlin. Napoleon, reinforced by Victor and Sébastiani, engaged battle on 20 May, crossing the Spree and taking Bautzen, in order to pin the enemy down and give Ney, who was hurrying up from the north, time to take them on the flank, and in the rear. The general attack was launched on the twenty-first. Once again, Ney arrived too late, manoeuvred clumsily, and restricted the movement that was to have overwhelmed the enemy. The Coalition forces were once more able to escape and retire to Silesia, along the mountains and beyond the Weistritz, abandoning Breslau to its fate. But they were badly off from the material point of view, and Napoleon, in spite of his losses, was still numerically superior. The *Landwehr* still needed some time to enter the front line, and the Austrian army far more. Fearing that Metternich would persist in his neutrality if they marched away from his frontier, they had made a risky move between the Riesengebirge and the Oder. Napoleon was thus given a last chance; he did not take it, but instead proposed an armistice.

Little did he know that the enemy were so weak, and Austria so unprepared. The intentions of Metternich had been communicated to him by Saxony, for Bubna had arrived on 11 May to confirm his master's conditions and propose a congress in Prague. Napoleon had agreed to the congress, but had made no offer; yet he was clearly ill at ease, for at the same time he was making unsuccessful attempts to enter into negotiation with Alexander. And so the unlooked-for retreat by the allies seemed to him to be a trap arranged with Metternich. Now he did not reckon himself for the moment to be capable of standing up to the three powers. His army was not in good condition; he could not manage to feed them; and the regiments were apt to melt away because of the excessive proportion of conscripts, who could not stand the incessant marches. There were thirty thousand on the sick-list, and the Third Corps, which had stood at forty-seven thousand on 25 April, now had no more than twenty-four thousand men. Munitions too were running short. An armistice would give a chance for reinforcements, particularly of cavalry; in fact, it did enable him to double the strength of his army. No doubt it would be useful to the enemy as well; but, given equal force, Napoleon felt he could win. Moreover, he did not give up hope of keeping Austria or winning round Russia by negotiation. In short, on 25 May Caulaincourt was commissioned to get in touch with the allies, and made proposals which surprised them. 'Do you realise that an armistice will be to our advantage? . . . If you are sure that Austria is with you, it would be better for you not to consider making peace with us.' They were only willing to suspend hostilities for a month, and only accepted the date of 20 July on the advice of Metternich, who needed this respite. The agreement was signed at Pleiswitz, on 4 June.

## THE AUTUMN CAMPAIGN

Diplomatically speaking, the armistice turned out badly for Napoleon. The English plenipotentiaries had just joined the allied sovereigns at Reichenbach. They signed treaties on 14 June with the king of Prussia and on the fifteenth with the tsar, under conditions fixed by Castlereagh, namely the restoration and enlargement of Hanover, the reconstitution of Prussia and no separate peace. Subject to these conditions, they promised a subsidy of £2 million – a third of it for Prussia and the rest for Russia, and guaranteed up to half a £5 million loan. From now onwards, Prussia and Russia could not treat without English consent, though England's intentions with regard to France had yet to be defined. Castlereagh's deep-laid scheme, which was not finally realised till 1814, was to unite in one unbreakable block all the enemies of France; and in this he had just scored a first success. But Austria still had to be won over.

Meanwhile, Metternich had brought his master to Gitschin, where Nesselrode saw them on 3 June. Francis was still averse to the idea of war, but he nevertheless consented to seek agreement on the conditions of peace, and to conclude an alliance in case his mediation should fail. Metternich went to Reichenbach, where the Prussians and Russians were obliged to agree to the stipulations Austria had made to Napoleon – the division of the grand duchy, the renunciation of Illyria and the Hanseatic départements, and the reconstitution of Prussia; the only point they added was to demand immediate evacuation of the Pomeranian fortresses. Metternich on his side promised to support the immediate dissolution of the Rhine Confederation, and admitted that once England was brought into the debate she might clearly put forward other demands. The alliance between the three continental powers was signed at Reichenbach on 27 June; but it was only to come into force if Napoleon refused the mediation of Austria. In that case, she would align herself with Prussia and Russia's maximum demands, resume her frontiers of 1805 and require the evacuation of the whole of Germany, Spain, Italy and Holland.

Metternich had not changed his position; for on the one hand he was still just as uneasy about the tsar, and on the other he was less and less convinced that it was possible to come to an arrangement with Napoleon. Napoleon summoned him to Dresden, where he saw him on the twenty-sixth. They had a stormy interview. To the offer of Illyria in return for neutrality, Metternich simply replied that Austria insisted on mediation, and would join the Coalition if her terms were rejected. On the thirtieth, as he was about to leave, Napoleon changed his mind. He accepted the mediation and the congress, and the armistice was extended till 10 August. This was only to gain time, for he gave Caulaincourt no instructions before 22 July, required him to claim the status quo ante bellum, and refused to give him full powers while he himself was away at Mainz up till 5 August, seeing Marie-Louise. When Caulaincourt at last appeared at Prague on the twenty-eighth, the allied plenipotentiaries refused to enter into any plenary conference and referred him to Metternich. The language he used was much the same as at Pleiswitz: 'Just tell me if you have enough troops to make us once and for all see reason . . . I am as good a European as you . . . Make us confine ourselves once more to France, whether it be by peaceful or by warlike means . . .' Metternich did not need any such encouragement, for he had made up his mind, and demanded an outright acceptance of the preliminary terms. On 5 August Napoleon resigned himself to asking for an official notification of them, which he received at three o'clock on the ninth. But his reply did not arrive till the thirteenth. He was willing to give up the duchy of Warsaw, except for Danzig, and accepted the re-establishment of Prussia, on condition that she compensated the king of Saxony by handing over to him half a million subjects. He was also willing to part with Illyria, except for Trieste and Istria. Yet even if Napoleon had given way unconditionally, the situation would have been completely changed, for on 5 July Castlereagh, spurred on by Wellington's victory at Vitoria, had espoused the maximum Russian and Prussian programme, reserving Sicily for Ferdinand and stipulating for Bernadotte certain advantages he had promised to him. But at midnight on 10 August Metternich pronounced the congress to be at an end; and on the twelfth he declared war. On 9 September the continental alliance was confirmed at Töplitz, and on 9 October England joined Austria, and made her a grant of £500,000.

All the belligerents had taken military advantage of the armistice. With part of the *Landwehr* coming into the front line, Prussia now had one hundred thousand men; the Russians had 184,000 and the Austrians 127,000. Bernadotte contributed twenty-three thousand, having lost all hopes of any further support from Napoleon since Denmark had once more ranged herself on the French side. In addition, Wallmoden was in command of nine thousand Anglo-Germans, and Mecklenburg provided six thousand soldiers. Against this total of 512,000 Napoleon could only set 442,000, without counting the twenty-six thousand men in the garrisons along the Elbe. But in the second line, his enemies' reserves were far superior to his own. All the same, he now had forty thousand cavalry.

The Coalition plan had been adopted on 12 July at Trachenberg, to which place Alexander had summoned Bernadotte. The first suggestion had been to enter Saxony in Napoleon's rear, Bernadotte and Blücher from the north and Schwarzenberg from the south. But as Blücher preferred to operate on his own, it was finally agreed to form three armies, the Prussians and Russians figuring in each of them so as to encourage Bernadotte and Schwarzenberg and also be able to keep an eye on them. To make up the Army of Bohemia, the 127,000 Austrians were joined by eighty-two thousand Russians and forty-five thousand Prussians, who crossed the frontier from 11 August onwards. The Army of Silesia, under Blücher's command, included sixty-six thousand Russians and thirty-eight thousand Prussians. Bernadotte took command of the northern army consisting of seventy-three thousand Prussians, twenty-nine thousand Russians and twenty-three thousand Swedes. The first army was to march on Dresden along the left bank of the Elbe; Bernadotte, covering Berlin, was to advance towards Wittenberg; Blücher would bear towards one or the other, depending on the movements of the French. It was moreover decided at the pressing request of Bernadotte that they should keep systematically out of the emperor's way and only give battle to his lieutenants. This strategy – which had nothing Napoleonic about it – can be explained by the Austrian and Prussian desire to protect their own territory, but also by the terror which the great warlord inspired. Instead of seeking for decisive encounters, they would have recourse to the eighteenth-century tradition of forcing the enemy back by manoeuvring so as to threaten his line of communications, thus wearing him down bit by bit. The astonishing thing is that this method succeeded. Although military writers have expressed admiration for the genius and vigour displayed by Napoleon in the course of various incidents in this campaign, it must be admitted that his grasp of the whole did not show its usual perfection – perhaps because the difficulties were insuperable.

The emperor's situation was now very like the one he had faced in August 1796, at the outset of his career, which he turned into one of his most brilliant triumphs. It might have been expected that he would fall with almost his entire strength on the northern army, which might have been taken in the flank by Girard setting out from Magdeburg, and Davout from Hamburg, as well as by the Danes. In that event, it would surely have been defeated and Berlin occupied. Blücher and Schwarzenberg would have joined forces, but this would not seriously have mattered. All the same, they would have captured Dresden; and this was what Napoleon, in his desire to spare the king of Saxony, could not bring himself to face. Moreover, he left Davout in Hamburg – the French having reoccupied it – and this deprived him of forty thousand men. In thus tying himself down to fortresses, which he had never done before, he reduced his freedom of movement, and this was the initial cause of the disaster. True, the distances to be covered between one enemy and another were two or three times greater than in 1796, and that with a much more numerous and much less seasoned army. The early events of the Russian campaign had perhaps convinced Napoleon that an offensive in the grand manner would exhaust his troops and lead to no result. Finally, there can be no doubt that he was mistaken as to the importance of the northern army, for he thought that Oudinot with seventy thousand men would easily contain it and would even be able to occupy Berlin. He himself took up a position that would allow him to wait for his enemies and yet take the offensive against the one that should prove to be the boldest. As he knew nothing of the massing of forces in Bohemia, he was not afraid of Schwarzenberg, imagining that to go to the help of Blücher he would come by way of the Bautzen gap. Two army corps were detailed to keep watch on him, while four others were disposed towards the Bober. He himself remained in reserve with the Guards and the cavalry in the neighbourhood of Bautzen. But Oudinot proved much too far off for him to be supported or recalled. Quite contrary to all his principles, Napoleon was infringing the rule of unified action. Besides, the formation of the large army in Bohemia and the attack delivered by it to the west of the Elbe deprived Napoleon's dispositions of all their effectiveness.

As always, it was the impetuous Blücher who first took the offensive. Napoleon at once fell upon him, and was surprised to see him hurriedly retreat. On 23 August, without having been able to engage him in battle, he suddenly learned that Schwarzenberg had driven Gouvion-Saint-Cyr back into the suburbs of Dresden. He immediately disengaged himself to go to the rescue of this city, leaving Macdonald seventy-five thousand men to keep Blücher in check, a step which made his own mobile forces too weak. His first plan was to advance by way of Pirna to take Schwarzenberg in the rear, a move that might well have proved decisive. But he heard that Dresden was about to fall! Yet he only sent Vandamme in this direction. At three o'clock on the twenty-sixth the redoubts covering the town had in fact just been taken when the Young Guard appeared and barred the enemy's path. On the twenty-seventh, the Army of Bohemia, with both its wings turned and its centre almost driven in, lost ten thousand men, and retired in disorder in several columns. Torrential rain was falling, and the French army was utterly spent. There was only a very ineffective pursuit, all the more so because Napoleon himself was ill and soon returned to Dresden. Vandamme, who had boldly pushed on to Töplitz to cut off the enemy retreat, suddenly realised at Kulm that he was surrounded, and surrendered with seven thousand men and forty-eight guns. This terrible reverse cancelled out the moral effect of the recent victory.

Nor was this the only reverse. Bernadotte, uneasy about his rear communications, and unwilling to risk a failure that would shake his prestige in Sweden, had not taken the offensive; besides, he was probably not very keen to fight his fellow countrymen as he had not given up hopes of being accepted as their sovereign if Napoleon were to fall. Nevertheless, since Oudinot had attacked Bülow at Grossbeeren on 23 August, Bernadotte had to support his subordinate. The forces of Saxony gave way, and Oudinot, finding himself driven back, had to retire behind the Elbe.

Macdonald, who had gone in to attack on 26 August on the Katzbach, saw his left flank and centre being threatened and thrown back by Blücher, and retired on the Bober, where one of his divisions was cut off and then destroyed, with a loss of twenty thousand men and one hundred guns. Napoleon sent Ney against Bernadotte and hastened to attack Blücher, who also retreated. Once again Schwarzenberg threatened Dresden, and once more Napoleon turned back to it, only to see the Austrians slip out of his way. During this time Ney, who had crossed the Elbe, was being beaten at Dennewitz on 6 September, with the loss of fifteen thousand men. Bernadotte marched southwards only with great deliberation and by a very roundabout route; nevertheless his cavalry entered Westphalia and on the thirtieth occupied Cassel.

The situation was becoming serious. The French army was dwindling at a frightening rate. This was not chiefly due to battles, but to the continual comings and goings and forced marches, and to hunger, for the soldier was only getting half a pound of bread a day and there was no more meat to be had. There were ninety thousand men sick, and the Third Corps, thirty-eight thousand strong on 15 August, was reduced to seventeen thousand by 1 October. The enemy's numerical superiority was gradually becoming a formidable factor. The emperor made one last but unsuccessful effort to reach Blücher; then he abandoned Lusatia* and retired behind the Elbe. Meanwhile the allies, going back to their original plan, were bearing down upon Leipzig, Bernadotte on the one side and Schwarzenberg on the other. The former crossed the Elbe on 4 October, pushing back Ney as he went; the latter bore down upon Chemnitz as early as 26 September, and Murat was told to harass his advance. As they were moving cautiously forward, Napoleon, covering eighty kilometres in two days, fell upon Blücher, who had also just crossed the Elbe at Wartenburg. But, once again, he failed. Blücher had escaped westwards, and, like Bernadotte, had taken shelter behind the Saale. For a moment, the emperor himself thought of crossing to the right bank of the Elbe, and switching his basis of operations; but when he learned of Blücher's movement, he made for Leipzig, where there was a risk of Murat being caught between two fires. Even then, however, he would not make up his mind either to evacuate Dresden, where he had left Gouvion-Saint-Cyr, or to recall Davout. And so he could only muster some 160,000 men around Leipzig against the 320,000 allies closing in on it.

* [Between the Elbe and the Oder.]

Nevertheless, the allied forces were very widely spaced. Blücher was approaching from the north, but Bernadotte only arrived on the eighteenth. Schwarzenberg, astride the Elster and the Pleisse, was in a most exposed situation. If the French had managed to mass their forces by the fourteenth, they could have crushed him the following day. But nothing of the kind took place. On the morning of the sixteenth Macdonald had still not arrived; and as Blücher with his usual zeal was pressing on Marmont to the north, Ney could not make up his mind to detach the divisions requested by the emperor. The battle was joined in the morning, on the heights of Wachau, to the south of the city. Schwarzenberg was the first to attack; but he met with a sharp counter-thrust, realised his danger and called on his reserves, while Napoleon was waiting in vain for reinforcements so that he could give the word for a decisive attack. Macdonald appeared at last – but it was too late: he could not turn the enemy flank, and the day ended with an unsuccessful frontal attack. Napoleon could still retreat, and this was his only chance of avoiding disaster. But he chose rather to stand and face the full allied attack. On 18 October his troops were thrown back right into the city. Bernadotte had debouched on the north-east, and the forces of Saxony deserted, thus hastening the defeat. The French only had one bridge they could use for retreat, the Lindenau bridge. On the nineteenth the attack was renewed and the bridge blown up, though this meant sacrificing the rearguard. The French had lost sixty thousand men, twenty-three thousand of them prisoners; the allies had sixty thousand killed and wounded.

After the conclusion of an armistice as from 17 September, Bavaria had gone over to the Coalition on 8 October by the Treaty of Ried, and Württemberg did the same on the twenty-third. But while Napoleon was moving by way of Erfurt and Fulda, Wrede lost time in reducing Würzburg and only blocked his advance at Hanau on 30 October. He attempted this most ineptly, and was driven back. What remained of the Grande Armée recrossed the Rhine at Mainz from 2 to 4 November, and to complete the disaster, typhus broke out. The German fortresses held another 120,000 men, uselessly blocked in.

At this moment Eugène, threatened by the Austrians, who had occupied Illyria and who were advancing by way of the Drave and the Tyrol, thanks to the defection of Bavaria, was completing his retreat on the Adige. On 15 November he scored a useless success at Galdiero; but the enemy proceeded to occupy the Romagna and the Marches. Murat, who had left Napoleon at Erfurt, resumed his talks with Metternich as soon as he had come back to Naples.

Spain was by this time as good as lost. In the spring of 1813 the insurrection had made headway in Biscay and Navarre and occupied the forces of Clausel. Joseph had no more than seventy-five thousand men, and they were scattered between Madrid and Salamanca. On 15 May Wellington took the offensive with seventy thousand men, and forced the French back on Salamanca with his right wing, while his left, crossing the Douro, joined hands with the Spanish from Galicia and turned the enemy front. Joseph evacuated Madrid and concentrated his forces behind the Carrion, but then retreated as far as the Ebro. By this clever manoeuvre Wellington had without striking a blow freed the whole Biscay coast, and thanks to the English fleet, who were cruising off the coast, he thus acquired a base of operations much nearer at hand. On 21 June he launched an attack with eighty thousand men against the fifty-five thousand French lined up behind the Zadorra, in front of Vitoria, and completely defeated them. The enemy retired behind the Bidassoa, where Foy and Clausel contrived to join them. Suchet, left on his own, managed to hold the Spaniards; but after Vitoria he had to fall back on the Ebro. Saragossa fell and Bentinck arrived from Sicily to attack Tortosa and Tarragona. Suchet retreated across Catalonia as far as Figueras.

This was the end of the Grand Empire; and as in 1723, France was now to experience invasion.

### THE CAMPAIGN IN FRANCE AND
### NAPOLEON'S ABDICATION

A bare sixty thousand Frenchmen formed a very thin screen from Switzerland to the North Sea. Having reached the Rhine with 140,000 men, the allies could march on Paris with practically no resistance. On the other hand, if they let the winter slip by, Napoleon would collect a new army and the whole situation would be changed. This was certainly the view of Alexander and Blücher; but others, moved by memories of 1792 and fearing a national resistance, did not wish to enter France except with overwhelming forces. Their advice was to call a halt till spring, so as to be able to bring up the reserves and wait for Bernadotte. Instead of marching on Holland, as the English had begged him to do, he entered Holstein on 14 January 1814 and forced the Danes to surrender

Norway to him. Besides, the troops were in an appallingly destitute state. All the sovereigns were short of money, for up till now England had supplied full consignments of arms and clothing, but no funds, because she was so afraid of weakening the pound as long as her trade with Germany was still suspended. The loan agreed upon at Reichenbach appeared to be impossible. During the summer d'Ivernois had studied the possibility of issuing a federal paper money, but without success, because he rejected the idea of an artificial rate of exchange recommended by Stein, and also because the English refused to give it complete backing, on the grounds that if it was thus put on a par with banknotes, it would have found its way back to England and ruined their own currency. In the end, England had agreed on 20 September to offer the allies bonds at six per cent, but the German banks had great difficulty in discounting them. In the council of war held on 7 and 8 November, Schwarzenberg obtained consent to a middle course. No date was fixed for an offensive, but it was agreed to begin it as soon as possible. This would mean a winter campaign – a decision that was to prove fatal for Napoleon.

Meanwhile, however, Metternich insisted on one more attempt to negotiate. On 17 October at Leipzig, Napoleon had conversations with General Merfeldt, whom he had just taken prisoner and was liberating for an express purpose. The emperor declared that he was prepared to give up the grand duchy, Germany, Holland, Spain, and perhaps even Italy, provided that England would give back the French colonies and restore freedom of the seas. He evidently still hoped to divide the allies and especially to win over Austria. Metternich himself got in touch at Weimar with Saint-Aignan, the French minister of finance, and on 9 November the Russians and Prussians reluctantly consented to send him with an offer of peace on the basis of the natural frontiers. Moreover, they seemed inclined to require some concessions and guarantees from England, whose ascendancy on the seas was not at all to their liking.

It will always be a matter of dispute how far Metternich was sincere: the probability is that he did not really know himself. His relations with the allies were bad; but he knew they could not get on without his help, and so openly pursued his personal policy, the prime object of which was to restore the power of the Habsburgs. In Germany, he was determined to bar the path of the revolutionary patriots by coming to an arrangement with the southern princes, and on 21 October he subordinated the work of the commission on the occupied countries presided over by Stein to a diplomatic committee set up in the chief allied headquarters. He was manoeuvring to make himself master of Italy, and during the autumn campaign he was continuously negotiating with Caroline in Naples. On 10 December he approved the decision to send Neipperg as an envoy to Murat. The ostensible aim was driving out Eugène; but Metternich's real purpose was to despoil the pope in concert with the Neapolitans. He likewise wanted to get a footing in Switzerland, bring about a counter-revolution, and establish his influence there, so making it possible to approach Italy from the north and cut it off from France by threatening Lyon. And finally, he was more than ever intent upon preventing Russian expansion in Poland and Turkey. His duel with Alexander was just beginning. The tsar had made a bargain with Prussia to give up Saxony, whose king was a prisoner, in return for the grand duchy. He was prepared to defend the Italian sovereigns, and at La Harpe's instance posed as the protector of the Swiss. While determined to dethrone Napoleon in order to satisfy his hatred, he fancied that he could replace him by Bernadotte, who would then become his underling. It only needed the barest suggestion of this kind to set Metternich planning the opposite and considering with some satisfaction how to save the emperor or at least his dynasty, using Marie-Louise's regency to tie France to Austria. He could hardly think it likely that Napoleon would be content with the natural frontiers, but it was an opportune offer, for at least it would involve the emperor in difficulties with his own subjects.

Napoleon received Saint-Aignan on 15 November. The next day he authorised Caulaincourt to negotiate, but he kept silence as to the conditions fixed by the allies. The rumour of this spread abroad and there was an outburst of feeling against him and against Maret, who remained to the last an advocate of war to the bitter end, sensing how flattering this was to his master's instincts. Either because he wished to spare Maret, or more likely because he hoped to gain time, the emperor appeared to change his mind. He replaced Maret by Caulaincourt in the Foreign Ministry and on 2 December the new minister accepted the preliminaries of Frankfurt.

But it was too late. On 16 November Lebrun had evacuated Amsterdam. On the seventeenth The Hague had risen in revolt, and the first concern of a triumvirate set up by Hogendorp was to ask for help from London and to recall the prince of Orange, who answered the call at once. On 4 December the allies, noting the silence of Napoleon, put out a proclamation in which they appeared to separate his cause from the cause of France. They again offered her peace, this time without mentioning the natural frontiers, which had already been invaded in Holland. As Metternich had reckoned, many Frenchmen held their leader responsible for the disasters. He would surely never consent to acknowledging his personal defeat, even if it cost the nation nothing. Yet even if he had resigned himself to this, what guarantee could be given him? Metternich's offer seemed even more suspect than his previous ones. The continental powers were tied to England, and could decide nothing without her; yet at this point she was avowedly opposed to these suggestions. The youthful Aberdeen had been accredited to Metternich in August, and proved fairly docile in his hands; but on 18 September Castlereagh, making Pitt's policy his own, had demanded that Holland should have a suitable barrier on the French side, and was giving a favourable hearing to the prince of Orange, who wished for Belgium. As England intended to keep several of the Dutch colonies, she would gain doubly by reconstituting the unity of the Low Countries. Castlereagh was also thinking of giving Holland part of the left bank of the Rhine, and refused on 5 November to allow this to go to France. Nevertheless, it may be presumed that at this point the French nation, negotiating under the wing of Austria, would have managed to retain some of the conquests made by the Republic.

The allied offensive was held up for a while by disagreement about Switzerland. At the urgent request of Alexander, Francis revoked the order he had given on 11 December to invade Switzerland. Metternich, however, was trying to persuade the cantons to make their own appeal to the allies. He did not succeed, but one of the agents, Senft by name, who had formerly been a minister in Saxony, induced General Watteville to make some rather ambiguous remarks, which provoked an aristocratic counter-revolution in Berne. The chancellor used this as a pretext for returning to the attack in agreement with Schwarzenberg, and on the sixteenth the latter was authorised to enter Switzerland. His army crossed the Rhine on the twenty-first, advanced from Schaffhausen and entered Basle. Bubna made for Geneva in order to attack Lyon while Schwarzenberg moved his troops forward towards Besançon, Dijon and Langres. On the twenty-ninth Switzerland renounced the Act of Mediation. At the beginning of January Blücher too crossed the Rhine, between Coblenz and Mannheim, penetrated into Lorraine and turned the Argonne by way of Bar-le-Duc. The marshals retired before the invaders, falling back upon the Marne. By the end of the month Schwarzenberg was marching on Troyes and Blücher was about to reach Saint-Dizier. Meanwhile, Caulaincourt had set out and wrote from Lunéville on the sixth to Metternich, expressing surprise that he had been left without information for a month. In reply, he was informed that the allies were waiting for Castlereagh, who arrived at Basle on the eighteenth – an event of the greatest importance.

In the year 1813 England had still taken only a very modest part in affairs on the Continent. She had kept contingents of any size only in Spain, and she had not sent any ready money. Up to the autumn, she continued to labour under great internal difficulties. But the evacuation of Germany and Holland, together with the excellent harvest of 1813, produced a tremendous change in the situation. The blockade was coming to an end and Central Europe was being reopened to colonial produce and to manufactured goods, which poured into it. Prices recovered, the index figure rising from 158 in 1811 to 185 in 1813 and 198 in 1814. A fever of speculation ran through the business world, in a recovery which put an end to unemployment and restored the level of wages. In 1814 the export trade produced more than £70 million, much more than in 1802 (£60.2 million), which had been the best year up till then. At the same time, the resumption of corn imports and the abundant harvest brought back the price of bread to the level of 1808, and working-class agitation died down. Thus reassured, England was now able to contemplate new efforts of financial aid. Under Vansittart new taxes were voted and in 1813 a loan of £105 million was negotiated. Expenses in that year were the greatest in this period, reaching £177 million; subsidies rose sharply from £3 million to more than £8 million, and payments abroad to more than £26 million. At this point, the national debt was nearly £834 million. The only difficulty was the rate of exchange, which remained low. In 1813 the Spanish piastre gained thirty-eight per cent, and in order to provide for Wellington's campaign, the Bank of England had to set aside £1,400,000 in gold from its cash reserves. Once again, the Rothschilds came to the rescue. Nathan in Holland, James in Paris and their brothers in Frankfurt drew heavily on their French funds, and thanks to what they made available, Wellington was able as he entered France to pay cash for all his purchases. In 1814 the Rothschilds also acted as intermediaries for transmitting the promised subsidies to the allies; and it was for these services that the Rothschilds of Frankfurt were raised to the nobility by the emperor of Austria in 1817. From now onwards England, although she lacked troops, could make her will prevail by arguing with good ringing coin.

In Castlereagh's opinion, it was high time for England to make her influence felt. Although the continental powers had promised not to treat without England, they had kept her out of their Prague and Frankfurt negotiations, and appeared to be ignoring her colonial and maritime claims. Metternich was negotiating with Murat without much regard for King Ferdinand. Several of the English diplomats were proving ineffective, and it was not possible at that distance to change their instructions in order to keep pace with the ups and downs of the war. The government were of the opinion that Castlereagh ought to be on the spot. He drew up his own instructions on 26 December. England was to demand that peace with France should be concluded in concert, in which case she would offer £5 million for 1814. She ruled out any discussion of the freedom of the seas, and would make the restitution of the conquered colonies depend upon the solution adopted for the Low Countries. Spain and Portugal were to be restored, and Ferdinand was to receive compensation. Nothing was said about the rest of the Continent, so that Castlereagh had a free hand, enabling him to pose as a mediator between the continental powers and to see that the traditional policy of the Foreign Office – in effect, Pitt's policy – should prevail. He now at last stood on the threshold of the career that was to bring him so much fame. On arrival in Basle, he at once set up a barrier against France. Holland should have Belgium under a European guarantee and Prussia should take possession of the territory between the Meuse and the Moselle, which would make it impossible for her in the future to have any underhand dealings with France. At this juncture, however, Castlereagh was still prepared for the frontier of France to advance as far as Trier if the military situation required it.

On 24 January, in company with the Austrians, he joined the Russians at Langres. Immediately he had to intervene between Alexander and Metternich. The general opinion was that Napoleon's cause was lost. The tsar refused to negotiate and wanted to dethrone him in favour of Bernadotte, while Metternich was willing to negotiate with the emperor, and wished to open the conference promised to Caulaincourt at Châtillon-sur-Seine. In any case, he ruled out Bernadotte in favour of a regency.* As to the wisdom of treating with Napoleon, the British government were divided.

* [On behalf of Napoleon's son, the king of Rome.]

Although Castlereagh would take no definite line, he knew that the prince regent and public opinion were becoming more and more hostile to the Corsican. He succeeded in turning down Bernadotte, and in exchange managed to persuade Metternich to give up the regency [proposal], in the firm belief that this would make the restoration of the Bourbons inevitable. In this way, he obliged the tsar to accept the conference, postponing its opening till 5 February in order to leave the way open for the decisive battle that was generally expected. Finally, he insisted on agreement about the conditions of peace, and on 29 January succeeded in reducing France to the boundaries of 1792. At this point, the diplomats left for Châtillon, just as the campaign in France was beginning.

This time Napoleon had neither the breathing-space nor the means to improvise a new army, though there was no absolute dearth of manpower. As from 9 October he called for 120,000 men from the 1808 to 1814 classes, who had already on 24 August provided thirty thousand for the army in Spain. There does not seem to have been any particular difficulty about this levy; but he had also called on the 1815 class to the extent of 160,000 conscripts, and this operation, which had scarcely begun when he came back from Germany, needed a good deal more time to complete. On 15 November he recalled 150,000 men from the 1803 to 1814 classes, plus 150,000 in the last resort if the eastern frontier was forced; and on the twentieth he added forty thousand to the quota from the 1808 to 1814 classes. The National Guard was set on an active footing in the fortified places on 17 December, and in Paris on 8 January 1814; and he then decided to form volunteer regiments that would take in the Paris unemployed, and even considered wholesale conscription. By the end of January, about 125,000 men had been collected in the depots, but were quite untrained. Most of them, moreover, were without equipment or weapons, for the magazines and arsenals were empty. As in 1793 requisitioning of arms, horses, fodder and corn was set in train in a rather haphazard fashion. Above all, there was a lack of money. In November and January Napoleon announced tremendous increases in taxation: but when would the money be collected? Even the receipts from indirect taxation were becoming almost negligible. There was no money coming into the treasury. Government stock had fallen from seventy-four to fifty-two francs after the Battle of Leipzig; money was being hoarded and the notes simply passed back to the Bank of France. Salaries and pensions above the level of two thousand francs were cut by a quarter, and contractors were now paid in sinking fund bonds which were nothing more than promissory notes, like the *assignats* of the Revolution. Enclosed once more within her old frontiers, the France of the Empire was on the same level as the much-abused Directory, and this was natural enough. No longer able to make war at the expense of the foreigner, Napoleon was reduced to seeking the wherewithal from his own nation.

The nation did not take at all kindly to this process, and for the first time there was resistance. The imperial aristocracy and the notables whose ranks the emperor had filled considered his downfall inevitable and were thinking how to snatch the political power he had always refused to give them by coming to terms with his successor, whoever he might be. When the Corps Législatif assembled on 19 December, it dared to ask that the allied conditions should be communicated to it, and the emperor gave way. In the name of the committee, Lainé declared that France would fight no more except to defend her independence and the integrity of her territory. At the same time, he asked the sovereign to guarantee his subjects' civil and political liberties. On 29 December the Corps Législatif gave its approval, and was at once adjourned. The pact that Bonaparte had made with the middle classes in Brumaire was finally at an end.

As for the people, they thought it monstrous that the emperor, after losing two huge armies in successive disasters, should presume to form another. In the course of a few months, Napoleon became downright unpopular. The nation wanted peace, and was rapidly coming to the conclusion that its master did not want to give it. With a running commentary from the royalists, the allied proclamation was having its effect. There was no thought of preferring the Bourbons to Napoleon, for they symbolised the *ancien régime*; but the French were weary and discouraged, and they began to offer passive resistance – the only right that he had left them. The malcontents, who had been growing in number since 1812, were now beyond computation. People stopped paying taxes; requisition orders were not obeyed. The population looked on at the invasion and took no action, at any rate, as long as the allies managed to hold their troops in check; and in the south-west the English were well received, for they could be relied upon to pay their way.

In normal times, the imperial administration would have had no difficulty in punishing the recalcitrant. But the overwhelming invasion left it no time to act, and – what was worse – paralysed its machinery. The officials who had rallied to Napoleon's cause realised how powerless they now were and foresaw the emperor's downfall. They were therefore anxious to provide for their future, and made common cause with the royalists or even came to terms with the enemy. Napoleon tried to get the machinery working again by sending special commissioners into the départements, as the Committee of Public Safety had done in its day; but the pitiable result of their efforts, as compared with the work done by the committee's travelling representatives, shows how low public morale had sunk. The royalists put the finishing touches to the disintegration. As in the days of the Republic, the country's misfortunes gave them new hope, and they did their best to help 'our good friends the enemy'. Their announcements and public notices spread discouragement and fostered the spirit of disobedience. Once again the West was stirring. In Flanders, Fruchart armed the recalcitrants in order to help the invasion, and everywhere the allies found guides, spies and traitors. By 3 December Count de Scey had reached Freiburg and in the name of the royalists of Franche-Comté was offering his province to Austria. On 12 March the mayor of Bordeaux handed the city over to the English, who had brought the duc d'Angoulême along with them. At moments, Napoleon would talk of once again becoming the soldier of the Revolution and rekindling the national spirit; but it was hardly more than words. How could he reconcile the memories of 1793 with the aristocratic monarchy he had undertaken to set up? His subservient ministers might remind him imperiously that it was his duty to see to the preservation of the social order and warn him against the 'dregs of the people'; yet the only national resistance was in Champagne, where in the heat of battle the foreign troops ran riot in appalling excesses. But the resistance had no time to develop, and no one came forward as a leader.

When Napoleon left Paris on 25 January, he handed over to the care of Joseph, as lieutenant-general, his wife and his son, whom he was destined never to see again. He had at his disposal only about sixty thousand men, and even these were not in a concentrated formation. He hastened to meet the Prussians, whom he thought to be at Saint-Dizier; but Blücher was already reaching the Aube, well on the way to linking up with Schwarzenberg. The emperor pursued him and beat him at Brienne on the twenty-ninth but was unable to prevent his joining up with the Austrians. On 1 February he was overwhelmed by a force three times as large at La Rothière. He fell back on Troyes, then on Nogent. But it was a hopeless contest: there was only one thing for him to do if he wished to save his throne – to negotiate unconditionally. During the night of 4 February he gave Caulaincourt a free hand; and on the seventh at Châtillon Caulaincourt was given the allied conditions, which reduced France to her frontiers of 1792. He protested, appealing to the preliminary negotiations at Frankfurt, though he had no illusions about the probable result. Here, then, was a unique opportunity offered to this statesman, who had always been a man of peace, and who was this time – most unusually – armed with full powers, to settle his country's destiny. But he dared not take the responsibility, not through fear of being a traitor, but because he was a little man: he referred the decision to his master. In the night of the seventh, after hours of anguish, Napoleon finally gave in. But by the morning he had changed his mind, for he had just discovered the enemy's military mistake. There was a new situation, and with it, new hope.

To satisfy Blücher and to facilitate their progress and their supplies, the allies had in fact once more separated. Leaving Schwarzenberg to follow the Seine, Blücher had advanced on 2 February by way of Sézanne and the Petit Morin valley, where his divisions were strung out in Indian file. He was aiming at cutting off the retreat of Macdonald, who was falling back before Yorck on the Marne and succeeded in reaching the Ourcq. During this time, Napoleon was hurrying towards them. On 10 February, at Champaubert, he routed Olsuviev's corps and cut the enemy's army in two. He then made for Montmirail, and on the eleventh completely defeated Sacken's corps there. Its remnants rejoined Yorck in front of Château-Thierry. Yorck was attacked and his front driven in on the twelfth, forcing him to recross the Marne with all speed, while Napoleon turned back against Blücher, who was pressing on Marmont at Vauchamps. On the fourteenth Blücher, finding himself under attack, retreated; but his forces were cut through in retreat, and he lost some ten thousand men. Napoleon had won a brilliant victory; but he had not destroyed the enemy, for their divisions managed to join up again at Châlons. Moreover, Schwarzenberg's troops were crossing the Seine, driving Victor and Oudinot as far back as the Yerres, where Macdonald joined them, and also on to the Yonne and the Loing, till he had reached Montargis and Fontainebleau.

By marching on Montereaux from Vauchamps, Napoleon could have carried out one of his favourite manoeuvres, but he lacked the necessary forces. He made for the Yerres, throwing the enemy back on the Seine, and on the eighteenth managed with difficulty to recapture Montereau. Schwarzenberg had time to reassemble his forces and retire on Troyes, continuing his retreat via Chaumont and Langres, although Blücher had already withdrawn to the Aube.

These checks disconcerted the allies. On the seventeenth the Austrians took it upon themselves to offer an armistice, and repeated the attempt on the twenty-fourth. In the letter he addressed to his father-in-law on the twenty-second, and in his instructions to Flahaut, commissioned to go and negotiate at Lusigny, Napoleon declared that he would only treat on the basis of the Frankfurt proposals, for he could not reduce France to smaller proportions than when he had assumed control. Moreover, Castlereagh had protested against the Austrians' separately taking the initiative. Although Schwarzenberg had sent fifty thousand men to the rescue of Bubna, who could not get the better of Augereau, final success was no longer in doubt now that Bernadotte's army was approaching. Bülow and Wintzingerode were already entering Champagne, while Langeron and Saint-Priest were bringing two fresh army corps from Germany. On 24 February Blücher set out again, this time with the valley of the Grand Morin as his objective. Castlereagh did not despair, but on the contrary pressed on with the final discussions. It had already been agreed on the fifteenth that if Napoleon would not negotiate before the fall of Paris, it might be necessary to consider a possible 'vote' of the capital in order to refuse to treat with him. It was agreed at Chaumont on the twenty-sixth to make a last communication of these conditions to Caulaincourt, fixing 10 March as the final date for reply. On 9 March, just as this fatal respite was about to expire, Castlereagh obtained the signature of a pact which bound the four powers together against France for a period of twenty years. In order to ensure respect for the new European order they intended to work out by themselves, they agreed each to provide 150,000 men. Only at this point did Castlereagh grant the £5 million he had offered for 1814 – now that he had at last formed the Coalition for which he had been hoping for over twenty years. On 10 March Caulaincourt, who had not succeeded in making Napoleon give in, asked for further time, and on the fifteenth produced a counter-plan, by which France would retain Eugène in Italy, keep Saxony in the hands of its king and have a voice in a congress to reorganise Europe. Negotiations were finally broken off at Châtillon on the nineteenth. Vitrolles, who had come from Paris, had already been received by the allies. They had authorised him to go to the comte d'Artois, whom he met at Nancy. Meanwhile, royalist demonstrations in the occupied areas were more or less openly encouraged. On 22 March the English government finally decided not to negotiate any further with Napoleon.

The drama was now drawing to its close. On 28 February Napoleon had once again dashed off in pursuit of Blücher, who was driving Marmont and Mortier before him until he was brought up short by the Ourcq on 1 March. Realising that he was in danger of being caught between two fires, he turned northwards to join Bülow and Wintzingerode, who were attacking Soissons. But he would not have escaped disaster if the place had not suddenly capitulated on the third, making it possible for his whole army to re-form behind the Aisne around Laon, while the French were compelled to look for a crossing-place at Berry-au-Bac. After repulsing an attack by Blücher at Craonne, Napoleon divided his forces into two columns and marched upon Laon, where the enemy had now massed one hundred thousand men. On the ninth, he was thrown back to the south of the town. Marmont, who had been held up to the east, was surprised during the night and put to rout. And now, on the tenth, the attack fell upon Napoleon, who withdrew towards Soissons, giving Saint-Priest's corps a pounding at Reims. Nonetheless, the manoeuvre had failed. Thereupon Schwarzenberg, who now only faced Macdonald and Oudinot, had slowly recovered all the lost ground. From the seventeenth to the nineteenth, Napoleon left Blücher and hastened from Reims to Méry in an attempt to take him in the flank. But once again his enemy made off, this time with even greater speed; and by the nineteenth he was in safe shelter between the Seine and the Aube.

At this juncture, Napoleon did not give up the fight, but ceased any attempt to prevent the allies marching on Paris. He decided to make for Lorraine, where he would regroup the garrison forces and cut the enemy's communications, after which he would come back and attack them under the walls of a beleaguered Paris. But Schwarzenberg suddenly made up his mind to act, and overwhelmed him on the twentieth and twenty-first as he was crossing the Aube at Arcis, while Blücher was also on the way via Châlons. Napoleon managed to cut free, though not without some difficulty, and retired to Saint-Dizier. Now that they had come together again, the two generals agreed to march on Paris side by side along the valleys of the two Morins. Mortier and Marmont, whose troops had been decimated on the twenty-fifth at Fère-Champenoise, fell back on the outskirts of Paris, which had just been abandoned by Marie-Louise on the twenty-ninth. After being attacked on the thirtieth and slowly driven back, they surrendered during the night. Napoleon was hurrying to their assistance in a state of agitation, and when he reached Fontainebleau on the thirty-first, he still would not admit defeat, but set about making arrangements for continuing the struggle. Already, however, he had been betrayed and deserted.

On 31 March an allied proclamation invited the inhabitants of Paris to pronounce on the kind of government France wished to have, and pointed to the example of Bordeaux, which had greeted the duc d'Angoulême with acclamation. The royalists went out to applaud the enemy's entry into the city and wore the white cockade, though they were few in number. On the evening of the thirty-first at Talleyrand's house, the sovereigns confirmed their resolve not to treat with Napoleon and required the Senate to set up a provisional government, of which Talleyrand naturally became the head. The municipal council and the various constitutional bodies immediately began to call for the return of the Bourbons. On 2 April the Senate decided that the emperor was deposed, and this was proclaimed on the third with the agreement of the Corps Législatif. The senators hastily patched together a constitution, taking good care to preserve their own hereditary status and endowments, and on the sixth they called Louis XVIII to the throne. Meanwhile, the marshals at Fontainebleau were refusing to follow their chief and were urging him to abdicate in favour of his son. Napoleon gave way, and on 4 April sent Caulaincourt, Ney and Macdonald to the tsar, picking up on the way Marmont, who had withdrawn to Essonne. Alexander would not give an immediate answer. But Marmont had accepted Schwarzenberg's offer to go over to the allies; and though he had put off taking this step, he went over to the enemy with his forces in the night of the fourth, thus leaving Fontainebleau undefended. There and then the tsar demanded outright abdication; and on the sixth Napoleon finally gave his consent.

But the war still went on in Italy and in the south. In January Murat had thrown off his mask and occupied Rome, then Tuscany, and had finally invaded the Romagna. He then hesitated, indignant at the actions of Bentinck, who had only agreed to an armistice with him on Castlereagh's orders, and, feigning ignorance, was landing troops at Leghorn in order to march on Genoa. Eugène was able to halt Bellegarde on the Mincio. In the hope of keeping the kingdom of Italy for himself, he began to negotiate with Murat. But no agreement was reached and on 13 April the king launched an offensive towards the Taro, and an insurrection broke out in Milan. On the sixteenth Eugène signed a convention allowing him to leave Italy. In the Pyrenees, Soult, after a fruitless attempt to free Pamplona and San Sebastian, had successively lost the line of the Bidassoa in October 1813, the Nivelle in November and the Nive in December. He had then fallen back on the Gave at Pau, leaving the road to Bordeaux open to Wellington. Though he was beaten at Orthez at the end of February, he manoeuvred around Tarbes for the whole of March, and then retreated on Toulouse, where he was finally defeated on 10 April.

The Treaty of Fontainebleau, signed on the eleventh, sealed the fate of Napoleon. He was given the island of Elba and an annual allowance, Parma was given to Marie-Louise and his son, and his relatives were granted an income in national funds. On the twentieth he said farewell to the troops that he had driven so relentlessly, who were yet the only people to remain faithful to the last.

# CHAPTER TEN

# The Restoration and the Hundred Days

T HE VICTORIOUS SOVEREIGNS assembled in Vienna to reorganise Europe according to their desires. In France, Louis XVIII confirmed the principles of 1789 and the institutions of Napoleon; but it was not long before the protests of a disappointed aristocracy began to be an embarrassment to his government. This was just what Napoleon had hoped for. He was incapable of resigning himself to his fate, and afraid that his conditions would be made worse; and so he resolved to try his fortune one last time. His return involved France in a fresh catastrophe, and led to his permanent captivity in St Helena.

## THE CONGRESS OF VIENNA AND THE SUCCESS
## OF THE COUNTER-REVOLUTION

The allies, who were now complete masters of France, began by imposing their conditions on the Bourbons. On 20 April the comte d'Artois, who had just been appointed lieutenant-general by the Senate, signed an armistice surrendering the fortified ports still held by the French, together with all their equipment and stores. Peace was signed in Paris on 30 May. As well as Montbéliard and Mulhouse, Talleyrand managed to save Chambéry and Annecy, together with part of the Saar region, where he had special interests. The allies did not ask for any war indemnity, and did not even claim the return of the artistic treasures removed by Napoleon from the conquered countries. As the boundaries of 1792 to which the allies had decided to confine France did not include the colonies, England took over Tobago, St Lucia, Mauritius, Rodrigo and the Seychelles, while Spain was given back her part of San Domingo. France accepted in advance any decisions the allies might make on the territories she had seized in the congress that would meet at Vienna.

This gathering was the most important that Europe had so far held, and aroused great hopes, first and foremost among the old 'legitimate'

authorities. The more important among the dispossessed princes resumed their places. Napoleon had himself set Ferdinand VII free by the
Treaty of Valençay as early as 11 December 1813, and had sent the pope
back to his Papal States in January 1814. The elector of Hesse, the king of
Sardinia and the dukes of Modena and Tuscany all went back to their
capitals, and the king of England resumed possession of Hanover, which
now became a kingdom. But would Napoleon's former allies restore what
he had given them? In Germany more especially, the *Ritterschaft* and
the ecclesiastical princes were asserting their rights. There was no less
anxiety on the part of the peoples who had fought for their independence, and not in order to re-establish the *ancien régime*, especially as they
had been promised their freedom. The German patriots claimed unity,
though without quite knowing how to define it, and from the beginning
of the year Görres had been conducting a vigorous campaign in the
*Rheinischer Merkur* against the selfishness of the princes. The Italians
were delighted to have got rid of the French, but were afraid the Aus-
trans might return. Moreover, the middle classes and peasants set free by
the French did not intend to sink back into a state of dependence. On 22
May 1815, on the eve of the new campaign against Napoleon, the king of
Prussia himself promised a constitution. But whether it was those who
adored the past, such as Baader, who urged the sovereigns to base the
new political order on the principles of religion, or those who looked to
the future, like Saint-Simon and Augustin Thierry, and who wanted at
last to organise a European society, there was common agreement that
what was required of the congress was peace – a long, if not an everlast-
ing, period of peace.

Castlereagh, Metternich and the Prussians did not look so far ahead.
Even the tsar, though he might listen to the vaticinations of Jung Stilling
and Madame Krüdener which reached him through one of the tsarina's
ladies-in-waiting, followed his usual habit of using the mysticism to further his ambitions. He was to say to Talleyrand before long: 'The habits
of Europe constitute its law.' The four powers intended the congress to
limit itself to ratifying their decisions, and before the congress England,
still claiming the right to mediate, invited the allies to come and settle
them in London. Alexander interposed in a lordly fashion, annoying the
Tories by flattering the Whigs, and offending the regent. The discussion
broke up without reaching agreement, and the September meeting in
Vienna was no more successful. The congress was then adjourned, and

although Talleyrand, with the support of Spain, won a moral victory by fixing the opening for 1 November, the congress never really came together. Everything took place in committee, and the important questions were decided by the four. The chief bone of contention continued to be the duchy of Warsaw, which Russia wanted to keep, and Saxony, which she intended to make over to Prussia. There was steady resistance from Metternich, while the English government showed itself indifferent, merely insisting on avoiding all discussion on the freedom of the seas and reserving its rights to decide the colonial question. England appropriated Malta and Heligoland, and took over from the Dutch the Cape, Singapore and a part of Guiana. She also obtained the condemnation of the slave trade, without however being able to secure its immediate abolition, owing to the non-cooperation of Spain and Portugal. On continental matters, she was prepared to leave Castlereagh a free hand.

Castlereagh did not think it possible for his country to stand aside: of all British statesmen, he was the most European-minded there had ever been. His first concern was to encircle France by organising the Low Countries, installing Prussia on the Rhine and settling Austria in Italy; yet he also thought it advisable not to allow the tsar to acquire hegemony. He thought it essential to fortify Germany against France and Russia by bringing Austria and Prussia together. At first, he seemed to be succeeding, and Metternich agreed to leave Saxony to Prussia if the Prussians would desert Alexander. But Frederick William, overwhelmed by his friend's reproaches, disowned his ministers' decisions. The situation seemed so serious that Castlereagh took it upon himself to sign a treaty of alliance with Metternich and Talleyrand on 3 January 1815. 'The Coalition has been dissolved,' wrote Talleyrand, who took the credit for this success, and has since persuaded a good many people to believe him. To be sure, he showed great adroitness; but the principles of territorial impartiality and legitimacy with which he made such play did not have as much effect as has commonly been believed. No one dreamed of granting him anything, and if he defended legitimacy, everyone knew that this was only in order to flatter Louis XVIII, who wanted to reinstate his relations in Naples and Parma. The truth is that he complied with Castlereagh and Metternich in order to get them to throw over Murat. Moreover, the allies had no intention of breaking up their coalition. Castlereagh was prepared to make concessions, and quickly persuaded Alexander to agree. Thorn and Posen were given back to the

Prussians, who had to be satisfied with a third of Saxony, and obtained only Eupen and Malmédy on the Dutch side. Failing any better offer, they accepted the Rhine provinces. Castlereagh thus followed Napoleon's footsteps in the unification of Germany. By agreeing with Talleyrand in his refusal to let the king of Saxony be brought on to the Rhine, he effectively prepared the way for him to come under Prussian influence. Once this matter had been settled, he left Vienna. Napoleon's return did not interrupt the work of the committees, and the final treaty was signed on 9 June.

This settlement has been looked upon as a masterpiece, but in fact it left the way open for rivalries in the East, which might well lead to further wars. The Turks had seized the opportunity to reoccupy Serbia between July and October 1813. Then in November 1814, as a result of a fresh revolt, they found themselves shut up in their fortresses. The tsar maintained that by virtue of the Treaty of Bucharest, the Serbs had a right to autonomy, while the sultan persisted in disputing the tsar's right to his conquests in the Caucasus. It was easy to foresee that some time or other the tsar would demand Constantinople in return for the services he claimed to have rendered to Europe. This was why Metternich had suggested to Mahmud that he should get the powers to guarantee his territories. But the Russians opposed the suggestion, and the English, oblivious of future dangers, also refused to give their consent.

Furthermore, it was natural that the diplomats of the *ancien régime* should be proud of their work, since they had divided the various lands and 'souls' according to their cherished principles of equilibrium. For that very reason, the work of the congress ran counter to the new European tendencies, for it completely ignored the feelings of nationality which the revolutionary wars had aroused. In spite of the Whigs' protestations, on this particular point Castlereagh was just as blind as Metternich. With the Lombards and Venetians handed over to Austria, the Belgians unwillingly subjected to the Dutch, Poland once again partitioned, and even the Germans brought together into a paralytic confederation torn between Austria and Prussia, it was obvious that the victims would not be long in reasserting their rights.

The political, administrative and social reaction was also taking its course. In May 1814 Ferdinand VII had annulled the constitution of 1812 before entering Madrid, and Ferdinand of Sicily followed his example. The pope and the Italian princes, and the sovereigns of Central and Northern Germany all set about destroying the work of Napoleon; while the king of Prussia suspended the agrarian reforms that were so hateful to the Junkers. Metternich reckoned that he would certainly also be able to make Southern Germany return to sound doctrine. In this respect, Castlereagh and the Tories agreed with him: freedom was a perquisite of the British aristocracy, and the continental rabble had no claims to it. They were soon destined to discover that the spirit of the Revolution, which had been carried abroad by Napoleon's troops, had survived their defeat. Even at the present moment, the aristocrats of Europe were furious to observe that the revolutionary spirit was being given its share of good things. Several usurpers were allowed to keep their thrones, which to the aristocrats seemed symbolic. True, Murat was condemned, because he obstinately insisted on retaining the Marches, thus alienating Metternich, who handed the matter over secretly to Castlereagh and Talleyrand in January 1815. But Bernadotte remained in possession of Sweden, and with English support compelled Christian of Denmark, who had been elected king by the Norwegians, to cede him the crown in November 1814. Bonaparte himself reigned over Elba, and his 'bastard', as Wellington called him, would one day be duke of Parma. The reactionary party considered it to be far more serious still that in the Low Countries, the Rhine provinces, Southern Germany and Switzerland there should be an apparent obligation to respect the whole or at least part of the French innovations. In order to oblige William of Orange to have some regard for the Belgians, Castlereagh had thought it necessary to make him give them a constitution. The tsar had also promised one to the Poles. In France, the legitimate king who had been restored with so much difficulty was very far from re-establishing the old absolutism and all its privileges. He had resigned himself to preserving the results of the Revolution and the Empire, and intended to share the work of government with the middle classes.

The lightning return of Napoleon was to be another proof of the frailty of this 'moderate' restoration regime.

## THE FIRST RESTORATION IN FRANCE
### AND THE RETURN FROM ELBA

Louis XVIII had reached Calais on 24 April 1814. It was hardly possible for him to accept the constitution drawn up by the Senate who had called him to the throne in the name of the nation. In a declaration made at Saint-Ouen on 2 May he treated it as no more than a preliminary sketch. He was prepared to keep its essential points, such as civil liberty and equality, the sale of national property, the retention of the imperial institutions and the principles of constitutional government; but the sovereignty of the people disappeared from the constitution, and in its place the king 'would grant a charter'. This was drawn up by a commission sitting from the twenty-second to the twenty-seventh. The political organisation was borrowed from the English. The king exercised executive power through respon-sible ministers. He also had sole power to initiate legislation. Taxes were voted and laws passed by a Chamber of Peers and a Chamber of Deputies, the first chosen by the king, with the possibility of hereditary seats, the latter elected by a suffrage based on property qualifications. Anyone pay-ing direct taxes of three hundred francs or more would have a vote, and at one thousand francs a man became eligible as a deputy. But for the time being, the Corps Législatif of the Empire became as it stood the Chamber of Deputies. The new aristocracy also provided the majority of the peers – eighty-four senators and several marshals. The Charter was read before the chambers on 4 June.

The upper middle classes received the new constitution with some sat-isfaction, for on the one hand it was a barrier against a counter-revolution, and on the other it deprived the common people of all political influence. All the same, it remained to be seen whether Louis XVIII would hand the government over to the notables, that is, whether he would choose his ministers according to the wishes of the parliamentary majority, like the king of England. Well, he intended to do nothing of the sort: he had reconstituted the old *conseils* '*d'en haut*' and '*des parties*', and his ministers were nothing but superior clerks who dealt with him separately and did not form a like-minded cabinet with collective responsibility. The middle classes were disappointed. And to make matters worse, Louis XVIII showed no interest in affairs, and foreign ambassadors – particularly Wellington and Pozzo di Borgo – aspired to have a hand in the game. The regime had no proper government, and consequently lost power.

The mass of the nation remained indifferent, for the Bourbons no longer counted for anything in their eyes, as the allies and émigrés had been astonished to note. After all, Louis had returned without their being consulted, and they only accepted him because foreigners seemed to be imposing him on them as a condition of peace and the evacuation of

French territory. Naturally enough, they were not at all grateful to him for this peace – quite the contrary, in fact: the white flag seemed to them to be a symbol of national humiliation. Nothing in the Charter could rouse their interest, for they did not care about the seat of political power once it had been decided not to reintroduce the ancient privileges, the tithe or the feudal dues.

This was precisely what the nobles and the priests could not resign themselves to accept. The latter in particular, having proclaimed the Catholic faith as the religion of the state, did not intend it to be a mere hollow formula. These two classes looked upon the Charter as a temporary concession, an opinion that was shared by the comte d'Artois. Louis XVIII, moreover, owed them certain satisfactions. To the nobles he dealt out places at court, in his household guard, in the administration and in the army, while thousands of officers found themselves discharged on half-pay, at a time when the financial state of the country was being made an excuse for maintaining the 'combined duties' which the comte d'Artois had promised to abolish. The clergy procured a decree requiring the observance of Sunday, the exemption of Church schools from all dues and all control, and the abolition of the office of grand master in the University of Paris. The government could hardly refuse to make certain symbolical gestures, such as the erection of a monument to the dead at Quiberon, and the elevation of Cadoudal to the nobility. There was all the more excuse for showing indulgence to the nobles' pleas and the priests' sermons; and all Frenchmen soon realised that nothing less than a return to the *ancien régime* would satisfy these interests. Resignation was now succeeded by anger, and the regime could certainly not rely on the loyalty of the soldiers.

Before long, there were conspiracies afoot. Fouché was confident that Europe would not tolerate the return of Napoleon and so was inclined to look to the duc d'Orléans, or a regency under Marie-Louise with the support of Austria. Maret, on the other hand, was working for the emperor, and in February 1815 sent Fleury de Chaboulon to inform him of the state of affairs. Some generals were preparing a military rebellion, and Lallemand and Drouet tried to provoke one in the north. They failed, but at the same moment the news spread that '*he*' had returned.

Napoleon, for his part, had never resigned himself to his fate, and he had good reasons for complaint. The authorities refused to give him back his son, and Marie-Louise had already taken Neipperg as her lover. Louis XVIII declared he would not pay him the allowance that had been promised. Napoleon probably knew that there was talk at Vienna of banishing him to St Helena. On 26 February, two days after Chaboulon's visit, Napoleon embarked for France, on an adventure which could only bring him new misfortunes.

On 1 March he reached the Gulf of Juan without let or hindrance. From there he marched upon Grenoble, where he was awaited by Colonel La Bédoyère, who surrendered the place to him. On the tenth the workers of Lyon greeted him in triumph. Ney, who had promised to recapture him, also went over to his side on the fourteenth at Lons-le-Saulnier and joined up with him at Auxerre. In face of this blow Louis XVIII, who up till now had appeared to be confident, came to the conclusion that the game was lost, and in the night of the nineteenth left for Lille, from which he reached Ghent. The eagle and the tricolour were flying once more from belfry after belfry, and even from the towers of Notre-Dame.

## THE HUNDRED DAYS

Napoleon met with no serious resistance. The duc de Bourbon and the duchesse d'Angoulême tried in vain to draw the troops away from the emperor. The duc d'Angoulême advanced from Languedoc as far as Drôme; but he was soon surrounded, and found himself being shipped off to Spain. Although Napoleon met with few avowed enemies, he found France considerably changed. During the Hundred Days political life gave signs of a revival that disconcerted Napoleon.

The spirit of the Revolution once more walked openly abroad and revived its traditions. In the course of his lightning journey, Napoleon had not scrupled to make use of it and to launch violent attacks upon the nobles and priests who wished to restore the *ancien régime*. 'I shall string them up to the lamp-posts,' he exclaimed at Autun. There was, in fact, a sharp popular reaction against both these classes. Moreover, the Jacobin bourgeoisie revived the federations, which proved successful in Brittany at the end of April, in Paris on 14 May, and more especially in the east – in Lorraine, at Strasbourg, in Burgundy and in Dauphiné. They brought back memories of the Committee of Public Safety and the army in Year II. There was even singing of the Marseillaise and the 'Chant du départ'.

The government took alarm and conscientiously set about measures to ensure that this revival did not have any practical results. But Napoleon gave it his approval, though without the least intention of restarting the Revolution. Hereditary and absolute monarchy had returned for good: all the people had to do was to keep quiet till they were required to fight.

But he did not dare to treat the liberals so cavalierly. From the moment of his arrival at Lyon he began to hand out lavish promises – no doubt at the instance of La Bédoyère, though probably without attaching much importance to them. But in Paris the newspapers, the constitutional bodies and even the Conseil d'État demanded a constitutional government. 'That blackguard has ruined France for me,' he remarked of Louis XVIII. But the king had in fact been powerless: he had had to bow in spite of himself to the power which the notables partly owed to the imperial policy; and Napoleon, reluctant to base himself on popular support, was obliged to do likewise. In order not to have to eat his own words, he merely agreed to promulgate a 'decree to supplement the imperial constitutions'. This supplementary decree was fairly close to the Charter, and was likewise a compromise. He signed it himself along with Benjamin Constant, who had as lately as 19 March published a violent article against him in the *Débats*, but had yielded to the emperor's first appeal. The liberal middle classes did not manage to retain the property qualification for the suffrage. Napoleon re-established universal suffrage and the electoral colleges; but he conceded hereditary peerage to the Senate, though he had refused it in Year XII. The results satisfied nobody. There were few voters at the plebiscite, and more than half the electorate failed to vote at the election of the deputies. The granting of hereditary peerages had frozen the zeal of the patriotic party and robbed them of all their initiative. As for the liberal middle classes, they did not trust Napoleon, and soon resumed the offensive against him. After the promulgation of the decree with all due pomp in a *Champ de mai* which had to be postponed till 1 June, the deputies undertook to transform themselves into constituent assemblies and to revise the decree. In short, Napoleon alienated the Frenchmen who were disposed to support him warmly, without managing to conciliate the notables.

The liberal opposition proved a source of annoyance to the government. Fouché, in control of the police, was lenient towards all parties, and was in addition secretly negotiating with Metternich. At the Ministry of the Interior, Carnot did not make many ministerial changes. The special commissions were no more energetic in their actions than in 1814. The censorship – which had been retained by Louis XVIII – had now been abolished, and the royalists took advantage of the fact to exploit the economic crisis, the fear of conscription and the inevitability of war. At the beginning of May the Vendée rose once again, and the *Chouans* reappeared in Brittany. The rebels took Bressuire and Cholet, and Napoleon had to put a western army in charge of Lamarque. The rebellion was quickly suppressed. The Vendéan leaders were crushed near Légé on 20 June and made peace on the twenty-fifth. Nevertheless, they had pinned down a force of thirty thousand, and had done good service to the Coalition, for Lamarque's troops would have made all the difference between victory and defeat at Waterloo.

Whatever interest the historian may find in these movements of opinion, Frenchmen themselves were more occupied during these months with the threats from abroad. During his march on Paris, Napoleon had given an assurance that he was acting in concert with Austria; but it is difficult to believe that he can really have been under such an illusion. When he reassumed the title of emperor, he sent the allies an offer of peace and despatched envoys to them. But he received no answer. As early as 13 March he was declared a European outlaw at Vienna, and on the twenty-fifth the alliance of Chaumont was confirmed. In this supreme and final struggle, the kings and the aristocracy once more posed as the defenders of popular independence and even the freedom of the French nation, which had been subjugated by a tyrant. They were in fact well aware that this was no longer the question at issue: the vital thing was to crush the Revolution once and for all by striking down the man who personified it in their eyes. Pozzo di Borgo had written:

> Napoleon is advancing on Paris, holding aloft the torch of revolution. He is accompanied by the dregs of the populace and by the army . . . The foreign powers must make haste to nip this evil in the bud, or it will once more undermine all the foundations of social order, for it represents the lust for pillage and violence pitted against the rights of property and law.

Europe was about to come down on France like an avalanche. She had from seven to eight hundred thousand men on foot, considerable reserves and all the resources of England at her disposal.

The Restoration had an army of 160,000 men, and there were another one hundred thousand at home, with or without leave. Napoleon called them all up and mixed them with the 1815 conscripts, who had been summoned to the ranks on 9 October 1813. He also appealed for volunteers and for officers of the reserve, preserved the organisation of the National Guard which he had initiated, and set a part of them to guarding the fortresses or forming reserve divisions. Unfortunately there was no great abundance of arms, munitions or horses, and still less money. The worst part of it was that the national spirit, though better than in 1814, did not show much enthusiasm. Those who were called up were slow to respond, and by no means all of them put in an appearance. Napoleon might perhaps have rekindled some enthusiasm if he had supported the federations. But he disclaimed the revolutionary ardour and the example of the Committee of Public Safety, and did not dare to restore either conscription or a mixed system which would have joined the National Guard in with the army and thus have made it easily possible to take two hundred thousand men to Belgium. It must, however, be admitted that he would not have had time to make better arrangements, for it was imperative to take the offensive and reconquer the Rhine before the Coalition was organised for action.

In his last army there was thus a breach with the traditions of the Revolution. It was composed of trained men, who had mostly already fought a campaign; it was more reliable than the 1813 army, and better provided with artillery and cavalry, but it was too small. Leaving out of account the National Guard and the forces assigned to the different frontiers, the northern army numbered only 126,000 men – that is, six army corps, the Guards and four cavalry groups. The staff and higher command did not prove to be of the first order, and on the very eve of Ligny Bourmont went over to the enemy. In spite of what has been said to the contrary, it would seem that the emperor's health, energy and confidence were no longer what they had been in former days.

Two of the armies that had evacuated France were still quartered in Belgium. One of these, composed of English, Hanoverians, Belgians and Dutch, numbered ninety-six thousand men; and Wellington had come to take command of it. The other – Blücher's troops – consisted of 124,000 Prussians. Between them, these two armies were therefore superior in strength; but they were still in scattered groups and there might well be a chance of surprising them, or at least defeating them one at a time: this at

any rate was the only card Napoleon had to play. Besides, even an overwhelming victory would not have decided the issue.

From 6 June onwards Napoleon began to move his troops from Lille
to Metz in order to concentrate them south of the Sambre, and on the
fifteenth he descended on Charleroi and threw himself between the two
enemy armies. But his orders were rather ineffectively carried out, and
Ligny and Quatre Bras were not taken. He for his part allowed the enemy
to retreat and lost the whole morning of the sixteenth. In actual fact,
Blücher and Gneisenau, having collected eighty-four thousand men, had
made up their minds to risk a battle. Wellington, who had made no move
until the twelfth and was still waiting for an attack from the Mons direction on the fifteenth, was quickly moving his divisions eastwards in order
to catch the French in the flank. At last, in the early afternoon of the sixteenth, Napoleon realised that the Prussians were present in force at
Ligny. He gave battle, instructing Ney and Drouet to fall back from
Quatre Bras on their right, but he had left Lobau's corps at Charleroi,
which did not rejoin him till the evening, and he had only sixty-eight
thousand men. Ney was under increasing pressure from Wellington, and
could not disengage himself. Orders were inefficiently passed on, with
the result that Drouet manoeuvred between the two battlefields without
being of any use in either. Blücher's army was driven in at the centre and
forced to retreat, though not destroyed. Napoleon was unwell, and left
the field of battle; there was no pursuit of the enemy until at the end of
the morning of the seventeenth, when Grouchy was at last sent to see
what had happened to their retreating forces. In the course of the night
he discovered that far from retiring on Namur, they were marching on
Wavre; and instead of crossing the Dyle and blocking their path he followed them, so that there was now nothing to prevent Blücher marching
to the assistance of Wellington.

Meanwhile, Wellington had retired northwards, and had taken up a
position in front of the forest of Soignes, on the Mont Saint-Jean plateau,
with sixty-seven thousand men, his right strongly protected by the
Château de Hougoumont and the Haye Sainte farm, and his centre well
covered. His left was more exposed, but he expected Prussian support
on this side. Napoleon turned back against him in the course of the
seventeenth with seventy-four thousand men; but rain impeded operations, and he did not launch an attack against him till about midday on 18
June, with the result that by one o'clock Bülow had appeared on the

French flank. The frontal attack on the English positions, which had been left to Ney, was deplorably carried out. Launched to begin with against the enemy's right, it was held up at the Château de Hougoumont; then it was transferred to the centre, where it was caught up until three-thirty in front of La Haye Sainte. After this, the infantry advanced in deep column and were mown down by grapeshot, then charged and thoroughly mauled. The cavalry, charging in its turn at the English squares, was repulsed; then in a final rally the infantry came back to the assault and shook the enemy line. Ney called for the Guards to deal a final blow. But Napoleon had been obliged to use a large part of them to support Lobau, who had slowly been thrust back by Bülow's growing forces, and was only able to send five battalions of the Old Guard, whose attack was held by the English Guards – Wellington's last reserves. At this moment Ziethen appeared on the extreme right of the French, and the English took up the offensive. The whole of Napoleon's army wavered, and then broke and fled in panic, losing thirty thousand men and 7,500 prisoners. Grouchy, who had been treated with some circumspection at Wavre, was able to disengage his forces; then the remnants of the army gathered together at Laon and retired behind the Seine.

Returning to Paris on the twenty-first, Napoleon wanted to organise further resistance. But the Chamber showed its hostility, and he abdicated the next day. An executive commission was elected, with Fouché as its moving spirit, and he succeeded in inducing Napoleon to leave Malmaison on the twenty-ninth. The Chamber declared against the Bourbons and sent a delegation to Wellington, who arrived outside the capital on 30 June. The general inclination was to substitute the duc d'Orléans for Louis XVIII, and Talleyrand (who had remained in Vienna) was inclined to assent. The allies had some difficulty in agreeing to restore the fallen king, and Alexander remained strongly opposed to him. But Alexander was not there: the unexpected disaster to Napoleon left the solution largely in the hands of Louis XVIII and Wellington. The king had set out at once, and from Cambrai on the twenty-eighth he promised to proclaim an amnesty. Wellington's reply to the deputies was that a change of dynasty would be a revolutionary act entailing the dismemberment of France, whereupon the Chambers and the commission broke up. Davout, who had been put in command of the army, signed the capitulation of Paris on 2 July, and then retired behind the Loire. Louis XVIII took possession once more on the eighth.

Meanwhile, Napoleon had arrived at Rochefort on the third. He had asked for frigates to take him to the United States; but the executive commission, intimating that there was an English cruiser in waiting, directed that he should go on board, and in fact held him as a prisoner. On the fifteenth, he surrendered to the captain on board the *Bellerophon*.

The English government, the Prussians and even Metternich were in favour of taking several provinces away from France. But Castlereagh, with Wellington's and Alexander's support, was firmly against this course. In the end, he won over Liverpool, while the tsar persuaded Austria to change her mind. The Prussians found themselves alone, and had to give way. The draft treaty, produced on 26 September, was rejected by Talleyrand; but Louis XVIII dismissed him and on 20 November signed the second Treaty of Paris, which took away from France Philippeville and Marienbourg, Sarrelouis, Landau and the Saar and all that was left of Savoy. An indemnity of seven hundred million francs was imposed upon her, in addition to 240 million in private claims; she was to be occupied by the allies for from three to five years; and this time she was also obliged to give back the art treasures she had taken from other countries. On the same day the allies confirmed their alliance and excluded the Bonapartes from the French throne in perpetuity. Castlereagh inserted the additional proviso that the congress should meet together from time to time to examine the situation in Europe. As from 26 September Alexander had concluded a mystical pact with Prussia and Austria, the Holy Alliance, to preserve peace and ensure good government in Europe according to the principles of Christianity.

Meanwhile, Napoleon was sailing towards St Helena, where the allies had decided that he should be interned. This tragic exile in a distant island, lost in the ocean, beneath a tropical sun, put the finishing touches to that romantic prestige which will always exercise such a fascination on the minds of men. It also helped to give birth to the legend which transformed the role he had played in history. In French eyes he became a victim of the kings, and was once again looked upon as the hero of a revolutionary nation. His captivity was not only due to the terrifying effects of his very name; it was also an expression of vengeance against the upstart soldier who had presumed to take an archduchess to wife.

With the last but by no means the least of his strokes of genius, he succeeded in dictating his memoirs with a complete forgetfulness of everything personal in his policies, seeing himself simply and solely as the leader of a revolutionary army come to set mankind and all the nations free, an army which he had in the end persuaded to throw away its sword.

## CONCLUDING REMARKS

The great Napoleonic achievement – the establishment of a new dynasty and the building of a universal empire – ended in failure. Hence the imagination of the poet has tended to see the emperor as a second Prometheus whose daring was punished by the heavenly powers, and as a symbol of human genius at grips with Fate. On the other hand, some have seen him as the sport of historical determinism, on the pretext that the Revolution was bound to lead to a dictatorship, and that the acquisition of her natural frontiers was bound to lead France on to perpetual war. Without rashly launching into metaphysical speculation, the historian would be inclined to agree with the former thesis. It would seem to him a fact that an authoritarian government was indispensable to save the Revolution as long as its enemies were in league with the foreigner, and that the middle classes needed Napoleon to give this authority. It would also seem at least probable that the annexation of Belgium and the left bank of the Rhine would expose France to new attacks. But a military dictatorship did not in itself necessitate the re-establishment of a hereditary monarchy, still less an aristocratic nobility. Nor was the best means of defending the natural frontiers to be found in expanding beyond them and so giving rise to coalitions in self-defence. Yet this was what Napoleon was personally responsible for setting in train. Circumstances were certainly favourable to his efforts, but they nonetheless arose from the depths of his own essential nature. Moreover, there is a widely held view that Napoleon's work was doomed to fail; and it would perhaps be salutary for all would-be Caesars and for the good of the human race if this judgement could be held beyond a doubt. But this cannot for one moment be admitted: Alexander's will-power might well have failed at Moscow, and the allied army might have been destroyed at Lützen. The only solid certainty is that the risks were tremendous, and that France, hazarding her all, lost all that the Revolution had conquered in her name.

Although Napoleon's individual ambitions were not realised, his actions have nevertheless left the deepest impress on society. In France, the new state had not yet taken definite shape, and it was Napoleon who gave it an administrative framework that bore the marks of a master hand. The

Revolution of 1789 had thrust the middle classes forward into power, but this power had then been disputed by a rising democracy. Under the protection of the emperor, the notables succeeded in recovering it, and grew in wealth and influence. Once they had got rid of the menace of the common people, they were prepared to govern and to restore liberalism. In Europe, the spread of French ideas, the influence of England, the advance of capitalism and the consequent rise of the middle classes, all tended in the same direction and resulted in a marked speeding up of evolution and the introduction of the modern order. The expansion of culture, the proclamation of the sovereignty of the people and the spread of Romanticism foreshadowed the awakening of nationalism, and Napoleon's territorial rearrangements and reforms encouraged these trends. Capitalism was taking root in the West, and the blockade provided protection for its early stages. Romanticism had long been fermenting in Europe, and Napoleon provided its poets with the perfect hero. But though Napoleon's influence was considerable, this was only in so far as it followed the currents that were already carrying European civilisation along with them. If historical determinism is to be brought into the picture, this is where its effects may be observed.

Since he was, in this respect, a man of his century, one can understand the swift growth of the Napoleonic legend, and the deep roots that it struck. Nevertheless, there is a glaring contradiction between his personal tendencies and the durable elements in his achievement, which only legend preserved. He had in fact become more and more hostile to the Revolution, to such a degree that if he had had the time he would in the end have partly repudiated even civil equality; yet in the popular imagination, he was the hero of the Revolution. He who dreamed of universal empire remained in the eyes of Frenchmen the defender of his country's 'natural frontiers' while the European liberals saw him as the defender of nationality against the kings of the Holy Alliance. He had instituted the most rigorous despotism; yet it was in his name that the constitutional reign of the Bourbons was opposed. The Romantics had idolised him, yet his methods of thought and his literary and artistic tastes ranged him on the side of the purest classicism. From the political and national point of view, this ambivalence was to lead in the end to Napoleon III.

Yet the Romantics were not wholly wrong about him, for his classicism was only one of culture and cast of mind. His springs of action, his unconquerable energy of temperament, arose from the depths of his imagination. Here lay the secret of the fascination that he will exercise for evermore on the individual person. For men will always be haunted by romantic dreams of power, even if only in the passing fires and disturbances of youth; and there will thus never be wanting those who will come, like Barrès's heroes, to stand in ecstasy before the tomb.

# CHRONOLOGY

| | | |
|---|---|---|
| 1789 | 14 July | Fall of the Bastille; start of the French Revolution |
| 1792–5 | | The National Convention; start of Revolutionary Wars |
| 1792 | 22 Sept. | France becomes a republic |
| 1793–4 | | Dictatorship of the Committee of Public Safety; Reign of Terror |
| 1794 | 27 July | Thermidor (fall of Robespierre) |
| 1795–9 | | The Directory – first phase of revolutionary imperialism |
| 1796 | 9 Mar. | Napoleon Bonaparte marries Josephine de Beauharnais |
| 1796–7 | | Napoleon's first Italian campaign |
| 1798–1801 | | Napoleon's Egyptian campaign |
| 1799–1804 | | The Consulate – Napoleon comes to power; second phase of imperialism |
| 1799 | 9–10 Nov. | *Coup d'état* of Brumaire |
| | 25 Dec. | Constitution of Year VIII – Napoleon appointed First Consul; reorganisation of administration (*préfectures*), taxes, civil service |

| 1800    | 14–23 May | Start of Napoleon's second Italian campaign – French army crosses the Alps |
|---------|-----------|-----|
|         | 14 June   | Battle of Marengo – French defeat Austrians |
|         | 3 Dec.    | Battle of Hohenlinden – French defeat Austrians |
|         | 24 Dec.   | Attempt to assassinate Napoleon by bomb in the rue Saint-Nicaise |
| 1801    | 9 Feb.    | Treaty of Lunéville between France and the Holy Roman Empire |
|         | 16 July   | Concordat signed with Pope Pius VII |
| 1802    | 24 Jan.   | Napoleon accepts presidency of Italian Republic |
|         | 25 Mar.   | Treaty of Amiens between France and Britain |
|         | 8 Apr.    | Law implementing Concordat with Pope Pius VII passed |
|         | 1 May     | Restructure of the French educational system – establishment of *lycées* |
|         | 2 Aug.    | Napoleon made Consul for Life |
| 1803    | 19 Feb.   | Act of Mediation in Switzerland |
|         | 3 May     | Louisiana Purchase Treaty – Napoleon sells Louisiana territory to the United States |
|         | 18 May    | Rupture of the Treaty of Amiens leads to the resumption of war with Britain |
| 1804–15 |           | The Empire – French conquest and loss of Europe |
| 1804    | Feb.–Mar. | Royalist plot to kidnap Napoleon leads to arrest of Generals Moreau, Pichegru and Cadoudal |
|         | 21 Mar.   | The Civil Code of the French People, |

|      |         | also known as the Code Napoléon, promulgated |
|------|---------|----------------------------------------------|
|      | 18 May  | Proclamation of Napoleon as emperor |
|      | 2 Dec.  | Coronation of Napoleon as emperor at Notre-Dame |
| 1805 | 18 May  | Napoleon crowns himself king of Italy in Milan |
|      | 9 Aug.  | Third Coalition formed – Austria joins Anglo-Russian alliance against France |
|      | 21 Oct. | Battle of Trafalgar – British fleet defeats French and Spanish |
|      | 2 Dec.  | Battle of Austerlitz – French defeat Austrians and Russians |
|      | 15 Dec. | Treaty of Schönbrunn between France and Prussia |
|      | 26 Dec. | Treaty of Pressburg between France and Austria |
| 1806 | 30 Mar. | Napoleon appoints his brother Joseph king of Naples |
|      | 5 June  | Napoleon appoints his brother Louis king of Holland |
|      | 12 July | Napoleon establishes the Confederation of the Rhine, effectively ending the Holy Roman Empire |
|      | 14 Oct. | Battles of Jena and Auerstädt – French defeat Prussians |
|      | 21 Nov. | Berlin decree initiates the Continental System |
| 1807 | 8 Feb.  | Battle of Eylau – French defeat Russians |
|      | 14 June | Battle of Friedland – French defeat Russians |
|      | 7–9 July | Treaty of Tilsit between France, Russia and Prussia |
|      | 27 Oct. | Treaty of Fontainebleau between France and Spain |

| | 30 Nov. | Napoleon begins French occupation of Portugal with General Junot occupying Lisbon – the start of the Peninsular War |
| | 17 Dec. | Milan decree strengthens the Berlin decree |
| 1808 | 1 Mar. | Organisation of the imperial *noblesse* |
| | 23 Mar. | French troops occupy Madrid |
| | 17 Apr. | Napoleon announces the Bayonne decree |
| | 2 May | Revolt in Madrid against French troops |
| | 7 July | Joseph Bonaparte appointed king of Spain; succeeded in Naples by Joachim Murat |
| | 16–19 July | Battle of Baylen – French surrender to Spanish |
| | 17 Aug. | Battle of Roliça – British defeat French in their first battle of the Peninsular War |
| | 21 Aug. | Battle of Vimeiro – British defeat French |
| | 30 Aug. | Convention of Cintra |
| | 27 Sept.– 14 Oct. | Congress of Erfurt between Napoleon and Tsar Alexander |
| | 4 Dec. | Napoleon recaptures Madrid |
| 1809 | 16 Jan. | Battle of Corunna – French held off by British |
| | 17 Jan. | Napoleon leaves Spain |
| | 29 Mar. | Battle of Oporto – French defeat Portuguese and capture city |
| | 12 May | Anglo-Portuguese army retakes Oporto |
| | 17 May | Napoleon annexes the Papal States |
| | 21–2 May | Battle of Aspern-Essling – Austrians defeat French |
| | 6 July | Battle of Wagram – French defeat Austrians |
| | 28 July | Battle of Talavera – inconclusive battle between Anglo-Spanish and French |

|        | 14 Oct.         | Treaty of Schönbrunn between France and Austria |
|        | 16 Dec.         | Napoleon divorces Josephine |
| 1810   | 17 Feb.         | Annexation of Rome confirmed by *senatus consultum* |
|        | 2 Apr.          | Napoleon marries Marie-Louise of Austria |
|        | 2 July          | Louis abdicates as king and flees from Holland |
|        | 9 July          | Holland annexed to France |
|        | 25 July         | French Empire's maritime trade put under state control |
|        | 27 Sept.        | Battle of Busaco – British defeat French |
|        | 13 Dec.         | North German territories annexed to French Empire |
|        | 31 Dec.         | Napoleon reopens his ports to neutral states |
| 1811   | 20 Mar.         | Birth of the 'king of Rome' ('Napoleon II') |
|        | 5 May           | Battle of Fuentes de Onoro – Anglo-Portuguese defeat French |
|        | 16 May          | Battle of Albuera – British, Spanish and Portuguese defeat French |
| 1812   | 19 Jan.         | British seize Ciudad Rodrigo |
|        | 16 Mar.–6 Apr.  | Battle of Badajoz – Anglo-Portuguese defeat French |
|        | 24–5 June       | Grande Armée crosses the River Niemen, beginning the Russian campaign |
|        | 22 July         | Battle of Salamanca – British, Spanish and Portuguese defeat French |
|        | 7 Sept.         | Battle of Borodino – heavy losses on both French and Russian sides |
|        | 14 Sept.        | Grande Armée enters Moscow |
|        | Oct.–Dec.       | Grande Armée retreats from Moscow, suffering huge losses |

| 1813 | 28 Feb. | Treaty of Kalisch between Prussia and Russia |
| | 16 Mar. | Prussia declares war on France |
| | 2 May | Battle of Lützen – French defeat Prussians and Russians |
| | 20–1 May | Battle of Bautzen – French defeat Prussians and Russians |
| | 21 June | Battle of Vitoria – British, Spanish and Portuguese defeat French, who start to withdraw from Spain |
| | 6 Sept. | Battle of Dennewitz – Russians and Prussians defeat French |
| | 9 Sept. | Alliance of Prussia, Russia and Austria |
| | 16–19 Oct. | Battle of Leipzig – Austrians, Prussians, Russians, Swedish and Bohemians defeat French |
| 1814 | Jan.–Mar. | Campaign of France – allies enter France |
| | 12 Mar. | Mayor of Bordeaux hands city over to the British |
| | 31 Mar. | Paris surrenders to the allies |
| | 2–3 Apr. | The Senate and Corps Législatif proclaim the deposition of Napoleon |
| | 6 Apr. | Napoleon abdicates |
| | 10 Apr. | Battle of Toulouse – French troops surrender; final battle of the Peninsular War |
| | 11 Apr. | Treaty of Fontainebleau exiles Napoleon to Elba |
| | 24 Apr. | King Louis XVIII returns to France |
| | 30 May | Treaty of Paris – Louis XVIII proclaimed king of France, restoring the Bourbon monarchy |
| 1815 | 1 Mar. | Napoleon lands in France after escaping from Elba |
| | 13 Mar. | Congress of Vienna declares Napoleon an outlaw |

| 19 Mar. | Louis XVIII flees from Paris |
| 20 Mar. | Napoleon arrives in Paris and takes control, marking the start of the Hundred Days |
| 16 June | Battles of Ligny and Quatre Bras – French force Prussians and British to retreat |
| 18 June | Battle of Waterloo – British and Prussian forces led by Wellington defeat French |
| 22 June | Napoleon forced to abdicate and leave Paris |
| 3 July | Paris surrenders to the allies |
| 8 July | Louis XVIII returns to Paris |
| 7 Aug. | Napoleon exiled to St Helena |
| 20 Nov. | Second Treaty of Paris, between France and the allies |

# FURTHER READING

It has been said that Napoleon's bibliography is second only in size to that of Jesus Christ himself, and certainly the number of books devoted to the emperor in the London Library alone, covering an entire floor-to-ceiling bookstack thirty yards long, would bear this out. Nonetheless, relatively few of these are full-scale biographies of Napoleon, so much as books covering every conceivable aspect of his political, military and amorous career. Here is a list of fifty of the more important works for further reading, chosen for their readability as well as their erudition. Do not be put off by the age of some of them: if a book is, say, half a century old it will be featured for a reason, such as fine prose style, penetrative insights or because it is a classic of historical writing. For the true Napoleonist, the splendid news is that the Fondation Napoléon, under its director Thierry Lentz, is publishing a completely new edition of Napoleon's *Correspondance Générale*, which will comprise some thirty-six thousand letters in all by the time of the completion of this immense and much-needed work of scholarship, edited by François Houdecek and Gabriel Madec.

## GENERAL BIOGRAPHIES

Asprey, Robert B., *The Rise and Fall of Napoleon Bonaparte*, 2 vols (London, 2000).
Castelot, André, *Napoléon Bonaparte* (Madrid, 2004).
Cronin, Vincent, *Napoleon* (London, 1990).
Dwyer, Philip, *Napoleon: the Path to Power, 1769–1799* (London, 2007).
Johnson, Paul, *Napoleon* (London, 2002).
Lentz, Thierry, 'Napoléon et la Conquête de l'Europe: 1804–1810', *Nouvelle Histoire du Premier Empire*, vol. 1 (Paris, 2001).
Markham, Felix, *Napoleon* (London, 1963).
McLynn, Frank J., *Napoleon: a Biography* (London, 1997).
Rose, J. Holland, *The Life of Napoleon I* (London, 1913).
Schom, Alan, *Napoleon Bonaparte: a Life* (New York, 1997).

Thompson, J. M., *Napoleon Bonaparte* (Oxford, 1988).
Tulard, Jean, *Napoleon: the Myth of the Saviour*, trans. T. Waugh (London, 1984).

## MILITARY AND POLITICAL HISTORIES

Adams, Michael, *Napoleon and Russia* (London, 2006).
Barnett, Correlli, *Bonaparte* (London, 1978).
Becke, A. F., *Napoleon and Waterloo. The Emperor's Campaign with the Armée du Nord, 1815: a Strategical and Tactical Study*, 2 vols (London, 1914).
Boycott-Brown, Martin, *The Road to Rivoli: Napoleon's First Campaign* (London, 2001).
Chandler, David G., *The Campaigns of Napoleon*, 3 vols (London, 2002).
—— (ed.), *Napoleon's Marshals* (London, 1987).
Coote, Stephen, *Napoleon and the Hundred Days* (London, 2004).
Englund, Steven, *Napoleon: a Political Life* (London, 2004).
Esdaile, Charles, *Napoleon's Wars: an International History, 1803–1815* (London, 2008).
Fisher, H. A. L., *Studies in Napoleonic Statesmanship: Germany* (Oxford, 1903).
Glover, Michael, *Warfare in the Age of Bonaparte* (Barnsley, 2003).
Herold, J. Christopher, *Bonaparte in Egypt* (Barnsley, 2005).
Horne, Alistair, *How Far From Austerlitz?: Napoleon, 1805–1815* (London, 1996).
——, *The Age of Napoleon* (London, 2004).
Ireland, Bernard, *The Fall of Toulon: the Last Opportunity to Defeat the French Revolution* (London, 2005).
MacDonell, A. G., *Napoleon and his Marshals* (London, 1934).
Palmer, Alan, *Napoleon in Russia* (London, 1997).
Riley, Jonathon P., *Napoleon as a General* (London, 2007).
Stendhal, *A Life of Napoleon* (London, 1956).
Uffindell, Andrew, *Napoleon's Immortals: the Imperial Guard and its Battles, 1804–1815* (Staplehurst, 2007).
Ward, A.W. and others (eds), *Napoleon*, The Cambridge Modern History, vol. IX (Cambridge, 1902).
Wilkinson, Spenser, *The Rise of General Bonaparte* (Oxford, 1930).
Zamoyski, Adam, *1812: Napoleon's Fatal March on Moscow* (London, 2004).

## FAMILY AND PERSONAL HISTORIES

Aronson, Theo, *The Golden Bees: the Story of the Bonapartes* (London, 1964).

Bernier, Olivier (ed.), *At the Court of Napoleon: Memoirs of the Duchesse d'Abrantès* (New York, 1989).

Bourrienne, Louis Antoine Fauvelet de, *Memoirs of Napoleon Bonaparte*, ed. R. W. Phipps, 4 vols (London, 1893).

Bruce, Evangeline, *Napoleon and Josephine: an Improbable Marriage* (London, 1995).

Delderfield, R. F., *Napoleon in Love* (London, 1974).

Fraser, Flora, *Venus of Empire: the Life of Pauline Bonaparte* (London, 2009).

Herold, J. Christopher (ed.), *The Mind of Napoleon: a Selection from his Written and Spoken Words* (New York, 1955).

Holland, Henry Richard Vassall Fox, *Foreign Reminiscences*, ed. Henry Edward Lord Holland (London, 1850).

Palmer, Alan, *Napoleon and Marie Louise* (London, 2001).

Rosebery, Archibald Philip Primrose, *Napoleon: the Last Phase* (London, 1900).

Smith, William H. C., *The Bonapartes: the History of a Dynasty* (London, 2005).

Thompson, J. M. (ed.), *Napoleon's Letters* (London, 1934).

ANDREW ROBERTS

*May 2009*

# INDEX